DRT MED £3 6/24

MALCOLM MUGGERIDGE. A BIOGRAPHY

Malcolm Muggeridge: A Biography

Gregory Wolfe

Hodder & Stoughton
LONDON SYDNEY AUCKLAND

For Suzanne

British Library Cataloguing in Publication Data
A record for this book is available from the British Library

ISBN 0 340 67139 4

Printed and bound in Great Britain by
Cox & Wyman Ltd, Reading, Berks.

Hodder and Stoughton Ltd
A Division of Hodder Headline PLC
338 Euston Road
London NW1 3BH

A little knowledge separates us from God,
much knowledge brings us back.
One should never be afraid to go too far,
for the truth is beyond.

Marcel Proust, quoted in Malcolm Muggeridge's diary

CONTENTS

ACKNOWLEDGMENTS

MY FIRST AND greatest debt lies with the subject of this biography. Malcolm Muggeridge was unfailingly kind to me over the ten years that I knew him, despite the large difference in years and experience that stood between us. Like so many other visitors to Park Cottage, I also came to know Kitty Muggeridge's self-effacing love and generous spirit.

I am grateful to the late Alec Vidler and to Lord and Lady Longford, who welcomed me into their homes and extended to me their gracious hospitality.

Warm thanks to the staff of Special Collections, Buswell Library, Wheaton College – Larry Thompson, David Malone and Judy Truesdale – for their tireless efforts on my behalf. Also, my thanks to the staff at the following libraries: Bodleian Library, Library of Congress, University of Kansas, Wichita State University and the Wichita Public Library.

I have benefited greatly from the encouragement and support of my colleagues at The Milton Center, Kansas Newman College: Harold Fickett and Virginia Stem Owens. The Milton Center weekly reading group helped me to improve this book in many ways. Special thanks must go to Richard Wilkinson, my colleague at *Image: A Journal of the Arts and Religion*.

For support along the way I wish to thank: David Bovenizer; Boyd Collins; David Dodds; Walter Hooper; Stan Mattson on behalf of the C. S. Lewis Foundation and its study centre at The Kilns; Barry and Margaret Oakley; William Oddie; Patricia Phelps; Jonathan and Brigitte Rowland.

For memories of Malcolm and Kitty Muggeridge and other valuable information, I am indebted to: Chris Barham; Richard T. Burress; Pat and Jenny Ferns; Myrna Grant; Ian Hunter; Fr John Kilmartin, F.D.P.; Russell and Annette Kirk; Andrew and Betty MacFarlane; Jack Muggeridge; John and Anne Roche Muggeridge; Leonard Muggeridge; Richard Nielsen; and Douglas L. Wheeler.

For grants that helped me to research and write this book, I am grateful to the Marguerite Eyer Wilbur Foundation and the Earhart Foundation.

Acknowledgment is made to David Higham Associates for permission to reprint copyrighted material from the works of Malcolm Muggeridge.

Acknowledgment is also made to William Heinemann Ltd. for permission to reprint copyright material from *To Keep the Ball Rolling*, by Anthony Powell.

Acknowledgment is made to the following for use of their pictures in the photograph section: to W. L. Bednarski for the picture of Malcolm with children from Fr. Bidone's home for mentally retarded children; to Western News for the picture of Malcolm with Andrew MacFarlane; to Jane Bann for the pictures of Malcolm in Whatlington Churchyard and of Kitty and Malcolm receiving communion after their rite of reception into the Roman Catholic Church; to Chris Barham for the pictures of Kitty in front of her mother's portrait, Kitty reading aloud to Malcolm, and Malcolm 'the pilgrim'.

My children – Magdalen, Helena, and Charles – have tolerated their preoccupied father with more grace than I had a right to. This book is dedicated to my wife Suzanne, whose love sustains me, and whose sense of irony delights me – and keeps me honest.

Muggeridge One, Two or Three?

I give you the end of a Golden String,
  Only wind it into a ball,
It will lead you in at Heaven's Gate
  Built in Jerusalem's Wall.
                                    William Blake

AS A MEDIA FIGURE for more than half a century, Malcolm Muggeridge understood the strange metamorphosis that turns an individual into an image. His face, his voice and his name were multiplied and reproduced innumerable times – on radio waves, television screens and in books and newsprint. For decades he had provided the news-hungry with dispatches from Our Own Correspondent in Cairo, Calcutta, Moscow, Washington and other points around the globe. At the dawn of the electronic age, he became one of the original Talking Heads – an interviewer, distinguished panellist, cultural critic.

While this public exposure appealed to his vanity, Malcolm also discovered the darker side of life as a creature of the media. "There is something very terrible in becoming an image ... You see yourself on a screen, walking, talking, moving about, posturing, and it is not you. Or is it you, and the you looking at you, someone else? ... Once, sleeping before a television screen, I woke up to find myself on it. The experience was quite terrifying – like some awful nightmare to which only someone like Edgar Allan Poe or Dostoevsky could do justice."[1]

And yet, despite this fear of confronting his electronic *doppelgänger*, Malcolm was his own favourite subject. Nearly all of his most engaging work was in an autobiographical mode. From his early novels to his memoirs, Malcolm conveys his experiences as chapters in his own spiritual and intellectual odyssey. At his best, Malcolm was an autobiographer whose honesty and capacity for self-criticism gave weight to his strongly-held opinions about God and man. At his worst, in old age, Malcolm repeated his story a few too many times, to the point of self-parody.

The first challenge that the biographer of Malcolm Muggeridge must face is the existence of Malcolm's own Authorised Version of his life. The two volumes of his *Chronicles of Wasted Time* have justly been called literary masterpieces. But if there can be no competition with Malcolm's eloquence, it is also true that Malcolm left ample room for the biographer to pursue his craft. His journalistic instincts led him to present various episodes from his life in over-simplified form – as if he were writing banner headlines without getting mired in long, compli- cated stories. Even one of his most sympathetic friends, the journalist Christopher Booker, felt disappointed by Malcolm's memoirs. With their "protestations of humility, confessions of weakness, eagerness for the joyful release of death and all", these memoirs began to read "just a little too much like a carefully prepared cover story". It was only with the publication of Malcolm's diaries, *Like It Was*, that Booker found himself moved by the unvarnished story of Malcolm's life.[2]

Despite his gregarious public persona, Malcolm was an intensely private person; he rarely confided to even his closest friends what was going on inside his heart. For example, his oldest friend, Alec Vidler, learned about Malcolm's 1943 suicide attempt more than twenty years after the fact, and then only because it was reported in a newspaper. There were moments of anguish in his life that even he could not face directly, much less put before the public eye. The most painful moment of all was the death of his son Charles, which he rarely ever mentioned, and then merely in passing. Malcolm's wife Kitty was his only real confidante, but their relationship was itself storm-tossed for decades before it achieved the harmony that struck so many people who met them in their later years.

Malcolm projected so many images of himself over the years that he has been accused of being little more than an incoherent collection of personalities and opinions. Sorting through these images and searching for the man behind them is the other task that the biographer of Malcolm encounters.

Perceptions about the significance of Malcolm's life and work vary widely. In Britain, he is often remembered as "the man on the telly", the "pop Socrates". Whether as interviewer, panellist or documentary host

Malcolm always had some outrageous opinion to offer or biting question to ask. An older generation can still recall his controversial editorship of the humorous magazine, *Punch*, and the infamous article he wrote on the royal family – "Royal Soap Opera" – which earned him temporary banishment from the BBC. While many Britons are aware of Malcolm's books of Christian apologetics, he remains fixed in the national imagination as a creature of the media rather than as a religious sage.

In America, where he is less well known, the opposite is true. The Americans who have heard of him know him as the author of *Jesus: The Man Who Lives* and *Confessions of a Twentieth-Century Pilgrim*. As "St Mugg", he is held to be a defender of the Christian faith second only to C.S. Lewis among modern writers. His papers have been acquired by the evangelical Wheaton College in America, where they join those of Lewis himself. His American readers know little or nothing of the man who battled the Fabian socialists and other sympathisers of the Soviet experiment in Communism throughout the 1930s and 1940s. Nor do they think of him as a satirist whose acid wit turned against institutional religion as often as it did against the principalities and powers of government.

"The man on the telly" or "St Mugg"? Such is the Atlantic divide over the significance of Malcolm Muggeridge. But this is not the only way in which aspects of Malcolm's career have been separated. If one were to move beyond popular perceptions to the assessments of his life and works among the leading critics on both sides of the Atlantic, one would still find a divided Muggeridge, albeit at a more sophisticated level.

Take, for example, the memoirs of Anthony Powell, *To Keep the Ball Rolling*. One of Britain's finest novelists, and for many years a close friend of Malcolm, Powell is known for his close observation of mores and manners. In his memoirs Powell pays tribute to Malcolm as a brilliant writer, faithful friend and literary colleague. But towards the end of *To Keep the Ball Rolling*, Powell writes of his growing unease with what he felt to be deep divisions within Malcolm's personality, which he facetiously calls "the Muggeridgean Trinity". Unlike the Christian notion of the divine Trinity, however, the three dimensions of Malcolm's personality, Powell holds, were ultimately at war with each other.

In the beginning ... was the sceptical wit mocking all, and the wit was with Muggeridge and the wit was Muggeridge. This First

Muggeridge – never wholly exorcised but undergoing long terms of banishment from the Celestial City of his personality – would sometimes support, sometimes obstruct, what then seemed his sole fellow, Second Muggeridge. Second Muggeridge, serious, ambitious, domestic ... with a strain of Lawrentian mysticism ... had a spell-weaving strain and violent political or moral animosities (animosity rather than allegiance being essential expression of Second Muggeridge's teachings), both forms of vituperation in the main aimed at winning a preponderant influence in public affairs ... In due course ... Third Muggeridge became manifest at full strength, hot-gospelling, near-messianic, promulgating an ineluctable choice between Salvation and Perdition. He who was not with Third Muggeridge was against him, including First and Second Muggeridge. In this conflict without quarter First Muggeridge, who treated life as a jest – now so to speak a thief crucified between two Christs – came off worst ... ending as a mere shadow of his former self.[3]

Powell's characterisation of the Muggeridgean Trinity sparkles with its own brand of wit, but it is impossible to avoid the conclusion that it traces the decline and fall of a brilliant and promising writer.

Powell's affection for First Muggeridge is evident; he is clearly the hero of the fable. His tragedy is that, delightful and coruscating though he is, he cannot avoid the dark *alter egos* who eventually crucify him. Lightness of touch and detachment are replaced by anger, intolerance and hysteria. One senses that, on a personal level, Powell increasingly felt that Malcolm was drifting away from him, a sad but inevitable loss.

What Powell describes in friendly and even elegiac tones, many leading critics, without personal ties to inhibit them, have put in a harsher and less forgiving manner. For critics such as Kingsley Amis, David Lodge, and Bernard Levin, the divisions in Malcolm are clear and, ultimately, damning. After a long career as a cynical gadfly – by his own admission a sensualist and a mocker of all commitments – Malcolm in old age suddenly gets religion and becomes a Grand Inquisitor bent on burning heretics. Whether the words "hypocrite" or "opportunist" are stated explicitly or not, they often seem to hover behind such critiques. Then to become a Roman Catholic at the end of his life – to join a Church which has an authoritarian structure, and which throughout most of its history has been as entangled with politics and corruption as it is possible to be – this is a total reversal. From revelling in uncertainty to a craven hunger for absolute certainties – First Muggeridge has indeed become less than a shadow. A Muggeridge divided against himself cannot stand.

It would be wrong to deny these charges categorically, since they contain insights into the complexities of Malcolm's personality, as we shall see. But in one sense the process described by Powell is familiar. In the twentieth century, the same lament has been made for other "lost leaders", including William Butler Yeats, T.S. Eliot, Evelyn Waugh and Aleksandr Solzhenitsyn. In each of these cases, the cry has gone up when an accomplished writer has emerged as an opponent of the prevailing secular, liberal consensus.

But in our efforts to understand Malcolm Muggeridge, it is well to remember the admonition of that first "lost leader", Wordsworth: "We murder to dissect." Analysis – even witty analysis of the kind practised by Anthony Powell – breaks things down into component elements. A life as complex and misunderstood as that of Malcolm Muggeridge needs more delicate instruments and an openness to the patterns that lie beneath the shifting surface images.

No true estimate of Malcolm Muggeridge's role in twentieth-century letters can be achieved so long as the focus remains on a very partial view of his career or convictions. Beyond the caricatures of Malcolm's life, beyond even his own autobiographical distortions and omissions, lies a more compelling story. Take, for example, his religious pilgrimage. Contrary to the myth of Malcolm as a late convert, he struggled with the Christian faith from the time he read the Bible secretly as an adolescent. As a first-year student at Cambridge University, he converted to Christianity and contemplated a vocation to the priesthood. In the 1930s, during the so-called First Muggeridge phase, he was publishing essays that upheld the Christian worldview as the only alternative to the collectivist regimes of the modern era. And late into the hot-gospelling Third Muggeridge epoch, his sharpest barbs were aimed at bishops and other Church leaders.

Malcolm's sense of being an outsider prevented him from being able to be unquestioningly loyal to any human institution or form of authority. But Malcolm did not begin his career as a "sceptical wit mocking all". His first forays into satire consisted of two novels, one an attack on a Liberal newspaper (the *Manchester Guardian*) and the other pointing out the West's blindness to Stalin's atrocities in the Soviet Union. From the outset of his career, Malcolm expressed his "political and moral animosities" through the medium of black humour. He knew the consequences of this public stance. "Such a disposition made one ostensibly irreverent, pessimistic, disloyal, and – the commonest accusation – destructive in attitude."[4]

In the 1950s and early 1960s, Malcolm's public persona as an irreverent cynic ("First Muggeridge") reached its height. First as editor of *Punch* and then as a television personality, Malcolm gained his reputation as debunker of myths and pieties, a verbal demolition artist. He knew instinctively that television lent itself to the staccato rhythms of debate and controversy rather than the careful accumulation and articulation of ideas. Malcolm's TV persona constituted only a part of his life, but it dominated the public's perception of him. If one actually reads Malcolm's writings from the 1930s to the early 1960s, one finds frequent references to Christianity and its greatest visionaries and mystics. These references did not perhaps counteract the image (largely self-created) of Malcolm as a cynical, worldly journalist, but they are an indication of an inner struggle that continued throughout his life. After an evening of witty conversation with friends like Powell or Hugh Kingsmill, Malcolm would go home and pore over Augustine's *Confessions*, or the mystical visions of Bunyan, Blake, Pascal, Kierkegaard or Dostoevsky. These writers all shared a profound sense of sin and suffering, and yet they showed that the City of God could be glimpsed from the City of Man by the passionate pilgrim.

When Malcolm was received into the Roman Catholic Church near the end of his life, he defended the decision by arguing that he had joined the one institution whose ultimate authority was divine, not human. To his critics, these two positions – the non-conformist and the believer in religious authority – could not be further apart. But for Malcolm, this action was the final reconciliation of his "political and moral animosities" with his desire for a transcendent communion. Like his contemporary Evelyn Waugh, Malcolm found that the Christian understanding of the two cities provided the perfect platform from which to undermine the pretensions of a fallen world. Malcolm, like Waugh, was something of a Christian deconstructionist.

What Anthony Powell and others have failed to recognise is just how consistent Malcolm's life and thought were. Powell's three characters – the satirist, the moralist and the Christian apologist – are inextricably woven together. Malcolm stands squarely in a tradition of Christian writers that includes Samuel Johnson, G.K. Chesterton, C.S. Lewis and Evelyn Waugh. Each of these writers produced satirical attacks on modern, secular progressivism from the perspective of Christian orthodoxy.

In the twentieth century, the intellectual elite has preferred religious figures to remain cloistered in a visionary world, rather than straying into the centre of the public debate. When C.S. Lewis dared to combine his religious writing with his academic career, Oxford was offended. And when Malcolm brought religion into the discussion of public affairs, he brought down upon himself the scorn of an even larger cohort of pundits and intellectuals.

In the face of such an onslaught, the ultimate temptation for the biographer of Malcolm Muggeridge may be to concede too much, to grant that Malcolm was perhaps nothing more than a "pop intellectual", and focus on him as a hilarious and memorable character. In that case, the temptation is to play Boswell to Malcolm's Johnson, concentrating on his innumerable witty retorts, *bons mots* and other examples of his dazzling sense of humour. This is a temptation that I have resisted. For all his brilliance, Boswell moves too quickly over the younger Johnson and does not delve deeply into the darker, more tortured side of Johnson's personality. In addition to Malcolm's wit, I have looked into the fierce inner struggles – the Augustinian battles between flesh and spirit – that formed his vision of the world in his early years. I have also paid careful attention to Malcolm's thought, because he was much more than a pop intellectual. Malcolm was neither an artist nor a scholar. But he possessed a powerful imagination that enabled him to see through the pretensions of those who pursue and wield power, and to record his commentary with astringent irony and, on occasion, with savage indignation.

At his best Malcolm Muggeridge achieved prophetic stature. He was prophetic not only in the sense of his moral criticisms of the West, but in the accuracy of his predictions. The prophetic gift is not so much an ability to see into the future as it is to sense the deeper currents flowing under present cultural trends. Malcolm sought to tear through the veil of fantasy that people place between themselves and reality. The collapse of the British Empire, the rise and eventual fall of Soviet totalitarianism, the commercialisation of a global culture, the pervasive influence of the media on all aspects of life, even the British royal family as an ongoing soap opera – in these and other historic developments, Malcolm proved his ability to see more clearly than most of his contemporaries.

Though his best writing is scattered through six decades of journalistic production, Malcolm's prose style is among the finest of his generation. Like Waugh and Chesterton, he had a highly developed sense of the absurd, and harnessed his own anarchic imagination to the defence of order. Above all, Malcolm's sense of the incongruous, of the disparity between human aspiration and human achievement, made him a supremely comic writer.

There was, of course, only one Malcolm Muggeridge. Among his favourite quotations was Blake's notion of the Golden String, which, if followed throughout one's life, will lead eventually to the gates of the New Jerusalem. Such a thread can be traced through Malcolm's own tumultuous life.

Fearful Symmetry

1903–1914

IN 1903, THE YEAR Malcolm Muggeridge was born, George Bernard Shaw published his play, *Man and Superman*. Malcolm's father, H.T. Muggeridge, would boast to his friends that he had published his own Superman in 1903. This witticism, full of a father's pride and affection, was typical of H.T.'s table talk. But he was not being merely witty. H.T.'s *bon mot* also concealed a world of hopes and ambitions for his son. It foreshadowed nearly all of the conflicts and tensions that would be played out in Malcolm's life.

Even as a boy, Malcolm knew that his father had made an enormous emotional investment in his future. H.T. was the "Man", but Malcolm was to become the "Superman". As a brilliant playwright and the leading socialist intellectual of the time, George Bernard Shaw symbolised everything that H.T. fervently admired. The title of his play echoed the radical ideas of Nietzsche; the play itself, an updating of the Don Juan story, was a witty debunking of traditional attitudes towards courtship, marriage and the relations between the sexes. Though H.T. was thoroughly conventional when it came to matters like sexuality and marriage, he nonetheless looked up to Shaw as the most sophisticated literary champion of the poor and downtrodden.

Malcolm would spend the first thirty years of his life struggling to enter the intellectual club run by Shaw and his associates. When he finally acquired membership in that club, through his marriage into a Fabian family and his own apprenticeship as a socialist intellectual, he found, to his disgust, that the other members were immersed in fantasy and hungry for power. This disillusionment not only set him at odds with his father, but intensified the struggle within his own heart and mind between cynicism and idealism.

H.T. Muggeridge's desire to live vicariously through his son was as much the result of his love and pride as it was of frustration and resentment against his own limitations. As a boy, Malcolm returned his father's love unreservedly. But as Malcolm entered the public realm, his father's expectations intensified and Malcolm's attempts to become a junior Fabian proved unsatisfying. When he came to see the naïveté of his father's idealism, Malcolm experienced the savage indignation that helped to make him a corrosive satirist and master of black humour. The idealism he inherited from his father was not so much abandoned as it was displaced. Out of this dialectic grew all of Malcolm's thought and writing.

In his autobiography, Malcolm confessed to a life-long habit of running away from unpleasant and onerous situations (something he called "the urge to be gone"). This impulse can be traced, in part, to his sense that he could not fulfil his father's expectations, but it also ran in the family. Malcolm's paternal grandfather, Henry Ambrose Muggeridge, was a figure who frequently had "the urge to be gone". Henry Ambrose was an undertaker in the London suburb of Penge. He fathered eleven children, of whom Henry Thomas was the eldest. H.T. was born in 1864, one of the seven children to survive the ravages of tuberculosis and live to maturity.

When H.T. was twelve, his father abandoned the family, reappearing only for brief interludes. Nine months after each of these interludes, it seemed to H.T., another child would be born. Once H.T. thought he saw his father with another woman in Victoria Station. Eventually he decided to put a stop to his father's furtive visits and ordered him to leave the house. It took courage and a powerful sense of responsibility for a teenage boy to bar the gates against his own father. There can be little doubt that his mother's desperation forced him to such a decisive action. H.T. would suffer pangs of guilt about this rejection of his father for the rest of his life.

H.T. made sure that his life bore no resemblance to that of his father. As he would later confide to Malcolm, H.T. had been financially responsible for others from the time he was thirteen. In the aftermath of Henry Ambrose's final departure, H.T.'s mother started a second-hand furniture business on Penge High Street. But this business would not have generated enough income to support a family of ten. In order to contribute to the family's income, H.T. passed an examination that enabled him to leave St John's School, Penge. He went to work as an office boy for a law firm in London. When it became clear to him that he would never achieve a position higher than that of lawyer's clerk, he decided to join the shirt manufacturing company of MacIntyre, Hogg, Marsh & Co. The year was 1880. He began by working as an office boy, then moved on to the "stock room", where goods were received, shelved and accounted for. Eventually he joined the accounting department as a ledger clerk. By the time he retired, a half-century later, H.T. Muggeridge had never worked for another company.

In *Chronicles of Wasted Time*, Malcolm Muggeridge describes his father's daily journey to London on the workmen's train, which he rode to save money. "It meant that he arrived an hour or so before his office opened, which he spent roaming through the City. In those days, he told me, he used to run more often than walk ... I have often imagined him darting about those streets like an excited sparrow."[1] Malcolm himself would become an inveterate walker. H.T. had plenty of time during these morning runs to contemplate his future. His prospects were limited. Having been forced to curtail his education, it was unlikely that he would ever be able to enter a profession or aspire to more than a lower-middle-class existence.

H.T.'s response to this situation established the pattern of his life and his political ideas. He accepted his place in the social order, but determined to work within the system to improve himself and his prospects. A true child of the Victorian era, H.T. believed in the inevitability of Progress and the virtue of Self-Help. He rejected violent political revolution, just as he refused to abandon his mother and seek his own immediate self-interest. But if H.T. was a gradualist, he nonetheless believed that at the end of his striving there would be a glorious new order, where young men like himself would have the education and social services he had gone without.

As it happens, H.T.'s progressivism and hunger for self-improvement had its roots in the Baptist Church he attended as a boy – an irony that his son Malcolm would later remark upon. Sitting in the chapel, H.T. heard the preacher use impassioned language to rouse the people to greater faith. Because the Nonconformist Churches were outside the Church of England and its institutions of education, the chapel often became an alternative source of learning. This spawned the development of Mutual Improvement Societies that offered courses, educational tours at home and abroad and other social and cultural activities.

The chapel's strong social focus often led to political engagement.

The Nonconforming Churches, including the Baptists, tended to gravitate towards the Liberal Party, rather than the Tories, who represented the Established Church of England and the privileges of the aristocracy. The Liberals pressed for a number of political reforms that were dear to the hearts of the Nonconformists, including the disestablishment of the Church of England and the creation of a national, nonsectarian educational system. The young H.T. became an ardent member of the Penge Liberal Association.

Though the Liberals were a potent force in nineteenth-century British politics, they experienced a growing number of internal conflicts and divisions as the century drew to a close. The origins of Liberalism were in the free market individualism of Cobden and Bright, which opposed the system of privilege that did not give the common man a stake in land ownership and enterprise. But with the rise of large industrial corporations and urbanisation, the Liberalism of Cobden and Bright came to be seen as outdated. Working-class Liberals felt that the industrialists represented a new class of privilege. They organised trade unions and adopted the collectivist ideas of William Morris.

Out of this political and intellectual turmoil arose organisations with explicitly socialist agendas, including the Independent Labour Party and the Fabian Society. H.T. became a founding member of both. He had been spending his free hours in educating himself through voracious reading. His favourite authors were the prophetic critics of the new industrial order: Thomas Carlyle, John Ruskin, William Morris, Charles Dickens, Walt Whitman, Prince Kropotkin, Edward Bellamy and the husband-and-wife team of Sidney and Beatrice Webb. Like so many self-educated men, H.T. hero-worshipped the intellectual class, men and women who used their pens and their wits to lay siege to the bastions of privilege.

The Fabian Society, which was to play such a large role in the lives of H.T. and Malcolm Muggeridge, was founded in 1884. It had grown out of an earlier society, the Fellowship of the New Life, a gathering of utopians who established their own experimental community. The Fellowship's first meeting, in 1883, ended with the following resolution: "That an association be formed whose ultimate aim shall be the reconstruction of Society in accordance with the highest moral possibilities."[2] In later years, Malcolm would make much of the secularised mysticism that surrounded these organisations of the Left. But when the young George Bernard Shaw brought Sidney Webb to a meeting

of the Fellowship, the balance of power shifted from the utopian mystics to the advocates of social science and rational planning. The Fabian Society took its name from the Roman general Q. Fabius Maximus, "the Delayer", who won his campaigns by slowly wearing down his enemies. Thus the Fabians signalled their commitment to working for reform within existing political institutions rather than through violent revolutionary action.

The philosophy of gradualism espoused by the Fabians reflected H.T.'s own temperament and ambitions. In 1892, when he joined the Fabian Society, H.T. had worked for MacIntyre, Hogg for twelve years. His steadiness and persistence would be rewarded the following year, when he was made head of the counting house.

The following year, 1893, marked another milestone in H.T.'s life, another reward for his patience. While on holiday on the Isle of Man, he met Annie Booler, a striking, fair-haired girl from Sheffield. In his autobiography, Malcolm imagines the encounter between H.T. and Annie as a scene out of one of H.G. Wells's novels of working-class life. "I imagine a Wellsian encounter, my father and the two office pals who were on holiday with him, in high spirits, and my mother flattered at being the object of the attentions of such sprightly young fellows."[3]

When the holiday was over, H.T. wrote ardent romantic letters to Annie, making clear his intentions. Within a few weeks, H.T. travelled to Sheffield to be presented to the Boolers. He was pronounced suitable and received their blessing.

Annie's father and several of her uncles worked in the cutlery business in Sheffield. As the young Malcolm would later realise, the Boolers were genuine working-class folk, representatives of what H.T. would call the oppressed masses. But on his visits to the Boolers, Malcolm never found them to be alienated or conscious of being downtrodden. Compared to his own rather spartan home, the Boolers' table was laden with good things to eat. A visit to Sheffield was always a treat for the Muggeridge boys.

Though Malcolm was raised to believe he would be one of the liberators who would rescue the likes of the Boolers, they refused to conform to their role in the socialist drama. Malcolm's maternal grandmother, who was widowed shortly after her daughter's marriage to H.T., would come down from Sheffield to take care of the Muggeridge children while their parents were on holiday. "She was a tiny, energetic lady who still wore a cap indoors, and bustled about the house, washing, brushing, polishing, cooking." One incident with this grandmother remained in Malcolm's memory. "Once . . . when I had been disparaging the story of Daniel in the Lions' Den, she shut me up by remarking with great emphasis: 'If Daniel isn't true, nothing is.'"[4]

It is unlikely that when Annie married the earnest, boyish H.T. she understood the intensity of his political and intellectual commitments. There is no evidence that she shared even a passing interest in her husband's philosophy. Her own attitude toward class distinctions was utterly conventional.

The Muggeridges' first home was on Broomhall Road in the village of Sanderstead, which would soon be absorbed by the larger suburban town of Croydon. They would only move once during Malcolm's youth, but that was merely to a different part of South Croydon. It is typical of the relationship between Malcolm and his father that despite their seeming intellectual agreement, they would experience the world of suburbia so differently. It was an article of belief for H.T. that suburbia was, in Marxist terms, *petit bourgeois*, and therefore to be despised. H.T. and his young disciple Malcolm agreed that the middle class was made up of complacent boors who stood in the way of positive social change. But as Malcolm grew up, he came to feel that H.T. was far more comfortable in his suburban environment than his opinions would lead one to believe.

Malcolm certainly came to hate the fraudulence and sentimentality of suburbia – the houses with names like The Elms, Chez Nous, The Nook, the mock-Tudor beams and gables, the snobbery of having a tradesman's entrance when there was scarcely room for a normal entrance. Croydon provided Malcolm with his first object lesson on the disparity between appearance and reality. These were the homes of the commuter-drones of the modern city – flowing in and out of London every day like the empty figures of T.S. Eliot's *The Waste Land*. The attempt of these suburbanites to sugar-coat their bland, routine existences with bucolic names for their homes and streets appealed to, and helped to develop, Malcolm's sense of the absurd. So powerful was his loathing for this world that when he found much of it destroyed in the Blitz, his first reaction was exultation.

Malcolm's extreme sensitivity to the difference between appearance and reality eventually was applied to his father. Despite their ideological agreement about the undesirability of the *petit bourgeois*, Malcolm suspected that his father had made his peace with the enemy. This was not something he would be able to articulate until he had become an adult himself. But in his first novel, *Autumnal Face*, written when he was twenty-seven, his parents are portrayed in language that is similar to that of Eliot. On the first page of the novel there appears a description of H.T.

> Dad was pottering about in the garden dressed in his gardening clothes – black suit now faded, but used once for the City; battered bowler that had made many journeys over London Bridge before its garden use. His clothes were unagricultural yet grimed with Croydon mud. On either side of Dad's garden there were other gardens, each a narrow strip enclosed between slight wooden fences, where other men worked – suburban peasants in black suits and bowler hats . . .[5]

With the uncompromising harshness of youth, Malcolm did not stop to consider whether his father's hard-won security might have had any emotional justification.

This struggle with his father was not to take place until Malcolm had reached adulthood. The more immediate effect of H.T.'s intellectual loathing for the *petit bourgeois* was on the formation of Malcolm's class-consciousness. "This attitude bred in us – or at least in me – a sort of social schizophrenia; we were snobs in relation to our neighbours, and anti-snobs in relation to those above and below us on the social scale."[6] Later in this passage from his autobiography, Malcolm goes on to compare his own background with that of George Orwell and Evelyn Waugh. They all shared a sense of embarrassment and loathing for their own middle-class origins, while at the same time feeling themselves to be "outsiders" in relation to the Establishment. To compensate, they identified with other social classes, Orwell affecting proletarian dress and habits, while Waugh pretended to be a country gentleman. Malcolm himself never went to such extremes of affectation, though at the peak of his media career, he enjoyed playing the dandy – cosmopolitan, cynical, world-weary and sensual. A long way from bowler hats and black suits caked with Croydon mud.

Thomas Malcolm Muggeridge was born in the house in Sanderstead ten years after his parents were married, on March 24, 1903. He was the third of five boys. His older brothers were named Douglas and Stanley; the younger, Eric and Jack. There must have been something remarkable about him as a small child, because H.T. wrote to a friend in the autumn of 1905: "I now have three youngsters. Little Malcolm, who is now two and a half, is the youngest and we think the most promising of all."[7]

His Christian name was given him by H.T. in honour of the Victorian social prophet, Thomas Carlyle. Carlyle was a critic of modern industrialism and mass society, dominated by what he called the "cash nexus". In his *Autobiography*, William Butler Yeats noted that Carlyle was "the chief inspirer of self-educated men in the eighties and early nineties". Even though the name Thomas was never used, except on official documents, Malcolm took his secular patron saint seriously. He read Carlyle as a young man, revelling in what one critic has called his "violent exclamatory rhetoric". Malcom once claimed that the first and most important influence on his literary style was Carlyle.[8]

When Malcolm was a young boy, his mother Annie still retained her good looks. But after bearing five children, she grew stouter and became a white-haired matron. Neither H.T. nor Annie were physically demonstrative parents. Annie was a practical woman whose household was governed by routine. While Malcolm looked on his mother as part of the landscape, his emotional life revolved around his father. Between his gruelling daily journey to London, and his increasing political activities, H.T. became a distant but romantic figure to the young Malcolm.

A photograph of Malcolm as a plump infant won a prize sponsored by the Mellins Food Company. As he grew up, Malcolm became extremely slim, a physical trait that would never alter through the course of his life. Photographs of the young Malcolm show a lean, blond-haired, blue-eyed boy with the same impish expression that would be instantly recognisable to millions of television viewers half a century later. He was a nervous, highly-strung child, given to sleep-walking and nightmares. For a time he slept with his two younger brothers in a large double bed that had been used by his parents. At night, Malcolm would frequently thrash about during his nightmares. Once he put his arm through a glass window, cutting himself badly, and leaving a permanent scar. There was one recurring nightmare in which Malcolm was trapped in a dark place, frenziedly attempting to get out into the light. When Malcolm sleepwalked, H.T. and Annie had to be wakened in order to steer him back to bed.[9] Though he eventually gave up sleepwalking, Malcolm suffered from insomnia and night fears for the rest of his life.

Malcolm learned his letters at an infant school run by two sisters named Monday who lived around the corner from the Muggeridge home on Broomhall Road. "The establishment had a faint aura of respectability, and represented a slightly superior alternative to the infants' department of the local elementary school," Malcolm wrote many years later. But the primary reason for going to the Monday sisters was that they were so close to home.

Following this, Malcolm was sent to a state elementary school. As a good socialist, H.T. felt that his son should not be sent to public schools, which he considered bastions of privilege and bourgeois values. There was certainly nothing at Dering Road Elementary School to suggest wealth or the trappings of social status. "No blazers or caps in those days at such schools; just classrooms and teachers and an asphalt playground." The classrooms were divided by wooden partitions that could be removed, creating a large assembly space. The day would begin by a careful registration of attendance, a prayer and a hymn. The headmaster was very particular that the children pronounce their aspirates, often having them repeat the Lord's Prayer several times before he was satisfied with their diction. Once Malcolm raised his hand to ask if God cared about whether his creatures dropped their aitches. He received no memorable answer.[10]

Malcolm's attitude towards his formal schooling signalled what was to become the pattern of his relationship to all institutions. Something within him resisted wholehearted participation in any form of collective activity. For example, when it came to singing hymns at school, Malcolm's voice did not swell the chorus. "Never having been able to sing in tune, I developed a faculty for appearing to be joining in eagerly, but actually making little or no sound ..."[11] The one hymn that sent thrills of delight through Malcolm was "Now the Day is Over", sung on Friday afternoons and heralding two days of freedom from school.

Passive resistance was not Malcolm's only tactic; he had an impulse towards active subversion. He frequently got into trouble for his habit of talking back. He also loved to devise tough questions that reduced his teachers to mumbles and polite coughs. Once he asked a teacher about the phrase in the Bible which indicated that something had to happen "in order that the prophecy might be fulfilled". How could it be an authentic prophecy, he asked, if words or actions were necessary to bring it to pass? This question proved to be beyond the range of his teacher's store of theological wisdom.

This teacher was actually Malcolm's favourite, a pretty young woman named Helen Corke, recently graduated from training college.

Though he didn't know it at the time, Miss Corke was carrying on a relationship with another teacher, from a nearby school, by the name of D.H. Lawrence. Like Malcolm's father, Miss Corke was a believer in progress and the need for liberation from conventional social forms. It is unclear whether she introduced any of these advanced ideas into Malcolm's elementary school education. Within ten years, Malcolm was himself to become an ardent disciple of Lawrence, preferring the passionate sexual creed of the messiah from Nottingham to the economics of his father's socialism. He would come to relish the irony of being Miss Corke's pupil. Half a century later, he sought out the elderly, white-haired Miss Corke for a television interview about D.H. Lawrence and his legacy. Towards the end of the interview, Malcolm turned to Miss Corke with that impish grin and asked her whether it was true, as he suspected, that Lawrence was obsessed with sex because he was, in fact, impotent. Miss Corke declined to be drawn on that issue. She told Malcolm's wife, Kitty, that she remembered him as "a very charming boy, but impossible".[12]

Miss Corke recalled Malcolm as being more than a rebel or troublemaker. She insisted that he had an exuberant and outgoing side to his personality. In his last term at the Dering Road school, she reminded him, she had written a play for the May Festival. It was "a fantasy of the months in which March is presented as having stolen May's rightful weather. The principals in this play were two gay and charming pupils named Madge Frost and Malcolm Muggeridge."[13]

Malcolm's real education took place outside the classroom. The only teacher to whom he ever really responded was his father. H.T., in turn, recognised that Malcolm was the only one of the five boys who had the intelligence and curiosity necessary for a political or literary career. The bond between them was their love of language, the way words could be used in the flashing repartee of debate, in the prophetic denunciation of social injustice, and in the depiction of the better world to come, the radiant realm of liberty, equality and fraternity. For Malcolm, the household shrine was the glass-fronted bookcase that contained H.T.'s carefully accumulated library. Here were the sacred texts of socialism, from Rousseau and Ruskin to Morris and George Bernard Shaw. In time, Malcolm would read most of these volumes, though he never felt impelled to brave Marx's *Das Kapital*. He often attempted to read these books before he was able to comprehend them. Once his mother found him trying to read Rousseau's *Confessions* when he was only ten or eleven.

Even more compelling to Malcolm was language when spoken aloud. H.T. read Shakespeare to the family on Sunday evenings, taking all the parts. Malcolm, however, found the blank verse rather hard to follow. Infinitely superior were the novels of Charles Dickens. H.T.'s own life had a touch of Dickensian melodrama to it: an abandoned child, the premature responsibilities of adulthood thrust upon him, the enormous effort to raise himself to another level of class and culture. H.T. and Malcolm relished Dickens' humour, his ability to create eccentrics and caricatures who encapsulated typical human foibles, his indignation at the plight of Britain's poor, his sentimental, idealised portraits of women. He began to sense that the dichotomies in Dickens corresponded closely to those of his father. "[Dickens'] capacity for turning on a passionate flood of righteous indignation at any time; his tears for the poor, and love of money and success; his scorn for his social superiors, and his passion to be like them; the sentimentality in which all his emotions, public and private, were drenched, and the corresponding humour which so incomparably expressed what he really felt . . ."[14]

At these dramatic recitals H.T. indulged his love of theatricality. In the protected world of his family, H.T. happily played the fool. As a child, Malcolm found his father's clowning funny and endearing. When the Muggeridge boys staged their own theatricals at home, Malcolm preferred to play ghosts or spirits.[15]

Malcolm loved his father's intellectual discussion groups, where language sparkled in witty debate, or ascended in flights of utopian visionary glory. Whisky and water would be served from a cabinet in H.T.'s study, and the talk would go well into the night. Malcolm would ensconce himself in a piece of furniture known in the family as the "cosy corner" – actually a "snuggery" from a pub. From the shadows of the cosy corner, Malcolm would listen to the conversation, often staying up until ten or ten thirty. Occasionally he would remind his father of his presence by attempting to join in the dialogue; this inevitably got him sent to bed, where he would strain to keep up with the muffled words rising from the living-room.

The "regulars" at H.T.'s Saturday evening sessions were mostly middle-class clerks and shopkeepers. H.T.'s tailor, Mr Jordan, was a faithful attender, as was a Mr Patterson, a Scottish accountant who went on to become a wealthy capitalist. Despite all the high-minded talk about the plight of the poor, no working men ever showed up at these gatherings. Malcolm enjoyed the conspiratorial atmosphere of these conversations, the sense that these socialist Davids would eventually slay the Goliaths of privilege.[16]

On occasion, the Muggeridge home would be honoured by visits from special guests. When a rising Labour politician would speak at a political meeting in Croydon, H.T. would generally preside and invite the speaker home for hospitality. Annie would dress Malcolm and his brothers in their best clothes, fussing over the inconvenience of these intrusions into her domestic life. Ramsay MacDonald, Philip Snowden, J.R. Clynes and Hugh Dalton – all destined to become leading Labour Party members and cabinet ministers – were among those who passed through the Muggeridges' living-room. Though they were ostensibly champions of the common man, Malcolm remembered them as already surrounded with the aura of power, condescending towards others and endlessly repeating slogans and clichés.

While H.T. welcomed these politicians into his home, he relished visits from his heroes, the Fabian intellectuals. In *Chronicles*, Malcolm describes these visitors as "careless, untidy, pipe-smoking men; ladies whose bosoms floated loose instead of being laced up like my mother's . . ."[17] Malcolm goes on to pinpoint the source of his father's worshipful attitude towards these intellectuals:

> They . . . had effortlessly acquired what he so desperately sought. They were what he wanted to be. Those hours at City libraries when he should have been eating or playing; the poring over French irregular verbs in order to be able to have a come-back if someone on the Croydon Council . . . quoted a Latin tag at him! – none of that for them. They were at ease in a world from which he felt he had been excluded, and which therefore seemed the more alluring – what he saw as the world of culture.[18]

Sidney and Beatrice Webb, the monarchs of the Fabian kingdom, held forth in the Muggeridges' parlour. Even H.G. Wells stopped by one evening. This was an intoxicating company, an inner circle which H.T. intended his son to enter on equal terms.

Early in his life, Malcolm got a taste for the way progressive social ideas might be put into practice. When he was about seven years old, Malcolm became ill, the symptoms appearing to indicate that he might have tuberculosis. H.T. had lost several family members to TB and decided to take no chances. Malcolm was sent for the summer months of 1910 to live with a spinster named Miss Lidiard in the Gloucestershire village of Sheepscombe. The connection came about because H.T.'s closest friend, Will Straughan, knew of a utopian community known as the Colony at Whiteway, just a mile from Sheepscombe. Though an ardent socialist, Straughan was not a wholehearted supporter of the Colony. Nor was Miss Lidiard. Perhaps this scepticism about the Colony brought them together, because Straughan eventually married her.

The Colony was essentially a "commune", inspired by the Tolstoyan gospel of pacifism and voluntary poverty. This early effort to go back to nature was also influenced by the daring new philosophy of "free love", which denied traditional sexual morality and encouraged individuals to change sexual partners. The Colonists dispensed with the use of money, using bartered goods to acquire all they needed. At the time when Malcolm knew the Colony, it was presided over by an eccentric Czech philosopher named Francis Sedlac, and his companion, Nelly Shaw, a formidable, if unattractive, feminist. Wracked by constant apostasy and dissension – including the stress of lovers afflicted by the archaic emotion of jealousy – the Colony never grew beyond a handful of members.

In his autobiography, Malcolm devotes several pages to the Colony. It made an indelible impression on him. One impression came from watching the Colonists bathing nude in a river; the sight, in general, was not that memorable, but there were a couple of adolescent girls who caught his eye. But Malcolm was also fascinated by the idealism and mysticism of this social experiment. As a young man, he adopted the theory – and practice – of free love, though it caused him, and the Colonists, a considerable amount of anguish. He would portray the Colony as "Beulah" in his satirical novel, *In a Valley of This Restless Mind* (1938).[19]

Malcolm shared his father's admiration for Will Straughan, whose genuine decency and compassion stood in stark contrast to the fraudulence and arrogance of the Colony and other intellectual coteries, such as the Fabian Society. Straughan receives the highest praise in Malcolm's autobiography: "a truly enchanting human being; gentle, humorous, quixotically generous, original . . ."[20] At any rate, Malcolm did not develop TB, and was soon back in the waste lands of suburbia.

Malcolm's experience in Sheepscombe left him with a lifelong desire for simple country living. This exposure to the countryside of Gloucestershire initiated his romantic affinity for nature. His first religious experience occurred during a bicycle ride into the country. H.T. and his five boys would pedal out from South Croydon into the rolling hills of Surrey and Kent, just a short ride away. One evening, riding near Chipstead as the sun set, Malcolm experienced an epiphany. "Suddenly I realised with a tremendous feeling of exultation that . . . the whole golden, glorious scene had some special significance in which I participated. That in its all-embracing beauty it conveyed a oneness, and that to identify oneself with the spirit animating it and giving it meaning, contained the promise of ecstasy."[21] Paradoxically, Malcolm's sense of oneness with the universe also made him feel a "stranger and pilgrim on the earth". His sense of the world's beauty was linked to a belief in its fragility. Like the Romantic poets, Malcolm could be intoxicated by natural beauty, while at the same time given to longings for the metaphysical truth beyond nature.

By the time Malcolm had returned from Sheepscombe, the Muggeridge family was settled into its new home, 17 Birdhurst Gardens, a large detached house in South Croydon. H.T. designed the house himself and had it built by a cooperative organisation, for a cost of £1,000, which included the cost of the land itself. It had a large living-room that ran from the front to the back of the house. In this room H.T. could hold political meetings with as many as fifty people in attendance. Though the design of the house was simple and austere, there were five bedrooms. The other half of the house was to have been occupied by Straughan, but he lost a great deal of money trying to save a shipping company and its employees, and did not move in.

The house at Birdhurst Gardens was clearly in a more respectable neighbourhood, a significant step up the social ladder for H.T. and his family. Not all the neighbours were pleased, however. Some of them thought that socialists ought to live in slums rather than respectable parts of town and took a rather dim view of the regular political meetings at number 17. Malcolm and his siblings became known as "those dreadful Muggeridge boys".

H.T. felt confident enough at this time to attempt his first bid for public office in many years. As early as 1895, he had contested a seat on the local council. But in 1911 he was elected as the first socialist member of the Croydon Council. Here, as in his job at the shirt manufacturer, H.T. was steady and reliable – he held his seat on the council until 1929, when he was elected to Parliament, and resumed it when he lost his seat in Parliament.

More than any of his childhood experiences, elections were for Malcolm the supreme events, charged with powerful emotions. Watching his father on the stump, seeking votes and approval, Malcolm sensed his father's vulnerability. He became his father's political acolyte; later he would think of these elections as similar in spirit to the pomp and ceremony of religious feast days. The family would appear beside H.T. when he gave his election address, red rosettes pinned to their clothes. Labour candidates had a special need, in the light of their reputation as dangerous radicals, to prove that they were traditional family men. The link between Labour politics and "free love" was usually left to rumours and innuendo, but in 1923, during H.T.'s third attempt to win election to Parliament, a brochure was circulated claiming that H.T. and Annie were not married, and that the children were illegitimate.[22]

In an early draft of his autobiography, written some time in the 1960s, Malcolm recalled an enduring image from these elections:

> How well I remember committee rooms, usually in an empty shop, or in the downstairs room of an unoccupied house; their very emptiness, unusedness, investing them with a lurid, stark quality, like unlighted empty streets in the early morning hours; the trestle-tables loaded with election literature, to be folded, and addressed, and posted; my father's face looking down on us from posters fastened on the bare walls as we toiled on his behalf . . .[23]

Going canvassing from house to house was also an emotionally draining activity. In *Chronicles*, Malcolm compares canvassing to another form of solicitation – the sexual variety. "Love me! Vote for me!"

His most poignant memory, however, was of his father standing on a fragile platform ("almost like a gallows against the evening sky") at the top of Surrey Street in Croydon, competing with the hucksters for the attention of passing shoppers. H.T. would try to work the crowd with some of his patented witticisms. In the aftermath of the public debate over building an expensive battleship, H.T. would say: "I'm interested in ships too! Hardships!" Malcolm's exultation in his father's sweeping language was dampened by his recognition that few passers-by were paying attention. But as H.T. gathered rhetorical steam, his voice rose in prophetic denunciation of the industrial monopolies and privilege-protectors. In those moments, Malcolm's attention was wholly centred on his father, even if the "crowd" had dwindled to a couple of party stalwarts and a group of curious children.[24]

But as father and son stood there in the failing light, united by love and mutual admiration, their experiences and emotions diverged. H.T., driven by his desire to bring about orderly progress, hoped to gain political power and see his son become a sophisticated Fabian intellectual. Malcolm, already feeling the pressure of his father's ambitions for him, thrilled more to the prophetic language that could tear down society's idols and illusions. As his father was running for a seat on Croydon Council, Malcolm received a birthday present of a toy printing set. He used the set to "publish" his first story, about a runaway train.

It was a story of a train going very fast and, to the satisfaction of the passengers, racing through the small stations along the track without stopping. Their satisfaction, however, turned to dismay, and then to panic and fury, as it dawned on them that it was not going to stop at *their* stations either when it came to them. They raged and shouted and shook their fists, but all to no avail. The train went roaring on.[25]

A Charming Boy, But Impossible

1914–1920

IF MALCOLM'S STORY about the runaway train was his first prophetic statement, the war that began in 1914 would soon fulfil it. Malcolm was too young to fight in the 1914–18 war, but the conflagration in Europe would affect him in a number of significant ways. In an unpublished autobiographical fragment, he wrote that the war constituted his first experience of the world outside his home. Later in the same passage, he wonders if his "sense of the inevitability of catastrophe" came from his youthful experience of wartime.[1]

The more immediate effect of the war on Malcolm was to inspire his romantic yearnings. His two older brothers enlisted, despite H.T.'s protests. He envied the dashing figures of Douglas, a subaltern in polished riding-boots, and Stanley, in the tunic and fore-and-aft cap of the Royal Flying Corps. When Malcolm was only fifteen he impulsively went to the recruiting office in Croydon, where he attempted to persuade the officer in charge that he was really seventeen.[2] Douglas would be captured in France and spend several months as a prisoner of war.

H.T.'s attitude towards the war was complex. As a socialist he was, in principle, a pacifist. Many of the Fabians argued that the "war party" consisted of industrialists who sought to profit from the sale of arms. Moreover, the whole concept of patriotism was an object of ridicule among socialists. Before the war broke out, H.T. and his friends hoped that the progressive German Social Democrats could prevent a conflict. But when the German Reichstag voted for war their illusions were shattered and they were forced into a grudging support of the war. They hoped that this would be the "war to end all wars", the prelude to the establishment of peace and socialism.[3]

At the war's end, however, H.T. did something that shocked

Malcolm. On November 11, 1918, Armistice Day, H.T. hung the Union Jack on the front of the house in Birdhurst Gardens. Aware that this patriotic gesture was out of keeping with his political commitments, H.T. felt obliged to deliver a "formal apologia . . . with an eye cast, especially, in my direction".[4] The flag-hanging reflected H.T.'s immense relief that both his sons had survived the war, but Malcolm, trained to ideological purity, was not able to understand his father's emotions on that day.

During this period of world war Malcolm found himself drawn into an ongoing domestic battle in which he felt impelled to act as peacemaker. Ever since his election to the Croydon Council, H.T. had been spending an increasing number of evenings away from home, at political rallies and council meetings. H.T.'s political activities not only took him away from Annie, but also struck her as unseemly. Because Annie was a retiring person, with next to no social life, these evenings were lonely. She had come from a large family and found an empty house to be depressing and frightening. In his first novel, *Autumnal Face*, Malcolm described the character who represents his mother in this way: "She always felt in need of some support when she was outside the house; the things indoors had been so pressed into her life that she could never be quite at ease without them."[5]

When H.T. went out for the evening, Annie would wait up for him, her knitting needles clacking rhythmically in the semi-dark. Whether through open conflict or her silent reproachful presence, Annie was determined to exact a price for H.T.'s independent life. Beside her, ensconced as usual in the cosy corner, would be Malcolm. He felt that if he was present, his parents would be less likely to have a row. If he had to go bed, he would nonetheless stay awake, straining to hear his father's arrival. When he heard the quiet sounds of his parents' feet ascending the stairs, he could rest easy.

At some point, Annie's resentment of her husband's life outside the home took the form of sexual jealousy. Clearly the Fabian women, whose bosoms floated free along with rumours of spouse-swapping at the Colony, had conjured up in Annie's mind images of sexual licence. As Malcolm recounts these episodes in his autobiography, it is hard not to laugh at the absurdity of Annie's lurid imaginings. The most bizarre accusation Annie made was that in the house behind theirs, "a maid-servant would sit exposing herself or otherwise sending my father erotic signals" while H.T. worked in the garden on Sunday mornings.[6]

Over the years, Malcolm himself encountered his mother's obsessive attitude towards sex first-hand. Annie was given to making cryptic comments that Malcolm struggled to decipher. When she caught him reading Rousseau's *Confessions* as a boy, she claimed that the author "had been born with his blood boiling". Since Malcolm was only ten or eleven at the time, he could not have made much of this pronouncement. She went on to tell her son that she "would rather see him dead at her feet than doing something or other – what I had no sort of an idea".[7]

In Malcolm's autobiography these anecdotes provide moments of droll humour, but they conceal the darker and more complex story of his sexual development. Growing up in a household of five boys, Malcolm had no experience of women outside what he knew about his mother. Annie, who was given to fantasising about her husband's sexual adventures, was not perhaps the best person to introduce him to female sexuality. Neither parent was physically demonstrative towards the children. H.T., whose attitude towards sex was formed by his own father's irresponsible and anarchic behaviour, was extremely shy about sexuality. There is an episode in *Autumnal Face* in which Dad worries about his daughter Minnie's relationship with a young man named Fred. He intends to explain the facts of life to her, but when the time comes he lacks the nerve. Minnie is left is ignorance.[8]

Malcolm confessed that as an adolescent the only resources he had to help him understand "affairs of the flesh and the heart" were literary: Keats's "The Eve of St Agnes" and Shakespeare's *Antony and Cleopatra*.[9] Of course, Malcolm was hardly unique in the context of his time. Michael Shelden, in his biography of George Orwell, wrote of his subject: "[Orwell's] sexual education was a jumble of misinformation, low jokes, and noble laments for lost love. A boy of his time and social class could not have expected much else."[10]

Malcolm's sexual awakening took place in an atmosphere of sexual repression, fear and ignorance. The result was that he came to associate sex with death, futility and guilt – the opposite of the "free love" ideal of healthy, carefree promiscuity. Like those of many English boys at this time, Malcolm's first sexual experiences may have been homosexual. Homosexual relationships for many boys meant an opportunity to release sexual tension without the complex dangers and emotional challenges posed by the female. From his unpublished diary entries, it would seem that Malcolm's first homosexual encounter might have taken place some time in his adolescence. The passages from this diary, written in India in 1934, are part of a series of recollections of his earliest sexual experiences. The references are ambiguous, leaving it unclear as to whether his first experience of homosexual sex took place when he went to Cambridge University or earlier. Here is one of the few instances where Malcolm, in his autobiography, does not tell the truth. In *Chronicles* he indicates that he never came closer to a homosexual encounter than when a young High-Church ordinand read to him from Swinburne's *Songs Before Sunrise*.[11]

Regardless of when his first sexual experience with another boy took place, there is little evidence from Malcolm's diary entries that any of his homosexual liaisons involved sustained, romantic relationships. He recalls one partner telling him "that I was not good-looking, but taking".[12] Later in the 1934 diary he discovers the homosexual community in Calcutta. This makes him realise that he still has "a touch" of the homosexual in him. As a *"type sympathique"*, he feels that he understands homosexuals quite well.[13]

One thing is not in doubt: throughout his adolescence Malcolm pursued relationships with girls. He even attended Sunday school at a Congregational church because he wanted to be with a girl named Winnie Hall. But the one romantic experience that overshadowed everything else was his encounter with Dora Pitman.

Malcolm met Dora when he was seventeen, shortly before leaving Croydon for Cambridge University.[14] Malcolm's first vision of Dora was burned into his memory. In *Chronicles* he describes the moment in almost Dantean terms:

> I happened to see Dora ... playing tennis on a public court, and instantaneously the whole of existence for me was concentrated on that one face, uniquely beautiful ... At the same time, the scene itself in which I saw her was glorified and became angelic; as though the wire netting of the court were golden mesh, the grass greener and softer than any grass ever before seen, the sound of the tennis ball against the racquets, and the laughter and shouts of the players, joyous and most wonderful. Whatever bodily stirrings accompanied these transports were merged and lost in this larger ecstasy, and I should have been outraged to think that what I felt could be reduced to the dimensions of schoolboy eroticism, with which, inevitably, I had become familiar.[15]

From the photograph of Dora that Malcolm preserved, it is not difficult to see why he might have been transfixed. She has the pert good looks of a "flapper" – heart-shaped face, large liquid eyes, and short blonde hair. She was only sixteen when they met. In the 1934 diary, Malcolm remembered Dora as "full of smiles (perhaps too full) and happy sensuality". Malcolm himself was quite "taking" as a young man: he too had a faun-like sensuality. A damaged photograph of him at sixteen or seventeen with his schoolmates shows Malcolm slouching back against a wall, his face drawn tight in a puckish grin. In the diary he recalled that Dora was so innocent when they first met that when they touched each other "she thought she might become pregnant".[16]

After that initial meeting at the municipal tennis court, Malcolm and Dora spent whatever free time they had together. She was a conventional middle-class girl without any ties to progressive politics. Malcolm liked Dora's father, who would call his wife "Peach Blossom" and play "The Lost Chord" on his cornet. In *Chronicles*, Malcolm describes idyllic outings to pick blackberries and the way his youthful love transfigured the dreary suburban landscape into something magical. She would play the piano, and they would sing the popular songs of the day: "Lean down, lean down, to the water", "There are fairies at the bottom of our garden", "Juanita" and "The Maid of Athens".[17]

The purity of those moments of joy always remained with him, precisely because they were so fleeting. In the event, schoolboy eroticism did insinuate itself into the relationship, as Malcolm acknowledged: "we exasperated one another with the sexual urges we mutually aroused, and then only partially and inadequately, or not at all, satisfied."[18] They never went beyond what might be called "heavy petting". Malcolm, of course, was hardly bound by the conventions of traditional sexual morality; Dora certainly was, and this was enough to prevent them from "going all the way".

Together they sampled a pleasure that Malcolm found delightful: the cinema. Despite his awareness of his father's disapproval of this frivolous medium, Malcolm lost himself in the vicarious passion and glamour of the silver screen. One of the most effective scenes in Malcolm's early novel *Autumnal Face* is a chapter depicting Minnie and Fred on a "date" at the cinema. "Deep in red plush they watched the pictures and listened to their talk. The air was heavy, slightly scented; and darkness enfolded them." Fred's physical advances in the darkness are gently, but persistently repulsed.

The pictures ministered to their exaltation. All they ever wanted was on the screen; the very passion they were miming through advance and repulse was there on the screen before them – vast magnified caresses, barely covered bodies interlocked, a Fred resplendent and a jewelled, lovely Minnie. What a world, they thought; what motor-cars, what dressing and undressing! Each planned a conquest of the world.[19]

In addition to the comedy of lower-middle-class manners, Malcolm has in this passage sketched out the earliest version of his attack on film and television.

After they emerge from the cinema, Minnie and Fred embrace on a bench beneath a statue of Queen Victoria. Fred's sexual desire is aroused, but he cannot satisfy it. Suddenly he fantasises about raping Minnie, forcing her to yield to him. However, with Victoria looking down on them, he manages to restrain himself. He carries on an interior dialogue with himself, full of self-pity and sexual frustration. Fred "was oppressed by that peculiar and devastating sense of futility that comes of inanely awakened passions, of passions that begin in nothingness and end in nothingness".[20] Sex and death, passion and futility, compulsion and guilt: these poles of experience would continue unchanged for the rest of Malcolm's life.

In 1915, when he was twelve, Malcolm had won a scholarship to the Borough Secondary School, which later became Selhurst Grammar School. Part of the examination for this scholarship included an interview with the local Inspector of Schools, "a portentous Scotsman with a mop of white hair whom I held in great awe". Malcolm recalled that his "enemies" hinted darkly that he had won the scholarship because this Inspector was anxious to ingratiate himself with H.T. Muggeridge, a Labour councillor and a member of the Education Committee. It was, he once said, the only examination in which he ever achieved any success.[21]

The Borough Secondary School was not an institution that he would remember with affection. When, fifty years later, Malcolm narrated a BBC documentary about his early life, one scene was shot before a class at Selhurst. Invited by the headmaster to address the class, Malcolm said that "School in my day was a place to get away from as soon as possible. Everything exciting, mysterious, adventurous, happened outside its confines, not within them ... No one ever seems to forget Eton, I easily forgot my Borough Secondary School."[22] What the headmaster and students made of this ill-mannered speech is not known, but it does indicate something of Malcolm's embarrassment at his schooling.

Even as a boy, Malcolm's eye for any disparity between the real and the ideal was acute, as his father knew. That a State school should engage in mimicry of the public schools – organising separate "houses" with prefects, colours and Latin mottoes – struck him, even at the time, as feeble-minded. Most of the regular staff were off fighting in the war, so Malcolm's teachers consisted of an assortment of people who were called to serve as replacements. One elderly mathematics master, who dyed his hair and wore a "frenzied moustache ... desperately flung chalk at us when, as frequently happened, we failed to get his point". One policy at the school for which Malcolm was always grateful was that sports were voluntary. Neither football nor cricket ever appealed to him, then or later in his life. He found all sports to be excruciatingly boring.

When in due course Malcolm was joined at the school by his younger brothers Eric and Jack, they became known as Muggeridge Major, Muggeridge Minor and Muggeridge Minimus. One incident from his schooldays earned Malcolm the admiration not only of his brothers, but of the entire school. The headmaster, a man named Hillyer, was known to have a sadistic love of caning boys. These caning sessions, held either in his study or in the library, became routine events for many of the boys. In order to prevent the boys from putting exercise books in their trousers to soften the blows, Hillyer would have them lower their trousers to the ground. One day, when a caning session was in progress in the library, Malcolm walked in, grabbed the cane out of Hillyer's hands, broke it, and walked out without uttering a word. Nothing was ever said about the incident, but it made him, for a time, the school hero.[23]

Throughout his adolescence, Malcolm's education took place largely outside the classroom. Literature provided solace and inspiration. In addition to his father's recitations of Dickens and Shakespeare, Malcolm read widely. For Christmas in 1914, he received a copy of *A Pageant of English Poetry*. In his autobiography, he also recalls his love for Bunyan's *Pilgrim's Progress*. When he read literature, Malcolm sought out the passages that attained mystical vision – the "timeless moments" of insight and transfiguration. This would remain the pattern of his appreciation for literature. Malcolm never developed a taste for literary form, which may explain why his own forays into fiction were such failures. But he would return, again and again, to the visionary writers: Bunyan, Herbert, Blake and Tolstoy. He cherished their epigrammatic wisdom and their ability to fuse a simplicity of image and diction with intense spiritual longing.

In these adolescent years, Malcolm was also reading something in secret, a book he did not want his father to know about: the Bible. This remarkable fact, which he mentioned only twice in his many autobiographical accounts of his life (and then only in passing), has been overlooked by most of the commentators on Malcolm's life and writings. In his last book, *Conversion*, he writes of himself in the third person, as "The Boy".

> The Boy acquires a Bible of his own and reads it surreptitiously, as it might have been some forbidden book like *Fanny Hill*. He puts a brown paper cover on it so that no one will know what particular book he is reading; he marks passages, and strangest of all, he takes it to bed with him, opened at some passage that has particularly impressed and moved him, as though it will protect and comfort him through the night hours when, as often happens . . . he is sleepless, turning over and over in his mind some dilemma or fear while on edge at the strange sounds the night holds. Years later he comes across this Bible among his books, and notes how crumpled and torn it is, and how the worst ravages are in the passages relating to the Passion – there, stains that might be from tears.[24]

In addition to the Bible, Malcolm also found himself strangely moved by the edition of Dante's *Divine Comedy* in his father's library. The lurid, often apocalyptic illustrations by Gustave Doré haunted his imagination.

Malcolm's decision to keep his Bible-reading secret was a natural one. H.T. felt that religion in general, and Christianity in particular, was a benign social force because its stress on compassion would lead in the direction of the welfare state. But he would have been shocked and concerned if he had discovered Malcolm reading the Bible with such intensity. To H.T. and his political comrades, Jesus was admired as a rebel who challenged the ruling class, a champion of the downtrodden. The main problem with Christianity, according to these tolerant socialists, was that it believed in an other-worldly heaven which the individual attains after a lifetime of spiritual pilgrimage. The Fabian heaven, on the other hand, was firmly grounded in this world – it merely lay in the future, and would be attained through a lifetime of political action.

Malcolm's only experience of organised religion as a youth – aside from his Sunday school attendance in pursuit of girls – came during his father's election campaigns. H.T. found political allies among Quakers and progressive clergymen. Because of their influence with their congregations, Church leaders were worth cultivating, especially because some people associated the Labour Party's progressivism with lax morality and godlessness. These clerics found common ground with H.T. because of their desire to "make the world a better place". In his autobiography, Malcolm recalled that there "was a sort of implicit pact whereby God was left out on the understanding that my father would accept the other's credentials as a progressive". He draws a verbal caricature of these clerics in which they call for "more money on education, slum clearance, welfare services, and so on. That's loving our neighbour, isn't it? As for loving God – we'll see about that in due course, ha! ha! ha!"[25]

It may be questioned whether Malcolm, as an adolescent, had developed such a sardonic view of the clergy. But it was just at this time that he might have been open to a sensitive minister or priest. He was poring over the Bible in his bed at night, aware of a very real struggle going on inside him between the flesh and the spirit. The emotional pressures of his confused sexual life – including his unconsummated desire for Dora and, quite possibly, the guilty release of his sexual liaisons with other schoolboys – were intense. It is hardly surprising that the passages in the Bible he underlined include St Paul's "For to be carnally minded is death, but to be spiritually minded is life and peace." And: "For the flesh lusteth against the spirit and the spirit against the flesh; and these are contrary, the one to the other, so that ye cannot do the things that ye would."[26] In the midst of this sexual crisis, Malcolm probably saw these politicised clergy as blind to their own mission: the care of souls.

H.T.'s ignorance of his son's struggles with sex and religion helped to open an emotional distance between them, but Malcolm's adolescence was not all morbidity and dread. Father and son remained close. When Malcolm was old enough, he would often travel to London to spend part of the day with H.T. Malcolm would make his way to the offices of MacIntyre, Hogg and up to his father's office.

> When he saw me, his face always lit up, as it had a way of doing, quite suddenly, thereby completely altering his appearance; transforming him from a rather cavernous, shrunken man into someone boyish and ardent. He would leap agilely off his stool, wave gaily to his colleague . . . and we would make off together. There was always about these excursions an element of being on an illicit spree, which greatly added to their pleasure. They were the most enjoyable episodes in all my childhood.[27]

Malcolm remembered one evening when H.T. brought him to a dinner meeting where the guest of honour was G.K. Chesterton. About twenty-five people gathered at an Italian restaurant in London for dinner and an address by the corpulent master of paradox and champion of Christian orthodoxy. Malcolm did not remember Chesterton's topic, though the evening was most likely a political one for, if G.K.C. was opposed to socialism, he was also a vocal critic of industrial capitalism. What Malcolm did recall was his awe before such an accomplished writer as Chesterton. "To be a writer, to have published books, far exceeded, in my eyes, any other kind of fame."[28] Within a few years, Chesterton's writings would help to shape Malcolm's understanding of the Christian faith.

In an early draft of his autobiography, Malcolm wrote that H.T. was given to "innocently showing off before me . . . In recounting this visit of mine to his dining club, he would describe how I had joined in the conversation with dazzling precocity. To the best of my recollection, I did not utter."[29] H.T. was not only proud of Malcolm, but encouraged him to participate in such occasions, and even to deliver stump speeches during electoral campaigns. It was at this time that H.T. set his political sights higher. He had been on the Croydon Council since 1911, and had been appointed Justice of the Peace in 1913. But in 1918 H.T. ran for Parliament for South Croydon. He was defeated by the Conservative candidate – the first of four consecutive failed attempts to achieve a seat in Parliament (the other elections being in 1922, 1923 and 1924, all losses to a Conservative candidate in what was essentially a safe seat). It would not be until 1929 that H.T. would realise his dream, and enter Parliament as Labour MP for Romford in Essex.

One of the epochal political events of this time was the Russian

Revolution, but ironically, few of H.T.'s circle paid much attention to the upheaval in the East. In looking back on this period, Malcolm tried to account for this blasé attitude. The Revolution occurred during the First World War, so Europeans were preoccupied with their own political and cultural catastrophes. Bolsheviks like Lenin were thought of at that time – even by Fabians and socialists – as little better than brigands; they were not taken seriously. It was only later, when the Soviet Union had hardened into a totalitarian regime, that intellectuals like Shaw and the Webbs became enamoured of the "Workers' Paradise".[30]

Lenin and his comrades did have one fervent young admirer in Croydon, however: Malcolm Muggeridge. Whereas his father was a gradualist, Malcolm was by temperament an anarchist; political revolution had an apocalyptic appeal that he found irresistible. He compared the Russian Revolution to the French Revolution, as described in the books of Carlyle and Dickens. He somehow ignored the negative portrayal of the French Revolution in these authors, and conceived of the Russian experience as a romantic struggle of noble peasants against cruel, sadistic masters. He dreamed of going to Russia to join in the struggle to make it a brave new world. It was a dream that would turn into a nightmare when Malcolm actually went to the Soviet Union as a reporter, fifteen years later.

As Malcolm's secondary school education was coming to completion, a decision had to be made about his future. Though he always spoke of his lacklustre academic performance, Malcolm was far more articulate and intellectually curious than the majority of those in his school. He had devoured his father's library and had already developed his capacity for public speaking at election time. Neither of his older brothers, Douglas and Stanley, had gone on to university. But Malcolm was different. H.T. may have resisted sending Malcolm to a public school out of egalitarian principle; he would have needed a full scholarship, in any case. But at this point in Malcolm's life, the usual route to the highest levels of intellectual and political life went through Oxford and Cambridge Universities.

In his autobiography Malcolm indicates that the decision to apply to Cambridge was made almost casually by his father. This is highly unlikely. Since his infancy, Malcolm had been his father's favourite, a Superman-in-the-making. It may be that H.T. did not want to appear too eager to send Malcolm to Cambridge: there are many occasions where Malcolm was quick to point out any discrepancy between his father's beliefs and his actions. But the decision was made; Malcolm studied for the entrance examination for Cambridge. The only subjects available for post-matriculation study at the Borough Secondary School were the "Natural Sciences" – chemistry, physics and zoology. Though Malcolm had little knowledge or interest in any of these subjects, they were his only option. He passed the examination, and was accepted at Selwyn College, Cambridge.

« 3 »

Outsider

1920–1924

MALCOLM NEVER REFERRED to his years in Cambridge with any emotion other than contempt. In describing his university career, he would use words like "tedium", "boredom", "inertia", "lacklustre", "decay" and "decomposition". Much of this is retrospective editorialising, but even at the time Malcolm was often deeply unhappy – lonely, confused, alienated. In his father's eyes, Cambridge was to be the training ground that would lead his son on to a brilliant career as a Fabian intellectual. But once again father and son perceived the world in vastly different ways. At Cambridge Malcolm felt himself to be an outsider, separated by his class and ideology from the social cliques and political inner circles. Without either the inner confidence or a public platform, he could not attack the insiders, so he withdrew into himself.

Malcolm's time at Cambridge, however, should not be seen only through his own retrospective distaste. Despite the darkness and confusion of these years, Malcolm found much to sustain and feed his imaginative and spiritual dimensions. Malcolm may have spent most of his time lingering in the university's shadows, but he also managed to make a lifelong friendship with Alec Vidler, experience a conversion to the Christian faith, develop his facility as a writer and speaker, and sharpen his critique of the modern era.

Cambridge was just recovering from the devastation of World War I when Malcolm came up in 1920. The colleges were full of veterans who had returned from the horrors of the Western Front to finish their education. Malcolm and others his age found these veterans to be almost a different species; their experiences made them seem older and more serious. Cambridge in the 1920s was also an institution finally emerging from the Victorian era. It was in this decade that many of Cambridge University's brightest young intellectuals would turn against the moral, spiritual and political traditions of their country and emerge as socialists or communists. In the case of figures such as Anthony Blunt, Guy Burgess and Kim Philby this led to their recruitment as Soviet agents and to their astonishing success in penetrating to the heart of the British secret service. Malcolm too considered himself a man of the Left, but his own social background and character led him to identify more with the specific causes and grievances of the working class than with the grand utopian schemes of aspiring intellectuals from the upper classes.

Selwyn College mirrored Malcolm's own position at Cambridge: it was a part of the university, but as a new foundation it lacked the social status of the oldest colleges, such as King's, Trinity and St John's. Founded in 1882, the college was named after George Augustus Selwyn, the first Anglican Bishop of New Zealand and "one of the heroes of the Victorian Church".[1] Designed by the Victorian architect, Sir Arthur Blomfield, Selwyn's red-brick, Tudor-style buildings have been described as offering "a typically sensible, modest contrast to Keble [College, Oxford]".[2] Another critic has written: "The pseudo-Tudor orthodoxy of Selwyn's buildings, manifested in a not very attractive brick, inspires a yawn."[3]

In 1920, when Malcolm came up, Selwyn was not yet officially a college; rather it was known as a "public hostel". But in fact the college was thoroughly integrated into the life of the university. Selwyn students attended lectures and tutorials given by dons at the other colleges, and participated in university sports and clubs.

Selwyn retained a distinct character, however. Though it was not a theological college or seminary, its student population had always included a large number of candidates for ordination. Selwyn also required attendance at more chapel services than any of the other colleges. The college was not restricted to members of the Church of England, but it expected all of its students to be baptised and confirmed. Malcolm had already passed an examination in "divinity", based on an eighteenth-century work of apologetics, Paley's *Evidences*.[4] But an element of mystery surrounds the circumstances of Malcolm's baptism and confirmation. According to the parish magazine of St Peter's, Croydon, Malcolm was baptised on June 19, 1920, before coming up to Cambridge. Several later issues of this parish magazine have been lost, so no record has been preserved as to the exact date of his confirmation. But there is also evidence that Malcolm went through a second service after he had already been at Cambridge for two terms. The service was held at Queen's College Chapel on March 6, 1921, and it certainly involved confirmation, and might also have included baptism. Why Malcolm would have gone through these rites twice – a theological redundancy – is unclear and likely to remain a mystery.

In addition to the education of ordinands, one of the founding purposes of Selwyn was to "provide for simple and inexpensive standards of living so as to enable less affluent parents to send their sons there".[5] This spartan regime certainly enabled H.T. to send Malcolm to Cambridge. But it also reinforced Malcolm's sense of being an outsider at the university. When the Dean of Selwyn addressed the college freshmen in the chapel, he said, in passing, that none of the students at Selwyn were "likely ever to be in want". Malcolm, who had inherited his father's insecurity about money, found the Dean's words startling.[6] Thrust into an environment where many of his peers could afford to entertain more frequently and lavishly than he, Malcolm determined that he would not be outdone. By the end of his first year, he had run out of money. It was an issue that would prove a source of tension and pain between Malcolm and his father.

Malcolm would later speak of the tedium of his Cambridge days, but in his first year, at least, he threw himself into the traditional habits and activities of a Cambridge student. Since he did not yet have a sense of his own identity, he began his university career by attempting to conform to the social and cultural norms that predominated at Cambridge. His letters to his new friend Alec Vidler are filled with gushing enthusiasm, their language marked by upper-class words like "topping", "ripping", "ever so jolly".[7] According to his brother Jack, Malcolm came home from Cambridge at the Christmas vacation a different person. "He had acquired a high-pitched affected accent, the parents were Pater and Mater and there were signs of being uneasy about our lower-middle-class status."[8] Despite his aversion to sports, Malcolm volunteered to row for Selwyn – the sport most clearly associated with the public schools. Finally, there is the fact that he took up another public school tradition: homosexuality. Once again, Malcolm was trying to join in, just as he appeared to be singing hymns heartily at grammar school.

In his first months at Cambridge, Malcolm continued his secret grappling with Christianity. H.T. would undoubtedly have felt at ease about Malcolm's baptism and confirmation, since they were requirements for his matriculation. But Malcolm took them more seriously.

Away at Cambridge, Malcolm no longer had to repress his spiritual longings. This led him to an intensely emotional, if solitary and idiosyncratic, acceptance of the Christian faith.

Because his autobiographical writings consistently misrepresent this period, it is important to establish the nature of his conversion. In his own autobiography, Alec Vidler wrote: "I do not consider that in his autobiography [Malcolm] has adequately assessed the sincerity and depth of his initiation into Christian faith and practice at this time ..."⁹ It is important to note that Malcolm did not meet Vidler until the Lent term, less than two months before the confirmation service took place in March. Though their friendship developed rapidly, it is clear that Vidler could not have single-handedly brought Malcolm to the faith. The ground had already been prepared in those nights in Croydon with the Bible wrapped in brown paper.

Malcolm's tutor in theology was S.C. Carpenter, a man described by Vidler as "amiable ... with a gracious style and liberal sym-pathies".¹⁰ It is doubtful that Carpenter's catechising had much of an impact on Malcolm's mind. He had never received any religious instruction as a boy, and he showed no inclination or aptitude for the study of theology. Rather, he was drawn to the "wild extravagances of faith".¹¹ He understood instinctively the war between flesh and spirit which afflicted St Paul; he was already wracked by sexual guilt and a confused sexual identity. Like St Paul, Malcolm yearned for an epiphany that would resolve the dualism in his soul.

Malcolm's faith had grown like an exotic orchid in a hothouse, without the usual contexts of family and Church. Though this faith would wither and bloom many times in his life, Alec Vidler played a crucial role in helping Malcolm sink roots that would survive. Vidler was a native of the picturesque town of Rye on England's south coast. His temperament and background could not have been more different from Malcolm's. Vidler came from a relatively untroubled middle-class background. He had attended a modest public school where he determined on a vocation to the priesthood in the Church of England. When they met in January of 1921, Vidler was in the third and final year of his theology degree. Vidler was a remarkably serene man, confident in his faith without appearing to be rigidly dogmatic or extreme in his views. Malcolm responded immediately to Vidler's self-assurance and untroubled faith, two characteristics he utterly lacked. At different times in his life, Malcolm would become deeply attached to a dynamic figure, older and more asssured than himself, someone who bolstered his own faith.

Vidler, on the other hand, sensed in Malcolm a restless, incisive and charming personality. "I also detected in those early days that potentially he had a kind of genius as a talker and writer and even as a seer."[12] They spent a great deal of time together in the Lent and Easter terms, playing tennis and attending concerts. Malcolm had to spend some time teaching in London as part of his degree requirements, and he wrote to Vidler about how depressing the city and the school had been. He tells Vidler that he has found consolation in meditating upon the "One Who Died".[13] Often in his letters to Vidler, Malcolm asks for prayers and guidance. "Pray for me Alec for sometimes I cannot pray – your prayers are so wonderful." Later in the same letter, Malcolm writes that "Jesus is still on his cross, I crucify him every day of my life."[14]

Vidler found Malcolm's political ideas intriguing. Unlike many would-be clerics, Vidler was not content to remain in an ivory tower. He had some sympathy for the younger breed of Anglican priests who were attempting to bring the gospel and social assistance to the poorest slums of London. When H.T. visited Cambridge in the Easter term, Vidler found himself entranced by the older man's vision of a socialist future. In his own diary Vidler wrote: "Mr Muggeridge I fell in love with right away – in fact I think I had done so long before I ever saw him" – thanks to Malcolm's descriptions. H.T. wrote to Vidler a few months later in the high-flown rhetoric that had so delighted him during the visit: "The next revolution must be a scientific one. The old barricade business is played out. Bombs only blow up – they don't build up – and the only successful revolution is the one that constructs. It must be based upon the enlightened Will of the mass of the people – and so more power to those who like you want to change the mental, moral, and industrial outlook of the individual minds!"[15] Malcolm, however, was no friend of gradualism. His own political inclinations were too anarchic. "Sometimes, Alec, I am a Bolshevik: it sometimes seems to me that the only way to wake these people from the rut that they are in, is to kill some, to give them a shock."[16] H.T. was grateful to Vidler not only for responding to his political idealism, but also because he felt Vidler would be a steadying influence on the moody, mercurial Malcolm.

Malcolm and Vidler visited each other's homes in the summer of 1921. At Rye, they bathed in the sea. One day they found the beach deserted, then stripped and went for a swim. No sooner had they entered the water than a woman and her adolescent daughter came and sat on the beach. The ladies seemed immovable, and forced the young men to swim for much of the afternoon.[17] When they came to the house in Birdhurst Gardens, Vidler loved to hear H.T.'s rhetoric and found himself supporting the Labour Party.

Vidler had passed his tripos examinations in May and had determined that he would attend theological college – the next step before ordination – at Wells. He could have gone to nearby Ely to continue his studies, but he felt that Ely was too closely associated with the Anglo-Catholic party in the Church of England. Though he was an Anglo-Catholic himself, Vidler decided it would be more prudent to go to Wells, which was more moderate and would not mark him as a proponent of a particular faction. The summer was a relatively happy time for Malcolm, but when he returned to Cambridge in the autumn, he felt devastated by the loss of Vidler's companionship. In fact, if Vidler had gone to Ely, he might have helped to prevent Malcolm from descending into moral and emotional chaos. But it was not to be.

One sign that Malcolm was possessive in his relationship with Vidler is that he did not tell his friend about his relationship with Dora Pitman for six months, and then only by letter. In July, just as Vidler was preparing to leave for Wells, Malcolm wrote: "Am fearfully in love with a charming little girl named Dora . . ."[18] Before Malcolm had gone up to Cambridge, his father had wanted him to sign an agreement that he would not see Dora for three months. He was worried that Dora was not an appropriate match for Malcolm and would only distract him from his studies at Cambridge.[19] Malcolm didn't sign the agreement. Though they had their share of quarrels and angry partings, Malcolm and Dora would remain romantically attached throughout Malcolm's years at Cambridge and beyond.

A few of Dora's letters from the period are preserved. They are effusive and affectionate, full of the same language (everything is "ripping" and "topping") that Malcolm had picked up at Cambridge. When Dora eventually got to know Vidler, she would write to him as well. After a visit to Cambridge in the spring of 1923, when she had tea with Malcolm's friends, she wrote to Vidler: "The ripping part is that they know Malcolm must not get excited, and they look after him in quite a motherly way. They gave M orders not to race down the platform when the train started."[20] There was some question at this period as to whether Malcolm had an "inflated" heart, and should avoid physical strain. Dora herself seemed to take a somewhat motherly approach to Malcolm, seeing herself as the steadfast woman who would care for the brilliant, rising literary man.

Dora appears to have been faithful to Malcolm, waiting for the time when he would be able to marry her, but it cannot be said that he was equally devoted to her. Because he was able to count on her devotion, he tended to take her for granted. Then there was, of course, the fact of his homosexual relationships. Whether he had sexual encounters with other boys in Croydon remains unclear. At Cambridge, however, he met young men from the public school culture who accepted homosexual sex as a normal practice, and he decided to join in. In his autobiography he notes: "The university, when I was there, was very largely a projection of public school life and mores, and a similar atmosphere of homosexuality tended to prevail."[21] Malcolm's faun-like good looks would certainly have been attractive to others. There is little evidence, however, that Malcolm's sexual relationships with other young men involved deep emotional involvements. With one of his partners – the "pretty boy of the college in my year" – he went to parties and expeditions to the countryside. But this liaison was short-lived.[22]

Given Malcolm's relationships to other men at Cambridge, the question naturally arises: was Malcolm's relationship to Alec Vidler homosexual in orientation? There is evidence, in the form of a letter, that Malcolm at one point did make overtures to Alec. The letter speaks in flowery language of Malcolm's desire to carry Alec off to a cottage by the sea.[23] Even by the standards of the time this letter seems to move well beyond the bounds of male friendship. But there is no evidence that Alec ever welcomed or encouraged a homosexual relationship. Though he was never to marry, Vidler lived his entire life as a celibate. It was common in those days for High-Church Anglican priests to emulate Roman Catholicism in certain respects, including priestly celibacy. It is clear that Malcolm and Vidler were drawn together – and remained together as friends – because of their intellectual and spiritual interests. Vidler was deeply concerned about Malcolm's volatile temperament and did his best to try to steady Malcolm.

Malcolm might well have wondered whether he had any identity at all in these years. To Dora he played the sophisticated university man, waiting to make his mark and sweep her off into a glorious future. To

Vidler he was a spiritual seeker, confessing his sinfulness and longing for enlightenment. To his father he was a Fabian-in-training, joining debating societies and stunning the crowds with his oratory. He lived secret lives, hiding something from each of those closest to him. He would never be entirely free from the sense that he was playing a role. Here, as in so many situations in his life, Malcolm's inner honesty about himself brought torment and depression and a desire for deliverance.

Fifteen years after he left Cambridge, in a fictional memoir, Malcolm wrote about this shifting sense of identity. The memoir is written by a fictitious Anglican clergyman who is clearly based on Alec Vidler. The description of Malcolm's Cambridge years is revealing:

> At Cambridge he was popular, but his friendships had a way of beginning very warm and then soon cooling. The first impression he made was of great amiability and cheerfulness; and it was only when his face was looked at closely that its background of irritability and restless melancholy was apparent ... He had been at a south London Secondary School, and spoke with a pronounced cockney accent, of which, however, he soon rid himself, except in moments of excitement ... It came as a surprise to me that he was morbidly class-conscious. Once he came into my rooms and burst into a flood of passionate weeping because an undergraduate had mistaken him for a laboratory attendant.[24]

By his second year, Malcolm had decided that he would not attempt to make a brilliant public career at Cambridge. H.T. paid for a life membership to the Cambridge Union debating society, but the Union was so thoroughly dominated by public school types that Malcolm did not have the will to try to break into that exclusive set. The high point of his career at Cambridge was a Union debate in which the proposition was "That the twentieth century shows a general improvement on the nineteenth". Malcolm proposed the motion and won. After this moment of glory, however, he spent most of his time in a discussion club known as The Friars, becoming its president in 1923.

The one ambition that never left him in these years was his desire to become a writer. There is no evidence among his papers that he published anything in university publications or elsewhere, but the feeling that he was destined to write was persistent and powerful. What he did begin to write was a series of sketches and short stories.

The first of these would not be published until 1928. As early as 1921, he wrote to Vidler about his impulse to stand up and "speak the burning words within me". Later he would write: "Alec, dearest, I have seen visions and felt calls lately that I dare not even face myself. God has some destiny mapped out . . ."[25]

In the summer of 1922, Malcolm came face to face with death. His older brother Stanley, who had served in World War I in the Royal Flying Corps, rode a motorcycle to work every day. On August 19, a policeman knocked on the door at Birdhurst Gardens, just as Malcolm and his father were finishing their breakfast. He told them that Stanley had had a serious accident and was in the hospital. It was decided that Malcolm and H.T. should go to him, but that Annie should stay at home. The version of this story in an early draft of Malcolm's autobiography is more raw and immediate than the published one.

> A policeman came to the house to tell us about it; a figure of doom, whose head, when he took his helmet off, looked like John the Baptist's on a platter . . . My father and I went together to the Croydon General Hospital, where my brother had been taken. On our way there, we passed a crossing-sweeper, whom I passed every day on my way to school. He was paralysed, and could only make indistinct noises impossible to understand. People threw him pennies, and we boys tormented him. When he saw my father and me that particular morning, his movements became convulsive, and words poured out of him in a flurry of troubled incoherence. I knew then that the accident had taken place at his crossing. In the hospital a screen had been put round my brother. When he breathed, he made gurgling noises in a tube inserted in his throat. These, as we waited, became as troubled and tumultuous as the crossing-sweeper's speech. Then [they] stopped.[26]

On the way back from the hospital, H.T. said to Malcolm in a "ruminative" voice: "I'm very resilient."[27] This phrase, so typical of his father's stoicism, brought tears to Malcolm's eyes for the first time that day. Within a few weeks, H.T. was running, for the second time, for a seat in Parliament. Malcolm was not especially close to Stanley, but the shock of this evidence of mortality affected him deeply.

In the summer of 1922, Vidler had returned from Wells to

Cambridge, where he had arranged to spend the last six months before his ordination to the priesthood. Vidler's return was to have several important consequences for Malcolm. It gave them a chance to cement their friendship; Vidler always had a steadying effect on the volatile Malcolm. But Vidler also acted as a sort of confessor and spiritual director. They discussed Malcolm's problems and ambitions. One topic that came up often was whether Malcolm might have a vocation to the priesthood. The idea had apparently occurred to Malcolm quite early. Back in Croydon, he had become an admirer of the work of the Reverend E. A. Phillips, who worked among the urban poor. With his skills as a speaker and budding social critic, the priesthood seemed to offer a spiritual outlet for Malcolm's idealism. Even at this age, Malcolm found more inner satisfaction at the idea of being a preacher than socialist academic or Labour MP. Malcolm even began going to daily Eucharist in Croydon while at home on vacation. When he told his father that he wanted to become a monk, H.T. encouraged him to do so as quickly as possible, since his university expenses would come to an end.[28]

When Vidler came back to Cambridge, he took up residence at the Oratory of the Good Shepherd on Lady Margaret Road. This too was to have a significant impact on Malcolm's life. The Oratory was an association of unmarried Anglican priests and laymen, founded in Cambridge in 1912. Though its name would seem to imply a religious order, the constitution of the Oratory was rather informal. According to one historian, the Oratory "was not, and is not, in fact a community at all, nor is it a guild, nor an order, nor could it have been in origin anything but English". They lived simply and ascetically, but maintained a good deal of common sense concerning practical matters. The "offices" of the liturgical day were said at the appointed times, and periods of silence were maintained. There was a Superior and a Chapter General, but meetings were rare. Many Oratorians lived in community, but others were spread out around the world, engaged in a variety of missions.[29]

The Oratorians were primarily scholars, writers, preachers and teachers. They balanced a love of traditional liturgy and sacraments with a strong sense of social involvement. Vidler would eventually become an Oratorian, and his subsequent career as a theologian closely followed the outlines of the Oratory's philosophy. The house on Lady Margaret Road was large enough to accommodate a number of students in addition to the Oratorians themselves. "It was an unbeautiful, inconvenient, poorly lit red-brick building, with very cold passages and a tangled garden."[30]

Vidler introduced Malcolm to the Oratory and was undoubtedly the one who persuaded him to consider living there himself. Given Malcolm's depression, guilt and lack of self-control, it would have appeared to both of them an ideal place for Malcolm to regain his spiritual and emotional bearings. As he wrote in his autobiography: "I fell into this way of life with great contentment, enjoying its remoteness from the University, and its relative austerity as far as food and domestic comforts were concerned. Austerity has always made me happy, and its opposite, miserable."[31]

Vidler would leave Cambridge at the end of 1922 for Newcastle-upon-Tyne, where he was to be ordained and given his first assignment. On the eve of Vidler's ordination, Malcolm sent him a note which stated: "You are a chosen vessel of the Lord."[32] Not long after this Malcolm moved into the Oratory. He missed Vidler's influence and companionship badly; it would be over forty years before they would live near each other, when they were white-haired and hard of hearing.

Malcolm found in one of the Oratorians a genial, if somewhat eccentric, spiritual figure who helped to make up somewhat for the loss of Vidler. The Revd Wilfred Knox was an Anglo-Catholic priest who shared Vidler's concern for the poor. He was one of four famous brothers, who included Ronald, an Anglican priest who converted to Roman Catholicism; Dillwyn, a genius in the art of cryptography, who broke enemy codes in two world wars; and Eddie, who would become the editor of *Punch*, a job that Malcolm would eventually take on. Wilfred was an eccentric but lovable figure, who would invariably be seen pottering in the garden of the Oratory House between 2 and 4 p.m. every day. When Malcolm first came upon Wilfred, he was "greeted with an almost unintelligible remark out of the side of the mouth, followed by a number of disjointed sentences. Could they connect? Well, that was just the fascination."[33]

Malcolm would frequently act as an altar server for Wilfred Knox. In the liturgy of word and sacrament, Malcolm found something close to peace. In journals and diaries kept towards the end of his life, he would return to those moments at the altar of Oratory House, sensing that a seed of faith had been planted then that would not flower for a long time to come. One day, raking leaves in the garden with Fr Knox, the older man raised the question of a priestly vocation. Malcolm felt uncomfortable and inadequate, asking what purpose he could serve. "You can persuade people to do things," Knox said. But when Malcolm pressed him about what things these might be, he let the matter drop.[34]

Life at Oratory House and his continuing friendship with Vidler and Wilfred Knox, though they might have had a calming effect, did not transform Malcolm's personality. It is not clear how long his homosexual activities continued, but other aspects of his life careered out of control, like that runaway train in his childish story. By the autumn of 1923 he had fallen badly into debt and quarrelled with his father, storming around the house at Birdhurst Gardens. He wrote to Vidler, asking for a loan, because H.T. had already paid off so many of Malcolm's debts. Vidler, who seemed to believe a firm approach was necessary in these matters, refused the request and suggested that Malcolm return to his father, like the Prodigal Son, and confess everything. After he had done so, he wrote back to Vidler: "My pater was very decent about it – didn't rave, just seemed resigned. That was gall to me."[35] Malcolm was torn between shame and rage. He knew that he was being unfair to his father, but he also recognised, as he wrote to Vidler, that he had a tendency towards self-pity that prevented positive change.

During his years at Cambridge, there was one thing Malcolm could do to show his love for his father. He could make speeches for him when he ran for a seat in Parliament. These were tumultuous years in British politics: the Conservative government was tottering under the inept leadership of figures like Bonar Law and Stanley Baldwin. A series of political crises forced elections in 1922, 1923 and 1924. H.T. contested each of these elections and lost every one to the Conservative candidate for South Croydon. As he grew older, Malcolm came to see his father's limitations more clearly, but he also found himself aware of his father's vulnerability and touching persistence. Don Quixote would be one of Malcolm's lifelong icons, symbolising an idealism doomed to failure, yet innocent and even mystical in its purity. In these elections, Malcolm could now step up on to the fragile platform at the end of Surrey Street, practise the art of rhetoric and feel his father's proud gaze.

In December 1923, Malcolm took his pass degree at Cambridge. He had persisted with the course in natural science even though he could have switched his subject at any time. By the time he discovered this, he had been too embarrassed and diffident to make the change. He had, however, worked to get a "Special" degree in English Literature.

In addition, he needed to spend a few extra months in order to obtain a teaching diploma. This was necessary because teaching was a requirement of the government grant he had received.

As the end of his time at Cambridge drew closer, Malcolm knew that Alec Vidler and Wilfred Knox were expecting him to enter the priesthood. Though Malcolm may have had some genuine impulse to move in this direction, it is likely that he went along with the idea in order to please Vidler and Knox – to tell them what they wanted to hear. Finding his bluff called, Malcolm began to distance himself from his friends and their staunch Christian faith. In November of 1923, Malcolm wrote a long letter to Vidler, setting out their differences.

> You're so lucky in a sense because having one great belief in life must be wonderful. I ask myself sometimes if I believe anything and then once again the guts question comes in; because it takes guts to believe – I suppose God willed that ... When anything happens you look at it through your belief and are strengthened. I see it naked and shudder ... I expect life to be unsatisfactory; I expect to sin and to hate myself but don't like being a worm.[36]

It was at this time that Malcolm built one of the arguments he was to use for decades as a reason to remain outside the doors of the institutional Church. In his critique of the decadence of bourgeois society, the hypocrisy and complacency of Churches and churchmen featured prominently. How he squared this with his concrete experience of Vidler, Knox and the Oratory is unclear. These men and their religious community were very much a part of the institutional Church, and yet they also manifested a freedom from rigid, conventional attitudes. Whether he decided to enter the priesthood or not, Malcolm could have found room in the Church for political engagement as well as sacramental life. But the call to commit oneself to the ordered life of the Church involved obligations that Malcolm felt unable to fulfil.

Malcolm wrote often of his lack of "guts", his indecisiveness. As late as the spring of 1924, he continued to vacillate about a vocation to the priesthood.

> All my thoughts and feelings about the injustices and sorrows of this world have come to a head so that I feel I must give my life to doing what I can. How I can best serve God at present I do not

know. I feel as though it will mean my giving up everything and being ordained and going into the slums. Of course I have had to tell Dora that I may not be able to marry her and she has been splendid about it. You see I feel that unless I do something extreme – burn my boats so to speak – I shall never do anything but talk.[37]

He went on a retreat with an Anglican monk named Fr Vernon, whose monastery was located in Stanford-le-Hope. Malcolm noted in one of his letters that he would obey whatever Fr Vernon commanded him to do. No record of Fr Vernon's counsel survives.

Dora was another factor. Her physical attractiveness and loyalty had not changed in Malcolm's years at Cambridge, but his perception of her had altered considerably. She seems to have represented a more conventional life that he could fall back on if he lacked the "guts" for boat-burning. His association with the Oratory gave him a ready excuse for telling her that he might not be able to marry her. Her fidelity in the face of this cavalier treatment is remarkable.

Then, in April 1924, Malcolm met W.E.S. Holland of the Church Missionary Society. One of the leading churchmen in the mission field, Holland had come to Cambridge in search of recruits to teach at Union Christian College in India. Malcolm immediately sensed a possible escape from the dilemmas that faced him: marriage, priesthood and the difficult question of how he should make his way in the world. According to his autobiography, his decision to accept this offer was immediate, but this is not quite true. He engaged in an intense burst of correspondence with Vidler on what he should do. At this point in his life, Vidler played a more crucial role than H.T. in Malcolm's decisions.

Malcolm set out the reasons for going. He needed to teach in order to repay his grant. English literature, which he would be teaching, was a "pet hobby" of his. Moreover, the college was an enlightened institution run by the Anglican Church – a Christian community not unlike the Oratory. He acknowledged that Vidler and Knox had great hopes that he would join the Oratory and help found an Oratory College. But he argued that the Oratory itself was still uncertain of its own identity: for example, would it allow married members or not?[38]

Vidler was not convinced by Malcolm's reasoning. When Malcolm announced his decision to take the position in India, Vidler wrote back in a harsh, uncompromising tone: "I do not disguise my regret. Your justification of the action you propose to take seems to me to be an excuse for doing something which has caught your imagination. Rather than as a rational case for doing your duty."[39] Vidler felt that Malcolm's lack of "guts" was leading him to shirk his responsibility. This exchange provides an insight into Vidler's somewhat paternal role in Malcolm's life, but it also shows the limitation of such a relationship. Malcolm, after all, had completed four years at Cambridge and proved his skills as a persuasive speaker. He needed Vidler's approval and guidance, but now that he was about to set out into the larger world, it was important for Malcolm to feel that he was his own man.

The decision to go to India cannot simply be put down under the category of Malcolm's "urge to be gone". A number of factors played a role in this decision. The relationship with Dora was static, but there seemed to be no reason to call it off; marriage to Dora was a fall-back position at best. He was clearly not prepared to make that lifetime commitment to the priesthood. Then, on the positive side, it should be noted that India appealed to Malcolm's imagination. Despite its being the "Jewel in the Crown" of a bloated and dying British Empire, it was also the home of an oppressed people with whom he could live and work. He needed to get away, to give himself some space to contemplate his hopes and ambitions.

In distancing himself from the Church and the idea of a vocation, Malcolm placed a strain on his relationships to Vidler and Knox. In the autumn of 1924, he explained to Vidler: "I should in many ways have loved to go back to the Oratory but you can see that it would have been very difficult. Of course, I still go and see Fr Wilfred and we're still friends but he has, rightly or wrongly, that type of mind and religion that make it almost impossible for him to accept me just humanly now that I have broken from him spiritually." To emphasise that he was breaking with Vidler as well, Malcolm made the following assertion: "I am coming to think that all one can do for God and humanity (terms so nearly synonymous to me) is to develop and to express all one has in one never selfishly but purely." This was to indulge in the kind of bland rhetoric practised by his father, but it served the purpose of sending a clear message to Vidler. As if to soften the blow, Malcolm added that each person had to work out their own religion. "The Catholic faith is, I believe, a right faith in essentials but it must grow up inside one. Evolve through suffering to have value."[40]

That human beings never learn except through suffering was one of Malcolm's themes throughout his career. As usual, this youthful comment turned out to be prophetic.

Malcolm turned for help to a fellow Cambridge student, a melancholy young man named Leonard Dobbs. Malcolm and Dobbs agreed to share rooms in a house at 46 Owlstone Road for Malcolm's final term in the autumn. Dobbs also provided Malcolm with his summer employment: working as a tour guide and factotum for Lunn's Tours in Belgium. Malcolm described Dobbs in his autobiography as "an unusual, rather sombre man, very gifted; a brilliant skier, a scientist of exceptional promise, curious about many things, enormously argumentative, and with a propensity for carrying every thought and notion to the extremes of fantasy".[41] Dobbs was not to become an intimate of Malcolm's – their personalities and interests were too divergent – but he would lead Malcolm to his sister Kitty, who would become his wife, and Hugh Kingsmill Lunn, destined to become his closest friend.

George Dobbs, Leonard's father, was an Irishman who had worked for Lunn's Tours since 1907. Mrs Dobbs, whom he had met and married in the course of his travels, was the sister of Beatrice Webb, the Fabian intellectual. Rosy Dobbs shared none of her sister's rationalism: the most eccentric member of the family, she was even more given to flights of fantasy than her son Leonard. Malcolm would later come to see her as a sort of batty angel, someone who could be irritatingly argumentative one moment, and then endearingly obsessed by spiritual questions, such as the immortality of the soul, in the next. His first encounter with Mrs Dobbs came that summer when he met her for tea. "'You are a friend of my son, Leonard,' she said and I nodded. 'I hear you have very left-wing views.' I nodded again. 'I take my political views,' she went on, 'from my sister Beatrice Webb and the *New Statesman*.'" Malcolm, whose love for the Russian Revolution made him despise such gradualists as the Webbs, tried to demolish their reputation, but Mrs Dobbs would have none of it.[42]

The other family that came to play an important role in Malcolm's life was that of the Lunns themselves. The paterfamilias, Sir Henry Lunn, was one of the founders of the modern business of tourism. Malcolm would relish the irony of the way this industry came about. Sir Henry, a high-minded Methodist, had been involved with one of the earliest efforts at ecumenism within the Christian Churches. In the course of preparing for an ecumenical conference at Grindelwald in Switzerland, Sir Henry discovered that if he guaranteed a large number of rooms, hoteliers would reduce their rates. With that profit margin in mind, he went from visions of religious unity to the business of travelling for pleasure. Though Malcolm recognised Sir Henry as a somewhat Pecksniffian character, he also felt that he had the "endearing traits of naïveté and absurdity".[43]

Thanks to their travel business, the Dobbses had the aura of the jet-set about them, travelling frequently on the Continent and particularly in Switzerland. Mr Dobbs, his sons and Kitty all became champion skiers when that sport was in its infancy. One day in the summer of 1924, Mr Dobbs mentioned matter of factly that his daughter Kitty had just returned from Switzerland. Malcolm met her later that day, when he went swimming with the rest of the family. Though he recalls having a sort of premonition about Kitty when her name was first mentioned, Malcolm left no impression of a dazzling first sight of her. Nonetheless, Kitty was a striking woman, tanned and athletic, with short, tiled hair in the fashion of the time. He undoubtedly found her sexually attractive and cosmopolitan in a way that Dora Pitman could never be. In the autumn she came to visit Leonard at Cambridge and Malcolm went for a walk with her along the River Cam. "I helped her over a stile," he wrote in his autobiography – a simple, ordinary gesture, but one that he would not forget.

There was one other significant encounter that Malcolm would make that summer, with Louis and Nan Wilkinson. Another "Lunn" man, Wilkinson was the first person Malcolm had ever befriended who actually lived the literary life, writing novels and literary criticism. He had met Oscar Wilde and knew John Cowper Powys and his literary brothers. With customary ambivalence, Malcolm admired Wilkinson for his ability to write and publish, but he also sensed that Wilkinson was a somewhat pathetic figure. His wife Nan was a frail woman who had tuberculosis. When he visited the Wilkinsons in London later, she climbed into bed with him one morning. But with Wilkinson himself singing in the shower nearby, Malcolm felt that he could not take advantage of the opportunity. In his early play, *Three Flats*, and in several short stories, Malcolm would satirise Wilkinson, who came to symbolise for Malcolm the danger of becoming a petty egotist who could not engage reality either in his writing or in his life.[44]

Malcolm's last term at Cambridge was relatively uneventful. He was relieved to be leaving an institution he had come to associate with pretension and sham. It was time to get away from a place where his sexual, religious and political identities had failed to cohere. He had made a gentle but decisive break with Vidler and Knox. Dora, patient and docile as ever, waited for Malcolm in Croydon. H.T., working hard to realise his dream of becoming an MP, remained doubtful about his son's character and education. Nonetheless he accompanied Malcolm to the dock at Tilbury on December 5, 1924, where he embarked on the SS *Morea*, bound for Colombo.

« 4 »
Passage to India
1924–1927

AS THE SHIP PULLED out of the dock, Malcolm waved goodbye to his father, guiltily relieved to be off. Cambridge, like Croydon, had been a prison, a place that had no room for someone who did not conform. He had conformed, but this had only brought sexual and spiritual confusion. He needed to escape to a place where he could work out his ideas and test his talents; above all, he needed experience of the world. India offered these prospects to Malcolm. It was a country that would haunt his imagination for the rest of his life, as it has for so many Western visitors.

However, the SS *Morea* "proved to be just a little bit of Croydon sailing over the high seas".[1] Though the British Empire would collapse in just twenty years, most of Malcolm's fellow passengers thought that it was a permanent institution, more like a law of nature than a fragile piece of political scaffolding. Malcolm noticed that the further the ship was from England, the more pronounced and shrill the imperialist attitudes of its passengers became. By the time the *Morea* reached Port Said in Egypt, the middle-class and lower-middle-class passengers had undergone a "strange transformation". "Now they were changing, the men becoming more assertive, the ladies more la-di-da; as it were, moving further and futher away from Bournemouth and Bexhill and nearer and nearer to Memsahib status and invitations to Government House."[2] The symbol of imperial status became the topee, the hat that protected pale English skin from the tropical sun. Malcolm bought a topee in Port Said, but he always wore it self-consciously.

Malcolm's reaction to this collective fantasy was to set the pattern for the rest of his life. He decided to offend his fellow travellers' feelings whenever possible – a policy of *épater les bourgeois*. Malcolm soon found a way to give offence. He shared a second-class cabin with an Indian clergyman, the Revd C.K. Jacob. After a few days at sea, Malcolm became aware that his association with Jacob was causing others to look askance. He overheard a conversation in which a man who worked in the Army Ordnance Department declared that Malcolm's association with Jacob "wasn't right". Malcolm's response was to spend as much time with Jacob as possible, strolling with him on deck in endless conversations. From Port Said, Malcolm mailed a letter to Vidler claiming Jacob to be "one of the most entirely charming and delightful people that I have ever met".[3] Later, Malcolm admitted that he often found Jacob tedious. But that was not to deter him from his purpose. Malcolm's tendency to act out his ideas in front of others, whether as clown, rebel or prophet, was already deeply ingrained.

The voyage from Tilbury to Colombo in what was then called Ceylon (now Sri Lanka) took five weeks. Because Alwaye, his destination, was located in the southern Indian province of Travancore (now Kerala), Colombo was the nearest port of call. He felt an enormous sense of relief in leaving the *Morea* and its "Empire Builders" behind.

In Colombo, Malcolm had his first experience of the East. He had a few days before he needed to continue his journey, so he wandered through the streets of Colombo, taking in this exotic new world. In his autobiography, the description of these moments retains the freshness of the original experience. Walking through the streets, Malcolm wrote, his senses drank in the new experiences.

Such a variety of faces and expressions! Whiskers and beards sprouting, eyes hooded or smiling; faces taut or withdrawn, or – as so many are in India – full of fathomless patience which is very beautiful and touching. Sometimes a face of rare serenity, so that you want to stop and offer thanks for it there and then. Or a face stamped with a lustrous beauty; momentarily glimpsed, then gone for ever. Or a beggar's face whining and cringing, mutely exposing sores or deformities, or holding up for inspection a wizened stunted child. Then, in passing rickshaws, with bells tinkling and the pat, pat of human feet sounding, some massive bearded merchant lost in his own thoughts and stratagems. Or a topee'd clerk or official. Or a minor Memsahib on her way to the Club. The unforgettable smell of spices, cow-dung, sweating flesh; the flies, the confused shouts; the little shops like opera boxes, exuding their own smells and tinkling sounds.[4]

Malcolm's impulse to melt into this crowd was, however, immediately frustrated. Blond-haired and blue-eyed, wearing Western dress and a topee, Malcolm was treated with the deference and distance accorded to a Sahib. With his sensitivity to class differences, Malcolm found this special treatment ironic. To the people in the streets of Colombo, a Croydon boy would appear just as exalted as an Etonian. Malcolm found people in queues stepping aside for him, leaving him embarrassed and uncomfortable. In his autobiography he claims that he soon came to count on this special treatment.[5] But over the course of the next two years Malcolm consistently refused to set himself above the Indians around him. It was an attitude that earned him trust and admiration.

To get a better sense of what British educational efforts in the East were like, Malcolm decided to make a trip inland from Colombo to Ceylon's other major city, Kandy. Trinity College for Boys stood on a hill overlooking Kandy. To get there, Malcolm was pulled in a rickshaw. He watched the man who pulled the rickshaw with fascination and then mounting horror, as the patch of sweat on his back expanded across his shoulders. Finally, after shouting and gesticulating, he persuaded the rickshaw driver to stop and let him out, so that only Malcolm's luggage rode in the rickshaw. When they arrived at Trinity College, the rickshaw driver caused a row over how much he should be paid. Malcolm was rescued by the Principal of Trinity, but he vowed that he would never ride in a rickshaw again, if he could help it.[6]

Trinity College proved to be an institution that would have warmed the hearts of the Empire Builders on board the *Morea*. It was as if a British public school had been transplanted to the tropics. "The boys wore blazers, played rugger, sang English songs and hymns heartily, though in fairly cracked tones because of the different scale in their own Indian music; they took cold showers and were taught to be manly and speak the truth."[7] He was appalled by the arrogance and insensitivity of this educational programme. In later years he would note that institutions like Trinity became the breeding ground for the nationalist rebels who would put a violent end to imperial rule.

Malcolm left Colombo in mid-January 1925. He had to travel by boat, bus and train to reach Alwaye, on India's southwestern coast, where he arrived a few days later. When possible he travelled third-class, to the astonishment of his fellow passengers; this was odd behaviour for a Sahib. But there were times when Malcolm's desire to live on equal terms with the Indians was frustrated. Once, on a train, the conductor demanded that Malcolm pay a first-class fare. When Malcolm asked where the second-class coach was located, the conductor replied that anywhere he sat would be first-class. This statement caused them both to burst into laughter, but Malcolm paid up.[8]

By contrast with Trinity, Union Christian College, where Malcolm was to teach, was a model of enlightened partnership between East and West. Founded in 1921 by a professor at Madras University, K.C. Charcko, it was intended to serve the community of Syrian Christians in southern India. At first the staff had been composed of Roman Catholic and Anglican missionaries, but by the time of Malcolm's arrival, twelve out of the fifteen lecturers were Indian. There were 214 students in 1924, primarily Syrian Christians, but also a number of Hindus and Muslims.[9] Within days of his arrival, Malcolm wrote to Vidler, boasting that "we are the only Indian-run college in India".[10] A few weeks later, he would enumerate the virtues of Union Christian College in more detail. It was an institution that was not only run by Indians, but had Europeans working under Indians. The students retained their native dress. The religion practised there was Syrian or Indian, rather than imported Anglicanism. And the staff, because they were not missionaries, were not obliged to spout a party line.[11]

Though he had been recruited by a clergyman, Mr Holland, Malcolm found that it was the founder, K.C. Charcko, who evoked his wholehearted admiration. Malcolm would often share an evening meal with Charcko, whom he regarded as a holy man. To Alec Vidler he wrote that Charcko "never evangelises. He never teaches. He never has prayer meetings. Yet by his life I know for a fact he has caused many a Hindu to look in a new way at Christianity."[12] To his parents he wrote that Charcko was "the most inspiring and unbodily person I have ever met".[13] For Malcolm, the evidence of Charcko's spiritual wisdom was not in his appearance, or in his abstemious habits, but in the unity he brought to the college. Under Charcko's direction, the different racial and religious traditions represented at the college came together in common worship and activity. Charcko's example, and others like it, led Malcolm to believe that secular schemes for the "brotherhood of man", marked by coercion or self-interest or violence, were vastly inferior to the freedom and unity of those who share a common faith.

Only weeks after his arrival at Alwaye, Malcolm encountered the greatest "holy man" of modern India, Mahatma Gandhi. This small wizened lawyer, who went about in simple peasant dress, had set India on fire with his campaign of resistance to British rule. Gandhi called his method of nonviolent resistance *satyagraha*, which he translated as "soul force". At the time of his visit to Alwaye, Gandhi was urging Indians to reject imported British goods. In particular, he encouraged the hand-production of native cloth. Malcolm went to the railway station at Alwaye, along with ten thousand Indians, and waited for hours for Gandhi's arrival. When he stepped off the train, Gandhi immediately went to a group of "untouchables", people whose shadow was thought to defile a caste Hindu. He sang a hymn with the untouchables before continuing on his tour, which brought him to the college. Many of Malcolm's students, their nationalist ardour roused by this visit, chanted "*Mahatma Gandhi Ki Jai! Mahatma Gandhi Ki Jai!*"[14]

Gandhi's "saintly style" of political action elicited Malcolm's praise in much the same way that Charcko's spirituality had. As he wrote to Vidler, Malcolm saw Gandhi as "a great man with a great message. I was thrilled with him. Like all extremists he gives the only practical plan; like all visionaries he talks common sense."[15] Malcolm wrote an impulsive letter to Gandhi after this visit. The letter, in Malcolm's typical fashion, combined respect and words of appreciation with a direct challenge. He urged Gandhi to accept the reality that manufacturing and technology were essential aspects of modern economies, and not to tie himself exclusively to such ideas as hand-spinning. Gandhi responded courteously, if somewhat evasively, to Malcolm's letter, and the correspondence continued. Gandhi later reprinted the exchange in his newspaper, *Young India*. To have agreed with Malcolm's arguments would have diluted Gandhi's message, but the young Englishman spoke the truth. Eventually, the nationalist forces in India had to join the twentieth century.

Soon after the encounter with Gandhi, Malcolm met another leading figure in the Indian nationalist movement: Rabindranath Tagore, the poet and painter who won the Nobel Prize for Literature in 1913. Malcolm went to hear Tagore speak, and then wrote to him as well. The subject of this correspondence, however, centred around the virtue of celibacy. Malcolm's concerns were not limited to the issue of population control, although there is some evidence that he advocated a policy of contraception and sterilisation to Tagore.[16] Behind these surface issues lay Malcolm's unresolved feelings about his sexuality. In the East, where holy men denied their bodies, Malcolm felt attracted to a life of self-denial. Because he found it so difficult to control his desires, Malcolm tended to ricochet between extremes of indulgence and asceticism. Within a few months of his arrival in India, he had become a vegetarian, a practice that would come and go for the next half-century.

Living in Alwaye, Malcolm revelled in the life of simplicity. Every morning he would get up at around six (he remained a lifelong early riser). His servant, Kuruvella, would bring him a cup of tea. Then Malcolm would go down to the muddy Perriar river to bathe. The river was often alive with activity, from those who were bathing to women washing clothes. He called the river "God's Chastity" because it seemed a place of purification, of baptism. After breakfast and a morning of teaching, he would take a nap in the afternoon. If it was not too hot, he would take a walk in the evening. He found great contentment in walking among the peasants, watching workers in the rice paddies and the passing traffic. Poverty and disease were in evidence on these walks, and yet Malcolm felt that these people, for all their suffering and deprivation, were somehow closer to nature and the basic truths of the human condition than the arrogant and powerful Westerners. After his walk, Malcolm would return to the river to bathe before settling down to reading, writing and, eventually, sleep. He also acquired a boat – little more than a canoe hollowed out of a tree trunk – which he often paddled from the college to Alwaye.

Malcolm's two closest friends at this time were Indians. Venketramen, a fellow staff member at the college, was a strict Hindu, a Brahmin, who lived the simple life that Malcolm loved so deeply. Mathail, a gaunt Christian sadhu or holy man, was also an ascetic to whom Malcolm was devoted. The power of Mathail's love, Malcolm wrote in his autobiography, had "a beatific half-wittedness about it". This was a pattern that would be repeated throughout his life: wherever Malcolm travelled, he always left the clubs and journalistic enclaves behind and sought friendship with natives. It was the way he got to know the places he visited.

With Venketramen he paddled around the backwaters of Travancore.

We loafed through cloudless mornings and afternoons in a little boat; and we had with us water in a stone pitcher and fruit and two books, one of verse and one of prose, from which we read to each other as the mood seized us. Nor did any single thing arise to mar either the scene around us – of endless cocoanut palms, with low, sandy shores before them and smooth water, blue as the sky, on all sides of them – water dotted everywhere with tiny boats, controlled by graceful, almost naked men, and curved at stern and prow – or the rhythm of our companionship.

When they went to Alleppey they stayed with Venketramen's friends, sleeping on the roof at night, and lulled to sleep by a woman named Sushila, who would play on an instrument called a *véna*.[17]

In the midst of such beauty and squalor, it is understandable that Malcolm often found his academic duties incongruous and somewhat absurd. He taught from a history of English literature written by a Victorian named Dowden. The book he used was an abridged version of this critic's writings, so it was known as "Little Dowden". In his autobiography Malcolm recalled quoting phrases from Dowden as if they had just occurred to him: "Dryden found English brick and left it marble." His students, blinking with incomprehension, would nonetheless copy all of these literary *aperçus* into their notebooks. They also struggled through such set texts as *Macbeth*, *Wuthering Heights* and Ruskin's *Sesame and Lilies*. There were times when Malcolm was overwhelmed by the absurdity of the situation.

> The sides of the classroom were open, as is the way with buildings in South India; as we droned on together, we could see the bright green paddy fields, and watch people working in them, treading round bamboo irrigation wheels which made them look like inflated daddy-long-legs, or bending in rows over the earth, singing as they worked. Looking at them from our classroom, I felt at times an almost physical anguish at being so preposterously engaged . . .[18]

One of Malcolm's other responsibilities – the staging of dramatic productions – led to the same sort of emotion. He was expected to put on such plays as Goldsmith's *She Stoops to Conquer* (in which he played Miss Neville), *Othello* and *The Way of the World*, the latter entailing "Indian students in home-made wigs trying to be Restoration gallants". "I felt a kind of inner shame and rage about all this."[19]

Union Christian College may have been one of the more enlightened institutions of education in India, but as these episodes show, it still suffered from what might be called cultural imperialism. Malcolm was grateful for the advantages of the college, but he felt impelled to press home his critique of its failures. This would be the pattern of all his relations with institutions: he would be tolerated or encouraged by his superiors, and then he would turn around and rail against the institution's follies and weaknesses. At Alwaye, he found a platform in the college magazine, which he was asked to edit. In the very first issue of the magazine, Malcolm satirised other faculty members for working "in the spirit of Mr Dryasdust, BA, BL, author of notes on this, and notes on that and notes on every possible thing except on life . . ."[20]

Despite his frustration at the incongruities, Malcolm threw himself into his job, earning the affection of many students. One sign of this was a parody of the Old Testament Book of Chronicles that Malcolm published in a later edition of the college magazine.

> And there dwelt in the N.E. Hostel a warden by name Malc, the son of Mug, a white man, and one who laughed with all his might, for he was very humorous.
> And he said to himself, I will buy unto myself a machine, for to speak with me: for I am very lonely.
> And he bought unto himself a machine, cunningly made, for to speak to him, and behold, it sang him songs . . .
> And the rest of the doings of Malc, are they not written in the book of the Chronicles of the staff, and in the hearts of the members of the College?[21]

Whenever possible, Malcolm encouraged his students to take more active and radical stands on behalf of Indian nationalism and the *swaraj* ("self-rule") movement. His letters to Vidler and H.T. contain accurate and realistic assessments of the political situation in India – an early sign of Malcolm's journalistic ability to grasp complex series of events and historical conditions, and to write about them concisely.

Malcolm maintained a number of contacts with his fellow country-men in the region. Not long after he arrived in India, he paid a visit to the British Resident, a man named Cotton, who lived on an island in the harbour of Cochin. Because Travancore was so far away from the main centres of political and economic activity in India, the British Empire seemed a rather distant and inconsequential presence. As Malcolm approached Cotton's tropical island, he could hear an Indian brass band playing "Sweet Hortense". "This is like the English; they always spoil everything by some giant incongruity."[22] Though this first impression might have roused Malcolm's indignation, he found that he liked Cotton. The British Resident took a cynical and ironic view of his situation, and had little pomposity – or ambition. The reason for Malcolm's visit was that Cotton wanted to find out whether he would be interested in becoming the private tutor to the Maharajah of Travancore. The job paid well and seemed pleasantly romantic, but it called for a six-year commitment, and would have constituted a breach of his contract with Union Christian College. It is tempting to wonder what changes might have taken place in the Maharajah's palace had Malcolm taken the position.

Three months after his arrival, in April 1925, Malcolm left Alwaye for Ootacamund, a small station in the Nilgiri Hills. When the heat and humidity at the lower elevations became intolerable, Europeans in the area would make the retreat to Ootacamund. There he lived in a hostel for missionaries which was run by a "zealous evangelical lady" named Miss Hopwood. He has written in his autobiography of Miss Hopwood's motherly care, which seemed to come from a different part of her soul than her stern Calvinist convictions. But many of the missionaries Malcolm encountered did not have Miss Hopwood's warmth to redeem them. In his letters from this period, he is constantly complaining about the shallowness of missionaries. What scandalised Malcolm especially was the spiritual smugness and superiority of Western Christians – Empire Builders with clerical collars. These missionaries were prime offenders in matters of incongruity. One day at Ootacamund he met a pastor handing out flyers, which said,"Holy Communion will be celebrated in the Cordite factory at . . . on . . ." Cordite is a form of explosive used in industry. Malcolm wrote that "no one laughed but me". Later he found that the railway station for this particular factory was called Lovedale.[23] Of one particularly vulgar missionary, an American, Malcolm wrote to his father: "Christ was his line, He boosted him."[24]

Malcolm wrote to his father that "India is a place in which it is impossible to avoid thinking." At this time, the subject that was never far from his thoughts was religion.[25] Though he loved and admired the Indian people, he never seriously considered Hinduism or Islam, nor did his exposure to Eastern religion lull him into a vague pantheism. Soon after he first set foot in Colombo, he wrote to his father about the images of Buddha he had seen. Buddha he calls "a nice god to worship . . . a sort of Mr Baldwin God". But he remained attracted to the "Christ-God" because "there is a wild-eyed fighting against God, a straining upwards. He gives no peace except very occasionally 'the peace of God which passes all understanding'."[26] In another letter he wrote: "I love the paradoxes and inconsistencies of Christianity. Christianity is to life what Shakespeare is to literature; it envisages the whole. It sees the necessity for man to have spiritual values and it shows him how to get at those through physical sacraments."[27]

The one Christian writer who captured Malcolm's imagination at this time was G.K. Chesterton. He found Chesterton's book *St Francis* delightful, not only for its verbal pyrotechnics, but for its fresh and arresting depiction of the Christian faith. Malcolm responded to Chesterton's image of St Francis as a medieval troubadour – a singer not of courtly love songs, but of hymns to the Blessed Virgin. Later in the book, Chesterton uses another analogy for St Francis. He recounts the medieval tale of the *jongleur de Dieu*, the poor juggler who had nothing to offer as a gift to the Virgin but a performance of his art. Malcolm called St Francis "a rough and tumble acrobat, horseplay jester for God". He wrote to his father that "this is the very spirit of Catholicism. We burn incense because it is fun – we wear vestments because they are gaily coloured – we go to the very heart of the common man's common happiness and love, we express it for him in worship."[28]

Malcolm did not find himself able to embrace Roman Catholicism, as Chesterton had, or institutional Christianity of any kind. He wrote to Vidler that he still loved Christ but was angry at fatuous missionaries and the institutional Church. "Wordy or 'creedy' religion kills the living beauty of God," Malcolm argued. "Its whole tendency is towards limitation." Away from Cambridge and Vidler, he returned to the notion that Christianity expresses the moral imperative behind socialism. In one of the sermons he preached at the college, Malcolm claimed that Christ was his hero, but denied that he atoned on the cross for the sins of the world. He railed against the tendency to make Christianity something apart from life.[29]

Faith must be based on doubt. Doubt is the rock on which a man must build up his religion ... We must dare doubts. We must risk mental and spiritual disorder for the true order that shall follow them. People seem so afraid of chaos and yet in reality it may be a most necessary thing ... There is many an individual who needs a conversion to disorder to awaken him to life ...[30]

The echoes of Chestertonian paradox are clear: faith must be based on doubt, order on chaos. In these sermons Malcolm was not only testing out his ideas; he was also testing the patience of the college authorities. By the summer of 1926, they had to call a halt to Malcolm's creative theology. He was barred from preaching because of his heretical opinions. In reporting this to his father, Malcolm seems pleased, noting that he remains on cordial terms with the college staff.[31] It may be doubted whether the staff felt quite so friendly to Malcolm.

The Nilgiri Hills provided Malcolm with the perfect setting for his religious search. Miss Hopwood had renamed these hills after John Bunyan's *Pilgrim's Progress* – the Delectable Mountains and Beulah. On his first hiking trip in 1925, Malcolm covered 160 miles in six days, encountering on his route only the occasional tea planter. In his autobiography he wrote that on journeys such as this, he felt that he was being pursued by God – the "Hound of Heaven", in the image of the Francis Thomson poem.

But Malcolm's intimations of immortality were not restricted to the natural world. Over the course of his time in India, Malcolm had met a few Christians who appeared to be messengers from above. They were exceptions to the missionaries who represented to Malcolm a sort of spiritual imperialism. One of these was the father of Stephen Neill, a young priest who had been at Cambridge with Malcolm. Neill, who would later go on to be a well-loved bishop, Malcolm found conceited. But Malcolm thought that Neill's father, a doctor who treated cholera sufferers in remote villages, was a heroic figure. Another encounter occurred on a train, when Malcolm met a Roman Catholic bishop travelling to a conference. The bishop possessed a spiritual intensity that transfixed Malcolm. They conversed in French, the only language they shared. The bishop concluded that without faith, one must remain earthbound. Malcolm replied that he would have to remain earthbound, but this protestation of agnosticism sounded hollow even in his own ears. When he wrote to his father about this incident he contrasted his own tendency to vanity, to "put on airs", with the bishop's humility. "My Bishop had no airs, only *la foi* – and I much prefer that. His attempt to shake hands with the drunk soldier was very beautiful – almost like the washing of the disciples' feet."[32]

Malcolm was determined to extend his talents beyond college sermons and magazines. He had come to the conclusion that his real vocation was to be a writer, and his letters from these years are full of worry about whether he will write well enough to rise above mediocrity and obscurity. "It's easy to say one must express oneself – that's the modern cant phrase and just now I'm almost tired of it – but suppose one's self isn't worth expressing!"[33] He wondered whether he had become a dilettante and was dissipating his energies.

Throughout his two years in India, he wrote poetry and worked on a number of short stories. As he later confessed, he had come under the influence of the Russian dramatist and short-story writer, Anton Chekhov, and his British emulator, Katherine Mansfield. Malcolm's stories were modelled on the portraits of sad, lonely figures found in Chekhov and Mansfield. But Malcolm's forays into short fiction only garnered rejection slips. They were also criticised by his father, who thought they were objectionable for their sexual content. This caused Malcolm frustration, because he felt that the stories were quite tame.

Malcolm had better success with non-fictional journalism. Gandhi had published his correspondence with Malcolm in *Young India*. Then Malcolm got a short piece published in the *Madras Mail*, for which he received a payment of fifteen rupees. He sent the money home to celebrate the first payment he had received for writing.[34] An article that Malcolm had written for the college magazine, "On the Loneliness of Being a Sahib", came to the attention of the editor of the *Calcutta Guardian*. It was reprinted in the issue of March 25, 1926, with an editor's note calling it a "delicious article . . . rescued from a comparative obscurity which is wholly undeserved". After describing the kind of special treatment Sahibs receive, Malcolm registers his indignation.

Of course, some of my countrymen may like their isolation. It may make them feel somebodies, but for myself I hate it. There are people, I suppose, that prefer all sorts of queer things. There may be men who prefer a roof to the sky . . . or who like money better than children, or clothes better than nakedness, but such people are freaks. So are Sahibs freaks who would sacrifice for a cheap kind of majesty, based on the vulgarity of money or the worse vulgarity of bayonets, three hundred million potential brothers or friends or lovers.[35]

The editor of the *Guardian* asked Malcolm if he would be willing to write a series of sketches about life in India. Malcolm was delighted. Several of these pieces show Malcolm's penchant for humour. "The Compleat 'Bus-Rider" tells, with relish, the antics of the crazed bus drivers who careen down dusty country roads.[36] "On Trains" extols this mode of transportation. Speaking of the guards, Malcolm writes that they have a "way of shouting in a loud voice even when other people are talking. It would be interesting to know how many guards have become members of parliament. One would imagine that this part of their work would fit them peculiarly for service in the House of Commons." The best things about trains, he argues, are the opportunities for conversations. This leads him to the conclusion that these conversations "have the further advantage that in them one may lie with impunity, for it is always a fair supposition to make that one will never again see those whom one meets on railway journeys".[37]

The best article that Malcolm wrote for the *Guardian*, "Along the Parur Road", describes his daily walk. One of the figures he sees regularly is a retarded boy who drives a flock of geese.

His chest is sunken, his face is vacant and his eyes are dull, yet he drives his geese skilfully; and ... he speaks to them in the soft, caressing voice a mother uses to a very little baby. He carries no stick to assist him in keeping order amongst them, but only a large leaf, which he waves slowly to and fro; and one might easily imagine that his speech was nothing but the wind through this, so like is it to the sound of a forest when, in the evening, a light breeze blows. With this he keeps his charges as a compact, disciplined company, not stupidly military in their orderliness, yet not by any means a rabble; rather they remind one of a band of pilgrims, or of workers working voluntarily together ... I realised how supremely successful he was at his work when, one day when perhaps he was ill, I saw another boy at it. The other boy was a bouncing, bumptious fellow, who carried a switch like a sergeant-major, and who shouted at the geese as Sahibs shout when they want something. The result was that they spread over the road in a screaming, cackling mob – some getting left behind; some getting run over by a passing motor; all of them lost and bewildered ...

... I envy the goose-boy. I feel that he has found the secret of happiness in that he has one useful thing which he can do superlatively well, and which he is content to go on doing from day to day until he dies. When his soul leaves the poor, puny body, with its gapingly vacant face, I believe it will be found to be a rare and beautiful soul, pleasing to its Maker. Sometimes I wonder about him, whether he will marry; whether he prays or has any kind of religion; whether he ever wonders about the meaning of things. All this is doubtful; what is certain is that he can drive geese efficiently; and that to do that is quite as worthy of praise as to write a book or bleat a lecture or drone a sermon or do any of the things we wretched intelligentsia preen ourselves on.[38]

The Muggeridgean themes are all here: the weakest members of society remind us that our civilised sophistication is built on the sands of vanity and pretension; simplicity is the road to spiritual vision; life is a parable that we must interpret. Forty years later, when he met Mother Teresa of Calcutta, Malcolm found someone who lived the simple life and ministered to the goose-boys of the world, someone who, like Gandhi, asked for nothing and yet received outpourings of love – a mystic who turned out to be the most practical of all.

Living in India, Malcolm could not avoid thinking. Some things began to become clear to him, others remained shrouded in uncertainty. In his weekly letters home, Malcolm sought reconciliation with his father. Freed from the claustrophobia of his Cambridge years, he opened up to H.T., thanking him for his sacrifices and patience. He confronted the worst in himself and paid tribute to H.T.'s endurance. "At least three times you paid my bills – you faced my examination failure at Cambridge – you faced my many and somewhat disgraceful 'amours' – you have faced my creative and impossible conduct – without any too bitter reproaches . . . I have all the elements that make a thorough wastrel."[39] Since H.T. had been aware of Malcolm's homosexual amours, it should not have been surprising to his son that he would worry about the sexual content of his writing. Given the tone of this and other letters, it seems clear that Malcolm had left that episode in his sexual life behind in Cambridge.

He was less clear about his own romantic life. He had neglected Dora towards the end of his time in Cambridge, but he continued to keep the relationship open as a kind of emotional fall-back position. Not long after arriving in India, he wrote to H.T.: "I had a letter from Dora last week and it completely unsettled me with half vague regrets and thankfulness and longings and a million and one other parts of a mood."[40] But the "mediocre" quality of the letter made him glad of the distance between them. Nonetheless, as late as the summer of 1926, Malcolm continued to speak of the possibility of marrying Dora.

There were few young white women in southern India. Malcolm

met and flirted with a few missionary daughters at the hill station at Ootacamund. Only one, a girl named Beatrice, caught his attention. In a letter to Alec Vidler, Malcolm claimed that he had fallen in love with her, but it came to nothing.

There was one other woman in his mind during this time: Kitty Dobbs. He had been fascinated and attracted by the bohemian lifestyle of the Dobbses. Their connection to Mrs Dobbs's sister, Beatrice Webb, and the intellectual aristocracy of the Fabian Society, also added to the allure. Toward the end of his time in India, he asked his father to send him a copy of Beatrice Webb's autobiography. His thoughts, when he read it, were linked to Kitty. "I am in the middle of Mrs Webb's autobiography. Pater, I like the book but I'm dashed if I like her. As Kit says, she's sentimental; and a shocking prig."[41] He did not want to go back to work for Lunn's Tours in Belgium, but he did hope to see Kitty again.

After a year in India, Malcolm decided that he would only stay for a total of two years rather than the three he had agreed upon. In April of 1926, he gave notice that he would leave in a year's time. There was undoubtedly something of "the urge to be gone" involved in this decision, but part of it had to do with his health. The climate and environment were not easy on Europeans. In the autumn of 1925 he developed a skin condition which in his autobiography he called "Delhi boils . . . little Etnas in my flesh, which went on persistently erupting". By the next summer he was suffering from two sorts of worms. His mood darkened, though he kept up a furious pace of reading and writing, in addition to his duties at the college.

As he looked to the future, he contemplated what sort of job he should seek when he returned to England. There were three options: become a secretary to a Labour Member of Parliament, launch a career in journalism or continue to teach, perhaps at a large secondary school in London. H.T. was at this time making a few approaches to editors on behalf of his son. But Malcolm's literary output was small, and he was too far away to interview. A more likely scenario came from Alec Vidler, who was always concerned about Malcolm and who missed his company. Vidler suggested that he come to Birmingham, where Alec was working in a parish. He could teach, and live at the rectory. It was to be the plan that he would adopt.

Malcolm's final days in India were clouded by a controversy he brought on himself. Not long before he was due to depart in the spring of 1927, Malcolm published a long article criticising the state of education in India. Though he did not single out Union Christian College, the staff felt implicated. The Principal of the college, A.M. Varkey, was upset and decided to cancel a send-off party for Malcolm. For his part, Malcolm felt "abashed", unaware that his passionate plea for a more realistic and nationalistic form of education would be taken personally at Union Christian College.

So he slipped off, as he often would in the future, without celebration or fond farewells. His two closest friends, Venketramen and Mathail, accompanied him as far as the coastal town of Alleppey. At first they had planned to come only as far as the town of Alwaye, but they insisted on coming as far as Alleppey. He was touched by their devotion.[42]

Though his prospects were dim and uncertain, Malcolm felt a kind of elation as he began his journey homeward. He sat in the river boat with Venketramen and Mathail, grading his students' final papers, and tossing them in the river as he finished them. No one failed.

« 5 »

Children of Their Time

1927–1930

MALCOLM'S RETURN TRIP went more quickly than his outbound voyage. By April 8, 1927, his ship had docked at Naples. There, on the quayside, stood H.T., who had arranged to meet Malcolm in Italy and share a brief holiday with him on the Continent before they returned to England. Malcolm's correspondence with his father from India had been regular, honest and had included frank confessions of his ingratitude to his father. H.T. felt relieved that Malcolm had restored their pre-Cambridge fellowship; his presence in Naples was intended to celebrate that restoration. H.T. was also proud of Malcolm's first efforts as a writer.

In his last letter to H.T. from India, Malcolm found another opportunity to keep his father on the straight and narrow path of socialist rectitude. H.T.'s employer, MacIntyre, Hogg, had offered him a directorship in consideration of his long service to the company. It would have entailed more money and a considerable enhancement of H.T.'s social status. But the offer came with a condition: H.T. had to pledge to give up his political activities. Despite this condition, H.T. had been tempted to accept. After failing four times to be elected to Parliament, H.T. might have felt that his political career was over. Malcolm, who had never suffered want or real insecurity, was appalled that his father was thinking of accepting. "I'm sorry to hear you're thinking of taking a place on the board of directors of your firm. It seems to me to be a great mistake . . ."[1] In the end, H.T. declined the offer.

From Naples, they travelled to Rome and Paris. A rather "progressive travel agent", as Malcolm described him, arranged for father and son to visit a club where women clad only in diaphanous scarves and high-heeled shoes would sit on patrons' knees and sip expensive drinks. When a rather startled H.T. gave his "girl" a pound note for a tip, she put it in her shoe. All the way back to their hotel, H.T. muttered to himself: "She put it in her shoe!" Malcolm marvelled at his father's innocence.[2] In an unpublished autobiographical fragment, he wrote that the incongruousness of the moment caused him to reflect on his relationship to his father. "I looked sidelong at my father – his head, as ever, a little tilted in defiance, the wings of his City collar whitely protruding, his outside bowler down on his ears – and felt a pang of deep, anguished affection for him. Did I then understand, as I do now, the reason for this anguish? I doubt it. Yet, in some vague way, even then I sensed that I must disappoint him, and cried inwardly to be spared this necessity of hurting someone so dear to me."[3] For that brief moment in Paris, Malcolm and his father were content to be on another of their escapades.

As planned, Malcolm went to Birmingham, where he became a supply teacher, ready to substitute for other teachers who had become sick. Alec Vidler had prepared the way for Malcolm's arrival, arranging the teaching job with the local education authority and offering a place to stay. Vidler was a curate at St Aidan's in Small Heath. The church was a bastion of Anglo-Catholicism, and its clergy were celibate. The Bishop of Birmingham, Dr E.W. Barnes, was a progressive both in politics and theology, and found the High Church practices at St Aidan's distasteful. Malcolm noted in his autobiography that Vidler stayed at this parish for seven years – longer than he really needed to – because he was locked in a series of battles with Dr Barnes.

Malcolm became a paying guest at St Aidan's rectory, suddenly finding himself, after two years in a tropical jungle, in an environment exactly like the Oratory of the Good Shepherd. There was a smell of

> tobacco smoke hanging about the curtains and upholstery, as well as in the lavatory, which gives an impression of being in constant use; like the crockery in a busy station buffet. No carpets, so footsteps echo up the wooden stairs and along the wooden corridors; the rustle of cassocks, and the fumes of plain cooking seeping through the service hatch; tea set ready for all and sundry in a large metal pot standing amidst an array of cups and saucers.[4]

Though Vidler had not lessened his commitment to the institutional Church, he did not place demands or conditions on Malcolm. He understood that Malcolm had declared his intellectual independence, and offered nothing more than friendship. Malcolm had by no means abandoned his religious search. It was at St Aidan's that Malcolm first read St Augustine's *Confessions*, a book that would haunt his imagination for the rest of his life.

Malcolm spent much of this period writing short sketches aimed at sharpening his writing skills and working out his own ideas about religion and politics. One such sketch argues that human beings need to achieve an inward, spiritual harmony as their ultimate goal. "Why then be a Socialist? – because even to make harmonies hands must be trained and fiddles mellowed. I am a Socialist because I believe that a gracious environment will help men to be good; and that only collectivism can create this."[5] But already he was finding himself out of sympathy with most of what passed for socialism. In a short story written at this time, Malcolm described a character named Anthony, one of his fictional *alter egos*:

> Most of his life he had found burdensome. A gloomy sense was with him always that the world of affairs in which he was forced to live was somehow hopelessly false and wrong. Even its better aspects – reform, progress, the new spirit of brotherhood breaking down barriers between race and race and man and man – filled him with loathing. It all seemed so irreligious, so Godless. The statistics were right, he knew, but somehow or other he felt that they missed out something essential; something which he wanted; this he could never find.[6]

Malcolm's teaching experiences in Birmingham were grim. By definition, supply teaching meant that he was constantly moving from school to school, never getting to know anyone well. One day he was called to the worst school in Birmingham, in the heart of the city's industrial district. In one of the sketches he wrote at this time, Malcolm described that day:

> The children were puny and, in feature, curiously aged. There was a weariness about some of their eyes, and lines in some of their faces, which one usually associates only with a world-weary middle-age. They seemed to have plunged into tragedy when most of us know only days of careless freedom in the forest of Arden. Winter, with them, had set in desperately early.

Yet even in the midst of this despair, Malcolm found children whose hearts seemed to possess an innocence and wonder totally out of keeping with their environment.

Just as I left three urchins from the top standard – louts of *Punch*'s vicious drawings – brought in a sparrow in a hat. It was injured and they were afraid that it might die. I fear I wept at this, for their kindness to the little bird made the world's unkindness to them seem the more cruel. "Strange," said the head, "that a creature with wings should come here."[7]

Malcolm felt these schools to be prisons, where the heads were wardens and the students inmates. Once again he sang "Now the day is over" on Friday afternoons with a longing for release.

Malcolm was grateful to Vidler for making his transition back to England smooth, but he knew that he could not go on working as a supply teacher during the day, and coming "home" to a group of celibate clergy in the evening. Rather than seek out a different job, however, his thoughts turned in the direction of the opposite sex. He had seen Dora on his return from India, but the reunion had not been inspiring. Once Dora's "happy sensuality" had been enough to invest her with romantic mystery, but all that Malcolm could see now was a conventional girl who hoped for a comfortable home and little else. She was *petite bourgeoise* in his eyes now. Yet he lacked the courage to break off the relationship.

Ever since the summer of 1924, when Malcolm had worked for Lunn's Tours in Belgium, his thoughts had returned frequently to the Dobbs family and to Kitty Dobbs in particular. Towards the end of his time in India he read the autobiography of Beatrice Webb to learn more about the Dobbs's Fabian connections. He was awed and somewhat dazzled by their cosmopolitan, upper-middle-class lifestyle and their association with the Fabian elite. He and Kitty might well have felt a *frisson* of emotion when they first met – perhaps when he helped her over the stile on that walk in Cambridge – but no romantic "understanding" had been achieved. They had not corresponded with one another while Malcolm was in India. But when he was finally able to leave Birmingham for the summer vacation in August of 1927, he travelled to Belgium.

It is not hard to see why Malcolm and Kitty should be attracted to one another. Kitty had a tomboyish sexuality that was exciting and unconventional. Having been educated on the Continent, she was a fluent French speaker. As a child Kitty had always been on the move: her father's work for Lunn's Tours required the family to move, according to the season, from winter to summer resorts. They would rent a chalet for a few months before moving on again and repeating the process. During the war they returned to England, where Kitty was enrolled at the progressive coeducational school, Bedales. She often visited the home of her wealthy uncle, Alfred Cripps, father of Stafford Cripps. When Stafford tried to make her say grace at tea one afternoon, she kicked him in the leg.

After the war, the Dobbses returned to the Continent. While her father hob-nobbed with the idle rich, her mother would spend hours painting water-colours and pausing occasionally to make grand pronouncements, often related to the opinions of her sister. Sitting on a terrace overlooking Lake Geneva, she would suddenly say: "My sister, Mrs Sidney Webb, does not believe in unearned incomes." Or, as she skated around a rink in the Alps, she would burst out with: "My sister, Mrs Sidney Webb, thinks that the playgrounds of the idle rich should not exist!" That she lived on unearned income and in the playgrounds of the rich did not seem to trouble Rosy Dobbs. Kitty would later write of her childhood that it was "a hit-or-miss kind of existence, complete disorder, and the dropping of everything at any time of day or night to consider a metaphysical point."[8]

Though her aunt was the formidable Mrs Sidney Webb, Kitty grew up without political convictions. Most of her time was spent skiing, dancing and acting in amateur theatricals. She had met her aunt Bo for the first time during the war, when she was eleven. Beatrice and Sidney arrived on a bicycle built for two. Tall, slender, elegantly dressed, Beatrice had "huge black eyes, set wide apart, a delicate Roman nose and arrogant mouth". Her beauty, Kitty wrote many years later, "was marred by a lack of tenderness, a kind of domineering masculinity and in the end could only be described as handsome". Sidney, by contrast, was short and thickset, with a large head, thick-lensed pince-nez and a goatee. He dismounted from the bicycle, perspiring, with a white knotted handkerchief on his head. "Sidney sweats," Beatrice noted, superfluously.

By the time Kitty had grown up sufficiently to interest her aunt Bo, she was summoned to her aunt's presence, evaluated, and told that she had been living a frivolous life. Aunt Bo set to work getting Kitty a job with the Parliamentary Labour Club as a secretary. Her first job was to take down several letters dictated by Hugh Dalton. When it came time to read them back, Kitty couldn't decipher a single word. After this fiasco, Aunt Bo insisted that Kitty study at the London School of Economics, which she had helped to found. Kitty's academic career there was brief.

When Malcolm turned up in Kitty's life, both her mother and aunt were charmed. Not only did Malcolm have solid Fabian connections through his father, but the charisma and intensity that had attracted Alec Vidler and others worked its magic on Kitty and her mother. Rosy Dobbs told Malcolm that he was a "genius".[9] He was humorous, witty and eager to try out his skills as a writer. Though he had few prospects for immediate advancement, he had travelled to India, corresponded with Gandhi and Tagore, and begun to publish essays and sketches.

After his arrival in Belgium in the summer of 1927, where the Dobbs were then based, things developed rapidly. "It somehow became understood that Kitty and I would get married. And quite soon. I cannot recall ever 'proposing' to her – something we should both have regarded as very bourgeois and conventional; terms of abuse in our vocabulary."[10]

Rosy was delighted; George was not. He had none of his wife's bohemian sensibility, and looked on a match with Malcolm as a considerable step down for Kitty, both financially and socially. He did not actively try to prevent the marriage, but he could not lend it his active support.

The marriage took place a little over a month after Malcolm had travelled to Belgium. The circumstances were hardly propitious. The marriage ceremony took place, not in a church, but in the Birmingham Register Office, and the only member of either family present was George Dobbs himself, who had arrived at the last minute. It was "a drab little scene in a dreary sort of place, where numerous couples were waiting about, though whether to be married or divorced or judicially separated their demeanour did not make clear".[11] When the Registrar put the question to those gathered, whether anyone saw any reason why these two should not be joined in wedlock, Mr Dobbs called out, "You can still get away, Kit!"[12] Then, when the ceremony was over, as if to make the furtiveness of the marriage even more evident, Malcolm inquired about the procedure for getting a divorce.

The scene would be farcical if it were not so touchingly uncertain. Despite Mr Dobbs's objections, the marriage need not have been quite so solitary and surreptitious. No family members were invited; Mr Dobbs showed up unexpectedly, hoping to prevent the marriage. Even Alec Vidler was away on holiday at the time. H.T. was deeply wounded when he found out that Malcolm had not asked him to the wedding. Explaining this in his autobiography, Malcolm wrote: "Incredible as it seems, I just didn't think of it; though there may have been some unconscious reluctance to have him there, some sense that his presence would have been awkward."[13] It is indeed hard to credit the notion that Malcolm simply forgot to invite his father; it would be truer to say that Malcolm was in a state of what modern psychologists would call "denial".

This helps to explain why the marriage was so furtive. Malcolm was insecure about his family's social status and he was embarrassed at the thought of his father appearing in the presence of the Dobbs. An egalitarian in theory, Malcolm found that in practice he could not bear the idea of his earnest but socially inept father coming face to face with the Dobbses. Rather than face such an emotionally awkward encounter, Malcolm chose the equivalent of eloping.

But there was a deeper insecurity involved, an insecurity revealed by his question about how to obtain a divorce. Though he and Kitty agreed that bourgeois conventions, such as monogamy and the permanence of the marriage bond, were outmoded, the fact is that Malcolm was terrified of the commitment involved in marriage. To have surrounded his marriage with witnesses and ceremony would have been to emphasise that commitment. He must also have had doubts about whether he would truly be accepted in the social and intellectual aristocracy epitomised by the Webbs. As he so often did, Malcolm made sure of his escape route.

H.T. was hurt and perplexed by his exclusion from the wedding. It was a match that brought him and his son closer to the Fabian inner circle. To make up this slight to his father, Malcolm and Kitty spent five days in Croydon immediately after the wedding. But Malcolm found a new way to wound his father. Rosy Dobbs had (rather injudiciously) shown Malcolm a letter from Beatrice Webb in which she wrote that she knew H.T. as "a Fabian and a very worthy person, though of modest means". Malcolm in turn told this to his father, who had to bear the knowledge that one of his Fabian idols looked on him with the same sort of class-consciousness that was supposed to be incompatible with socialism. Passing this story on may have been Malcolm's way of explaining to his father that he wanted to spare him the snobbery of the Webbs. H.T.'s response was far more generous and funny than it had any right to be: "And to think that I gave up a directorship!"[14]

Kitty, on the other hand, began the marriage by showing her solidarity with Malcolm's principles. The couple had received a wedding present from Sir Henry in the form of a cheque for fifteen pounds. In the presence of the clergy at St Aidan's rectory, Kitty proceeded to tear the cheque into shreds, arguing that Sir Henry was a "despicable figure". The clergymen stooped down and picked up the pieces and managed to put them back together, but for all their efforts, the cheque was never cashed. Malcolm, aware of his precarious financial situation, must have felt a twinge of doubt about Kitty's high-mindedness, but he went along with her wishes.[15]

After the stay in Croydon, Malcolm and Kitty went on to spend a week in Paris, followed by a few days at the Dobbs's home in Montreux, near Geneva. On their return they paid their respects to a number of Kitty's relatives from the aristocratic Potter side of the family. The portraits that Malcolm draws of Lady Courtney and the Webbs in his autobiography are prime examples of his brilliance at the short personality sketch. Malcolm approached this new social milieu with his characteristic ambivalence: he was attracted to the aura of power that attended the Potter family, with their titles, wealth and progressive political crusades. At the same time, his eye for hypocrisy remorselessly hunted out the weaknesses and inconsistencies in their personalities.

Sidney and Beatrice Webb were the king and queen of Fabian socialism, the objects of H.T.'s fervent admiration. Meeting them was a momentous event for Malcolm, but he was prepared to be sceptical.

Mrs Webb was waiting for us in the sitting-room, standing, as she so often did, with her back to the fire, and swaying slightly to and fro. So completely different from her sister Kate [Lady Courtney]; frail and white, almost ghostly, by comparison with the other's solidity. She rushed at Kitty in a way the Potter women had, hurling herself upon her with a kind of avidity, as though to assure herself that Kitty was indeed there in her bodily presence ... The thing that struck me about her at once was her beauty, so reminiscent of Kitty's. A beauty of bone rather than of flesh. She was also, I sensed, tragic ... Webb came toddling in. He really was a ridiculous looking man, with tiny legs and feet, a protruding stomach, and a large head. A sort of pedestrian Toulouse-Lautrec.[16]

Visitors to Passfield Corner soon learned that rigid hierarchies were enforced there. One's place at the dinner table was determined by one's social status. Sidney and Beatrice would recount their anecdotes and make their pronouncements employing the royal We.[17]

Even before he met the Webbs, Malcolm had built up a strong aversion to their sort of rationalist, bureaucratic approach to social problems – the approach which became the foundation of the modern welfare state. From India, Malcolm had written to his father that the ability to say "'Dadda' to God is what people need even more than minimum wage".[18] In an attempt to articulate his political sensibility to H.T., he wrote that "more and more I see how we need sacraments and symbols; how in fact we live by them."[19] Malcolm became convinced that the most effective political action grew out of a religious and mystical view of human nature – Gandhi being an unassailable example. He believed that a figure like Gandhi, for all his religiosity, was more in touch with concrete realities than the Webbs, immersed as they were in abstractions that seldom corresponded to anything in the world around them.

While Malcolm and Kitty were making their social visits, Kitty's father, George Dobbs, was thinking that his son-in-law could do better than working as a supply teacher. Soon after their wedding, Mr Dobbs pointed out to Malcolm that the Egyptian government was advertising for teachers of English language and literature, and that these jobs paid better than his situation in Birmingham. The job had no future, but the pay was acceptable, and it would give Malcolm the opportunity to travel again, to experience yet another outpost of the British Empire, and perhaps to continue his writing. Malcolm agreed, sent in his application in October 1927, and was hired immediately. He was to teach at the Government Secondary School in Minia, Upper Egypt.

Malcolm and Kitty travelled by way of Paris, Montreux, Genoa, Naples, Syracuse, Alexandria and Cairo, arriving at Minia by the middle of November. The city of Minia is located on the Nile, in Upper Egypt, south of Cairo. From Minia Malcolm wrote to Vidler: "Kit and I are settled here for the time being. I doubt if we shall ever be settled anywhere long. A restless movement from place to place is only the outward sign of an inward unsettlement. And we are both children of our own generation – the more so because we so constantly criticise it."[20]

There was much to remind him of his time in India: the teeming life of the streets, the attempt to impose Western education on a subject people, the faint echo of the imperial presence in a distant outpost. But Malcolm never fell in love with Egypt the way he had with India. He was more attracted to the lush jungles and the spirituality of India than he was to the desert and to Islam. A married man now, his friendships with Egyptians were naturally less intense than his relationship to Indians like Venketramen and Mathail. But the political situation offered plenty of opportunity for commentary and the light workload enabled him to write.

His teaching duties involved him in the same bizarre incongruities that he had known at Alwaye. He found that his Egyptian students were far more indolent than his Indian students had been. Often by late afternoon the sound of snores could be heard in Malcolm's classroom. His students were not captivated by their textbook, *Man and His Work*, an assortment of facts and statistics that might have strained the endurance of the most unimaginative utilitarian.

These early days in their marriage were among the most idyllic for Malcolm and Kitty. From the beginning of their marriage they proved to be wonderfully companionable: they loved to read out loud to each other, play chess and go for long walks. Though their marriage would be rocked and nearly shattered by rows and infidelities, Malcolm and Kitty were in a fundamental sense good friends, comrades-in-arms. It was this bedrock of friendship and trust that enabled their relationship to weather the gale-force winds that would soon sweep down upon them.

Early in 1928, Kitty discovered that she was pregnant, something they had not intended. As Malcolm wrote to Vidler: "The real joke, Alec, about birth control is that there is no such thing. And I'm rather glad."[21] Malcolm and Kitty both revelled in the joy of new life, following closely the changes in Kitty's body. Here too they established a pattern that would not alter substantially for the rest of their lives. Though both of them claimed that they believed in the idea of an open marriage, and they would indeed put that theory into practice for much of their lives, they nonetheless felt an instinctive antipathy towards the practice of birth control. It is important to recall that at this time, birth control was still considered by many people to be an immoral practice. In the Christian community, contraception would only become acceptable after 1930, when the Anglican Lambeth Conference approved of the practice. The Muggeridges looked on contraception as a form of artificial sterility, though not for religious reasons.

After only two terms at Minia, Malcolm was invited to join the English faculty at Cairo University. The head of the English department at the time was Bonamy Dobree, a "man of letters" who became a highly successful literary critic and historian. This was a welcome move, enabling them to leave a provincial backwater and live in the political and cultural heart of Egypt. They found a house in Helmia Zeytoun, a suburb of Cairo on the edge of the desert. After a time, Malcolm managed to acquire a battered old Chevrolet in which to drive around the city.

Though Cairo was an improvement on Minia, it did not change Malcolm's lack of affection for Egypt. "Cairo gave an impression of being inflammatory. In the dry burning heat, after weeks and weeks without rain, one expected the place to catch fire; as, indeed it did some years after I left . . ."[22] The one haunt that Malcolm recalled with pleasure was known as "Old Groppi, a garden café in a courtyard with trees growing in it, and tables set under their shade or under coloured umbrellas".

> There, all day long sat the Pashas and Beys and Effendis consuming their tiny cups of sweet Turkish coffee, and keeping the flies at bay with their whisks; occasionally rising to greet one another with many courteous bows and gestures, but mostly, like my students, seemingly sunk in a long brooding reverie . . . Their inertia gradually became infectious, and one would likewise sit on and on, as the sun moved across the courtyard, with only the snores of a sleeping Pasha, the rhythmic gurgle of a hubble-bubble, the incursion of a newsboy, to disturb the scene's somnolence.[23]

Malcolm's experience at Cairo University was not appreciably different from the secondary school in Minia. The university was housed in the Zaffaran Palace, which had once been used to house the Khedive's harem, a fact that lent itself to much ironic commentary on Malcolm's part. His students here were also sleepy, though this was not so much due to the textbook as to the widespread use of hashish. Aside from this drug, the only other enthusiasm Malcolm detected in his students was for the nationalist party, the Wafd, which was engaged in a struggle for power with the British imperial machine. This political activity often led to student strikes, which served to further lighten Malcolm's teaching burden.

The Muggeridges decided to spend the summer vacation of 1928 at a small town in Austria named Melk, on the banks of the River Danube – a cool alternative to Cairo's climate. There Malcolm wrote his most ambitious literary work to date, a play called *Three Flats*, which would be performed in London in 1931. As the title indicated, the action takes place in a building divided into three flats, all of which are represented on stage. In the bed-sitter upstairs live Dennis Rhys, a young, struggling writer, and his lover, the neurotic Maeve Scott. One of the flats is occupied by two unmarried schoolteachers, Miss Capel and Miss Edwards. Mr and Mrs Mason, a middle-aged, lower-middle-class couple, inhabit the other flat.

Three Flats is a quirky play that doesn't quite live up to the promise of its clever stagecraft. The central theme is a simple one: that people in the modern era are living lives of quiet desperation. Malcolm offers glimpses of the inane, hollow world of contemporary London – the world depicted in T.S. Eliot's *The Waste Land*. The tone of the play veers from melodrama to farce to grim social realism. But if the parts never add up to a convincing whole, the play is written with a brisk confidence that is engaging.

Dennis and Maeve are caricatures of Malcolm and Kitty, or what they might become if their worst characteristics were taken to an extreme. Described in the stage directions as a "wordy politician" or "oracular professor", Dennis is indolent and emotional, a self-absorbed artist.[24] Maeve accuses him of always "playing a part"; later we discover that he actually comes from a wealthy family and see him sneaking off to have an expensive lunch with his mother. Maeve is liberated but extremely vulnerable; her relationship to Dennis is going nowhere, but it has stigmatised her as a "loose" woman. Having run away from a solid middle-class family, she knows she cannot return to that world. She tells Dennis that they lack roots: "We've nothing in the present that's continuous."[25] After Dennis goes off to his secret lunch, Maeve commits suicide by drinking poison, ironically reciting Cleopatra's dying words from Shakespeare's *Antony and Cleopatra*. The second and third acts of the play take place with the audience aware that Maeve is lying dead upstairs.

Mr and Mrs Mason are loosely based on Malcolm's parents. Mrs Mason is a shrill, angry woman who has become hardened through a lack of love in her life. Mr Mason, on the other hand, is a romantic dreamer who has fallen in love with the schoolteacher next door, Miss Edwards. Though Miss Edwards sees clearly that Mr Mason will never leave his wife for her, she has her own dreams. She sublimates her sexual yearning into utopian political causes. Later, Rhys enters Miss Edwards' flat, rather drunk from his expensive lunch, and attempts to seduce her. They discuss the virtues of "open marriage", which Dennis says has done away with "the old property idea" and brought about true freedom.[26] But before this seduction can go anywhere, the discovery of Maeve's body brings the whole play to a macabre conclusion.

At the heart of this play is Malcolm's indictment of the human impulse to dwell in self-indulgent fantasy rather than have the "courage and faith", as Mr Mason puts it, to face the truth. Malcolm was a much better writer than his fictional character, and there were many truths which he did face up to, but he would use the notion of "open marriage" to enact his own macabre melodramas again and again.

The following year, on a vacation visit to England, Malcolm told Beatrice Webb that he had written a play. She invited him to read it aloud at Passfield Corner. Alec Vidler was also invited for the occasion. In her diary Beatrice wrote: "Malcolm Muggeridge, Kitty's husband, is an extremely clever young Cambridge graduate ... *Three Flats* was unexpectedly brilliant. But it was grossly coarse in incident and language – so indecent that I went hot all over and wondered whether I ought not to stop it..."[27] Beatrice respected Malcolm's abilities sufficiently to send a copy of the play on to George Bernard Shaw for criticism, acting as an intermediary between them. Shaw also found the sexual frankness of the play distasteful. Malcolm defended his interest in sex in terms derived from his hero D.H. Lawrence: in a deracinated industrial society, he argued, the only possible "contact with the earth" is sex. Shaw retorted that "Sport and Art ... are the safety valves of sexual pressure." Malcolm thought that an incredibly naïve response. He replied that Shaw "doesn't see beneath the blazers and flannel trousers and tennis frock: and doesn't see that these only hide what Lawrence calls – The Dirty Little Secret."[28]

The summer of 1928 nearly ended in tragedy. Towards the end of their vacation in Melk, Kitty fell over a wash-tub and hurt herself. As

Malcolm wrote to his father, "a miscarriage was feared. She had to be taken into Vienna in a motor ambulance. She stayed in hospital there for three days, and thank God, it was found that no harm was done."[29]

Soon after their return to Cairo, Kitty gave birth to a healthy boy, whom they named Leonard, after Kitty's brother. Malcolm and Kitty were elated. In a letter to H.T., Malcolm was full of good humour, recounting how he had been reading aloud to Leonard from *Antony and Cleopatra*. "When I came to 'I am dying, Egypt, dying,' he burst into tears, which seems to show a certain sensitiveness of feeling and at the same time a measure of artistic appreciation."[30] Before Leonard was a year old, Malcolm and Kitty gave him the nickname "Pan", which they continued to use for many years in preference to his given name.

As the new year, 1929, began, Malcolm considered his situation. Aware that the Labour Party in England was at last on the verge of electoral victory, he volunteered to work for his father, if he were to be elected. He thought that he would be happy with any sort of "pseudo-political" job.[31] In June, the Labour Party did achieve a majority in Parliament, with Ramsay MacDonald becoming Prime Minister. On his fifth attempt, H.T. Muggeridge was elected to Parliament as the representative for Romford. After all the emotional memories of elections from his boyhood, Malcolm was not able to be with his father for his greatest triumph. This victory did not, in fact, induce him to return to England. Oddly, part of his response to his father's election was to write another play, called *Expense of Spirit*, which centred around a newly elected MP, John Ramsden, another pathetic character based on his father. But this play was far less intriguing than *Three Flats* and was never per- formed.[32]

Though he speculated about getting a political job, Malcolm was far more industrious when it came to his writing. Late in 1928 he had the pleasure of seeing two of his pieces published. "An Elderly Teacher", a story first drafted in India, appeared in the *New Statesman* for December 1, 1928. This was a Chekhovian story of a melancholy, pathetic secondary school teacher on the day of his retirement. Far more assured and convincing was an essay published in a publication called *Young Men of India*. "Subject Peoples" is an all-out attack on Western imperialism. At a time when most Westerners felt that the colonial system was part of the natural order of things, Malcolm confidently predicted its imminent collapse.

We have to face the fact that there is today a stirring of subject peoples all over the world. They are demanding the right to govern their own destinies in their own way ... There can be no doubt that the subject peoples will go on demanding concession after concession, and that the Powers will be forced to give way to them. The only thing is that the more graciously they give way the better it will be for all concerned. And the half-way houses will be dangerous and uncomfortable. They always are. There is that amount of truth in the contention of the die-hard as against that of the sentimental liberal – it must be a steel frame or nothing; wooden scaffolding is useless. And nothing it will, of course, be in the end ... Reaching this end, however, would seem to be a weary, wrangling process, full of hartals and strikes and wars and bloody revolutions.[33]

Malcolm saw himself as a die-hard. This explains why he wrote to his father at this time about his continuing desire to travel to Russia to witness the experiment of Soviet communism at first hand. The Soviet Union, he thought, was not mired in sentimental liberalism.

Taking advantage of his own firsthand view of the political turmoil in Egypt, Malcolm began to write news commentaries and send them off to a number of newspapers and magazines. Though the British grip on Egypt was ostensibly much looser than in India, Malcolm recognised that London called nearly all the shots in Cairo. By the time Malcolm had arrived in Egypt, Zaghlul, the charismatic founder of the Wafd, had died and was replaced by a less effective figure, Nahas Pasha. Egyptian politics were complicated because in addition to the Wafd, the other source of power was King Fuad, a monarch who preferred to dream of autocratic rule rather than the development of a true Egyptian democracy. Fuad, however, had little real power, though he could sometimes act as a spoiler in the complex political manoeuvrings of the time. Malcolm found Fuad a rather comic figure; after he was shot in the throat in an assassination attempt, Fuad's voice sounded like a dog barking.

Malcolm's sympathies were clearly with the Wafd, despite their use of street violence and political murder to advance their nationalist cause. In his autobiography, Malcolm singled out his defence of the Wafd as an example of his own naïveté – a form of radical sentimentality. One of his articles from this time argues that "a certain amount of street turbulence, in any case greatly exaggerated in some of the reports, should not blind us to the vitality and vision of Egyptian nationalism, or induce us to think yet again in terms of conqueror and conquered, with the inevitable consequence of struggling on for a few more years towards predictable disaster."[34] As was often the case, Malcolm was too hard on himself in retrospect. True, there is a tendency evident in this article to excuse the use of violence, but his point is valid: if the British were to use the excuse of rioting to harden their position and fall back into the mode of enlightened conquerors, they would only prolong the bloodshed and political stalemate in Egypt. This, of course, is precisely what happened.

Malcolm sent one of these articles to the *Manchester Guardian*, which had long been associated with the progressive strain in Britain's Liberal Party. With the decline of the Liberals and the rise of the Labour Party, the *Guardian*, while not espousing socialism, was clearly situated on the Left. Malcolm's article was accepted, and was duly published, being attributed to "A correspondent in Cairo". Malcolm was elated. The *Guardian* was an august institution, one of the pillars of the Left in Britain. His excitement was multiplied when he received a letter from the editor asking for more articles about the situation in Egypt. Then, "to complete my happiness", he was informed that the *Guardian*'s roving correspondent, Arthur Ransome, would be travelling to Egypt in December of 1929 and would like to meet Malcolm.[35]

Ransome travelled to a number of countries for the *Guardian*, but he could not be enticed to join the staff in Manchester. That was because he had his own personal ambitions as a writer of children's stories. Soon after he met Malcolm he published *Swallows and Amazons*, the first in a series of highly successful children's books. Malcolm found Ransome "an amiable and attractive man, with a luxuriant blond soup-strainer moustache, a rubicund complexion, a large mouth from which more often than not a pipe protruded, and a hearty disposition". The two men immediately took to each other. Malcolm was awed by the fact that Ransome had travelled to Russia and witnessed the Revolution. The older man was obviously pleased by this interest, but he also responded with genuine enthusiasm to Malcolm's obvious talents. He wrote to the editor of the *Guardian*, Ted Scott, with the following report.

Calls himself Labour but considers Labour better served by the M.G. than by his own representatives. Wants to write. Has a

congenital interest in politics. I asked him how long it took to
write the sort of articles he has been sending us. He said he never
has time to give more than a morning to doing an article.
Concealing my respect behind a pompous manner, I did not let
him know that I considered him one of the heavenborn . . . He is
extreeeeeemly [*sic*] young, but decidedly nice in feel, altogether
unlike some other rabbits whose diseased livers and swollen
spleens affect the corridor atmosphere. I think he is the sort of
lad you would find it refreshing to have about and one who, as his
articles show, has a natural instinct for the M.G. attitude. The
feel of the fellow is thoroughly simple, eager and pleasant, and
free from any kind of intellectual cockiness while at the same time
he is extremely clever and has crammed a lot of experience into
his 26 years.[36]

Ransome's glowing report – not unlike Beatrice Webb's diary entries
about Malcolm – was all that Ted Scott needed to make his decision.
He wrote to Malcolm inviting him to join the editorial staff of the
Guardian for a probationary period of three months.

It was a triumphant moment for Malcolm. After the confused,
alienated years at Cambridge and the obscure exile as a teacher in the
far-flung corners of Empire, he had written his way into a position
with one of the leading institutions of public opinion in Britain. "I
believe I have never received a letter which gave me so much delight;
waving it triumphantly in the air, I rushed to tell Kitty, and then to
the post office to telegraph my acceptance of the offer."[37] He still had
to finish his teaching assignment at Cairo University, but would be
able to begin at the end of the summer of 1930. Kitty and Leonard
went ahead in the spring. Then, in the summer, Malcolm was able to
leave the heat of Cairo behind and head for the wet but solemn and
high-toned world of Manchester.

« 6 »

Picture Palace

1930–1932

AS MALCOLM TRAVELLED from Cairo to Manchester, he was moving from the outside to the inside, from a minor teaching position in a foreign country to the editorial staff of one of Britain's most influential newspapers. He had ample reason to feel pride and excitement. He had been offered the job primarily on the basis of his abilities as a writer and political critic, not through any connections with the Webbs or the Cambridge old-boy network. During his time in Egypt, he had published several articles in the *New Statesman*, the leading magazine of the intellectual Left. The Webbs considered him a brilliant new star on the Fabian horizon, and George Bernard Shaw had thought it worth his while to comment on Malcolm's as yet unpublished and unperformed play, *Three Flats*. He was married to a beautiful and intelligent woman, and had a healthy young son.

Yet, in spite of these personal triumphs, the two years ahead of him would also see his marriage nearly destroyed and a hurried departure from Manchester, once more to become an outsider. Like a character from a Dostoevsky novel, Malcolm could swing from agony to ecstasy and back again with a dizzying suddenness.

But when Malcolm's train pulled into the smoky industrial city of Manchester he felt only elation and curiosity. The *Manchester Guardian* (today known simply as the *Guardian*) was in those days one of the citadels of political righteousness in Britain. The paper had its origins in the labour unrest that accompanied the Industrial Revolution, and had become a venerable institution not only in Manchester but throughout Britain. It grew out of the movement within the Liberal Party that opposed the concentration of power in large industrial corporations – the same movement that had inspired H.T. Muggeridge when he was a young man. Championing the rights of the common man, Liberalism stood against privilege and the dangers of oligarchy. The *Guardian* had, for example, led the struggle to give women the right to vote. It had also maintained an anti-imperialist position, denouncing British involvement in the Boer War and fighting success-fully for Irish Home Rule.

By 1930, the year Malcolm joined the *Guardian*, Liberal institutions had been eclipsed by the growth of trade unionism and the collectivist politics of the Labour Party. The last Liberal government that had gained a parliamentary majority without a coalition had been in 1910. The *Guardian*'s relationship to the two parties in this era of political transition was at times confused and uncertain. The *Guardian* was not prepared to endorse socialism outright, but it was nonetheless on the Left and continued to possess considerable moral authority and influence in British politics. Malcolm came to see that the underlying link between the Liberal and Labour viewpoints was the belief that most human problems could be solved through education and various forms of social engineering. Progress, according to this worldview, was inevitable, but it was retarded by ignorance, prejudice and a blind allegiance to the status quo. If only men of reason and moderation could be brought together, most social ills could be eliminated or drastically reduced.

The *Guardian* represented the philosophy of gradualism that had guided Malcolm's father throughout his life. Malcolm, however, being a "die-hard" by temperament rather than a gradualist, was bound to clash with the forces of moderation and caution. When that confron-tation came to pass, Malcolm took revenge by writing a satirical novel about the *Guardian*, *Picture Palace* (a title chosen by the publisher, which he never liked). When the novel was printed in 1934, the *Guardian* threatened to sue Malcolm and his publisher for libel, so the book was pulped.[1] Both *Picture Palace* and Malcolm's first novel, *Autumnal Face*, written in Manchester, provide fascinating glimpses of his life at this time.

Malcolm had received the invitation to join the *Guardian* staff from the editor, Ted Scott, but the paper was at that time still dominated by Ted's father, C.P. Scott. For nearly fifty years C.P. Scott had edited the *Guardian* – the paper was little more than his lengthened shadow. He had officially retired in 1929, in favour of his son Ted, but in fact he continued to dominate all aspects of the paper until his death in 1932. In his autobiography Malcolm recalled being ushered into C.P. Scott's presence on his first day at the *Guardian*. He was "sitting at his desk staring fixedly in front of him, his eyes bright blue, his flesh rosy, his beard white and truculent; a high-minded Sir John Falstaff, looking, as the old and famous often do, a little mad."[2] Malcolm found the elder Scott to be full of contradictions: vague and genial in manner, but capable of being sly and Machiavellian; an advocate of liberation for the oppressed who ruled his own business like a tyrant; an intellectual egalitarian who lived the life of a pampered Victorian magnate. Kingsley Martin, the long-time editor of the *New Statesman*, overlapped briefly with Malcolm at the *Guardian* and had a similar reaction to C.P. Scott.

> The world in which C.P. Scott lived was very different from anything I ever saw afterwards ... It was a rich, cultured world, and not at all the ascetic type of life which many people imagined. His must have been one of the few remaining Victorian households of the best upholstered period. The furniture was massive; everything was solid and expensive, designed to last many lifetimes. C.P., as Ted ... remarked, never had any notion of equality; he lived in the world of benevolent masters who had no difficulty about getting servants.[3]

Malcolm's portrait of C.P. in *Picture Palace* is sharply drawn and devastating. The opening scene of the novel introduces us to Old Savoury, the much-lionised editor of the *Accringthorpe Courier*. Sitting alone in his office, Old Savoury reads press cuttings about himself, as if to reassure himself that he is still alive and vigorous. Gathering strength, Old Savoury contemplates some grand gesture.

> Can't we send someone from country to country, all over the world, with a message from the *Courier*? Our contribution to the solution of contemporary problems. A message of hope. A restatement of first principles ... I'd appeal for peace, for the putting aside of national animosities, for co-operation in the great task of making good the ruin that has been left by war. I'd appeal in the name of freedom, justice, democracy ...[4]

The heart of Malcolm's moral indictment of the elder Scott, and of the *Guardian* in general, was the assertion that the paper survived on the profits of the *Manchester Evening News*, a tabloid that was anything but high-minded. Scott refused to acknowledge this fact. In his novel,

Malcolm describes the *Evening News* as containing "the ecstatic statements of charwomen who had won sweepstake prizes, rows of bathing girls, angelic film stars, turf lore, salacious sweepings of the police courts and divorce courts".[5] Old Savoury passes on the letters about the relationship between the two papers to his son, forgetting that the correspondence files contained nothing about this accusation.

> Other moral problems in plenty – the rights of subject peoples, the duties of colonial administrators, religious instruction in the schools – an infinite number and variety of moral problems treated at length, and with zest. He had fed on moral problems, fattened on moral problems, jumped out of bed in the morning to struggle with them, reluctantly extricated himself from their clasp when he went to bed at night. His life had been one moral problem after another. Was he to be expected, then, to interrupt these great labours because tactless correspondents brought up the question of the curious, and profitable, ownership of the *Evening Gazette?* A trifling matter, he thought; of no importance. And, anyway, it's been dealt with before – several times.[6]

When the *Guardian* threatened to sue Malcolm over *Picture Palace* they singled out this charge as the most libellous. But Malcolm was right, of course. The balance sheets could have been consulted, but Malcolm's publisher was too timid to press the matter.

Malcolm and C.P. Scott actually got along quite well. The satirical portrait of Old Savoury in *Picture Palace* has more than a touch of affection for the old man. Preposterous and pathetic though he might be, he comes off better than the younger generation of political and intellectual climbers.

If there was one thing about the elder Scott that Malcolm could not forgive, it was his domination of his son, Ted. Though he had worked for the *Guardian* since 1912 and was the heir apparent, Ted was never able to step outside his father's shadow. Malcolm's fictional persona in *Picture Palace*, Pettygrew, tries to set out his feelings for Old Savoury's son, Arthur. "A rare man, not as coarse and insensitive as the common run, and not as cruel; a man who was bullied, and whose nature, hurt by bullying, turned into itself; a man sacrificed, like a Hindu widow, on his father's funeral pyre . . ."[7] But despite C.P.'s all-consuming nature, Ted was affable, humorous and ironic. Though he tended towards cynicism, Ted had made his peace with his role in life. Malcolm took to him immediately and the feeling was reciprocated.

The friendship between Malcolm and Ted Scott was the source of much envy and resentment, particularly from senior writers on the staff. One of Malcolm's friends from this period, then a young history professor at Manchester University, was A.J.P. (Alan) Taylor. In his own memoirs, Taylor spoke of Malcolm as the "spoilt child of the *Manchester Guardian*".[8] According to Taylor, Malcolm got special treatment. The normal working hours for a leader writer were from 5 p.m., when assignments would be given out, to 11.30 p.m., when proofs were read. Taylor reported that Malcolm would ask Paddy Monkhouse, a young, unmarried writer, to read his proofs for him. Monkhouse, who, like Ted Scott, admired Malcolm, was willing to perform the task.

Kingsley Martin, though six years older than Malcolm, had not fared well at the *Guardian*; his writing for the paper had been rather pedestrian, and he had given C.P. Scott the impression that he was a dangerously radical Leftist. Compared to Malcolm's mercurial rhetoric, Martin's earnestness seemed lame and one-dimensional. Malcolm's arrival made it easier for the Scotts to let Martin go, and early in 1931 the twenty-seven-year-old Malcolm became the paper's chief leader writer. Precisely because Ted saw through his father's high-mindedness, he was drawn to Malcolm's gloves-off, die-hard style.

Whenever he wrote about his time at the *Guardian*, Malcolm singled out the hollowness and pomposity of the paper's house style – a style that he claims to have parroted. But Malcolm had a tendency to be excessively harsh on himself in retrospect, allowing himself to be implicated in sins he did not commit. He was sensitive and honest enough to realise that the business of leader writing often involved the summoning up of artificial indignation and bogus principles – something he discovered on his first day at the *Guardian*. His first assignment was to write a leader on corporal punishment. Since it was not a subject, like India or Egypt, that had a clear political implication, Malcolm wandered over to Paddy Monkhouse. "What's our 'line' on corporal punishment?" he asked. "Without looking up, or stopping his typing, [Monkhouse] muttered: 'The same as capital, only more so.'" In his autobiography, Malcolm brilliantly deconstructs the typical editorial, using his leader on corporal punishment as his example. He highlights the invariable patterns: "First the originating observation ... Then the qualifying counter-observation ... Followed by a touch

of facetiousness . . . Preparing the way for the ascent to total seriousness . . . and working up to the moral point on which every leader
must hinge . . . Finally, a note of hope, on which all good leaders must
go out . . ."[9]

Because Malcolm had an almost obsessive passion to reveal any
disparity between appearance and reality, he quickly became disgusted
by the *Guardian*'s abuse of language. There was, of course, a humorous
side to the absurdity of the rhetoric, the fatuous crescendos at the end
of each leader: "It is greatly to be hoped . . . Surely wiser counsels will
prevail . . ." Malcolm found this "non-language" all too tempting at
times. His *alter ego* in *Picture Palace*, Pettygrew, finds himself falling
into this trap, making some comment on the beauty of nature as
opposed to the ugliness of the city. Pettygrew is then upbraided by the
character based on Ted Scott. "You're a prig, too," Arthur says to
Pettygrew. "Why can't you leave it alone? Just like father. First a
contrast – black, satanic mills. Then a moral, an ideal, an aspiration.
Thinking leading articles, speaking leading articles, living leading
articles."[10]

But Malcolm was not so cynical and detached about this issue that
he could remain satisfied with irony and jokes. He sensed that the
Guardian worldview was based on sentimentality and fantasy, a refusal
to accept that the gritty, unpleasant facts of life could not be solved by
political fiat. When Arthur tells Pettygrew about Old Savoury's plan
to send a message to the world, Pettygrew laughs. "Strange that he
should still believe in principles as principles. Strange that he should
still look at them, their abstract statement, to resolve conflicts, order
chaos."[11]

Malcolm's leaders for the *Guardian* rarely fell into the falsity of
abstraction. Rather, they are urgent, passionate pleas for political
realism. He returned frequently to the argument first made in his
article on "Subject Peoples":

We simply cannot afford to allow Mr Winston Churchill to stage
a new and improved version of the Black and Tan drama in India.
No doubt it would be thrilling enough and the eyes of all the
world would be upon it. But the cost is too great – in money, in
blood, and in shame – and even if we were less squeamish about
investing in murder, massacre and demoralisation we should like
a better guarantee than Mr Churchill's for the profits to be
derived from his sanguinary speculations.[12]

In his history of the *Guardian*, David Ayerst wrote about the impact of Malcolm's leaders on the paper's staff and readers. "A reader might feel that here was a man who could perceive that the King-Emperor wore no clothes. Or he might consider that Muggeridge was a wild and dangerous fanatic."[13] According to Ayerst, both views were held about Malcolm. But he was no political fanatic. He could also call for political compromise. As he wrote on the situation in India:

> Yet compromise, in one form or another, is the only policy that is immediately practical. We can neither govern nor "get out", and so it is necessary to devise a Constitution that seems in India like self-government and in Westminster like the British Raj. The sooner it is done the better. No more gestures, no more oratory, no more picturesque assemblies; an India Bill, Provincial Autonomy, an All-India Federation.[14]

Ayerst writes of the "innocence" of Malcolm's vision, but this leader on India, which is representative of much of Malcolm's output, could serve as a textbook example of *realpolitik*.

Malcolm also contributed an occasional piece on a literary subject. For Shakespeare's birthday he wrote a leader entitled "This Side Idolatry", which concludes that

> his essential greatness lay in the fact that he showed human life to be a splendid thing despite its limitations and its chaos. He showed men and women living and dying; loving one another and hating one another; possessed by ambition, lust, by jealousy, by all the passions that waste and yet glorify human beings. And always they were real. Hope cannot quite die because a poet who dared to consider the worst, the most terrible, still saw a dignity and an ecstasy in human life.[15]

Though he was at this time an ardent disciple of D.H. Lawrence, Malcolm had little time for Catherine Carswell's book on Lawrence, *The Savage Pilgrimage*. At the end of his review, Malcolm wrote: "How sick one gets of Don and John Patrick [Mrs Carswell's husband and son]! How sick one gets of Lawrence himself. How sick, how unutterably sick, of Mrs Carswell!"[16] Since Mrs Carswell was a long-time, valued contributor to the *Guardian*, Malcolm had managed to offend a large number of readers.

Not long after Malcolm arrived at the *Guardian*, he met a writer who was to play a pivotal role in his life: Hugh Kingsmill. Kitty had known Kingsmill since her childhood, because he was the son of Sir Henry Lunn. They knew Kingsmill's brother, Brian Lunn, quite well. Kingsmill had a stormy and complex relationship with his father; dropping his surname was part of Kingsmill's rebellion against Sir Henry. Much of their struggle related to money and dependency. Sir Henry had put all his sons on the payroll of the firm, without demanding much work from them. Kingsmill took advantage of this for many years, but when he came into conflict with his father over the breakup of his first marriage, Kingsmill was let go, and had to fend for himself for the first time in his life. Though he was a talented novelist and biographer, he was not a practical man and had little interest in working a steady job at a magazine or publisher. Constantly in need of money, he had used his connection with Kitty to approach Malcolm about the idea of getting a regular book review column for the *Guardian*.

Malcolm recounted his first meeting with Kingsmill many times.

He arrived quite late on a Friday night, and we went to the station to meet him. You know that curious feeling one has of meeting someone with whom one is going to be intimate. You feel as though you had known them already. Features, tone of voice, gestures, are all at once familiar. Thus I remember, in the dark, cavernous Manchester station with people streaming through the barrier, picking out Hughie without the slightest difficulty and greeting him as though we were old friends instead of strangers.[17]

Kingsmill had an exuberance for life that Malcolm found stimulating, precisely because of his own tendency towards depression and morbidity. But this hearty, confident manner often had the effect of making others uncomfortable. When Malcolm took Kingsmill to the *Guardian* offices, the literary editor, Alan Monkhouse, was not impressed by Kingsmill. The reviewing job did not materialise.

Returning to the Muggeridges' flat in the village of Didsbury, a prosperous suburb just south of Manchester, Malcolm and Kingsmill talked for hours. Without directly attacking the *Guardian*, Kingsmill pointed out the absurdity of the ideological rhetoric used in its pages – the catch-phrases about wiser counsels prevailing and men of goodwill drawing together. Malcolm had already begun the process of turning his back on this brand of cant, but Kingsmill demolished it with a playfulness that Malcolm found liberating. "Political Leftism, he said, was 'Dawnism' – that is, a propensity always to see a new dawn. Just by that one word he showed how absurd it all was, because, obviously, there can be no new dawn, but only dawn, leading in its invariable way to another afternoon and another evening. The word remained with me, like so many of his words and phrases."[18] Kingsmill was fourteen years older than Malcolm; he was just old enough to be something of a mentor, but not so old that he could not be a friend.

On Sunday, Kingsmill endeared himself to Malcolm even more with an example of his legendary absent-mindedness. Kingsmill got the notion that his friend, the actor and writer Hesketh Pearson, was going to be passing through Manchester on the train and would meet them on the platform at Stockport station. No trains came, but Kingsmill spoke so warmly of Pearson that Malcolm was touched. "We walked up and down Stockport platform for half an hour or so, and then he reluctantly reached the conclusion that what he had imagined to be a carefully arranged rendezvous was not as definite as he had supposed. We went off, however, feeling quite satisfied. If we had not met you, we had gone to meet you . . ."[19] When he got to know Kingsmill in later years, he came to believe that this absent-mindedness was not merely eccentricity, but a sign of mystical unworldliness.

While Kingsmill was struggling, Malcolm's own literary fortunes were prospering. His play, *Three Flats*, was performed by the Stage Society, opening at the Prince of Wales Theatre in London on February 15, 1931. The cast included several actors who would become well known on the London stage; one of the extras was the young Anthony Quayle. With Kitty, he took his father and mother to a Sunday evening performance. "It was an occasion of delirious happiness; there were shouts for the author, and I took a curtain with the cast. My father's pleasure was a great satisfaction to me, and I hope it offset some at least of his disappointments. His eyes were shining." Also in the audience were George Bernard Shaw and the Webbs, who had already discussed the play at length while Malcolm was living in Egypt. The reviewer in *The Times* noted the play's melancholy themes, but concluded that it was "a play distinguished by the sureness of its detail and the economy of its writing". He also learned that Universal Pictures had bought an option on the play, but a film of it was never made.[20]

Though his agent, Walter Peacock, Malcolm found a publisher for

Three Flats, G.P. Putnam's Sons. The managing director of Putnam was an American named Constant Huntington – a "Europeanised New Englander", as Malcolm described him, in the mould of Henry James and T.S. Eliot. Huntington admired Malcolm's talent and invited him to write a novel. This was the sort of offer that a young writer longs for, and Malcolm quickly agreed. He worked on the novel in the mornings, and completed it in less than a year.[21]

Autumnal Face, published in November 1931, is, like most of Malcolm's novels, eccentric, occasionally brilliant, but deeply flawed. It is an autobiographical novel, set in the Croydon of his youth, with characters based not only on his own family, but also on Dora Pitman and Kitty. The world it depicts is that of the lower middle class in a dreary modern suburb, where the routines of work and the home are only interrupted by equally predictable trips to the seaside. Unlike Evelyn Waugh, the rising literary star at the time, Malcolm was not interested in writing about the Bright Young Things of the upper classes. *Autumnal Face* is not a political novel, but Malcolm's decision to explore this part of the social landscape was deliberate. In this he was probably influenced by H.G. Wells and Arnold Bennett, whose novels discovered drama and dignity in the lives of working-class folk.

The story centres on the Pill family – Dad, Mum, Gran, Uncle George and daughter Minnie. If the novel has a protagonist it is Mum, a timid, but sensitive woman who no longer loves her husband. She is filled with inarticulate longings that Dad cannot perceive or fulfil. The character of Dad is a cruel caricature of H.T. as a suburban peasant who shuttles between his London counting house and his vegetable garden. In the second half of the novel, Dad loses his job and becomes completely disoriented; he wanders over the countryside, catches a chill and dies. Malcolm's feelings for his father at this time continued to be dominated by embarrassment and shame. When he read *Autumnal Face* H.T. experienced, once again, the bafflement and pain of his son's rejection.

The tone of the novel is established by the title: all of his characters are tired, worn out, in decline. The pervasive sexual metaphors in the story are those of impotence and sterility: Dad's awkward lovemaking ("a mountain in legitimate eruption"[22]), the voyeurism of the crippled Uncle George, and the ill-fated encounter between Minnie and her boyfriend Fred. After their evening at the cinema (recounted in chapter 2), Minnie and Fred go on a Sunday school excursion to the countryside. They go to a damp hollow, where once again their sexual urges bring only frustration and shame. Fred leaves and Minnie catches a chill and dies, a sterile virgin: this was Malcolm's epitaph on his relationship to Dora Pitman.

In the second half of the novel, Fred, now older, meets and marries an attractive, ultra-modern young woman named Phil. Here Malcolm translated his early married life with Kitty into the novel. Fred and Phil make love, but it does not bring physical or spiritual satisfaction.

> "Love makes us like one person," Fred whispered. He had whispered it so often. It was not true. They were never as separate as when their bodies were twined together. Sitting in the two-seater car they had a kind of union, or fox-trotting over a polished floor, or partners at tennis; but there in bed together, together in a dark bed, they were utterly separate. Phil abandoned herself to passion as she had abandoned herself to speed. She closed her eyes and let passion sweep through her. Then she carefully washed away Fred's sperm with disinfectant.[23]

Fred and Phil, unlike Malcolm and Kitty, seek nothing more than a bourgeois existence. Their modern bungalow has all the modern conveniences. They drug themselves by driving fast in their car, pacified by the "speed and rhythm" of the machine. This was the world that Malcolm and Kitty scorned and wanted to avoid at all costs.

Autumnal Face is a novel that attempts an unblinkered social realism, but at the same time it is marred by a large number of sudden deaths and accidents – the type of events that belong in a mediocre Victorian romance. Malcolm did have enough distance from the action to let the story unfold more naturally. He grants a certain stoic dignity to the character of Mum, but he finds it necessary to kill off the characters representing Dora and his father. There are moments in the novel of acute observation and black comedy, but they never fuse into a whole.

The critical reception of the novel was positive. The reviewers admired the frank and direct engagement with the working-class, suburban milieu. Malcolm got the greatest satisfaction from the headline in a publication called the *Sunday Referee*: "A YOUNG NOVELIST TO WATCH".[24] Coming on the heels of his success with *Three Flats* and his privileged position at the *Guardian*, this was one of the brightest moments of Malcolm's literary career.

As the scenes with Fred and Phil in *Autumnal Face* suggest, not all was well with Malcolm and Kitty. To their friends, however, they were a vibrant young couple, mildly bohemian, fun to be with. Kingsley Martin remembered one sign of their modern attitudes: "Kit had hung her pyjamas out of the window as a flag of defiance . . ."[25] Alan Taylor, who thought Kitty was "staggeringly beautiful", wrote in his memoirs of a summer afternoon when he and his wife went with the Muggeridges to "a remote field by the River Dane". The historian Lewis Namier was also with them. "We and the Muggeridges bathed in the river and ran naked along its bank."[26]

Back in their Didsbury flat, however, things were less exuberant. There were several different causes of tension between Malcolm and Kitty. But the two most explosive issues were undoubtedly sex and Kitty's isolation and increasing restlessness.

In his autobiography, Malcolm described the beginning of his marriage in these terms: "Marriage . . . begins, not with setting up house, counting wedding presents, blowing kisses, looking at wedding groups, but with two bodies confronting one another like two wrestlers."[27] Like Fred and Phil in *Autumnal Face*, the Muggeridges experienced the frustrations and emotional strains that attend any long-term sexual relationship. Kitty was certainly a modern woman in her candour about her own sexual needs and desires. This led to feelings of inadequacy and resentment on Malcolm's part. He reasoned to himself (and perhaps aloud to Kitty) that his absorption in his writing tended to drain him of sexual energy.[28] At his most self-pitying, he thought of Kitty as a sexual vampire with a voracious and endless need.[29]

The other issue that became a constant source of contention was Kitty's boredom and longing for some form of fulfilment besides motherhood. The relationship between Pettygrew and Gertrude in *Picture Palace* provides a number of vividly drawn scenes that were transcribed directly from experience. In this novel Malcolm did not spare himself.

[Pettygrew] was only able to keep their marriage afloat by scrupulously avoiding all reality. The moment even a particle of reality crept in, he was frightened, and wanted to run away. If he found himself saying something to Gertrude that he really meant, still worse letting her stir his feelings, his heart grew heavy with foreboding . . . Hate was as much an enemy as love. He avoided both, sustaining his relationship with his wife, as he sustained the leading articles whereby he earned a living, on the shiftless play of his mind.

This atmosphere of unreality oppressed Gertrude. She half expected the furniture, when she cleaned it, to be brittle and break in her hands, and would look down at her baby sucking at her breast and half wonder how he came to be there. Boredom accumulated in her, making her sometimes sad and sometimes resentful. Pettygrew was pompous about her discontent.[30]

As Pettygrew strides around the room, uttering platitudes about the glories of motherhood, Gertrude turns to him and says: "I wonder how you would like it ... sitting here every day and every evening with nothing to do except look after a baby and a miserable little flat. How would you like it?"[31] This leads Pettygrew to even wilder forms of rationalisation, then to apologies and pleas for reconciliation. But Gertrude retreats into herself. "He felt that she was a more serious and a more dignified person than he was. She seemed, he thought, to be independent of him. Her life was too sensitively organised to join itself on to his. In the end she would leave him, and he wanted her to go, and, when she had gone, be broken-hearted for ever."[32]

This kind of argument precipitated a crisis. Alan Taylor was present when Kitty "announced that she was leaving for London in order to become an actress. We saw her off at London Road station, Malcolm running along the platform as the train went out and calling, 'Good-bye Kitty. Perhaps our paths will cross again some day.'" The following day, when Malcolm was having tea with the Taylors, Kitty phoned to say that she would be returning that evening. Malcolm put the incident into *Picture Palace*, but there Gertrude does not come back. It is up to Pettygrew to search her out, after he becomes distraught with loneliness and sickened by his own tendency to seek out casual sex with other women.

Kitty's brief flight to London was the worst that Malcolm's friends saw, but there was more. Malcolm's insecurity was not merely sexual, but also related to Kitty's own personality and upbringing. She had a confidence and self-possession that were independent of him. She was, after all, the daughter of a cosmopolitan, upper-middle-class family; she could retreat into that world at any time. Malcolm could not, it would appear, think of any career that Kitty might pursue. To be fair to Malcolm, it has to be said that Kitty herself did not have a strong sense of what she wanted to do beyond the fleeting desire to become an actress.

Malcolm's reaction to these troubles was not to find ways to bind himself and Kitty closer together, but to argue in favour of an "open marriage". There is a passage in *Picture Palace* that explains Malcolm's reasons for avoiding intimacy.

> To be close to anyone was to make separation inevitable. He had been close to Gertrude. Creating happiness was like creating a home – something to destroy, to burn down, to pull to pieces. He shrank from happiness as he shrank from love ... The prospect of happiness was terrifying because it meant unhappiness, being vulnerable, exposing himself.[33]

So he suggested to Kitty that they both be free to have affairs. In his 1934 diary, Malcolm looked back to their time in Manchester, only two years earlier. "Some years after I'd been married to Kit, when we were first in Manchester, I suggested she should go to town for a few days. She didn't want to go, but I pressed her. 'Go and enjoy yourself,' I said. 'Have an affair.' I suppose it was just my crooked way of preparing the ground for having an affair myself."[34]

Once again, Malcolm was probably shocked by Kitty's independence, because she took him at his word and had an affair with a socialist writer named Ernest Davies, who worked for a magazine called the *Clarion*.[35] Of course, Malcolm was intensely jealous and there were angry confrontations, accusations and shouting matches. Malcolm was all too aware of his own hypocrisy. In *Picture Palace*, a character named Rattray, based on Alan Taylor, wants to have an affair with Gertrude. "'You've buried your pear-shaped head and your blond beard in Gertrude's body,' Pettygrew wanted to say, 'and I hate you for it.' Actually, he said, 'Possession is a negation of everything. It's a negation of life as we know it ... So far as I'm concerned, jealousy's inconceivable.'"[36]

There seems to be little evidence that her affair with Davies or any of her future affairs meant much to Kitty. In fact, the evidence points the other way. Kitty's affairs tended to be a form of retaliation, a desire to show Malcolm just how hypocritical and weak he was being, a challenge that would force him to declare himself. It was not in her nature to endure Malcolm's evasive behaviour passively. This sexual warfare was not resolved during their time in Manchester, but would continue for over a decade, leaving a battlefield scarred by heartbreak and tragedy.

A major turning point in Malcolm's life came in the autumn of 1931. Britain and the West had been suffering from the economic devastation of the Depression for two years, and these pressures had taken a toll on the Labour government that had been elected in 1929. Unemployment was reaching staggeringly high levels, and the Labour government's schemes of public works seemed too little and too late. Without emergency measures, including new taxes and cuts in government programmes, the nation seemed headed for financial catastrophe. On August 24, 1931, Ramsay MacDonald and the Labour government resigned. The following day, a National government was formed, which included Conservative and Liberal cabinet members, though MacDonald retained the post of Prime Minister. The majority of the Labour Party rank and file rejected the National government, considering it a massive betrayal on the part of MacDonald. A general election was held on October 27. It confirmed the National government, but the Labour Party went from the 288 seats it won in 1929 to a mere 52 seats in 1931.

Among those who lost seats in Parliament was H.T. Muggeridge. His election in 1929 had been the reward of decades of effort, a moment of bright promise for the Labour Party and the future H.T. wanted to bring about. Suddenly his parliamentary career was at an end, and because of a Judas-like betrayal of the Labour Party leader. H.T. had asked Malcolm once again to come and help him with the campaigning just before polling day. Malcolm drove to Romford from Manchester and gave a series of stump speeches for his father. In his 1934 diary, Malcolm recalled that his father "was proud of me because I spoke with an upper-class accent." Malcolm's feelings about his father continued to be a mixture of embarrassment and anguished affection. The diary entry continues with an account of H.T.'s final speech. "He had the air of a silly old boy arriving in a brothel ... I heard his harsh voice, watched him gesticulating, almost crying with I don't know what feelings. He was so game and so pathetic and so preposterous."[37]

On polling day, October 27, Malcolm uttered a panegyric for the Soviet Union. In his outrage at MacDonald's betrayal, Malcolm decided that he would become a Communist. The sentimental liberals had abandoned principle and proven themselves to be nothing more than cowards and opportunists. Only die-hards who did not stop at half-measures – such as the leaders of the Soviet Union – earned Malcolm's approbation. In the days before the election, Malcolm watched his father campaign valiantly, but H.T. was "scarcely aware of the way things were going". Malcolm drove back to Manchester late on the evening of the election and poured out his feelings to Kitty. "Back in Manchester I told Kit about the election, and about Dad speaking to the little crowd outside the pub, and cried as I told her. I suppose feeling must have been accumulating in me."[38] H.T. was sixty-seven years old, and everyone knew that it would be his final parliamentary campaign. He returned to the Croydon Council, which he would serve faithfully until 1940.

The government crisis of 1931 also affected Malcolm in another crucial way: it split the editorial staff of the *Guardian* and contributed, to a great extent, to Malcolm's departure from the paper. On the side of the National government were the two senior men on the staff, A.P. Wadsworth and W.P. Crozier; on the other side were Malcolm and Paddy Monkhouse. To add to the confusion, the crisis of August 1931 came during Ted Scott's summer vacation. There were no clear guidelines on how to respond to these novel political circumstances. Crozier and Wadsworth determined to support the new government. Crozier, in his long leader for August 25, wrote: "The National Government, formed for a specific purpose and for a limited time, should be warmly approved by a country which is, as a rule, suspicious of a Coalition ... There is to-day an emergency of peace which is comparable with that of war."[39]

When Ted Scott returned, he found his staff locked in a civil war. Malcolm had no time for Crozier's tergiversation. In the midst of the debate Scott wrote to a friend: "I am afraid we may not be able to keep Muggeridge very long, and even [Monkhouse] may find it difficult to associate himself permanently with a paper that will remain bourgeois to the last."[40] Scott managed to prevent the younger men from resigning. When, at a luncheon at Scott's home, the editorial staff had their chance to put forward their arguments, Malcolm felt that Scott was coming over to the anti-government position.[41] Scott's own editorial line began cautiously, but over the ensuing weeks became more embittered and critical of the National government. In the end, his position became almost identical with Malcolm's, even though it cost the paper advertising revenue from some of the larger businesses in Manchester. Malcolm's affection for Scott grew even stronger.

The death of C.P. Scott on New Year's Day, 1932 seemed to herald a new era on the paper. Malcolm rejoiced in what he saw as a liberation for Ted, and looked forward to a more principled and honest editorial line.

But the new era was fated to come to an abrupt and tragic end. Four months after his father's death, Ted Scott went with one of his sons for a brief holiday to Lake Windermere in the Lake District. On April 22, he took a dinghy out on the lake, presumably because he was going to board a yacht. About three hundred yards from the shore the dinghy capsized. His son Richard decided to cling to the overturned boat, but Ted began to swim to shore. He never made it there. In the cold water he suffered a heart attack and drowned. When Malcolm received the news by telephone from Mrs Spence, in whose home Ted and his son were staying, he could not believe what he was being told. "I found some difficulty in registering what she had said . . . 'You mean it's all over; that Ted is . . .' 'Yes,' she said, in a flat definitive voice."[42]

The news came as a hammer blow to Malcolm and all of Scott's many friends and admirers. To Malcolm there was a fearful symmetry in Ted Scott's death. It was as if the old man had so sucked the life out of his son that he could not possibly last long on his own. Crozier asked Malcolm to write the obituary. Rushing to meet the copy deadline that evening, Malcolm wrote that Scott was "a man among the most charming who ever lived. He was one of those in whom one is constantly finding new depths and new qualities. He did not reveal himself easily. He was somewhat shy and reserved. But those who were privileged to get beneath the reserve found a character that was at once simple and strong, gentle and shrewd – incapable by its very nature of any form of insincerity or self-deception."[43] These were all qualities that Malcolm, in his personal life at least, lacked. Scott was his "better angel" and now he was gone.

As he sat writing Scott's obituary, handing each sheet to Crozier as he finished, Malcolm could not resist praising Scott for reversing the paper's stand on the National government. This slap at Crozier was another example of Malcolm's habit of burning his bridges. But the damage had already been done, when Malcolm had convinced Scott to repudiate Crozier's position. Crozier, who had worked for the *Guardian* for many years, and who had been passed up for the editorship in favour of Ted Scott, now succeeded to the position. There would be no more special treatment for Malcolm. At best, he would be tolerated, given inferior topics to write on. The only mitigating factor was that the surviving heir, John Scott, had instructed Crozier to follow in Ted

Scott's footsteps. This enforced an uneasy truce between Malcolm and his editor. But Malcolm could not endure the reduction in his own status. He was also thoroughly disgusted with sentimental liberalism. So his thoughts turned to the East, to the experiment in Communism that had evoked his admiration since he was an adolescent.

When the *Guardian's* Moscow correspondent, William Henry Chamberlin, notified the paper that he intended to go on a six-month leave of absence, Malcolm immediately applied for the position. Crozier, only too happy to have Malcolm out of the office in Manchester, agreed.

Kitty, who was probably just as eager as Malcolm was to leave the scene of so much pain and frustration, went with Leonard to her parents' home in Vevey, Switzerland. Beatrice Webb arranged for Kitty to go to Moscow during the summer of 1932 to scout for possible jobs for herself and to obtain a long-term resident's visa. According to Mrs Webb, who was in the Soviet Union herself that summer, Kitty "had come in the same boat as the Fabians – travelling 'hard' in a party of ninety, mostly workers of humble station. She was staying at the river-front hostel for sailors, sleeping ten in a room, and roughing it . . ."[44] She not only obtained the visa, but signed on with the *Moscow News* as a writer. But when Kitty returned to England, she brought with her stories of terrible hunger and want in the Soviet Union. Despite Kitty's unsettling preview, she and Malcolm were determined to continue with their plans.

Leonard, now four years old, was placed in a school at Windermere, until such time as Malcolm and Kitty had settled in Moscow and could send for him. "It was an arrangement hateful at the time, and seems even more hateful in retrospect," Malcolm wrote in his autobiography.[45] They spent their final days in England at Passfield Corner with the Webbs. The Fabians had got over their loathing of the Soviet regime and now hailed it as the Workers' Paradise. Once again, Malcolm found himself at Tilbury, boarding a ship for a distant destination and a new beginning. He and Kitty sailed on the Soviet ship *Kooperatsia*, bound for Leningrad.

« 7 »

Death of a Die-Hard

1932–1933

MALCOLM SPENT ONLY seven months in the Soviet Union, but the experience proved a major turning point in his life. The standard version of this episode, recounted in Malcolm's many autobiographical accounts and repeated by others, is that he and Kitty went to the USSR as earnest, naïve, committed Marxists who fully expected to spend the rest of their lives as Soviet citizens. But Malcolm's emotions and convictions were never monolithic or naïve; he was too self-conscious and sceptical for that.

With the death of his friend and patron, Ted Scott, Malcolm knew that the *Guardian* was not likely to change from an utterly predictable source of high-minded progressive ideas. Ramsay MacDonald's betrayal of the Labour Party was yet another example of the hypocrisy and insincerity of the gradualist school of political reform. Malcolm came to feel that the Communists might be the only group willing to deal with social and economic problems with decisive, harsh, but realistic measures. And only in the Soviet Union had Communism come to power.

Malcolm's train of thought was not much different from that of many other Western intellectuals. The 1930s were to become the decade when Communism would have its greatest appeal to writers and artists. After the cataclysm of World War I, many intellectuals had been appalled that the Western nations had returned to the bourgeois materialism of the Roaring Twenties. The advent of the Depression seemed to confirm the instability and injustice of the capitalist system. When supposedly progressive leaders like MacDonald ended by capitulating to the established order, gradualism itself no longer seemed tenable. Perhaps it would require a violent revolution to pull down the rotten, thoroughly compromised institutions of the West –

the kind of catastrophic event that Communist theory called for. In the Soviet Union, the Communists, under the leadership of Josef Stalin, were undertaking drastic measures to ensure full employment, economic justice and social equality.

The notion of the USSR as a promised land had a particular appeal to Malcolm. He had always been attracted to the mystical streak in Russian culture, the spiritual intensity so vividly captured by the writings of Tolstoy and Dostoevsky. To join the Soviet experiment also had the aura of the Simple Life to which Malcolm was drawn. Another factor was the guilt Malcolm felt because he tended to be an observer, rather than a direct participant in events. He and Kitty knew that life in the Soviet Union would be rough, but they willingly embraced this form of asceticism, selling off their few trinkets and pieces of fancy clothes before boarding the ship to Leningrad.[1]

The best insights into Malcolm's experience in the Soviet Union come from his third novel, *Winter in Moscow*, written immediately after his experience in Russia. Malcolm portrays himself as the journalist, Wraithby, whose name suggests his lack of connection with the world around him. The initial character sketch of Wraithby provides a fairly honest portrait of Malcolm on the eve of his journey to the Soviet Union.

He was a dim, fitful person. Floating loose on society; making little darts, like a bee in search of honey, at newspaper offices and literature and politics and love affairs, and then hastily withdrawing into himself; interested in the world and in human affairs but having no contact with either; carried this way and that by changing emotions and convictions, he had observed from afar the Dictatorship of the Proletariat and had felt it to be substantial. He knew that it was brutal and intolerant and ruthless. He had no illusions about its consequences to individuals and to classes. Only, he thought, it offered a way of escape from himself. It was *Brahma*; an infinite; and by becoming one with it he would cease to be finite. It would relieve him of the burden of his appetites and opinions, and give him peace and humility. It would make it unnecessary for him to formulate points of view about pictures and books and social problems and relationships. His tired mind, everlastingly grinding into his soul like a dentist's drill into a tooth, would be able to sleep on its bosom. It was a sea that would cradle him. A baptism and a rebirth. He longed to lose himself in the Dictatorship of the Proletariat as Lawrence longed to lose himself in the loves of gamekeepers and gipsies.[2]

This is hardly a picture of an earnest, naïve Marxist. The religious language of this passage points to a common desire among the intellectuals of this period: the search for clear, unambiguous authority, which exercises power without hesitation or apology. Defenders of the Soviet regime acknowledged that force – sometimes brutal and ruthless – was the order of the day. But it was argued that Russia was only just emerging from a period of barbarism, and that desperate measures were necessary in desperate times. But on his way to Moscow, the one hope to which Malcolm clung was for a regime that understood the real world and would act decisively to remedy social ills.

In travelling to the Soviet Union, Malcolm was calling his own bluff. That would account for the absolute and somewhat brittle quality of his statements to his friends and colleagues. Alan Taylor told Malcolm, "If the Russians do not come up to your expectations, don't take it out on them." But Malcolm had replied, "No, no, it will be Utopia. I must see the Ideal even if I am unworthy of it."[3] It was one thing to call himself a Communist in Manchester, amidst the fecklessness of liberals, but now he was about to test his credentials as a die-hard. In the preface to *Winter in Moscow*, he acknowledged that he did not find the mystical source of political order. Rather, "I might almost say that at the ultimate source, at the place where water was bubbling up from the earth, I found myself."[4]

Disillusionment began on the voyage to Leningrad. The passengers were travelling to the Soviet Union more as pilgrims than as tourists or fact-finders. Malcolm recognised the type immediately: "They had the shambling gait, the roving eye, the air of being the elect or chosen ones, which I had come to associate with those who knew the answers, and could steer us aright to peace, prosperity and the everlasting brotherhood of man."[5] These were, of course, precisely the people Malcolm was leaving Britain to get away from. With his eagle's eye for any disparity between theory and practice, Malcolm watched his fellow passengers' attempts to socialise with the ship's crew as social equals. The crew were addressed as "Comrades" and instead of tipping them – a vulgar capitalist practice – the travellers decided to purchase books for the ship's library. This did not elicit much enthusiasm on the crew's part.

Towards the end of the voyage, it was decided that the passengers should put on a theatrical production for the benefit of the crew. To prove their ideological credentials, they staged a tongue-in-cheek version of a medieval mystery play about the creation of the world. Once again, the comrade crew members failed to appreciate the gesture. They "retaliated by offering a musical evening at which *Stenka Razin* and *Ochi Chornye* were sung; two songs that were to become all too familiar in the months ahead".[6]

Leningrad appeared to Malcolm to be only a shadow of its former glory. He and Kitty travelled on directly to Moscow. Sensing the historic importance of the time and place, Malcolm began a diary when he arrived in Moscow. The very first comment in the diary was: "Already I have made up my mind to call this the *Diary of a Journalist* and not the *Diary of a Communist*."[7] Malcolm had decided to reserve judgement, to remain an observer rather than a participant. For the first two months of his stay, the diary entries contain a running internal dialogue between the side that was growing uneasy about the Soviet regime and the side that struggled to make excuses for it.

In his characteristic fashion, Malcolm got to know his new environment by walking incessantly around the city. He was fascinated by Red Square and the Kremlin, which appealed to his sense of paradox. The stern authority of the Kremlin fortress contrasted with the fanciful towers and onion-shaped domes of churches like that of St Basil. Lenin's tomb fascinated him. He thought of the embalmed, immaculately preserved body of the great dictator as being like the displays of medieval saints, whose bodies were supposed to be incorruptible. A nearby church had been turned into an anti-God museum, its main exhibit a large pendulum, which was supposed to show that the theory of gravity had made God obsolete. Malcolm noted the Soviets' use of ceremony and ritual to create their own peculiar form of political theatre.

The Muggeridges found that the transition to their new life in the Soviet Union was not as smooth as they had hoped. While they stayed at the Nova Moskovkaya Hotel, they searched for a flat. What they found was that most Moscow flats were inhabited by two or more families, privacy being supplied by makeshift walls of blankets. Malcolm, of course, needed a quiet place to write, but there was another reason to want some space and privacy: Kitty was pregnant with their second child. When the manager of the hotel told them that they could no longer stay there, they began to panic. They were rescued, not by the Soviets, but by a wealthy German businessman, who had a dacha just outside Moscow in a town called Kliasma. He and his mistress only used the dacha at weekends, and were willing to share it with the Muggeridges. The house, made of wood, was reminiscent of a Swiss chalet. Though Malcolm hated the commute in and out of the city on crowded trains, he enjoyed walking on the long, straight paths in the pine woods near the dacha. Nestled in the midst of the forest was a small, abandoned church which had been turned into a tool shed. Malcolm noticed that it had not been totally abandoned because it had been repainted – surreptitiously, by some faithful Russians – in bright blue and white.

Malcolm decided that he needed to learn Russian as soon as possible. He studied the language with an eccentric woman named Klavdia Lvovna, whose age, he thought, could have been anywhere between twenty and forty. She asked to be paid with food, rather than money, because the rouble was increasingly worthless and foreign currency in the hands of a Russian was considered suspicious. Translating articles about the mighty deeds of Stalin and the Party made her nervous. Klavdia clung fiercely to her Russian Orthodox faith, despite the increasing religious persecution by the authorities. Eventually she confided to Malcolm that she had passed the food he gave her to a nun, who in turn sent it along a network that reached nuns who had been imprisoned in labour camps.

It did not take Malcolm long to fall into the rhythm of being a foreign correspondent in Moscow.

Being a newspaper correspondent in Moscow, I found, was, in itself, easy enough. The Soviet press was the only source of news; nothing happened or was said until it was reported in the newspapers. So, all I had to do was to go through the papers, pick out any item that might be interesting to readers of the *Guardian*, dish it up in a suitable form, get it passed by the censor at the Press Department, and hand it in at the telegraph office for dispatch.[8]

He could always embellish the material somewhat, looking for some local colour to add interest to the dispatch, providing that the censor would not find it objectionable.

If Malcolm thought that an air of unreality permeated the *Guardian* offices in Manchester, he soon discovered in Moscow an even greater atmosphere of deceit, fantasy and gullibility. The perfect symbol for this syndrome was Stalin's Five Year Plan, a highly-touted blueprint for industrialisation and economic redistribution that had just been completed when Malcolm arrived in Moscow. Many Western intellectuals had, in the light of the Depression, come to believe that capitalism involved intolerable boom-and-bust cycles, so the idea of a planned economy had become immensely popular. Stalin's Five Year Plan was hailed by these intellectuals as a bold stroke of statecraft that Western politicians were too timid to follow. The foreign press in Moscow was by and large uncritical of the unending stream of facts and figures which the Soviet ministries proclaimed were evidence of stunning success.

For the first few weeks Malcolm attempted to reserve judgement, hoping that beneath the propaganda and inflated statistics put out by the Soviet government, there was at least real progress towards economic equality and an acceptable standard of living. But he carried on a fierce inner debate on these issues in the pages of his diaries. Soon after his arrival in Moscow he wrote in his diary:

> These people are starving – that's a fact; they're building up, with some measure of success and a great deal of waste – a number of great industries; the country is governed by the stiffest dictatorship I've ever come across so there is no way of estimating what measure of popular support this grandiose Five Year Plan has – entailing terrible sacrifices, particularly on the part of the poorest people (the peasants) – however to find out I must learn Russian.[9]

A few days later he continued to struggle with the Plan:

> There is a vile kind of sentimentality in my whole reaction to Russia. But what I hate in it is just what I expected not to hate – the plan and all that doesn't conform, that's not mediocre, crushed out of existence. To me, tyranny and cruelty are little things ... But the plan is ghastly ... At the moment [the Plan] seems to me to be the characteristic product of the minds of a number of revolutionaries ... mad to impress themselves on their times, mad to be somebodies.[10]

Then, a week later: "I've suddenly realised that, after all, I'm civilised and that certain obvious kinds of cruelty are unexpectedly abhorrent."[11]

Malcolm's first real experience of the Soviet propaganda machine came in early October, when he and the rest of the foreign reporters were taken on a rail journey to see the newly completed Dneprostroi Dam in the Ukraine. The dam was the perfect incarnation of Stalin's policy of industrialisation, proof of the Soviet Union's determination to become a world power. The press delegation was shepherded by the head of the Soviet Press Department, Constantine Oumansky, an unctuous Party official whom Malcolm disliked intensely. Travelling through the beautiful rolling countryside of the Ukraine, Malcolm and the other correspondents were treated to fine food and a well-stocked bar. Malcolm found himself attracted to the svelte American photographer, Margaret Bourke-White, who had come to record the event. On occasion they would pass through stations where peasants had gathered to stare at their train. In his satirical version of this trip in the novel *Winter in Moscow*, Malcolm wrote: "At the stations peasants collected in wistful groups to stare at such magnificence; and occasionally one of the more soft-hearted amongst the journalists would toss them a piece of bread or a leg of chicken which they gobbled up voraciously on the spot."[12] As with nearly all of the events in the novel, this was a direct transcription from his actual experiences.

When they arrived at the dam in the evening, Oumansky took them to the site, where searchlights played over the huge concrete structure. A huge illuminated sign proclaimed: "ELECTRICITY PLUS SOVIET POWER EQUALS COMMUNISM". The following day a crowd of ten thousand people gathered to hear interminable speeches by representatives of the Party. Military bands played the Internationale at various times in the proceedings. Malcolm found himself talking to an American engineer named Cooper who had helped the Soviets to build the dam. When asked how he had found the working conditions at the dam, Cooper was enthusiastic: "No labour trouble!" he said. It didn't take long for Malcolm to realise that the Soviets had employed forced labour to complete the dam. Cooper appears as Camshott in *Winter in Moscow*: "You can do what you like here. Build what you like, as big as you like. The bigger the better. No restrictions on anything. Only get on with the job. Get it finished no matter what it costs; no matter how many hours you or anyone else has to work. Yes, I like it. It's a big country; and these boys have got big ideas. I'm proud to work with them. Yes, sir, proud to be in on this show."[13]

On arriving back in Moscow, Malcolm complained in his diary that the trip had been "unreal". But he had not completely abandoned his hopes. According to the American journalist, Eugene Lyons, who was also a Moscow correspondent at the time, Malcolm had not yet given up on the Soviets. Lyons recalled Malcolm's behaviour on the Dneprostroi trip. "I remember," Lyons wrote, "how he and another young Londoner defended their dream against the doubts and criticisms of the more seasoned correspondents."[14]

In fact, Malcolm had already befriended one of the most seasoned and cynical of the foreign correspondents, an Englishman named A.T. Cholerton, who was at that time writing for the *News Chronicle* and would later work for the *Daily Telegraph*. Cholerton had been living in the Soviet Union since the mid-1920s and had married an Austrian woman named Charlotte. Cholerton had the qualities of detachment, scepticism and a dark, ironic sense of humour that Malcolm always found appealing. Cholerton would be "habitually stretched out on a couch, having a lung infection which made him subject to sudden temperatures; often with a bottle of red Caucasian wine beside him. He had a way of lining up bottles in the morning for the day's consumption. With his untidy beard, incessant conversation, wide-ranging, inconstant but scintillating mind, he was the very image of the Russian intellectual as portrayed by Dostoevsky."[15] Cholerton's cynicism about the Soviet regime was epitomised in a comment he made to one of the many liberal pilgrims to the USSR. Were the accusations made against the Old Bolsheviks in Stalin's show trials true, the pilgrim asked. "Yes," Cholerton replied, "everything is true except the facts."

Malcolm spent many evenings talking with Cholerton. He also frequently went to the theatre with the Cholertons, even though he couldn't understand the language. The only play that impressed him was Chekhov's *The Cherry Orchard*, performed at the Stanislavsky Theatre. The rest of the productions he saw were absurd morality tales about earnest Marxist heroes fighting bourgeois villains. Each of these plays seemed to end with a large tableau depicting industrial machinery turning smoothly, followed by a speech extolling Communism and the playing of the Internationale.

Despite the enormous amount of new information and experience Malcolm encountered in those early weeks in Moscow, his attention was concentrated primarily on the dacha in Kliasma. On his return from Dneprostroi he found that Kitty had become ill, running a high fever and remaining confined to her bed. After nearly a week, a German doctor diagnosed the illness as typhus. Kitty was relieved when she was told that typhus would not be harmful to the baby in her womb. Malcolm, who had been distraught at the idea that Kitty might die, was also relieved. He nursed her faithfully, even sleeping on the floor in her room to be near her. Several times a day he would take her temperature, feeling elated or depressed with every little change up or down. Kitty's illness convinced them both that she should have the baby in England. When asked about the hospitals in the Soviet Union, the German doctor had shuddered. It was decided that she should leave in December.

Malcolm was writing *Picture Palace* at this time. He wrote at a tremendous rate, completing the novel in only three months. In it he poured out not only his scorn for the sentimentality and fantasy of the liberalism represented by the *Guardian*, but also some of the personal traumas of his years in Manchester. The novel, he thought, was well written, but he did have some lingering doubts. One of those doubts, that the parallels with living persons and institutions was so close as to be libellous, would prove to be well founded.

Picture Palace is deeply flawed as a novel, but its theme is central to Malcolm's philosophy. "The thesis of my book becomes more and more the unhappiness and ineffectualness of the intellectual in contact with passionate realities; his inability to manage his affections, his helplessness politically and economically; and yet at the same time the power that he has in a Capitalist, or, for that matter, in a Communist country."[16] Here Malcolm was once again ahead of his times, for the 1930s were pre-eminently the decade of the intellectual: from the older generation, including Shaw, Wells and the Webbs, down to angry young poets like W.H. Auden and Stephen Spender, the intellectual was hailed not only as political crusader but as architect of a new order. As Beatrice Webb had said to Malcolm just before the Muggeridges left for Moscow: "Sidney and I have become ikons in the Soviet Union."[17] With characteristic honesty, Malcolm realised that he too was an intellectual. He believed that he could only redeem himself by refusing to get into the "power racket" and by writing books that would show up the fraudulence of the intellectual class.

Malcolm recognised that his style would be criticised. "As usual with my work, there is a tendency towards the grotesque."[18] Actually, *Picture Palace* begins promisingly. The opening scenes about Old Savoury and Pettygrew are reminiscent of the early novels of Evelyn Waugh; there are the same elements of black comedy, satire and a flair for the absurd that can be found in novels like *Black Mischief* and

Scoop. Unfortunately, Malcolm had little sense of literary form; he lacked the patience needed to stick to one story. So the novel veers in several different directions, from an election day sequence based on his father's recent defeat to Pettygrew's marital problems and affairs. *Picture Palace* shows Malcolm's talent for satire, but like all of his novels it fails to cohere.

After finishing *Picture Palace*, Malcolm set to work on a play, "Too Much Venus". It is written in much the same vein as *Three Flats*: a drawing-room comedy revolving around progressive ideas about sex and politics. Unlike the earlier play, however, "Too Much Venus" is less interested in depicting the life of the working class than it is in satirising the pretensions of the intellectual class. Wilfred Eggers is a literary dilettante who translates the works of others. He lives with a lower-class tart, Molly Hollands, but has become engaged to Eleanor Law, a beautiful, sophisticated advocate of idealistic causes. The farce associated with this love triangle is outweighed by the satire on progressivist eggheads. Sibil Rackham-Smith, a novelist and *grande dame* among the freethinkers, is eloquent on the advanced mores in the Soviet Union: "The first thing, then, to notice about sex-life in Wussia is the sepawation of mawiage and pwocweation from sex. This sepawation is possible because, with birth control information available for all, and abortions in case of accidents, there [is] no danger of one invading the pwovince of the other . . ."[19] The dialogue in the play is snappy and charged with wit, making it at least as good a play as *Three Flats*. But "Too Much Venus" took aim too directly at its targets to be staged in England. The real Sibil Rackham-Smiths, not to mention the Bernard Shaws, wouldn't stand for it. Malcolm planned to write yet another play at this time, "Foreign Correspondent", but it came to nothing.

When Kitty recovered her strength, Malcolm realised just how precarious their life had become. He had made an agreement with Crozier at the *Guardian* that he would be paid as a free-lancer and he had not filed many reports in his first weeks in Moscow. True, they had been able to move into the Moscow flat of the *Guardian* correspondent William Henry Chamberlin by mid-November, but no money was coming in and their savings were quickly running out. Now Kitty, who had been terribly ill, was returning to England to give birth. Added to this was Malcolm's own struggle to reserve judgement on a regime that increasingly seemed to be evil and barbaric. There had even been some question about whether Chamberlin would be taking his leave of absence, but he finally did leave Moscow, allowing Malcolm to begin writing for the *Guardian*.

Malcolm attempted to make contacts at the British Embassy. One of the embassy officials, William Strang, was friendly and occasionally provided Malcolm with helpful information. Malcolm did get to know one of the young embassy staff, a man who would play a major role in the Muggeridges' future. His name was Michal Vyvyan, and their first encounter was not auspicious. Malcolm had come to the embassy to interview Vyvyan. After they had been engaged in conversation for some time Vyvyan got up rather abruptly, made a perfunctory excuse, and left. Malcolm found this behaviour offensive, but what made it especially galling was that Vyvyan was upper-class and this made him feel that he had been snubbed. A couple of days after this meeting, Malcolm thought of turning it into a plot for a short story called "Class". The Vyvyan character has a "sprouting moustache, silky eyes, immaculate clothes, louder than I would care to wear. There is an immediate antagonism between the two men. The one is aggressive, the other is insolent. Vyvyian [*sic*] does something vaguely insulting. It is not a conscious insult; it may even be all the other's imagination. Yet class hate flares up inside him because of it."[20] Malcolm considered Vyvyan a "nincompoop", his public school education having taught him nothing but superficial ideas.

Though their initial encounter had been so disastrous, Malcolm did not attempt to avoid Vyvyan – they met at receptions, parties and meals taken at the embassy. After a few weeks they became friendly. One night, shortly before Kitty was scheduled to leave for England, Malcolm and Kitty dined at the embassy. During the course of the dinner, Malcolm became convinced that Vyvyan was "amorously inclined" towards Kitty.[21] He was right. Vyvyan had fallen in love with her. Since Kitty was about to depart, Vyvyan could not act on his feelings. He said nothing to Malcolm, and continued to socialise with him while Malcolm was still in Moscow.

With Kitty gone and *Picture Palace* completed, Malcolm could devote his attention to the search for the truth about the Soviet Union. Soon after he had arrived in Moscow, Cholerton had given him a copy of the French historian Taine's *Origines de la France Contemporaine*. Taine provided Malcolm with an important insight into the nature of ideological abstractions: "Nothing is more dangerous than a general idea in narrow and empty minds; since they are empty, it would not encounter any knowledge that would be an obstacle to it; since they are narrow, it does not linger to occupy them totally. Consequently, they are no longer their own master. They are mastered by it; it acts in them, and by them; in the proper sense of the word, man is possessed."[22] Taine had spoken of the French Revolution, but Malcolm found this insight equally applicable to the Russian Revolution. As Malcolm tried to piece together the various elements of the Soviet regime – the use of propaganda, forced labour, the constant references to the so-called threat of "counter-revolutionary" forces, the "disappearances" and the pervasive sense of fear – he began to understand the nature of totalitarianism. Stalin was not merely a traditional "oriental despot", but a master of a new political system: the ideological, totalitarian regime. The tyranny of the "general idea" made Tsarist repression seem liberal by comparison. Not long after he had arrived in Moscow, Malcolm had written in his diary: "The Theory hangs like a cloud over Russia. Those who believe in the Theory, and who at present have power may be able to shape the future. They may build up a new civilization. If so, the rest is dead wood. But should they fail, then they will leave a desert behind them, a vast desert. Marxism may replace European civilization; in any case, as far as Russia is concerned, it will destroy it."[23]

Malcolm's uneasiness about the Soviet Union and the uncritical admiration of Western intellectuals for it quickly grew into outrage. It was in the figure of the *New York Times* Moscow correspondent, the British-born Walter Duranty, that Malcolm saw the *reductio ad absurdam* of the intellectual's hunger for power. In 1932 Duranty was at the peak of his influence: he had just won America's prestigious Pulitzer Prize for his reporting of the Five Year Plan. Like Cholerton and Eugene Lyons, he had been reporting from Russia for years, but he was far more influential than them. His popularity at this time can be gauged from the story told by Alexander Woollcott. At a banquet celebrating the United States' recognition of the Soviet Union in 1933, an honour roll of people who had helped to bring this event to pass was read. All received polite applause, "but the one really prolonged pandemonium was evoked by the mention of a little Englishman ... Indeed, one quite got the impression that America, in a spasm of discernment, was recognizing both Russia and Walter Duranty."[24]

When, nearly sixty years later, a full-length biography was written about Duranty, the estimation would be vastly different: the book is entitled *Stalin's Apologist*. Malcolm recognised immediately that

Duranty was obsessed with power. Malcolm wrote in his autobiography that Duranty "admired Stalin and the regime precisely because they were so strong and ruthless. 'I put my money on Stalin,' was one of his favourite sayings. It was the sheer power generated that appealed to him . . ."[25] Malcolm's judgement was so harsh because he recognised in Duranty something that he himself had come dangerously close to accepting. Malcolm, after all, had written in his diary: "To me, tyranny and cruelty are little things." Unlike Duranty, however, Malcolm found himself unable to worship the ideological overlords. He also found himself less and less enamoured of collectivism and more and more concerned with the fate of the individual.

Duranty is satirised as Jefferson in Malcolm's novel, *Winter in Moscow*. In one scene, Jefferson and the other foreign correspondents rush to write their telegrams about an interminable speech by a Party official named Kokoshkin. Malcolm himself had sent many such telegrams. Jefferson, an old hand, taps away almost unconsciously.

last night addressing collective farm shock-workers kokoshkin stressed necessity ruthlessly crushing opposition elements to governments collectivisation policy stop bolsheviks determined harmonise agricultural economy with industrial development plan stop admittedly involves cruelty and casualties like other forms war but dash putting it brutally dash impossible make omelettes uncracking eggs . . .[26]

Of the omelettes and eggs metaphor, Duranty's biographer notes: "The phrase did seem to take on a life of its own, turning up again and again in Duranty's work – and in the work of others. It was to become the historic rationale for the whole process of modernization as epitomized by the Five Year Plan."[27]

The group of correspondents in Cholerton's camp despised Duranty and others like him. They developed a dark sense of humour about the barbarism of the Soviet regime and the gullibility of Western intellectuals. At one point the Cholerton group held a contest "to see who could produce the most striking example of credulity among this fine flower of our western intelligentsia". Malcolm won an honourable mention by persuading Lord Marley "that the queuing at food shops was permitted by authorities because it provided a means of inducing the workers to rest when otherwise their zeal for completing the Five

Year Plan in record time was such that they would keep at it all the time . . ."[28]

But Malcolm, despite his penchant for black comedy, found himself unable to laugh off the events taking place in the Soviet Union. "I am now completely disillusioned," Malcolm wrote in late November. A few weeks later something occurred that turned disillusionment into a more active phase of investigative journalism. One day a man showed up at Malcolm's door offering to give him some information. Klavdia Lvovna, frightened by the implications of this, refused to interpret to Malcolm. Later in the day he went to Cholerton, whose secretary also declined to interpret. But Cholerton asked the man to come back in the evening.

> He was, he said, from the North Caucasus where people were starving and being shot for storing grain. He left us a pile of notes. They told an appalling story. The treatment of the peasants by the Soviet Government is, in its way, one of the worst crimes of history. I shall send an account to the *Manchester Guardian*. 'Ask them abroad not to buy our food,' he kept saying, 'Tell them to stop buying. Otherwise we are ruined.'[29]

Ever since the Dneprostroi trip, Malcolm had found Stalin's obsession with heavy industry to be at odds with the need of the people to increase agricultural production in order to eat. The two primary aims of Stalin's agricultural policy were the forced transition to collectivisation and the elimination of the kulaks. Collectivisation entailed the end of private property and the establishment of large-scale factory farms, known as *kolkhozes*. Stalin called this the "revolution from above" and it was intended to break down the resistance of stubborn individuals and keep them in controlled environments. Kulak was the name given to a relatively prosperous peasant, but the term was manipulated by the Soviet leadership to create a "class enemy" to Communism. The kulaks, essentially "middle peasants", accounted for a large percentage of the agricultural production in the country. A third, unstated goal of Stalin's plan was the destruction of the Ukraine, a fiercely proud nation with its own language and culture that had been dominated first by the Russian Empire and then by the Soviet Union. Tsars and commissars alike wanted to destroy the spirit and identity of the Ukraine, which always remained a threat to the regimes run by ethnic Russians.[30]

Malcolm had arrived in the Soviet Union at the outset of the "terror-famine" of 1932–1933. Robert Conquest, the outstanding Western historian of this episode, begins his book, *The Harvest of Sorrow*, by comparing Stalin's genocide to the Holocaust (symbolised by the Nazi concentration camp at Belsen) that would take place a decade later:

> Fifty years ago as I write these words, the Ukraine and the Ukrainian, Cossack and other areas to its east – a great stretch of territory with some forty million inhabitants – was like one vast Belsen. A quarter of the rural population, men, women and children, lay dead or dying, the rest in various stages of debilitation with no strength to bury their families or neighbours. At the same time, (as at Belsen), well-fed squads of police or party officials supervised the victims.[31]

What made this famine practically unique in history was that it was not the result of drought or any other natural cause, but was brought about deliberately by the systematic efforts of the Soviet regime. Grain harvests were taken from the famine area and anyone caught hoarding even the smallest amounts of grain was shot. The countryside was covered by the rotting corpses of animals and people. It is estimated that between seven and ten million people died in the famine.

The first Western reporters to witness the effects of the famine themselves were Ralph Barnes of the *Chicago Daily News* and William Stoneman of the *New York Herald Tribune*. They had received information from Eugene Lyons that the GPU (the precursor to the KGB) had gone on a "rampage" in the Kuban district. Barnes and Stoneman, knowing that their reports would never make it past the Soviet censors, sent their dispatches out through "an obliging German Jewish fur buyer" who was returning to Berlin. According to S.J. Taylor, the publication of these articles alarmed Soviet officials, who immediately banned foreign journalists from travelling outside Moscow. "As early as the beginning of March 1933, the British Embassy reported to the Foreign Office in London that travel into the afflicted area had now been suspended for all members of the foreign press."[32]

Malcolm, who had already got himself into trouble with Oumansky for writing an article about the Lubianka prison run by the GPU, began to write boldly critical pieces for the *Guardian* on the failure of

Soviet agriculture. In an article entitled "The Price of Russia's 'Plan'", Malcolm noted that collectivisation was taking a terrible toll on the farmers, threatening food supplies in the towns. The acidic tone of his dispatches at this time can be gauged from this comment on a Soviet journal: "A few numbers of *Bezboghnik* (the *Atheist*) are calculated to make the austerest Puritanism seem, by comparison, full of humanity and tolerance and the Wahabis overflowing with charity and neighbourliness . . . To say that there is no religious persecution in Russia is like saying that negroes have the vote in the United States. Both statements are technically true but actually false."[33]

Malcolm was now thoroughly depressed. His disgust for the Soviet leadership had become intense. The manuscript of *Picture Palace* had been rejected by his editor at Putnam as libellous. He missed Kitty badly but made love to one of his fellow correspondents' daughters. "Again I feel ready to die," he wrote in his diary. "Dictatorship of the Proletariat. Anyway I don't want to dictate. Never, never to dictate. Russia has set me irrevocably against a dictatorship by Muggeridge. Better to suffer than to make suffering. I lay down to sleep, tired out with nothing. Another day was over."[34] At the end of January, he gave up writing in his diary altogether.

In early March, Malcolm decided to find out about the famine for himself. Despite the official ban on travel, enacted after the Barnes and Stoneman excursion, Malcolm simply went to the railway station, bought a special ticket to Kiev and Rostov-on-Don that allowed him to stop off along the way, and boarded the train. He told no one where he was going and there was no one to stop him. It was a courageous act, but Malcolm felt he had little to lose. He no longer wanted to spend the rest of his life in the Workers' Paradise, so he decided to gamble on a fact-finding trip that would confirm the rumours of famine and brutality in the Ukraine and surrounding areas.

The journey to Rostov was, as he put it in his autobiography, a "nightmare memory". Travelling in comfort along with minor Party officials, he found that none of them would talk about the conditions in the area of the famine. He resisted the temptation to simply stay in the relative comfort of the train, disembarking several times to have a closer look at the conditions in the villages. He saw "abandoned villages, the absence of livestock, neglected fields; everywhere famished, frightened people and intimations of coercion, soldiers about the place, and hard-faced men in long overcoats". One scene was unforgettable. He came upon a group of "peasants with their hands tied behind them being loaded into cattle trucks at gun-point ... all so silent and mysterious and horrible in the half-light, like some macabre ballet".[35]

Malcolm then went to Kiev. Finding that it was a Sunday, he sought out a church. This too proved to be an unforgettable experience, almost mystical in its intensity. After having witnessed the horrendous privations of the countryside, he was deeply moved by the faith he felt in that church service, with men, women and children gathered before the priests chanting and swinging censers before the altar. "[T]he sense conveyed of turning to God in great affliction was overpowering ... to God they turned with a passion, a dedication, a humility, impossible to convey. They took me with them ..."[36] One could ascribe psychological terms to this sense of spiritual exaltation, considering the circumstances. But there is no question that Malcolm himself felt that a truth had been vouchsafed to him. Decades later, in some autobiographical jottings, he remembered that it was at this service in Kiev that he had, for the first time, come to feel the absolute truth of the Easter proclamation that "Christ is Risen".[37] In the years after his time in India, Malcolm had drifted away from religious speculation, but this moment revived his spiritual longings.

After reaching Rostov, Malcolm travelled to the Kuban district of the North Caucasus to see one of the agricultural concessions that had been granted to the Germans. The order, efficiency and plentiful food at the concession were such that he felt he had suddenly arrived in a different country. The German farmers – experts in agricultural techniques – admitted that starving peasants continually begged them for work and food. That evening, while the Germans entertained him with food and song, someone turned on the radio. The broadcast, from Germany, announced that Adolf Hitler had just been named Chancellor. Malcolm's first reaction was horror, but the agricultural experts welcomed Hitler's rise to power. They argued that even though their own class might lose everything, as they had in World War I, Hitler would restore Germany's strength and dignity. It was as if Malcolm had been given a secular revelation. "Thenceforth, I never doubted that another war was inescapable."[38]

On his return to Moscow, he found a telegram from Kitty announcing that their second son, John, had been born. The news of this new life, so full of promise and hope, contrasted with the death and destruction he now had to report to the world. Malcolm gave a full account of what he had seen to the British Embassy in Moscow and then immediately set about writing a series of three articles on the famine. They were smuggled out of the country in diplomatic bags and published, in a somewhat edited form, in the *Guardian* on March 25, 27 and 28, 1933. The writing was impassioned but meticulous. Malcolm reported the "fields choked with weeds, cattle dead, people starving and dispirited, no horses for ploughing or for transport, not even adequate supplies of seed for the spring sowing".[39] In the last of the three articles, he concluded: "To say that there is a famine in some of the most fertile parts of Russia is to say much less than the truth; there is not only famine but – in the case of the North Caucasus at least – a state of war, a military occupation."[40] Crozier, who had cut some of these articles, placed two of them on page 9 and one on page 13 of the *Guardian*.

The response to these articles was not long in coming, either in the West or in Moscow. Malcolm knew that it was only a matter of time before the Soviets would declare him *persona non grata*, so he prepared for his departure. Before he left, however, another newsworthy event occurred. Two British employees of the Metropolitan-Vickers Electrical Company had been arrested and charged with industrial sabotage. The arrest and trial of two foreign nationals in the Soviet Union was a major event, but at first Oumansky and the Press Department refused to admit that the arrests had been made. One of the accused men was Allan Monkhouse, a cousin of Paddy Monkhouse at the *Guardian*. The articles Malcolm sent back on the Metro-Vickers affair, as it was known, were once again cut by Crozier. This was the last straw for Malcolm as far as his connection with the *Guardian* was concerned. He wrote Crozier a fierce letter, effectively ending his association with the *Guardian*: "From the way you've cut my messages about the Metro-Vickers affair, I realise that you don't want to know what's going on in Russia, or to let your readers know. If it had been an oppressed minority, or subject people valiantly struggling to be free, that would have been another matter. Then any amount of outspokenness, any amount of honesty."[41]

Malcolm was quite surprised to receive, on the eve of his departure, an invitation from Oumansky to dinner. The setting for the dinner was the Spirodonovka, once the home of a rich merchant, filled with marble and mirrors, candelabras and heavy drapery. Sitting in this relic of the pre-Revolutionary past, talking politely with men who were systematically distorting and repressing the truth about a murderous and genocidal regime, Malcolm was overcome by the irony and surrealism of the moment. There was a question that Malcolm kept trying to put to Oumansky, a question derived from Lenin. "Who whom?" It is the ultimate question of political power: who will rule whom? Malcolm was never sure whether he ever got an answer, but he thought that Oumansky eventually whispered: "I they!"[42]

On his way out of the country, Malcolm decided to break his journey at Leningrad. There he sought out the cemetery where the great Russian writer Dostoevsky was buried. The grave was untended and overgrown, of course, because Dostoevsky had been banned by the Soviet authorities. He had written prophetically of atheistic ideologues who would create a form of tyranny unknown in human history. Dostoevsky also professed a passionate, if tortured, Christian faith. He was, at that moment, an appropriate patron saint for the young man who was heading back to his wife and family, and to a new and more bitter form of exile than he had yet known.

« 8 »

Black Moments

1933–1935

THE MALCOLM MUGGERIDGE who left Moscow in the spring of
1933 was an angry young man. Malcolm was angry at the gullibility of
the entire Leftist establishment, from his father to the *Guardian* to
Fabians like Shaw and the Webbs. He was furious at the cowardice of
the foreign correspondents in Moscow, epitomised by Walter Duranty.
He loathed and despised the thugs who ruled the Soviet Union
through a never-ending Reign of Terror. Above all, he was angry at
himself – for allowing himself to become stranded and isolated, without
money or prospects for employment, without positive convictions or
hopes. Instead of a widening horizon of opportunities, he felt that he
had been backed into a corner from which he could not break out.

His first expression of this anger came on the train journey out of
the Soviet Union. The train was headed for Riga, the capital of Latvia,
which was then an independent nation before its absorption into the
Soviet Union after the Second World War. Along with his fellow
passengers, he had waited with eager anticipation for the border
crossing out of the USSR. "Then, when we were safely in Latvian
territory, we all began spontaneously to laugh and shout and shake our
fists at the sentries. We were out, we were free. It was one of the
strangest demonstrations of the kind I have ever been involved in."[1]

Malcolm decided to break his journey in Berlin so that he could see
for himself what Hitler's Nazis were like. Having heard in Russia that
Hitler was now Chancellor, he needed to test his intuition that the
Nazis were about to create their own brand of totalitarian state. The
storm-troopers swaggering around Berlin were all too familiar. The
hedonism of the Weimar era, he thought, was giving way to the
puritanism of National Socialism. In his letter to Crozier, severing his
ties with the *Manchester Guardian*, he wrote: "It's silly to say the

Brown Terror is worse than the Red Terror. They're both horrible. They're both Terrors. I watched the Nazis march along Unter den Linden and realised – of course, they're Komsomols, the same people, the same faces. It's the same show."[2]

After only a couple days in Berlin, he travelled on to Montreux, Switzerland, where he had agreed to rendezvous with Kitty. She approached him on the platform, holding Leonard by the hand and John in her arms. The safe arrival of John into the world and the relief of having put the Russian episode behind them blotted out any discord at this reunion. There was only joy at this moment, the two self-described "vagabonds' clinging to each other once more.

Thanks to the Dobbs family, the Muggeridges were able to stay in a chalet in Rossinière, Switzerland, owned by the Workers' Travel Association. The Chalet de la Colline, as it was called, had been built by an Englishman, but when he ran out of money it had been bought by the WTA. The first guests were not due to arrive until the end of the summer, so Malcolm and Kitty had it all to themselves. Kitty knew the area well; she had been born in the nearby village of Château d'Oêx. Over the course of the summer, the Muggeridges were dependent on the Dobbses for money. Malcolm felt deeply embarrassed and frustrated at this arrangement, but for the time being he had to accept it. He had a story to tell, and he needed some time not only to report his experiences in the form of newspaper articles, but to put those experiences into a novel.

His first article, "The Soviet's War on the Peasants", appeared in May in the pages of a relatively obscure journal known as the *Fortnightly*. It was similar to his *Guardian* dispatches, but set out the history of collectivisation and the elimination of the kulaks in a remarkably dispassionate manner. He wrote of the "circus" staged by Stalin and his henchmen to expose the "counter-revolutionary" forces working to undermine the progress of the Soviet plan. "The reality behind the circus," Malcolm wrote, "is the GPU and the army . . . 'Political Departments' have been established in every machine tractor station and state farm – that is, all over the country – and will be responsible for executing the Government's agricultural programme . . . It is an important stage in the evolution of Soviet Russia into a huge and centrally organised slave state."[3]

Malcolm went on to write a series of seven articles on the situation in the Soviet Union. Obviously, they could not be sent to the *Guardian*. Even if he had not broken with Crozier, the March articles on the famine had brought many angry denunciations and attacks in the letters column. He decided to send them to the *Morning Post*, a "reputable" if right-wing Tory paper. The *Morning Post* accepted five of the articles, running them under the title of "Russia Revealed". Perhaps because some of his earlier reports had been mocked and dismissed, the tone in these articles is angry and argumentative. Decrying the gullibility of those who live in the "Fabian Fairyland", Malcolm repeated the story of the man-made famine in the Ukraine and North Caucasus. "The particular horror of their rule is what they have done in the villages. This, I am convinced, is one of the most monstrous crimes in history, so terrible that people in the future will scarcely be able to believe it ever happened."[4]

Several of the *Morning Post* articles explored the institutions and ideology that constitute a totalitarian regime. Malcolm noted that the Soviet regime, despite its claim to be a "classless society", was in fact run by an elite class of Party officials (a class later known as the *nomenklatura*). The Bolsheviks could only maintain themselves in power, however, through a campaign of terror that set every man against his brother. "This is worse than a civil war. It is a people making war on itself." Malcolm understood that this was not merely a rebirth of Tsarist repression, but an abstract, modern ideology that could seduce people into acquiescence. He called it "a kind of mysticism". Citing an obituary in *Pravda* for Dzerzhinsky, the founder of the Soviet secret police, he noted the "lyrical" quality of the prose.

> It had a rhythm like a religious chant. I thought, and still think, that I had found in it the quintessence of revolution; and I hated this quintessence because it was a denial of everything that has been gained in the slow, painful progress of civilisation; because it was beastly, because it idealised and spiritualised evil; because it glorified destruction and death; and, going beneath the animal, beneath hate, beneath lust, beneath every kind of appetite, founded itself on impulses which, though they have in the past sometimes been organised into abominable, underground cults, have never held sway over a hundred and sixty million people inhabiting a sixth of the world's surface.[5]

In the last article, Malcolm defended himself against the charge that his critique of the Soviet Union made him a "reactionary". He argued that he had every sympathy with the working class. Then he made a point that would not be acknowledged by scholars and commentators for decades. Malcolm pointed out that the Soviet regime was itself reactionary – not an avant-garde, egalitarian paradise, but a xenophobic, autocratic regime rigidly opposed to the individualism and freedom of the modern era.[6]

The two articles not accepted by the *Morning Post* included one on the pressures brought to bear on foreign correspondents by the Soviets, which was also rejected by *The Times*. The other article contained another prophetic vision that seemed so bizarre that not even the right-wing *Morning Post* would take it. In a piece entitled "Red Imperialism", Malcolm predicted that the Soviets would return to the old expansionist vision of the Slavic imperialists, the kind of men who spoke of opening a "sea route to the south" through Afghanistan. At the time he wrote this, the Soviets proclaimed their desire for total disarmament and were embraced by every pacifist organisation in the West.[7]

Precisely because the majority of readers were not prepared to hear such harsh accusations, Malcolm decided to make them more believable by putting them into the form of a novel. As with his previous two novels, *Winter in Moscow* was written rapidly, taking only the summer months to complete. The novel is composed of brief episodes, with a constantly changing cast of characters, though a few recur from chapter to chapter. But there was an advantage to this episodic technique: like the "documentary novel" pioneered by the American John Dos Passos, *Winter in Moscow* takes a panoramic view, from starving peasant women in the Ukraine to the endless round of parties in Moscow for diplomats and journalists. The cumulative impact of these snapshots of life in the Soviet Union, which alternate between absurdist black comedy and abject pathos, is substantial.

By writing an argumentative preface, added just before the book's publication in March of 1934, Malcolm undermined the whole point of using fiction to sneak past the reader's prejudices and preconceptions. Once or twice in the novel Malcolm also breaks into the narrative to attack some aspect of the Soviet Union in his own voice. Malcolm's anger was such that he literally could not contain himself, straining the reader's patience and willingness to suspend disbelief. There is one other serious problem with *Winter in Moscow*: a virulent anti-semitism. Many of the officials in the Soviet bureaucracy in the early 1930s were Jews, and in the novel Malcolm combined a typical prejudice of his day with a critique of these bureaucrats. When he witnessed Hitler's treatment of the Jews on his brief visit to Berlin in 1933, he suddenly found that he had to rethink his prejudices. It would take several years before he sloughed off the remnants of his earlier anti-semitism.

Despite the many flaws in *Winter in Moscow*, there are a number of darkly humorous scenes, particularly of gullible intellectuals and jaded correspondents. Some episodes come almost directly out of Malcolm's diary, such as the trip to the Dneprostroi Dam. There is a parody of an interview with Stalin's mother ("If there's any more of this victimisation of kulaks, I'll really have to give Jo-Jo a talking to") that appeared in an American publication. Malcolm also demonstrates that he is capable of a light touch, as in a conversation between two correspondents. Roden asks Muskett if he knows about the shootings, internal exile and other practices of the secret police. "'Don't make the mistake,' Muskett interrupted, indicating at the same time to the waiter that he wanted another bottle of beer, 'of fastening onto details. Keep in mind the main objective.'" Jefferson/Duranty enters the conversation, stressing the need to see the "broad outline". "'Besides . . . it's a big country,' Jefferson concludes."[8]

Malcolm took a story about the famine that had reached Moscow and turned it into a gruesome interlude in *Winter in Moscow*. It seems that a peasant family was discovered to be hiding some grain. When the Soviet officials took the husband and the grain away, the wife, in her madness and despair, shot each of her children and stuffed them into grain sacks. She then called the officials back, confessing that she had hoarded several sacks of grain. When the chief Party man looked into the sacks and froze with horror, she buried an axe in his head. She was, of course, shot for her crime. Malcolm then shows how a human tragedy becomes distorted in the ideological cauldron of a system based on terror. In the mind of Kokoshkin, the GPU chief, the incident is transformed.

The dead bodies of Comrade Babel and the peasant woman, rotting underground, sprouted and produced a rank crop; hate and fear and suspicion, that was harvested by the Dictatorship of the Proletariat. In Kokoshkin's mind, a ferment; little bubbles stirring, and engendering thoughts and words that sped along corridors and telegraph wires, and collected in typewriters and roll-top desks, and in separate minds; at last in a collective mind. Action followed; swift movement by night; searches; a tearing open of mattresses and a turning over of papers; motor-cars

> coming and going; long interrogations in rooms so silent and
> remote that they seemed just space.[9]

The peasant woman is transmogrified by Kokoshkin into a conspiracy
of counter-revolutionary forces and appropriate actions are taken.

Winter in Moscow is filled with thinly veiled portraits of correspondents, diplomats and Party officials. When the novel was published,
the press corps in Moscow enjoyed spotting each other in its pages.
Eugene Lyons, the journalist who had been on the Dneprostroi trip,
called Malcolm's chapter on that event "unforgettable" and the novel
as a whole "brilliant".[10] S.J. Taylor, the biographer of Walter Duranty,
uses Malcolm's descriptions of the character of Jefferson to probe
Duranty's psychology and motivations, praising them as highly accurate. In his history of England in the first half of the century, A.J.P.
Taylor, though a political enemy of Malcolm's, called *Winter in Moscow*
a "masterpiece".

When the novel was published in the spring of 1934, however, it
met with few words of praise. Nearly all of the reviewers focused on
Malcolm's anger, calling the book hysterical, obsessive and poisonous.
Most of the book's critics assumed that Malcolm was simply wrong
about the Soviet Union. Perhaps the most painful and embarrassing
response to the novel came in a newspaper article about H.T.
Muggeridge's reaction entitled: "Father and Son. Piquant Difference
of Opinion on Russia". After a brief introduction, H.T. is given two
columns to criticise the novel in his own words. Referring to Malcolm
as "a son of mine" and "my gifted relative", he grants that the novel
may have some value in debunking false impressions, but concludes
that the book is "the outcrop of an obsession". Because Malcolm makes
everything look so awful, H.T. argues, he neglects the fact that many
earnest men in the Soviet Union are striving for a better world. H.T.'s
language is characteristically obtuse: "I cannot believe that out of a
population of 160 million souls no decent person can be found or that
a system however successfully it may conceal its ultimate intent under
repellent phrases is one gigantic fraud and pretence."[11]

None of Malcolm's attacks on the Soviet Union made much of an
impact on the intellectual defenders of the regime. The Webbs were
impervious. Malcolm had in fact written impassioned letters to
Beatrice Webb as early as February 1933, imploring her to reconsider
her support of the Soviet Union. "I know your premises are wrong. I
know you've been deliberately misled. Your own intellectual integrity

and courage have been the means of deceiving you, and through you, others. Can you imagine, Aunt Bo, a government taking by force from millions of peasants every scrap of grain they produced, leaving them without any food at all, and then announcing that the standard of life of the workers and peasants has risen?"[12] When their book, *Soviet Communism: A New Civilisation?*, went into a second edition, the question mark was removed. George Bernard Shaw remained fervent in his adulation of the Soviet regime. Typical of Shaw's pronouncements on the Soviet Union was his comparison of English gaols to those in Russia. "In England, a delinquent enters [the gaol] as an ordinary man and comes out a 'delinquent type', whereas in Russia he enters . . . as a criminal type and would come out an ordinary man but for the difficulty of inducing him to come out at all. As far as I could make out they could stay as long as they liked."[13] And Walter Duranty could write to a friend in June 1933, that "the 'famine' is mostly bunk."[14] As he wrote those words, the peasants in the Ukraine and North Caucasus were dying at the rate of twenty-five thousand people per day. When Duranty did eventually concede the existence of the famine, he pointed out the moral of the story: "Those who do not work do not eat."[15] Malcolm's conclusion about Duranty could not have been simpler: he was "the greatest liar of any journalist I have met in fifty years of journalism".[16]

Malcolm became fascinated with the gullibility of Western intellectuals when confronted by the Soviet Union. A few months after arriving in Switzerland, he wrote an essay, "To the Friends of the Soviet Union". Like all of his writing in this period, the essay is a mixture of anger, ridicule and penetrating insight. He confessed that he could not understand why intellectuals who condemned oppression and injustice in India or Japan or the United States would not do the same for Russia. "You are indulgent towards the dictatorship of the proletariat because . . . you are, or would like to be, a dictatorship of the proletariat yourselves." What appeals to the intellectual about the totalitarian regime is that "it shows you an attainable bridge between the abstract and the concrete. It shows a means of putting your ideas, not approximately, but exactly into practice; how you can become men of action without having to compromise or to lay yourselves open to the reproaches of your less successful, and therefore more consistent, comrades; a way of enjoying unrestricted power without sacrificing one iota of your faith."[17] The same arguments would soon by made by scholars such as the psychologist Karl Mannheim, but Malcolm once more was ahead of his time. It was not until 1949 that a number of Western intellectuals published *The God That Failed*, admitting that their infatuation with the Soviet Union had been utterly misguided.

It was only when Khrushchev came to power in the Soviet Union that Malcolm's account of the famine was officially recognised. Khrushchev himself had been one of the Party thugs carrying out the Soviet agricultural policies. But in the West it would take even longer before voices were raised in defence of Malcolm's efforts in the 1930s. Only in the last ten years have scholars such as Robert Conquest paid tribute to Malcolm's courage and determination. Duranty's biographer, S.J. Taylor, put it this way: "But for Muggeridge's eyewitness accounts of the famine in the spring of 1933 and his stubborn chronicle of the event, the effects of the crime upon those who suffered might well have remained as hidden from scrutiny as its perpetrators intended. Little thanks he has received for it over the years, although there is a growing number who realize what a singular act of honesty and courage his reportage constituted."[18]

Malcolm's fierce opposition to the Soviet Union remained a constant in his life, even though it brought him the reputation of being an obsessed, fanatical cold-warrior. It was one of the few causes that would induce him to put aside his role as observer and take action, whether in the form of writing articles, signing petitions or marching in protest. He did so not because he had a better "general idea" to advance against his fellow intellectuals, but because he would never forget those Ukrainian peasants being loaded into cattle trucks.

As Malcolm wrote furiously in the summer of 1933, the idyllic reunion with Kitty and his children soon gave way to tension and depression. Malcolm was not only angry, but embarrassed and despondent as well. His promising career as a writer had been jeopardised by his outspoken attacks on the USSR. It was only natural to feel that he was, in essence, an exile or fugitive living abroad in disgrace. Though it would never occur to him to mute or change his opinions, he still had a natural desire for success and the approbation of his peers. He had almost no money – the twenty-five guineas he received from the *Morning Post* was soon spent – and had been forced to accept financial support from the Dobbs. All of this tended to make him withdraw from Kitty. He found himself fearful of meeting Kitty's sexual needs. As so often happens in marriage, sex became the battleground where many other conflicts were played out.

Malcolm's depression was serious enough to lead him to thoughts of suicide, though he admitted in his diary to a tendency to self-pity and self-dramatisation. "I have reached the state of life when I have no convictions, only an appetite for information, a fondness for literature, and a determination to write."[19] When he was depressed Malcolm also tended to hypochondria, imagining all sorts of illnesses and wasting diseases. A real effect of his tension was a recurrent stomach ailment that gave him a great deal of pain. He made another of his periodic attempts to live the Simple Life, eating and drinking less. By denying his body he could to some extent balance his inner emotional excesses. So he continued to withdraw into himself. "I know I love the children; and yet I know, too, that I don't take much notice of them unless someone's about. Then I play up to the loving tender father role. Life is not very nice. Men are not very nice."[20]

Things became more complicated when Michal Vyvyan arrived in Rossinière in August. As a secretary to the British diplomat William Strang, Vyvyan had followed Strang to a new assignment at the League of Nations in Geneva. In Moscow Malcolm had noticed Vyvyan's infatuation with Kitty, and now he was near enough to pursue her. Whether Malcolm realised it or not, pulling back from Kitty gave more room for Vyvyan to present himself as an emotional and sexual alternative. It is doubtful that Malcolm knew right away that Vyvyan would become his rival, but over time it would become unmistakable.

Two events that took place late in the summer reveal Malcolm's continuing preoccupation with Christianity. He and Kitty went to a church in Rossinière one day and read to each other from the Bible. Then, a few days later, Alec Vidler came to visit. Malcolm asked him on an impulse if he would baptise the children. Vidler interpreted the request as a gesture of defiance to the official atheism of the Soviet Union. But as Malcolm's mystical moment in the church at Kiev and the Bible-reading episode in Rossinière indicate, he continued to long for faith. Vidler asked if Malcolm would promise to raise the children in the Church, but that was precisely the kind of commitment that Malcolm was temperamentally unwilling to make. Vidler refused to perform the baptism.[21] Malcolm might have felt rejected and angry at this, but precisely because he criticised others for any disparity between their "faith" and their "practice", he retained his respect for Vidler. They parted as friends.

Malcolm knew that he had no creed or convictions. Both in diary entries and in a few scattered essays at this time he assailed the rootlessness of modern society. People were losing a sense of place and of history; they also lacked a vital link with the moral and spiritual traditions of the West. Thus the modern world, he noted in his diary, was forced into three different directions: "1) Bolshevism (lawlessness and terror); 2) Fascism (artificial and forced return to old standards); (both 1 & 2 are reactionary) and 3) Cynicism (rule of expediency, sharp practice everywhere; sex-cinema world)." The best response Malcolm could come up with at this time was a vague call for a renewal of "standards". A modern man himself, he was not prepared to recite old creeds.

A phone call from a friend, David Blelloch, offered Malcolm the chance to get out of his self-absorption and depression. There was, it seemed, a job opening at the International Labour Organisation for someone to carry out a study of the world's cooperative movements. Malcolm desperately needed the money and the distraction, so he took the job and moved the family to Geneva. The purpose of the ILO was to parallel the work of the League of Nations itself, "the intention being to reinforce the League's machinery for promoting social justice, on a basis of fair wages and humane working conditions".[22] Though there was a faint connection to Malcolm's youthful desire to help the working classes, he recognised that the ILO, like the League, was one of those modern abstract schemes that had little relationship to the real world. His superior, a "pedantic Frenchman" named M. Prosper, was the quintessential modern bureaucrat, a mindless cog in a large machine. When asked to make policy decisions, M. Prosper would blurt out, "*J'ai mes règles! J'ai mes règles!*" On the other hand, when it came to matters of salary and promotions, he would become articulate and forceful.[23]

The job was excruciatingly boring. Malcolm attempted to point out that the information they relied upon came from governments, and therefore was likely to be doctored to appear more favourable. Shouldn't some corroborating evidence be found? This proposal was roundly rejected. Malcolm naturally found Geneva itself to be the world capital of fantasy. The League, with its constant talk about disarmament and other grand schemes for peace and harmony, was just another form of intellectual abstraction. Though it might seem harmless when compared to the brutality of the Soviets or the Nazis, it was dangerous precisely because it could not deal appropriately with such totalitarian regimes. To Malcolm the posturings and pronouncements of politicians like Litvinov, Briand, Ramsay MacDonald and the young Anthony Eden were like a macabre puppet show played out against the backdrop of a crumbling Europe – a Europe which he was convinced would soon be at war.

Malcolm made an effort to keep up his journalistic contacts by spending time at the Café Bavaria, a favourite haunt for journalists. But depression and despair continued to dog him. He confided to his diary: "There's nothing before me but failure. I've got a great pile of failures on my back."[24] He and Kitty fought incessantly. The thought of abandoning the family occurred to him. But even in his darkest moments he recognised Kitty's virtues. "Kit has gone to town because she promised Pan he should have a birthday party. She is amazing. She works like a horse; and this evening, though she was utterly exhausted, she went to Geneva to buy crackers and toys."[25] Malcolm decided that Kitty and the children should go back to England, and that he would follow after a few more weeks of work. This caused another row, because Kitty suspected that Malcolm was preparing to leave them. Nonetheless, the plan went into effect.

Alone in Geneva, Malcolm's hypochondria increased. He went to a stomach specialist and worried about having a venereal disease. Then a crisis occurred when a cheque he had written could not be deposited and Kitty was left in England without money. This shocked and upset him. "Underneath my insincerity there's a tiny core of sincerity which belongs to her. If the whole of humanity died tonight, and I lived on, I should have no feeling in the matter except about her loss ... I'm ashamed and afraid."[26] He tried to put his emotional crisis in perspective. "Like any other disintegrated man I am a nerve for instruments to play on; sex, success, failure, pain, loss – all producing their reactions. No order. No foundation. A nerve stirred this way and that as my way of life listeth. I see religion as so important and necessary. Reason is nothing: intellect is nothing (at least to me): faith alone gives a human being coherence and stability. I have, and can have, no faith."[27] As the year 1933 drew to a close, Malcolm thought his diary should be called "Chronicles of Wasted Time". It was the title he would give to his autobiography some forty years later.

Finally, Malcolm left Geneva and joined Kitty in London, where she had found a flat in Parliament Hill Fields. Once again, a reunion with Kitty filled him with happiness. "Kit is pregnant again. I hope it will be a daughter. Our two children are delightful ... Kit seems fairly happy, but tired, as well she may be after all she's done. I love her more and more seriously; that is, better. She has more good qualities ... than anyone else I know ..." But money continued to be scarce.

Malcolm had placed only a few articles and essays on a free-lance basis. "I badly need some money, and feel cynical enough to do nearly anything to get it."[28] He applied to most of the major newspapers, including *The Times*, the *Morning Post* and the *Week-End Review*. None of them had openings, or so they said. Malcolm had already gained a reputation as a hothead, and his political incorrectness could not have been more pronounced. As the weeks progressed, he began to panic.

The publication of *Winter in Moscow* provided some distraction in the spring, but the reviews were mixed. Then he received another offer, this time from the book publisher, Jonathan Cape. Over a meal at the Etoile – a restaurant haunted, Malcolm once wrote, "by the ghosts of the books I haven't written and the contracts I haven't fulfilled" – Cape asked him to write a book about Samuel Butler, the Victorian author of *Erewhon* and *The Way of All Flesh*. The publication of the book was to coincide with the centenary of Butler's birth in 1935. Malcolm knew little or nothing about Butler, but put on a display of enthusiasm and confidence for Cape's benefit. A book contract meant an advance and Malcolm was overdrawn at the bank. Cape, having heard a little of Malcolm's past history, imagined that he would find the iconoclastic Butler a sympathetic figure. It was a reasonable conjecture: Butler's books had satirised Victorian hypocrisy and cruelty, taking aim at the Church, public schools, marriage and the family. What Cape couldn't have known – what Malcolm scarcely knew himself then – was that Malcolm was beginning to formulate a critique of liberalism as a decadent and destructive philosophy that threatened civilisation itself. Meanwhile, a contract was signed and an advance paid out.

A modest advance would not stretch very far, so Malcolm had to continue his search for work. Scanning the "situations vacant" section of *The Times*, Malcolm noticed that the position of assistant editor at the Calcutta *Statesman* was open. He applied and was hired. Once again Malcolm found himself taking a position in a far-flung part of the globe, running from a situation gone sour, going into exile. There was, of course, a pressing financial need and a major inducement for taking the job was money; he thought the salary "princely". It enabled him to take "a pleasant little Regency house in Grove Terrace, overlooking Hampstead Heath". Once again Kitty had to move the family, and she had only just given birth to their third child, the daughter they had hoped for. They named her Valentine.

In September of 1934 Malcolm found himself on a ship – the *Viceroy of India* – steaming to India, ten years after his first trip. He could not help but make comparisons. The intervening ten years had put an end to the youthful idealism that had led him to offer advice to Gandhi and feel mystical inspiration in the "Delectable Mountains" of Travancore. Now, of course, he was writing for a major newspaper, not the college magazine. Before leaving London he had met Lord Reading, the former Viceroy and Lord Chief Justice of India, and Sir Samuel Hoare, the Secretary of State for India. Sir Samuel had in fact asked Malcolm to write to him privately from India to provide unvarnished reports on the situation there. Ten years earlier he would have envied someone in such an influential position, but now it was little more than the taste of ashes in his mouth. Malcolm was in retreat and he knew it. On the ship he met someone he had known in Egypt. "'You've changed,' he said. I realised with a start, a little fear, that I had."[29] He began his new diary: "I feel full of foreboding; as though, somehow, I'd sold my soul. I shouldn't be at all surprised, or much mind, if I died quite soon. Now that I've digested my repudiation of dawnism, and reconciled myself to doing nothing about anything, but writing, it seems as though I'd shot my bolt."[30]

Unlike his arrival at the *Manchester Guardian*, which was so full of eagerness and a sense of triumph, Malcolm came to the Calcutta *Statesman* with few hopes and no ambitions. Despite the general atmosphere of *Guardian*-style liberalism at the paper, Malcolm recognised that it was the "organ of British business interests" in Bengal and elsewhere. The *Statesman* inhabited an impressive building on Chowringree Street. None of his associates there made a lasting impression on him. He shared a room with a man named Wordsworth, "a funny dissatisfied man, with an inferiority complex but a kind heart".[31] Wordsworth, a gentle soul who earnestly believed in the League of Nations and other progressive causes, exasperated Malcolm frequently.

For a brief moment, early in his time at the *Statesman*, Malcolm became engrossed with the notion that he might "take over" the paper. He had long talks with a certain Mr Kelly, an assistant to the paper's manager, Alfred Watson, about this prospective coup. But within a few days the plan evaporated and was forgotten.

Though he wrote dutifully about the situation in India, Malcolm's leaders were often about the political and intellectual upheavals in Europe and Russia. A leader entitled "Towards a Repetition of 1914" returned to Malcolm's conviction that a war in Europe was inevitable. Wordsworth's blue pencil took much of the edge off the piece: he added "Herr" to Hitler's name, and his deletions included the sentence: "A child can see what Hitler intends, and knows what will be the consequences for the whole world if he has his way."[32]

Malcolm was an early critic of the policy of appeasement – the policy that led to Neville Chamberlain's famous declaration, in Munich, of "peace in our time", just before Hitler's *blitzkrieg* ripped through Poland. One leader, entitled "Herr Hitler's Cold" (referring to an excuse given to postpone a meeting with British Foreign Secretary Sir John Simon), included this statement: "Europe has got used to an England which at one moment trails along behind France, at another accepts a Nazi bluff at its face value, and always shows a pathetic readiness to trumpet meaningless internationalist platitudes at Geneva, so that any expression of emphatic opinion on her part is an occasion for surprise . . ."[33]

Malcolm also delved into the larger cultural and intellectual issues behind these events. He reviewed Leonard Woolf's book, *Quack! Quack!*, which interpreted contemporary events as a struggle between civilisation and savagery, where figures like Hitler and Stalin represented a "return to magic and the witch doctor".[34] And in a leader on "Totalitarian Religion", Malcolm argued that both the Nazis and the Soviets had created false religions. He concluded: "One remarkable fact should be noted: organised religion seems alone to be able to offer any serious opposition to the Totalitarian steamroller which has already flattened out a large part of Europe; humanitarianism, liberalism, every sort and description of loose idealism, goes under it at once."[35] Here was another prophetic statement that was well ahead of its time. Over fifty years later, the Iron Curtain would come down, according to many scholars, because of a Polish Pope and the strength of organised religion in Poland and East Germany.

He worked at the book on Samuel Butler in a desultory fashion. Butler, he came to believe, was one of the founders of the progressivist mentality that rejected religion, the family, and other traditional institutions. By throwing off these "relics of the past", Butler and his intellectual fellow-travellers believed that men and women would be freed from the shackles of repression and hypocrisy and liberated into a new life of pleasure, honesty and humanitarian works. Thus Butler was idolised by Shaw and the Fabians. Malcolm now believed that instead of liberation, Butler and Co. had only brought about a rootless, alienated culture. "Butler, more than any other 19th-century writer, is us. The empty space he cleared has been our heritage."[36]

When he wanted to escape Butler, the *Statesman* and the Anglo-Indian "philistines" who inhabited the clubs and party circuit, Malcolm did what he had done in 1924: he sought out Indian friends. Brian Lunn, the brother of Hugh Kingsmill, had recommended that Malcolm get to know a professor of fine arts at Calcutta University, Shahid Suhrawardy. Though he was from one of the leading Moslem families in Bengal, Suhrawardy was a worldly man. Malcolm did not take to him at first (contrary to the impression given in his autobiography): Suhrawardy seemed to be one of those Indians who had become Westernised "badly", tending more to eccentricity than to cosmopolitanism. But Malcolm was quickly won over by Suhrawardy's warmth and enthusiasm. Through Suhrawardy, Malcolm met three other Indians: Apurbo Chanda, a civil servant and a Hindu; Tulsi Goswami, a member of the Indian National Congress, and despite his wealth, a faithful follower of Gandhi; and Sudhindranath Datta, an urbane man of letters, Bengal's greatest poet and the editor of a literary journal.

The four men decided to dine together on a weekly basis, a welcome respite for Malcolm. He felt himself drawn most to Datta, who was, like himself, melancholy, literary, a shrewd observer of men and events. In a separate memoir of Datta written after the poet's death, Malcolm wrote: "His elegance, his sardonic wit, his subtle and perceptive intelligence, the perfection of his manners, and the grace which gave his person and his words a particular charm, all endeared him to me." Malcolm felt that Datta was, at heart, a mystic.[37] He kept in touch with Datta over the years, meeting him both in India and in England.

In November Malcolm received bad news: his novel, *Picture Palace*, had met an untimely end. He had known from the moment he sent the novel off that it might be considered libellous; its characters were modelled directly on the living and the recently deceased. He made the same gamble with *Winter in Moscow*. What he had not reckoned with was that the greatest danger to *Picture Palace* came not from individuals like Kingsley Martin and Alan Taylor, but from the *Manchester Guardian* itself. When Arthur Ransome had read it, he was horrified, and on his recommendation Malcolm's first publisher, Putnam, had turned it down. It had eventually been accepted by Eyre and Spottiswoode. The book had been printed and bound and review copies sent out before Malcolm heard that the *Guardian* was seeking an injunction and threatening to sue for libel. Malcolm's publisher had no desire to risk its own money on such an uncertain outcome and asked Malcolm if he could put up £2,000 in advance against the costs of a trial. Obviously, Malcolm could do no such thing and so the book was withdrawn and all but a very few copies destroyed.

"This was the heaviest blow I had received as a writer, and it came just when I was least equipped, financially or in any other way, to withstand it."[38] What hurt Malcolm more than wounded pride or frustration at wasted effort was the blatant hypocrisy of the great bastion of liberalism suppressing free speech. Another galling aspect of the incident was that the one part of the book the *Guardian* had singled out as actionable was the assertion that its existence was subsidised by the profits from the *Manchester Evening News* – a fact that was absolutely true and verifiable.

Malcolm's sense of isolation and despair deepened. It was in moods like this that he became morbidly preoccupied with sex. His diary from this time is filled with reminiscences of his sexual life, from his early homosexual experiences to seductions in Manchester and Moscow. Those who have accused Malcolm of a Manichean dualism – a tension between unbridled lust and disgust with the body – could find in these diary entries ample evidence for their claims. One entry contains a sketch, "The Sun Bathers", which is Swiftian in its obsession with the grotesqueness of human flesh.[39] A couple weeks later, he contemplated writing a story called "The Vampire" about a woman's insatiable sexual desire.[40] He returned often to his belief that his own alienation and despair were part of the modern disintegration. "I saw it all like a pageant – girls in short skirts and hats askew, frenzied sexual dancing, idealism (a rank word that thrives on disintegration) sprouting up into my own little corner of the mess, my own little 'be free and fuck' movement, my own little world fit for golden youths and maids (only they were soon, soon, frowsty, generally unsatisfied, careworn with being careless) to be themselves in."[41]

At the same time, his yearning for faith continued. "If God would help me to overcome my body with my spirit so that these tortured days of illness came to an end, and zest for life returned, I'd believe in God."[42] But God did not intervene directly, so Malcolm continued to be dominated by sex and hypochondria. His stomach problem flared up again. This led to the darkest and most absurd episode in this time, a moment of black comedy. A doctor had asked Malcolm to bring in a sample of his stool. This called for a rather delicate operation with a cigarette tin that did not go well. The resultant mess was bad enough, but the last straw occurred when the toilet overflowed. One sign that Malcolm was profoundly unhappy at this time is that he recorded this incident without a trace of humour.[43]

In the midst of these diary entries Malcolm wrote: "Often I blush to think of this diary, yet, as diaries go, it's rather honest."[44]

Eventually Malcolm found a focus for his sexuality beyond his memories. Through Suhrawardy, he met a Parsee woman named Khurshed, whom he found "ravishing despite her hardness; lovely eyes and a long straight nose and a golden skin". He was aware that she was attracted to him as well, thinking him an *homme du monde*.[45] Khurshed was married, but she had had lovers before, as she told Malcolm a few days later in her garden. She told him to be patient, that they needed to begin their affair well. He found her a fascinating mixture of sophistication and naïveté, but he recognised a certain artificiality in the affair, as if it was more of a sexual meeting of East and West than an affair of the heart.

As was his habit, Malcolm immediately began to miss Kitty after parting from her. Two weeks after his arrival, he wrote to her, asking her to spend six weeks with him in Calcutta in the winter. She wired back to say that she would come early in the new year. Malcolm's diary entries in the days before her arrival are full of anxiety and foreboding about the visit. He was involved with Khurshed by this time. His feelings of guilt, anger and embarrassment at living in virtual exile in India had not dissipated.

Malcolm's worries proved amply justified. Kitty arrived on January 19, 1935. They fought furiously from the beginning of the visit to the end. It was Kitty, however, who dropped the largest bombshell. She confessed to having an affair with Michal Vyvyan and to being pregnant with his child. Malcolm pretended to be unaffected by this news, acting as if he was above jealousy and rancour. But he was of course deeply wounded. His first reaction to Vyvyan in Moscow had been rage at the upper-class superiority of the man with the absurd sprouting moustache. Now he had been cuckolded by this very man. Malcolm never forgot that Kitty had grown up in a higher social class than he had, and the affair with Vyvyan went straight to the heart of his social insecurity.[46]

Kitty claimed that Vyvyan was a "beast" and that the affair meant nothing. She told Malcolm that she planned to return to London to have an abortion. "This did not touch me at all," he wrote in his diary, "but, like a lawyer, I saw how it strengthened my case and seized on it. We lay side by side, heads aching, mouths dry, still fighting."[47] It is unlikely that Malcolm could have remained untouched by the prospect of his wife having an abortion. He and Kitty had often shown an instinctive aversion to contraception and abortion, often mocking them as evidence of a decaying social order. One of the recurrent motifs in *Winter in Moscow* is that abortion is readily available in the Soviet Union, a symbol of the totalitarian culture of death, and very appealing to the progressive visitors from the West. It is doubtful that Malcolm would have encouraged her to have the abortion.

They fought for nearly a month, until Kitty's departure on February 14. On the eve of their separation, she turned to Malcolm and said quietly: "You'd better stick to me. No one'll love you as I do."[48] It was true and it stuck in Malcolm's mind, but Kitty's statement did little to resolve the immediate crisis. They continued to fight in their letters after Kitty had returned home.

Malcolm was close to the end of his tether. He was haunted by his own sense of failure and by the news Kitty had brought. "I keep thinking of Kit having Vyvyan's child and know in my heart that all that's finished for me."[49] He had a nightmare in which he had returned to their flat at 19 Grove Terrace and found his son Leonard and a little girl on the front step. "We've been waiting and waiting," Pan said, "and nobody answers when we ring." My heart sank. I knew what had happened, went into the house and found Kit dead. She'd written me a letter before she died. It began: "It doesn't often come to a human being to want nothing; I want nothing now – not even you.' Marvelling at the beauty of this sentence, I woke up, feeling afraid."[50]

When Malcolm found that he had been assigned by the *Statesman* to cover the British government in its summer residence at Simla, he was relieved. Calcutta had been a swamp for him, both literally and figuratively. The image he retained of this period was of a dank, humid place. The prospect of going to the coolness of the mountains, where Simla was located, was the kind of change he needed.

After a brief stop in Delhi, Malcolm went directly to Simla. His autobiography contains several lively pages painting a portrait of the social and political life of the British in Simla, but his experience at the time was not that of the eager observer. It was closer to that of the sleepwalker. He had seen it all before – the fantasy of the British Raj, with its pomp and circumstance, and its utter detachment from the stark realities of life in India.

Simla was, as Malcolm later put it, "an authentic English production; designed by Sahibs for Sahibs, without reference to any other
considerations – not even Maharajahs".[51] There, amidst the band-
stands, government buildings and the Mall, with its theatre, Malcolm
went about in search of news – and distraction from his unhappiness.
Eventually he was invited to the Viceregal Lodge, where he met the
Viceroy, Willingdon, and his wife. The Lodge, of course, was the
"focus of attention" in Simla, not just politically, but socially as well. To
receive an embossed invitation to the Lodge ("Their Excellencies
request the pleasure . . .") was an enviable privilege. Willingdon "looked
tremendously like an old beau in a Restoration comedy", Malcolm
thought, a man who merely drifted along in office rather than an active
shaper of events. "People were inclined to think that India was difficult
to govern," he told Malcolm, "but he'd found it almost ridiculously
easy. You just had to be nice to these fellers, and they responded."[52]

He spent much of his time in the company of two other correspondents: Sandy Inglis, a Scot, who reported for *The Times*, and Jim
Barnes, who wrote dispatches for Reuters. The two men could not
have been more different: Inglis an earnest believer in the possibility
of liberal reform and an enlightened Raj, Barnes an uncompromising
fascist, denouncing British weakness and decadence while holding up
Benito Mussolini, the Italian dictator, as the kind of strong man needed
in dangerous times. Both men, in their opposite ways, exemplified the
almost fanatical belief of the time that politics could solve human
problems. Malcolm was becoming more convinced than ever that the
power of the state to reform society was limited at best and at times
horribly counter-productive.

The one lasting friendship Malcolm made in Simla began with a
nasty fight. Malcolm had written several articles for the *Statesman* on
the fiscal policies of the British government in India. The Finance
Member, P.J. Grigg, took exception to the articles, and began to tell
the other journalists that Malcolm had fallen under the influence of
Jim Barnes and the Italian trade commissioner. Malcolm thought this
was a particularly egregious form of character assassination and wrote
a cutting letter to Grigg. Grigg wrote back pompously, and Malcolm
began to consider legal action. The tempest blew itself out rather
quickly. He and Grigg met and agreed to bury the hatchet.[53] He found
himself drawn to Grigg, whose combination of irascibility and spiritual
restlessness resonated with Malcolm's own personality.

The argument with Grigg was the last political event in Simla that caught Malcolm's attention. On the day of his reconciliation with Grigg, May 22, he had seen a young woman named Amrita Sher-Gil, who was half Indian and half Hungarian. Like Khurshed, Amrita had given off a strong erotic charge when he first met her. "I smelt emotional entanglement," Malcolm wrote in his diary that evening. Sandy Inglis had gone to Quetta to see the results of a devastating earthquake, but Malcolm chose to stay and pursue a relationship with Amrita.

Her father was a Sikh noble, Sardar Umrai Singh. A disciple of Tolstoy, he was a quiet man, spending much of every evening looking at the stars through a telescope. Amrita's mother was a Hungarian named Antoinette, a large, red-headed woman who wore a great deal of jewellery, and who played the piano with a ferocious intensity. In this rather unusual household, Amrita had grown up as a free spirit. She spoke French as well as English, having studied at the Ecole des Beaux Arts in Paris. She was a talented painter, and would later be recognised as one of the most accomplished artists of twentieth-century India.

Amrita was only twenty-two when she met Malcolm, nearly ten years younger than him. She had an animal sensuality that was combined with what Malcolm called a certain inner "hardness". She dressed in colourful saris made of exquisite materials. Her face was round, with full lips and large almond-shaped eyes. Malcolm was mesmerised.

Amrita had already had several lovers and an abortion by the time Malcolm met her. She was less hesitant and entangled than Khurshed, but more demanding. Malcolm was ripe for such an affair. He wanted to extinguish his tortured consciousness in a perfect, self-contained sexual relationship. Neglecting his duties at the *Statesman*, he spent all his time at the Sher-Gils' home in Summer Hill, just outside Simla. He sat for Amrita, and the portrait she painted of him hangs in the National Gallery in Delhi. In it, Malcolm leans back against a wall, a large elongated hand across his stomach, with a cigarette holder held lightly between his fingers. He looks at the viewer with one eyebrow arched ironically, his lips large and sensual. Amrita captured the youthful, satyr-like Malcolm – a look that was rapidly changing under the stress of recent years into the harder, more tightly stretched look of his mature years.

For a time, Malcolm did lose himself in what he would often call, later in his life, "carnality". His diary chronicled his love-making with

Amrita, including the number of orgasms they both achieved. But he failed to find the forgetfulness he wanted. In the margin of the diary entries about his love-making he wrote: "This is dead."[54] Soon their egos began to abrade each other. "She is a demon," he wrote, early in their relationship. "I get a sense of someone entirely egocentric, coarse, petulantly spoilt, almost to the point of physical nausea."[55] Amrita fascinated Malcolm because she was so completely amoral. But Malcolm's conscience never left him alone for very long. On the same day he was recording their sexual achievements, he also set down a quote from Samuel Johnson: "When I survey my past life, I discover nothing but a barren waste of time, with some disorders of the body, and disturbances of the mind very near to madness, which I hope He that made me will suffer to extenuate my many faults, and excuse many deficiencies."[56]

In all of his autobiographical writings, Malcolm used this affair with Amrita Sher-Gil as the one affair that he discussed publicly. It was as if this episode were to stand for all his other infidelities. It was a good choice, of course, because Amrita was such an exotic figure, more interesting than most of his other lovers. But this affair was not much different from the rest. By early August, it was coming to an end.

Malcolm managed to finish a draft of his book on Samuel Butler late in the summer. It is difficult to imagine a book written in more adverse or unpropitious circumstances. When, after his return to England, he gave the manuscript to his two friends, Hugh Kingsmill and Hesketh Pearson, they counselled him to tone it down, telling him that it suffered from a pervasive feeling of "nausea".[57] What they did not appreciate fully was that all of Malcolm's books to this point were characterised by nausea. There were times when Malcolm could turn this sense of world-weariness and Swiftian disgust with humanity to his satirical advantage, but there were other times when the nausea got in the way of his artistic and intellectual purposes.

The Earnest Atheist: A Study of Samuel Butler is a sustained attack against its subject and the progressivist liberalism he represented. Malcolm had once again declared war, although this time it was against a popular literary figure rather than a newspaper or a totalitarian regime. During his own lifetime, Butler was known only for his utopian fantasy, *Erewhon*, and a few minor books and essays. It was only after his death in 1902 that his novel, *The Way of All Flesh*, was published and he became a posthumous celebrity. George Bernard Shaw hailed it as a masterpiece. After the horror of World War I, the novel fed the younger generation's anger against the fathers who had sent them to war. An Erewhon Society was formed and annual dinners held. Butler's notebooks were then published and widely admired for their supposed profundities, witticisms and *bons mots*. Malcolm set himself the task of pricking this inflated balloon of a reputation.

The Earnest Atheist, like Malcolm's novels, is a poorly organised book, but brilliant in parts. It begins with a portrait of Butler, not as a liberator, freeing the repressed and inhibited from humbug, but as an ideologue.

> Like his fellow-Victorians, the deepest need of his nature was to escape from the reality of his own existence; only he escaped by means of ideas, and they by means of emotions. He was a pioneer idealogue [*sic*]. His mind was his refuge; and he lived secure amongst its shadows and fantasies. Where for instance Dickens shaped his turbulent appetites into creatures of darkness and light, making a melodrama of them, Butler shaped his into thought and made a utopia of them. His utopia was Erewhon, Nowhere, a quiet twilit place where banks were churches, doctors priests, and disease alone evil. It has very largely come to pass. Waiting at a bank-counter faces are reverent; and angels glow with health, not holiness – airmen or potent gamekeepers; and the psycho-analyst, or, as Butler called him, Straightener, ministers to all who travail and are heavy-laden; and virtue is assessed in public health statistics.[58]

Butler's ideology, Malcolm argued, was parallel to that of Marxism: both believed in inevitable progress – or evolution – towards Utopia; both placed evil, not in men's hearts, but in institutions which must be overthrown; both substituted materialism for religious faith. Though liberalism might seem less dangerous than totalitarianism, Malcolm believed that the social and moray decay of the West could be as stifling a prison as the Iron Curtain. To Malcolm, Butler's worship of money made him even more contemptible than a straightforwardly power-hungry figure like Lenin.

The bulk of *The Earnest Atheist* attempts to show how Butler came to create his ideology and how badly this system worked in his actual human relationships. Thanks to some adroit research done by Kitty and forwarded to India, Malcolm was able to deconstruct the myth Butler had erected around his life in *The Way of All Flesh*. He showed how Butler exaggerated his father's monstrousness and his own victimhood. In examining Butler's relationships to Charles Pauli, Hans Faesch and Festing Jones, Malcolm pointed out how Butler's fantasies led him to be duped and swindled, just as Ernest Pontifex, the hero of the book, had been. Butler, according to Malcolm, had been the quintessential Victorian: timid and repressed about his sexuality, longing for material success and living a fastidious, ordered life. "No one ever took such pains as Butler to let posterity know the sort of man he was ... He swept himself up, the minutest crumbs; he dissected himself; he embalmed his spirit and laid it out, like a Pharaoh's body, to last for all time; he – this would have appealed to him – put himself in the bank to multiply at compound interest forever."[59]

There is an edge to Malcolm's writing in this book that comes not just from his own depression at the time he was writing it, but from his recognition that he had the makings of a Butler in his own personality. Certain sentences and paragraphs in the book could be applied directly to Malcolm. Had he not often resented and feared H.T., who was an embarrassment to him? "Looking back on his childhood, he saw himself being delivered into the hands of the enemies, irretrievably cut off from all he most admired – self-confidence, good-breeding, ease of manner, charm, good looks."[60] These were the attributes of Michal Vyvyan and his world. The tortured duality of Butler's personality was described by Malcolm: "All he was able to do was to impose an outside orderliness, but inside the conflict continued to the end – the conflict in his nature between ... mind and flesh, between extravagant self-depreciation and extravagant egotism, between a sense of sin and a conviction that there was no sin."[61] This led to a state of morbidity and nausea. "He was one of those who smell death in life and hate in love. Decay was always in his nostrils, and beauty's scaffolding, dry bones, broke through its flesh. Faces were masks, and passion a harlequinade."[62] Butler feared that he would be looked on as a man who carped at society because of his own ugliness, as Thersites had carped against Odysseus, Agamemnon, and the other Greek warriors in the *Iliad*. "Of Thersites's rôle Butler had a particular horror, because he knew it was his, and that he was fated to rail against all who were in authority, not to care what he said so long as he might raise a laugh, and to be regarded as ugly and graceless."[63]

Whether all of these characterisations apply to Butler or not, they add to the book's intensity. Butler stood as a warning to Malcolm. Writing about Butler, he attempted to exorcise some of his own demons.

Just as he had completed a draft of his book and his relationship with Amrita was coming to a conclusion, he received a telegram from Percy Cudlipp, the editor of the *Evening Standard*, asking Malcolm if he would be interested in writing for their feature, the Londoner's Diary. It was little more than a gossip column, but Malcolm clutched at it like a drowning man, and he wired off his acceptance of the job.

Amrita came to the station to see Malcolm off early on a September morning. In his second volume of his autobiography, *The Infernal Grove*, he recounts that she told him through the train window that they "had some *beaux moments*" together.[64] What he didn't say in that passage was that she had also reminded him that they had had some "*moments noir*".[65] Malcolm's entire year in India had been filled with black moments, and he would not soon leave them behind. He was returning to a marriage that was in ruins, a wife pregnant with a child that was not his, and a position as a gossip columnist.

« 9 »

The Bewildered Soul
1935–1938

RETURNING TO ENGLAND did little to alter the basic conditions of
Malcolm's life. He had exchanged the unreality of reporting on the
British Raj in Simla for the unreality of a writing a gossip column for
a London tabloid. Working on the Londoner's Diary, pursuing gossip
about aristocrats and establishment figures, did nothing to alleviate
Malcolm's feeling of being marginalised. On the domestic front, he
and Kitty continued their epic struggle of wills, their pitched battles
interspersed with brief cease-fires. Malcolm's stomach still gave him
pain; he saw a number of doctors and worried that he had become a
hypochondriac.

Nonetheless, the year in India was undoubtedly the nadir of his life
up to this time. Whenever Malcolm was alone he tended to withdraw
even further into himself, and his old obsessions – sex and death –
would dominate his waking moments. The return to England had the
virtue of bringing him back into contact with people who drew him
out of himself. With the help of friends like Hugh Kingsmill, and the
strength he drew – despite the drag of marital strife – from Kitty and
his children, Malcolm would emerge in these pre-war years from the
blackness of despair to renew his search for religious and imaginative
truths that he could affirm. It was a period that saw some of his best
writing, a sharpening of his satirical sensibility and the beginning of
his love for the rolling downs of the Sussex coast. It was one of the
few periods in his life that he would look back on with nostalgia.

Immediately after his plane landed, Malcolm went home to Croydon
to see his parents. There Kitty and her father joined him. In her arms
Kitty carried a new-born child, Charles, whose father was Michal
Vyvyan. Before Malcolm had returned to England, Kitty had broken
off her relationship with Vyvyan. Since she had travelled to India

when she was only a few weeks pregnant, no suspicions about the paternity of Charles were raised and Vyvyan was never told. Back in India, Malcolm had wondered whether the birth of this child would provide him with the impetus to leave Kitty. But Malcolm proved true to the pledge made by his fictional counterpart, Pettygrew, in *Picture Palace*. In that novel, Pettygrew had told his wife Gertrude that he would accept any child she conceived, regardless of the child's paternity. Malcolm treated Charles as his own child and watched the progress of his son's brief life with as much interest and affection as he did any of his children.

The family resumed its life at Grove Terrace, Highgate. Now the mother of four children, Kitty could no longer entertain the idea of working as a journalist or an actress. Leonard ("Pan") was seven years old, but John, Val and Charles, who had been born so close together, were infants and toddlers, and required constant attention. Malcolm and Kitty could not afford nannies or maids, so the entire burden rested on Kitty. She never begrudged her role as a mother, but her ample intelligence and talent had to wait for thirty years before they emerged in her autumnal career as writer and translator. Everyone who knew her, from Malcolm to the childless Beatrice Webb, acknowledged that she was a devoted and loving mother. "It gave me a great sense of peace and happiness to be back with Kit and the children. Nothing much else seemed to matter, does matter."[1] From their home in Grove Terrace, Malcolm took a tram daily to Holborn, where he continued on foot to the Fleet Street offices of the *Evening Standard*.

Within days of his arrival at the paper, he complained that it was a "nightmare". His first impression of the *Evening Standard* was not promising. He hated the way the editorial staff were spread out in one large room, without walls or offices. But first impressions worked both ways. On the day of Malcolm's arrival at the paper, his immediate superior on the Diary, a Scotsman named R.H. Bruce Lockhart, wrote in his diary: "Malcolm Muggeridge, the author of an anti-Bolshevik book on Russia and of a suppressed novel on the *Manchester Guardian*, joined us today. Clever, nervous and rather 'freakish' in appearance. Holds strong views."[2]

The Diary was a collection of paragraphs, printed opposite the main leader for the day, that took note of new appointments in government, education and the diplomatic corps, passed on gossip about aristocrats, actors and magnates, and commented on trends in culture and the arts. Although the tone of the Diary could be, on occasion, somewhat tart,

Malcolm thought that it was, in general, sycophantic and trivial. Another irritant was the fact that his material had to be overseen by editors who would cut and rewrite at will. This was not something the former chief leader writer for the *Guardian* took very well.

At this point, Malcolm did what he always did when rebelling against an institution: he veered from the extremes of either asserting his own will, regardless of the paper's ground rules, or playing the game all too well and going "over the top". An example of the former would be the serious and intense paragraphs he contributed one day on the state of Europe. The first paragraph asserts that the League of Nations must prove its ability to restrain aggression by preventing the Italian conquest of Abyssinia (the country now known as Ethiopia). "If the League works on this occasion it will work all the better if and when Germany kicks over the traces. If it does not work, then its impracticability will have been demonstrated once and for all." A few paragraphs later, he takes on Mussolini, comparing him to the ill-fated Russian Tsars. Mussolini is like a Tsar, "like any individual in whom has been vested absolute authority. Self-confidence becomes a mania rather than a source of strength. An ominous glitter comes into the eye, not betokening vitality and strength of purpose but brooding egotism."[3]

On the other hand, Malcolm took to making up dialogue and stories about the high and the mighty, rather than making the effort to gad about town to parties and events. "I found that no objections were ever raised so long as what appeared in the Diary ministered to the subject's self-esteem; not even to purported quotations given in direct speech." Once he wrote of "a newly ennobled Scottish peer that his grandfather had been a poor crofter, and he wrote in to deny that this was so. Honour was satisfied when I made the necessary correction by stating in a subsequent paragraph that his grandfather had been a rich crofter."[4]

The men who wrote for the Diary, both the regular staff and the stringers, constituted a remarkably talented group, many of them at the outset of their careers. John Betjeman, the paper's film critic, helped out with "architectural and ecclesiastical news"; Patrick Balfour handled cultural matters; Randolph Churchill, the eccentric son of Winston Churchill, dealt with politics. Malcolm liked most of these men, especially Randolph Churchill, whom he thought a doomed son, not unlike Ted Scott. But the most sympathetic person on the staff to Malcolm was Leslie Marsh, "the real pillar of the Diary". Malcolm immediately warmed to Marsh's ironic detachment from his work, as he had to similar figures in the past, such as Cholerton in Moscow. He also had a dry sense of humour. "If one asked him whether he had enough paragraphs, he would never admit to more than: 'I can fill'; if one sought his help in finding a subject, more often than not his only response would be: 'Have you looked at the stiffs?'"[5]

Neither his friendship with Marsh nor his proximity to such talented colleagues could prevent Malcolm's rapid alienation from the *Evening Standard*. More offensive than the actual gossip writing was the atmosphere at the paper, which he attributed to Lord Beaverbrook himself. Few figures in twentieth-century British history have been quite as controversial as Beaverbrook. From Evelyn Waugh's satirical portrait of Beaverbrook as Lord Copper in such novels as *Scoop* to A.J.P. Taylor's adulatory biography, the Canadian-born press baron has evoked every kind of response. Born Max Aitken in Ontario, he grew up in the small New Brunswick town of Newcastle. A typical self-made millionaire of the era, he attempted several business ventures before making his fortune selling bonds – and then companies. He came to England before World War I and began dabbling in politics. After a brief period as an MP, Aitken decided that he could wield more power as a press baron than a politician and made his debut on Fleet Street by taking over the *Daily Express*. Later, he started the *Sunday Express* and acquired the *Evening Standard*. When he helped to bring down the Liberal government of Asquith, a grateful Lloyd George offered Aitken a peerage, making him Lord Beaverbrook.

To Malcolm, Beaverbrook represented the vulgarity and decadence of a materialistic age. Beaverbrook was given to pronouncements such as that he stood for "more life ... more money ... more work ... more happiness". Malcolm compared him to C.P. Scott of the *Guardian*. Both men tended to dominate the daily affairs at their papers. Beaverbrook did his domineering by telephone and telegraph; editors would receive phone calls from the man himself, with the phrase "You've gotta say" as the frequent refrain. But at the *Evening Standard*, Malcolm almost became nostalgic for the *Guardian*. "The essential difference between Scott's control of the *Guardian* and Beaverbrook's of his papers was that Scott had views and attitudes which, however distasteful, were fairly consistent, and could be cogently expounded; whereas Beaverbrook, when you got down to it, really had no views at all, but only prejudices, moods, sudden likes and dislikes, which his newspapers have to keep abreast of and reflect ..."[6]

Many of Beaverbrook's causes were utterly ephemeral, such as the crusade for Empire Free Trade and his backing of a political nonentity like Bonar Law. Malcolm once heard a writer at the *Evening Standard* respond to a question about which part of the paper's large readership he aimed at in his writing. "'I write', he said majestically (and it seemed an historic pronouncement which thoroughly deserved to be recorded), 'for one little old reader – Lord Beaverbrook.'"[7]

Malcolm recognised Beaverbrook's genius at creating newspapers that were appealing to a huge readership, but that was part of the problem. Like Scott, Beaverbrook offered a bland optimism that could only be maintained by immersing itself in fantasy. The most egregious case of this was Beaverbrook's insistence, throughout the 1930s, that there would be no war. The ultimate expression of this fantasy, according to Malcolm, was in Beaverbrook's religiosity. The son of a Scottish Presbyterian minister, Beaverbrook tended to fret about questions like immortality. He asked the Anglican theologian Dean Inge to write for his papers. Malcolm remembered seeing an advertisement of an Inge column on one of the delivery vans: "IS THERE AN AFTER-LIFE? SEE TOMORROW'S EVENING STANDARD."[8]

After six months at the *Evening Standard*, Malcolm's objections to the paper were, in his mind at least, a matter of conscience. The four five-pound notes that he collected each week could not induce him to do such things as write editorials endorsing certain charities, giving them exactly the amount of space that they took in paid advertising.

> This well-paid and unexacting servitude to Beaverbrook's way-ward fancies and malign purposes was more spiritually burden-some than might have been supposed. There was a steady and insidious process of corruption going on all the time, which I could observe working in others, and, in moments of candour, in myself. Underneath all the buffoonery, I detected a whiff of sulphur; a transposing of values, whereby whatever was most base was elevated, and the only acceptable measure of anyone and anything was money, the only pursuit worth considering, worldly success.[9]

During the late winter and spring of 1936, Malcolm looked for a way out.

Eventually, he found such a way, though it involved the kind of financial and emotional risk that he had avoided in the past. He decided to work as a free-lance writer. The only assurance of regular income that he had was an agreement he made with the *Daily Telegraph* to review several new novels every week for five guineas per review. But he was ready to take the risk this time. Part of his motivation was the conviction that Britain would become involved in a war within a matter of years; he had certain literary and intellectual ambitions that he wanted to fulfil in the intervening time.

At the same time, Malcolm and Kitty decided to move away from London. The expense of living in London would be difficult now that Malcolm had so little regular income. There was, first and foremost, his own geographical schizophrenia: after living in the city he became restless and longed for the country, and vice versa. There were other inducements for the Muggeridges to move out to the country. After his return from India, Malcolm had renewed his acquaintance with Hugh Kingsmill, who was at that time living in Hastings on the Sussex coast. Ever since his visits to Rye with Alec Vidler, Malcolm had loved the rolling downs and coastline of Sussex. Malcolm and Kitty found an old inn that had been converted to a home in the small village of Whatlington, near Battle. A recent suicide in the Mill House, as it was called, helped to bring the price down to £800, which Malcolm could just manage with a mortgage.

The final weeks before the move were marred, however, by a crisis that would leave permanent scars on both Malcolm and Kitty. Kitty had become pregnant once again, but this time she did not bring the child to term: she had an abortion. Malcolm's diaries are somewhat cryptic about this event. It is unclear whether Kitty was suffering from some illness that made pregnancy dangerous to her own survival or not; he only notes that the abortion was "necessary in her case". By today's standards, Kitty might well have chosen abortion because she felt overwhelmed by the four children she had already borne. Malcolm's diaries do not reveal the ultimate reason for the abortion. "She is to have an abortion, and is frightened about it. Getting an abortion in England, in her case absolutely necessary, is an amazing business. It has to be called by another name, all the circumstances of getting it are frightening, and it's fabulously expensive."[10] The tone of this diary entry is rather detached and neutral, but it is hard to believe that Malcolm felt anything less than fear, pain and ambivalence, whatever the reason for the abortion. Throughout his books, both birth control and abortion are used to symbolise the self-indulgence of modern materialism, so the fact that Kitty was to undergo such a dangerous – and illegal – procedure must have been terrifying.

The diary entry for the following day betrays a little more emotion, on both their parts. "Kit was better, the operation finished. When I saw her she was a bit dazed, because the chloroform hadn't quite worked off. 'Have they really done it?' she kept saying. She also told me that when she first came to she could only remember my name and the children's, and kept saying them over and over. I shall never forget this."[11] This passage was reprinted in Malcolm's published diaries, *Like It Was*, but without reference to what kind of operation Kitty had undergone. In the light of her abortion, the repetition of "Have they really done it?" takes on a whole new, tragic meaning. The abortion itself was a trauma that they never spoke about for the rest of their lives. It does, however, give a certain emotional resonance to the anti-abortion activism that Malcolm and Kitty both engaged in during the 1970s and 1980s.

Within a year, Kitty was to become desperately ill again. Malcolm refers in his autobiography to a dangerous illness of Kitty's while they were living in Whatlington. In his diary entry for June 11, 1937, Bruce Lockhart noted that Malcolm had come up to Fleet Street to work for a couple of months in order to pay for Kitty's "serious operation (gall stones) . . ."[12] Her medical situation was complicated by the discovery that she also had an ulcerated liver.[13] The operation was successful, but Kitty lost so much blood that she needed a transfusion. Malcolm asked if he could be a donor. His blood was tested and found compatible. Malcolm put this episode into his novel, *In a Valley of This Restless Mind*:

With difficulty the doctor squeezed a drop of blood from the woman's wasted finger, then a drop of blood from mine. He tested these drops of blood and found they would mix. Then my living arm was laid beside her dying one, and both our arms were pierced and connected by a glass tube. The doctor pumped, and red blood flowed from my arm to hers. I understood that this red blood was life, revivifying, like rain falling on parched earth. The woman's parched veins sucked it up and she gained strength. It flowed between the two of us making us one flesh. Our other unions had been partial, but not this one, with the same blood flowing through our veins, one bloodstream.[14]

Here at last was an example of a symmetry that was not fearful: a brief scene symbolising everything that their love ought to be.

A month after the operation, they made the move to Mill House in Whatlington. It was a time of retrenchment, an effort by the two vagabonds and their brood to sink roots into the Sussex soil. Malcolm had opted, once again, for the Simple Life. "It was a fairly austere existence; water came from a well which had to be pumped by hand, and drinking water from a spring some little distance away. Each day I fetched two bucketsful. Bathing was done in a small metal bath in front of the kitchen stove; there was no heating apart from fires and, of course, we had no car. The nearest shopping-centre was Battle, some two miles away; and we would usually walk or cycle in and out."[15]

To support himself, he had to do more than review novels for the *Daily Telegraph*. He contributed a number of essays to *Time and Tide*, a magazine published by Lady Rhondda and staffed primarily by women. One of the more thoughtful magazines of the era, it also published the writings of several imaginative Christian writers, including C.S. Lewis and Charles Williams. On a lesser level, Malcolm found himself ghosting part of a translation of Caulaincourt's *Memoirs*, and writing two stories for *The Fifty Most Amazing Crimes of the Last 100 Years*, a book used to boost the circulation of the *Daily Herald*. But the most important financial boost he received was a £300 advance from Jonathan Cape for a book which surveyed contemporary religious denominations and practices. Malcolm had recently been reading the philosopher William James's *Varieties of Religious Experience*, and offered Cape a similar survey. This was the second time that Cape had commissioned a book from Malcolm and the second time he was to receive something very different from what he had expected.

The first book that Cape had commissioned from Malcolm, *The Earnest Atheist*, was published by Eyre and Spottiswoode in August of 1936. Malcolm's attack on Samuel Butler and his legacy earned him the most savage reviews he had received up to that time. Desmond MacCarthy, an influential member of the liberal establishment, devoted two articles in the *Sunday Times* to defending Butler against Malcolm's charges. (It was said that MacCarthy had thrown the book into the Adriatic in disgust.) E.M. Forster speculated that Malcolm must suffer from a guilt complex to have written such a book. Many of the reviewers, including Stephen Spender, singled out the harsh tone and barbed rhetoric of the book as its own worst enemy. This is certainly true, although it is doubtful that a more subtly argued attack would have enjoyed a better reception. Butler's reputation was then at its height. Since that time, critical opinion has moved closer to Malcolm's position.

Malcolm dedicated *The Earnest Atheist* to his father, "With Gratitude and Affection" and inscribed a copy with the words: "To Dad and Mother, who gave so much and got so little". H.T. responded with unstinting praise of the book – the first time he had done so to any of Malcolm's literary productions. Malcolm's book was, after all, a critique of a man who had loathed and rejected his father. Butler was not the kind of intellectual figure with whom the practical and political H.T. associated himself, so he did not feel personally challenged by Malcolm's attack. He wrote to his son: "I can scarcely express my joy over your new book – somehow it seems my triumph because in spite of (not because of) your other books I always believed in you and your calling someday to do something great that will help our bewildered and lost world. This is it."[16] Like H.T.'s hero, George Bernard Shaw, Malcolm had proved that he could debunk with the best of them. H.T. was no closer to understanding Malcolm's attitude towards politics or other matters, but that did not detract from this moment of reconciliation. Father and son had found an opportunity to express their love for each other. When they did so, it was with a sense of relief.

As the months wore on, Malcolm suffered fits of depression and boredom that never stayed away for long. His greatest consolation in these years leading up to the war was his friendship with Hugh Kingsmill, who was then living near by in Hastings. Not long after his return from India in the autumn of 1935, Malcolm had sought Kingsmill out. He remembered the feeling of predestined friendship when he had met Kingsmill in Manchester six years earlier. In writing his book on Samuel Butler, Malcolm had drawn on the chapter on Butler in Kingsmill's book, *After Puritanism*.

Kingsmill was forty-six years old when Malcolm renewed their acquaintance. He was stocky but not overweight, his unruly hair having gone prematurely grey. His financial troubles had continued unabated, as they would until his death. Malcolm noted that Kingsmill treated publishers as if they were banks. An example of this occurred one day when Malcolm and Kingsmill were walking along a London street and noticed the offices of an obscure publisher. "'Do you think,' Hughie asked eagerly, 'if I went in now he'd give me an advance?'"[17] Malcolm was doubtful, so they did not pursue the matter. At times, Malcolm loaned Kingsmill money, even though he was desperately hard up himself. The money was occasionally repaid, but more often it was not.

Because his fiction had not been successful, Kingsmill confined his writing primarily to biography, for which he could get advances from publishers. He had written the lives of Matthew Arnold, Samuel Johnson, Frank Harris and Charles Dickens, and was working on a biography of D.H. Lawrence when Malcolm met up with him in Sussex. Kingsmill also had a knack for putting together anthologies on various subjects; his reading was so wide and his memory so retentive that he could assemble much of the material for these books in his head. He also collaborated with several other writers, including Hesketh Pearson, William Gerhardi and Malcolm. None of Kingsmill's books sold well, but he always convinced himself that the *next* book would be a huge success.

One of the reasons for Kingsmill's failure to sell books was that he was impossible to categorise. He belonged to no literary group or movement. This was one of the things about him that Malcolm understood and admired. Unlike Malcolm, however, he had no interest in public affairs or politics whatever. Though he had mocked "Dawnism" when he had first met Malcolm in Manchester, he had no political philosophy except an aversion to collectivist solutions to social problems. His great love was literature, and his heroes were Shakespeare, Cervantes, Johnson, Blake and Wordsworth. Kingsmill hated sentimentality, which was why he clung to the humane realism of writers like Shakespeare and Johnson, who balanced a belief in human dignity with an understanding of evil and folly. Malcolm believed that Kingsmill had a mystical streak, although it was manifest more in a love for writers like Blake and Wordsworth than in any ascetical "dark night of the soul".

Those who knew Kingsmill respected him as a writer, but they loved him as a talker. He was at his best in the company of one or two friends, carrying on a conversation that would sparkle with wit, anecdote, literary allusion and a torrent of provocative ideas and epigrams. Though he rarely told jokes, his conversation was always humorous. Kingsmill's private life was hidden from his friends: Malcolm rarely saw his second wife, Dorothy, and his children. But with his friends, Kingsmill became expansive and delightful. After his move to Whatlington, Malcolm saw Kingsmill constantly.

His visits were the high point of my week. I would usually go into Battle to meet him. Theoretically, we were supposed to meet half way, but actually, it nearly always happened that I had passed the half way point by a good stretch before I saw his burly figure coming along the road. Never have I seen him without a warm rush of happiness ... Then, of course, the rest of the afternoon was devoted to talk ... [at] our dear old Mill House, out of doors in the summer and snug by a log fire in the winter, one of Kitty's delicious suppers preparing, a climb up the hill to the Royal Oak and an hour or so in its cosy bar ... and then the regret as the time for the last bus drew near.[18]

Kingsmill's trademark greeting, – "Hullo, old man, hullo!" – was always a delight to Malcolm's ears.

Malcolm and Kingsmill were frequently joined by Hesketh Pearson, a former actor who, like Kingsmill, survived as a man of letters by writing biographies. Pearson was also older than Malcolm, and had known Kingsmill since 1921. Malcolm became quite possessive with Kingsmill and resented Pearson's intimacy with him. This caused tension between all three men. Kingsmill wrote to Malcolm to ask him to relent: "What has upset me is the amount of will you put into your friendships. There is bound to be will in every relationship, but there oughtn't to be much in friendship."[19] Part of the problem was that Pearson was a humanist, an admirer of freethinkers like Tom Paine, with no interest in religion or mysticism. Pearson and Kingsmill shared a love of literature and a hatred of cant, but Malcolm felt that Pearson simply could not see Kingsmill's mystical side. While Kingsmill was alive, they generally maintained an uneasy truce. When Malcolm wrote to apologise for referring to Pearson's hero as "poor besotted Tom Paine", Pearson's response was disingenuous. "All that I can say in reply is that my opinion of your intelligence is lowered and that I am sorry you should think me a deluded ass, but I remain as fond of you as ever I was."[20]

A great deal has been written about the relationship between Malcolm and Kingsmill, but most of it is rather misleading. Both the biographers Michael Holroyd and Richard Ingrams, and even Malcolm himself, have characterised the relationship as being that of master and disciple. "In Malcolm Muggeridge," Holroyd has written, Kingsmill "saw perhaps his one and only disciple ..."[21] According to Ingrams:

If Kingsmill and Pearson were like Holmes and Watson, the Kingsmill-Muggeridge relationship had perhaps more in common with that of Johnson and Boswell . . . No schoolmaster or don had inspired Muggeridge during his time at school and university. Now Kingsmill appeared, late in the day, as a teacher of genius, to introduce him to literature and to show how it was not a means of escaping from life but was in itself one of the most important things in life . . . All this Malcolm absorbed to such an extent that afterwards he could never be sure when he was quoting Kingsmill and when speaking for himself.[22]

Malcolm himself made similar statements.

There is no question that Kingsmill played a crucial role in Malcolm's life, but the statements above simply do not do justice to Malcolm's intelligence, his maturity and his originality as a thinker. Malcolm did in fact have a mentor at university in the person of Alec Vidler. Like Vidler, Kingsmill was intellectually self-confident, cheerful by disposition, but also drawn to Malcolm's dark genius. Unlike Vidler, however, Kingsmill did not make so many demands on Malcolm; because he was outside the institutional Church, Malcolm did not feel somewhat guilty, as he did with Vidler, that his religious commitments were not more settled and defined. Malcolm tended to overlook the core of sadness and tragedy that haunted Kingsmill, preferring to cling to his friend Hughie's better side – the exuberant, witty, endlessly curious conversational partner.

Kingsmill did not introduce Malcolm to either literature or the critique of "Dawnism". Malcolm had read many of Kingsmill's favourite authors, including Blake and Johnson, for years. In his novels and other literary projects, Malcolm had demonstrated his conviction that literature, far from being an escape from life, could be a more realistic way of grappling with life than any other form of discourse. Malcolm's understanding of the modern trend toward collectivist and ideological politics was well developed before he met Kingsmill and was in fact more wide-ranging and penetrating than that of his friend. Malcolm's religious and political convictions were already formed by the time he got to know Kingsmill well. The myth of the master-disciple relationship was really begun by Malcolm himself. Though he could be scathing about his enemies, Malcolm was always extremely generous toward his friends. Acknowledging his debt to Kingsmill was the best tribute he could pay to his friend.

What, then, did Malcolm derive from his relationship to Kingsmill? Essentially, Kingsmill gave Malcolm hope. Kingsmill helped Malcolm to feel that there was a deep and inexhaustible strain of sanity in the best literature. He had encountered that sanity in the Chesterton books he had read in India in the mid-1920s, as well as in St Augustine's *Confessions*. Believing in this sanity was a necessary balance to Malcolm's tendency toward a Swiftian disgust at the human condition. Again and again, Malcolm thanked Kingsmill for helping him to rejoice in the mundane, ordinary things in life. In his company, waiting for Pearson,

> I discovered, for the first time, that Stockport Station was full of interest. There was never any need to go sightseeing with Hughie ... Either everything is interesting or nothing is ... Of all the many truths I learned from him I count this the greatest – that to go searching out for what is interesting is a confession of not having detected life's interest. As he often said, action is exciting but not interesting; and the only thing in life which is admirable is goodness.[23]

This passage is an example of how Malcolm often preserved and made memorable the kind of things that Kingsmill said more in spontaneous conversation than in his prose.

The other gift that Kingsmill gave Malcolm was the idea that human life consists of a perpetual struggle between the will and the imagination. As with many of Kingsmill's insights, it had the effect of clarifying for Malcolm what he already knew in his bones. It explained not only the conflict within his own soul, but the mystique of political power that had proved so intoxicating in the modern era. He summed up the opposition in this way: "The imagination generated love, serenity, literature, faith, laughter, understanding; the will, appetite, in the individual for sensual satisfactions and in the collectivity for power."[24] When Kingsmill reproved Malcolm for imposing his will on their friendship, it was an argument that the younger man had to concede. There were other ways to apply this idea to his own life. Malcolm had rejected the elevation of the will in the political realm, but he did not have the strength to renounce his will to enjoy sensual satisfactions. "To live in the will was to be imprisoned in the dark dungeon of the ego; the imagination was a window, to look out of, and dream of escaping ... The will belongs to time, the imagination projects time into eternity."[25] One of the legacies of his friendship with Hugh Kingsmill was that Malcolm now believed more firmly that the life of imagination was possible – not because Kingsmill wrote about it so well, but because he lived it so intensely.

It was inevitable that Malcolm and Kingsmill – two highly imaginative men – would want to collaborate on a series of literary projects. If none of these efforts came to much, they at least provided a reason for spending time in each other's company. The first project was conceived soon after they had renewed their friendship. Kingsmill thought that Britain needed a witty, independent magazine that could bring humour, satire and critical insight to bear on the increasingly chaotic times. The British press, Kingsmill argued, seemed more timid and more staid than it had been in the early Victorian period, when a magazine like *Punch* provided witty, critical commentary on the follies of the era. With Malcolm's enthusiastic support, Kingsmill drew up a prospectus for a magazine called *Porcupine* that began: "The critical press of England is in a poor state to-day. *Punch* is losing its sales because its ultra-respectable prosperous atmosphere no longer corresponds to the temper of the age. There is no critically humorous paper in England to-day." The publication would not subscribe to any of the popular ideologies or schemes of the moment, but would be written "from the commonsense standpoint of the 18th century, the century of Swift and Johnson, before the world was laid waste by Rousseau, the French Revolution, and all the doctrinaires of the 19th century, ending in Marx, the inspirer of Lenin, and Nietzsche, the inspirer of Hitler."

Financial support was needed to launch such an ambitious project. Neither Malcolm nor Kingsmill knew anyone likely to back such a venture, so they rather naïvely placed an advertisement in the personal columns of *The Times*: "A group of writers who believe that there is room for a weekly which would deal wittily and honestly with the modern world would be glad to hear from anyone interested in financing such a venture."[26] The response was hardly inspiring. Someone in a Home for Indigents wrote wishing them well, adding that he had no money and admonishing them to place "honesty before wit". The next letter came from a man who proposed a scheme for raising capital; he required that they send him £25 in order that he could turn that amount into £1000 or £2000. They let that offer pass. A letter from Zurich told them to launch the project by subscription, "the way people do who make potato chips, or soap, or substitute butter . . ." The most promising response came from a publisher of a magazine for badminton players. Malcolm and Kingsmill travelled to their offices, where the publisher told them that he had succeeded by finding a specialised market for his product. "If, by the same token, we could indicate to him where circles interested in humour were to be found, he felt sure that he would be able to meet with a corresponding success with a humorous publication."[27]

From the ashes of *Porcupine* rose the more practical idea of collaborating on a humorous book. Malcolm and Kingsmill had cemented their friendship back in 1930 when they had laughed over the absurd rhetoric of the *Manchester Guardian*, so they conceived of a book that would contain a series of parodies of the British press. *Brave Old World: A Mirror for the Times* was published in 1936, with humorous illustrations by Sydney Maiden. The book, though ostensibly a collaboration, bears the imprint of Malcolm's mind and interests. This was inevitable, since Kingsmill had no interest in public affairs and the book was entirely about such matters. The stories, printed in the same type as their original sources, are divided into the twelve months of a year. Many of the leading politicians, journalists and intellectuals of the day are satirised, including John Maynard Keynes, J.L. Garvin of the *Observer*, the Webbs and Ramsay MacDonald. Feature articles deal with an American starlet who switches husbands every two months and the testimonies of those who have been "changed" by Frank Buchman's Moral Rearmament crusade.

The central thread running through *Brave Old World* is the rise of the dictator Tamerlane, also known as Al Rak, who sits atop the Union of International and Equal Totalitarian Republics. A composite of Hitler and Stalin, Tamerlane is less absurd than his fawning Western admirers, such as the Anglican Dean of Kensington, who eagerly hopes for the "harnessing of the dynamic energies of Mr Tamerlane to constructive rather than expansionist policies". The Dean, in his New Year Broadcast, goes on to say: "The world was becoming a wiser world. It was becoming a happier world. Above all, it was becoming a more honest world. The keynote of the age was a mistrust of phrases, an almost alarming sincerity in word and deed."[28]

Though Kingsmill believed, with his eternal optimism about his books, that *Brave Old World* would become a best-seller, sales of the book were disappointing. Critics, including Malcolm himself, have noted the inherent difficulty in parodying the press. Michael Holroyd thought the book failed because "all newspapers contain their own parodies and those who see nothing funny will never appreciate such a book; while those who are amused are already supplied with a never-ending and daily source of such humour."29 While this is undoubtedly true, it tends to miss the way the book wittily undermines many of the fads and ideologies that a large percentage of the population believed in earnestly or at least accepted passively.

Undeterred by the lukewarm reception of *Brave Old World*, Malcolm and Kingsmill wrote a second book in the same vein, *Next Year's News*, published early in 1938. Once again, the book is clearly Malcolm's. The conceit of this book was that the authors were chronicling the events that would take place that year. Here Hitler and Stalin appeared under their own names. One of the set-pieces of the book is the posthumous trial of Lenin by Stalin, a send-up of the Soviet show trials of the 1930s. Lenin is condemned and, for his sins, is buried in consecrated ground. Then Marx himself is discredited. *Pravda* comments: "Our ever loving Leader and Father, Stalin, tirelessly uprooting all enemies of the proletariat now tears the mask from the Jew-bourgeois-emigré face of the arch-Leninist-Trotskyist-Bukharinite Marx." One piece of prophecy in *Next Year's News* that stands out was contained in the following item:

HITLER–STALIN MEETING

The meeting between Hitler and Stalin yesterday on King Carol's yacht, *Hannibal*, in the Baltic took place in conditions of great secrecy. The dictators were together for three hours and twenty minutes. On parting they shook hands warmly.

Though both of these books dealt "honestly and wittily" with the modern world, they were too out of tune with the times to be widely appreciated.

Malcolm and Kingsmill collaborated on one other project. A little over a year after their proposal for *Porcupine* fizzled, a magazine called *Night and Day* began publication in London. *Night and Day* was remarkably similar to the proposal for *Porcupine*. The literary editor of *Night and Day* was Graham Greene, who was known at the time for his novels *Stamboul Train* and *A Gun for Sale*. Though it only lasted six months, from July to December 1937, *Night and Day* was an impressive magazine, counting among its contributors Anthony Powell, Evelyn Waugh, V.S. Pritchett, Elizabeth Bowen, Herbert Read, John Betjeman, Cyril Connolly, Stevie Smith and William Empson. A number of these contributors, including Greene himself, were just beginning their literary careers. Some of the leading cartoonists and illustrators of the day graced the magazine with their talent and humour. *Night and Day* had the independence that Kingsmill had called for in his prospectus. Urbane and witty, it could also be acerbic and satirical. Ironically, this satirical sharpness was to hasten its downfall. After Graham Greene reviewed a film starring the child star, Shirley Temple, in which he commented on the sexual undertones to her childish coquetry, a libel suit was brought on her behalf against the magazine. Since its finances were already shaky, the entire venture collapsed.[30]

Among the contributions that Malcolm and Kingsmill made to *Night and Day* were excerpts from their book-in-progress, *Next Year's News*. They also did a series of "Literary Pilgrimages by H.K. and M.M." in which they would visit a site with some literary association – an association that did not necessarily show the author in a favourable light. These pieces consisted of a narrative introduction which gave way to a rather droll dialogue between H.K. and M.M. on the significance of their discoveries. The first pilgrimage was to the house in Handel Street where Samuel Butler and his friend Festing Jones would visit the same prostitute, although on different days of the week. The second was to Paris to visit the great-great-granddaughter of William Wordsworth – the descendant of the child he had fathered with Annette Vallon. They also went to the house in Wimpole Street where Alfred Tennyson had spent a week with Arthur Hallam not long before Hallam's death. To prepare for the visit, they went to a Turkish bath the night before. As in all their literary collaborations, there is an unmistakable sense that Malcolm has done the lion's share of the writing. In fact, there can be no doubt that these efforts were one way that Malcolm could give something to Kingsmill: splitting advance payments for books that Malcolm was to write.

The writing that Malcolm did for *Night and Day* helped to introduce him to several writers with whom he would develop friendships, including Anthony Powell and Graham Greene. Much as Malcolm enjoyed his life in Whatlington, spending delightful evenings with Kingsmill and Pearson, he still wanted to know writers who were more at the centre of the cultural stage. It would be wrong to attribute this need merely to a secret longing to be accepted by the establishment. Like Wyndham Lewis, whose books he had read and admired, Malcolm had declared himself "The Enemy" of the establishment. Writers such as Powell and Greene and George Orwell were beginning to be successful and influential, but they had not compromised their critical stance to the state of Western culture. They were independent thinkers, and that attracted Malcolm to them.

It was in these pre-war years that Malcolm's search for religious faith emerged more forcefully than at any time since his Cambridge years. Kingsmill certainly played a role in this, with his Wordsworthian mysticism. Unlike Kingsmill, however, Malcolm struggled fiercely with the concrete beliefs and moral demands of the Christian life. He had renewed his friendship with Alec Vidler, spending summer holidays with him in Ireland in 1936 and France in 1937. Though Vidler was tolerant of Malcolm's refusal to join the Church, Malcolm always knew where Vidler stood. In fact, Malcolm admired and sometimes envied Vidler's faith; he took comfort in its steadiness and wisdom.

Malcolm had only to contemplate his recent past to realise that he needed to consider the state of his convictions, and of his soul. He had recently been through a season in hell: the despair of his year in India, the crisis in his marriage with Kitty and the birth of a son that was not his own. He had descended into a personal and emotional chaos that had frightened him. He had little or no faith in himself; he thought that faith in God might release him from the burden of his own desires and vanities.

Malcolm may not have pursued his religious search with an absolute and unwavering commitment, but the struggle was genuine. He tried to reform his behaviour. He confided these resolutions to his diary. "I want to give up smoking, arguing, reading newspapers, losing my temper."[31] His underlying love for Kitty was undiminished, but now he challenged himself to care for her more sensitively. "Kit had one of her black fits, but now it's passed. I tried to think what I ought to do to help her, and only felt myself a prig. I must love her, I thought. (I see now that I'm only at the very beginning of the road I thought I had got well along.) This was false. My falsity to blame, I thought." He decided that Kitty ought to go on a holiday to Switzerland by herself, and agreed to take care of the children for the two weeks she would be away. "Looking after the children makes me love them more," he discovered afterwards.[32] One day he could write in his diary: "I still ... plan a surreptitious fuck." But then ten days later he threw a packet of condoms into a river.[33]

In a series of essays written for *Time and Tide*, Malcolm tested and developed his religious convictions. The central problem of human nature, he writes in an essay entitled "What Is My Life?", is desire. Are human desires naturally good and deserving of gratification? Is the satisfaction of desire the end of human existence? Malcolm's response is to point out the insatiability of desire, that it is a constant of human nature. He goes on to note that many modern thinkers have argued that human desires can be satisfied only when they are satisfied collectively, through the agency of political change. In this approach, some social phenomenon is blamed for the world's ills – capitalism or war or a lack of adequate education. The search for a collectivist solution, which he calls idealism, is based on a hope for Utopia. But utopian politics is just as illusory as other means for satisfying desire. "It is as impossible for an individual to achieve serenity through perfecting his environment as through satisfying Desire, since his environment is only a projection of his Desire. Thus trying to satisfy Desire by creating a Utopia is like trying to finance a new company with debts in the hope of thereby being able to pay them off."

The essay concludes rather weakly, asserting that since desire cannot be satisfied by any means, what remains are the mystical moments when one senses the "Oneness" of creation. The enemy of these moments of vision is the Self, which hankers after desire. But Malcolm refuses to say how the individual might prepare himself for these visions: no religious or ascetic practices or acts of will can evoke them.[34]

Other essays from this period fill out Malcolm's argument a little more fully. In "Faith", he attacks the idea that science can provide certainty in an age of doubt and despair. Science itself, he says, has become dogmatic, asserting its theories as a kind of pseudo-metaphysics. But science and poetry are not interchangeable; only poetry can nourish our souls.

Bishop Barnes may scoff at the miraculous and call sacramentalism magic, but if one still sees God as a father and mankind as His children he is being as unscientific as any witch doctor since this conception rests not on scientific but on imaginative or poetic truth. However powerful telescopes may become they will never be able to prove or disprove the existence of heaven; Blake reached conclusions from a grain of sand which would not have been affected had he been shown the whole vast extent of the universe . . . and it is doubtful if Christ would have seen fit to alter any syllable in the Sermon on the Mount in the light of quantum or relativity theory or both.[35]

Malcolm held that religious faith was the only source of true individuality; it enabled one to avoid both the isolation of materialism – man as hedonistic consumer – and the false brotherhood of totalitarianism – man as creature of the state. To the objection that religion only focused attention on a transcendent world and left the pain and misery of this world untouched, Malcolm responded:

> those in whom [the religious] sense is strongest have been most persistent and effective in championing the weak and helping the unfortunate. To feel that men are all children of God, and so brothers, is a more effective spur to effort on their behalf than either a personal or a vicarious grievance. Envy and hatred may make revolutions, and, incidentally, counter-revolutions, too, but charity . . . has been the mainspring of all true disinterestedness.[36]

Malcolm's belief that truth could not be embodied in creeds or institutions was hardly original. It was, in fact, a quintessentially liberal position, but he did not press the question too far. But he did acknowledge that religious institutions had a role to play.

> Even when religions as embodied in institutions become depraved, as they all do and must, they still serve a purpose, since they keep alive a necessary sense of Man's littleness and at the same time of his infinite worth as one of God's creatures. If I hear a clergyman whom I despise, who I know draws his stipend from slum property, toadies to the rich and despises the poor, who is idle, ignorant, parasitic, an enemy of good causes and a friend of bad, say, "Except a man be born again he cannot see the Kingdom of God," it is still more invigorating than a visit to the most perfectly equipped anti-God museum. A savage grovelling in front of a garlanded stone fills me with more awe and hope than the most powerful hydro-electric plant under the sun.[37]

In writing these essays, Malcolm had worked out his thoughts about religion more clearly than he had ever done. But, as he was all too aware, he had not reached the end of his search. He was still on the road and had to make choices about which paths to take. His criticisms of institutional Christianity were unquestionably true so far as they went. He had made the unassailable point that religion was not alive unless the individual had a personal experience of faith. But if religion, as the etymology of the word would indicate, involves a "binding together", then how could Malcolm stay aloof from the community of believers? If one of the central tenets of religion is the belief in human brotherhood, it is difficult to see how the practice of religion can be solitary and individualistic. But Malcolm told himself that getting down on his knees with others would be to abandon the necessary detachment of the writer and critic.

Malcolm was too honest about himself not to be aware that his resistance to Church and creed arose out of his fear that he could not live up to such commitments. Nonetheless, he was to spend the next thirty years living in the tension between his private religious yearnings and the public life of the Church. He had a number of mystical experiences at this time, but they did not involve a direct sense of contact with a personal God. One occurred on a walk with Kingsmill. They were on the cliffs above Hastings.

> It was an autumn evening, slightly misty and very still, with a sharp chill in the air. From the chimneys below, wreaths of smoke were rising into the sky; from each particular chimney, pale smoke, briefly separate, then becoming indistinct, and finally, lost to view; merging into the grey, gathering evening. I was suddenly spellbound, as though this was a vision of the Last Day, and the wreaths of smoke, souls, leaving their bodies to rise heavenwards and become part of eternity. At the same time, I felt full of an inexpressible tenderness for these fellow-humans, sending up smoke-signals to me from their separate hearths, and an inexpressible joy at sharing with them a common destiny.[38]

Another mystical moment took place in the churchyard in Whatlington, where he felt a great sense of peace amid the gravestones and the massive yew tree.

His attitude toward the idea of Christ's divinity shifted constantly. He could write in his diary at this time: "It is inconceivable to me now that I should ever believe either in a personal God, or that Christ's claims to be God's son in a special sense were, in so far as he made them, anything but bogus."[39] Then, a few days later, he would read the Sermon on the Mount or the opening chapter of the Gospel of St

161

John or I Corinthians 13 to Kitty and be profoundly moved. Once again, he and Kitty wondered whether they should have the children baptised.

As he had done so often before, Malcolm transformed this agonised spiritual search into autobiographical fiction. The book surveying modern religious beliefs and practices he had promised Rupert Hart-Davis at Cape was turning into a dark, picaresque tale – a tortured pilgrim's progress. He had originally called it "The Bewildered Soul", but he found a better title in Shakespeare's sonnets, a title more reflective of his inward condition at the time: *In a Valley of This Restless Mind*.

« 10 »

Lost in the Darkness of Change
1938–1941

IN 1933, Malcolm was one of the few political commentators confidently to predict the coming of another European war. By 1938, however, it did not require prophetic powers to see that Neville Chamberlain's proclamation of "peace in our time" was premature. Malcolm understood that fascism and communism were militant ideologies that would not rest at political domination within their own borders; they were inherently expansionist. The signing of the Nazi-Soviet Pact in 1939 could not come as a surprise to the man who had foreseen it as a piece of "next year's news".

Since moving to Whatlington, Malcolm had made a deliberate effort to withdraw from the political preoccupations of journalism and work out his religious and literary ideas. At a time when most Western intellectuals were looking for political solutions to human problems, Malcolm was moving in the other direction. While literary figures from Shaw to Auden were praising Stalin and idealistic youth was going off to fight for the Republicans in the Spanish Civil War, Malcolm was writing essays that addressed what he considered to be the underlying spiritual crisis of the West.

But as the world careered towards Armageddon, Malcolm worried that he was too detached. The outbreak of the war itself broke the tension of this paradox and enabled him to become a participant rather than an observer – for a time. But as the war progressed, Malcolm, like his contemporary Evelyn Waugh, grew ambivalent about the notion that the Allies represented the triumph of civilisation over barbarism.

It had become clear to him that neither individuals nor nations could live without religious faith. He argued that the Judeo-Christian vision of a fallen world offered an antidote to the utopian fantasies of the modern era. By proclaiming the death of God, modern man had sought to become his own source of order. Thus politics had supplanted religion and acquired an almost sacred status; in short, the Church had been eclipsed by the State. Malcolm believed that this process of secularisation led either to the progressivist liberalism embodied by his father and the Fabians or to totalitarianism, whether of the Left or the Right. What separated liberalism from totalitarianism was not principle but degree: both ideologies turned to the state to remake the social order. The fatal flaw in this way of thinking, Malcolm believed, was the idea that human nature could be changed by education or welfare or any other political scheme.

Malcolm was not alone in formulating this religious critique of modern ideologies. A number of Western thinkers, including T.S. Eliot, Christopher Dawson and Jacques Maritain, were articulating the same ideas, often in philosophical terms that were of little interest to Malcolm. But Malcolm chose to remain an outsider. He had come close to professing the Christian faith in his essays and articles, but he had not taken the final step. Writers like Eliot were more comfortable with institutional Christianity than Malcolm was; they were, in his mind, part of a Christian establishment from which he was excluded. He continued to work out his religious search in his own terms.

Malcolm poured the full emotional intensity of that search into *In a Valley of This Restless Mind*, a book that ranks among Malcolm's best, and that deserves to be considered a classic. Jonathan Cape must have had a moment of *déjà vu* when once again he received a manuscript that was very different from the one he had commissioned. Instead of a survey of contemporary religious ideas and practices, Cape found a tortured spiritual autobiography. Rupert Hart-Davis, Cape's editor, argued for publication, calling the book a "masterpiece", but Cape was unmoved, and the book was eventually published in 1938 by Routledge.

As Evelyn Waugh wrote in his perceptive review of *Valley*: "It is not an easy book to describe. It has affinities, in form, with *Candide* and, in temper, with *Voyage au bout de la nuit*. It is a highly symbolized and stylized autobiography whose range includes satirical reportage and something very near prophecy."[1] Another reviewer suggested that it should have been called *The Pilgrim's Regress*.

Malcolm's original intention was to make it an even more autobiographical book. He planned to publish it under the pseudonym of T. Wildish, and wrote an introductory "Memoir" of this fictitious *alter ego*, who has died at age thirty-seven after finishing *Valley*. Malcolm's publisher rightly rejected the pseudonym and memoir, arguing that they were too cumbersome and confusing. But this discarded chapter does contain a revealing self-portrait of Malcolm.

The memoir describes Malcolm's career in exact detail, from India and Egypt to the *Guardian* and Moscow. It is ostensibly written by an Anglo-Catholic priest who had been a friend of Wildish – an unmistakable allusion to Alec Vidler. The device of the memoir was Malcolm's attempt to come to terms with Vidler – one sign that Kingsmill was not the only important influence on Malcolm at this time. Vidler, though a gentle man and a theological liberal, continued to be critical of Malcolm for refusing to make a commitment to the life of faith.

The portrait of Wildish painted by the fictional Vidler is focused on Malcolm's inner life. The language is unsparing:

> What was there in his personality, I ask myself now, that made it somehow vivid and striking, if often disappointing? His intellectual gifts were not great; his conversation was sometimes lively, but often tediously earnest as well as irritating. The sincerity on which he prided himself, however real it might be at a particular moment, was subject to bewildering fluctuations. How often with him have I found today's enthusiasms become tomorrow's abominations.[2]

Of Malcolm's ability as a writer, the comment is even harsher: "His gifts were demagogic rather than artistic."[3] The priest then goes on to describe his conversation with Wildish's wife Gertrude after the funeral.

> "He had a bit of genius," Gertrude said.
> I wondered if this were so.
> Aware of my doubts, she went on: "Oh yes, he had a bit of genius. What is genius? – it's exuberance mitigated by disinterestedness, or disinterestedness enlivened by exuberance. A woman tenderly looking after an idiot child is [a] genius. He had that sort of quality, along with much that was showy and cheap and greedy."
> In the now quite dark room we both cried, not so much because we should never see Wildish again or hear his voice, as for the strangeness of human life; love lavished on an idiot child, its sublimity and its horror, its incomprehensibility.[4]

In a Valley of This Restless Mind, like *Candide* and *Rasselas*, is the story of a young man in search of enlightenment about the eternal questions. Like its eighteenth-century predecessors, it is not so much a novel as a fable or allegory that unfolds in a series of tableaux. But unlike the tales of Voltaire and Johnson, Malcolm's hero has no Dr Pangloss or Imlac to dispense words of wisdom or set him back on the right path. The protagonist of *Valley* is a bewildered soul (to use the original title of the book), afflicted by the fever of lust, prone to nausea, doubting everything, yet longing for faith, hope and love. Because the nausea and the spiritual longing are kept in tension, the reader follows the shifting scenes with a sort of horrified fascination and just a touch of sympathy for the protagonist.

Though the story is told in the first person, the narrator goes by three different names: Motley, Flammonde and Wraithby. The first comes from a Shakespeare sonnet: "Alas, 'tis true I have been here and there/And made myself a motley to the view," a poem that ends: "Mine appetite I never more will grind." The second derives from a poem by Edwin Arlington Robinson: "And women young and old were fond / Of looking at the man Flammonde." Wraithby, a name used in *Winter in Moscow*, alludes to Malcolm's fear of moving through the world like a detached, ghostly observer. Malcolm once suggested that the three identities were "Motley the womanizer, Wraithby the anti-hero and Flammonde the returned traveller from over the hill", but they are only three aspects of one personality.[5]

Valley opens on a note of spiritual longing.

> Looking for God, I sat in Westminster Abbey and watched sightseers drift by. The Cross on the altar was covered with grey cloth, like chairs at spring-cleaning ... Thinking of it now my heart melted, I scarcely knew why. Even covered with grey cloth, and with sightseers shuffling to and fro and whispering, it was poignant, seeming to promise an alternative to the Will's arrogance, the Flesh's passion, and Time's inevitable corruption.[6]

There are many traces in *Valley* of the original plan of writing a survey of religious practices and beliefs. Malcolm did have breakfast with an archdeacon in gaiters, attend a mass meeting of Buchman's Moral Rearmament at Albert Hall, and visit "Fr Boniface" at an Anglo-Catholic monastery. These episodes enabled Malcolm to satirise the hollowness of traditional Christian institutions and their more eccentric offshoots.

Secular substitutes for religion do not come off much better in *Valley*; they are all depicted as forms of bogus spirituality, from the psychoanalysis of Dr Appleblossom to the political utopianism of the left-wing journalist, Wilberforce. Then there is the Lawrentian sex-mysticism of the novelist Flavell: "The bit he did yesterday about Amyas not being able to wait for Enid until he had taken off his pit clothes, and having her on the stone kitchen floor while the bath she had prepared for him got cold – needed re-touching."[7] A character named Friend represents the Establishment, and the false comfort of merging into the respectable bourgeois world. Sidney and Beatrice Webb show up at the Bretts, and Malcolm takes another swipe at their godlike pretensions as social engineers. He imagines himself partici-pating in this power, the language parodying that of God in the Book of Job:

Now to cut away the dead wood! I cut away the angry dart and the shrinking fear and the tremulous fornication. I made old life bud new as coolly as old thought budded new. I regulated the seed's ardour, and reinforced the young shoot's frailty, and tempered the honeysuckle's passionate scent. I said to the bacillus, "Be patient!" and to the worm, "Take thought." Then I looked at what I had done, and in place of Earth I saw principles, abstractions, unresponsive to the sun's heat, unthirsty for the rain's wet, unfearful of the frost's grip. There was death in my touch. I touched the sky and it unrolled like a blind; I touched plants and creatures and they died. Even the sun went out like a fused bulb, and there was darkness.[8]

Malcolm threw many of his personal experiences into the story. The utopian community he encountered as a child, the Colony, appears as Beulah, a commune wracked by sexual jealousy and a lingering attachment to private property. There are allusions to his sexual life, from the frustrated adolescent groping with Dora to the decadent sophistication of his affair with Amrita Sher-Gil, who shows up as Palmyre, reclining on her bed and lacing her conversation with French phrases.

Most of *Valley* is taken up with what Waugh called the process of arriving at "negative truths". There are only a couple of moments where a more positive truth makes a fleeting appearance. One such moment occurs in a small village in the country, where the narrator accosts the local rector on his lawn. When he questions what the rector believes, the priest begins simply with the Apostles' Creed. To the fevered questions of "What am I to do now?" the rector replies mildly, "Really . . . I scarcely know." But after a quiet tea on the lawn, they go to the church for Evensong.

> Kneeling there together . . . we sent up our souls to seek God's face, and knew for a moment without any possibility of doubt that Will and Appetite were unsubstantial . . . The Rector knelt on in his place after the Benediction. How strange a chance, I thought, that had dressed him in a white surplice to stand in front of an altar . . . So quavering a priest, so quavering a church, washed by Time as a shore by the tide, accumulating Time's deposit, scarcely recognizable, greed growing to it like thick ivy, abomination enjoying its shelter; so corrupt a church, yet miraculously passing on its uncorrupt Word as seed was passed on generation after generation, uncorrupt, by corrupted bodies."[9]

The other glimpse of grace occurs at the end of the book, when the narrator is able to watch his blood being transfused into his wife's body, the momentary image of what their marriage ought to mean.

The book concludes not with an affirmation of faith, but with the sense that faith is something that the narrator can long for but never attain. The final image is of Whatlington churchyard, where the narrator hopes to be buried; he will at least lie in the shadow of the church he cannot enter.

Malcolm was deeply gratified by Evelyn Waugh's review of *Valley*. Waugh not only praised the content of the book, but reserved his highest compliments for its mastery of English prose. Malcolm and Waugh were exact contemporaries, and had much in common, from ambivalence about their social origins to their capacity for Swiftian satire and their loathing of modern secular ideologies. Ironically, throughout their lifetimes, they could only admire each other from afar; social prejudices and personal jealousies kept them from ever becoming friends. But in this review, Waugh paid tribute to Malcolm's vision. In writing about Malcolm's attitude towards lust, Waugh wrote that it "is that of a surfeited and rather scared Calvinist". Given Malcolm's poor self-image, and his perpetual fear of being left outside

– whether of Establishment or Church or Heaven itself – this is a strikingly accurate description. Waugh also went on to note that: "His is that particularly English loneliness of a religiously minded man suddenly made alive to the fact that he is outside Christendom."[10] It was a loneliness that Waugh had known before he had been received into the Roman Catholic Church. Malcolm would take the same step, but only after thirty more years of wandering in the valley of the restless mind.

By the beginning of 1938, the events occurring in the world beyond the Sussex coast began to pull Malcolm's attention away from his spiritual preoccupations. He received a commission from the publisher Hamish Hamilton to write a book on Britain in the 1930s. His primary research tool was *The Times*; he acquired every issue printed during the decade. As he wrote in his autobiography, his study was literally walled in by stacks of *The Times*.

He continued to write articles critical of the Soviet Union. One such article, printed in the *Daily Telegraph* in March of 1938, attacked the show trials that Stalin was then staging in Moscow. As he had argued in 1932, the Soviet regime required a continuous process of ideological warfare which identified "enemies of the state". One of the most insidious forms this warfare took was the toppling of high-ranking officials. The purge of 1938 had claimed such leading figures as Radek, Zinoviev and Bukharin. Malcolm's articles in the *Telegraph* elicited a rambling letter from the Irish playwright Sean O'Casey defending Stalin and attacking Malcolm. When the *Telegraph* declined to publish this long letter, O'Casey sent it to the Communist paper, the *Daily Worker*. Malcolm thought the letter was so flimsy that he did not bother to reply. O'Casey then accused Malcolm of being a "cock that won't fight". Malcolm responded by saying that he would be willing to debate with O'Casey at any time on their views about the Soviet Union.

Mr O'Casey is so fine a dramatist that I cannot help being surprised at such folly in him. He, an Irishman, with a vigorous independent mind, not to be brow-beaten by authority in any guise – he, of all people, comes forward and insists on the validity of a series of charges, so fantastic that if they were made in a British or a German, still more an Irish court, he would be the first to laugh them to scorn; insists that confessions often containing obvious absurdities (as at the Ramzin trial, when interviews were confessed to with men dead at the time the interviews were supposed to have taken place), unsupported by documentary or other evidence, are to be implicitly believed . . .

The Dean of Canterbury, Professor Laski, the Duchess of Atholl, Sir Bernard Pares, the Webbs – these I can understand; but the author of *Juno and the Paycock* – I admit I was surprised.[11]

The debate then shifted to the pages of *Time and Tide*, where Malcolm argued that the French tradition of allowing those attacked to reply should be adopted in the British press. O'Casey responded yet again, this time in the company of Idris Cox of the *Daily Worker*. Malcolm's final contribution concluded with these words to O'Casey:

If you have decided to plump for Stalin and throw in your lot with his comintern sycophants inside and outside the U.S.S.R, then cut out talk about fair play and freedom. That kind of cant I expect from Idris Cox, but not from you, who must know that if you went through a *Daily Worker* file, and through a file of every Soviet newspaper ever published, you would not find one single word criticizing the Soviet government, its acts or policies or extant personnel.[12]

Malcolm's warnings about the Soviet Union largely fell on deaf ears. It was Hitler, rather than Stalin, who was grabbing the headlines at this time. The *Anschluss*, or annexation, of Austria had taken place in March and Hitler was pressing for territory in Czechoslovakia. War – its probability, nature, and effects – was the subject that everyone was discussing. As early as 1936, Malcolm had made clear that he would fight. In an essay, "Why I Am Not a Pacifist", Malcolm severed yet another tie with his socialist past. He looked upon disarmament conferences and "peace ballots" as further evidence of the fantasy that had come to dominate the political crusades of the 1930s. Unless one is willing to renounce the protection and freedom provided by one's nation, Malcolm argued, one must defend that nation when it is threatened. That England is guilty of numerous sins does not invalidate one's obligation to defend her. He offered this analogy: "A husband who deserts his wife when she is in difficulties, even though he thinks they are of her own making, is despicable. He has enjoyed his wife's companionship when things go well, and then, when they go ill, asserts his moral right to go his own way." The notion that one can separate oneself from the wrongs of society and exist as a solitary, pure individual, is both misguided and irresponsible.

> Killing is evil, and war is a senseless, terrible calamity. Like many other human activities it reflects, not the divine, but the beast in Man. As a rash manifests measles war manifests mass hysteria and hate. I might pledge myself to take every care to avoid becoming infected with measles, but it would be absurd as well as dishonest to pledge myself never to have a rash. War is but one aspect of the whole horror of human behaviour. It cannot be isolated. It belongs to Evil, which, like Good, is one and indivisible.[13]

The war finally arrived in the form of a radio broadcast by the Prime Minister, Neville Chamberlain, on Sunday morning, September 3, 1939. The Muggeridges, who could not afford a wireless, listened to the broadcast at a neighbour's home. Outside they saw an Anglican clergyman muttering to himself, "We're in God's hands now, we're in God's hands now." Malcolm recalled Kitty looking for the children, a new vigilance in her eye. Sirens were sounded and barrage balloons raised, but the war would take some time to manifest itself in the Sussex downs.[14]

The story of Malcolm's experience of the war is complex and ambiguous. The war years take up about three-quarters of the second volume of his autobiography, *The Infernal Grove*. War offers an endless supply of anecdote, farce and set-pieces, ranging in tone from the sublime to the ridiculous, and Malcolm took full advantage of this in his autobiography. He does recount some of his darker moments during the war, but the narrative is so interesting that it conceals just how disastrous these years were for him. The war marked the end of the relatively happy and productive years in Whatlington, where he had produced two of his finest books, *In a Valley of This Restless Mind*, and his soon-to-be-published *The Thirties*. Except for the first months, he would not write anything during the war, nor did it provide the basis of any creative work in the future. Cast adrift in the anarchy of war, it was as if Malcolm had returned to his black year in Calcutta: once again he became mired in ennui, attempted to compensate with a series of sexual entanglements, all the while haunted by a desire to end his life. Above all, his religious search stalled and was not to return to its former intensity for many years. Like Bunyan's pilgrim, he fell into the Slough of Despond and only slowly extricated himself from its marshy pull.

The day after war was declared, Malcolm announced to Kitty that he was going to join the army. "She did not, as I half expected she would, reproach me, but just accepted what was, given my age, circumstances and family responsibilities, an intrinsically foolish and egotistic thing to do."[15] He made the dramatic gesture of packing a bag in case he was to be sent off immediately to camp. He travelled to Hastings, only to find that there was no recruiting station there. So on Tuesday he set off for Brighton. Malcolm found that there was already a long queue of middle-aged men trying to join up. When it was his turn to present his form, he was told that as a journalist he was in a "reserved occupation" and that he was best occupied behind his typewriter. Undeterred, he tried several other tables, each time listing a different occupation – author, schoolmaster, book reviewer and unemployed. He was turned down every time. Defeated and embarrassed, he returned to Whatlington and wrote an article for the *Daily Telegraph* on how difficult it was in this war to enlist – somewhat like getting a ticket for the Royal Enclosure at Ascot. Soon after it was published, Malcolm received a letter from a Lieutenant Colonel Davies, whom he had known slightly in Egypt. Davies asked Malcolm if he was merely being facetious or really meant what he said.

In the weeks that followed, Malcolm wrote to every influential person in the government with whom he had even a casual acquaintance in order to get a military posting. He asked Lord Lloyd to help him become an RAF pilot or rear-gunner. He even wrote to Lord Beaverbrook and Brenden Bracken, but to no avail. The period known as the "phoney war" had begun: despite the declaration of war, not much seemed to be happening. Malcolm found this limbo particularly difficult to endure because his only regular source of income was the weekly book review for the *Daily Telegraph*. He did, however, receive an offer from a publisher to write a book about the war. The publisher wanted it to be modelled on *The First Hundred Thousand*, by Ian Hay, an account of the British Expeditionary Force in 1915. Despite the offer of a temptingly large advance, Malcolm turned down the project. It would have forced him to remain an observer at the very moment he was desperate to become a participant.

It wasn't long before the *Telegraph* wrote to tell him that the war had put an end to his book reviewing. But the same day he also received a letter inviting him to join the newly-formed Ministry of

Information. This was hardly what he wanted: it would force him to remain an observer and it would require him to spend the week in London, away from his family. On the other hand, he had no source of income and his advances had all been spent. He had little choice but to accept the offer. In his autobiography he comments rather harshly on this decision. "I did this, not under compulsion, not from any genuine sense of duty, but just out of vanity and foolish bravado; ultimately, I suppose, because I wanted to get away on my own, and behave as I liked. Something that wars make permissible, practicable and even praiseworthy."[16] These words apply with more force to Malcolm's later decision to leave the Ministry of Information and join the Intelligence Corps. But this admission does point to the syndrome that would make the war a lonely, emotionally chaotic time for Malcolm, a return to the black moments he had known in the past.

The Ministry of Information had been hastily put together for the purpose of creating and disseminating propaganda to the Allies and their friends around the world. It was the obvious place for writers to put their talents to work, and Malcolm soon discovered that his colleagues at the Ministry included such figures as Graham Greene, George Orwell and the young socialist intellectual R.H.S. Crossman. Malcolm found that his years at the *Guardian* put him in good stead for the sort of uplifting material he was supposed to turn out; he became, once more, an apostle of hope. He also did a little work for the religious department. The workload, however, was fairly light. Malcolm found himself spending most of his time drinking tea and talking incessantly with Greene and Crossman.

Malcolm shared an office with a writer named Palmer, a man who must have brought back memories of Wordsworth at the Calcutta *Statesman*. Like Wordsworth, Palmer was a supporter of the League of Nations, where he had worked for many years as a minor bureaucrat. Malcolm found that Palmer had no complaints about the lack of work. He had "developed in himself a sort of Buddhistic power of contemplation as he sat at his desk staring in front of him; expenditure of energy being reserved for things like getting stationery, paper-clips and other clerical impedimenta together, taking control of the opening and shutting of our window, and seeing that his blotter was changed from time to time ..." Palmer, it turned out, wrote thrillers with a colleague of his at the League, a man named Hilary St George Saunders. Palmer evidently thought Saunders was a man of superior talents, though Malcolm detected in his office mate "a strain of envy, and perhaps resentment".[17] The relationship between these two men would eventually germinate in Malcolm's mind, forming the plot for a murder mystery of his own, published as *Affairs of the Heart* in 1949.

Walking through the blacked-out streets of London in the evenings, Malcolm threaded his way back to his flat in Bramerton Street in Chelsea. In spare moments he laboured to finish *The Thirties*. Occasionally he would have dinner with Graham Greene, the main course being sausages, which were at that time still available. Striding through the murky city streets, as he had done in Cairo, Manchester, Moscow and Calcutta, Malcolm found himself repeating a single phrase over and over again, like a mantra: "Lost in the darkness of change".

Soon Malcolm found change coming to him in the form of an invitation to go to Mytchett Hutments, Ash Vale, part of the large military base at Aldershot in the Hampshire countryside. There he was to present himself to join the Field Security Police. Lieutenant Colonel Davies, who had responded to Malcolm's *Telegraph* article on the difficulty of getting military postings, had taken action. Malcolm was not obliged to make this move. He had just been offered a promotion at the Ministry of Information, which entailed a raise in pay. Now that he had the opportunity to become a soldier, something he had eagerly sought only weeks earlier, he wondered whether he had made another impetuous and impractical decision. But he was duly inducted into His Majesty's armed forces. "I ... filled in yet another prodigious form, stripped for the purpose of being medically examined, wandered about naked holding a phial of my urine; then swore on a dog-eared Bible to fight loyally for King and Country as and when required. Thus the matter was settled; the Ministry of Information knew me no more, and I became a private, acting unpaid lance-corporal, in the shortly-to-be-formed Intelligence Corps."[18]

It is difficult to imagine anyone less suited than Malcolm to the collective enterprise that is life in the armed forces. A nonconformist in wartime is liable to end up either in comic situations or in trouble – or, as in Malcolm's case, in both. The first thing that Malcolm noticed about army life was the way it tended to reinforce the class structure of society. When Malcolm was a private, he was looked upon with contempt by the regular Military Police at Aldershot; something about him rankled with them. But when he was rapidly promoted, achieving the rank of lieutenant by May, 1940, he was suddenly treated with respect: his rank and his class were now matched appropriately.

"Hostility turned into amiability; I found myself quite a favourite when I condescended to visit the sergeants' mess, being regarded as a card, an odd fellow, who said preposterous things but needed to be cherished and protected."[19]

Whenever Malcolm attempted to prove himself the perfect soldier, the result was invariably comic. To his way of thinking, the exaggerated, punctilious salutes and other rituals which the NCOs and warrant officers indulged in became so important precisely because the war was so far away; they were an end in themselves. Nonetheless, he became the object of attention whenever he tried to mimic these actions. He served for a brief time as a warrant officer and realised, "rather to my surprise, that I could emulate these old pros in volume of voice if nothing else; shouting out 'Squad, Abbbbout turn!', or 'Staand eas ... y!' as to the manner born. My performance was so unexpected that it attracted attention; a little crowd would gather to hear me at it; drawn, I suppose, by the ludicrous disparity between what I looked like, and perhaps was, and what I was doing."[20] When he was assigned to meet an important officer from the War Office at the railway station, Malcolm spent hours polishing buttons and other fittings, shining his boots with a hot spoon and otherwise making himself immaculate. When he met the officer at the station, Malcolm saluted smartly, took the officer's bags, and got into the car beside the driver. But when he looked into the rear view mirror, there was something familiar about this exalted officer. He too cast furtive glances at Malcolm. Finally, Malcolm recognised that the man was one Edward Crankshaw, a neighbour from Sussex and a Kremlinologist. They "began to laugh long and uproariously ... Somehow, thenceforth, I was never again able to take my military duties, such as they were, quite seriously; like other exercises of the will, they required dressing up and histrionic skills to be convincing."[21]

Even the most serious parts of their military activities had a touch of absurdity about them. The Field Security Police was evolving into the Intelligence Corps, but its training methods were antiquated. At the centre of their training was a course on Security Intelligence, which was almost unchanged from the course given during the 1914–18 war. Perhaps the most ludicrous element of the course was the *Dames Blanches* organisation, "which consisted of Belgian ladies who counted the carriages of troop trains rumbling past as they knitted at their windows, thus making an estimate of the forces the Germans were moving up to the front."[22] There was also a lecture on creating a ring of informers, with emphasis placed on barbers and taxi drivers. Malcolm in turn became an instructor and faithfully passed on the course as he had received it.

Through the months of the "phoney war" Malcolm drifted along, falling into the rhythms and routines of army life. His efforts to get posted to France, Norway or the Middle East had all come to naught. Most weekends he spent with his family. The pass he carried with him on these trips home had the ironic notation, "for the purpose of going to Battle".

Kitty had been left to manage four small children on her own. When Malcolm first enlisted, she received only £1 19s od per week, with only modest improvements as he rose in rank. Malcolm recognised that he had placed Kitty in an impossible situation and decided that he needed to raise some cash. He wrote to a wealthy acquaintance, asking for money. He ended up doing what he had laughed at Hugh Kingsmill for doing: he went to several publishers, seeking advances for various book projects. He contracted with Hamish Hamilton to write an "autobiographical work" for an advance of £200. With Methuen he signed on to do another book with Kingsmill: *Backwards to the Future*. Eyre and Spottiswoode signed him on to write a book on journalism, *Guilty Pens*, but advanced him only £40 for expenses. Hamish Hamilton also signed Malcolm to a three-novel contract. Of all these projects only one novel, for Hamilton, was ever written and published.

One piece of good news that Malcolm received at this time was that his book *The Thirties* had been named a Book Society choice. This brought a desperately needed infusion of money. It was also the closest Malcolm had come to being accepted in the cultural mainstream. He had finished the book at Mytchett Hutments, scrawling the final pages on notepads and sending them off to the publisher. Completed in the shadow of the war he had predicted for nearly a decade, there was something fitting about the book's timing. Malcolm thought of it as a study of a phoney decade, appearing in the midst of a phoney war.

A number of critics believe that *The Thirties* is Malcolm's best book. Certainly it is his most sustained and accomplished effort at social criticism. *The Thirties* is nothing less than a social, cultural and intellectual history of a crucial decade in modern history. Neither scholarly nor dispassionate, *The Thirties* contains its share of errors and questionable generalisations. But few works of history have ever been written with more passion, or glitter with so many brilliant epigrams, extended metaphors and mordant insights. Malcolm himself had written nothing like it and, despite plans for sequels, would never write anything like it again. The scope of the book is comprehensive: from wars and financial crises to Mr Sponge, a hapless dog sentimentalised in the British press.

The Thirties was a book he was supremely well qualified to write: he had first-hand experience of the British Empire's decline in Egypt and India; he had witnessed the true nature of Soviet totalitarianism in the streets of Moscow and the Ukrainian steppes; he had observed the workings of the League of Nations; he had been a leader writer for the leading newspapers of the Left and the Right. At the beginning of the decade he had been an ardent admirer of D.H. Lawrence and a somewhat independent but sincere socialist. His disillusionment with the ideologies of the time was more rapid and more complete than that of his contemporaries, but he had known many of these passions from within.

The tone of *The Thirties* is that of an amused and ironic observer. Gone are the anger and "nausea" of *Winter in Moscow* and *The Earnest Atheist*. The assertions are confident, sometimes aggressive, but more often than not they seem to emerge from a consistent vision of the world. The book opens with a brilliant survey of the beginning of the decade, "Yesterday and Yesterday and Yesterday". Early on, Malcolm focuses on Lenin's all-important question, "Who Whom?" Though he notes that most of the ruling parties and classes remained in command of their populations, one of the central themes of the book is that authority itself was being undermined.

> Authority still resides in Lords and Commons. They must take decisions, they must govern. Nothing can be done without their approval; patronage is theirs to bestow, and the framing of policy their responsibility. It is not power which Parliament lacks, any more than Louis XVI or Nicholas II lacked power; rather the will to exercise it. Power without resolution is as vain as desire without virility and evokes as scant respect.[23]

He goes on to refine his theory of authority in the next chapter, which begins: "It is impossible for one man, however determined and cunning he may be, to impose his will on other men for long unless they recognise themselves in him. This applies just as much in an absolutist as in a democratic state." Projecting their hopes, fears, and desires on to their rulers, the people get the kind of government they deserve.

"The blind lead the blind because there are none who see. And if there were, would the sightless deliver themselves over to them? Rather gouge out their eyes, too. There is no leading astray, since Leaders are made in the likeness of the led."[24] The crisis of authority, Malcolm argues throughout the book, is ultimately a moral crisis; the tendency to prefer fantasy to unpleasant truth leads to indecision and superficial solutions.

The prevailing fantasy of the decade, according to Malcolm, is that of liberalism, or the belief in "progress without tears". A host of politicians and writers touted this philosophy, but for Malcolm the epitome of liberalism was Ramsay MacDonald, whom he calls "Mr High-Mind". Puffed up with the rhetoric of righteousness, MacDonald was formidable in opposition. But when it came time for him to govern, the balloon began leaking. The end result was the financial crisis leading to the National government, the event that had trauma-tised Malcolm when he was at the *Guardian*. With a marvellous shift to bathos, Malcolm compares MacDonald in this crisis to the play-wright Noël Coward. "Both MacDonald and Mr Coward had reached the climax of their careers. By routes how different, they had arrived at the same point, the one purveying sentimental idealism, the other sentimental cynicism; sweetly bitter and bitter sweet, my working-class friends and my idling-class friends. This was their supreme moment, higher than this they were not to go."[25]

Liberalism, Malcolm argued, was a philosophy grounded in materialism, the notion that the satisfaction of man's physical needs was the goal of human existence. The materialist refuses to believe in anything that cannot be empirically observed and proved. This accounts for the modern cult of scientific rationalism, the elevation of "facts" and the denigration of metaphysics. For those obsessed with facts, it is only natural that the camera becomes the conduit of truth: it captures the outward appearance of things and thus cannot lie.

> To keep to the facts is ever the despairing hope of those who feel their lives disintegrating, whose feet are in shifting sand ... Prostrating themselves before facts, appealing to facts for guid-ance in time of trouble, they credit them with a validity they do not possess, and lay themselves open to deceptions greater than any the imagination can practise. The camera cannot lie, they assure themselves, and when it does lie quite succumb to its falsehoods. An imaginative symbol like the Cross may delude; but

because it is imaginative – that is, a product of an understanding of life's totality, and because it is a symbol, with no pretensions to be more than reality seen through a glass darkly, its power to delude is less than that of a photograph, which bears no relation to life's totality, and which purports to be definitive. Propagandists and advertisers find the camera their most useful instrument, and are more beholden to mathematics than to mysticism.[26]

Elsewhere in the book he points out that the modern era was witnessing a shift from a verbal to a visual culture. "Cameras were all-seeing eyes, and telephones all-hearing ears ... Words lost their force; leaded, staring, becoming ever bigger and ever fewer. It was the eye which required, and was given, sustenance."[27]

Facts cut off from the imagination become abstractions, and abstractions become dangerous when they are imposed on people by political means. Social scientists like the Webbs had reduced man to an abstraction – a statistical Everyman who could be satisfied with the requisite amount of food, clothing, shelter, sexual satisfaction and entertainment. The premise common to both liberalism and totalitarianism is the idea that people can be grouped into collectives and brought to a materialist promised land. Malcolm noted that in the case of Hitler's National Socialism many Westerners had recognised a deadly foe. But that recognition was vitiated by their inability to see Stalin's brand of totalitarianism as equally evil. Because collectivism is based on abstractions, it loses touch with real human needs and ends by turning into the raw exercise of power. Malcolm had seen the results of such power in the desolation of the Ukrainian famine.

Though most of *The Thirties* is preoccupied with a critique of these ideologies, Malcolm does provide glimpses of his own position. In opposition to materialism, he takes his stand with a religious vision of the world, though he does not make his arguments in explicitly Christian terms. In discussing the trend towards increasing narcissism and self-preoccupation, Malcolm writes: "If men represent creation's only endeavour, and human life its whole range, then each individual man must be remarkable, and each individual life a unique drama. Men can only be humble if they have a God, only content to be alike if they feel themselves children belonging to one family with a father in Heaven. Without a God they must be arrogant to be able to go on living at all, unique or they are nothing."[28] Near the end of the book, as he touches on the war that has just begun, he says that the "functionless" looked to the war to give them purpose in life. But war itself cannot be the source of an individual's identity. "To be alive is a little thing, merely alive, unless in living passion is expended, fruitfulness achieved. What if the functionless are endowed or fed, still they are functionless, standing aside. The only brotherhood is of work, the only sisterhood of procreation – except membership of a family whose father is in Heaven; and if Heaven has been abolished, how shall that be attainable?"[29]

In a section on the rise of sensational journalism, with its constant focus on celebrities and the British monarchy, he writes: "It used to be confidently assumed that as society became more theoretically equalitiarian, so it would inevitably become less snobbish. The reverse has been the case. Social position and wealth have come to have an almost mystical significance; to be observed with the same superstitious reverence as religious relics, and to focus the same curiosity as haunted houses or murderers."[30] On the personality types that tend to do well in politics: "English politicians . . . to succeed must look and speak like bookies or like clergymen."[31]

Published in the first months of the war, *The Thirties* found a large number of readers who were anxious to reflect on what had led them to the current crisis. It was widely reviewed. Rebecca West, writing in *Time and Tide*, spoke for many in attacking the book's negative tone; her first reaction was of "infuriation" with Malcolm's conviction that "all human proceedings are hideous in all respects". But later in the review she writes: "When Mr Muggeridge is not writing arrant nonsense he is exquisitely intelligent, bright with Arielesque wit, and with a keen eye for the authentic history that rarely gets written."[32] It is somewhat ironic to find Graham Greene and George Orwell, both known for their dark visions, complaining in their reviews that Malcolm was too negative. But both men were deeply impressed by the book. Greene thought it was "a poem, for it has the unity of a mood and the general effect is personal". Malcolm's prose, he noted, is "peppered with present participles", as in Carlyle's *French Revolution*.[33] Orwell thought *The Thirties* read like "the Book of Ecclesiastes with the pious interpolations left out". But he admired Malcolm's willingness to bash both Left and Right, noting that Malcolm had joined the army, "a thing which none of the ex-warmongers on the Left has done, I believe".[34] Greene and Orwell went beyond admiration to establish firm friendships with Malcolm.

Meanwhile, Malcolm was getting his first taste of action. His depot was transferred to Sheerness on the Isle of Sheppey, in the Thames Estuary. Their assignment was to interrogate French troops who had fled from the Germans, keeping an eye out for German spies who might have infiltrated the ranks of these refugees. Malcolm found the Frenchmen deeply demoralised, and attempted to rally them "with a sort of sub-Churchillian address in my bad French". It failed to impress. Malcolm and the others in his unit also had to patrol the island, which, they realised, was one of the first places a German invasion force would land. Each man was issued a rifle with twelve rounds of ammunition, but supplies were so short that they were not allowed to fire a single practice shot. One night, as they were patrolling the shore, they heard the sound of aircraft overhead. The officer in charge, a Captain Partridge, told his men to throw themselves on the ground. Malcolm did as commanded, but as he hit the ground his rifle discharged. "This caused near panic; everyone thought the invasion had begun. One lance-corporal insisted that he heard church-bells ringing – the agreed signal that the invader had arrived – another that he clearly saw the outline of a boat approaching the shore. It was a case, Captain Partridge explained, of fighting to the last man and last round of ammunition; which in my case would now be the eleventh round instead of the twelfth."[35] It was also the only shot he fired throughout the war.

After this inglorious episode, Malcolm managed to get himself posted to General Headquarters, Home Forces, which was located at Kneller Hall in London. He thought it would be a relief from the endless round of lectures and drills, but it turned out that there was even less to do at GHQ Home Forces. The feared invasion had not materialised, so the phoney war continued for a few more months. At first, due to a lack of space, Malcolm had to camp in a tent outside Kneller Hall – the only time, he noted, that he was "under canvas" in the war. They soon moved to the larger premises of St Paul's School, Hammersmith, where they set up their gear amidst blackboards and specimen jars. Without much to do, Malcolm and his fellow officers would go on long pub-crawls, which they could justify as an effort to explore the locality for suspicious characters. Malcolm could not participate in these evenings without self-consciousness, and often tried to drink away his depression.

Malcolm's immediate superior at this time was Colonel Ross-Atkinson, a career army officer in his late fifties. Though he travelled in establishment circles – his club was the exclusive White's – Malcolm found him to be unpretentious and melancholy. They became friends, and Malcolm was frequently asked to drive Ross-Atkinson around London to various appointments. "Occasionally, he lost his temper with my nihilistic views, and bawled me out, but something in him, despite his *Burke's Landed Gentry* credentials, responded to them."[36]

One sign that Ross-Atkinson respected and trusted Malcolm was an assignment that he asked Malcolm to undertake early in his time with GHQ Home Forces. It seemed that the Commander-in-Chief of British Forces, General Ironside, was spending a great deal of time at a private residence in Holland Park, sometimes for hours on end. Ironside was said to have had contacts with representatives of certain fascist organisations, so Malcolm immediately recognised the explosive nature of the assignment. With great trepidation, Malcolm conducted his inquiry, concluding that these lengthy visits to Holland Park had more to do with the general's sexual appetites than with treasonous plots. Malcolm, of course, was hardly in a position to criticise that sort of behaviour. Still, he realised General Ironside's behaviour was highly questionable, given the all-absorbing nature of the Commander-in-Chief's duties. But when Malcolm considered what Ross-Atkinson's reaction to this awkward piece of intelligence might be, he feared that the matter would simply be dropped.

He decided to consult a friend from Mytchett, Bobby Barclay, about what to do. Barclay suggested that they make a private visit to his step-father, Robert Vansittart, who was a high official at the Foreign Office. To Malcolm, Vansittart reeked of a faded upper-class milieu. He sat impassively as Malcolm recounted his story, giving no indication at the end what he might do with the information he had received. Malcolm, all too aware of his own failings, found his feelings about General Ironside mixed. Was he betraying another fallible human being, exposing him to ruin? Though Malcolm was accused at different times of his life of being holier-than-thou in his moral condemnations, he rarely approached individual situations smugly. For example, at one point during the Ironside episode, Malcolm was playing chess while serving as the duty officer. When the phone rang and Malcolm was asked what should be done with a deserter, he said, without looking up from the chessboard, "Let him go." This caused a great deal of amusement at the time, though Malcolm later realised he could have been court-martialled for the action.

The day after their meeting with Vansittart, the evening paper had a banner headline: "GENERAL IRONSIDE SACKED". Barclay was delighted, but Malcolm's feelings of ambiguity were only intensified. With his penchant for the theatrical gesture, Malcolm wrote an account of the incident just before he was to leave the country in 1942. As it turned out Ironside was given a peerage and made a field-marshal.[37]

Another assignment Ross-Atkinson gave Malcolm was to attend the trial of an American diplomat, Tyler Kent, and Anna Volkov, the daughter of a Russian admiral. Kent, who had been stationed in Moscow for a time, and Volkov both had reasons to hate the Soviet Union. Kent thought that President Franklin Roosevelt was secretly scheming with Churchill to enter the war, something he claimed was unconstitutional and intolerable. Volkov had become a fascist in reaction to the horrors the Communists had perpetrated on her family and Russia. They were charged with passing secret documents from the American Embassy in London to the Axis governments. Some of the information in those documents showed up in the broadcasts from Berlin of William Joyce, an Englishman in the employ of Hitler and popularly known as Lord Haw-Haw. There was also the question of the communications between Churchill and Roosevelt; if revealed, these exchanges might have delayed or prevented America's entry into the war. As Malcolm soon realised, there was little reason for him to attend the trial, which was being held at the Old Bailey, except to provide daily instalments of the drama to Ross-Atkinson. But the trial had the effect of immersing him, for the first time, in the murky world of espionage.

The phoney war officially came to an end in August, 1940 with the commencement of the Blitz. The Blitz appealed to Malcolm's anarchistic temperament: "I felt a terrible joy and exaltation at the sight and sound and taste and smell of this destruction; at the lurid sky, the pall of smoke, the faces of bystanders wildly lit in the flames." As the bombs dropped and broke apart the physical structures of London, the fragile bonds of the moral and social order were loosened or severed. "The Blitz was a kind of protracted debauch, with the shape of orderly living shattered, all restraints removed, barriers non-existent."[38]

Malcolm, like others of his generation, felt a powerful curiosity about the spectacle taking place outside, and decided to prowl about in the darkness as the bombs fell about him. His most frequent companions on these strange walkabouts were Graham Greene and Andreas Mayor. Mayor was the son of Kitty's cousin, Beatrice Mayor. Malcolm found his melancholy temperament congenial; Mayor, too, was an observer of life. He was also well-connected: his sister Tess was soon to marry Lord Rothschild. Andreas took Malcolm to a number of furtive parties that took place during the Blitz. One such party centred around the writers associated with *Horizon* magazine: Cyril Connolly, its editor, Stephen Spender and others. But the one social gathering that remained in Malcolm's memory was even more exclusive: the upper-class intellectuals of the Left, John Strachey, J.D. Bernal, Anthony Blunt and Guy Burgess. Blunt and Burgess, of course, would later be revealed as Soviet agents and traitors. It was Burgess, though, to whom Malcolm reacted most violently: "he gave me a feeling, such as I have never had from anyone else, of being morally afflicted in some way. His very physical presence was, to me, malodorous and sinister; as though he had a consuming illness . . ."[39]

Graham Greene held a special fascination for Malcolm because he was a convert to the Roman Catholic Church. Greene's faith, however, was not the "muscular Christianity" of the confident apologist, where all moral questions became black and white. Rather, his faith coexisted with an awareness of the ambiguities of the human condition; the cross was a reminder that we lived in a fallen world and that suffering was a necessary part of our sanctification. Greene's vision was imbued with the "tragic sense of life", a phrase taken from the Catholic philosopher Unamuno, whom he much admired. Malcolm had been deeply impressed by Greene's novel, *The Power and the Glory*, which had just been published.

Malcolm was drawn to Greene's vision, as he was to that of another Catholic convert, Evelyn Waugh. But he could not imagine himself entering into that community. During the Blitz, when Greene made an act of contrition before going outside and risking death, Malcolm felt excluded. "It made me feel uneasy, and even envious; like travelling in a first-class railway carriage with a first-class ticket holder when one only has a third-class ticket oneself. I imagined Graham being carried away to paradise, and I left behind in purgatory, or worse." This did not make Greene a puritan, however. One of the places he took Malcolm was to the Windmill Theatre, famous for its nude dancing revue. It was not particularly appealing. Years later, Malcolm said that Greene was a saint trying, unsuccessfully, to become a sinner, while he was a sinner trying, equally unsuccessfully, to become a saint.[40]

Despite this camaraderie and the strangely exciting spectacle of the Blitz, Malcolm was deeply depressed. Anarchy may have seemed to him an alternative preferable to a decayed social order, but his feelings of manic exultation were shortlived. One night, in anarchic high spirits, he drove around and around a deserted Piccadilly Circus in the wrong direction. But another night, after a bout of drinking, he drove his camouflaged Austin into a traffic island on Blackfriars Bridge. He emerged, dazed, from the car, brushed broken glass from his head and clothes, hailed a passing taxi, and eventually passed out in his room. Only the offices of a friendly lance-corporal enabled him to escape serious punishment.

In April 1941, Malcolm was transferred to 5 Corps Headquarters, which was located at Longford Castle, near Salisbury. His job was to serve as an intelligence officer in Department l(b), Security Intelligence. The commander of 5 Corps was General Bernard Law Montgomery, already called Monty by his men, who would go on to become one of the most successful Allied commanders in the war. Malcolm was later to get to know Montgomery well through their mutual friend, P. J. Grigg. Once again, Malcolm applied to Montgomery to be sent into action – any action – but his petition was ignored.

As he had in earlier assignments, Malcolm coasted along in his job at 5 Corps. For much of his time there, he was little more than a glorified messenger boy. As a liaison officer with other units, Malcolm was given a motorcycle and spent hours roaring over country roads between different headquarters, delivering papers and messages. He went on a course with a Motor Reconnaissance unit and enjoyed meeting the young officers in charge there. A request to transfer to that unit, which would have put him in combat, was denied.

He was able to visit his parents, whose home had been destroyed in the Blitz. They had lodgings nearby in Christchurch. It was clear that his father's health was failing. Malcolm wrote to Kitty: "He is almost blind and his heart is very weak indeed. He has become very childlike, worries about getting his tea and how his flowers are arranged. Milder weather may revive him a little but I doubt if he has very long to live."

Malcolm found it impossible to participate in the collective activities of army life. He wrote to Kitty about one evening when "the men got very noisy and (would you believe it?) pulled off each other's trousers and pulled each other around by their ties. Most of the men were around forty. I went up to bed and lay there thinking somewhat sombre thoughts."[42] When he was asked to make a dummy of a German soldier, with all the correct insignia, some devil entered into him. "I felt an irresistible impulse to make him wounded and bloody;

with his arm in a home-made sling, and a blood-stained bandage around his head. Thus, warming to the work, I put him on a crutch, and finally amputated one of his legs." He was let off with a reprimand. Malcolm developed a friendship with the camouflage officer, Victor Stiebel (in civilian life a distinguished dressmaker), but this association came to an end when Malcolm was thrown out of the house where they were billeted. The Mess President, an Irishman named McNally, told Malcolm that he was being expelled because of Malcolm's "talk", which had caused numerous complaints. When Malcolm pressed McNally to find out what had given offence, he was told that it wasn't anything specific; it was the just the way he talked, "the whole tenor".[43]

Rather than fight, Malcolm simply accepted this verdict. Late in 1941 he had received a mysterious letter summoning him to an address in London, where he was to be interviewed about the possibility of his taking on "special intelligence duties". It was an opportunity once again to plunge into the darkness of change, and with his usual impulsiveness, he took it.

« II »

Espionage in a Hot Climate
1942–1943

MALCOLM'S INTERVIEW, held at the Savage Club in London, turned out to be with a man named Alan Williams who was, in civilian life, a thriller-writer. For Malcolm, it was not surprising that writers should be drawn to intelligence work. The writer, like the spy, must be observant, imaginative, alert to motives and capable of "trafficking in lies", as Malcolm would put it many years later. Malcolm's entry into the spy business was the result of a scheme he had hatched with another writer, Graham Greene. Early in the war, Greene mentioned that his sister Liz worked for an important officer in the secret service. The two men asked her to work on their behalf, seeking a posting overseas. The summons Malcolm received in late 1941 was the delayed result of that plan.[1] Greene entered the secret service at the same time.

When he arrived at the Savage Club, Malcolm found that Williams, like the protagonist of his novels, had a club foot and a boyish delight in the dangers of intelligence work. He hinted darkly to Malcolm that agents whose cover was blown would have to be "discarded". Malcolm wondered what types of discarding might be employed, but he assured Williams that he was prepared for the perils of spying. Williams, like many of the men he encountered in the secret service, revelled in espionage because it was, in essence, an elaborate game, with endless rules and a taste for secrecy. When, after the war, the master spy Kim Philby was revealed as a double agent and defected to the Soviet Union, Malcolm was relatively mild in his criticism. He refused to believe that Philby was an evil man, bent on the destruction of Western civilisation. Rather, Malcolm argued, Philby was a "boy scout who had lost his way".[2]

Soon after the interview with Williams, Malcolm heard that he had been accepted. Early in 1942 he presented himself at an address in

Broadway, across the street from the St James's Park Underground station. He had assumed that he would be sent to a safe house, or some other type of "front", but he discovered that the office in Broadway was in fact the headquarters of the British Secret Service (or SIS, as it was then called). The division that Malcolm joined was known as MI6, which dealt with the work of espionage, as opposed to its counterpart, MI5, which dealt directly with intelligence work. Here he encountered the same sort of World War I era mentality that had characterised his intelligence course at Mytchett Hutments. There were older agents sporting monocles and even, at times, spats. He also thought he spied several false beards, although in the case of one former trade unionist, he discovered the beard to be genuine; it had been specially grown, however, for intelligence work.

Malcolm's first contact within MI6 was Leslie Nicholson, a genial man who had formerly been the Chief of Station for Riga in Latvia. Nicholson briefed Malcolm on his assignment. At this point in the war, Allied convoys travelling around the African coast, from the Indian Ocean to the Atlantic, were being devastated by German U-boats, causing a catastrophic loss of matériel and human life. MI6 was busily setting up a network of agents in Africa to attempt to counteract this threat to the Allied war effort. Graham Greene was to be posted to Freetown, Sierra Leone, on the west coast of Africa, and Malcolm was to be stationed at Lourenço Marques (now called Maputo), Mozambique, on Africa's east coast. Their chief mission was to penetrate and subvert the enemy spy networks that were providing information about the routes and movements of Allied shipping. As a colony of Portugal, Mozambique was officially neutral in the war; in addition to Britain, Germany and Italy maintained consulates in Lourenço Marques. Malcolm was to undertake his operations under the cover of his position as vice-consul.

In order to place Malcolm in Lourenço Marques, it was necessary for him to obtain a civilian identity card. He was given a passport that said he was a businessman living at the St Ermin's Hotel. The story he was to give to the authorities issuing the identity cards was that he had only just returned from abroad, having recently landed at Liverpool. He dropped by St Ermin's Hotel to bolster his story and found it the sort of place where progressive conferences of the League of Nations sort might be held. He showed up at the appropriate office, fearful that he would be closely questioned and his story picked apart. As it happened, no questions were asked and the card was duly issued. It occurred to him that if he could be given a passport by MI6 he could just as easily have been given a civilian identity card. There seemed to be a principle in the secret service that if something could be done clandestinely and with difficulty, it should be done that way.

The same note of fantasy was struck when he went for a one-day intensive course in the use of invisible ink, a staple of the spy business. At a house in Hans Crescent, Malcolm met his instructor, "a sad-looking man with a large rubicund face, thinning black hair, and short fingers". They went over the techniques for mixing the inks, which could be made from milk, wine and a variety of chemical compounds, such as a brand of headache tablets. If Malcolm ever found himself in an emergency, his instructor intoned, and none of these substances were available, he could resort to the use of BS. After a few minutes of explanation, Malcolm deduced that this stood for "bird shit". Malcolm should not assume, his instructor continued, that dropping breadcrumbs on a windowsill would obtain the necessary samples: he himself had tried this, only to find that the birds ate the food without leaving any deposits. Instead, Malcolm ought to go to a public park and, when he spotted an adequate amount of BS, drop his handkerchief casually and scoop up the stuff. Several other techniques were then explained and practised. Malcolm performed these rather clumsily, deepening the dolefulness on the instructor's face. "You'll never make a spy at this rate," he said, at last, and Malcolm felt that he might be right. When he left late that evening, Malcolm was struck by the absurdity of two grown men spending their time in such a bizarre manner.[3]

Malcolm spent the first weeks of 1942 familiarising himself with the workings of MI6 – putting himself "in the picture". Section 5, the section responsible for counter-espionage abroad, was then located at St Albans. The nominal head of the section was Felix Cowgill, but Malcolm immediately noticed that the commanding presence there was Kim Philby. Malcolm had met Philby once, during his stint at the Londoner's Diary of the *Evening Standard*. Philby's father, St John Philby, was a well-known Arabist who had travelled extensively in the Middle East and written about his experiences. During the war, St John Philby was interned on the Isle of Man under regulation 18B because he had told his friend, King Ibn Saud of Saudi Arabia, that he should not enter the war on the British side, as Hitler was bound to win. Malcolm later said that Kim Philby's personality was shaped by a need to emulate his father's buccaneering spirit. When Malcolm interviewed David Ben-Gurion many years later, the Israeli Prime Minister said: "The father became a Moslem, so why should not the son become a Communist?"[4]

When Malcolm met Philby again at St Albans, he was not mesmerised by him. But in retrospect he acknowledged that Philby had an intense and charismatic personality and that this prevented anyone suspecting him of being a Soviet agent. Philby had a stutter that made most of his utterances tortured affairs; Malcolm thought it was closer to a fit than a speech impediment. Philby drank rather heavily, but he never discussed politics. He had been at Cambridge a decade after Malcolm and there had embraced Communism. Like Malcolm, he rebelled against the decay of the British Empire, but whereas Malcolm had rejected the Soviet experiment as an alternative, Philby maintained an ideological commitment to Communism, an unwavering belief in political solutions to human ills.

It soon became clear to Malcolm that the art of cracking enemy codes was at the centre of the British intelligence effort. He travelled to Bletchley Park in Buckinghamshire to learn more about the process. Bletchley had been chosen because it was equidistant from Oxford and Cambridge. It did not take Malcolm long to sense the donnish atmosphere there and he soon fell into "my Cambridge state of mind".[5] In 1941, with the help of Dillwyn Knox, the brother of Fr Wilfred Knox, the priest Malcolm knew at Cambridge, the British had broken the most important enemy code: the Spy Enigma Variation. The code involved the use of a machine that looked like a rather complex typewriter. Because of its bulk, the Enigma machine could not be used by enemy agents in the field. It could only be located at German embassies in occupied territories or in neutral countries.[6] Mozambique, to which Malcolm was headed, was just such a neutral country.

The final errand Malcolm had to run before embarking was a visit to the head of MI6. To preserve secrecy, the man holding this position was known within MI6 only as "C" At this time "C" was Sir Stuart Menzies, a leading figure, to Malcolm's mind, in the cult of secrecy for secrecy's sake. There was a light outside "C"'s office which had to be illuminated before one could enter. "I made my way into the inner sanctum where I found two sedate, middle-aged secretaries who gave an immediate impression of being exceptionally well-bred. Readers of the Bond books [by Ian Fleming] will recognise the scene, but, of course, glamorised in Fleming's version; the secretaries more alluring,

'C' more steely, the office more daunting." During their conversation, Menzies placed his overcoat over the telephone to prevent any attempt at eavesdropping. Malcolm heard that he also answered the telephone from underneath the overcoat.[7] Their conversation, as it turned out, was brief and superficial, touching briefly on the conditions in Mozambique. In his autobiography Malcolm commented on this meeting. "On such occasions as this, I always find myself torn between a desire to please and a resentment at so desiring, and have to confess never having worked out a basis for harmonising the two states of mind."[8]

Malcolm was granted a few days of leave before his departure, which he spent at Whatlington with the family. He could not, of course, divulge his destination, so Kitty had to be satisfied with vague allusions. He felt guilty at leaving his family behind while bombs continued to rain down on Britain. The "urge to be gone", to escape from the pressure of his responsibilities, had led him once again to another impulsive scheme. One morning, during this brief respite in Whatlington, Kitty turned to Malcolm in bed and told him: "Only death can part us."[9] This was another of Kitty's sayings that would be for ever burned into his memory.

In order for Malcolm to establish a cover, he had to travel to Mozambique through the Portuguese capital of Lisbon. He left on a flying boat from Poole harbour in Dorset on March 18, 1942. The passengers, most of whom were destined to carry out military, diplomatic or intelligence missions, kept to themselves, sombrely considering what lay ahead of them.

The first thing that struck Malcolm about Lisbon was the light. In contrast to the darkened, blitzed streets of London, Lisbon was brilliantly lit and full of consumer goods. Initially he was dazzled by this abundance, but he found the contrast only heightened his rejection of materialism. He found himself going into several Catholic churches, watching services and feeling "very envious of the devout".[10] Later, in his diary, he reflected:

Not through having, or through satisfying, desire, comes happiness; not in the indulgence, or in the deprivation, of appetite; not in the ecstasy, or in the forgetfulness, of the flesh; not in the quick, or in the slow, passing of time. Happiness comes unaccountably, mysteriously, through a sense of belonging to all creation and of participating in its significance; through surrender to, rather than through affecting to direct, the process of living. It comes when the ego is put to sleep.[11]

The SIS section at the British Embassy proved to be a highly efficient unit. Whereas in London monocles, spats and false beards could still be seen, the agents in Lisbon dressed casually. They represented the younger generation of intelligence operatives who respected and emulated Kim Philby. Malcolm was told that he would have to apply for a visa to Mozambique, but that this process could take some time – weeks or even months. After a few days, he found a room with a Portuguese family, where he took his meals and tried speaking the language. During the days he would spend some time with a language tutor, but the rest of the day he would wile away either sitting in cafés or pounding the streets. He watched Walt Disney's *Fantasia* in a movie theatre and found it intriguing but a rather ludicrous mixture of high and low culture, Stravinsky and hippos in tutus.

Into this limbo of inactivity came the news that his father had died on March 25. Malcolm did not receive the news until April 12, when he received two letters from Kitty. The first described H.T. on his deathbed. "Your father now is dying ... He has lost his angry expression, and I don't think he any longer has any fear of death. He does not eat or open his eyes, and his hands lie on the bed very lifeless. He can with difficulty speak names – Douglas, Malcolm. Your mother is distressed because he does not look at her, and she tries to lift his eyelids and kisses his brow, but he cannot make the effort at recognizing her." In the second letter Kitty wrote of the funeral in Whatlington churchyard, with about a dozen people in attendance.[12] Just before his final turn for the worse, H.T. woke up and noticed how distraught his wife was. "Sitting up and seeing my mother's tears falling," Malcolm wrote in his autobiography, "he turned on her one of his splendid grins, and then with a wink slipped out of bed, and offered her his arm. 'Come on, Annie,' he whispered gaily, 'we're off to the Greyhound!', and swaggered down the passage with her. It was, Kitty wrote, a glorious wink; knowing, and joyous and infinitely reassuring."

Malcolm's grief at his father's death was mixed with guilt. He had not turned out to be the witty, sophisticated Fabian intellectual of his father's dreams; he had, moreover, attacked many of the ideas and institutions his father regarded with reverence. Their temperaments had been almost diametrically opposed: H.T.'s optimism, conditioned by his own difficult youth, could not comprehend Malcolm's deep pessimism about the human condition. The idealism he inherited from his father was channelled into religious rather than political longings. The irony was that H.T. was not a domineering or manipulative father. But the very innocence and intensity of H.T.'s hopes were such that Malcolm felt condemned to disappointing him and appearing to be guilty of ingratitude.

Malcolm could not look on the circumstances of his father's death with anything but sincere pity. A man of habit and routine, H.T. had been displaced by the war, his and Annie's home bombed into dust. The war itself contradicted all those hopes that wiser counsels would prevail, that a programme of gradualism would lead to a better world. Malcolm's intuition of anarchy and apocalypse had proved to be more accurate. But even in his grief, Malcolm was flooded with affectionate memories.

> His presence seemed very near, and once more I was waiting at East Croydon station, anxiously scanning the commuters' faces as they came off the trains; catching sight of him at last, well to the fore. An indomitable figure, striding out, bowler hat a shade too large, somehow low down on his ears; wearing the City's livery, yet so evidently not of it. So evidently a man on his own, a man apart; serving parties and movements and causes loyally and ardently, but without ever being wholly committed to them.[13]

That was H.T.'s most important legacy to his son: not his gift for rhetoric or his exhibitionism, but his willingness to be "a man apart". Malcolm drew more strength from this than perhaps even he knew.

After the war, Malcolm asked his son Leonard what should be inscribed on H.T.'s gravestone. Leonard suggested the words used in the New Testament to describe Joseph of Arimathea, also a town councillor: "A good man, and a just".

Malcolm moved out to the town of Estoril to be near the coast, where he could swim every day. He explored some of the historical and cultural sites in the area, fixing his attention most intently on religious buildings and ceremonies. He walked around a ruined monastery in Cintra and saw priests blessing the fishing fleet with candles and ancient songs. His thoughts often turned to Kitty and the children. More than ever he found it impossible to sleep peacefully until morning. One night he woke up and thought he heard Kitty sobbing bitterly.

On May 6, 1942, he was finally granted a visa to Mozambique. It was decided that he should travel by boat down the west coast of Africa, so that he could deliver a number of large diplomatic bags to British representatives in the larger ports of call. Ten days later he left Lisbon on the *Colonial*. "The scene when the boat left Lisbon was very touching," he wrote to Kitty, "hundreds of people waving handkerchiefs at each other and finally breaking down and sobbing. I had no one to wave to, but participated in the emotion of the others."[14] He was under strict orders not to let the diplomatic bags out of his sight, but he almost immediately lost track of them, only to find that they had been stored deep in the hold. He decided they would be safe enough there.

On board the *Colonial* Malcolm met two men *en route* to Tokyo, a French naval officer and a Swiss diplomat, with whom he carried on marathon conversations about the war. At first Malcolm's ascerbic views – including the notion that the war was little more than "theatre" – scandalised the men, but soon they became friendly. Malcolm developed a fondness for the Frenchman in particular, a melancholy man loyal to the Vichy government, but rejoicing in every German defeat. At each port, Malcolm would go ashore and have a drink with the British representative. He found that the diplomatic bags were largely filled with material from the Ministry of Information – hardly top secret material.

Three weeks after his departure from Lisbon, the *Colonial* docked at Lobito in Angola, where Malcolm disembarked. He was to travel overland by train to Elizabethville in the Belgian Congo, where he would fly on to Nairobi to meet the MI6 director for East Africa. The train ran only once a week, and Malcolm found that the Europeans in the interior would come out to meet it at different stops in order to have some contact with the outside world. At the Angolan border he chatted with a number of missionaries from the Plymouth Brethren sect. When he reached Elizabethville he wrote in his diary: "Arrived here after long journey, dust, immense distances of desolate land, chilly mornings, tepid afternoons, still evenings and nights when, like a swimmer, my soul dipped under the surface of things, treading profundity, treading, and finding no bottom, emerging again to the surface, half suffocated, to spit water and gasp for breath."[15]

Nairobi in Kenya reminded him of India: the Empire at its most resplendent, with an impressive Government House, flags flying, black troops saluting, but rotting from within and doomed to collapse. "C"'s man in Nairobi "turned out to be a kindly avuncular figure whose attitude toward me was rather like that of a bishop briefing a curate for work in some distant and possibly hazardous mission field." He told Malcolm that he had been stationed in Cairo before the war and that Malcolm's name had appeared on the list of "undesirables" back in 1928–1930. This revelation gave Malcolm unalloyed pleasure.

Despite a stomach ailment that had left him in bed for three days and weakened him, Malcolm took a flying boat from Nairobi to his final destination, Lourenço Marques, arriving at the end of June. His first impression was of a Mediterranean resort, with seaside hotels, beaches, restaurants, souvenir stalls, casinos and cabarets. He soon discovered that Lourenço Marques was a more cosmopolitan and sensual resort than any in South Africa, where the influence of the Dutch Reformed Church had created a puritanical regime. As a result, quite a few South Africans came to Lourenço Marques, many of them intending to take advantage of the local brothels.

It is impossible to consider Malcolm's time in Lourenço Marques and not notice that it bears an uncanny resemblance to a wartime *film noir* like *Casablanca* – tropical climate, ceiling fans whirring, a cat-and-mouse spy game, corrupt local officials, even the existence of one or more Ingrid Bergmans. But Malcolm was to find his role in this drama a great deal less romantic than that of Humphrey Bogart.

He moved into the Polana Hotel, where he quickly came into contact with his two opposite numbers in the espionage game. The German *Abwehr* agent was named Leopold Wertz. His appearance was far from threatening. In his diary, Malcolm noted that Wertz was "a Bavarian, rather pleasant looking, plays piano, heard him playing German sentimental music to celebrate fall of Sebastopol. Has his small circle of Portuguese hangers-on; comes and goes, on Saturdays appearing in shorts with small Bavarian green coat."[16] The Italian, Campini, a large, vivacious man, was given to sporting a flowing cloak in imitation of Mussolini. Malcolm would meet these men in the corridors of the Polana – or in the lavatories – and they would exchange stiff bows and cold stares. Inwardly, Malcolm found these antics silly, but at the same time he enjoyed playing the role of intrepid master spy. The very essence of the spy business is to play games with the relationship between appearance and reality. Malcolm could laugh at the sillier manifestations of this game, but it also contributed to a depression that would deepen over the course of his year in Lourenço Marques. Malcolm found that he was wearing a mask so constantly that he was unsure of whether he had a real face left.

His office at the British consulate was furnished with a typewriter and a safe, in which he kept the paraphernalia for deciphering coded messages. The consul, a man named Ledger, was sceptical about the value and necessity of Malcolm's activities, but tolerated his presence. The first telegram that Malcolm received was from his boss, Kim Philby. It began by recounting the intelligence situation in Lourenço Marques. It also included information from the telegrams of Wertz and Campini, telegrams that were intercepted and decoded at Bletchley. Thus Malcolm had the opportunity to see his opponents' dispatches. Wertz portrayed Malcolm as a cunning spy with a huge network of informers who he, Wertz, was defeating at every turn. Malcolm had no aptitude for the process of decoding his telegrams from MI6: using a "one-time pad" he would subtract certain numbers in the incoming message in order to arrive at the correct letters. A single mistake would force him to start from scratch, often causing him to stay up until late into the night.

Philby's advice was that Malcolm concentrate on penetrating Campini's operation, as he was the more vulnerable of the two enemy spies. Malcolm wasn't sure how to go about this. He looked at Campini's wife in the hotel restaurant and wondered if an affair with her would yield a rich trove of her husband's secrets. He tried following the two men around – at a discreet distance. Unfortunately, he never managed to overhear their conversations, although he did discover that in his room at night Wertz wore a hair-net.

The advantage Malcolm had of Bletchley's code-cracking was more than offset by the fact that he still spoke little Portuguese and had no network of informants at all. His first job was to acquire such a network and the method for doing that involved mastering the art of bribery. Within a few days of arriving, he met Camille, a Polish Jew who had escaped from the Gestapo and had ended up in Lourenço Marques, where he survived by playing bridge at the casinos. Camille insisted on his own particular role: that of the "cavalry officer, who, through the fortunes of war, found himself in strange, if not disreputable, company, towards whom his attitude was one of tolerant condescension, as I, a fellow *chevalier*, would readily understand".[17] Malcolm had reason to understand why such a role was so important to Camille, whom he came to love.

It was through Camille that Malcolm made his first important breakthrough. One day Camille ushered Malcolm into the presence of a high-ranking police inspector. "He had one of those bashed-in faces which look as though lumps have fallen off them here and there; like a plaster bust which has been left exposed to the weather." Since the inspector had only a spotty knowledge of English and French, Malcolm laboured to convey that he would be grateful if the inspector might be willing to pass along information of interest to the British consulate. Suddenly the inspector broke out into a broad smile and Malcolm sensed that it was time to pass across the table his first bribe. He gave an envelope to Camille to give to the inspector, but when Camille opened it, he gave a look of dissatisfaction with Malcolm. Taking Malcolm aside, he said that Campini and Wertz paid much more than a mere one hundred escudos. After Malcolm suggested another three hundred escudos, Camille's "lips soundlessly formed the word *cinq*, and *cinq* it was". Malcolm came to the conclusion, after he had been at it long enough, that bribery has "as many subtleties and diversities as seduction".[18]

The inspector, as it turned out, played a crucial role in several successful operations. The first opportunity arose when a troopship carrying South African soldiers to North Africa was torpedoed off the coast of Mozambique. Malcolm and the other consular staff went out to the beach and watched as the cold, exhausted soldiers staggered on to dry land. It was evident that the soldiers were going to be interned by the local authorities in appalling conditions, so Malcolm devised a plan to get them back home. With the help of the inspector, he informed the troops that they would be strolling along the road to Swaziland on Sunday afternoon. Malcolm then went in search of transportation. The business community, fearful of conflict with the authorities, was not forthcoming. In the end, it was the taxi drivers of Lourenço Marques who agreed, unanimously, to form the convoy. The inspector having cleared their path, the troops were duly driven across the border to Swaziland, and then to South Africa.

The threat to Allied shipping remained Malcolm's top priority. He discovered the identity of a man who was providing shipping intelligence to Campini and decided that he had to be neutralised, preferably by abducting him and spiriting him out of the country. Malcolm discovered the weakness in the man's situation that he could exploit: he was in love with a South African girl who did not return his affection. The girl wanted to return to South Africa, but the authorities in that country refused, on the grounds that she had been living an "immoral life". Malcolm promised her that he would intercede with the South African representative in Lourenço Marques in order to get her a return visa.

The girl was to ask her would-be lover to take her for a drive down a certain road. The police inspector was waiting, and the man was taken away, first to Mbabane, and then on to England. When he was captured, notes about Allied shipping movements were found in his pocket. Back in Lourenço Marques, Malcolm had to deal with the aftermath of the incident. The man's disappearance had sent minor shockwaves through the community, so Malcolm started a rumour that the man had been in serious financial difficulties. But Malcolm's conscience could not deal as easily with the South African girl's situation. He had promised her something that he had no idea whether he could deliver. He cursed himself for making what he thought of as a "shabby bargain" with her, but he did meet with the South African Consul General and pleaded her case. The man told Malcolm with a knowing look that he was well aware of how the abduction had taken place. But he refused to make any promises. To Malcolm's intense relief, he received a note from the girl a few days later, informing him that she had obtained the visa and was going home.

Malcolm's greatest coup as a spy was the capture of a German U-boat, a direct blow to the very menace he was sent to combat. Another informant, an East European Jew named Serge, told Malcolm that he had found a Greek sailor who had mentioned that he worked on a ship that ran supplies to a U-boat in the Mozambique Channel. It was decided that a rendezvous with the Greek sailor should be made at Marie's Place, a local brothel he frequented. Malcolm and Serge duly arrived at the building, the traditional red light shining over the front door, and reminding Malcolm of the light outside "C"'s door. After a brief discussion with Madame Marie, they were introduced to Monique, the sailor's favourite girl. "She turned out to be an exceptionally amiable woman, well, even heavily, built, rough featured, with a pleasant smile and smooth, pleasant voice ... Yes, she knew our Greek quite well; a nice boy, but young, naïve, inexperienced – the last slightly accentuated." She said that he had told her about their clandestine supplying of the German subs and that by passing the information on to Serge she hoped to help the Allied cause. They thanked her, and no sooner had she left than the Greek sailor arrived. He proved to be amenable to a plot to capture the sub; the first officer, he said, could also be counted on. Once the captain and one or two members of the ship's crew had been disposed of, the ship could be sailed into the South African port of Durban. Malcolm asked what the sailor meant by the word "disposed". "He smiled. That was optional; they could be thrown to the sharks, or, alternatively, secured and handed over the the Durban authorities." Much to the disappointment of Serge, Malcolm opted to have the captain and his henchmen arrested rather than made into shark bait.

The plot was executed pefectly: the ship was commandeered and sent on to Durban. With the exact coordinates of the rendezvous in hand, it was a simple matter to capture the sub intact. Despite the brilliance of the operation, Malcolm received a reprimand for going directly to Naval Intelligence with his information, rather than consulting MI6 in London. But a few days later he received a congratulatory telegram from "C" – a "considerable accolade in Secret Service circles".[19]

After a few months, Malcolm acquired something of a staff. The first addition was Miss Stewart, who took over the draining task of coding and decoding and typing the message traffic with MI6. Next came an odd little man named Steptoe, who had been interned in Japan and who arrived in Lourenço Marques as part of a prisoner exchange. Steptoe

> was a little cock-sparrow of a man, with a bristling moustache, a high voice, a monocle and a lot of suits, ties, hats and shoes . . . A real pro, I felt, to whom every encounter, however innocent, was clandestine, every letter – even bills – needed to be tested for invisible ink, and everyone near him, in a café or restaurant, in a railway carriage, or just happening to pause in his vicinity to light a cigarette or do up a shoelace, was keeping him under surveillance.[20]

Malcolm was also joined by a representative of the new American intelligence agency, then known as the Office of Strategic Services (OSS). Huntington Harris was a tall man with a "dry drawling wit" part of a generation of American agents who were eager to learn from the British. "They came among us, these aspiring spy masters, like innocent girls from a finishing-school anxious to learn the seasoned, demi-mondaine ways of old practitioners – in this case, the legendary Secret Service." The awe in which the Americans held the British soon disappeared, he thought, but he and "Hunt", as Harris was called, decided to move to a house on the outskirts of Lourenço Marques, and pool their resources. There was a door into the house from a garage which enabled people to enter unseen. Hunt also had a good deal of American cash to help keep Camille, Serge and the inspector happy.[21]

There was one other member of the British intelligence team in Mozambique whom Malcolm does not mention in his autobiography. John Mockford was an MI6 agent assigned to the counter-intelligence section in Lisbon, where he worked as a case officer. About halfway through Malcolm's time in Lourenço Marques, Mockford arrived to assist his efforts. He was appalled that Malcolm held regular nightly meetings with several of his local agents during which they would go over the cipher intercepts from Bletchley. To Mockford, this was a dangerous breach of security, since anyone who attended the meeting could decide to become a double agent.[22]

In his autobiography, Malcolm plays down his achievements as a spy, just as he understated his independence as a writer for the *Manchester Guardian* and the integrity of his performance in other jobs he took on over the years. He was, in fact, an outstanding secret agent, not because he was dashing and patriotic, but because he was a shrewd and sympathetic observer of human nature. In the shadowy and ambiguous world of espionage, where the difference between loyalty and treachery is hard to ascertain, Malcolm knew exactly what cards to play. But he drew very little sustenance from his successes as a spy. For one thing, he was tortured by the moral implications of some of his actions. He had chosen for the ship's captain to be captured rather than thrown to the sharks, but he could have had it the other way. Even though he took the humane and moral course, he felt wracked by the kind of power he had been given. "So the Greek [captain] lived, and I knew that I was a fraudulent belligerent, with no passion like Serge for victory and vengeance – the same thing, really; no sense of being engaged in a life and death struggle against the forces of darkness."[23]

Malcolm was, in fact, quite close to his friend Graham Greene in his sense of the ambiguities of loyalty and patriotism. He and Greene exchanged long, coded letters to each other to pass the tedious days. In November 1942, he wrote to Kitty that he had read Tolstoy's *Anna Karenina*, and found it the greatest novel ever written. "Like all great books it gave me a passionate longing to write again. I bought a notebook, got as far as that . . . I sometimes try [to write] but it always ends in nothing."[24]

In the midst of this depression and isolation, Malcolm returned to the pattern of sexual obsession and guilt that had marked the other black moments in his life. There were three women in Lourenço Marques with whom he became involved.

Malcolm first saw Bibla da Costa when she entered the lobby of the Polana Hotel. A young Portuguese woman who exuded intelligence and sensual grace, Bibla (who is called Anna in the second volume of Malcolm's autobiography *The Infernal Grove*) was married to a German businessman named Leidenburg. Without thinking, Malcolm approached her and said "Hullo!" Rather than rebuff him, Bibla returned his greeting and their relationship was initiated. He soon discovered that she and her husband were in the process of getting a divorce. They stayed in separate rooms at the Polana and spent little time together. Since she was still married to a German, and sat with Wertz at dinner, Malcolm told himself that he had a professional interest in Bibla. Her sister was, in fact, Wertz's mistress. Malcolm stationed himself at the end of the hotel terrace, hoping that Bibla would pass by after dinner. After a time, she did come, and they sat and talked. It was the first of many such conversations. She told him about her divorce, but she also told him that she was in love with, and hoped to marry, another German – Baron Werner von Alvensleben, whom Malcolm calls Johann von X in *The Infernal Grove*.

Despite her intention to marry Werner, Malcolm pursued Bibla and she yielded. It seems that she carried on affairs with both men at the same time. Though this made for high tensions, Malcolm became quite fond of Werner, who was ten years his junior. An aristocrat, Werner had joined the Nazis as a young man, though he was assailed by doubts about the movement from the beginning. He came to work with such high-ranking Nazi officials as Heinrich Himmler. Werner volunteered to carry out a plot to assassinate a minister in the Austrian government in order to destabilise the regime and prepare for the German annexation of Austria. The plot failed, and Werner was arrested. He eventually returned to Germany in a prisoner exchange. But it became clear that he was in danger from the Nazis, so he sought refuge in Africa. When the war began, he was interned in Rhodesia as an enemy alien, but he managed to escape to Mozambique, the nearest neutral nation. Malcolm felt that Werner's story was a typically modern one, paralleling in some ways his own: a youthful involvement in a totalitarian ideology, disillusionmentl and exile. He intended to write a book, "Letters to an Enemy", with Werner, but, as with all of his literary projects during the war, the project was abandoned.

Werner and Bibla often went out with Malcolm on excursions, for picnics by the beach and drives into the countryside. There came a point, however, when Werner discovered that Bibla was sleeping with Malcolm. Werner confronted them and they agreed to end the affair.[25]

On the rebound from his relationship with Bibla, Malcolm found himself turning to Andrée, the French wife of a British intelligence officer, whom Malcolm calls "Nero" in *The Infernal Grove*. Nero worked for the Special Operations Executive, another division of the secret service that specialised in various forms of sabotage. Nero and Andrée had two daughters, and Malcolm enjoyed visiting them when he could. In his diary he noted that Andrée was "sensual, but religious". She was off limits.[26]

Toward the end of his year in Lourenço Marques, Malcolm did find a woman who was in a position to return his attentions. Through his informant Serge he met a dancer at a night club known as the Café Penguin. Her name was Diane (Hélène in *The Infernal Grove*), and Serge thought that her ability to speak French, Spanish and Portuguese, and the type of contacts she could make at the night club, would be of some use to them. Half Belgian and half Greek, Diane had a face with a "large nose and small chin", which reminded Malcolm "of one of those Egyptian heads in the Cairo Museum. Her voice was rather hoarse, her clothes cheap-looking and flashy; but there was something bright and brave about her that I found appealing."[27] Diane was not a Bibla or an Andrée; he felt somewhat embarrassed to be seen in her presence. But he began to frequent the Café Penguin to be near Diane, who would come and sit with him after she had performed her dance. Diane complained that she was being treated by the night club management as if she was a *papillon* or taxi-girl, rather than an *artiste*.

One night, after driving Diane home, he made a pass at her in the car. "She was astonished, truly astonished: '*J'avais beaucoup de considération pour vous,*' she said in a flat, sad voice. It was not exactly a reproach; much worse than that. No words ever spoken to me, I think, have echoed more wretchedly in my ears, and made me feel more sick with myself."[28] It is not clear whether Diane remained astonished at Malcolm's intentions. They continued to spend time together. Once, while they were driving together, Malcolm lost control of the car and nearly crashed head-on into a tree. Later it was discovered that a vital part of the car's steering mechanism had been removed. Malcolm then remembered that he had had the car serviced by an Italian mechanic, probably one of Campini's men. After the war, when Italy had fallen, Campini said under interrogation that "when he was driving his car by the sea and saw me walking along, he had a strong impulse to run me over".[29]

Whether Diane yielded or not, Malcolm plunged into deep despair. He wrote in his diary: "In the mornings, going into the sea with [Huntington Harris], I thought of the night before with groans, and complained to the wide sky that I continued to live, and ruefully surveyed scratches on my shoulder, dishonourable wounds." He was bored, unable to write or imagine a future for himself, filled with sexual frustration, and wracked by guilt about Kitty and his family. Once again he contemplated suicide. He wrote a love letter to Bibla, even though he knew what her answer would be. Andrée rebuffed an advance. He thought he was showing the first signs of syphilis. He got drunk. "Then," as he later wrote in his diary, "the whole horror of life brought upon me; that evening's happenings, all I'd said, all I'd done, the falsity, the words I'd spoken, the emotions I'd seemed to feel, the expense of passion in a waste of shame. I felt I could live no more; I felt I'd reached the end. No other day could be endured; the next morning I could not face."[30]

How should he kill himself? There were no drugs available on which he could overdose. Shooting himself would only bring shame and horror to his family. Then the idea came to him that if he drowned in the sea it might look like an accident.

I drove to the further point along the coast road, some six miles from Lourenço Marques, and there got out of the car and undressed. The lights were still on in Peter's Café and Costa da Sol. As the tide was far out, I had to wade on and on before there was enough water to swim in. So this was the end of my life, my last little while on earth. I kept on trying to think of the French word for "drown". Everything seemed to me unreal – had there been a single moment in my life when I had truly lived? Everything false – love, hate, happiness, despair, all equally false. Even this dying seemed false. Was it me, wading on to the open sea? Was it really happening? The bottom I trod on was muddy now, the water creeping up and cold, the air damp. At last there was enough water to swim in. I started swimming, the dark water churning white as my arms beat through it. Soon I was out of my depth, and still swam on. Now I felt easy, now it was settled. Looking back I could scarcely see the shore; only the lights of Peter's Café and the Costa da Sol, far, far, away. I began to tremble, all my body trembled; I went under the water, trembling, came up again and reposed myself as though on a bed. I could sleep on this watery mattress, sleep. Then, suddenly, without thinking or deciding, I started swimming back to shore. I was very tired, and kept feeling if I was in my depth again, and wasn't; I shouted foolishly for help, and kept my eyes fixed on the lights of Peter's Café and the Costa da Sol.

They were the lights of the world; they were the lights of my home, my habitat, where I belonged. I must reach them. There followed an overwhelming joy such as I had never experienced before; an ecstasy.[31]

Exhausted, Malcolm stumbled ashore in a river estuary, some distance from where he had parked his car, and went home.

In his autobiography, Malcolm notes that he immediately reported the event to MI6 as another piece of "deception material" (what today would be called "disinformation") calculated to delude Wertz into thinking that Malcolm had failed as a spy. Wertz took the bait and wired his superiors that he had thwarted the intrepid British agent. "In the end I began to wonder whether, after all, it *had* been a ruse." When the historian David Irving found a reference in a telegram by Wertz to the suicide, he made it public in 1966. At that time, Malcolm denied that he had wanted to kill himself. "It was purely a matter of deception. I never tried to commit suicide. It was staged as a plot to fool the Germans."[32] But less than a decade later, in his autobiography, he asserted that it was not only a genuine suicide attempt, but a spiritual turning point in his life – a watershed event.

Even at the time Malcolm recognised that his motives could not be distentangled, that the suicide attempt was also an act, more melodramatic and self-pitying than tragic. In a diary entry written not long after the event, he noted that everything in his life seemed false, even the suicide. But his emotional crisis was real enough: he had returned to the "black moments" that had characterised his year in India in 1935. This time, however, he had no willing Amrita Sher-Gil to distract him. When Graham Greene, who had returned to London from Africa, read Malcolm's telegram about the episode, he told his colleagues at MI6 that the suicide attempt was undoubtedly genuine.

The other question that lingers is what the consequences of this event really were. In Malcolm's autobiography, the decision to live, to swim for the shore, was surrounded by an ecstatic affirmation of goodness over evil, life over death. It was, he said, the moment when he emerged from his spiritual adolescence, and knew that he would, from that point on, always be on the side of life. But like so many significant episodes in Malcolm's life, such as his Christian conversion at Cambridge, there was no clear-cut Before and After. He may have felt some inward assurance about being on the side of life and goodness, but even this suicide attempt did not constitute a Damascus Road experience.

Malcolm's days in Lourenço Marques were quickly drawing to a close. He had been summoned to Cairo in the spring of 1943 to be instructed on how to spread "deception material". While he was in Cairo, however, he noticed a newspaper headline proclaiming that the Germans were in full retreat from Africa. He knew then that his job in Lourenço Marques would soon be over, because Allied shipping would once more be able to use the Mediterranean, instead of having to go around the southern tip of Africa and up the Mozambique Channel.

Malcolm left Lourenço Marques in July 1943. When he arrived at Kampala in Uganda, he was stricken with acute abdominal pains. He was brought to the hospital, where an appendectomy was performed. After only five days of recuperation, he was able to fly on to Lagos in Nigeria. There he stayed at a Special Operations Executive house, and was booked on to a flight to England the following day. But when he was ready to board the flight, he found that he had been bumped off by a wooden-legged colonel, whose rank entitled him to priority seating. Later, he heard that that flight had crashed in the mountains around Shannon airport in Ireland. Since Kitty had been informed that Malcolm was to be on that flight, she thought he had been killed. When he eventually arrived, it was "as one risen from the dead. My welcome would, I am sure, have been warm in any case, but in the circumstances it was positively ecstatic . . . It was tempting to regard my ejection from the crashed plane as a kind of miracle . . . but on reflection such a view seemed disrespectful to the memory of the one-legged colonel, who would certainly see the incident in a different light."[33]

Liberator
1943–1945

WHEN HE returned to England, Malcolm needed to rest and recuperate. He had just experienced three close brushes with death: a suicide attempt, an emergency appendectomy and the crash of a plane that he nearly boarded. All of these incidents had taken place at the end of Malcolm's assignment in Mozambique. Despite his triumphs as a spy in Lourenço Marques, he had once again plunged into the "black moments" that always left him drained and listless. It is well that the assignments he received in the last years of the war did not force him into the isolation of his year in Mozambique. Acting as a liaison officer enabled him to do what he did best: observe the people and places around him and search out the larger historical and moral truths about them.

After two months of rest at Mill House, Malcolm reported back to MI6 on the first of October. The offices had moved from St Albans to Ryder Street, off Piccadilly, in London. He discovered that his exploits in Lourenço Marques had earned him prestige, but he felt no desire to exploit this and become ambitious to rise within the intelligence community. Most of the senior officers in MI6 were, to Malcolm, creatures of the Establishment; he preferred to remain an outsider.

Returning to MI6 brought him back into contact with Kim Philby. He visited Philby's new flat in Chelsea, finding, to his surprise, that it was luxuriously appointed. Given what he knew about salaries at MI6 and the general state of wartime conditions, Malcolm concluded that Philby's wife Eileen had private means. After Philby defected to the Soviet Union, Malcolm realised that Philby must have been receiving money from the Soviets by 1943. Another thing that Malcolm noticed in 1943 was that Philby rarely joined in political discussions. The one exception to this occurred in a debate over whether intelligence from Bletchley about the German Eastern Front should be passed on to the Russians. Malcolm held that the current policy of withholding this information was the only prudent course, since there was a possibility that the Soviets might find another occasion to betray the Allies. He went on to argue that Stalin had acted in a typically irrational manner in the past, rejecting offers of intelligence from the British, even when they proved true. Uncharacteristically, Philby broke into the debate, declaring loudly that it was the duty of the British to help their Soviet allies in whatever way they could, even if it meant risking the flow of information coming from Bletchley. While odd, this intervention by Philby did not raise any suspicions in Malcolm's mind about his being a double agent.[1]

Malcolm's next assignment was determined by his contact, earlier in the war, with the French resistance forces, and his ability to speak the language. He was sent to Algiers, in what was then the French colony of Algeria. Throughout the war Algiers served as Allied headquarters for North Africa, and it also became the rallying point for the French freedom fighters. Charles de Gaulle was the leader, along with Henri Giraud, of the French Committee of National Liberation, based in Algiers. Malcolm's role was to serve as liaison officer between MI6 and its French counterpart, the *Securité Militaire*. Algiers was also the base for British intelligence missions to Italy and the Balkans. Since there was no need for Malcolm to retain a civilian identity, he was reinstated into His Majesty's armed forces at the rank of major.

His arrival in Algiers did not begin auspiciously. On his second day the car in which he was travelling was involved in a traffic accident. Malcolm suffered concussion and awoke in a hospital. When he came to, he told Kitty in a letter, he felt a sensation of complete freedom, from his body or anything else. It was as if he was suspended "between time and eternity belonging to neither. In a way I understood and felt quite reconciled. But of course the next morning the noise of life began again – and I began to plot to get out of the hospital and about again."[2]

Malcolm's first job was to get to know the leading figures among the French forces. The chief of the *Securité Militaire* was a man named Paiolle, whom Malcolm found to be stiff and formal, though a conscientious officer. More attractive to Malcolm was de Gaulle's intelligence director, Jacques Soustelle. A brilliant anthropologist who had been named director of the *Musée de L'Homme* in Paris when he was only in his twenties, Soustelle proved a congenial friend. Many years later Malcolm would write of Soustelle that he was "an intellectual, an instinctive anarchist; a poacher, not a gamekeeper".[3] Malcolm also found Soustelle sympathetic because he was an articulate defender of de Gaulle. The French forces at this time were divided between supporters of de Gaulle and those who maintained loyalty to the Vichy government in France, which had been set up in 1940 under Marshal Pétain, and which controlled unoccupied France and its colonies. The divisions he observed in Algiers were just a foretaste of the violent and often tragic clashes between these factions that would erupt during the liberation of France.

The MI6 head of station in Algiers, and Malcolm's immediate superior, was Trevor Wilson, one of the few intelligence officers who earned Malcolm's respect. "He was a short, unaccountable man with a toothbrush moustache, who had been a bank-manager in France; knew the language perfectly, but spoke it in a strange muttering whisper, with his head bent down, and usually a cigarette in his mouth which got affixed to his upper or lower lip, wagging with his words."[4] Wilson was a man of extremes, from his political opinions (staunchly conservative) to his quirky sense of humour. From his office in a spacious Arab house high above the city of Algiers, Wilson directed a wide variety of intelligence operations.

Malcolm's duties included intelligence briefings for senior officers and working with the local police to pick up informers. By far the most interesting task was the promulgation of deception material, or disinformation, through "turned-around" agents. This false information, known in MI6 as "chicken feed", was intended to sow confusion in the enemy ranks. What fascinated Malcolm was not the outcome of the process – who won the battle – but the process itself. Why was it that an agent could provide the Germans with patently false information and yet continue to be believed, against all reason? Because, he concluded, the German intelligence officer, or "control", in charge of the informer had made an investment and did not want to lose face by repudiating his source.

Malcolm was always amazed at human capacity for self-deception. In the spy business, where hard-nosed realism was supposed to prevail, he found the most bizarre examples of credulity imaginable. His favourite case involved a French colonel who was dishing up ample amounts of chicken feed for his German control. Malcolm's French colleagues dreamed up ways to make a profit from the colonel's activities. They had him inform his control that he must be paid in specie, rather than notes, because paper money was more detectable. In due course, the colonel went out to an agreed-upon location, and found that a box of coins had been air-dropped for him. Once, when there was a shortage of tyres, the colonel requested to be paid in tyres. Sure enough, the tyres floated down from the sky. Malcolm noted that they were Dunlops. He joined in the spirit of the occasion.

> I made the suggestion that the colonel should send a message complaining of being troubled by his sexual appetites, to the point that it was impossible for him to concentrate on his work, and that he hesitated to avail himself of the local facilities for fear of giving himself away. I had a picture in my mind of Rhine maidens floating down from the sky, but our French colleagues were more sceptical. The most that could be expected by way of response, they insisted, would be a supply of bromide.[5]

Games of this sort, however, failed to provide much in the way of distraction. Malcolm descended quickly into depression and alienation. He wrote to Kitty at Christmas, 1943, describing himself lying on his bed, "full of hateful thoughts and images; a sense of being imprisoned, of being diseased and distorted, of corruption".[6] The war had forced him into a limbo from which he thought he might never emerge. He told Kitty of his deepest fear. "My nightmares of never being able to write again continually haunt me."

He was relieved when his immediate French superior, Paiolle, offered to take him on a tour of North Africa. They drove along the coastal roads, visiting French army installations. Seeing these far-flung outposts of the French colonial empire reminded him of the Raj in India, but they were more sympathetic. "Other people's empires tend to seem more tolerable than one's own."[7]

If Malcolm could not write, at least he could seek out the company of writers. There were a surprising number of them in Algiers. Perhaps the most famous was the French author, André Gide. The British Council representative in Algiers was able to arrange a meeting with Gide. Malcolm thought of Gide as a typically modern intellectual, a critic of traditional morality and institutions and an advocate of homosexuality. But Malcolm had reasons for not condemning Gide entirely. Gide had been among the intellectuals, like Shaw and the Webbs, who had been enamoured of the Soviet Union and had been an "icon" there. When he learned enough about the inhumanity of the Soviet regime, however, he had proven to be more independent in his thinking than the other political pilgrims: he had retracted his endorsement of the Soviet experiment. Later, he would contribute an essay to the collection *The God That Failed*. Malcolm found Gide sitting by an open window on the Rue Michelet, watching American soldiers passing by.

> For Gide, the spectacle, for obvious reasons, held a special attraction. I was aware at once of his grey, coldly luminous face; almost priestly in style – an impression enhanced by a skull-cap that he wore. But priestly on the Devil's side; the sanctity somehow foetid, the luminosity unearthly without being heavenly ... Nonetheless, there was something enchanting about his words, as he chose them and used them, the timbre of his voice: so clear and so true, like the bells of those little Swiss churches sounding out on a Sunday morning in the chill mountain air.[8]

In the course of his duties, Malcolm came to know Duff Cooper, who was then the British emissary to de Gaulle's provisional government. Cooper and his glamorous wife, Diana, were one of Britain's most celebrated society couples, the staple of the gossip columns. At a cocktail party held by the Coopers, Malcolm ran into Evelyn Waugh, who had recently survived a plane crash. As Malcolm later noted, their every encounter seemed ill-fated. Waugh was evidently shaken by the crash and, like Malcolm, he had become dispirited by the war and his inability to write. Malcolm thanked Waugh for his perceptive review of *In a Valley of This Restless Mind*. But the conversation faltered and trailed off.

Algiers had become such an important base of Allied operations that Malcolm ran into several old friends. Bobby Barclay turned up, as did Colonel Ross-Atkinson. On a brief trip to Cairo, Malcolm even ran into his old friend from Moscow, A.T. Cholerton, whom he found "much fatter, still bearded, drinking ... We spent a couple of evenings together precisely as so often in Moscow, piecing together his muttered incoherence so full of humour and sagacity. Of the German invasion of Russia he said: 'Hitler had to make his best-seller come about.'"[9]

But the most interesting encounter Malcolm had in North Africa was with a fellow MI6 officer, a man whose face had struck Malcolm as being older and more mature than the others, who went by the name of Adrian Hunter. Malcolm soon learned that the man was Austrian, not English and that "Adrian Hunter" was a *nom de guerre*. Hunter was none other than von Strachwitz, the Austrian spy who had been exchanged with Malcolm's friend from Lourenço Marques, Werner von Alvensleben. Hunter, a devout Catholic and a man of culture, shared Malcolm's conviction that Stalin would be one of the chief beneficiaries of the war. They spent many evenings together lamenting the naïveté of the younger intelligence agents, who tended to favour Communist or Leftist factions in war-torn nations like Yugoslavia. This willingness to support those who despised Western values seemed to Malcolm and Hunter to be a sort of cultural death-wish.

> We sat talking in this strain, looking down on the lights of Algiers, and on the Mediterranean beyond – the same coast from which Augustine of Hippo had watched the collapse of Rome as we were now watching the collapse of Christendom. Adrian's face, with its ironical creases and wrinkles, its tired eyes, which yet, behind their tiredness, held an impregnable serenity, was like a veritable map of what we were talking about.[10]

As the Allied campaign in Italy progressed, Malcolm travelled to the southern Italian city of Brindisi to continue his duties as a liaison officer. There he found another provisional government, headed by Marshal Badoglio, and ensconced in the Hotel Imperiale. The Marshal appeared somewhat bemused by his new role as the shadow leader of Italy. In the evening, the Marshal, along with a group of intelligence officers, gathered around a radio, which was supposed to link them to their man in German-occupied Rome. They were to listen to the message from the agent and determine whether he seemed to be under enemy control or operating freely. The message eventually came through: it should not be thought, the agent said, that all loyal Italians were in Marshal Badoglio's government; there were many good men in Rome as well. Malcolm argued that such a statement was too authentic to have been concocted by an agent of the *Abwehr*, and so the agent in Rome was approved.

Malcolm continued up the Italian peninsula in the wake of the victorious Allied armies. Furnished with a car marked "International Control Commission" (he never found out what, exactly, was being controlled) and a driver, Malcolm kept on the move. In Naples he picked through the rubbish left behind in what had been Gestapo headquarters. There he came across propaganda and pornography: the eroticism of power and of the body. "Violence, sentimentality and porn, and finally, to round things off, sheer imbecility, in the form of a propaganda record lying about which played a Lili-Marlene-type song into which a soft, persuasive voice broke from time to time, saying, in English: 'You know you're losing the war . . . You'd far better give in . . .'"[11] He and his driver drove north, through Capri, Pompeii and Caserta, eventually ending up in liberated Rome. There Malcolm was billeted in the Bank of Rome, a splendid building that he thought of as a cathedral devoted to money. Though it was desolate and empty when Malcolm stayed there, it would not be long, he thought, before the marble would shine again and money once again have its rites.

After the Normandy invasion, it was only a matter of time before Malcolm continued his assignment with the *Securité Militaire* in liberated Paris itself. On the morning of August 12, 1944, Malcolm flew from England with Paiolle and another French officer to France. Because fighting was still going on near the Paris airport of Le Bourget, the plane was forced to land seventy miles from the capital. They got a lift on a truck carrying French troops. Being officers, they were given seats in the front, so all the way to Paris they received the ecstatic praises of the crowds that lined the road. "[W]e responded officially, saluting and waving like royalty, on behalf of the others, many of whom were already fairly drunk, and very wild and excited; shouting, dancing about, and even occasionally letting off a gun. In time, we, too, became infected with the prevailing excitement; the more so because every time we were brought to a halt, swigs of cognac and glasses of champagne were pressed upon us."[12]

The city was in a state of chaos, without basic services. Malcolm made his way through the confusion and found Trevor Wilson, who had managed to obtain a car and driver and other amenities. They went off to a café on the Left Bank, where a man with a "large, sad clown's face" was recounting to the patrons all the sufferings he had endured in the course of the war. "*Et maintenant*, he concluded, with an expression of infinite woe, through which he struggled to break into a wry smile – *Et maintenant, nous sommes libérés!*" The play of expressions on the man's face seemed to Malcolm to encompass the truth of the liberation far more accurately than a barrage of patriotic pieties. As he commented in his autobiography: "Only clowns and mystics ever speak the truth."[13]

Malcolm soon found himself ensconced in luxurious accommodation. The British had requisitioned the Rothschild mansion on the Avenue Marigny. The head of the family, Victor Rothschild, was married to the sister (Tess) of Andreas Mayor, Malcolm's friend. Victor invited Malcolm to stay in the mansion while he was stationed in Paris. Malcolm grew fond of the *maître d'hôtel*, M. Felix, who stood guard at the porter's lodge. M. Felix was resourceful and ironic, and Malcolm enjoyed chatting with him. The mansion and its contents were in remarkably good shape, considering that the Nazis had only recently departed. According to M. Felix, the German general who had lived in the house had behaved impeccably. When Malcolm questioned M. Felix on this, he replied: "Hitlers come and go . . . but Rothschilds go on for ever."[14] Living in the Rothschild mansion seemed to Malcolm just another surrealistic episode in his life. From the richly upholstered, hushed interior of this imposing edifice Malcolm sallied forth into anarchy – a city wracked by gunshots, shrieks and drunken shouting.

The conflicts between the Gaullists and the defenders of the Vichy government, between the "collaborators" and the "liberators", became acute. In the anarchic conditions of liberated France, revenge and retribution were the order of the day. As an intelligence officer, Malcolm saw the results of this surreptitious civil war at first hand. Those accused of collaborating with the enemy endured various punishments, from having their heads shaved to being shot in cold blood by roving vigilantes. For a time Malcolm went about with a group of young FFI (*Forces Françaises de l'Intérieur*) members. He watched, appalled, as they confiscated valuables, made arrests and treated people with a harshness that seemed the more horrifying because of their youth.

It quickly became evident to Malcolm that almost everybody who had lived in France during the war could be accused of collaboration. Restaurant owners had fed German officers, barbers had cut their hair, whores had made love to them. Without authority or law, the populace was retreating into brutishness. In the daytime it wasn't so bad. "Then, as night came on, sounds of scurrying feet, sudden cries, shots, shrieks, but no one available, or caring, to investigate. It is unknown to this day how many were shot down, had their heads shaved, piteously disgorged their possessions in return for being released, but certainly many, many thousands."[15]

Malcolm's primary assignment was to sort out the cases of British agents who had been accused of collaboration. He later felt that this task was easily the most worthwhile thing he had done in the war. But he found himself emotionally caught up in a number of other cases. There was the French criminal, Laffont, who had worked closely with the Germans. The French authorities were eager to prosecute him, but that thought made Laffont suicidal and he pleaded to be tried by the Allied command, where he said he would get a fair trial. Malcolm was called upon to hear Laffont out, which he duly did. He found his reaction to this desperate criminal, an egotist who had lost touch with reality, was more sympathetic than judgemental. The worst part of the experience, however, was Malcolm's awareness that his conversation with Laffont was a charade. Later, he heard that Laffont had been executed in a manner that had some precedent in French history – he was guillotined.

The most famous case that Malcolm took on was that of the comic writer P.G. Wodehouse. The creator of Bertie Wooster and his valet Jeeves had been living in France before the war. When the Germans occupied France, Wodehouse and his wife Ethel were brought to the prison camp at Tost as enemy aliens. The conditions at Tost were fairly mild, though they had to subsist on small rations. With his strange blend of innocence and detachment, Wodehouse managed to write five novels at Tost, turning out his daily quota of words. He and Ethel were released a few months before his sixtieth birthday, the customary age for prisoners to be given their freedom. They travelled to Berlin to stay with some American friends (America not having entered the war yet). Wodehouse was invited by a man from the Columbia Broadcasting System to deliver a series of talks about his experiences at Tost. Rather naïvely, Wodehouse agreed and broadcast a number of innocuous descriptions of life in the camp. He had hoped that the broadcasts would let his family in England know that he and Ethel were alive and well. It never occurred to him that these talks would be seen as serving the purposes of German propaganda. Though Wodehouse said nothing to indicate he sympathised with the Germans, the broadcasts caused outrage in Britain. He was stripped of his membership of various clubs and organisations, and taken off the honour roll at his old school, Dulwich College.

Wodehouse and his wife had been living quietly in Paris after the liberation, but Malcolm was ordered to keep an eye on them. Malcolm first met them when they were living in the Bristol Hotel. They got on famously. Malcolm was charmed by the essential innocence of Wodehouse's vision. Wodehouse took to Malcolm immediately. "When I got to know him better," Malcolm wrote later, "I asked him what sort of person he had expected to come into his room. 'Oh, I don't know,' he said, 'but not you.' This, I must say, greatly pleased me."[16] It is interesting to note that Wodehouse's greatest fans included three of the most biting satirical writers of the twentieth century: Muggeridge, George Orwell and Evelyn Waugh. Malcolm actually arranged for Orwell, who had come to Paris as a correspondent for the *Observer*, to meet Wodehouse.

Some time after he met the Wodehouses, he was called upon to rescue them from trouble. Wodehouse had been denounced to the authorities as a "notorious British traitor" and had been taken to a police station. Malcolm secured the release of Ethel and her dog Wonder immediately, but it took a few days to get Wodehouse released. As usual, Wodehouse found something about his environment to amuse him: in this instance, it was the fact that his prison was located in a maternity ward. Some time later, a British bureaucrat was sent to investigate Wodehouse. Though he concluded that the writer was hardly guilty of treason, it was decided that he should stay out of Britain. Wodehouse elected to move to America, where he lived into his nineties. He never set foot on English soil again, but he remained grateful to Malcolm and entertained him whenever he came to New York.

The most unsettling episode of these months in Paris concerned a young French girl who had been accused of collaboration. The story went like this. A German officer had been billeted in her family home during the occupation. At first, she had resented his presence, but over time he demonstrated to the girl and her family that he was honourable and decent. The girl responded to this, and eventually they became lovers. With the German retreat from Paris, the officer had been forced into hiding and she had been branded a collaborator. Malcolm found her case emblematic of the darker side of the liberation. "After all, she said to me, his being a German didn't make him not a man, and her being French make her not a woman. The sentiment was commonplace enough in itself, but her words continued to echo in my mind."[17]

Malcolm was able to help the girl, but the incident sparked his only creative effort of the war years: a play, entitled *Liberation*, written soon after he had left France. The themes in *Liberation* are reminiscent of Graham Greene's fiction: the complex mystery of the human heart, poised between loyalty and betrayal, sincerity and hypocrisy, love and hate. The ill-fated lovers are Françoise and Karl. Françoise's father, M. Dubois, a Gaullist soldier, returns to Paris during the liberation, only to find that his dreams of joyous, unified occasion are torn asunder by suspicion, recrimination and violence. Françoise's grandfather, M. Bernard, is in danger of being imprisoned. A man of letters who supported the Vichy government, M. Bernard has been thrown in prison by every group that had been in power. Though Malcolm did not especially like the defenders of Vichy, he makes M. Bernard his spokesman in the play.

The plot thickens when Françoise is denounced to the police for her relationship with Karl. As it turns out, the informer who denounced her was none other than her own brother, Gerard, a young man full of political hatred and ideology. The hapless M. Dubois is unable to cope with the harsh realities that lie beyond his sentimental patriotism. Only M. Bernard sees into the heart of the matter. He addresses Gerard:

> Poor Gerard! You think you're a fanatic! A hero of our time, like Stendhal's Sorel ... The fever of action has got into your blood – like desire, extinguishing reason, drying up compassion. The Nazis were just like you. They, too, were full of adolescent ambition, adolescent romanticism. For them, it's all ending in gas chambers and rubble. With you, in denouncing your sister ... If you'd been born in Germany you'd have been a Nazi, and probably by now have found the death, which is what you're really looking for.[18]

M. Bernard, though he supported the Vichy regime for a time, is no fanatic. He is based, of course, on Malcolm himself, a writer who tries to tell the truth but who falls foul of the dominant political ideologies of the day. Chided for not keeping his opinions to himself, he responds: "Arguments, the right to have arguments, is what the war is all about. Civilisation develops the individual, barbarism depends on the herd. It is not unity we need so much as tolerance. The diversity of innumerable individuals, who are alike only in that they are made in God's image, and united only in that they belong to one family whose Father is in heaven."[19]

By the end of *Liberation*, Karl has been shot by vigilantes from the FFI, M. Dubois is stunned into silence, and Gerard is filled with guilt and hate. Only Françoise, who has to go to the hospital and identify

Karl's body, has achieved a sense of detachment from the follies surrounding her. She, alone, has been liberated.

Liberation was never performed professionally; it ran counter to the patriotic myths and sentiments of the time. Years later, Malcolm turned to the successful playwright, Christopher Fry, hoping that he might be able to promote the play. Fry made a number of editorial suggestions, but no producer he contacted decided to bring it to the stage.

Despite his awareness of the dark side of the liberation, Malcolm retained his respect for the political leaders of Britain and France. When Winston Churchill came to Paris in November 1944, Malcolm wrote to Kitty: "I saw him walking down the Champs-Elysées with de Gaulle and I must say felt most moved. He looked so pink and happy as the crowd cheered him; even de G. melted somewhat and waved his arms in the air in his ungainly way."[20] When, later in his life, Malcolm was asked who were the greatest political leaders of the twentieth century, he replied without hesitation: Gandhi, de Gaulle and Stalin.[21] It would be difficult to think of three more dissimilar figures, but Malcolm defended his choice. Each of these men had a sort of unworldly spiritual charisma – in Stalin's case, the source being evil – that rallied men to their standards. Back in 1924, Malcolm had witnessed Gandhi's power at the station in Alwaye. Like Gandhi, de Gaulle was a somewhat comical figure, large and ungainly compared to the Indian, who was small and ungainly. Malcolm responded to de Gaulle's inner confidence, moral rectitude and sense of history. Early in the liberation, Malcolm witnessed a symbolic demonstration of de Gaulle's character. During a thanksgiving service at Notre-Dame cathedral, a shot was fired. The effect was immediate and dramatic: the entire congregation flattened themselves to the floor, with the exception of one man. De Gaulle alone remained standing, "tall and alone", as Malcolm would always remember him.

As the months wore on, and things began to settle down in Paris, Malcolm became increasingly bored and restless, in danger of falling into his "black moments". He became involved with a French woman whom he calls "F" in his diary. Could this have been the "Françoise" who had been denounced for her affair with the German officer? It is impossible to say. In his diary Malcolm wrote:

One night when I was sleeping in the flat in the Avenue Henri Martin I woke up to hear a man being murdered, and his last cry was exactly like the cries that F and I had made earlier in the night. An awful horror of the flesh gripped me, and then I thought that after all passion was innate in life, that in one form or another this experience had to be gone through or life was not life at all, but that as one understood so one wished ever more intensely to be released from its bondage.[22]

After he returned to England, "F" continued to write to Malcolm for some months, but the relationship did not survive the end of the war.

The other form of distraction he pursued, as he had in Algiers, was the opportunity to meet some of France's leading writers. Some were disappointments. Henri de Montherlant, whose novel *The Bachelors* Malcolm had enjoyed, was morose and given to the sort of Lawrentian sex mysticism that Malcolm now scorned. Perhaps the most impressive of these writers was the Catholic novelist, François Mauriac. Graham Greene, who had left MI6 to join the publishing firm of Eyre and Spottiswoode, commissioned Malcolm to meet Mauriac and obtain permission to have his books translated into English. "Mauriac proved to be a frail, intense man of a kind often found among French writers and intellectuals, who seem to shake themselves to pieces with the vigour and urgency of their thoughts and words; like some ancient rickety old car which shakes and shivers when the engine is started up, so that one constantly marvels that it can hold together at all."[23] For all Mauriac's intensity, his Catholic vision of redemption through suffering, he had a dry but lively sense of humour. When Malcolm asked him if there was any truth to the rumour that Gide was thinking of becoming a Catholic, Mauriac groaned and said that, if it were so, he prayed it would come only moments before he expired. Malcolm's admiration for Mauriac grew when he learned that the writer had adamantly opposed the spirit of revenge and intolerance that character-ised the liberation. Many years later Malcolm would find another occasion to be grateful to Mauriac, when the Frenchman waged a successful campaign to have the Nobel Prize for Literature awarded to the Russian dissident, Aleksandr Solzhenitsyn, one of Malcolm's heroes.

After he had been stationed in Paris for some months, Malcolm had been informed that Kim Philby was now in charge of a newly formed unit whose purpose was to gather information on Soviet intelligence activities. As the war was coming to a conclusion, it became clear to the Allies that the Soviets would revert to being their enemies. Philby, a Soviet agent himself, made a successful power play to direct this anti-Soviet unit within MI6. One of the first requests Malcolm received from this unit was to discover where the headquarters of the French Communist Party were located, and who served as party chairman. When he passed this request on to his French counterparts, they laughed. Why not look the headquarters up in the phonebook, where it was undoubtedly listed, they asked? A brief phone call would reveal the identity of the party chairman.

Easily the most bizarre moment of these months in Paris took place in the company of Kim Philby. One day Philby turned up in Paris and invited Malcolm to dinner. With his taste for the good life, Philby ate a large, rich meal, while Malcolm only picked at his food. They did, however, drink an equally large amount of spirits. When the meal was over Philby suddenly announced that they should go to the Rue de Grenelle. Malcolm was not aware that this was the location of the Soviet Embassy. As they approached the building, Philby began to complain in a loud voice how difficult it was to penetrate the embassy staff, who were all imported from Russia. It was nearly impossible, Philby bellowed, to plant bugs in the place. "He carried on in an almost demented way; not exactly shaking his fists, but gesticulating and shouting at the hermetically sealed embassy . . ."

Malcolm, drunk as he was, knew that he was not dreaming up this strange scene. Not suspecting that Philby could have been a Soviet agent, he had no clue as to why Philby should jeopardise their security by putting on this display in plain view of the embassy. Malcolm never came up with an adequate explanation, except to say that Philby's behaviour that night probably derived from the identity crisis that every double agent suffers.

Philby himself never revealed what was going on in his mind. But he always remained fond of Malcolm, in part perhaps because Malcolm defended him when the initial investigations into Philby's Soviet connections began some years later. In his autobiography, *My Silent War*, Philby wrote: MI6 "even survived . . . corrosive imports, such as Graham Greene and Malcolm Muggeridge, both of whom merely added to the gaiety of the service . . . [Malcolm] was despatched to Lourenço Marques, too far away for my liking . . . I was glad when . . . Malcolm was brought back to deal with various aspects of French affairs. His stubborn opposition to the policy of the day (whatever it was) lent humanity to our lives."[24]

By the spring of 1945, Paris was returning to a semblance of order and Malcolm's workload dropped off to almost nothing. The Roths-child mansion was soon to revert to its rightful owner, as M. Felix tactfully reminded Malcolm. With the same impulsiveness that had led him to try to enlist in 1939, Malcolm decided that he would simply go home. This was, strictly speaking, illegal, since he had to apply officially for his demobilisation. But Malcolm was in no mood to present himself to the authorities. In the confusion at the end of the war, he actually got away with it, though he would receive his official discharge from His Majesty's armed forces in August 1945.

Before he left for England, however, he decided to see Berlin. He had last been there in 1933, right after his departure from Moscow, when he saw the storm-troopers marching up and down the Unter den Linden. Now Berlin was little more than rubble, pulverised by countless bombing raids. As he walked through the devastation he was amazed to see that human beings were actually living amidst the wreckage, setting up lean-tos in walls that remained standing, foraging for what little food and drink could be scrounged. Faced with the enormity of this destruction, Malcolm wondered what purpose had been served by the war. Hitler was gone, but Stalin was now "Uncle Joe", and the West was busily congratulating itself and reverting to the same fantasies that had marked the pre-war era.

He had chided his father for putting out a Union Jack on Armistice Day in 1918. When V-E Day was celebrated in 1945, he also refused to join in. Malcolm's war seemed to come to a conclusion when he and his family attended a performance of Shakespeare's *As You Like It* at the bomb-damaged Old Vic theatre in London. Arriving late, he looked at his family sitting in their seats. Parts of the stage and seating were still roped off as unsafe. The actors were students from the Royal Academy of Dramatic Art. Malcolm watched Kitty and the children from the back.

> There they were, caught up, compacted, by the enchantment of Shakespeare's comedy; and there was I, looking at them, and recalling that it was thirty years since I had likewise sat in that auditorium as a child, and been enthralled by *As You Like It* . . . After all, then, something *had* been salvaged from the world's wreck, as there still might be something to salvage from my life's wreck. At the back of the Old Vic auditorium I had my own private V-E day, and then, when the lights went up, joined the others.[25]

« 13 »

Terrible is Earth

1945–1947

THE END of the war brought with it a sense of disorientation. Malcolm, like so many others returning from the war, was emotionally drained and uncertain about the future. Ironically, the experience of disorientation was often heightened by the very lack of change in daily life. Aside from the destruction wrought by the Blitz and the shortages of food and other goods, life in Britain was not radically different from what it was before the war. The anarchist in Malcolm had revelled, during the Blitz, in the destruction of respectable bourgeois structures and institutions. They rose, slowly and inexorably, from the rubble, undying. Life went on and he had to find his place in it.

Kitty had moved the family once again, this time to a part of a flat on Buckingham Street, overlooking the Embankment and the Thames. (Malcolm was later to stare out at the Festival of Britain on the South Bank a rather feeble attempt, in the aftermath of the war, to bolster patriotic feeling by mounting a large exhibition lauding British achievements. In an unpublished fragment of the third volume of his autobiography, Malcolm wrote: "At the Empire Exhibition in the Thirties they presented the Prince of Wales in butter; in the Festival of Britain the lions were stuffed with straw.")[1] Soon Malcolm's ambivalence about city living would increase. By November of 1945, Malcolm records in his diary that "we have taken a little house" in Battle. The flat in London was maintained, giving Malcolm the option of moving back and forth.

Faced with the need to start again, Malcolm experienced a crisis of identity. At forty-two he was entering middle age. That he was a writer – a "vendor of words", as St Augustine had once described himself – was not in doubt. But what kind of writer? The two books Malcolm had published on the eve of the war, *In a Valley of This*

Restless Mind and *The Thirties*, were far and away his best. But circumstances had blunted their impact. *Valley* was not the kind of book that Malcolm could easily repeat. It had embodied his tortured spiritual journey at the time, but it did not point him in the direction of a more coherent theological vision. Besides, his religious and mystical impulses had become submerged in the chaotic unreality of the war years. *The Thirties* promised to be his breakthrough book, but the war and the patriotic feelings it evoked quickly diverted attention from the sardonic insights of Malcolm's social history. The post-war years would not be any more hospitable to astringent cultural criticism. Here, too, Malcolm was not alone. George Orwell, an admirer of *The Thirties* and now a friend of Malcolm's, confronted the dilemma of how to launch an attack on the social and intellectual trends of the day. He chose to couch his two great post-war books in the form of a fable (*Animal Farm*) and science fiction (*1984*).

Anthony Powell, who had met Malcolm in 1937, but only got to know him well after the war, wrote in his autobiography that Malcolm appeared to him to be a man without ambition. That was true enough if ambition is defined in the sense of seeking wealth and advancement within institutions. Malcolm's ambitions were strictly literary, but they were powerful and weighed heavily on him. Powell was a little closer to the mark when he pointed out, in the same passage from his autobiography, that Malcolm was still not well known in literary circles. His books and his journalism, being out of step with the time, failed to build him a reputation. Powell felt that there was a fundamental disparity between Malcolm's involvement in journalism and the seriousness and subtlety of his mind. When he compared Malcolm to other journalists, Powell thought that "Muggeridge's whole approach to life seemed remote from those determined to achieve that sort of ephemeral fame as quickly as possible."[2]

Malcolm wondered whether he should return to free-lancing and concentrate on writing books. But in a period of post-war austerity, it would be even harder to survive on the erratic income of a free-lance writer. Malcolm desperately needed money to support his family: his army pay had just covered the bare necessities and the advances he had received from publishers in 1940 had been spent long ago. Journalism seemed to be the only practical outlet available to him.

Malcolm approached the newspaper which had published his book reviews and anti-Communist articles before the war, the *Daily Telegraph*. He hoped to obtain a position on the literary and cultural side

Henry Thomas Muggeridge, Malcolm's father. Known to his friends
and colleagues as "Harry" or "HTM".

One of the Selwyn College, Cambridge, rowing teams, 1921. Malcolm is
standing, second from right. Alec Vidler is seated, centre.

Malcolm with two Indians, Union Christian
College, Alwaye, India, *c.*1925.

Malcolm in the early 1930s, when he
worked for the *Manchester Guardian*

Malcolm, Amrita Sher-Gil and her parents, near Simla, India, 1935.

Hugh Kingsmill, left, and Hesketh Pearson.

Malcolm during the
Second World War, when he had
attained the rank of major in MI6.

An undated photograph
of Kitty Muggeridge,
probably taken in the 1940s.

"Does the panel think...?" A somewhat weary Malcolm,
seated far left, on a BBC radio panel.

Malcolm during his editorship
of *Punch*, mid-1950s.

This photograph, from a television
programme, has become known as
"Malcolm savours a point".

Malcolm with three children from Fr. Bidone's home for mentally
retarded children, 1971.

Malcolm sharing a moment of hilarity with Andrew MacFarlane, the Dean of the University of Western Ontario School of Journalism, 1978.

Malcolm standing in Whatlington churchyard, where his parents were buried, and where he and Kitty were also, in time, to be buried.

Kitty standing in front of a portrait of her mother, Rosalind Potter Dobbs.

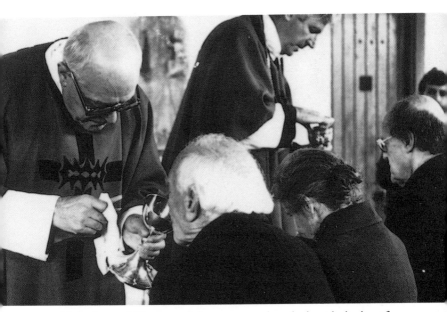

Malcolm and Kitty receiving communion during their rite of
reception into the Roman Catholic Church, November 27 1982. To their right
are Lord and Lady Longford. Administering the chalice is Fr Paul Bidone.
To his left is Bishop Cormac O'Connor.

Kitty reading aloud to Malcolm, a regular part of their evening routine.

The pilgrim.

of the paper. On May 18, 1945, he went to the *Telegraph* to see George Bishop, the literary editor. Bishop had nothing to offer Malcolm, but he took him down to see the editor, Arthur Watson. Watson asked Malcolm if he could write leaders; he replied in the affirmative. The next question that Watson put to Malcolm was whether he believed in "private enterprise". To the son of H.T. Muggeridge, this was not an easy question to answer. Malcolm's anti-Communism had perforce led to associations with conservative publications, but he would never be able to identify himself with conventional Tory politics or the world of big business. His critique of progressivist liberalism was, in essence, conservative, but he never became an advocate for capitalism. He hedged Watson's question, but this lack of enthusiasm for the free market did not interfere with his job prospects. A couple of days after the interview, he was offered the job and started work on the first day of June.[3]

Malcolm worked for the *Telegraph* in various capacities for the next eight years, the longest continuous term of employment in his career. This longevity can be attributed, in large part, to Malcolm's feeling that the *Telegraph* was devoid of the pretentiousness of the other papers he had worked for. The owner of the paper, William Berry, Lord Camrose, compared favourably with C.P. Scott and Lord Beaverbrook. Camrose, it appeared to Malcolm, was a relatively simple man, content with his wealth and his aristocratic title. Unlike the other two proprietors, Camrose did not set himself up as a political prophet or wire-puller, nor did he seem haunted by unfulfilled ambitions. "He told me once," Malcolm wrote in his autobiography, "how, travelling in an American plane, a fellow-passenger, hearing he was a lord, asked him where his castle was. I could quite see his point; Camrose looked like a man who lived in a castle."[4]

Arthur Watson, it turned out, was the brother of Alfred Watson, the former editor of the Calcutta *Statesman*. Malcolm found him a sympathetic figure, provincial perhaps, but in some ways an innocent.

He was a large, benign man, with a shining, pink face, abstemious in his ways and measured in his speech; a superb newspaper technician, with, beyond a vague [free-market] liberalism, no particular views on anything. He had never travelled, sought no tête-à-têtes with the great, wrote legibly, read little, and sat patiently in his editorial chair without a break from the early afternoon till he had seen the first edition through the press.[5]

Malcolm always remained grateful for the kindness Watson showed him.

The other three colleagues with whom Malcolm worked most closely were Colin Coote, J.C. Johnstone and H.D. Ziman. Coote had come to the *Telegraph* from *The Times*. Unlike Watson, Coote was someone Malcolm never felt comfortable with, especially when Coote eventually became editor and Malcolm served as his deputy editor. Coote was, to Malcolm's mind, "an exile from *The Times* ... his demeanour sometimes suggested a regular officer from a crack regiment ... who had strayed into a run-of-the-mill wartime mess."[6] He undoubtedly had a more competitive relationship with Coote than with the older and calmer Watson.

J.C. Johnstone, on the other hand, appeared to Malcolm as a more colourful and eccentric figure. He had arrived at the *Telegraph* when it absorbed his former employer, the *Morning Post*. Johnstone was the most ideologically fervent conservative on the editorial staff, and would argue his points with ardour. Malcolm shared an office with Johnstone, who had a habit of pacing up and down as he composed his next leader in his head. Malcolm also had a cordial relationship with H.D. Ziman, known affectionately in the office as "Z". Malcolm described Ziman as "articulate and loquacious, but with the air of a displaced person lost between the playing fields of Eton and Jerusalem's Wailing Wall".[7]

When Malcolm arrived at the *Telegraph* the editorial staff were deeply concerned about the parliamentary election of July 1945. Winston Churchill and the Tories had brought Britain through the war, but the martial virtues of Churchill were not what the people wanted in the post-war years. Many factors led the to huge Labour Party majority in this election, with Clement Attlee as the new Prime Minister. The social changes brought about by the war effort were enormous, most of them leading in the direction of collectivism and egalitarianism. Rationing and other acts of government planning had accustomed people to the idea of a welfare state. After the privations of the war years and growing resentment against the privileges of the upper classes, the British people were ready for a government that promised the redistribution of wealth. The covenant offered by the welfare state was that everyone's health and income would be guaranteed "from the cradle to the grave". The intellectual groundwork, of course, had been laid by the Fabians and engineered by the redoubtable Webbs.

Malcolm had lived to see his father's dream of a socialist government come true, but he felt neither enthusiasm nor horror. He was still enough of a social outsider to retain his belief that the class system in Britain was moribund, and he continued to hope for a better life for the working class. But he never endorsed the welfare state. There was an element of absurdity in the grand promises of the welfare state that reminded Malcolm of the League of Nations and all the "peace ballots" it passed just prior to the carnage of World War II. Increasingly he had come to believe, in the words of his hero, Samuel Johnson, "How small, of all that human hearts endure, /That part which laws or kings can cause or cure!" Malcolm preferred saints to social engineers when it came to bringing about lasting social reforms. He admired leaders like Gandhi and de Gaulle because they led people more through the imagination than by the will: they appealed to the moral and spiritual wellsprings of the social order.

The one member of the Labour government that Malcolm held in high regard was the Foreign Secretary, Ernest Bevin. A leader of the trade union movement in England, Bevin had served with distinction in the War Cabinet. He was an ardent opponent of both the Nazi and Soviet regimes, precisely because they did not allow free trade unions. When he became Foreign Secretary under Attlee, Bevin pursued a consistently anti-Soviet policy. At first he hoped to keep England outside America's sphere of influence, but he quickly concluded that Britain needed American help to offset the Soviet threat. Malcolm preferred Bevin to Anthony Eden, who had been involved with the League of Nations and the disarmament fantasies of the 1930s and was pro-Soviet after the war. In his diary, Malcolm noted his approval for a speech Bevin had made. "Such simplicity and honesty, really finely put, a touch of imagination, almost of poetry about it. A really great man, who makes someone like Eden seem infinitely insignificant."[8]

On Malcolm's first day at the *Telegraph*, Lord Camrose came down to the editorial room and said he needed two leaders, one on Burma and one on Syria. "On Burma I duly tapped, writing almost automatic, after so many years easily coming, complete rot."[9] Malcolm soon discovered that his workload was rather light: for many months after the end of the war, the *Telegraph* consisted of only six pages, thanks to the restrictions on the use of newsprint. In the mornings he laboured over his play, *Liberation*, for which he had high hopes.

To earn some extra money, Malcolm took on the task of editing the diary of the late Italian foreign minister, Count Galeazzo Ciano. The offer had come through the publishing firm of Heinemann, where

Malcolm would soon become a literary advisor. Ciano, who was the son-in-law of dictator Benito Mussolini, had kept a diary during the war years, recording in detail the inner workings of the Italian regime. Ciano's personality, a strange combination of narcissism, naïveté and guile, struck Malcolm as providing an ideal window on the follies of power and its devotees. Fascinating as the Ciano diary was, Malcolm found himself unable to concentrate on the project. It would be two years before the volume was completed and published.

In these months of disorientation and emotional apathy, Malcolm found consolation in his newly-established friendships with Anthony Powell and George Orwell. The three men would meet for lunch at least once a week, often joined by Julian Symons, a young friend of Orwell's. Their favourite haunts were the Bodega in Bedford Street and the Bourgogne on Gerrard Street. Conversation ran on literary lines, primarily, but politics often entered in. Powell was not, on the surface, the type of man Malcolm would have found attractive. Educated at Eton and Balliol College, Oxford, Powell was a Tory – very Establishment of very Establishment. But despite this background, Powell was in fact an independent thinker, capable of the detached but acute social observation that characterised his Proustian masterpiece, *A Dance to the Music of Time*. Powell, like Graham Greene, had first noticed Muggeridge through the short-lived magazine, *Night and Day*. Later he became intrigued by Malcolm's fearless campaign to tell the truth about Soviet totalitarianism. He struck Powell as someone whose mind penetrated the surface of public affairs; he was clearly someone who understood "how politics work". At the same time Powell was amazed at Malcolm's indifference to the arts (outside literature). Above all, he found Malcolm a delightful talker: stimulating, witty and original. "Unlike most good talkers, Muggeridge needed as a rule not the smallest warming-up process."[10]

Malcolm's friendship with George Orwell, though less intimate, was nonetheless heartfelt. They had much in common. Both had lived in the East as young men, and had identified themselves as socialists championing the cause of the lower classes. They had experienced a period of disillusionment with Communism, the Soviet regime and the blindness of Leftist thinkers in the West to the threat of totalitarianism. Orwell, like Muggeridge, wrote novels, but neither man created densely textured, imagined worlds; rather, their novels tended to provide an occasion for satire and the exploration of political ideas. In addition to being serious thinkers, both men were able journalists who wrote to deadlines.

Orwell had admired *The Thirties* and introduced himself to Malcolm in Paris in 1944. But Orwell never fully understood Malcolm. In one of his "As I Please" columns, Orwell characterised Malcolm as a "neo-reactionary", along with such writers as Evelyn Waugh, Wyndham Lewis, T.S. Eliot, Aldous Huxley and, somewhat surprisingly, Graham Greene (presumably because of the latter's conversion to Catholicism).[11] Placing Malcolm in the company of these writers indicates the level of Orwell's respect for Malcolm as a writer, but the notion of Malcolm as a "reactionary" is far-fetched. Like Eliot and Waugh, Malcolm had argued that the eclipse of Christianity by secular ideologies had brought about a state of social and moral decay. But unlike those writers, he never looked back into history with nostalgia for the Middle Ages or some other period of religious integration. Orwell made a similar mistake in an essay, "Notes on Nationalism", where he classified Malcolm, along with Hugh Kingsmill, Waugh et al. as "Neo-Tories". The quintessential Neo-Tory, according to Orwell, was an "anglophobe who suddenly becomes violently pro-British".[12] Here too there is a strange misunderstanding of Malcolm's worldview. The notion of Malcolm as "violently pro-British" is so wide of the mark as to shade into the bizarre.

Malcolm tolerated these crotchets of Orwell because he admired Orwell's willingness to criticise his own political allies on the Left. He saw Orwell as a somewhat naive idealist who often tilted against windmills, but who possessed courage and honesty. He also responded to Orwell's melancholic temperament. Malcolm wrote in his diary: "Lunched with Tony Powell and George Orwell, the latter exactly like Don Quixote, very lean and egotistic and honest and foolish; a veritable Knight of the Woeful Countenance."[13] Orwell's habit of dressing and acting as if he were a proletarian, instead of an Eton-educated child of the middle class, provoked more mirth in Malcolm's mind than contempt. The corduroys and heavy boots worn by Orwell seemed all too similar to Don Quixote's rusty armour.

Malcolm recognised that Orwell was an outstanding writer. Orwell gave him the manuscript of *Animal Farm* to read and Malcolm immediately sensed that it would be a classic, even though it was to be rejected by a score of publishers before being taken on by Warburg. Malcolm suggested to Orwell that at the end of the fable, when the animals begin to walk on two feet, a herd of fellow-travellers, such as the infamous "Red Dean" of Canterbury and writers such as Kingsley Martin, should come on the scene on all fours. Orwell laughed at the idea, but declined to insert it into the manuscript.[14]

The weekly lunches with Powell and Symons were lively affairs. Malcolm delighted in goading Orwell into making some of his silly generalisations. According to Julian Symons, Malcolm played an "impish, mischievous role ... luring Orwell away from his sensible empiricism to wild flights of political fantasy, such as his view that the Labour government might induce the British electorate to accept a lower standard of living in exchange for an end to colonialism. 'Freedom for the Colonies, and a Lower Standard of Living for All', that would have been his election rallying cry."[15] Another favourite moment of Malcolm's was the time when Orwell shouted out: "All tobacconists are fascists." For a moment, Malcolm recalled, one would consider the probability of such a statement, imagining these men in their kiosks muttering fascist slogans. Then everyone except Orwell would suddenly roar with laughter.

Despite the emotional release afforded by these friendships, Malcolm began to feel cornered once again. The arrival of Christmas and the New Year prompted him to a personal stock-taking. He had finished his play, *Liberation*, but feared that it was "hurried and mediocre". It seemed to him that he ought to write a book, but he had neither the subject nor the drive to write it. On Christmas Day, 1945, he also took stock of his family. Kitty, he thought, always knew what the children needed. "In buying Christmas presents for the children she knows exactly what they want because her life is centred on them. I have no such knowledge. To me, they are interesting. I watch their development critically but affectionately." He watched his family listening to Schubert's "Unfinished" Symphony on the gramophone, a present from Kitty to their eldest, Leonard.

Leonard was now seventeen, "delicate and sensitive ... very religious, reads the Bible every day and goes to Communion every Sunday". Shy and introspective, Leonard would soon discover and join the evangelical Christian sect known as the Plymouth Brethren. John, now twelve, was the child Malcolm could most easily relate to. "John loves information. He is enthusiastic, and turns over the pages of books eagerly ..." Valentine, or Val as she was called, was eleven, and, being the only daughter, evoked a special tenderness in Malcolm. Charles had just turned ten. Malcolm noticed that he was quite different from the other children. "Charles is consumed with ambition and must be first in everything. Of his football, his report said that if his skill equalled his courage he would be unbeatable. 'Courage' was the wrong word; they meant determination or will. In the charade they did yesterday, he was radiant when he had the part of King Canute and ordered the waves to recede."

Malcolm's relationship with Kitty continued to be marked by dissension. Again and again in his diaries he praises her devotion to the children, her hard work and the moments of delight he has felt in their companionship. A few weeks before Christmas, they had even thought Kitty might be pregnant again. But Malcolm continued to feel unhappy and restless. "Alas, I can't seem to be happy. Each night I lie awake for several hours full of dark thoughts and foolish regrets, and my old longing to cease to be. Although I've often been happy, I've never felt at home in the world, and know now that I never shall."[16]

One source of tension between Malcolm and Kitty at this time was his decision to become the *Telegraph*'s correspondent in Washington, DC. Late in the autumn he had heard that the post was coming open and was given the assignment. He was feeling stifled as a leader writer, because Lord Camrose kept a fairly tight rein on his editorial staff. The "urge to be gone" had come upon him and he had acted on it. The decision involved sound journalistic instincts, of course. By the war's end it had become clear to almost everyone that there were only two "superpowers" in the world, America and Russia, and that the sun had set on the British Empire. Since he had been to Moscow, it seemed right that he go to Washington, DC, to determine what would be the shape of things to come. But in his diary he asked himself: "Is going to America really flight?"

After he had spent nearly six years away from the family, often living alone in London during the week, Kitty undoubtedly felt that Malcolm was fleeing. He told her that she and Val could join him in the autumn; the boys would be in school by then. But this plan did not solve the emotional crisis. By the early spring of 1946, the conflict between them took the same pattern it had in the past. Kitty had been having an affair with Hesketh Pearson since the early years of the war. As with Michal Vyvyan, Kitty's choice was perfectly calculated to find Malcolm's point of emotional vulnerability. Malcolm had always been jealous of Pearson because of his friendship with High Kingsmill, and he disliked Pearson's secular rationalism intensely. On the eve of his departure for America in late March, he finally sensed that Kitty and

Pearson were having an affair and confronted Kitty about it. "It all came out when I came back rather tight with her and suddenly accused her and she admitted. It gave me a great feeling of melancholy . . ."[17]

Kitty accompanied Malcolm to Liverpool, where he was to board ship, but it was a strained trip. Once the ship had set sail, Malcolm found that the seas were smooth and his cabin commodious. He passed the time reading thrillers and playing chess. But his thoughts kept returning to his failures as a writer and a husband. Perhaps because he was on the ocean, he recalled his suicide attempt in Lourenço Marques. He wrote a number of letters to Kitty while on board ship, but tore them up. There were moments, however, when he felt stabs of joy and a feeling that his existence was part of a divine plan.

In such moods I recite the Lord's Prayer to myself, finding great comfort and delight in its words. Then I see passion in all its forms as a foolish, far-off thing, and wonder at the strange noises and grimaces it has evoked. Human love seems like thin smoke rising into a vast sky, soon dissolved, and human aspiration, whatever form it takes, no more substantial. I love this mood and would ever live so, but of course cannot on this earth. Each little ego seeking in some way to record itself, to sustain itself. "Terrible is earth" is a phrase Hughie Kingsmill quoted to me once – terrible because of passion, which means the same as suffering. The realization that it is so implies a promise of release – to be patiently awaited, like sleep, and not angrily sought. I cannot really be interested in anything except this reality, and if I had the courage I should now give myself wholly to its pursuit.[18]

Writing this last sentence, Malcolm might have remembered what he wrote about the school report on his son Charles. "'Courage' was the wrong word; they meant determination or will."

Malcolm disembarked at New Brunswick, Maine, where he took a train to Boston. Within hours, he was exposed to some of the idiosyncracies of American culture. The conductor on the train explained that he had written a book for children on railroads; he handed a card to Malcolm which identified him as a "Christian Railroader". Waking up the following morning, he looked out of the window and thought the New England seacoast looked beautiful. In

Boston he got his first real experience of culture shock. Having left a country suffering under rationing and shortages of every kind, he gasped at the huge plate of bacon and eggs he was given for breakfast. Along with his breakfast, he read a sixty-two-page Sunday newspaper – more than ten times the size of the six-page *Telegraph*. As soon as he could, he got presents for his children and nylons for Kitty. Other packages would follow on a regular basis.

He continued to New York, where he was to spend three weeks acclimatising himself to America and getting to know the *Telegraph*'s New York correspondent, Alex Faulkner. The skyscrapers and commercialism of the metropolis brought out his hatred of materialism. He thought that each of these tall buildings could be labelled "First Church of Christ Capitalist". "Somehow I think this whole show is a fraud, in its own way as total and grand as Moscow."[19] To Kitty he wrote that America was rather like a Dickens novel: "tingling with energy, sparkling with humour, destitute of any authentic emotion, false and superficial and deplorable".[20] A few weeks later he would write to Hugh Kingsmill: "In no country that I've been in have I felt so completely an outsider as here . . . I miss talk. There is no talk here at all."[21] But like many European visitors, Malcolm soon found himself revising his negative first impressions. He was baffled and intrigued by the intense interest in religion and spirituality that coexisted with the material plenty of America. He grew to appreciate the hospitality and openness of his American friends.

Pacing the streets of New York, he listened to the bells tolling for Good Friday. On Easter Sunday he walked up and down Fifth Avenue, watching the crowds coming in and out of the stately Gothic churches. He did not step inside any of these churches, but they stirred up longings and regrets. He wrote to Kitty: "I think of you all constantly, and worry about how you're getting along, and regret we're not together, and wish that I'd arranged things differently, and know that if I had it wouldn't have made any difference."[22] Now that he had committed himself to this stint as Washington correspondent, he became depressed. "I have an awful feeling when I wake up in the night that I made one of the great mistakes of my life when I didn't just settle down and write on leaving the army."[23] He asked Kitty for photographs of the children.

Washington, DC, proved to be a more congenial city. Its warmth and humidity were pleasant and reminded him of Lourenço Marques. In 1946, Washington was still a quiet Southern town, not the sprawling metropolitan area it is today. After a few months in Washington apartments, he moved across the Potomac river to the Virginia countryside, which he came to love.

His cubicle at the National Press Building, on the other hand, was claustrophobic: a desk, a typewriter and two tickertape machine which spewed endless amounts of yellow paper on to the floor. "In my little office, ninth floor, I sit with the ticker machine, watching it spell out the news, then myself spell out news to send to London – this ticker, moving finger which writes and having writ moves on, now an integral part of my life."[24] Malcolm soon developed a routine. He had no legman to help him gather information, so he had to go round to Congress and each government department himself. In a BBC documentary many years later, he recalled: "I used to think of my passage from one government department to another – State, Commerce, Treasury, Interior – like the Stations of the Cross, pausing at each one to beat my breast and mutter, 'Mea Culpa! Give us this day our daily story'; then on to the next."[25] Most awesome and disconcerting of these seats of power was the Pentagon, the nerve centre for America's military forces. Its huge, cavernous corridors seemed to go on for ever: which, in fact, they did, since they had no beginning or end.

As he had in Cairo, Moscow and Calcutta, Malcolm quickly discovered – and extracted pleasure from – the most absurd aspects of his assignment. In the endless hunt for news, Malcolm found that an old stand-by was what he thought of as Transatlantic Tennis. This is how it worked: "James Reston in Washington picks up a story from London, dishes it up as from 'State Department sources', or 'informed circles in the White House', and bashes it back to London. In London they pick it up, and back it comes to Washington, where you are waiting for it at the net to smash it down – fifteen all!"[26] Malcolm also developed a taste for "minor ceremonial occasions", such as the unveiling of a portrait of the First Lady. The staging of these events, with their artificial sentiments, vacuous rhetoric and journalistic obsequiousness (as cameras flashed and reporters asked innocuous questions), never failed to amuse Malcolm.

But if the minor ceremonies provided him with the occasional treat, the spectacle of power was his meat-and-potatoes. He explained this fascination in a letter to Kingsmill: "Isn't there a sexual aberration called being a voyeur? ... Well, I'm a voyeur as far as politics are concerned, peeping with fascinated disgust at the obscenities of power." Malcolm's understanding of the relationship between the media and power in the latter part of the twentieth century was already acute. He wrote in his diary:

> Curious contemporary phenomenon, I thought, the politician or individual in power followed around by journalists notebook in hand – as though they were a kind of Greek chorus, his heralds who, instead of blowing trumpets to announce his presence, tap words. Most characteristic, I thought – a marionette man with microphone, camera, pencil, etc. the wires which manipulate him. Take away those wires and he sags, lifeless. He no longer exists. Publicity creates its own manipulations. It is the mystique of the Century of the Common Man – with rites and mysteries of its own, and priests and devotees.[27]

Americans, he thought, were capable of an unselfconscious naïveté that was by turns endearing and grotesque. A perfect illustration of this was the Air Force's testing of an atomic bomb in the Bikini Islands. "The airplane that carried it," he wrote to Kitty, "was called Dave's Dream and a pin-up girl was painted on the bomb before it was dropped. Apparently scarcely any damage was done at all. A flock of goats left on the island appeared unperturbed afterwards." Malcolm later heard that the pin-up girl was Rita Hayworth, who had wept for joy at the honour done to her. As part of the publicity manipulations for this event, the Bikini goats were brought to Washington, along with some pigs and rats who had lived through the nuclear ordeal. Malcolm went to see them. "They were receiving blood transfusions and vitamins in air-conditioned pens. A press handout answering criticism of humane societies that it was cruel to submit animals to atomic explosions contained the delightful phrase: 'They have not died in vain.' I suggested there should be a tomb to the unknown pig on which visiting statesmen might lay a handful of acorns."[28]

In the early days of Harry S. Truman's presidency, Malcolm tended to underestimate the Missourian's political savvy and resilience. Malcolm was delighted when he found out that the President's middle initial "S" stood for nothing, so that he became known as "Harry S. (for nothing) Truman". But he did not take a facetious attitude to what he considered the most serious issues of American involvement in world affairs. He was surprised and impressed by America's willingness to take up the mantle of power in the world. After World War II, the strain of isolationism in American politics had given way to an internationalist perspective.[29] Congress passed a number of foreign policy bills, including loans to Britain and the Marshall Plan, which brought needed aid to Europe. However tempted he was to satirise American pretensions, Malcolm remained firm in his belief that American power had to be deployed throughout the free world to counter the threat of Soviet expansionism. Malcolm was one of the few political commentators who knew that the Cold War had not started in 1945. Back in 1933 he had written an article on "Red Imperialism", which no one would publish. Here, as in so many other issues, Malcolm was ahead of his time, and his time vilified him for it.

He discussed these issues with sympathetic American friends, some of whom were old acquaintances. William Henry Chamberlin, the Moscow correspondent Malcolm had replaced in 1932, flattered Malcolm by being able to recall entire passages from *Winter in Moscow* verbatim. The American spy Malcolm knew in Lourenço Marques, Huntington Harris, was living in Virginia and became a frequent conversational partner. Most surprising of all was his reunion with Sir James Grigg, whom he had known in India back in 1935. After their initial row in India, they had warmed to each other. Meeting Grigg in Washington renewed a friendship that would last until Grigg's death.

Malcolm experienced little help or encouragement from the British Embassy, which was then presided over by Lord Inverchapel, "a curious figure with a rather large nose, and naturally very rubicund . . ." At one point, Malcolm had been "warned off" the embassy because he had been "unhelpful". Translated, this meant that Malcolm was guilty of "letting someone else's cat out of [his journalistic] bag . . ." Not long after this, he had a chance encounter with Inverchapel in a Turkish bath, where he had gone to seek relief for a lung ailment he was suffering at this time. The place had the unfortunate name of Ringworm Hall.

> Nonetheless the place had considerable social cachet, and when I came to and began to peer through the steam I saw quite near me the familiar features of . . . Lord Inverchapel . . . I thought it best to divert my eyes – exchanging a wink, however, with his private secretary, who was being steamed beside him, presumably to be on hand if some prescient thought or remark was steamed out of His Excellency. It all seemed, somehow, very symbolic of this federal capital whose only industry is government, and whose

only output is words. Words ceaselessly produced, like steam, and then distilled into heavy drops of information, which in turn are evaporated again into steam.[30]

The one member of the embassy staff with whom Malcolm came in most frequent contact was Donald Maclean, a Russian spy like his comrade Kim Philby. Maclean was then passing military and technical secrets on to the Soviets and would eventually make a successful defection to the USSR.

Malcolm's first months in Washington were lonely and depressed. He regretted that he had not decided to devote himself to writing books after the war. The result was a drift back into his "black moments". As he wrote in his diary: "When I concentrate my thoughts and write I'm happy and yet what resistance inwardly to doing this – the most boring company, futile conversation, weary trudging through the streets, foolish lechery preferred."[31] In his restlessness and uncertainty he contemplated leaving the *Telegraph*, or at least trying to get a different assignment. "I'd like if possible to quarrel with the D.T. and get something on the book side of the paper out of them, then settle down to do a book on the forties which really is my genre more than imaginative writing. I don't believe I've got much imagination really."[32] This last remark is clearly the overstatement of a man struggling to find the literary form that best suited his talents. Malcolm was close to the realisation that his skills as a writer did not lie in fiction. He was soon to make a final attempt at writing a novel; the result would confirm his suspicions. That he was a brilliant – and imaginative – cultural and social critic was evident to many, including such admirers as Orwell, Powell and Greene. But he had yet to discover what form this sort of writing could take.

Kitty and their daughter Val arrived in the autumn of 1946, to Malcolm's tremendous relief. He had felt remorse at leaving Kitty and the family so soon after his return from the war and pledged to her that he would never again take a position as a foreign correspondent. This was one promise he lived up to: Washington was his final extended assignment abroad. But the notion of going abroad resurfaced in a different form. He and Kitty discussed the idea of emigrating, perhaps to Canada or Australia, in order to establish a new life for themselves.

With Kitty and Val beside him, Malcolm settled down to his journalistic duties. The staff at the *Telegraph* thought his work was exemplary. He proved not only to be an astute observer of politics and culture, but also a possessor of prophetic insight. Several of his key predictions later came to pass, such as that General Dwight Eisenhower would eventually emerge as the Republican candidate for the presidency. Malcolm also predicted that Henry Wallace, the former Vice President under Roosevelt who had been replaced in Roosevelt's last term by Truman, would split off from the Democrats and run for the presidency on a third party ticket.

Having settled down, Malcolm was able to bring some order into his life. His edition of Ciano's diaries was completed and published in 1947. In the introduction he developed some of his ideas about the modern worship of political power. Using the pre-war policy of appeasement as his example, Malcolm drew a distinction between power and authority. Authority involves the responsible use of power; it is undergirded by clear principles and an unblinkered realism about human affairs. The policy of appeasement, though it purported to be "reasonable and considerate", was in fact the manifestation of Britain's inner confusion and lack of conviction. "Appeasement in this case, as it always will, only made war more certain. Those who exercise authority irresponsibly suffer from the disability that they cannot understand authority in any other terms; no traffic is possible with them except in terms of power. Inability to understand this has already cost the world most dearly, and may yet cost it more dearly still."

Malcolm insisted that the Axis powers suffered from the same decadence and confusion. Mussolini, he argued, despite his reputation as a man of action, was just as confused and vacillating in his actions as a Neville Chamberlain. Il Duce was in reality nothing more than a heightened reflection of his time: glorying in power rather than authority, and in the semblance of order rather than in order based on moral truth. Mussolini, according to Malcolm,

> was entangled in events beyond his control which shaped him rather than being shaped by him; he also became eminent only because there existed in his heart a confusion which matched the confusion without. A disintegrating civilization racing like the Gadarene swine to destruction was personified in him, in his arrogance and cupidity and shifting purposes and vanity and folly. For a little while he led the rush, and then was trampled underfoot, others struggling to the fore to be first over the cliff.[33]

Malcolm was not quite through with Ciano. After the publication of the diaries, he was also asked to edit *Ciano's Diplomatic Papers*, published in 1948. Then, a few years later, when an earlier, pre-war diary of Ciano's was discovered, Malcolm once again agreed to write an introduction. *Ciano's Hidden Diary* (1953) was translated by his good friend Andreas Mayor.

By the summer of 1947, Malcolm felt that it was time to bring his American stint to a close. Kitty and Val returned to England in August 1947. Malcolm's plan was to spend a few weeks finishing off his Washington assignment, then travel across the United States, and on to the Far East before coming home. The pressures of work for the *Telegraph* meant that he had spent all of his time in either Washington or New York. Now, with the support of the *Telegraph*, he could see America on an expenses-paid trip, and go to report on the latest developments in Japan and the rest of Asia.

Malcolm set out on his cross-country drive in early November. As he drove mile after mile through Tennessee, Alabama and Arkansas, he listened to an unceasing babel of radio preachers. The Christian Scientist preacher, he noted, claimed that Christ, "though of humble station, was 'highly successful and influential'". On the other hand, a Roman Catholic priest made a "clever pessimistic analysis of the present situation". He sensed the massive influence of undiluted Protestantism in the South. The "two great permitted indulgences" in this part of the world, he concluded, were "eating and domestic fornication".[34] In Little Rock, he attended a speech given by General Eisenhower to a group of veterans. The blaring trumpets and patriotic rhetoric left him flat.

While in New Mexico, he couldn't resist trying to extract some gossip about his former hero, D.H. Lawrence, who had lived in the state for some time. Lawrence's widow, Frieda, was still living there, with an Italian who was apparently a demon with the ladies. "Seems fitting," Malcolm wrote in his diary, " that royalties of *Lady Chatterley's Lover* should have subsidized fornication of Lawrence's successor." Through vast stretches of desert he drove on to Las Vegas, Nevada, where he went to witness the state's two major industries – gambling and divorce. He noted that in addition to these two "mysteries", there was a third sacred to Americans: speed. Speed, he thought, was "celebrated everywhere with its immense human sacrifice of blood which all accept as righteous ... [the] day when driving licence first granted to juveniles treated very much as first Communion." This, in turn, led to gloomy musings about the state of Western civilisation. Malcolm was inclined to agree with Clemenceau, who had said that Americans were the only people who had gone from barbarism to decadence without ever having passed through the stage of being civilised.[35]

After a few days in Los Angeles and San Francisco, Malcolm flew, with a refuelling stop in Alaska, to Tokyo. Japan too was experiencing the dominance of America, from the atomic bombs dropped on Hiroshima and Nagasaki, to the military and political reforms which the victors were bringing to the vanquished. He went to the Japanese legislature, or Diet, where democracy was in the process of being born. Another strange experience was a visit to the war trial of General Tojo and his cronies. The defendants were as solemn and inscrutable as statues; from the expressions on their faces, they could just as easily be the judges as the accused. Malcolm found it a grim, tedious spectacle.

Malcolm was able to join an official visit of the Japanese emperor, Hirohito, to Hiroshima to witness the destruction wrought by the atom bomb. The emperor was not a physically impressive man. As Malcolm wrote in his diary, Hirohito's "method of acknowledging cheers of crowd lifting of homberg hat and putting it back; nervous, shy, stuttering, pathetic figure, formerly god." The efforts to reconstruct the city had done little to alter the utter devastation wrought by the bomb. Malcolm was able to chat briefly with one of the few survivors, a Jesuit priest.

The single biggest journalistic coup of Malcolm's time in Japan was the exclusive interview he was granted with General Douglas Mac-Arthur, who presided over the American occupation of Japan. He found MacArthur a ludicrous figure. Smoking a large black pipe, he spoke interminably about the glories of democracy and Christianity that America had brought to Japan. "He spoke of the Sermon on the Mount," Malcolm recorded in his diary, "producing exceptionally large number of clichés ('Freedom is a heady wine,' etc.). I was bored and embarrassed." MacArthur's flow was unstoppable. "Occasionally I made feeble efforts to check the flow of words, but with no avail. It had to run irresistibly on ... An inconceivable performance."[36]

After the interview, Malcolm made the mistake of recounting the performance to an American State Department official. The official was amused, but a member of MacArthur's staff who overhead the conversation was not, and a miniature scandal ensued. Malcolm suffered no ill effects, but the State Department man was sent back to the States.

The marathon journey home took Malcolm to Hong Kong, Bangkok, Rangoon, Calcutta and Cairo. India brought back many memories, good and bad. At the airport he was able to see his old Moslem friend, Shahid Suhrawardy, who filled him in on news of his other Bengali friends. On the verge of independence, India was in a state of turmoil. The end of British colonial rule was something that Malcolm had long hoped for, but he and Shahid were both pessimistic about the nation's prospects for the future. In his diary he concluded: "Twilight of Empire. Now the night."[37]

« 14 »

The Art of Non-Conforming
1948–1952

MALCOLM SLIPPED back into his routine in London with remarkable ease. Despite having been abroad for nearly two years, and having recently traversed the globe, Malcolm barely broke his stride on returning to England. He and the family had moved to yet another address – 5 Cambridge Gate, near Regent's Park. The rhythm of his day rarely changed – writing in the mornings, eating lunch at the Authors' Club, strolling in the park with his neighbour, Anthony Powell, in the afternoons, stopping in at the *Telegraph* in the evening to write his leader, often dining out late or entertaining guests at the flat.

Malcolm, it seems, had finally settled down. Even the tone and character of his diaries changed at this time: they became longer and more detailed, more focused on recording personalities and events, less tortured and introspective, and much more discreet. Malcolm had his own pet theory for this shift to a calmer, more regular pattern of life. It was his belief that "highly imaginative people are invariably miserable when they are young, and on the whole, grow progressively happier."[1]

The proprietor and editors of the *Telegraph* had been delighted with Malcolm's dispatches from Washington, and on his return he was given something of a promotion. His chief assignment continued to be leader-writing, but he was awarded a broader and more serious range of topics, including the job of covering the House of Commons. Malcolm found this a mixed blessing: it was better than writing leaders on subjects like Burma, but it required him to comment on yet another parliamentary body at a time when he felt that democratic institutions were losing their authority and meaning. Like many of his literary friends and contemporaries, including Orwell, Waugh and Powell,

Malcolm feared that the Labour Party's efforts to create a welfare state and also to appease the Soviets would lead to a catastrophic loss of freedom. He wrote in his diary after a visit to the House of Commons: "Thought as I watched that there appears to be no middle position between a free and a slave totalitarian economy, and that all attempts, such as the Labour Party has been making, to find and hold a middle position, are doomed to failure."[2] This sort of comment cannot be written off as the paranoia of a political reactionary. Orwell, who remained to his death a man of the Left, had the same fears and put them into his novels, *Animal Farm* and *1984*.

Malcolm hoped to land a less journalistically demanding position, something that would enable him to write more about culture and ideas, and give him greater responsibility. In the years after his return from America Malcolm was told that he was being considered for the editorship of both the *Spectator* and the *Daily Mail*, but neither of these positions was ever offered to him. Within the *Telegraph*, he lobbied hard to take over the job of chief reviewer of non-fiction books from Harold Nicolson. Early in 1949 he was given the post. Under this new arrangement, he was still expected to write a few leaders each week, but he was given the larger cultural portfolio that he had desired. Under the new arrangement, he needed to come into the *Telegraph* office only on Fridays and Sundays.

Not long after his return to London, Malcolm embarked on a whole new career, though he did not know it at the time. He was invited by the British Broadcasting Corporation to take part in a radio programme known as *The Critics*. The purpose of the programme was to have several critics review books, art exhibitions, films and theatre performances. Each member of the panel prepared a brief review which they read, but they were also expected to participate in a lively, wide-ranging conversation following the review segment. Malcolm signed up for a series of six programmes, for which he was to be paid twelve guineas per programme.

This was not Malcolm's first experience of radio broadcasting. Back in 1936 he had written a short story, "Summer in Simla", that was read (by an actor) on the BBC. Then, during the war, while he was stationed in London with the Field Security Police, Malcolm had broadcast a short essay on the Romantic poet, William Wordsworth. In this first broadcast in his own voice, on New Year's Day, 1941, Malcolm managed to inject a note of political controversy. He focused on Wordsworth's rejection of the French Revolution – the event that had once filled him with utopian longings. Caught up in the ideological abstractions of the era, Wordsworth, like many of his contemporaries, had overlooked the bloody, totalitarian dimension of the French Revolution. Malcolm took aim at those in Britain who were guilty of the same blindness about the Russian Revolution and its consequences. There were those in his own time, he said, who also "hoped to see a new world come to pass because an old tyranny had fallen, and were ready to forgive much violence and bloodshed".[3]

It is not difficult to see why radio broadcasting would have appealed to Malcolm in the post-war years. With his book-writing career stalled, his only audience consisted of readers of the conservative *Daily Telegraph*. Radio broadcasts, on the other hand, reached a huge and diverse public, generating a tremendous amount of publicity for the personalities they featured. During the war, a single broadcast of the programme *Any Questions?* had catapulted the scientist Julian Huxley and the philosopher C.E.M. Joad to national prominence. The medium was perfectly suited to someone like Malcolm, a brilliant talker with a mordant wit and a rich sense of irony. As a journalist he had mastered the technique of condensing his thoughts into pungent, epigrammatic phrases. On many of these panel discussions, Malcolm was a stiletto, while the others were butter-knives.

The routines for recording panel programmes were fairly similar. The BBC producers invited the panellists to a meal – lunch or dinner, depending on the recording schedule at Broadcasting House. Over the meal the producers would explain the format of the programme and ask the contributors to give their arguments a dry-run. At some of these meals, Malcolm noted, producers attempted to steer the conversation away from areas of controversy. But they were usually genial occasions where many BBC producers got to know and admire Malcolm. When the meal was over and the panellists had been given a short break to gather their thoughts, the recording began.

For many years Malcolm thought of his radio broadcasts largely as a means to an end, a source of publicity that would create a larger audience for his writings and make him more eligible for a job as a newspaper or magazine editor. Though he always considered his radio and television work to be inferior in value when compared to his writing, he became fascinated by the challenge these media presented. Early in 1948 he wrote in his diary: "Rather intrigued by the idea of mastering broadcasting technique, which is entirely different from journalism or public speaking."[4]

Malcolm's ambivalence about the BBC as an institution, however, was equally strong. Though the extra income he received from these broadcasts was helpful, Malcolm never attempted to tone down his rhetoric or opinions on the BBC; he spoke his mind from the beginning. After only two or three broadcasts of *The Critics*, Malcolm found himself in hot water. "Donald Boyd delivered a short lecture, saying that in last week's programme some of my remarks had had to be cut out because they were too strong. There is something peculiarly oppressive and depressing about the whole atmosphere of Broadcasting House. It reminded me of being in Russia."[5] Because *The Critics* was pre-recorded, anything that the producers considered offensive or excessively controversial could be edited out, as Malcolm quickly discovered.

The next conflict with the BBC came only a month later, when Malcolm read a talk on Sidney and Beatrice Webb for the Third Programme. Ostensibly a review of the Webbs' book, *Our Partnership*, this piece is marked by the familiar blend of intellectual critique and damaging personal anecdote that would become the hallmark of Malcolm's career as a media commentator. Beatrice, he recounted, used to order Sidney to go for a walk after lunch, while she rested on her bed. But Sidney, he continued, "was liable to employ what might well be described as Fabian tactics, and go only as far as the nearest convenient haystack, where he too, would have a nap." He attributed to Beatrice Webb the statement: "Old people take to pets, and mine is the USSR." A tabby or a pekinese, Malcolm adds, "might have been easier to handle and certainly better house-trained". He concludes by comparing Beatrice to Don Quixote: "she finished up enmeshed in her own self-deception, adulating a regime which bore as little relation to the Fabian Good Life as Dulcinea del Toboso to the Mistress of Don Quixote's dreams."[6]

Several of the Webbs' friends and relatives voiced their objections to the broadcast. But no one was more outraged than the chairman of the BBC himself, Lord Simon. He immediately drafted a memorandum cancelling the rebroadcast of the programme:

I listened to this broadcast with growing horror, incredulity and anger. The Webbs were personal friends of mine, so I am not an impartial judge. But nobody can doubt that they were very great public servants; after all they were buried in Westminster Abbey. The Muggeridge broadcast expressed only contempt and derision, mocking their personal characteristics, mental and physical, with practically no regard for truth and decency. It was the most disgraceful piece of bad taste that I have ever heard. Why was he chosen in view of his past career? How did any producer come to pass such a scandalous script?"[7]

Despite Lord Simon's indignation, opinion within the BBC was divided. The head of the Third Programme, Harman Grisewood, sent a congratulatory letter to the head of the Talks department, calling the programme "one of the best we have had recently".[8] When the controversy erupted, Grisewood wrote to the Director of the Spoken Word, George Barnes, in defence of Malcolm's broadcast. Barnes concurred and sought to reverse Lord Simon's decision. When it became clear that Lord Simon was adamant, Barnes reluctantly wrote to Malcolm:

> We have learned that your talk on Beatrice Webb's Journal has given some pain to friends and admirers of Mrs Webb's and, in the circumstances, we have decided not to repeat it Monday. We will, of course, pay in full the fee which you were offered for the repeat, and we shall merely make a substitution of another programme. I regret very much if this decision of ours causes you disappointment, and I hope that you will agree with us in regarding any pain caused to living people about a friend recently dead as overriding other considerations.[9]

Rather than debate the issue, Malcolm wrote Barnes a three-word letter: "I quite understand." In his diary, Malcolm mused: "Imagine that this is the end of my brief connection with the BBC."[10]

Contrary to several of Malcolm's later, somewhat misleading, statements, the flap over the Webb broadcast did not keep him off the airwaves for a long period of time. Three months later he was back on the air doing another series of *The Critics* broadcasts. In fact, Malcolm was one of the most popular contributors to BBC radio programming over the ten years from 1948 to 1957. According to a scholar who has researched Malcolm's radio career, he participated in at least 144 programmes in this decade. The actual number is undoubtedly higher, because the overseas broadcasting services were not required in those days to keep written records of their programmes."[11] Since this was before Malcolm became an interviewer, nearly all of these programmes called for a substantive contribution from him.

Malcolm felt from the outset that the BBC was not independent and objective. In a review of Lord Reith's memoirs, published in 1949, Malcolm criticised the paternalistic attitude of the first Director-General. Reith's lofty demeanour, he argued, masked the plain fact that the BBC was a largely unregulated monopoly. Conflicts "between Governors responsible for policy and a Director-General responsible for executing it are endemic in publicly controlled enterprises. They represent a recurrent, and perhaps fatal, defect in a socialised society."[12] A decade later, Malcolm extended his critique by pointing out the intellectual conformism of the BBC. "By appearing to be free of governmental control, its subservience is the more effective. The Corporation may be relied on always in the last resort, to operate on the side of conformism. The Party Line does not have to be formulated; it beats naturally in the hearts, speaks in the mouths, wanly illumines the eyes of those . . . ultimately responsible for its direction." George Orwell once told Malcolm that Broadcasting House gave him the idea for the Ministry of Truth in his novel, *1984*.[13]

During the war, the BBC had achieved a high level of public approval and admiration. But it wasn't long before a reaction to the paternalism of the BBC set in. The Corporation, in line with its educational mission, tended to air programmes that were organised like lectures; this gave the impression that it was talking down to its audience. Hence the nickname "Auntie BBC". The Corporation came under increasing pressure to create programmes that were more democratic: these included the use of panels representing multiple viewpoints, as well as programmes that involved audience participation.

Malcolm benefited directly from the change in BBC policy. In addition to *The Critics*, he also became associated with *The Brains Trust* (originally, and confusingly, titled *Any Questions?*), a programme that featured a panel responding to questions from the audience. In time, *The Brains Trust* would move from radio to television, and from the studio to locations all over Britain. Malcolm was asked to take part in dozens of BBC programmes, on both the home and overseas services, including *Friday Forum*, *Woman's Hour*, *Fifty-one Society*, *Frankly Speaking*, *At Home and Abroad* and many others. Myrna Grant, an expert on Malcolm's radio career, concluded that "Muggeridge was not merely a favourite of a small number of staff producers within a department but [of] men and women throughout the Corporation

[who] facilitated his controversial career and enabled him to have national exposure." In an interview with Grant, Malcolm explained this broad support within the BBC as a direct result of his candour: "One Christmas I had, I think without exaggeration, fifty Christmas cards from the BBC people, most of them quite high up, really saying to me in effect, 'I'm glad you said [one thing or another] . . . of course, I can't agree with you in the circumstances, but I'd like you to know I am really happy to think that you did that.'"[14]

It is worth stressing the controversial nature of Malcolm's commentary on the BBC from the beginning of his broadcasting career because the most enduring and damaging criticism of him over the years is that throughout his life he was guilty of "biting the hand that fed him". Malcolm certainly found the extra income he brought in as a result of his broadcasts helpful; it enabled him, for example, to buy new suits for his children.[15] But from his Wordsworth broadcast of 1941 Malcolm spoke his mind. In his essay, "My Life with the BBC", he acknowledged that the Corporation "disposed of enormous patronage", and that many contributors were "easily induced to be compliant" because of their fear of losing the fees they were paid.

There is a broader interpretation of the "biting the hand" judgement against Malcolm, which says that his attacks on the media were hypocritical, coming as they did from a man who owed his fame to radio and television. But that argument has been used in a highly arbitrary and selective fashion. A good many writers and scholars have owed their fame and popularity to the broadcast media. That is hardly a disqualification for criticising the media. Malcolm became an expert practitioner in the new technologies of radio and television; he knew the enormous power they had, the radical change they were bringing about in modern culture, and the temptations they offered to those who produced them and those who consumed them.

In the late 1940s, however, Malcolm's media career was only in the embryonic stage. Having come to a standstill in his book-writing career, Malcolm found himself in the painful position of watching the careers of his contemporaries begin to flourish. Graham Greene had already published *The Power and the Glory* and *The Heart of the Matter*, he had just written the screenplay for the highly-regarded film *The Third Man*, starring Orson Welles and Joseph Cotten. Anthony Powell shared with Malcolm the manuscript of his novel, *A Question of Upbringing*, which would become the first volume in the twelve novels known collectively as *A Dance to the Music of Time*. George

Orwell would soon become famous as the author of *Animal Farm* and *1984*. In his diaries, Malcolm admitted that these successes led to pangs of envy and self-pity.

He decided to write a novel that would satirise an obscure, frustrated writer like himself. Since many of the best-selling novels of the day were thrillers or murder mysteries, he chose to write in that genre. Malcolm's strategy for the novel was to have his cake and eat it too: the book would be marketed as a thriller, but one of its primary intentions was to parody – and thus undermine – what Malcolm thought of as an inferior genre of fiction. The result is *Affairs of the Heart* (a title forced on Malcolm by his publisher), which came out in 1949. It is Malcolm's last published novel, by far the most conventional in terms of plot and characterisation, full of epigrammatic wit, recognisable caricatures and flashes of insight, but failing to develop into a convincing story.

The protagonist, once again called Wraithby, is a struggling writer who takes advances from publishers but fails to produce much. At the office of his literary agent he sees a pair of writers, Ossian Routledge and Philip Ambrose, who write popular thrillers under the pen name of Anthony Anstruther. It is evident that Routledge is the dominant member of the pair, socially and culturally superior to Ambrose. The next morning, Wraithby visits the British Museum to do some research. There he again sees Routledge, who appears agitated, and who then collapses and dies after suffering a seizure of some kind. Soon afterwards, Wraithby is summoned back to the office of his agent. It seems that Routledge's widow thinks her husband has died in suspicious circumstances, despite the coroner's verdict of "natural causes", and she wants Wraithby to investigate. The prime suspects, of course, are Philip Ambrose and Mrs Routledge herself, but Wraithby also learns that Routledge was having affairs with four different women. Any one of them might have had a motive for killing him.

The plot of *Affairs* was suggested by Palmer, the man in the Ministry of Information with whom Malcolm shared an office in the first months of the war. The earnest, politically engaged Palmer wrote thrillers in collaboration with a man named Hilary St George Saunders. Palmer's adulation of Saunders is reflected in Ambrose's admiration for Routledge. Malcolm thought he detected an undertone of envy and jealousy in Palmer; these darker traits are brought out in the character of Ambrose.

As with his other novels, *Affairs* is filled with thinly veiled caricatures. The literary agent, Elphinstone, was modelled directly on Malcolm's agent, David Higham. Elphinstone is depicted as sycophantic to his successful writers and condescending to failures like Wraithby. When Wraithby mentions his need for money, he causes offence. "A mention of ready cash produced the same disagreeable impression as the use of the word 'poor' instead of 'under-privileged' at an American discussion group or of 'abortion' instead of 'curettage' in the consulting-room of a Harley Street gynaecologist."[16] But Higham was so pleased to be in the book that he pointed it out to everyone he met and bragged that *Affairs* was easily the best thing that Malcolm had ever written.

Perhaps the most effective caricature is of Evelyn Waugh, who appears as the Catholic writer Gerald Manifold. Waugh later paid tribute to Malcolm's satire when he came to write an autobiographical novel, *The Ordeal of Gilbert Pinfold*. The humour at the expense of Gerald Manifold had stuck in Waugh's mind.

Despite the clever caricatures and epigrams, most of the reviewers were tepid in their reaction to the novel. They complained that at the end of the novel Wraithby simply gives up, leaving the reader hanging just at the point when the mystery should be solved. Some commentators have assumed that this was due to Malcolm's laziness. But such criticisms miss the point: *Affairs* is a parody of a mystery novel, and the protagonist's lack of interest in a factual solution is meant to deflate the reader's hunger for superficial answers. By the end of the novel, Wraithby has made a more important discovery; in the words of Samuel Johnson, he has learned "the vanity of human wishes".

Affairs is really about the emptiness of the passions of lust, greed and ambition. The closer Wraithby comes to the truth about Routledge, the more he realises that there is a hollowness at the centre of this mystery. Despite Routledge's worldly success, he lived an utterly superficial existence. His four mistresses – the sensual rector's daughter, the bohemian writer, the naïve Woolworth's sales girl, and the sleek but chilly socialite – appear to indicate a connoisseur's taste for richness and variety. But when he meets each of these women and learns their stories, Wraithby realises that each new affair is a monotonous repetition, the same *danse macabre* of lust and vanity.

Though it appears to be his least autobiographical novel, *Affairs* is as focused on Malcolm's own experience as anything he ever wrote. Just as he had written about Samuel Butler, who represented to

Malcolm an extreme version of some of his own worst tendencies, so the character of Ossian Routledge is an exaggeration of Malcolm's obsessive need for sexual entanglements. The London flat used for trysts, the reconstruction of Routledge's pick-up lines and tactics, the women themselves – they were Malcolm's own experiences. Routledge's cheerful amorality, however, contrasts with the guilt and self-loathing that characterise Wraithby. Once again, Malcolm gives himself the name of Wraithby, the ghost who inhabits a body, the stranger in a strange land.

Affairs also contains a brief but revealing encounter between Wraithby and his wife, Laura. Like Kitty, Laura is homely and simple in her tastes, preferring her garden in the country to the sophisticated life of London. In the novel, Laura has taken the step of becoming a Catholic, something Kitty had not done. According to Beatrice Webb's diary, Malcolm was seriously considering converting to Catholicism as early as 1944.[17] But Wraithby thinks that Laura's conversion has made her "complacent". There is more than a hint of self-justification in that judgement. His own explanation for not converting was that joining the Church would rob him of his intellectual independence and questing spirit. A year after the publication of *Affairs*, his friend Auberon Herbert asked Malcolm if he was considering becoming a Catholic. The answer was negative, as he recorded in his diary: "I see the force and importance of the Catholic Church, but I could not, in honesty, accept its dogma."[18]

Wraithby acknowledges that he deceives and neglects Laura. But she is depicted as having an inner peace and strength of character that is not merely complacent. That inwardness is something he cannot penetrate. Wraithby feels himself to be an outsider in relation to his own wife, but his respect for her is clear. In a highly rhetorical fashion, Wraithby claims that the decay of Western civilisation makes individual actions insignificant. But Laura is not so willing to absolve the individual of responsibility. Her comments on Wraithby's investigation are direct and incisive. Of Mrs Routledge, she says: "'Well, it seems to me that she was in love with her husband.' Then, sensing the possibility of an interruption from me, 'It can happen, you know.'"[19] It does not take a prodigious feat of imagination to sense the sting Malcolm felt when Kitty herself said these words to him.

There can be no doubt that Malcolm's love for Kitty was genuine. He counted on her forgiveness. His diaries contain a number of spontaneous moments of affection and gratitude for Kitty's love: "My darling looks anxiously at all our brows to see if they are troubled, soothes them gently with her love, and sends us calmly away. Sometimes I wonder fearfully how I can have deserved such good fortune as to have her love and compassion."[20]

Aside from Kitty, the one person whom Malcolm counted on for friendship was Hugh Kingsmill. Early in 1948, however, he was shocked to realise that he might lose his beloved Hughie. Kingsmill's health had been deteriorating after the war. He was suffering from a duodenal ulcer, an affliction that undoubtedly reflected the intense stress brought on by constant financial difficulties. On March 30, 1948, he suffered a haemorrhage and was admitted to the Royal Sussex County Hospital in Brighton. Malcolm could not get away to see him immediately, but his first thought was to ask the editors at *Punch*, for which Kingsmill wrote book reviews, to continue paying him while he was in the hospital. From Kingsmill's daughter he heard an anecdote about Hughie that delighted him. Not long after he had arrived at the hospital, a doctor, flanked by a number of nurses, told him that he could wait a week to see if he was, indeed, suffering from an ulcer. What would happen at the end of that week, he asked. "You'll probably die," was the reply. What other choice did he have? "You can be operated on at once to find out if you've got an ulcer." What would happen if he chose that option? "You'll probably die at once." Kingsmill said he'd have to consult his wife, but the doctor reminded him that the decision was really his alone. "Well, as there seems nothing in it, and I'd prefer drastic measures, I'll be operated on at once." Sadly, the operation did not discover the ulcer, a mistake that would prove to be fatal.[21]

After the operation, Kingsmill regained his strength, to Malcolm's great relief. Malcolm came to visit on April 17, where he found a "haggard and old-looking" Hughie.

> He was asleep when I got there, but when he woke up and saw me sitting by his bed such a smile of happiness came on his face that I was deeply moved. We talked for about two hours and he was quite up to his old form . . . He had been reading Sherlock Holmes stories which, as he said, with all their inherent absurdity, never quite lose their charm, especially when one is ill or fatigued. He quoted a line from Browning's *Andrea del Sarto*: "I am often tireder than you think" and said that it was one of those everlasting remarks which can be described as "husbandly".[22]

When Kingsmill was released in early May, he and his wife Dorothy stayed for a week at the Muggeridges' flat. Malcolm and Kingsmill sat on benches in Regent's Park and spent the afternoons talking. Malcolm sensed that he might not have Kingsmill around for much longer and made a concerted effort to see him often in the ensuing months.

Kingsmill suffered several attacks towards the end of 1948, but he recovered sufficiently to carry on. On January 20, 1949, Malcolm recorded in his diary:

> Hughie came to lunch, and we were much amused by an extract from Archbishop Lang's memoirs in the *Sunday Times*, particularly the statement that on a stalking expedition, in order to protect the King from a heavy shower 'the Archbishop, claiming the privilege of a subject to cover the person of his sovereign, lay down on top of him'. On this awesome picture Hughie dwelt at great length, imagining what would have been the reaction of some Highland gillie who had come upon the monarch and the archbishop thus disposed under an overhanging rock.[23]

A few days later, after another lunch with Kingsmill, Malcolm and Kitty discussed why Hughie's conversation was more enlivening than anyone else's. They decided that it was because "his interest in people and things is, as far as it is possible for a human being's to be, detached from his own personal interests."[24]

Kingsmill was readmitted to the hospital in Brighton on April 10. From there he wrote to Malcolm: "Balmy spring breezes blowing in from the sea outside, and all past springs revive, but I hope that this decaying old husk will release me at not too long a date to recover all the beauty of those old days in some other form."[25] He was too weak to be operated on, and was kept alive by constant blood transfusions. Malcolm, visiting on May 7, was touched to discover that Kingsmill had read all his articles and was able to talk about them. They discussed what books Malcolm could send him. Kingsmill wanted Samuel Johnson's *Lives of the Poets*; he felt that Johnson's stoic acceptance of suffering and lack of rancour were what he needed then. He kept begging Malcolm to stay, but after two hours he had to leave. Malcolm and Hesketh Pearson were to go down to Brighton the following day, but Dorothy called to say that Hughie had become gravely ill. On Sunday night, May 15, she called again to say that he had died. She said that his final vision, on Good Friday, was of Christ coming to him and passing to him all of his pain.

Malcolm wrote a moving obituary for the *New English Weekly*. With Pearson, he arranged a memorial service, held St Paul's Church, Covent Garden, on June 9. He and Pearson read the lessons. They also set about trying to get a Civil List pension for Dorothy Kingsmill, who was destitute. It was a cause that would require a great deal of time and effort over the next several months. Malcolm spent many hours in the offices of bureaucrats lobbying for the pension, a torture that he endured out of his love for Hughie.

In order to preserve their memories of Kingsmill, Malcolm and Pearson decided to write a book about their friend in the form of an exchange of letters. *About Kingsmill*, published in 1951, was not a book destined to reach a large audience. Kingsmill's books had themselves sold poorly, but he was too important to his two friends for them to calculate the cost of paying tribute to him. Precisely because Kingsmill had played such an important role in Malcolm's spiritual development, his death elicited the most vigorous and persuasive writing that Malcolm had produced in a decade. Whereas Pearson's letters are chatty and anecdotal, Malcolm's letters are impassioned, championing Kingsmill as a man with mystical insight into the meaning of life. The only issue where the two men clash is over Kingsmill's religious life. Pearson, himself an agnostic, stressed Kingsmill's powerful reaction to his father's hypocritical Methodism. But Kingsmill had revealed his continuing attachment to the Christian faith to Malcolm.

Malcolm upheld Kingsmill as a mystic who was far more deeply in touch with reality than modern materialists. "That scepticism which, contrary to the generally held conviction, is characteristic of the religious temperament, led him to examine critically and then dismiss both scientific utopianism and apocalypse-ism." In fact, he continued, Kingsmill rejected materialism because it was more credulous and naïve than a belief in transcendence.[26]

In one of his last letters, Malcolm confessed that he could never see any of Kingsmill's faults, though he knew his friend had his fair share. A true friendship, Malcolm declared, had its own standards. "Friendship is the most delightful of human relationships. Passion is not disinterested, but friendship is as nearly so as is possible in human beings. One wants nothing of a friend except the delight of his company. The satisfaction of appetite, the pursuit of power – these are, in the end, sombre activities which cannot but imprison the spirit. Friendship is their converse, and brings release."[27]

Not long after Kingsmill's death, Malcolm lost another, but quite different, friend, George Orwell. After Malcolm had gone to Washington as the *Telegraph*'s correspondent, Orwell had left London and gone to live on the island of Jura, off the Scottish coast. Originally, Orwell had been invited merely to have a brief vacation on Jura at the home of his friend David Astor, a writer for the *Observer* and the son of a lord, but he became so taken with the idea of living there that he bought his own house on the island. There he had completed *1984*. But his deteriorating health forced him to retreat to a tuberculosis sanitorium in the Gloucestershire village of Cranham. Malcolm and Anthony Powell went to visit him there in February 1949. Malcolm found him "the same old trusty, lovable egotist", but was acutely aware that Orwell did not have much longer to live. Orwell himself seemed to understand that his days were numbered, but he eagerly described his plans for the next ten years. The conversation went on for over three hours. At one point Orwell, who smoked cigarettes despite his TB, produced from under the bed a bottle of rum, which the three of them promptly consumed.

Orwell gave Malcolm a copy of *1984* in typescript, prior to its publication. Malcolm's first reaction to this negative Utopia, or "dystopia", was highly critical. *Animal Farm*, a satirical fable, was more congenial to him than the bleak future world of Big Brother. It seemed to him too close to the preposterous fantasies of H.G. Wells to be convincing; apparently it didn't occur to him that *1984* was just a different sort of fable, not an attempt to make accurate predictions. However, he told the book's publisher, Warburg, that it would be a best-seller. Soon after *1984* appeared, Malcolm recorded a review of it for the BBC Third Programme with T.R. Fyvel, a Jewish writer and editor, who was a friend of Orwell. Fyvel recalled the programme in his own memoir of Orwell: "Because we knew that Orwell would be listening from his bed, Muggeridge suggested that after paying due tribute to his grim vision of the future . . ., we should make our conversation as lighthearted as possible." They singled out the scene near the end of the novel, where Winston Smith is tortured by having a cage full of rats placed over his head. Malcolm and Fyvel observed that the scene was reminiscent of a room full of boys in a boarding-school concocting the worst tortures their imaginations were capable of. "In the end one boy says: 'I'll tell you what's the worst thing. You're all tied up and a cage full of stinking rats is put over your face. First one rat bites your eye. Then another bites your lips. Then another starts eating your nose.' At this point the dormitory prefect calls out, 'Silence, all of you! Lights out.' . . . We heard from Orwell that, listening in bed, he had laughed out loud. A crumb of solace, anyway."[28]

In September of 1949, Orwell was moved to University College Hospital in London, which meant that Malcolm and Anthony Powell could visit him more often. Malcolm found him "inconceivably wasted", with "a queer sort of clarity in his expression and elongation of his features". Looking more than ever the Knight of the Woeful Countenance, he evoked Malcolm's sympathies. Orwell was about to get married to Sonia Brownell, an attractive and vivacious woman who worked at the literary magazine *Horizon* with Cyril Connolly. Orwell, who always thought of Malcolm as worldly-wise and well travelled, had a habit of asking him to find him clothes. When Malcolm went off to Washington as a correspondent, Orwell had asked him to send him a good pair of boots. From his bed in the hospital he said he wanted a bed-jacket to wear for his marriage ceremony. Powell took on that assignment and came back with what Malcolm described as "an elaborate velvet smoking jacket".

For a brief time after his wedding, Orwell seemed to improve, but his condition soon deteriorated. His eagerness to go on living, to travel to a Swiss sanitorium, to plan books that he wanted to write – all these desires struck Malcolm as touching, but also as sad. Unlike Kingsmill, who had died with a spirit of acceptance and grace, Orwell seemed to be entangled in the will. Malcolm continued to boggle at some of Orwell's more bizarre ideas, such as the notion that capital punishment was still legal in Britain because judges derived an erotic thrill from it, or that an advertisement for underwear which referred to the Greek god Mercury was, to him, more blasphemous than any mockery of Christianity.

On Christmas Day, Malcolm and Powell visited Orwell, who looked "deathly and wretched". Malcolm last saw Orwell on January 19, when he realised that his friend was at the "last gasp". Two days later, he heard that Orwell had died. In his diary Malcolm wondered about Orwell's strange combination of romanticism and an interest in the "dreariest aspects of life".

All the same, there was something very lovable and sweet about him, and without any question, an element of authentic prophecy in his terrible vision of the future. His particular contribution to this sort of literature was his sense that a completely collectivised State would be produced not, as Wells had envisaged, in terms of scientific efficiency, not, as Aldous Huxley had envisaged, in terms of a heartless but vivid eroticism, but to the accompaniment of all the dreary debris and shabbiness of the past — mystique of materialist Puritanism . . .[29]

The arrangements for Orwell's funeral were handled by Malcolm and Powell. Though he was not a believer, Orwell had requested that he be buried according to the rites of the Church of England. The funeral service was held on a cold morning in an unheated church near Regent's Park. The small group of people gathered there, Malcolm noted, seemed to consist entirely of Jews or unbelievers. Powell had chosen one of the lessons from the Book of Ecclesiastes, and one verse struck Malcolm as particularly moving: "Man goeth to his long home, and the mourners go about the streets." After lunching with the Fyvels, Malcolm read the many obituaries of Orwell, seeing in them "how the legend of a human being is created . . ." He himself was to get caught up in the politics of Orwell's posthumous fame when, in the early 1960s, his wife Sonia asked him to write the official biography of Orwell. Malcolm agreed, more out of loyalty to Orwell's memory than from a desire to undertake the project. Apparently Sonia was counting on Malcolm's indolence, because she really did not want anyone to write a biography of Orwell. So long as Malcolm could be held up as the writer working on the authorised biography, other would-be biographers could be held at bay. After a few years, the pretence was dropped and other biographers laboured to overcome the barriers put up by Sonia and tell the story of Orwell's life.[30]

Having lost two friends whom he considered to be, in their different ways, honest and courageous seekers, Malcolm pondered his own accomplishments and remaining ambitions. He knew that *Affairs of the Heart* was little more than an "entertainment", as Graham Greene called some of his novels, and that his book on Kingsmill would appeal to only a small audience. The BBC asked him to take part in an ever-increasing number of programmes, but broadcasting, while pleasing to his vanity, was not on the same plane as serious writing.

Malcolm did in fact conceive a number of ambitious literary projects. He began a novel with the working title of "A Hero of Our Time", which was to trace the life of a Welsh liberal who got involved in many of the grand political causes of the twentieth century, only to find himself mired in fantasy and futility. Only a few thousand words of this novel were written. Another discarded product of the time was a play, "Comrade Caliban", for which Malcolm had high hopes. This, too, never appeared on the stage or in print. He even considered writing a study of the intellectuals who had created the utopian ideologies that had plagued the modern world. The culprits were to include Rousseau, Shelley, Whitman, Tolstoy and Nietzsche. Malcolm wanted the title of the book to be "The Green Stick", from a story Tolstoy told about his brother Nicholas. As a boy, Nicholas thought he knew where there was buried in the ground a magic green stick which had an inscription telling how the welfare of mankind was to be achieved. Malcolm's book, unfortunately, remained buried in his mind. But he would later use the title for the first volume of his autobiography.

The most compelling of these projects was an obvious choice: a book to be called "The Forties", which presented him with the chance to repeat the success of *The Thirties*. He worked at "The Forties" in a desultory fashion, in scattered bursts of effort, between 1948 and 1950. The diaries for these years contain a number of admonitions to himself to work harder on the book and build some momentum, but eventually even these fade away. "The Forties" was never completed.

How to account for such a wasted opportunity? Part of the reason is that the decade was dominated by the war, and Malcolm found writing about war tedious and unrewarding. He once wrote: "War is collective passion, and its true horror is, not so much its bloodshed and destruction, as the emotional falsity it imposes. Its language is like old love-letters – the fraudulent words which accompany desire."[31] His life was also far more frenetic than the days in Mill House at Whatlington, where he could spread out ten years' worth of *The Times* and master a huge and unruly set of facts. Nevertheless, it is a shame that he did not complete "The Forties", because it would undoubtedly have secured his reputation as an incisive social critic and might have opened up new opportunities for him as a writer.

In April 1950, Arthur Watson retired as editor of the *Telegraph*. His successor was the deputy editor, Colin Coote. When Malcolm heard the news, he wondered who would be selected as the new deputy editor. Discussing the matter with his office partner, J.C. Johnstone, Malcolm urged his friend to put himself forward for the position. But Johnstone said he wasn't interested, as Malcolm noted in his diary. "Johnstone, as I said to him, has less desire for power than any human being I've ever met. He refused to regard this as a compliment, and said it was purely because he was an introvert by nature, but I didn't agree. There is a kind of innocence about him in relation to life which is most charming." Malcolm was summoned to the office of Lord Camrose, the owner of the *Telegraph*, and told that he had been chosen to become the new deputy editor. The promotion meant an extra £500 a year in income, but it also entailed new responsibilities. Whenever the editor was not in the office, Malcolm would have to sit "in the chair" as acting editor. It was also clear that as second-in-command, he was automatically positioned to inherit the editorship of the paper. Malcolm was flattered, of course, and pleased with the money, but he also had "mixed feelings" because he feared his own writing would suffer.[32] There was really no choice but to accept: three of his four children were still at school, and he and Kitty maintained an active social life in London that placed a strain on their finances.

Aside from the book reviews that Malcolm wrote for the *Telegraph*, his primary theme was anti-Communism. It was during these tense years – the years of the Berlin Crisis, when the Soviets first began to threaten the West, and the Communist coup in Czechoslovakia – that Malcolm became widely known as an indefatigable Cold Warrior. In this Malcolm was profoundly out of step with the intellectual class that was dominant in academic and literary circles. There were some important exceptions to this. A collection of essays by disillusioned former adherents of Communism was published in 1949 under the title *The God That Failed*, and included such eminent contributors as Arthur Koestler, Ignazio Silone and Stephen Spender. But the prevailing climate of opinion was, as one liberal put it, "anti-anti-Communist". Those who vigorously opposed the Soviet and Chinese regimes were frequently accused of being paranoid crypto-fascists, looking for spies and traitors under every bed. Malcolm had been vilified in just such a fashion before the war; he was inured to it.

As Malcolm had feared ever since the start of the last war, Stalin emerged from the conflict with a hugely expanded area of influence and, despite the Nazi-Soviet Pact, continuing goodwill in his role as "Uncle Joe". Malcolm considered the Yalta Conference, where Churchill, Stalin and Franklin Delano Roosevelt redrew the map of post-war Europe, a travesty that conceded far too much to the Soviets, including most of Eastern Europe. The fundamental fact of post-war foreign policy was the urgent need to oppose the expansionist goals of the Soviet Union, Malcolm thought. This was the subject of his article on "Red Imperialism" that he could not get published in 1933, and he would not deviate from it. His most frequent target was not the Politburo in Moscow, but the British government, which he thought was just as indecisive and inept in the face of Soviet power as it had been when Neville Chamberlain had to face Nazi power. The Labour government under Clement Attlee, he argued, had retreated ignominiously from India and Palestine, leaving behind political vacuums that would turn into civil wars and smouldering regional conflicts.

Moreover, the notion, propounded by the leaders of the Labour Party, that their Soviet policy would benefit because "Left would speak to Left", Malcolm thought of as foolish and deluded. "As far as Stalin was concerned, the Leftism of Mr Attlee and his colleagues was about as congenial as ginger beer to a congenital drunkard." An example of the government's confusion, he wrote, was its reluctance to deal with France, because its current ruler had been tainted by his association with the Axis powers. "Yet Stalin, to come to terms with whom they would make any sacrifice, was not only an instrument but an active participant in Axis policy; Tito, whose regime can scarcely be described as parliamentary, can always safely rely on sympathetic treatment from them; and Mao Tse-tung, no Gladstone, is, next to Mr Nehru, their particular favourite."[33]

What of Malcolm's own consistency in the area of foreign policy? Back in 1928, he had written as a socialist in support of oppressed "subject peoples" yearning to break free from the yoke of imperialism. Now an intransigent Cold Warrior writing for a conservative newspaper, he was arguing that Britain was not projecting its power throughout the world with sufficient force. When examined carefully, however, the difference between these two positions turns out to be superficial rather than substantive. Malcolm believed that the British, who had thought only a few years ago that the empire would be eternal, had suddenly and irresponsibly pulled up stakes and left India. The aftermath of this withdrawal was the eruption of fierce conflicts between Hindus and Muslims, which in turn led to the partitioning of Pakistan and rioting in which more than a million people were killed. Having repressed these conflicts through the police power of the

Empire, the British walked away, leaving just before the pressure cooker exploded.

Malcolm's concern for subject peoples was precisely what drove his attacks on the world's newest empires: the Communist totalitarian states of Russian and China and their satellites. He had seen for himself the kulaks being loaded into trucks to be executed. Now Eastern Europe was being swallowed whole, and the war in Korea threatened to extend Communist rule even further. In his 1928 article on subject peoples, Malcolm had pointed out that "sentimental liberalism" was incapable of facing up to the harsh realities of life, and that this immersion in fantasy would lead to suffering on a massive scale. The leaders he wrote for the *Telegraph* and the increasing number of speeches he made for anti-Communist organisations, grew out of the same critique of liberalism. Collectivism, based on social scientific abstractions made popular by the Webbs, treated men and women as members of classes or categories, rather than as individuals. The result, Malcolm was convinced, was that the individual would lose his freedom and be submerged by a paternalistic state. That was why liberals and socialists failed to see that millions of men, women and children were being added to the ranks of "subject peoples".

Malcolm was amazed and appalled by the continuing appeal of Communism to Western intellectuals. He had long argued against intellectuals like Shaw and the Webbs, but there was one individual in these years who particularly galled him: the "Red Dean of Canterbury", the Reverend Hewlett Johnson. To Malcolm, the Red Dean embodied everything that was most fatuous in liberalism. Preaching from the pulpit of Britain's most ancient and venerable Christian shrine, Johnson waxed eloquent about the glorious social experiment taking place in the Soviet Union. "As a symbol, from the Communists' point of view, the Dean is incomparable. All their ridicule of Christianity, all their confidence that its day is done, seems to come true in his very person. Moscow newspapers, in their cartoons, present the Christian Church in just such a guise: gaiters, cross, white locks, and seeming venerability, adorning absurdity."[34] That Johnson and others like him could maintain these ideas in the face of Communism's rejection of religion in theory, and persecution of it in practice, struck Malcolm as so perverse that it had to have a deeper explanation. Liberalism, he began to think, was driven by a death-wish, a profound alienation from the Western tradition that led its adherents to worship those who would pull that order down.

When the issue of Communist infiltration of Western governments arose at the beginning of the Cold War, Malcolm was in favour of efforts to bar present or former members of the Communist Party from holding positions of responsibility. For example, he and Anthony Powell decided to become more involved with the National Union of Journalists, when they realised that its Communist members were close to taking over the leadership of the union. They attended meetings more regularly and voted against various propositions made by the more extreme members. This stance often led critics to charge that Malcolm was guilty of paranoia, hysteria and a callous disregard for civil rights. But Malcolm embodied none of these traits. When he heard, in 1948, that Claud Cockburn, a journalist who belonged to the Communist Party, had been "black-balled" for membership in the Author's Club, he was indignant. He recounted in his diary an argument with J.C. Johnstone on the subject. "I contended that this was wrong – indeed I had supported Claud's candidature – because a club was a purely social organization. I said I'd be prepared to go further than anyone in the way of depriving Communists of access to State secrets and means of sabotaging economic recovery, but that I differentiated between this and barring them from ordinary social intercourse."[35] Later, when Kim Philby was under investigation for being a Soviet agent, Malcolm was one of his staunchest defenders.[36] Malcolm even wrote a satire against the infamous Communist-baiting US Senator, Joseph McCarthy, entitled "Senator McCarthy McCarthyised, or The Biter Bit". In this *jeu d'esprit*, the Senator is himself grilled by a committee and becomes outraged by the same techniques of innuendo and illogicality that he employed.[37]

One way that Malcolm fought the Cold War was through a continuing association with MI6. After his return from Washington, Malcolm had been approached by several SIS staff members about his willingness to give lectures on the geopolitical implications of the struggle with the Soviet Union. For several years, Malcolm gave a large number of lectures for MI6 and other branches of the intelligence services. One lecture was titled, "The Strategy of World Political Warfare". He was even approached on occasion by an MI6 operative who wanted a legitimate "cover" from the *Telegraph* before going on an assignment. Malcolm looked on these efforts not as a chance to continue playing the spy, but to communicate clearly about the threat posed by totalitarianism.

With his promotion to deputy editor of the *Telegraph* in the spring of 1950, Malcolm became more than a mere leader writer. One evidence of this was that he was sent on several newsgathering trips overseas. In 1951 he made an extensive tour of the Middle East, including stops in Israel, Lebanon, Jordan, Iran and Iraq. Another trip took him to Yugoslavia, Austria and Germany. He also travelled to the Far East early in 1952, where he visited the Federation of Malaya, which was then very much in the news. After World War II, Britain had consolidated several territories in the area into a crown colony, which they called Malaya, but a rebel force, inspired and financed by China, carried on a campaign of terror and guerilla warfare that posed difficult challenges to the British authorities. On each of these trips, Malcolm proved to be a diligent and hard-working journalist. He not only drank in the local atmosphere, but assiduously gathered information from government officials, businessmen and fellow journalists, and turned it into a series of carefully written articles.

His position at the *Telegraph* was now important enough for various politicians and public figures either to seek him out or to welcome a meeting. By doing so, they could try to get their "message" across and improve their chances of positive coverage in one of the country's leading newspapers. Malcolm's diaries from this period are filled with memorable portraits of these men of affairs. The person he got to know best was Field Marshal Montgomery, or Monty as he was known around the world. They had first encountered each other when Montgomery was commanding 5 Corps in Salisbury. He had gone on to become the hero of the North African campaign and Britain's most victorious general. When Malcolm gave a lecture at a military college, he got into a conversation with General Bernard Paget, who mentioned that Monty was writing a book attacking Eisenhower. Malcolm said that this would be a mistake, and General Paget asked him if he would be willing to make that case directly to Montgomery. Malcolm said he would, and a little more than a week later the meeting was arranged.

Montgomery was installed in a large office in Dover House, overlooking the Horse Guards Parade. Attired in full military regalia, with all his ribbons and two wristwatches, Montgomery did not make a good first impression on Malcolm. "Funny little wizened face, which is slightly disagreeable because it is much too fat for its framework, eyes are glazed over and mad-looking. In fact, his whole attitude suggested to me that the strain of his fame might have cracked his wits a bit." Instead of listening to Malcolm's insights, he spent most of their hour together talking. "A clear case of advanced megalomania . . .

reminded me of my interview with General MacArthur." However, Malcolm was impressed with Montgomery's conviction that the West was now "at war with Communism" and that the Western nations had to work together to develop a defensive alliance.[38] Through his friend, P.J. Grigg, Malcolm visited Montgomery again, six months later. His reactions on this visit were more positive: "really rather charming in his odd way . . ." When Montgomery got on to the subject of the North African campaign, he described it with a mastery and intensity that Malcolm found appealing. He was also a source of malicious gossip about figures like Churchill and Attlee, recounting the sort of anecdotes that Malcolm relished. Though he was not particularly intelligent or charming, Malcolm reflected, Montgomery had a sort of greatness, "greatness being, I suspect, a kind of vitality and singleness of purpose more than anything else".[39]

Malcolm was able to make use of his conversations with Montgomery in the *Telegraph*, often printing his stories as from the "diplomatic correspondent". Monty's efforts to help establish the North Atlantic Treaty Organization (NATO) took him to Paris, so Malcolm saw less of him. But when Malcolm was about to leave for Malaya in 1952, Montgomery heard about it and at the last minute summoned him to Paris in order to share some information that would prove helpful to Malcolm. Montgomery welcomed him to a chateau near Fontainebleau, where he even provided pyjamas for Malcolm, who had left too quickly to pack his own. Malcolm was touched when Monty put the pyjamas in front of the fire to warm. By this time their admiration was mutual. As he was driven away, Malcolm concluded that Montgomery was "a good man who understands much in essentials but little in detail; the precise converse of an intellectual".[40]

One day in the summer of 1950, Malcolm was summoned to a meeting with Winston Churchill at his country home of Chartwell. Malcolm had always been ambivalent about Churchill: impressed at times by his rhetoric, but convinced that he was living in the past rather than the present. Chartwell was a "large, not very attractive house, part of it old, much added to, like the residences of all power addicts (the Webbs, Monty) curiously impersonal, nothing individual about it at all, comfortable without being cosy". Malcolm was told that Churchill was somewhere in the gardens. Then he walked in, "wearing his famous siren suit and smoking a huge cigar – a quite astonishing figure, very short legged, baby faced, immensely thick neck, and oddly lovable". A servant arrived with a tray of whisky and sodas, rather than tea. They discussed Churchill's memoirs, which he was then writing. Malcolm told him to write the last volume immediately, in order to make the truth known about the Yalta Agreement. Churchill said that he could not do so without alienating the Americans, since he was convinced that they had refused to recognise the Soviet threat.

After a few more trays had been brought in, Churchill got up and began to rehearse a speech he was to give in Cologne. It was, Malcolm thought, "a bizarre spectacle, the great wartime Prime Minister, rather tight, walking up and down reciting his speech which he proposed to give to a German audience from whom he expected warm applause". Malcolm thought that Churchill treated him with great respect, occasionally looking out of the corner of his eye to gauge Malcolm's reactions to him. He was taken down to a room full of Churchill's own paintings, which were surprisingly colourful. Then he was shown Churchill's office, which included a poster printed during the Boer War, in which he had fought. The poster, signed by the Boer statesman, Paul Kruger, offered a £25 reward for the capture of Churchill, dead or alive. "It's more than they would offer for me now," Churchill said.

Churchill particularly wanted to show Malcolm his goldfish pond. The fish, he said, knew the sound of his voice and would come to be fed when they heard him. But, despite his best rhetorical efforts, the fish would not come. He then produced some maggots, which immediately attracted the attention of the fish; the fish, he said, were supposed to associate the sound of his voice with the provision of maggots. Malcolm commented that Churchill was in the same situation with his constituents: they too associated the sound of his voice with a provision of maggots. Rather than take offence at this, Churchill laughed. As Malcolm bade farewell to Churchill, he was suddenly struck by the thought that the politician was like King Lear. He felt a moment of "pity for him, imprisoned in the flesh, in old age, longing only for a renewal of the disease of life, all passion unspent". Ten days later, he was surprised to receive a phone call from Churchill, who wanted to discuss whether he should respond to a speech made by the Prime Minister, Clement Attlee. Malcolm advised him against it, and Churchill agreed.

In addition to these political figures, Malcolm also met two literary figures from the Edwardian era, Max Beerbohm and Hilaire Belloc. Malcolm and Kitty spent their summer holiday in 1949 at the French Riviera, in the seaside town of Roquebrune Cap Martin. (They liked the place so much that they would return there nearly every year for the next twenty-five years.) Beerbohm lived in Rapallo, on the Italian Riviera. A brilliant satirist, essayist and illustrator, Beerbohm had lampooned the Victorians and Edwardians with wit and a genius for parody. With Auberon Herbert, Malcolm and Kitty went to have tea with the Beerbohms in Rapallo. Dressed in an old-fashioned linen suit, the diminutive Beerbohm greeted them on the roof of his house, his face "very old, somehow shaggy . . . affectionate, gentle, sad eyes; head bald, very browned from the sun". Beerbohm mocked the development of a profession known as "interior decoration" and said that he now hated all change. There were frequent references to his old literary cronies, "dear Belloc" and G.K. Chesterton. He mentioned the curious news that George Bernard Shaw's wife had included in her will a large sum of money to establish institutions for "improving the manners of the Irish". Beerbohm thought this extraordinary, but Malcolm "suggested the purpose was clear enough – to prevent any recurrence of Shaw. This vastly amused Max." Beerbohm's gentleness and manners touched Malcolm. He thought of Hugh Kingsmill's phrase, that in old age Beerbohm was like a good ham, "mild and cured".[41]

Auberon Herbert was also responsible for taking Malcolm to visit Belloc, who provided an extreme contrast to Beerbohm. "Belloc came shuffling in, walks with great difficulty because he has had a stroke, inconceivably dirty . . . mutters to himself and easily forgets what he said, heavily bearded, fierce-looking and angry." Malcolm saw Belloc as a bitter old man, showing little evidence that the Catholic faith he had championed for so long made any improvement in his life. Belloc did, however, have a somewhat manic and ribald sense of the absurd. He was given to humming or singing old music hall songs, Malcolm noted in his diary, songs such as "'Chase me girls, I've got a banana, oh what a banana!' This song pleased him hugely." When two of his family went out of the room, Belloc turned to Malcolm and Auberon and said: "'They're longing for me to die,' and then laughed gleefully."[42]

In the autumn of 1952, Malcolm was approached by Christopher Chancellor, the head of the news agency, Reuters, who asked if he was interested in becoming the editor of *Punch*. It was not a position he would have ever desired. Back in the late 1930s, he had written for the short-lived *Day and Night*, a magazine established to supply the sort of biting wit and intelligence that was clearly not appearing in *Punch*. Though it had a venerable history, *Punch* in the early 1950s was a rather blasé publication, and Malcolm was intrigued by the opportunity he was being given, as an outsider, to bring about a revolution. It was as if an anarchist with a bomb had been ushered into Buckingham Palace and told that he was now the monarch. This was an offer he couldn't refuse.

Malcolm's colleagues at the *Telegraph* were genuinely sorry to lose him. As a leaving present, they gave him a large, elaborate silver inkstand of Punch and two Judies, which had once resided in the Royal Horse Artillery mess. He went down to the composing room of the *Telegraph* to say goodbye. All the workers there in the beating heart of the newspaper banged on their machines by way of applause and farewell.

« 15 »

That Idiot, Laughter

1953–1957

IN HIS YEARS AS editor of *Punch*, more than one commentator pointed out the odd similarity between the grinning, crescent-moon-shaped face of Mr Punch, and that of Malcolm Muggeridge, with his strong chin, large, fleshy nose and expansive forehead. As Malcolm's face became increasingly well known in these years through the medium of television, the comparisons would become more and more plausible – another example of Blake's "fearful symmetry". Both Malcolm and Mr Punch seemed to share a ribald sense of humour that refused to take human institutions and pretensions seriously. And like Mr Punch, Malcolm seemed ready to play the clown in order to call attention to the foolishness in the world around him

Malcolm's appointment as the eighth editor of *Punch* was unprecedented in a number of ways. The ancient tradition at *Punch* was that editors were chosen from within the magazine's staff. Bringing in an outsider like Malcolm was a clear sign that times were changing, and that he was to be the agent of change. This would be no easy task, because *Punch* was a national institution. Founded in 1841, *Punch* began as a sharply satirical magazine, full of brilliantly drawn caricatures by cartoonists such as John Tenniel, George du Maurier and John Leech, and pungent articles by writers such as William Makepeace Thackeray. As early as 1843, *Punch* became the centre of a national controversy when it published Thomas Hood's poem on the plight of women garment workers, "The Song of the Shirt". In its first decades, *Punch* was unrepentantly political and always topical. But with the advent of the twentieth century and the trauma of World War I, *Punch* retreated into a pastoral world that catered for the escapist fantasies of the middle and upper classes. As Malcolm would put it, many years later: "Its cartoons of funny servants, comic schoolmasters, and its professed aim of making 'a little gentle fun about the garden mower', no longer seemed relevant even in dentists' waiting rooms."[1]

Just as the BBC looked to Malcolm to open up the stuffy, conformist atmosphere of its programming, so the proprietors of *Punch* recognised that their magazine had to become more attuned to the complexities of post-war Britain. In particular, there was the question of class. *Punch* was written and edited largely by those who had been to the public schools. Many of the magazine's contributors had been recruited right out of Oxford or Cambridge and had little experience of the world. Malcolm's social origins were more humble than the majority of *Punch*'s staff and contributors. Having travelled all over the globe as a journalist, however, his range of experience was in stark contrast to that of his insular staff. This disparity would lead to simmering tensions that would plague his five years as editor.

The conventional wisdom for some time had been that the typical reader of *Punch* was a "retired colonel living in Cheltenham". This figure of Colonel Blimp had become a figure of dread to editors and owners: if anything controversial was inserted into the pages of *Punch*, the Colonel would go to his desk, red-faced with indignation, moustache bristling, and cancel his subscription. Since the Colonel and his ilk constituted a large percentage of the subscription base, this was an event to be feared. There was more than a grain of truth in this, as Malcolm was to learn to his dismay, but even the cautious proprietors of *Punch*, Bradley, Agnew & Co., recognized that the Colonel's day was passing: the magazine would have to appeal to younger, less traditional readers in order to survive.

Malcolm's arrival at *Punch* was marked by what some people thought to be an ill omen and which has subsequently passed into legend. At the centre of the magazine's editorial life was something known as the Table. Membership in the Table was reserved to those who had earned a place there after many years of distinguished service. Since the middle of the nineteenth century, the Table met for lunch on Wednesdays, where food and drink were always plentiful. The Table was a large mahogany structure, almost as old as *Punch* itself. Those who gained admission to it were invited to carve their initials on the Table. Thackeray's monogram can be seen on the Table, as can the initials of A.A. Milne, Ernest Shepard and the American humorist James Thurber. Legend has it that when Malcolm carved his initials into the Table, he made such a botch of it that part of the Table had to be sent away for repairs. Actually, Malcolm had only begun to carve; he allowed his son, Charles, to finish the job. Charles pressed so hard that the knife went right through the Table.[2]

When Malcolm was made editor, the offices of *Punch* were located at 10 Bouverie Street, just south of Fleet Street. His own spacious office was beautifully appointed, but had a rather poor view. From his window, Malcolm could see trucks unloading huge rolls of newsprint on which the *News of the World* was to be published. On the wall was a portrait of Owen Seaman, a dour, even priggish, man who had been one of *Punch*'s least popular editors. Malcolm quickly replaced it with the more soothing visage of another former editor.

The atmosphere in the office, Malcolm thought, was strangely sombre and furtive. This was a complete contrast to the historic image of *Punch* as a place of raucous Falstaffian laughter. Malcolm was not alone in this opinion. Anthony Powell, whom Malcolm persuaded to join the staff as literary editor, wrote in his memoirs: "[O]thers as well as myself were struck by the peculiarly muted atmosphere of the *Punch* office, the apparent physical enervation, the inward-looking personal exchanges; a surrounding despondency alleviated only by an unusually charming team of girl secretaries."[3] The arrival of such a thorough-going outsider as Malcolm tended to increase, rather than decrease, the insular atmosphere among the regular staff.

One of Malcolm's first actions was to give *Punch* a large transfusion of talent from other outsiders. He turned to a number of old friends whose writing and characters he admired. In addition to hiring Powell as literary editor, he asked his old friend from the *Evening Standard*, Leslie Marsh, to become the chief copy editor. Since members of the Table had for many years had the privilege of sending their articles directly to the printer, instead of having to submit them for editorial scrutiny, the acquisition of Marsh was widely resented. But Marsh became an essential part of the new regime. Malcolm's insistence that *Punch* carry more topical material meant that deadlines were now mad scrambles. As *Time* magazine reported a few months after Malcolm's appointment: "[P]utting *Punch* to press – once a quiet, timeless ritual – now has all the excitement of a city room covering a fast-breaking news story."[4] Marsh made this possible.

Malcolm also made a concerted effort to attract leading writers into the pages of the magazine, which had hitherto been dominated by a small cadre of scribblers who wrote exclusively for *Punch*. Within the first year of his editorship, he published articles by literary luminaries such as Stevie Smith, Angus Wilson, Antonia White, Noël Coward,

Julian Symons, Dorothy L. Sayers, Lawrence Durrell, Elizabeth Bowen, Kenneth Tynan, Joyce Cary, J.B. Priestley and Robert Graves. There were internal critics who sniffed at what they saw as an effort to publish literary "celebrities", but Malcolm wanted more out of these new contributors than their fame. His goal was to invigorate the writing and broaden the magazine's range of experience. Some of Malcolm's new recruits became regular contributors. Christopher Hollis was given the political beat, to which he brought a wit and forthrightness that had been missing from the magazine for decades. John Betjeman, another former colleague of Malcolm's at the *Evening Standard*, was invited to write on architecture. Perhaps most satisfying to Malcolm was his successful campaign to coax P.G. Wodehouse once more to become a regular contributor to *Punch*. Though Wodehouse would never return to Britain from his American exile, his regular presence in *Punch* was an important part of the rehabilitation of his reputation. Eight months into his editorship, the *World's Press News*, a British trade publication, noticed "a wonderfully fresh vitality [in] *Punch*".

One of the new outside contributors to *Punch* was Claud Cockburn, who was then living in Ireland. He was invited to write for *Punch* by Anthony Powell, who encouraged him to be "somewhat astringent". This request came as something of a surprise, since Cockburn had never known *Punch* to be astringent, nor was he even aware of the new editor's identity. After he had written several pieces for *Punch*, Powell invited him to stop by the office the next time he was in London. When he did so, Powell mentioned rather casually that the magazine's new editor was Malcolm Muggeridge. Cockburn's first reaction was one of extreme nervousness. After all, in his Communist days, Cockburn had locked horns repeatedly with Malcolm at meetings of the National Union of Journalists. Powell managed to agitate Cockburn even further by suggesting that they visit Malcolm immediately. This reduced Cockburn to near incoherence. "I have every reason to suppose," he said to Powell, "that [Muggeridge] detests me as deeply as I detest him. Let us keep this whole thing as far as possible in the old boy net – let me deal exclusively with yourself. A meeting with Muggeridge can end only in bitterness and disaster."

Powell's only response to this was to laugh and then to guide Cockburn down the hall into Malcolm's office. "Of that first conversation I remember very little," Cockburn wrote in his memoirs, "except that it was from the start tumultuous and at the end – hours later –

hilarious."[5] Their friendship was cemented in those moments and remained intact until Cockburn's death. In Cockburn Malcolm found a kindred spirit: a former Leftist who had become disillusioned with political solutions, but whose ideas were not easy to categorise. Like Kingsmill, Cockburn had a vivid sense of the absurd in human affairs, and also had something of a mystical streak. He and Malcolm used to have long talks about Christianity, to which they were both attracted, but from which they held aloof. Malcolm and Kitty went to visit Cockburn in County Cork, Ireland, and frequently entertained him on his trips to England. Once, Malcolm received an urgent call from Cockburn's wife, saying that one of his children had suddenly become seriously ill. Malcolm immediately swung into action, locating Cockburn and helping to get him on a night flight to Dublin. "[T]here has never been a man on God's earth who would do more for you when the chips are down, and he has seen a number of chips down in his life," Cockburn wrote in his autobiography.[6]

Cockburn was one of Malcolm's staunchest allies in the effort to return *Punch* to its heritage as a bitingly satirical and topical magazine.

> I began to have the feeling that with this fiercely gentle, chivalrously ungentlemanly man on the far side of the grandiose editorial desk, jerking and flashing his eyes, from time to time cackling out a cacophony of furiously raucous expressions like a sailor's parrot loose in the Mission Hall, something new and special in the way of clowning and satire might yet be made of this ancient publication, once so rowdy, later so often muffled nearly to the eyes in old school scarves. The room at large was as dead as a white sepulchre, but you could feel some life crackling behind the desk, as though someone, for a joke, had thrown a fire-cracker into the mausoleum.[7]

Not long after taking over the magazine, Malcolm made two editorial changes that, at the time, were considered radical. The first was to have all his contributors sign their full names to articles, rather than going by their initials. The use of initials was for many years tied to an arcane system of seniority: only the most senior writers were allowed to sign their full names. This change was one of Malcolm's more popular decisions, since it enabled some of the younger writers to get credit for their work. The other, more controversial decision, was to change the magazine's front cover. Drawn by Richard Doyle, and printed in black ink with a little highlighting in red, the *Punch* cover had been in continuous use for 109 years when Malcolm decided to vary it. The occasion was an issue devoted to satirising television, and the only actual change was to substitute contemporary figures, such as Lord Reith, for Doyle's caricatures. But this action was so controversial that the change was only temporary. For the next four years, the traditional Doyle cover remained on most weeks, alternating occasionally with four-colour covers illustrated by contemporary artists. Only in Malcolm's final year as editor was Doyle abandoned for good.

Another part of Malcolm's campaign to modernise *Punch* was the elimination of the taboos that had been in place for some time. The most controversial of these was the taboo on sex. Ever since his first play, *Three Flats*, had been staged, Malcolm had sought to write frankly and realistically about the sexual habits and obsessions of the twentieth century. Humour, of course, was one of the few ways Malcolm could gain some perspective on his own tortured sexual life. The protagonists of his novels all suffer from the restlessness of lust and their inability to remain faithful to their wives, giving rise to a particular brand of sexual black humour. By the 1950s, Malcolm had come to the conviction that Christian sexual morality was crucial to the survival of the social fabric. He had, in fact, accepted this sexual morality before he was prepared to live according to its teachings. *Punch*, under Malcolm's editorship, was soon commenting on the sexual mores of the day.

Malcolm also increased the number and pungency of the parodies published in *Punch*. Among the publications he and his staff parodied were *The Times*, the *New Yorker*, the Soviet equivalent of *Punch* known as *Krokodil*, the *Radio Times*, the *New Statesman*, and a fictional composite of several women's magazines. The *New Statesman* parody took aim at the editor, Kingsley Martin, Malcolm's old co-worker at the *Guardian*. Malcolm often jibed at the way Martin seemed to change his mind, and the editorial stance of the *Statesman*, on policy questions. The parody contains a pseudo-column about a dancer named King Slee Mah Tin, known for his "Paradise Dances". "These are based on *sans-culottist* tradition, to which they bring, I'm told, a suppleness and refinement rare in that art ... His repertoire will include, no doubt, that old favourite the *crank-hop*, with its accompaniment of gaffes and jitter-bones, in which King Slee runs to and fro in all directions before a couple of columns before standing on his head in order to (as the programme note puts it) 'settle a policy.'"[8] But Malcolm soon found the effort to create parodies was doomed, precisely because the absurdities of the real world always outdistanced what the *Punch* editors could imagine. When the *Punch* staff attempted to parody the BBC, they came across a Third Programme lecture on "The Place of the Potato in Folklore" and despaired of coming up with anything to rival it.[9]

Above all, Malcolm stressed to his editorial staff that he favoured writing in a plain style, and that he had little time for flowery prose. In a tribute to the famous editor of the *New Yorker*, Harold Ross, Malcolm wrote that Ross "instinctively distrusted pretentious, mannered writing, and, in matters of taste, followed his flair rather than any conformist (or anti-conformist) system".[10]

Soon after he had taken over the editorship, Malcolm flew to the United States to open a travelling exhibition of art from *Punch*. There he explained to the *New Yorker* that *Punch*'s role was to be something more than a collection of jokes. Rather, its role "should be social history – to record the age". But Malcolm confessed that he was not entirely sure how to effect the change from escapism and nostalgia to satirical realism. "I've been working very much in the dark," he told the *New Yorker*.[11] In his diary he admitted to uncertainty about whether he was up to the job. One representative entry reads: "Alternate between despondency and confidence."[12]

His first efforts went too far in the direction of straightforward journalism. In addition to commissioning articles on current political events, Malcolm himself wrote a series of serious editorials that were almost indistinguishable from what he had been writing at the *Telegraph*. The election of General Eisenhower in America, the death of Stalin, the purges in Communist-dominated Eastern Europe, the debate over the proposal to introduce commercial broadcasting in Britain – Malcolm approached these topics in his most earnest and combative manner. But it must have become evident to him that he was being far too grim, because he gradually began to write in a more deliberately humorous and ironical manner. "Advice to Diplomats" contains these admonitions:

1. When an international agreement is unilaterally denounced, ensure that any formal protests you are instructed to make are as hesitant and equivocal as possible. Remember that the contravention of one agreement provides for the negotiation of another, which may well bring you fame and promotion . . . 4. Remember

that nowadays the glittering prizes are given for feats of demolition, not of construction. Lord Mountbatten was made an earl for getting us out of India in record time; Lord Halifax founded a career of immense distinction on a capacity to be on good terms alike with Gandhi and with Goering. Every diplomat carries a peerage in his knapsack, provided only that he keeps retreating ... 6. In politics you should incline to the Left. If you can combine this with ample private means and socially distinguished circumstances, so much the better. The contrast between your private circumstances and your political professions will serve to draw attention to you and to recommend you equally to Conservative and Labour Governments.[13]

This was followed by "Advice to MPs" and a series written by a historian from the future about the decline and fall of Western civilisation in the late twentieth century. To ridicule the opposition to the establishment of commercial broadcasting, Malcolm wrote a piece advocating the nationalisation of the advertisements alongside the escalators at Underground stations. If only a cultivated, public-spirited man like Lord Reith could erect a series of edifying messages, society would be infinitely better off. For example, the "wise sayings of contemporary statesmen like Mr Nehru and Dr Nkrumah might have been set forth in some striking and memorable manner, while at another station the available space could have been devoted to national heroes, climbing up, as it were, to those of modern times, like Asquith, Bonar Law and Ramsay MacDonald, and descending to those of the past like Chatham, Marlborough and Warren Hastings."[14]

If Malcolm was learning to unbend somewhat and make his satire more imaginative, he also helped to bring out the best in others. It has been said that Malcolm had little appreciation for what made *Punch* cartoons funny, and it is true that he had little interest in art forms other than literature. He brought on a man named Michael Cummings to put the punch back in the cartoons that accompanied the articles on Parliament. But in Ronald Searle he recognised a supremely innovative style harnessed to sardonic wit. When Malcolm arrived at *Punch*, Searle was illustrating the regular articles on theatre and film. Searle was an able caricaturist, but Malcolm felt that his talent was being wasted. In his diary Malcolm wrote: "Suggested to Ronald Searle he should do some satirical work in Hogarth manner." This gave rise to a series of full-page cartoon spreads updating Hogarth's eighteenth-century work, *A Rake's Progress*. Searle's thoroughly modern rakes – poets, politicians, and actors – rise from obscurity to success, only to succumb to "temptation" and experience "ruin". Malcolm was delighted with the results.

The most important cartoon in each issue of *Punch* was the political cartoon, printed opposite the lead editorial. During Malcolm's tenure at *Punch*, this was the responsibility of Leslie Illingworth, whom Anthony Powell described as a man with "gnomelike features, body, and demeanour".[15] Illingworth was also the chief editorial cartoonist for the *Daily Mail*, which often espoused views diametrically opposed to those which Malcolm propagated in *Punch*. But according to Powell Illingworth was completely apolitical and encompassed these contradictions happily. Illingworth would often ask for detailed instructions for his next assignment and follow them closely. A few of Malcolm's ideas can be traced through Illingworth's cartoons, including several that utilise Malcolm's favourite image for the modern era: the Gadarene swine, possessed by demons, flinging themselves off a cliff.

Malcolm worked with Illingworth to make the political cartoons as pointed and relevant as possible. About a year after his arrival at *Punch*, Malcolm set off the first major controversy of his editorship with an Illingworth cartoon depicting a tired, and perhaps senile, Winston Churchill, his eyes staring into space, a pen dropping from tired, swollen fingers. The caption underneath, from the Bible, read: "Man goeth forth unto his work and to his labour until the evening." By 1954, Churchill was again serving as Prime Minister, but at the age of eighty, he was clearly failing, physically and mentally. In the editorial that accompanied the cartoon, Malcolm described the decay of a fictional Byzantine ruler, Bellarius, who "clung to power with tenacious intensity. His splendid faculties began to falter. The spectacle of him thus clutching wearily at all the appurtenances and responsibilities of an authority he could no longer fully exercise was to his admirers infinitely sorrowful, and to his enemies infinitely derisory."[16]

Before this issue even went to press, Malcolm knew that a firestorm would erupt. When he arrived for a visit with Claud Cockburn in Ireland just prior to publication, he told his friend that the next issue was "likely to get us all into a lot more hot water".[17] Sure enough, the angry letters and cancelled subscriptions from red-faced colonels arrived at the offices of *Punch*. It was Malcolm's first major run-in with the proprietors, Bradbury, Agnew & Co. Though he was protected to some extent by his contract, the friction from this incident began a process that quickly eroded Malcolm's desire to edit the magazine. Powell writes in his memoirs that he witnessed several meetings between Malcolm and the management of the magazine. Though Malcolm eventually allowed Powell to skip these meetings, Powell was glad to have a glimpse of the pressures exerted on the editor by people who have little understanding of the literary character of the publication. Powell remembered one department head urging Malcolm to run a series of articles on the subject of "How to Build a Boat".

While Powell was correct in thinking that Malcolm was "perfectly capable of dealing with snipers from behind his own lines", he forgot just how quickly Malcolm lost interest in editing *Punch* after the Churchill cartoon incident.[18] By the spring of 1954, Malcolm's own signed contributions to *Punch* had become more sporadic, and by 1955, they had nearly ceased altogether. He continued to preside over the Table, and suggest topics and authors. Malcolm "throws off ideas like a catherine wheel", one of his staff told *Newsweek* magazine in 1956.[19] But by that time Malcolm's close friends could tell that his heart was no longer in the magazine. Claud Cockburn sensed Malcolm's disengagement. "With you," he told Malcolm, "the tendency to become bored has the quality of a vice."[20] When, not long after this, Cockburn suggested to Malcolm in a phone call from Ireland that they ought to discuss the subject of Cockburn's next article, Malcolm replied: "Hell, my dear boy, I leave all that to you. Write anything you like." Cockburn eventually learned that Malcolm had reverted to the old *Punch* tradition of having material sent directly to the printer, at least in the case of Cockburn and a few trusted contributors.[21] It seemed to Cockburn that Malcolm's days at *Punch* were numbered.

During his years as editor of *Punch*, Malcolm found diversion in his increasing number of appearances on radio and the relatively new medium of television. This caused widespread resentment among the staff of *Punch*. When the most recent historian of *Punch* asked an ancient maintenance man there about his memories of Malcolm, the reply was: "Muggeridge, now, I didn't see it myself, but they say he got in at nine and was gone by five minutes after, off to do some television programme."[22]

Before Malcolm's television career was even fully launched, he found himself at the centre of a major debate about the medium itself. The debate concerned the proposal for allowing commercial television to break the BBC's monopoly. When the Tories under

Churchill returned to power in 1951, the advocates of commercial television gained considerable ground. A government White Paper suggesting that competition might be an option touched off the controversy.

Malcolm, who had already suffered at the hands of those in the higher echelons of the BBC who disliked controversy, threw himself into the debate on the side of commercial TV. In a 1951 article criticising the conformist mentality at the BBC, Malcolm had contrasted the British situation to commercial broadcasting in America: "In this strange limbo it is possible sometimes to sigh for the harsh unrestrained accents even of a Walter Winchell, to find a certain poetry even in the voice which breaks into a Beethoven sonata to ask: 'Is your romance slipping?' and then recommend some brand of toilet soap as a corrective."[23] When the possibility of commercial television was raised two years later, Malcolm fought actively for the breaking of the BBC monopoly.

He faced a formidable set of opponents, including such Establishment figures as Lord Hailsham, Lord Reith, Lord Halifax, Lord Radcliffe, the Labour MP Christopher Mayhew, Randolph Churchill and Lady Violet Bonham-Carter. On the side of commercial TV, Malcolm was joined by the Earl of Derby and an assortment of writers and actors, including Rex Harrison, A.J.P. Taylor and Somerset Maugham. Malcolm used the pages of *Punch* to carry on his campaign, writing ironic editorials against commercial sponsorship of Underground escalators, and publishing parodies of BBC programmes.

One of the final episodes in the controversy, for Malcolm and perhaps for much of the British public as well, came in a debate broadcast on the BBC radio programme, *Fifty-one Society*. Held in late January 1954 in Manchester on the eve of parliamentary consideration of the Television Bill, the debate featured Malcolm and Violet Bonham-Carter and was chaired by Norman Fisher. In his opening statement, Malcolm focused on the issue of freedom. He began by reminding the audience that the dictators of the world all had state-controlled media, and that the BBC monopoly, however disinterested it claimed to be, was open to pressure from government. Commercial TV, he argued, promised an alternative that would promote the free exchange of ideas. "I want non-governmental – which means non-BBC – television, and the more varied and more diverse, in purpose and control, the better pleased I'll be." He then alluded to the way Churchill had been barred from appearing on the BBC prior to the war, when he had opposed the disastrous policy of appeasement pursued by his fellow Conservative, Neville Chamberlain.

The most persuasive part of Malcolm's case concerned the analogy he drew with the press. "What keeps newspapers truthful (in so far as they are truthful) is one another – the fact that their exaggerations, their special pleading, their distortions, will necessarily be exposed, explicitly or by implication, in the columns of their rivals." Competition, he concluded, offers the best check to the monolithic, quasi-official pronouncements on the BBC. To the argument that advertising revenues would bring their own lies and distortions, Malcolm responded again with the example of the press. "High-mindedness wouldn't carry the *Manchester Guardian* along unless fortified by the cotton trade . . ." "Advertising," he continued, "is the price we pay for freedom of the press, and I am quite prepared to pay a like price for freedom of the air. If there were some other way of procuring freedom of the air, so much the better. It's the freedom I want, not the advertising, which is only a means (and a very imperfect, and sometimes distasteful, means) to an end."[24]

Lady Violet's response was full of the high-mindedness and paternalism that Malcolm associated with liberalism in politics. Competition, she held; was not a guarantee of freedom; only "public service corporations" could rise above all interests, including the profit motive. This was the same logic behind the effort in these years to nationalise many of Britain's leading industries. The underlying assumption in such an argument, Malcolm believed, was the notion that the state would be the unbiased judge, the good father, who would give everyone their due. Like George Orwell, however, Malcolm feared any form of state paternalism: there was less of a gap separating Auntie BBC from Big Brother than many people imagined. Also like Orwell, he was also concerned with the way that society was susceptible to manipulation by the media.

After laborious scrutiny in Parliament, the Television Bill was passed in July 1954 and commercial TV, heavily regulated, was introduced in Britain. Five years later, Malcolm would lament the fact that, to his mind, the Independent Television Authority had caved in to the same conformist pressures that had been dominant at Broadcasting House: "Two BBCs have been made to grow where there was only one before."[25]

Ironically, Malcolm would be associated primarily with the BBC, rather than ITV, for the next thirty years of his broadcasting career. Despite his prominent role in the fight for commercial TV, the BBC not only continued to employ Malcolm but also helped to make him a celebrity. In 1954, not long after he had debated with Lady Violet, he was invited to appear on *Panorama*. Malcolm's assignment was to provide commentary on a sermon delivered by the American evangelist, Billy Graham, and then to conduct an interview with Graham. Up to this time, Malcolm's role on radio had been that of commentator, or, on occasion, of intellectual sparring partner for prominent thinkers and politicians, such as Bertrand Russell and Aneurin Bevan. With this assignment on *Panorama*, Malcolm's talent as an interviewer was recognised, both by the BBC staff and by the British public. In fact, it would not be an exaggeration to say that Malcolm helped to pioneer the adversarial style of television journalism. As an interviewer, he felt free to challenge those he faced, expecting them to field difficult or embarrassing questions and justify their actions and opinions.

Michael Barsley, who worked for several years on *Panorama* with Malcolm, recalled the Billy Graham interview and its significance. "Once, when Muggeridge made one of his penetrating thrusts about the evangelist's showmanship in religion, Dr Graham replied solemnly, 'I think only God can answer that, Mr Muggeridge.' Malcolm said, 'And unfortunately, we haven't got Him with us tonight, have we?' adding, after a glance upward, 'Or have we?'" It was this sort of knowing wink at the absurdity of things that provided some balance to Malcolm's aggressive style of presentation.

Malcolm became a television personality with the same ease and mastery that he had brought to newspaper journalism and radio broadcasting. He adapted himself to TV as a visual medium, learning, as he later recalled, the three cardinal rules of TV: "talk quietly, never shout, and look at the camera."[26] One example of Malcolm's capacity for absurdist humour came when a surgeon who had separated Siamese twins was put on to a *Panorama* programme at the last minute. Malcolm was completely unprepared for the interview. Casting about for something to say, he asked: "Supposing the twins wanted it, could you join them up again?" When he ran out of questions for Salvador Dali about art, he found himself asking whether his moustache stayed upright in bed at night, or drooped.[27]

Perhaps the most obvious example of Malcolm's tendency towards clowning was in a *Panorama* programme from 1956 where he was given the job of interviewing the editor of *Tailor and Cutter* magazine, the publication of Britain's clothing industry.

MUGGERIDGE: I've got here tonight Mr John Taylor, who's the editor of the *Tailor and Cutter*, a very eminent journal, supreme in its field, and I'm going to ask him, if he'd be so kind, without being unduly insulting, to comment on my appearance.

TAYLOR: Well, as long as you have no solicitors secreted about you, Mr Muggeridge, I would say that the thing that mainly worries me about you is a sort of greyness that you present –

MUGGERIDGE: It's drab you think?

TAYLOR: No, not necessarily, but rather unimaginative – the grey shirt, the grey tie, the grey suit –

MUGGERIDGE: Shabby?

TAYLOR: No, no, no, but coupled with the grey hair and the grey eyebrows it's rather a formidable experience you know. The jacket is very nice, it's short, which of course is a fashionable thing, but I rather feel that you've had that one long enough for the fashion to come round again –

MUGGERIDGE: Mr Taylor, you're dead right – but that was no question of a feeling for fashion, it was just simple poverty.

TAYLOR: Of course when we get . . . may I?

MUGGERIDGE: Oh do, take anything off you like – do you want me to take my trousers off?

TAYLOR: No – no – no – not at the moment.[28]

When Kingsley Amis came to write about Malcolm in his memoirs, the one TV appearance that remained in his mind, twenty-five years later, was this discussion with the editor of *Tailor and Cutter*.

The other piece of television foolery that has passed into legend concerned an interview that Malcolm did on *Panorama* with the Irish playwright, Brendan Behan. It was in the spring of 1956, a week after Behan's play *The Quare Fellow* had opened in London. Behan arrived early at the Lime Grove studio in a state of mild inebriation. There he was offered a bottle of whisky, the contents of which he quickly consumed. When the interview began it became clear that Behan could only answer Malcolm's questions with incoherent mutters. Malcolm, who was enjoying himself enormously, went on to answer his own questions. "Toward the end of our time," Malcolm later recalled, "remembering that the intoxicated can sometimes sing when they can't speak, I asked him if he would care to give us a song. In a thin, reedy voice he managed to give a rendering of a song in his play . . . It was the pleasantest and most rewarding evening I ever spent in Lime Grove."[29]

Malcolm's physical appearance and manner were essential to his success as a television performer. Peter Black, the historian of British broadcasting, wrote that Malcolm presented a striking figure on television, with "his delicate, ascetic features, his cigarette holder . . . his extraordinary accent in which Oxford and Wimbledon struggle for mastery, and his quick and lucid mind . . ."[30] A frequent epithet for Malcolm in these years is that he looked "gnomish", the living embodiment of Mr Punch, with his jutting chin, round nose and broad forehead that would wrinkle in a variety of ways, from quizzical laughter to profound contemplation. His hands were expressive and constantly in motion. After a couple of years on TV, Malcolm began to dress and look like something of a dandy, with his cigarette holder, well-cut suits that would have made *Tailor and Cutter* proud, the ubiquitous white handkerchief emerging from his breast pocket.

Within months of launching his television career, Malcolm noticed that he was being referred to in the newspapers as a "TV star". "Always in two minds about TV – half pleased, half disgusted, though, must confess, tickled to be described in *Tribune* as TV star."[31] There was something intoxicating about this new-found fame that went well beyond anything he had known. He had spent so many years writing books and articles that went against the spirit of the age – living in a sort of intellectual internal exile – that his television fame must have felt like compensation that was long overdue. As a TV personality, he could continue to be a gadfly and yet at the same time be at the centre of attention – the outsider camped in the halls of the Establishment.

Inevitably, Malcolm became a "talking head", known to millions by a variety of epithets, including "Telly Mugg", the "pop Socrates" and "the poor man's Voltaire". His habit of asking the most difficult questions, of probing at the weak spots, provoked delight and outrage among his viewers. At his best, Malcolm knew how to zero in on the central issues. Asking an evangelist like Billy Graham about the showmanship in preaching may have seemed like bad taste to some, but the question goes to the heart of the matter: how much of such performances comes from religious inspiration and how much from human vanity? Asking a cardinal about the existence of the afterlife, pressing a cloistered nun about her vow of chastity, daring Bertrand Russell to defend the idea of progress – Telly Mugg was unabashed.

For many, he was "the man you love to hate", but many more simply hated him. It became a commonplace that Malcolm Muggeridge himself hated everyone and everything. His friend Claud Cockburn thought such accusations to be misguided. The successful satirist, he wrote in his memoirs, "cannot run on the fuel of hate alone. He has to have something of Dante in Browning's description – 'Dante who loved well, because he hated, hated wickedness that hinders loving.' And although a lot of television viewers and *Punch* subscribers claimed they saw no signs of it, it was a quality very marked in Malcolm's make-up. He positively loved people unless he thought them fraudulent or cruel."[32] Those who are less friendly to Malcolm would argue that this latter category was rather abnormally and irrationally large in Malcolm's case.

The very unpredictability of Malcolm's opinions became a trademark. That was why he raised the ratings of almost any programme he appeared on. But here again there was a major drawback. Malcolm's lack of attachment to political parties and ideologies seemed to many people to be irresponsible and perverse. Describing himself, as he did on *Any Questions?* in 1954, as a "complete anarchist" did not help him much. But to Malcolm the modern era suffered from an excess of credulity and conformism. The real danger to society, he believed, lay not in too much cynicism but in arrogant, misguided earnestness. Malcolm cherished the line from Shakespeare's *King John*, when the king bemoans the way humour gets in the way of his political intentions – "that idiot, laughter, so hateful to our purpose".

Malcolm had a way of suprising audiences with insights that cut across party platforms or cherished ideological principles. When asked about nationalised health care in Britain, Malcolm responded by questioning the egalitarian ethos underlying the rhetoric of the politicians. "On the one hand, we are telling people that it is absolutely wrong that there should be any inequality, and any honest man must assent to that. On the other hand, we are asking people to save, to provide for their future, to pursue their own interests and ends. Now, these two things are in fact incompatible . . ."[33] When a union leader, Ted Hill, was criticised in 1957 for saying that he was only concerned with the interests of his members, Malcolm responded: "To tell you the truth, I rather liked Mr Hill's remark . . . because it was scrupulously honest and because [it] brushed away a great deal of cant

... The fact is that in an acquisitive society this is precisely what people do and I cannot for the life of me see how we can pick out Mr Hill for particular blame."[34]

The type of comment that got Malcolm into hot water could be exemplified in this response to someone who said those who don't vote should lose the right to vote. Not only should they not be disenfranchised, Malcolm said, but they "are the absolute flower of our community. They are the élite, they are the people who have realised the only fundamental truth, which is that though these politicians in their personal capacity are nearly always the most enchanting people, in their public capacity they're a lot of rogues, and equally rogues, and the realisation of that point naturally induces one not to vote for either of them."[35]

Privately, Malcolm experienced uncomfortable moments when he suspected that his television career was little more than a Faustian bargain; he wondered whether he would pay a heavy price for spending so much time in front of the camera. The nature of the medium drove its most frequent stars to develop a persona for the screen, which tended to have the exaggerated features of a caricature. Then there was the relentless trivialisation that TV gives rise to. Malcolm accepted almost every invitation indiscriminately, and so he appeared on ephemeral programmes that valued short, witty "sound bites" or acrimonious debates over reasoned discussions. At the outset of his TV career in 1954, he noted in his diary that "constant appearance on such programmes would be degrading. One would be forced to build up a synthetic, vulgar personality . . ."[36] Three years later, he would write in the same diary: "Remorse over so much time lost in foolishness or nothingness ... I survey my activities, such as they are – TV, articles in papers, fragments of writing, unfulfilled projects – with contemptuous despair."[37]

One of the dispiriting truths he was learning was that most television viewers, from charwomen to Sir Kingsley Amis, remembered episodes like the *Tailor and Cutter* interview rather than the more serious and profound discussions, such as Malcolm's encounter with Trevor Huddleston, then an Anglican priest in South Africa, in 1956. Here Malcolm, who personally loathed the South African regime of apartheid, challenged Huddleston's decision to oppose the policies of that regime publicly. The basis of the challenge was Malcolm's belief that when clergymen became political, they compromised their allegiance to supernatural things. He raised the issue of St Paul's refusal to condemn slavery, and quoted Christ's statement: "Render unto Caesar the things that are Caesar's and unto God the things that are God's." Huddleston agreed that Christianity should not be equated with political movements *per se*, but held that defending human rights often forced one to come into conflict with governments and their definition of political rights. The entire discussion was illuminating; Malcolm was challenging but respectful, Huddleston was discriminating, compassionate and articulate. Clearly, an interview of this kind is among the best things that television can do. Malcolm undertook a number of similar interviews, but they were not what people remembered him for.[38]

As with any persona built up by constant media exposure, Malcolm's mask began to crack. Anthony Powell noticed the stress that Malcolm was undergoing in these early years of his success on television. "The role of television personality," Powell wrote, apropos of Malcolm,

> seems to impose an intense strain on its virtuosos ... The actor is governed by the disciplines of art, the politician by the exigencies of political survival. The television personality is positively encouraged by the condition of existence to be answerable to no one but self, under no sort of restraint other than remaining a recognised "personality". The impression often given is that prolonged expenditure in that manner of the personality ... is cruelly hard on mind and body.

Television tended to filter Malcolm's personality in such a way as to obscure the deeper parts of his mind, both literary and religious, distilling him down to a fairly corrosive mixture of venomous wit and absolute statements. Meditative discussions about Pauline theology were simply not as memorable as goading Billy Graham, or offering to drop his trousers in prime time.

Malcolm was aware that his role as media gadfly entailed, as Powell put it, a lack of responsibility to anyone but himself. As he had many times before in his life, Malcolm longed to be more than a mere observer and critic; he wanted also to be a participant, to make a direct contribution to some cause. Because Malcolm's attitude towards religion was still complicated and ambivalent, he devoted his energies to the campaign against Communism. In the spring of 1956, he found an occasion to mount a major protest. The two leaders of the Soviet Union, Nikita Khrushchev and Marshal Bulganin, had been invited by the Prime Minister, Anthony Eden, to make a state visit to Britain. That Bulganin and Khrushchev should be asked to Britain and given all the courtesies of a state visit was galling to anti-Communists. The two Soviet leaders had only recently visited Burma and India, where they had denounced Britain as an imperialist power. Eden's invitation was not based on any particular issue that required urgent negotiation; the Soviet leaders were to be treated like the heads of friendly nations, touring various sites in Britain and being photographed shaking hands with officials of state.

By the early 1950s, Malcolm had made contact with a number of organisations representing Eastern European nations suffering under the yoke of Soviet rule. At a rally staged by Roman Catholics, Malcolm gave a speech at the Albert Hall, on December 3, 1953, in his capacity as president of the Anglo-Polish Society. "The conflict, as I see it, is between Christianity and Materialism," he concluded. He also became associated with something called the Congress for Cultural Freedom, which had been founded by Polish expatriates. The Congress was funded in large part by money supplied by the American CIA, but few people knew it at the time. Perhaps the most lasting accomplishment of the Congress was the founding of *Encounter*, a magazine edited by Stephen Spender and Irving Kristol. Malcolm had frequent meetings with Spender as *Encounter* was in the process of being launched.

When the Khrushchev-Bulganin visit was announced, British anti-Communists and Eastern European exiles were outraged. Malcolm took the leading role in organising nation-wide protests, which included signing petitions, making speeches and sending letters to the editors of Britain's leading publications. The culminating event was to be a major rally, which would demonstrate the strength of British opposition to the visit of the Soviet leaders. Working through the Polish newspaper, *Dzennkik Polski*, Malcolm booked the Albert Hall for the rally, which was to be held on Palm Sunday, March 25, 1956. But ten days before the event, the Albert Hall cancelled the booking. According to an article in *The Times*, the management of the Hall "quoted a clause which enabled them to refuse the letting of the hall if it was considered that there was danger of damage to their property, or the meeting was likely to cause a disturbance".[39] The next day, Malcolm wrote a letter to *The Times* to clarify the purposes of the protest rally. "The project originated in an informal talk between myself and a few friends, some fellow-countrymen, and some exiles from behind the Iron Curtain, some Roman Catholic and some

Protestant, some Conservative, some Labour, and some, like myself, nondescript." He admitted that the Albert Hall was within its rights to cancel the booking, but he said that the cancellation reminded him of a similar event, "at the time of Munich, and the object of the banned meeting was to enable Sir Winston Churchill and others to protest against the disastrous agreement which Neville Chamberlain had just made with Hitler".[40]

After efforts to secure another location in London proved unsuccessful, Malcolm booked, at his own expense, the Free Trade Hall in Manchester for March 26. A crowd of nearly three thousand gathered for the event, forcing many people to be turned away at the door. Telegrams in support of the event arrived, including some from behind the Iron Curtain. Malcolm declared from the podium:

> It is possible to guess who was behind the Albert Hall cancellation – after all, guessing has not yet been nationalized ... What we are protesting against is not so much a visit, or an ill-conceived or fatuous diplomatic initiative – although expecting B. and K. to reform their ways as a result of seeing our free way of life is like asking two professional ladies from the Moulin Rouge to attend Roedean in the hope that they will marry Archdeacons and settle down to a life of quiet respectability; no, what we are protesting against is evil itself.[41]

Malcolm was followed by other speakers, including Fr McGrath, a Catholic priest, and Christopher Hollis, his colleague at *Punch*. The rally concluded by adopting a resolution, as *The Times* reported: "Amid a disciplined enthusiasm a resolution was passed unanimously declaring that 'however much the people of Britain may long for friendship with the Russian people, there can be no mutual trust while the Soviet Union remains Communist, retains prisoners of war, maintains slave labour camps, and continues to hold in thrall the nations of eastern Europe.'"[42]

During the actual visit, Malcolm travelled around the country, making speeches against the Soviet regime. The *News Chronicle* quoted him, after an appearance in Coventry, as saying that he felt "a brief pang of pity" for B. and K., who had to spend so much time "talking to the greatest bore in Christendom", Anthony Eden.[43] Malcolm was challenged to debate his position against an MP. He duly went to the Oxford Union and carried the motion "This House refuses to believe that there has been any change in the Russian policy of world domination" by a vote of 237 to 173. The most impressive event of the protest campaign came when Malcolm led a march of twenty thousand people to the Cenotaph in Whitehall. He then went on to present a petition signed by sixty thousand people to the Prime Minister's residence at 10 Downing Street.

The visit went off exactly as planned, and the only immediate result of the protest was considerable nervousness on the part of the owners of *Punch*, who disliked their editor becoming embroiled in political controversy. In the ensuing months, as the revolt against Soviet rule in Hungary was brutally crushed, and Anthony Eden initiated the disastrous Suez Canal crisis, Malcolm's views would appear a great deal less shrill.

Immediately after the protest, Malcolm was distracted by the sudden intrusion of tragedy into his life. His son Charles had gone on a skiing trip in Switzerland with some friends in April 1956, rather late in the skiing season. On April 27, late in the afternoon, Charles insisted on going on a final run. He was caught in an avalanche and thrown down the three-hundred-foot cliff face of Peak Brévent, near the town of Chamonix. He was killed instantly.

Charles's death devastated Malcolm and Kitty. One sign of just how deeply they were wounded was that the death of their son was something neither of them spoke about in public, and rarely in private. Some parents feel the need to objectify their grief by sharing it with others. But for Malcolm and Kitty it remained too painful for words. Malcolm, whose writings were so thoroughly autobiographical, referred to his son's death once – in his memoirs, and then only in passing. But even after his conversion to Christianity, Malcolm never brought the death of a child into his books and essays dealing with human suffering and grief.

That Charles was not Malcolm's biological son inevitably complicated his and Kitty's feelings about his death. He had always been treated as an equal member of the family, but Malcolm could not help noticing that he was different. In a 1948 diary entry, Malcolm noted: "Charles' birthday – he's the oddest little man, quite different from the others; fond of getting into my bed in the mornings and reading the papers, and going for long walks on his own about London."[44]

Malcolm's diaries contain as many affectionate references to Charles as to the other children. Both Charles and his older brothers had attended Cranbrook, a public school in Kent, where Malcolm would occasionally visit them. At Cranbrook, the boys did well, at least as far as Malcolm could tell, and he was immensely proud of them all. Leonard, shy and serious, struck Malcolm as being other wordly – already a religious pilgrim. John loved knowledge and information and, when he returned from a trip to Kenya as a young man, wrote an account of his time there which was published in *Encounter*. Charles also did well at Cranbrook. In Malcolm's diaries he noted that Charles was "top of his class . . . a schoolmaster's dream".[45] He was the most athletic and physically outgoing of the children, not only playing sports at Cranbrook, but skiing in Switzerland. He had joined the Royal Navy after finishing at Cranbrook, and had achieved the rank of a sub-lieutenant at the time of his death. When he graduated from the Naval Academy, Dartmouth, Charles had won the highest award given to a midshipman.[46] One photograph of Charles, taken shortly before his death, shows a ruggedly handsome young man dressed in Navy whites, blond and confident. Another shows him in profile against the Swiss mountains where he would shortly meet his death.

Though their conscious minds told them that Charles's death was nothing more than a terrible accident, Malcolm and Kitty could not avoid wondering about the meaning of their son's death. Was there not a fearful symmetry here? Charles had been conceived in Switzerland twenty years before, only miles from where he died. He had been born at a time when Malcolm and Kitty were fighting and wounding each other, engaging in affairs and counter-affairs. Was Charles's death a message from God, a punishment for the sins of the father and mother? It is difficult to imagine that Malcolm and Kitty did not ask themselves these self-lacerating questions, and envision a variety of answers to them.

The impact of Charles's death on Malcolm may not have been visible in his writings or public utterances, but it took a toll on his health. He was not keeping a diary when Charles died, but early in 1957 he took it up again. "Resume journal after long interval during which I was ill, troubled, etc., etc. Have decided that climacteric now passed, and henceforth my life must be quieter, more industrious. After being ill, gave up drinking, smoking and am gradually giving up taking dope for sleeplessness."[47] It was around this time that Malcolm also decided that he should become a vegetarian. The death of his son made the indulgence of his own appetites repugnant. As many of his contemporaries remarked, to use the words of Peter Black, Malcolm was for many years "the all-drinking, all-smoking boon companion", cigarette holder in one hand and drink in the other.[48] Having felt the shock of mortality, he decided once again to purge himself, to live the Simple Life, as he had done in India after his turbulent time at Cambridge, and at other intervals throughout his life. Over the next few years he found it easier to stick to vegetarianism than to abstinence from drinking and smoking.

Malcolm also made an effort to extend his abstinence to his sexual life. This took the form of giving up a long-running affair with Pamela Berry. She was the wife of Michael Berry, the son of Lord Camrose, owner of the *Daily Telegraph*. Her father was the famous Conservative lawyer and politician, F.E. Smith, who had served as Attorney General, Lord Chancellor and Secretary of State for India in Conservative governments. "F.E.", as he was known, was a celebrated wit, thoroughly at home in high society, and later became the Earl of Birkenhead. His daughter inherited many of his qualities, becoming one of the leading hostesses in London. She was active in supporting museums, and was president of the Incorporated Society of Fashion Designers. According to her obituary in *The Times*, the Berry home "was often regarded as virtually the last private political and intellectual *salon* in the classical tradition".[49]

Malcolm had known Pamela Berry since he joined the staff of the *Telegraph* after the war. In 1954, he noted in his diary that she was "not witty, but immensely droll; not clever, but shrewd and tough . . . Dresses always exactly like a gipsy with heavy, glittering metal on her dress."[50] He was not alone in admiring her qualities. Anthony Powell told Malcolm that she would turn up as a legendary figure in memoirs written by those of their generation. She was the opposite of Kitty – outgoing, fashion-minded, moving at ease in high society and in the public eye. She represented the Establishment from which Malcolm had always felt excluded. It may be that part of his attraction to her was precisely that she was the ultimate insider.

Malcolm's affair with Pamela Berry began soon after the 1954 diary entry, but it was stormy from the beginning. When Malcolm went to a party at the home of Pamela's brother, Freddie Birkenhead, he went over to Pamela, whom he hadn't seen for some weeks. "She said she'd given me up for Lent, but missed me and I said I'd missed her. So all was repaired."[51] After Charles's death, Malcolm insisted that they stop seeing each other. In the spring of 1957, however, Malcolm had received a letter from Pamela Berry that threatened to reopen the affair. "I wrote back briefly that if we saw each other again the same situation would arise, which I couldn't and wouldn't endure. Felt relieved when this was over."[52] But her hold on him was far from over. Two days later he wrote in his diary: "Thought much about P, mostly, alas, with shuddering and dread – Beware, beware, her flashing eyes, her floating hair ... the last convulsive twitch of a dead passion ..."[53] Within a few weeks, they were seeing each other again. The affair would continue, off and on, into the 1960s.

The sudden irruption of tragedy into Malcolm's life, though it triggered another episode in his Augustinian civil war between flesh and spirit, did not bring about a religious conversion. Malcolm's tortured spiritual life remained a secret to almost everyone except Kitty and a few friends like Claud Cockburn who were also religious seekers. To someone like Anthony Powell, not known as a religious man, Malcolm gave no indication of his spiritual yearnings. On the other hand, he did not confide fully in Alec Vidler, because his friend would say what he had said ever since their Cambridge days: that Malcolm should make an act of will and embrace the faith, something Malcolm did not feel ready to do. But to those, like P.J. Grigg and Cockburn, who were not conventionally religious but who had what he thought to be a mystical streak, he spoke of his desire to embrace Christianity.

What friends like Powell did not know was that after spending an evening as the "all-drinking, all-smoking boon companion", Malcolm would come home and read the works of Christian mystics late into the night. Grigg gave him *The Wandering Scholars*, by Helen Waddell, an expert on the early and medieval Christian ascetics and poets. There he discovered the story of Paulinus of Nola, a wealthy Roman who converted to Christianity and lived as a hermit. What Malcolm found particularly compelling about Paulinus was that his retreat from the world, far from ending his impact on the world, actually had a positive influence on his culture. Malcolm felt that Paulinus, like Gandhi, had discovered a profound secret: an absolute commitment to spiritual values had more practical benefits for society than the pursuit of power and political change. Reading Gerald Bullett's book on the English mystics, Malcolm noted in his diary that "political, social, and other such categories all break down completely where mystics are concerned – e.g., some, like Bunyan, proletarians; others, like Law, fanatical Royalists, etc."[54]

He reread Augustine's *Confessions*, which he had first encountered in Birmingham in 1926. In it he found a personality deeply akin to his own – sensual, intoxicated by the power of words and his success in using them, haunted by the feeling that God was pursuing him and demanding that he surrender his ego and embrace the life of faith. As he wrote in his diary, Malcolm was "convinced, more than ever that St Augustine, and those like him, alone have found the answer to life, which is to 'slaughter our self-conceits like birds, the curiosities by which we voyage through the secret ways of the abyss like the fish of the sea, our carnal lusts like the beasts of the field' in order that 'you, O God, you the consuming fire, should burn up those dead cares and renew the men themselves to immortal life.'"[55]

In his own family, Malcolm had examples that pointed him in the direction of the Christian life. Kitty's increasing serenity, her ability to endure suffering and to care for those who were experiencing suffering themselves, evoked Malcolm's continuing admiration. When their daughter Val was going through a difficult time, Malcolm observed Kitty: "When she goes to bed she puts on a pink bed jacket which Val knitted for her, her face exquisitely resigned; then she lies quite still, not sleeping, but with her whole being concentrated on Val and her trouble; all immobile lest I should worry about her not sleeping, her eyes glowing like two steady stars. This is love."[56] There was also his son Leonard, who had joined the Plymouth Brethren. Malcolm thought that Leonard's gentle spirit, his lack of egotism, set him apart from others. At a dinner with Natasha and Andrew Ronalds, whom he had known in Lourenço Marques, Natasha gave him something of a start. "Natasha perhaps has second sight, makes strange uncannily perceptive observations in the midst of wild chatter. She said that Pan was a saint to make up for all my sins."[57]

A year into his editorship of *Punch*, Malcolm wrote in his diary: "Bad night full of dark fears. While shaving suddenly thought with infinite longing how, of all things, I'd most love to live a Christian life. This the only wish now I'd ever have. And yet other satisfactions, known to be spurious, still pursued."[58] The death of his son Charles shocked him into an attempt at asceticism, but he could not bring himself to profess the Christian creed. There were several reasons for this. To get down on his knees with others in the pew would force him to become a full participant, thus compromising his stance as the outsider. Then there was the simple fact that he did not yet trust himself to be able to give up "spurious satisfactions". He knew that if he made any public confession of Christian faith his behaviour would immediately be scrutinised and held against him. Finally, he was deeply ambivalent about the state of the Christian Churches. The

Anglican Church, he thought, was accommodating itself to secular trends and causes and abandoning its supernatural message. Not only were there clerics like Hewlett Johnson, the "Red Dean", who seemed to worship Stalin rather than God, but there were others who called for the Church to relax its moral stands on such issues as marriage, divorce and sexuality. Malcolm's own behaviour contradicted many of these teachings, but that did not alter his conviction that to abandon these standards would inevitably lead to the unravelling of the social fabric. The Roman Catholic Church continued to exercise a strong attraction on Malcolm, but he could not see past the institutional dimension of the Church, with its many fallible guardians, to the Church as a transcendent reality. Unable to resolve his feelings, habits and convictions, Malcolm remained an outsider.

The other change that Malcolm made around the time of Charles's death was to move back to Sussex, where he and Kitty had their happiest memories. Their country home since 1952 had been located near Sevenoaks in Kent, a huge old rectory they shared with the writer Douglas Jerrold and his wife. But in 1956 the family moved to Salehurst Farmhouse in Robertsbridge, nestled in the Sussex downs near the town of Battle. The farmhouse was situated on land that had been used in the cultivation of hops. To all intents and purposes, this was to be their last move. Within a few years, when their children had all left home, they would leave the big farmhouse and settle into the smaller and more convenient Park Cottage, a beautiful seventeenth-century structure, located only a few hundred feet away from the farmhouse.

As Malcolm's five-year contract with *Punch* drew to an end in 1957, he realised that he no longer had the heart to edit the magazine. He had brought *Punch* into a new era, but he had lost his desire to struggle with the proprietors over editorial issues. For their part, Bradbury, Agnew & Co. had lost their enthusiasm for an editor who spent so much time on television and on controversial political causes. Circulation had begun to fall to the level it had been at when Malcolm had taken over, erasing the gains of recent years. The immediate cause for Malcolm's parting of the ways with *Punch* is said to have been the breakdown of negotiations for a Canadian edition of the magazine. There were also some controversial pieces, such as an article called "A Taste in Wine", which contained offensive statements about the Roman Catholic Mass. Malcolm apparently did not even read the piece before it was published. Several jokes made at the expense of Cheam, the school which the young Prince of Wales attended, did not go down well. One of the Agnew sons was also at Cheam.[59]

Rather than tender his resignation, Malcolm wanted to be sacked, which would entitle him to tax-free compensation. After what has been called "a clever skirmish with the management", Malcolm was offered a £5,000 severance payment and ceased acting as editor in the summer of 1957.[60] "It was with a sense of infinite relief that I went downstairs, past the figure of Mr Punch, and out through the door for the last time. A sense of almost mystical exhilaration seized me at the thought that I should never again cross that threshold, never again enter the twilit world within, or find myself under the professional necessity of trying to be funny."[61] He had now become such a regular fixture on television that he hoped to support a renewed effort at serious writing with the income he would receive as a media personality. Both the exhilaration and the plan would soon come to an abrupt end, but he could not know that as he stepped out into Bouverie Street for the last time.

« 16 »

Talking Head
1957–1962

"AMERICA PRINTS AMAZING ROYAL ATTACK BY ENGLISH TV IDOL."[1] This banner headline, printed in the British tabloid the *People* in the autumn of 1957, was the first shot fired in what was to become the nastiest and most infamous controversy of Malcolm's controversial career. By the time the smoke had cleared, Malcolm had received threatening phone calls and letters containing excrement and razor blades; he had been spat upon, his home had been vandalised and his media career had seemingly come to an abrupt end.

From the perspective of the present, however, the hysteria generated by the "royals scandal" seems almost quaint. The vicissitudes of the House of Windsor have sustained hordes of journalists and pundits for over two decades now, with no end in sight. That Malcolm should have been vilified for calling attention to the development of a "Royal Soap Opera" is almost incomprehensible today, a tempest in a Royal Doulton teapot. Malcolm himself would have preferred to be embroiled in a controversy over something more substantial than the state of the British monarchy, but he had little choice in the matter. As he often said when commenting on the problems of political leaders, Malcolm was in this instance a "victim of history". Here, as in so many issues, Malcolm suffered for his prophetic insights. We may take his opinions for granted today, but little has been done or said to give him credit for having the courage of his convictions.

The first act of the royals scandal began with a short essay in the *New Statesman*, entitled "Royal Soap Opera", published in 1955. In it, Malcolm bemoaned the vast amount of media attention being paid to the royal family. He pointed out that the attitude of "adulatory curiosity" towards the royals was a relatively recent development. Throughout the nineteenth century, *Punch* and other publications had

293

satirised the failings of monarchs and their families. But the twentieth-century tendency "to put them above laughter, above criticism, above the workaday world, is, ultimately, to dehumanise them and risk the monarchy dying of acute anaemia." The royal family was in danger of becoming a media sensation on the level with Hollywood film stars. But "their role is to symbolise the unity of a nation; to provide an element of continuity in a necessarily changing society. This is history, not *The Archers*, and their affairs ought to be treated as such." It was crucial that the royals and their advisers decide how they were going to position themselves: "do they want to be part of the mystique of the century of the common man or to be an institutional monarchy; to ride, as it were, in a glass coach or on bicycles; to provide the tabloids with a running serial or to live simply and unaffectedly among their subjects like the Dutch and Scandinavian royal families. What they cannot do is have it both ways."[2]

When this essay appeared, it stirred little controversy. Only the Beaverbrook papers took any notice of it, and their attack on Malcolm did not spread outside their own pages. In response to the attack on "Royal Soap Opera", Malcolm wrote a scathing piece on Beaverbrook himself, in which he accused the man of being an expert at "conducting vendettas by remote control", phoning and telegraphing his minions from different spots on the globe, giving them orders to go on the offensive. Malcolm told the old story of his colleague at the *Evening Standard* admitting that he wrote, not for the public, but "for one little old reader – Lord Beaverbrook".

In the spring of 1957, not long before he left *Punch*, Malcolm travelled to New York. While there, he was approached by the editors of the *Saturday Evening Post* for an article. Malcolm's essay, "Royal Soap Opera", had not gone unnoticed. The editors of the magazine asked Malcolm if he would write a longer, more elaborate piece on the same subject. The *Saturday Evening Post* was one of America's leading magazines, read by the affluent middle classes and fairly conventional in content and editorial policy. Knowing the American fascination with the British monarchy, the editors sensed an occasion for a controversial article that would make their readers sit up and pay attention. Malcolm returned to England, wrote the essay and promptly went on to other things.

When the editors at the *Post* learned that Queen Elizabeth would be making state visits to the United States and Canada in the autumn, they decided to delay publication of Malcolm's article until that time.

Aware that the article would make as big a splash in Britain as in America, the *Post* released the complete text of the article prior to its publication. The British press got hold of it and wasted no time. A week before the *Post* even published the essay, Beaverbrook's *Sunday Express* and the *People* ran news articles about it, accompanied by editorial denunciations of Malcolm. The *People* condemned Malcolm's essay as "ruthless, shocking, patronizing, gruesome" and as nothing more than a "diatribe".

In their headlong rush to lynch Malcolm, these papers distorted and falsified the arguments presented in the *Post* essay. The extracts from the article were brief and taken out of context. Malcolm, it was said, had called the monarchy "a club for snobs and a drain on the British taxpayer". In fact, Malcolm put forward the argument that the rise of egalitarianism in the century of the common man had, ironically, caused many people to become more snobbish and class-conscious than they had in the past. As to the monarchy being a drain on the taxpayer, Malcolm criticized the "sour-faced journalists" who made such arguments: "Compared with the cost of atomic submarines or guided missiles, the monarchy cannot be considered expensive . . ."[3]

If the press accounts ignored Malcolm's historical survey of the British monarchy and his arguments about the way celebrities have become the secular equivalent of saints or mythic figures, they were quick to pounce on his more acerbic comments. He took aim at the BBC commentator, Richard Dimbleby, whose "hushed and reverent" tones when describing royal events Malcolm found unctuous. With a certain amount of rhetorical playfulness, he imagines previous monarchs confronting Dimbleby. They would have seen his commentary as so much "gibberish", not to mention "unnecessary, bewildering, and absurd". "Queen Victoria would, we may be sure, not have been amused." A few paragraphs later, Malcolm notes that the upper classes are in fact more critical of the monarchy than the working classes. "It is duchesses, not shop assistants, who find the Queen dowdy, frumpish and banal."

The public response to these news reports about Malcolm's essay – which was still not published – was one of hysterical outrage. Sir George Clark, at a Unionist rally, told his audience that Malcolm should be horsewhipped. One reporter had been told by the vicar of Cholsey in Berkshire that Malcolm "has a face it would be most satisfying to poke – the sort of face one just wishes to flatten out . . .

My study will be at Mr Muggeridge's disposal and I will gladly provide a steak for his black eye."[4] While walking by the sea at Brighton a man came up to Malcolm, spat in his face and continued on his way. Their house in Robertsbridge was vandalised, and their garage and a nearby barn were spray-painted with loyalist slogans, which included a demand that he apologise. The League of Empire Loyalists proudly claimed responsibility for the spray-painting. The yellow paint reminded Malcolm of the yellow markings which the Nazis had placed on Jewish homes and businesses in Germany before World War II. The *Sunday Dispatch*, which had only just signed Malcolm as a weekly columnist – touting him as "the most controversial writer in Britain today" – decided they no longer required his services.

A particularly bizarre episode took place when Malcolm travelled to Scotland to take part in the elections for the Rectorship of Edinburgh University. The Rector is elected by the students, and Malcolm was one of eleven candidates nominated for the position. When he arrived at Waverley Station, he had to be escorted by police through a crowd which included demonstrators chanting: "God Save the Queen" and "No Mercy for Muggeridge". On the eve of the election, the two leading supporters of Malcolm's candidacy were kidnapped and left, bound and gagged, in an abandoned hostel. When the results were announced, Malcolm had come in fifth.

Then there were the phone calls and letters. In addition to the letters containing razor blades and excrement, there were others that made the same point verbally. A sampling of the letters Malcolm received includes such statements as: "Were you born ugly and smug? . . . We are all fed up with your egotistical ideas . . . Your damn ugly face that you have, and your snooty talk, with your stinking nose . . . I noticed you received rather more than the thirty pieces of silver paid to your predecessor . . . and he, Judas, did at least have the decency to go out and hang himself." Then there were two letters which were in a category all by themselves. The first included these sentiments: "With reference to your son who was killed . . . it was all for the best. Eventually he would have found out that not only did you not know who the father was, but neither did his mother . . ." The second letter simply said: "The world is better off now he [Charles Muggeridge] has gone: what about joining him?"[5]

As soon as the news about the article broke, the BBC invited Malcolm to appear on the next *Panorama* to explain his position and defend himself against the mounting number of attacks. The invitation had come from the young producer of BBC talks programmes, Michael Peacock. But Peacock was told by his superiors to cancel the invitation. A mere five hours before the programme was to be broadcast, it was announced that Malcolm would not be appearing. A BBC official explained: "We have come to the conclusion that we should not give further publicity to a matter which has already had enough." When pressed, the BBC spokesman admitted that there had been only about a dozen phone calls objecting to Malcolm's scheduled appearance.[6]

The decision to bar Malcolm from *Panorama* was made by the head of the BBC, Sir Ian Jacob, though there was some speculation that the order had come directly from the Prime Minister, Harold Macmillan. According to a British television historian, Sir Ian, whatever his many positive achievements may have been, "made a mess of the BBC's public relations . . . his regime seemed memorable for excessive concern with a narrow definition of propriety in broadcasting."[7] Henceforth he would be known as "Sir Ban". When the cancellation of Malcolm's appearance on *Panorama* became known, Sir Ian attempted to protect himself from accusations of censorship. He and Malcolm met a few days later, ostensibly to discuss Malcolm's future with the BBC. After the meeting, a "corporation spokesman" announced: "There is no ban on Mr Malcolm Muggeridge, who will continue to appear in BBC programmes."[8] This was a disingenuous answer at best, because six weeks later, when the time came to renew Malcolm's contract with the BBC, his agent, David Higham, received a brief letter stating that the contract would not be renewed. Even the commercial television company, Associated Rediffusion, announced that, contrary to a news report, it was not prepared to "offer engagements to Mr Muggeridge at the present time". The ranks had closed: Malcolm had been quietly but effectively banned from the airwaves.

His final assignment for the BBC was to interview the painter Augustus John, who had been a *bon vivant* and fixture in London society for many years. Malcolm found John a refreshing change from the politicians and bureaucrats he normally had to interview. Malcolm's one serious concern about the split from the BBC was the fate of a documentary series he had worked hard to produce, called *The Thirties*. He met Sir Ian again to discuss the fate of the programme. Sir Ian's initial reaction was to avoid the issue: he suggested postponing the broadcast for three months. Malcolm, sensing that this might give Sir Ian room to shelve the programme, insisted that a decision for or against be made immediately. Sir Ian relented, and the series was broadcast. It was Malcolm's first effort at a more constructive and creative use of the medium than he had engaged in to this point: the documentary. Several years would elapse before he could return to making television documentaries.

If he could not defend himself on British television, Malcolm had the opportunity to do so on an American programme. He accepted an invitation to appear on *The Mike Wallace Interview*, to be broadcast live on October 19, the day the *Saturday Evening Post* article was published. In deference to the Queen, who was in Washington, DC, with her entourage, the network blacked out the broadcast in Washington. When Malcolm arrived at Mike Wallace's house, where he was to spend the night before the programme was to take place, he discovered that Wallace was under pressure to cancel the broadcast entirely. At one point the phone rang, a long-distance call from California. It quickly became clear that Wallace was becoming involved in a long, drawn-out argument. He motioned to Malcolm to listen in on the other phone extension. "The voice I heard (belonging, as I subsequently learned, to one of the chief executives of the TV network for which Mr Wallace then worked) was raucous and deeply perturbed as it rebuked Mr Wallace for interviewing me at all, and appealed to him, if the interview must take place, not to be 'soft' with me. 'Don't you realise,' it said, in a final effort at persuasion, 'that this Queen is the only bulwark against Communism?'"[9] Wallace was undeterred by this line of reasoning.

The British-born American journalist Alistair Cooke wrote an article describing the interview. "Like a proconsul summoned to Rome to explain the riots in East Anglia Mr Malcolm Muggeridge flew into New York last night to account for his views on the British monarchy to Mike Wallace, the public prosecutor of American television." To Cooke's mind Malcolm gave a bravura performance. Even though "strong men have quailed and wept" when interrogated by Wallace, Malcolm handled him with ease.

Mr Wallace came at him like the Hound of the Baskervilles, and Mr Muggeridge said, "There, there." Mr Wallace bayed to heaven to bear witness to Muggeridge's *lèse-majesté*, to his "carefully designed attempt to create a sensation". Mr Muggeridge said not so, and mocked him with a roguish smile. Mr Wallace leaped to his full height to maul the abominable no-man, and Mr Muggeridge tugged his ear. No matter how threateningly Mr Wallace shifted his inflections, narrowed his eyes, drained smoke from his nostrils, he still was as adorable as a puppy to Mr Muggeridge. In the end he was eating out of the enemy's hand.[10]

Cooke's description certainly conveys the ease and composure with which Malcolm, an old hand at television interviewing, handled Mr Wallace. There were plenty of roguish smiles, such as the moment when Wallace quoted the British MP, Michael Astor, to the effect that Malcolm's "genius is for disliking [his] fellow human beings". To which Malcolm replied: "Well, if my fellow human beings were all Astors, there might be some element of truth in that, but fortunately for us all, the Astor family is a large one, but not so large that it's occupied the whole human race . . ."

Lost in the midst of Malcolm's coruscating wit were his more serious observations, including his insistence that "the essence of a free and civilised society is that everything in it should be subject to criticism, that all forms of authority should be treated with a certain reservation, and . . . that once you have produced . . . a totally conformist society in which there were no critics, that would in fact be an exact equivalent of the totalitarian societies against which we are supposed to be fighting in a cold war." Wallace, in obvious frustration, asked whether Malcolm accepted any higher authority than himself, such as religion. Malcolm replied that "because I regard the temper of my mind as religious, I am profoundly sceptical about any form of human authority, any form of human self-importance. You see, the hallmark of religion is to distrust claims made for mortal men. It is in ages of great religious faith that great scepticism can find expression."

In the final segment of the programme, Wallace simply asked Malcolm's opinions about several world leaders. Churchill achieved greatness in the war, but he was an "appallingly bad politician" who "hung on to power long after he should have done". Eden: "the most disastrous Prime Minister in our history". Macmillan "achieved power too late" and was out of touch with the times. American Secretary of State John Foster Dulles: "portentous, sincere, honest and rather stupid". The Russian launching of the Sputnik satellite did not depress him, Malcolm said. "[S]upposing that the founder of the Christian religion, who, after all, has dominated art, thought, literature, law for 2,000 years of western European civilisation; supposing that He had been on a conducted tour of Rome or had known that the world was round instead of flat – or had flown in a jet aircraft. I do not believe that the Sermon on the Mount would have been either more or less profound than it is. Sputnik is just . . . a firework, a rocket, a new invention." By this point Wallace could only "look wistfully at the camera", as Cooke put it, and thank Malcolm for coming and exercising the "ancient British tradition of free speech".[11]

Back at home, a few voices began to speak up in Malcolm's defence. The *Sunday Mirror*, for example, proclaimed: "If all views must agree with the BBC (Better Be Careful) censors, nothing worthwhile will ever be said."[12] Jo Grimond, the leader of the Liberal Party, urged a protest against the ban. "I disagree with many of Mr Muggeridge's views, but we cannot tolerate the BBC putting any institution above criticism. We allow atheists and Communists on the air. We must surely allow responsible discussions of the Crown and Court."[13] Even the *Manchester Guardian* stood up for its wayward son: "Anti-Muggeridgism has recently taken on the appearance of pre-war anti-semitism . . . Muggeridge has been exposed to a campaign which the mildest supporter of Voltaire would have to oppose."[14]

Despite his public display of detached amusement, Malcolm was deeply shocked and wounded by the whole affair.[15] Aware that his future as a journalist was in jeopardy, he decided to fight back. He went to an eminent lawyer to find out whether he had grounds for a libel suit. The lawyer, pacing up and down his quiet office, agreed that Malcolm had been libelled. The problem, he said, was that, "in the circumstances", it was unlikely that Malcolm would find a judge or jury who would be unprejudiced. "It was eerie, and a little alarming," he later recalled, "to have the theory of 'People's' justice, as administered in Communist countries, thus expounded by this Dickensian figure . . ."[16]

A less risky gambit was to file a complaint with the Press Council. This was a supposedly independent body, which handed down rebukes to editors and journalists when they offended against the canons of fairness and civility. Malcolm was told that the Council could not take up the matter until their next quarterly meeting, some three months hence. When he offered to appear before the Council to clarify his position, the offer was declined, on the grounds that the editors of the *Sunday Express* and the *People* would have to be summoned as well, adding another three months to the process. These bureaucratic and secretive policies did not bode well for Malcolm, and when the verdict was finally reached in late January 1958, the Press Council ruled that

Malcolm had not justified his complaint. The statement concluded: "The Press Council does not think the considerable misfortunes of which Mr Muggeridge complains were due to the alleged 'gross falsification' but were the outcome of the disparagements which he deliberately put in his article."[17] In contrast to the sanctimonious bombast of the Press Council, however, the National Union of Journalists issued a concise report that concluded that Malcolm's article had indeed been distorted.

With these conflicting judgements, the royals scandal came to an inconclusive and ignominious end. Or so it seemed. In fact, Malcolm would continue to suffer from the after-effects for many years. In 1964, the executive committee of the prestigious Garrick Club, to which Malcolm belonged, decided to launch an "investigation" into "the propriety of a member of the Club speaking against the Monarchy". Once again the Establishment was closing ranks, launching a witch hunt under the guise of propriety and highmindedness. Rather than endure another round of persecution at the hands of the highminded, Malcolm resigned from the club.[18]

More than two years after the affair had ended, when Malcolm was just resuming his television career, he was given encouragement and comfort in an unexpected fashion. While he was staying at the Midland Hotel in Manchester, a man walked up to him in the lobby and said: "Never forget that only dead fish swim with the tide."[19] Malcolm immediately decided that this piece of wisdom should become his personal motto.

In one sense, the royals scandal fitted the familiar pattern of Malcolm's career: he would speak the truth before most of his countrymen were prepared to hear it, suffer ostracism and ridicule, only to be proven right years later. By the time his prophetic insights had passed into common currency, his prophetic role was usually forgotten and little or no credit was added to his reputation.

There can be little doubt that in this episode Malcolm was a "victim of history". The emotions unleashed by the controversy ultimately had a lot more to do with Britain's declining role in the world than anything Malcolm thought or said. Having recently experienced the fiasco of Anthony Eden's disastrous Suez expedition, many Britons were increasingly sensitive about their marginal role in world affairs. The middle class suffered the most intense identity crisis at this time, and it was this class that clung most desperately to the monarchy as an emotional prop. Malcolm found this borne out by the most hysterical reactions to the reports of his essay on the monarchy. "The abusive letters, though largely illiterate, suggested, by their notepaper and manner of address, rather genteel than proletarian origins. The voices which screamed insults down my telephone had about them likewise a faint flavour of gentility."[20]

Malcolm's willingness to deride the Establishment seemed to many to be just another form of negativism and even of treachery. But to Malcolm's mind it was precisely because of Britain's decline in real power and influence that the institution of the monarchy, which was purely symbolic, became invested with a disproportionate amount of adulation and reverence. This is where his point about royal-watching being an ersatz religion comes in. Without faith in God, he believed, people tend to invest the rich and the famous with a mystique formerly reserved for saints and martyrs. Abetted by the media, and especially television, modern men and women were increasingly living vicariously through the soap operas staged from Hollywood and Buckingham Palace. Treating the royal family like movie stars, he said, would trivialise the institution. His consistent argument had been that focusing on the personal characteristics of the monarch or any member of the royal family would, in the long run, backfire. The all too human foibles of the individuals would bring the *office* of the monarchy into disrepute. The rest, as they say, is history.

Of course, Malcolm was not merely a victim in this controversy. The monarchy row was the first intimation that Malcolm's Faustian pact with television was close to dragging him down into the jaws of media oblivion. What television gave, television could take away. But Malcolm's continuing popularity through the years was not simply a function of his being "the man that millions love to hate". As one writer put it: "A lot of Malcolm's popularity with the general public came from [the fact] that Malcolm was never afraid to say what he thought. Malcolm never held back. Sometimes, well, the people thought he went just a bit too far ... Malcolm always went in, sometimes where angels fear to tread, and I think a lot of people admired him because he was prepared to state the facts clearly and in depth."[21]

But the image of Malcolm as the consummate hater persists to this day. Some of the reasons for a backlash against Malcolm have already been discussed, including the sheer number of programmes he appeared on, and the fact that many of them inclined to short satirical answers rather than serious explorations of important subjects. Radio and television tended to filter out his positive convictions, particularly in the area of religion; these beliefs did not fit the Muggeridge persona and failed to register. Then there was his physical appearance. Malcolm's manner and facial expressions could be delightfully wicked, but they could also be smug and pompous. When in later years Malcolm watched film footage from his early television career, he was abashed. "It appals me now, but I used to look uncommonly self-satisfied, and not a little arrogant."[22]

Malcolm denied that he was a pathological hater. He was, rather, a nonconformist, prepared if necessary to point out that the emperor was not wearing any clothes. The reason why censors like Sir Ian Jacob preferred to ban Malcolm from the airwaves was that "the assumptions on which our institutions and values are based have come to seem so dubious that any questioning of their validity appears indefensible and intolerable. In other words, accusations of bad taste are in reality no more than a means of evading disagreeable truths . . . To the Scribes and Pharisees the Christian Gospel as preached by its Originator appeared in the worst possible taste."[23]

The true nonconformist knows the importance of humour. "A totally conformist society never laughs – laughter itself being a kind of criticism, an expression of the immense disparity between human aspiration and human performance. As such, it is intolerable to all orthodoxy-enforcers, from Torquemada to Stalin."[24] Humour is thus subversive and anarchic, turning the pretensions of those in authority on their heads. Humour and ridicule help keep in check the tendency of those in authority to extend their power and privilege. Without the anarchic force of humour, power becomes arrogant and monolithic. Humour literally frees us; it is the opposite of servility. "The grinning, unsightly gargoyles that stand below Salisbury Cathedral's exquisite steeple, in underlining its inadequacy, heighten its sublimity. They represent, on the part of their medieval creators, a deliberate gesture of bad taste, which, in relation to the rest of the edifice, adds to its glory."[25]

Along with the gargoyle, Malcolm frequently commented on the role of the clown, and in particular the Shakespearean Fool, in relation to the larger social order. This was an image that had come to have a strong personal meaning for Malcolm, because he had come to feel that his public role had developed into that of the clown – a development that arose as much out of necessity as of choice. "The circus clown," he wrote is made to look different from his fellow-performers. He falls over, he stands on his head, he grimaces and rides absurd bicycles. Yet what would a circus be without him? How especially the children would miss him, however daring the trapeze artists, however majestic the lion-tamer! It is worth noting, too, that Shakespeare's Fools are given some of his most sagacious and poetic lines. The non-conforming Fool proved, in the end, King Lear's most tender, understanding and faithful friend, when all the conformists had abandoned him to his fate.[26]

But if the fool could be a noble and humane character, Malcolm knew that he was still a figure of ridicule, tolerated but rarely loved. He frequently recalled the line in the Shakespearean sonnet about making oneself "a motley to the view". His appearance and manner had, by the time of the royals scandal, became part of Britain's cultural consciousness, and gave rise to many funny cartoons by artists like Trog, to impressions by comedians like Mike Yarwood, and, eventually to a Malcolm Muggeridge figure in Madame Tussaud's Waxwork Museum in London. The role of clown was, at best, bittersweet. The emotional cost – to his dignity and to his sense of his literary potential – was higher than Malcolm was prepared to admit. He might well have remembered that many clowns have sad faces. Or that Lear's fool leaves the stage early, well before the play is done.

In the aftermath of the royals scandal Malcolm did what he had done several times before: he fled public criticism, seeking solace and distraction abroad. Just as he had left England for India in 1924 and 1935, after intense personal crises, so he now accepted an invitation from the *Sydney Morning Herald* to spend three months in Australia. His plan to support himself through television appearances had fallen apart, making such an invitation difficult to turn down. The only regular income he had came from his weekly column for the *Sunday Pictorial*. But going abroad was not his only alternative. He could have sought an advance from a publisher and written a book, something he had not done for ten years. Despite the pangs of guilt that he was not writing something more substantial, Malcolm's "urge to be gone" won out, and he boarded a plane for the far side of the world.

The offer by the *Sydney Morning Herald* was a generous one. He was to come to Australia and travel wherever he wished, writing articles about subjects that interested him. For his first topic he inquired into the reasons people emigrated to Australia. He went on board ships that had only just docked at Sydney harbour, and sought out other immigrants just making the transition to their new life. He was most impressed by the simple answer given to him by a Hungarian, who did not hesitate in answering Malcolm's question about liking Australia. "Of course I like it. I like freedom." Far less appealing were the British immigrants who complained of having to give up their social security benefits. "The welfare state," Malcolm concluded, "is a kind of zoo which provides its inmates with ease and comfort but unfits them for life in their natural habitat. Mangy and bleary-eyed, they grumble and growl as they walk up and down their cages wailing for slabs of welfare to be thrown to them at mealtime."[27]

He stirred up the most controversy by attacking the notion that the British Commonwealth was any more substantial or unified than the Empire had been. On a television series broadcast under the title, *Malcolm Muggeridge Meets Australians*, he confronted the tendency of some Australians to revere and imitate the British. Sir Arthur Fadden, the deputy leader of the government, spoke of "what I am still old-fashioned enough to call the British Empire". When Malcolm said this was like calling a Rolls-Royce a coach and four, Sir Arthur was not amused.

Malcolm also visited the Geelong Grammar School, which called itself the "Eton of the Antipodes". He found that graduates of this school, like its counterpart in England, tended to end up in the Foreign Service. Malcolm called them "the funeral mutes who have followed the hearse of British policy from one disaster to another, without ever losing their breath, their composure or their infinite complacency".[28]

Despite its remote and exotic location, Malcolm felt that Australia was, like most places on the globe, conforming to a mass culture (predominantly American) that knew no boundaries. In Melbourne he spent some time with the rebellious youth, known locally as "bodgies" (boys) and "widgies" (girls). Sporting sideburns in honour of their hero, Elvis Presley, these delinquents described to Malcolm their "police convictions and undetected misdemeanours with quiet pride – breaking and entering, larceny, carnal knowledge. They might have been going over cricket scores." More offensive to Malcolm than their casual attitude towards crime was the "amount of whining mixed up with their boasting". The bodgies and widgies, he concluded, were "waifs of a materialist society . . . over rather than underprivileged". The gyrations of rock-and-roll dancing left the "tang of adolescent sex" in the air, something he found revolting.[29] Ironically, he thought that this youth culture was marked by a weariness and ennui that made its adherents prematurely old.

He kept up a furious pace of activity throughout his three months in Australia. Articles, book reviews, a television series, speeches and interviews followed each other at a dizzying rate. He had ruffled as many feathers as he could find, bringing down upon himself a new set of angry denunciations. But at least one Australian felt that Malcolm's visit had been a tonic. Malcolm "is interested in everything and everybody. He writes to shake his readers out of their sunny hypocrisy, out of their placid habits and out of their horrible acceptance in having their thinking done for them. His name is on every lip and we think and talk about his wickedly witty words with varying degrees of warmth. He has slapped us awake."[30]

Thanks to the intervention of Dr H.V. Evatt, the leader of Australia's opposition at the time, Malcolm was able to obtain a visa to visit the People's Republic of China. En route to China, he made a series of lightning trips to, among other places, Japan, Indonesia, Thailand, Ceylon (now Sri Lanka) and Hong Kong. He passed on his impressions of these places in a series of articles for the *Sunday Pictorial*. He managed to cause another furore by calling Hong Kong "a museum piece of old-fashioned colonialist government, capitalist economy and speculator's paradise" – another comment that, from this distance in time, would hardly raise an eyebrow.[31]

From Hong Kong he took a train to the border with China. The railway ended just before the border, and passengers had to walk to the border post where they were to be processed. He actually felt his spirits lightening as he approached the border: China evoked Malcolm's curiosity and respect, as Russia and India had in the past. The people, he thought, were "infinitely charming". His mood was temporarily deflated when the first thing he saw was a "poster showing some idealized workers looking at television. However, I thought, it's only a poster. They haven't actually got it."[32] Contrary to the image of Malcolm as a fanatical anti-Communist, he was actually prepared to be impressed by China. As he travelled north to Peking by train through the rich South China countryside, he concluded that China had experienced a "smiling revolution", as opposed to the grim regime in the Soviet Union. "I did not feel that the Communist regime had laid a very heavy hand on this part of China."[33]

Peking itself seemed ordinary, compared to the "Xanadu" he had imagined it would be. On the way to his hotel, he saw several hideous statues and bas-reliefs of heroic, larger-than-life proletarian – "the Festival School which is standardized throughout the world – dedicated to the Unknown Common Man". He was met by the Reuters correspondent and whisked off to a party at the British Embassy. The experience was like a "strange dream". He was driven through a huge red gate into the embassy compound, which was a small world unto itself, cut off from everything. The sense of claustrophobia continued, as a Norwegian lady explained to him that the Westerners in Peking spent all their time together, showing one another "cine-camera films" of the last May Day parade. Not long after he had been told this, the British Consul, Cedric Mabey, summoned everyone to watch film footage of his recent trip to Cambodia. Malcolm found the whole atmosphere at the embassy pathetic. His attitude had not changed since he was a twenty-year-old stepping ashore in India: he found the Westerner's capacity to insulate himself from the rich, multifarious life of other nations disgusting.

The Forbidden City had more than a touch of Xanadu about it, but the rest of Peking was more prosaic. He was impressed by the "propriety" of the Chinese and the "total absence of coloured filth and sadism which is to be seen wherever Freedom reigns and Western Values prevail". Businessmen from the West, he noticed, lost no chance to do business with the Chinese; their only criterion was the profit motive. But Malcolm had not been completely seduced by the Chinese. Though the people were charming and intelligent, he recognised a totalitarian regime for what it was. In his diary he noted that social and political control in China was exerted differently from that in the Soviet Union. Instead of the ubiquitous presence in Russia of uniformed police, the Chinese Communists used a complex system of "surveillance based on the street, the residence, the floor, and, finally, the individual apartment".[34]

He flew on to Shanghai, where he was taken to meet one of the few surviving Chinese capitalists. As it turned out, this gentleman had been to Cambridge University, where he read economics. His conversation was liberally interspersed with the phrase "I don't mind telling you." He told Malcolm that he was highly satisfied with the current Communist regime under Mao Tse-tung, but somehow Malcolm wasn't convinced. "His face was oddly tormented – but the torment below the surface ... I felt sorry for him and drawn to him. He went on and on telling me how happy he was, and thereby conveying his truly appalling unhappiness."

Malcolm's interest in religion drove him to seek out churches and attempt to gauge their condition. At an Anglican service, held entirely in Chinese, and with the Red Flag prominently displayed behind the pulpit, he sat next to an Anglican clergyman who explained the rules governing religious practice in China. His reaction to the Anglican clergyman was typical of his feelings about that Church as a whole: "a bit too smooth for me". The Catholic service, which he attended later, was altogether different: "much less prosperous, no Red Flag, a kind of tatterdemalion defiance about it". The Catholics were putting up a fight, he thought. But he feared that Christianity had no roots in China and would eventually wither away.[35]

Summing up his thoughts about China in an article, Malcolm gave a balanced report. While he did not deny the oppressiveness of the regime, or the monotony of life under it, he pointed out that social maladies such as drug consumption and prostitution had been virtually eliminated, that the people were relatively well off and that the government was well respected. He predicted in that article that China's relations with the Soviet Union would become strained and that China would eventually seek closer ties with the United States – a prediction that Richard Nixon would fulfil in the early 1970s. It was time, he argued, for the United States and the United Nations to formally recognise China: "The simple fact is that the Peking government rules all China and will continue to rule it in the foreseeable future."[36]

From China he flew on to the Soviet Union. To his surprise, he had had no difficulty in obtaining a visa. His flight made several stops, giving him brief glimpses of several cities. Gone were the signs of famine and grinding poverty that had burned themselves into his mind back in the winter of 1932–3. "It was extraordinary," he noted in his diary, "to be back in this country after twenty-five years. I had never really expected to see it again, and now there I was, walking about, looking."[37] When he finally reached Moscow, he felt neither exaltation nor desolation. Staring at Stalin's embalmed corpse, lying in the mausoleum in Red Square next to that of Lenin, he realised that he was no longer emotionally involved in the shifting political fortunes of the world, as he had been twenty-five years before.

Extending his voluntary exile, Malcolm travelled on to the Middle

East, visiting Israel, Egypt and several other Arab nations. This too was territory he knew well. But then this trip was never really about exploring new ground; it was about movement itself, the "urge to be gone" raised to a fever pitch. Malcolm was killing time. Photographs of him from this trip show a pale and exhausted man, with dark hollows under his eyes. He returned home from the Middle East, but only for a few weeks. By the autumn of 1958, he had taken on another temporary assignment covering the proceedings of the United Nations in New York. He thought of the UN as a reincarnation of the League of Nations – another utopian scheme that was perpetually bogged down in ideological rhetoric. The UN headquarters building in New York he called "that huge symmetrical glass tombstone ... whose occupants specialize in throwing stones".[38]

He kept moving. On to Little Rock, Arkansas, where the governor, Orval Faubus, was refusing to allow Blacks to attend public schools, in direct opposition to federal desegregation policies. Malcolm's suggestion that the larger social and historical forces of the time were working against him failed to register with Governor Faubus. Back to England, and then over to Berlin, where he surveyed a city divided by two opposed cultures, though not yet divided by a physical wall. He felt then much as he had when he went from Hong Kong to Peking. To the East he saw dialectical materialism, which had created a puritanical slave-state, where people scrabbled for the perks that come with Party membership; to the West he saw individualist materialism, where Everyman was enslaved by the relentless, narcissistic pursuit of happiness.

In February of 1959, Malcolm added a final coda to the travels that had taken him away from England for the better part of a year. He returned to Russia, this time to cover the mission of Prime Minister Harold Macmillan to the Soviet Union. Malcolm considered Macmillan to be the last feeble representative of British upper-class rule, a man who "looked more than ever as though he had come out of a tattered old volume of the *Forsyte Saga*". The whole purpose of Macmillan's visit was misguided Malcolm thought. Macmillan and his advisers believed that Britain might be able to defrost the Cold War by showing Soviet premier Nikita Khrushchev that the West was willing to deal with him. The problem, according to Malcolm, was that Macmillan had no real power and no concrete offers to make. It was "a diplomatic Suez – an effort on the part of the Conservatives to show that they were capable of an independent diplomatic initiative, as, at

Suez, they tried to show that they were capable of an independent military initiative". The truth was that Macmillan was "tethered to Washington and can graze but not wander".

Nonetheless, Malcolm found much to amuse him on the trip. Hearing Macmillan utter statements like "across the Steppes the furnace glow of industry beckons to a promised land" or "over the broad plains of the Ukraine there ranged the same spirit of self-reliance as over the hedged fields of England" sent Malcolm into spasms of laughter. Perhaps the most unforgettable moment was the day that Macmillan spoke at Moscow University, standing under a gigantic banner that said: "Welcome to the Glorious Red Army". Macmillan, he thought, looked "so like the chairman of the governors at a school speech-day that I fully expected him to ask for a day's holiday".

Malcolm stayed, along with the other journalists, at the Hotel Ukraine, a building of "inconceivable architectural hideousness". There he met a young Russian journalist named Vladimir, who had a highly developed sense of the absurd. Watching Macmillan refer to the number of motorcycles manufactured in the United Kingdom on Soviet television, Malcolm and Vladimir could hardly contain themselves. Later in the trip, on the train from Leningrad to Moscow, Vladimir went off to find out what one high Soviet official had said in a speech. By the time he made it back to Malcolm, Vladimir had forgotten what the official told him, with the exception of an old English proverb he had quoted: "Leave and Let Leave". At a cocktail party Malcolm encountered another delightful Russian, a scientist known as Dr Kapitza, who had been to Cambridge University in the 1920s. After reminiscing about those days at Cambridge, Dr Kapitza explained the etiquette that Communist underlings had to observe before they could approach the Top Brass. He, however, did not intend to fraternise with the commissars. It was a good principle, he said to Malcolm, "to keep as far away from the boss as possible, and as near as possible to the kitchen, and when in doubt to go to sleep".[39]

Perhaps Malcolm's most intriguing encounter during the visit was at that same cocktail party. Lady Reilly, the wife of the British ambassador, brought Khrushchev himself over and introduced him to Malcolm, who was himself introduced as the former editor of a humorous magazine, *Punch*. Through an interpreter, Khrushchev said that he didn't care for the Russian humour magazine, *Krokodil*. His grandchildren made him read it, and had to explain the jokes to him.

Malcolm replied that he too had found himself having to explain jokes, and that nothing could be more painful or melancholy to the professional journalist. Khrushchev disagreed.

> "It's all right for you," I said, "to be funny, as indeed you are. But just imagine having to do it for a living. And anyway life is funnier than anything you can think of. Take this reception, for instance . . ."
> "Life is good," Khrushchev said.
> I agreed that it was good but also funny.
> As he left, he said: "In your article write the truth."
> "Such," I replied, "is my constant endeavour."[40]

After the trip with Macmillan, Malcolm actually began a correspondence with the editor of *Krokodil*. In December 1959, *Krokodil* asked Malcolm to write a sketch about the funniest thing that had happened that year. The piece he wrote described a ludicrous speech Macmillan had given in Kiev, and went on to compare the old Etonian to Don Quixote, assigning the role of Sancho Panza to the Foreign Secretary, Selwyn Lloyd (who was in fact a rather short man). Not long after sending it on to *Krokodil*, Malcolm received an apologetic telegram informing him that they could not run the piece because they held Macmillan in high esteem and did not want to make him the object of ridicule. "The world's present insecurity," Malcolm reflected, "is liable to create an exaggerated respect for authority. In the shadow of the mushroom cloud, we draw together, hush our voices, and keep in step. Such order as exists seems too frail to be subjected to the blasts of ridicule. Like an invalid, it has to be wrapped up, kept from the draughts, and fed on pre-digested food."[41]

Malcolm's year of wandering had been a way of marking time while the emotions generated by the royals scandal slowly subsided, but on those long plane and train journeys, he had thought a great deal. It was on his visit to Berlin at the end of 1958 that Malcolm passed an intellectual watershed that signalled a permanent shift of attention. Since 1932, his deepest passion and most consistent subject had been the struggle of the West against Communism and its associated ideologies. But there was a moment in Berlin when he realised that in the future he would have a new focus of attention. Whereas only a few years before he would have stressed the differences between the freedom of the West and the tyranny of the East, he now felt that the differences were less dramatic and less urgent.

> The Cold War itself has no more reality than the wars between the Big-enders and the Little-enders in *Gulliver's Travels*. It is about nothing. The very words which express it are becoming, on both sides, emptier and emptier, more and more turgid, laboured and tedious. By contrast, whenever one of the huge motor cars used by the United States embassy in Moscow stops, it is at once surrounded by a little crowd of awed admirers. So would a sputnik be if it were on show in New York.

Now that the Cold War had settled into a protracted conflict, Malcolm's attention turned away from the grand political fantasies of socialism and Communism to the fantasies of the individual – wealth, ambition, celebrity, sexual liberation. He had always been a moralist, but up to this point his moral critiques had largely been directed against social and political sins, such as snobbery, Leftist ideology and the pretensions of those in power. But now he had come to believe, as his old friend Hugh Kingsmill had believed, that the underlying problem of modernity was materialism. Once God had been declared dead, modern men and women inevitably chased after strange gods. His travels had convinced him that the world was indeed becoming a global village, in which desires and appetites were more uniform. Recalling the neon signs he had seen in many American towns – "Gas, Drugs, Beauty, Food" – Malcolm concluded that they represented "the *logos* of our time, presented in sublime simplicity. It was like a vision in which suddenly all the complexity of life is reduced to one single inescapable proposition. These signs could have shone forth as clearly in Athens, Greece, as in Athens, Ohio. They belonged as aptly to Turkestan or Sind or Kamchatka. All the world loves Lucy."[42]

This shift in focus was not immediately recognised or understood by the majority of those who knew him, including some of his oldest friends and closest observers. They identified Malcolm as an anti-Communist crusader, an incisive cultural critic and a devastating satirist. But as he began to write and speak about the moral implications of issues such as sexual liberation, illegal drugs, heart transplants and, eventually, birth control and abortion, he caused surprise and anger. This was Third Muggeridge, according to Anthony Powell, the "hot-gospelling" fanatic. As far as Malcolm was concerned, however, there was no radical change in his sensibility. He was now focusing more intently on the moral issues that had always been at the heart of his thought.

There was one other important effect of this shift in Malcolm's attention. Implied in the conviction that materialism is the prime sin of modernity is the idea that ultimate truth is spiritual and transcendent. The more Malcolm thought about lust, greed, selfishness and vanity, the more he had to think about the opposite virtues of faith, hope and love, and their source in Christian belief. Occasionally he would write sentences like: "To me the Christian religion is like a hopeless love affair. I carry its image about with me, and look at it from time to time with sick longing."[43] He omitted to say that the affair was hopeless because he was the one who could not make a commitment. But the more he thought about the moral decay of the West, the more he agonised about his own recalcitrant sins. "The only wish I have left in this life," he confided in his diary, "is that there should be burnt out of me all egotism, all pride, all lechery, all greed . . . I want my being's dwindling flame to burn clearly and steadily, with no smoky spurts, until it flickers out."[44] His continuing efforts to give up smoking, drinking and meat progressed and regressed. "Just now I am in love with abstemiousness," he wrote in his diary. "One should not give up things because they are pleasant (which is Puritanism) but because, by giving them up, other things are pleasanter."[45]

Malcolm was not yet such a critic of popular culture that he could turn down an offer to appear in a feature film. He was approached by the film-making team of John and Roy Boulting, who wanted him to play himself in their new film, a comedy entitled *I'm All Right, Jack.* The Boulting brothers were among the most distinguished film-makers in Britain. Their films included the most successful adaptation of a Graham Greene novel ever made, *Brighton Rock*; social criticism, as in *Fame is the Spur* and *The Guinea Pig*; and several comedies that satirised the legal profession, the army and the red-brick university in *Brothers in Law*, *Private's Progress* and *Lucky Jim*.[46] Their new film, *I'm All Right, Jack*, was to be easily the most topical and controversial comedy they ever made, dealing as it did with the conflicts between industry and labour unions. The film featured Ian Carmichael as a gullible upper-class twit tricked by his unscrupulous relatives into helping them pull off a profitable, and highly illegal, scam. Sent to work in a factory, Carmichael's character falls foul of the shop steward, Fred Kite, brilliantly played by an up-and-coming actor named Peter

Sellers. An earnest if small-minded Marxist, Kite wears a Hitler moustache, and comes home to a wife and daughter who prove to be far more formidable than the corporate bosses. Though Sellers was not the star of the film, his performance stole the show, presenting a comic figure who nonetheless had just enough real human vulnerability to engage the viewer's sympathy.

I'm All Right, Jack contained the sort of hard-edged satire that Malcolm loved. He was called upon to play himself in the film's climactic scene, in which he moderates a television panel discussion that includes union and management representatives, along with the sinned-against Carmichael. When Carmichael upends a briefcase full of pay-off money, the studio audience rushes to grab some for themselves. In the ensuing mayhem, there is a brief shot of Malcolm furtively slipping out of the back of the studio. It is a delicious moment of anarchy, the sort of comic fantasy that Malcolm probably day-dreamed about.

Sensing an opportunity, Malcolm sought to capitalise on his new contact with the Boulting brothers. Since they had not yet made a film that took aim at the Church, Malcolm offered them a story. A few months after the premier of *I'm All Right, Jack*, he signed a contract with their production company, British Lion Films, to produce a screenplay entitled "The Parson's Nose". The film that grew out of this project was called *Heavens Above!*, and premiered in 1963. It bore very little resemblance to the story that Malcolm produced, though the screenplay, written by Frank Harvey and John Boulting, was listed on the credits as having come "from an idea by Malcolm Muggeridge". By the spring of 1961, Malcolm could tell that few of his ideas would make it to celluloid. He wrote in his diary:

> Talking with John Boulting about my *Heavens Above* film story, I realized that the producers didn't understand the theme at all. They're caught up in the almost universal fallacy that the good Christian is one who tries to behave in the Christian way, not the "changed" man, the man who's put away the old Adam, and tries in the flesh to be reborn in the spirit. Dropping the conversion from my story ... is St Paul without the Damascus Road, or a story of adolescent love without adolescence – the *change*.[47]

Malcolm's original story was about a vicar who had served the Church diligently for many years, without much emotion or real faith.

Suddenly he finds himself actually believing in the Gospels; he experiences a true conversion. In the film *Heavens Above!*, the vicar, played by Peter Sellers, is presented from the start as a holy fool, a humble, trusting, otherworldly man already living out the Gospel injunctions. Speaking with a Liverpudlian accent, Sellers is uncomfortably close to the working class for most of his fellow clerics. The Boultings were less interested in the inner development of the vicar than they were of the havoc he would create in Church and society by practising Christianity in a literal and uncompromising way. Sellers is lovable and convincing as the vicar, but he is a catalyst: he doesn't change, but everything around him does.

Though little of Malcolm's original story survived, *Heavens Above!* is a funny film, with the satirical edge characteristic of the Boulting brothers at their best. Malcolm was given a brief cameo appearance as a bishop, complete with gaiters and broad-brimmed hat. The scene is set in a cathedral cloister, where a worldly archdeacon is recounting his latest trip to the Riviera, dwelling with particular relish on his time on Lord Buckley's yacht, "with the sun pouring down on my naked body". Malcolm, as the bishop, turns to him and says: "Most interesting thought, archdeacon." There are a few Muggeridgean moments in the film, as in the scene where the Prime Minster (a Harold Macmillan look-alike) has to deal with a national crisis caused by the vicar's good deeds. "Obviously we have to do something," the PM says, "but it's absolutely vital that we appear to do nothing." Some of Malcolm's favourite targets – Freudian psychology, the welfare state and the absurdity and eccentricity of the upper class – all come in for a drubbing.

Malcolm developed the *Heavens Above!* story into a novel that was never published. He struggled in the 1960s to write creatively, despite the number of failed novels and unperformed plays that had accumulated in his filing cabinets. When the obscenity prosecution of *Lady Chatterley's Lover* was brought to trial, Malcolm wrote a play called "Too Much Venus", the same title he had used for a play written in Moscow in 1932. He also signed a contract to produce a book with the working title of "Contemporary History: 1918 Until Today", but it too joined the list of unfinished projects.

But if his book-writing career remained stalled, television beckoned once more. Not only had the monarchy row faded from memory, but times were changing at the BBC. The first sign that the Muggeridge ban might be ending was the broadcast of several interviews Malcolm had done in New York with veteran American journalist Edward R. Murrow. Then, in January 1960, Sir Ian Jacob left the BBC and was replaced by Hugh Carleton Greene, the brother of novelist Graham Greene. Hugh Greene was far less repressive than Jacob had been, and opened the BBC to the winds of change that were blowing through society as a whole. Malcolm had a great deal of respect for Greene, who in turn gave Malcolm an increasingly free hand.

It was in 1960 that Malcolm also went beyond the BBC for the first time, signing a two-year contract with ITV's Granada to produce a series of one-to-one interviews. The programme, entitled *Appointment With:*, paired Malcolm with some of the leading politicans, writers and celebrities of the day, including Arthur Miller, Jacques Soustelle (whom Malcolm had known in the war), Lord Chandos, J.B. Priestley, Sir Harold Nicolson, Professor J.D. Bernal and Marian Anderson. One of the more memorable programmes in this series took place in March 1962, when Malcolm was able to reunite four writers who had all made their reputations in the 1930s: W.H. Auden, Stephen Spender, Cyril Connolly and Christopher Isherwood. Though Malcolm was utterly opposed to their Leftist ideas, he was quite gentle with them. When he looked at that interview many years later, for a BBC retrospective called *Muggeridge: Ancient and Modern*, he confessed that he had wanted to ask a more controversial and emotionally charged question. He wanted to ask Auden and Isherwood why they had fled to America during World War II, rather than stay behind, as other writers, including Eliot and Malcolm himself, had.[48] In his interviews, Malcolm may have gone for the jugular, but he rarely went for the groin.

Malcolm did not always come out the winner in his television interviews. When he asked the society hostess, Elsa Maxwell, the question, "Have you ever met any unimportant people?" her response was: "Not until tonight." In 1961, he received a telegram from the painter Lucian Freud, with whom he was scheduled to do an interview. The telegram cancelled the interview, stating merely: "Life too short to talk to Muggeridge."[49]

By the early 1960s, Malcolm was able to settle down to a more stable life in Robertsbridge, travelling abroad only for shorter, more specific assignments. On a trip to Hamburg, Germany, in 1961, he dropped into a "teenage rock-and-roll joint". He noticed that the

band were English, from Liverpool, and recognized me. Long-haired, weird feminine faces; bashing their instruments, and emitting nerveless sounds into microphones ... One of them asked me: "Is it true that you're a Communist?" No, I said; just in opposition. He nodded understandingly; in opposition himself in a way. "You make money out of it?" he went on. I admitted that this was so. He, too, made money. He hoped to take back £200 to Liverpool.[50]

The band, of course, were the Beatles, who were just on the verge of becoming rock-and-roll superstars.

Malcolm was himself basking in stardom as his media career resumed its course. He was no longer on the run – in a literal sense, at least. But he remained inwardly restless and depressed. His affair with Pamela Berry was sputtering out. The TV appearances and newspaper columns came out of him effortlessly, and that very fluency increased his guilt about not doing more serious writing. He could challenge anyone he wanted, from prime ministers to movie stars, to live up to higher standards, but he was plagued by the knowledge that he was not challenging himself, either intellectually or morally. He wanted to do something more substantial and lasting, but he wasn't sure how to go about it. He was haunted by the figure of Christ, and pursued him through the writings of the mystics, but he could not yet profess the Apostles' Creed, or contemplate joining the institutional Church.

When the cameras stopped rolling and his typewriter was at rest, Malcolm still wrestled with despair, his sleep as disturbed and fearful as it had been since his childhood. "Woke up with that feeling of being a castaway," he wrote in a typical diary entry. "The night still in my head; a sense of being lost and alone in an inhospitable universe." But that same morning he began to reread the *Pensées* of Blaise Pascal. He marvelled at how closely the seventeenth-century scientist and Christian thinker had diagnosed his own paradoxical condition. Without faith, Pascal wrote, man remains a mystery to himself, subject to a perpetual war between flesh and spirit – bored, anxious, uncertain. The cause of inconstancy, Pascal wrote, was "the consciousness of the falsity of present pleasures, and the ignorance of the vanity of absent pleasures". Malcolm saw himself again and again in these crystalline insights, such as: "We run carelessly to the precipice, after we have put something before us to prevent ourselves from seeing it." The truth of *Pensées*, though bitter, filled him with joy. He wrote in his diary: "Such is the power, across three hundred years, of one clear, true mind on another which, however inadequately, is striving after clarity and truth. No other specific can work this transformation; no pill, potion, headshrinker's incantation, etc ... The only uplifting I ever want is from ecstasy. Nothing else will do."[51] That ecstasy would remain elusive, but Malcolm was beginning to feel that his search for it would have to intensify in the time that remained to him. Again, it was Pascal who provided him with the encouragement he needed: in the *Pensées*, God speaks these words to the anxious soul: "You would not seek me if you did not possess me. Therefore be not troubled."

« 17 »

The Third Presence
1963–1968

EARLY IN the 1960s, Malcolm made another unsuccessful attempt to write a stage play. Like every other such effort since the staging of *Three Flats*, the play, "Life and the Legend", was relegated to the filing cabinet. But the metaphor on which the play is based had a deeply personal meaning for him, and it showed up in several of his journalistic pieces throughout the decade.

In the play the stage is divided into three areas. The area in the centre – Café Limbo – is equipped with a TV set and juke box; it represents the "workaday world where we live our daily lives, earning a living, reading newspapers, exchanging money, recording votes, chattering and eating and desiring". To the left is a darkened space, where a housing estate can be dimly seen, its television aerials set against a twilit sky. This is Life, where the ultimate realities of love and suffering are enacted. But the realm of Life is covered in shadows, so that truth can be perceived only dimly and fitfully. On the right is a television studio, illuminated by powerful arc-lamps. This is Legend, "where history is unfolded and news is made; this is where we live our public, collective lives, seat and unseat rulers, declare wars and negotiate peace, glow with patriotism and get carried away with revolutionary zeal, enact law, declaim rhetoric, swear eternal passion and sink into abysses of desolation." Life is reality, but its activities are shrouded in mystery and their significance is apparent only to the imagination; it requires the sustained effort of the saint, mystic or artist to dwell in Life and perceive its meaning. Most of us prefer the bright lights of Legend, which transforms the stuff of life into fantasy. Legend is dominated by the will, and is thus interested only in power and pleasure. "In Life there is suffering, deprivation and sanity; in the Legend, happiness, abundance and madness."[1]

319

The protagonist of the play, a television journalist known as Cuthbert Graveley, is yet another fictional incarnation of Malcolm. Making his living in the realm of Legend, Graveley spends most of his time lounging about Café Limbo, where he casts an occasional, longing glance towards Life. He has long since emerged from Life to be transformed by Legend. One of his more inglorious jobs is to host a "queen for a day" programme, sponsored by "Eezit, the pill that stops the pain". Trapped in trivial programmes of this sort, Graveley/Muggeridge suffers from despair and ennui, which he tries to stave off with sex. He is described as "a sexual exhibitionist, and it is generally assumed that one of his perks as compere is to take his pick of the girls chosen. Actually, his reputation for assaulting them is greatly exaggerated. When he does have an affair with one of them . . . he is liable to become emotionally, as well as sexually, engaged. His vision of himself as a gay, heartless seducer is unrealised, like all his visions."[2]

The play has almost no plot, but it does dramatise Malcolm's anxiety over the moral and spiritual impasse in his life. When he had set aside the play, he developed the metaphor in an essay, also titled "Life and the Legend". Though the language of the essay is impersonal, its autobiographical relevance is unmistakable. Malcolm focuses on the plight of the person who passes from Life into the Legend, becoming in the process a larger-than-life image. He is "character-typed, his public persona is fixed. He is in an iron lung of publicity, and there must live for ever, unless he can manage (which happens rarely) to escape back to life and anonymity."[3]

Malcolm recognized that this dilemma had its humorous side, as he discovered after conducting a television interview with a Russian Orthodox bishop, Anthony Bloom, in 1963. The subject of their extremely thoughtful discussion was the problem of pain. The next day, when Malcolm got into a taxi, the driver turned around and said: "I saw you yesterday with that bloke with a beard – you knocked hell out of him."[4]

But Malcolm recounted such incidents with a heavy dose of irony. In his more honest moments, he knew that no one had forced him to become a denizen of Legend, and that his own vanity and indolence were largely responsible for keeping him there. The danger for anyone in this position, as Malcolm recognised, was that he would *become* the persona, a prospect that truly frightened him. As the 1960s progressed, Malcolm's efforts to escape from his persona intensified. This was an enormously complicated process, for a number of reasons. First, he did not know where to escape *to*, because he continued to be wracked by his own unresolved intellectual and spiritual conflicts, which could have driven him in several different directions. His emergence, by the end of the decade, as an ardent defender of the Christian faith was far from inevitable. Then there was the fact that anonymity was not really an option. He would have to change his public persona in public, an extremely hazardous and difficult feat. Once a persona is established, even if it is a controversial one, audiences come to expect it – and they tend to be resentful of change. There were many instances in these years when the changes in Malcolm's character and opinions outpaced the public's perception of him, leading to further controversy and, occasionally, to hilarity.

A classic case of Malcolm moving on just as others were catching up with him concerned what has been called the "satire boom" of the early 1960s. Just three years after Malcolm had suffered through the monarchy row, satire became the rage in Britain. The "boom" began with the success of a satirical revue, *Beyond the Fringe*, first staged at the Edinburgh Festival in 1960. The sarcastic wit of the Cambridge University students who produced *Beyond the Fringe* became so popular that the revue went on to successful runs in London's West End and on Broadway, and propelled several of its stars, including Jonathan Miller, Peter Cook, Alan Bennett and Dudley Moore into acting careers. Soon after, the Establishment, "Britain's First Satirical Night Club", opened on Greek Street in Soho. Eight months later, it had a membership of eleven thousand. Even the BBC decided to get on the bandwagon. Under the leadership of Hugh Greene, the BBC launched a new Saturday night programme, *That Was The Week That Was*, on November 24, 1962. Greene was confident that *TW3* (as it was abbreviated), though it was a "minority programme", would nonetheless have a substantial audience. By the end of its first season, *TW3* had over twelve million viewers and had launched several careers, including that of David Frost. Finally, there was the publication of the satirical magazine, *Private Eye*, whose inaugural issue appeared on cheap orange paper on October 25, 1961. After six months, the circulation was up to fifteen thousand and would, with a few temporary setbacks, continue to rise throughout the decade.[5]

To say that Malcolm had single-handedly made the satire boom possible would obviously be a wild exaggeration. Larger social forces were at work, as he would have been the first to acknowledge. The monarchy row, he came to realise, was practically the last gasp of Victorian propriety; henceforth, the public forum would be more open and raucous. Nor was Malcolm the only literary satirist practising. Writers with greater artistic gifts than Malcolm, such as Evelyn Waugh, Anthony Powell and Kingsley Amis, had been writing incisive satirical fiction for years. The leading figure of the satire boom was not Malcolm, but Michael Frayn, whose work appeared on the feature pages of the *Observer*, and who would go on to become a successful playwright. But the fact remains that Malcolm was both a forerunner and a continuing inspiration to a younger generation of satirical writers, particularly in the world of journalism and political commentary. His editorship of *Punch* and the monarchy row had earned him the status of a John the Baptist, a voice crying out in the wilderness – losing his head in the process, perhaps, but making straight the way for incisive social criticism laced with humour.

Malcolm's influence can be traced most directly in the circle that produced *Private Eye*. The magazine had grown out the association of three men – Richard Ingrams, William Rushton and Christopher Booker – who had been at Shrewbury School together and had written for the school magazine. In their university years there had been other joint efforts and their circle of friends had expanded. After dispersing to different occupations, the original three came back together to launch *Private Eye*. The magazine was characterised by unremitting attacks on political figures, irreverent cartoons (by veterans like Trog and brilliant newcomers like Ralph Steadman and Gerald Scarfe), malicious gossip and thorough-going bad taste.

Booker was known as the "intellectual" of the group. In a manner reminiscent of the precocious Malcolm Muggeridge, Booker, at the age of twelve, had found Malcolm's *The Thirties* among his father's books and devoured it. "I was so haunted by this shrewdly mocking way of looking at the personalities and events which make up contemporary history that if there was any one book which made me want to become a writer it was this."[6] Booker would go on to write a social history of the 1960s, *The Neophiliacs*, that owed much of its style, as well as its content, to *The Thirties* and Malcolm's other writings.

Of the *Private Eye* group, it was Richard Ingrams who would become the most personally devoted to Malcolm. They were introduced to each other by Claud Cockburn, whom Ingrams had invited to edit an issue of *Private Eye*. Ingrams then asked Malcolm to guest-edit the issue of August 7, 1964. Malcolm protested that he was too much of a "fuddy-duddy" to edit such a youthful production, but was persuaded to accept the offer. The cover of that issue through drawing of a gnome-like figure riding a donkey, clasping a woman with one hand and his own enlarged phallus with the other. The origin of this ribald drawing was, in fact, a detail from the original Doyle cover of *Punch* that had been overlooked for over a century. The illustrator Ronald Searle also paid tribute to Malcolm in the issue through his "Rake's Progress" series, this time chronicling the rise and fall of *Punch* itself. One panel depicts Malcolm departing from the ship, HMS *Bouverie Street*, which contains a corpulent and obviously senile Queen Victoria. The caption reads: "Muggeridge appointed editor. Queen Victoria disgusted. Advertisers disgusted. Editorial office disgusted. Regular readers disgusted. Paper improves. Advertising drops. Muggeridge dropped."[7] Ingrams and his editorial staff referred affectionately to Malcolm as "Muggo, or the Guru". After his guest editorship, Malcolm would regularly be consulted about some tricky question relating to a potentially controversial cover, or a threatened libel action.

Malcolm's first impressions of *Private Eye* had been mixed. Writing in the *New Statesman* in 1962, he commended the magazine for being "delightfully and offensively rude to one and all". He also pinpointed what he considered to be the magazine's discovery of a new and appropriately modern form of satire: the news photograph, with comic captions enclosed in bubbles. "The camera, not pencil or brush, is the young satirist's instrument; it almost appears that he needs no inventiveness; mimicry and press-cuttings will suffice. He holds nature up to the mirror; all the stage is a world." But Malcolm wondered if *Private Eye*'s satire was sufficiently focused: the editors, it seemed, "fire a bazooka rather than . . . poisoned arrows". With his sharp eye for matters of social class, Malcolm also noticed the public school ambience at *Private Eye*, the tendency to snigger at the "Pseuds" rather than transcend human follies through laughter. The magazine treated those in authority like "a schoolmaster, who, when his back is turned, can be pelted with paper darts and mocked with mimicry and funny faces". By the time of Malcolm's guest editorship, the satire boom had ended – the Profumo scandal in Britain and the assassination of President John F. Kennedy seemed traumatic enough to cause a backlash against the purveyors of bad taste. But *Private Eye* survived. Its chief editors, Ingrams and Booker, had become disciples of guru Malcolm.

Malcolm's comments on the satire boom betray a certain uneasiness. Perhaps there was a touch of resentment at all the attention being lavished on younger satirists while an old, battered warrior like himself remained unrecognised. The Establishment, he noted, was lapping up the satire against itself. "Laughter is as bold as brass. Indeed, it is the Brass who laugh. Decaying societies, like decaying teeth, invite the tongue to probe, and touch the exposed nerve."[8] But, as with so much of his writing, Malcolm was sending a message not only to the editors of *Private Eye* but also to himself. In his essay on satire, Malcolm had invoked the spirit of Jonathan Swift, arguing that Swift's satire – laced with "savage indignation" – rose above trivial or "sick" humour because it was the "obverse of an elusive perfection". He was acutely aware of his own tendency, particularly on television, to descend into trivial clowning. At the same time, he was increasingly interested in pursuing the vision of "elusive perfection" directly. Throughout the 1960s, the inner struggle between the satirical and the mystical strains in Malcolm's personality would rise to the surface.

The conflict was played out, appropriately enough, on television, where his role was beginning to change, or at least expand. By 1964, Malcolm was an old hand at television, and was finally rewarded with assignments he had wanted for some time. Increasingly, he was being called upon to make documentaries and extended personal narratives. If brief *Panorama* interviews and instant-answer programmes were the television equivalent of junk food, a documentary was a steak dinner. It was an opportunity to do something more substantial, more reflective of his own passions and convictions. Malcolm was not without some experience in this genre: he had written the commentary for *The Thirties* in 1957 and a two-part programme, *The Titans*, about America and the Soviet Union, in 1962. The first documentary he was asked to present himself, *Twilight of Empire*, was autobiographical, dealing with his years in India.

Having turned sixty in 1963, Malcolm was ready to tell the story of his life, a story that some critics would complain would become all too familiar over the next two decades. *Twilight of Empire* was only the first instalment of a series of autobiographical television programmes, essays and books. Many of these memoirs were commissioned by BBC producers and others who admired the extraordinary range of Malcolm's experience. But Malcolm's emotional and spiritual restlessness increasingly drove him to look back and search out the patterns of meaning in the story of his life.

Twilight of Empire displayed Malcolm in a gentle, elegiac mood. The first half of the programme dealt with his years in Alwaye, which had always been been a source of happy memories. He began by going back to the waterways of south India that he had loved. Talking to one of the boatmen that still plied these waters, he decided to go for a swim, as he so often had back in 1924. At Union Christian College, he found a few people he had taught. One former student reminded him of the time when a Brahmin scholar had come to the college and lectured on Shakespeare. This man had written extensive annotations on Shakespeare's plays, the student recalled.

> INDIAN: And in your presidential address, you said something like this: "If I go to heaven, which I very much doubt, I shall ask of God one favour. And that is to send Shakespeare down to earth again, and make him sit a Madras University examination, just for the fun of seeing him fail."
>
> MUGGERIDGE: Well, I'm sure Shakespeare would fail.
>
> INDIAN: Yes, I'm sure too.
>
> MUGGERIDGE: The question is: whether God would pass an examination in theology? What do you think about that? It's an awkward question.

The second half of the programme dealt with Malcolm's second trip to India in 1935, "a different me and a different India". In Calcutta and Simla Malcolm's account of the doomed Empire was done with a light touch, focusing more on the absurdities and pretensions of the British than on their crimes and injustices. The most surreal episode was in Simla, where Malcolm and his film crew found the Viceregal Lodge still standing, but empty, carpets rolled up, and marks on the walls where paintings had once hung. But the thrones – for the Viceroy, Vicereine and Governor of the Punjab – remained intact. Sitting on the Viceroy's throne, Malcolm read from his diary entry recounting his first dinner there. "The end of power," he concluded, speaking in the present, "is always more exhilarating than its beginning. I much prefer Napoleon on St Helena to Napoleon being crowned by the Pope in Notre-Dame, Hitler in his tank-tangled bunker to the sieg-heils of Nuremberg. In the days of its functioning, I used to hate this popinjay court up here. Its disappearance into furniture vans is one court the less. Let the bell which summoned the Viceroy's guests to dinner toll for it now." Malcolm, in this case at least, was able to have the last laugh.[9]

Two years after *Twilight of Empire*, Malcolm went back even further into his own past for a BBC documentary entitled *A Socialist Childhood*. Here Malcolm's mood was not elegiac, but world-weary and cynical. The story of his youth was subordinated to Malcolm's ideological animus against socialism. This was the programme where Malcolm was invited to speak to a class at Selhurst Grammar School, which he had attended as a boy. He proceeded to run down the school in his most arrogant fashion. One television critic noted that "*A Socialist Childhood* allowed its inventor far too much rein for indulgent capering", but admitted that "as always with Mr Muggeridge, it was witty and verbally dextrous." The only moment that caught the critic's attention ("a touch of inspiration") was a scene in which Malcolm, standing in a Croydon back garden, conducted an imaginary choir.[10]

The same unpleasant disparity between Malcolm's scorn and the topic addressed was evident in two documentaries he made about America in 1964 (though not screened until 1965). Since 1960, Malcolm had been a regular on the American lecture circuit, travelling in the early autumn, when the academic year began, to address schools, universities, civic organisations and ladies' clubs. *Ladies and Gentlemen, it is my pleasure* . . . was based on footage from his lecture tour of 1964. Once again he served up a few witty, arresting statements along with a large dose of condescension. It was not difficult for him to make the eager, earnest and rather simple Americans waiting for his words of wisdom look foolish, but the inevitable reaction to such "capering" is to wonder why it is necessary to smash flies with a sledgehammer. "The day has come round again," he began. "From every corner of the globe, we, the L men [lecture men], are converging on New York . . . Ladies in Eau Claire Wisconsin await my coming. Santa Maria California, do not lose heart – I'll be with you soon. Jewish ladies in Los Angeles – Executives in Seattle – Art lovers in Chicago – I'm on my way." Even the comments that seem to cut closest to the truth came out in too extreme a form: "Americans often seem like a looting army. They, as it were, invade and occupy their own country, gorging their own provisions, sacking their own cities, grabbing their own treasure, raping their own women."[11]

The American Way of Sex also suffered from overkill. That "sex is the mysticism of materialism" is an insight that bears scrutiny. But Malcolm quickly left that thought behind. The assertion that "sex sells anything from deodorants to bulldozers" points to a cultural trend worth reflecting upon. But why should the Americans be singled out, in the era of Twiggy and the Beatles? "Oh, vestal virgins of Madison Avenue," Malcolm intoned. "Oh, Aphrodite, rising so fragrantly, so exquisitely out of the mist of universal desire. Even the dolls must have reached puberty to be interesting. The bra precedes the breast."[12] What makes statements like this so irritating is not so much the element of exaggeration – all satire and large-scale generalisations require a certain amount of caricature – but the very immaturity that he criticised in *Private Eye*. Even a satirist has a responsibility to the standard of truth from which he launches his attacks. But the cynical persona that Malcolm cultivated at this time too often seemed not to care whether his arrows had even hit home.

Actually, there was much in America that Malcolm loved, and his American connections were multiplying in these years. Late in 1963, Harold Hayes, the editor of *Esquire* magazine, invited Malcolm to become their regular book reviewer. *Esquire*, a sophisticated monthly "magazine for men", was something after Malcolm's heart – irreverent, satirical, urbane without being precious. It had no equivalent in Britain. In addition to long essays on politics and culture, *Esquire* published fiction by the leading writers on both sides of the Atlantic. It was also the spawning ground for what became known as the New Journalism – a far more stylised and imaginative form of reportage epitomised by the writings of Tom Wolfe. For Malcolm, who had always resented the sharp distinction academic critics drew between literature and journalism, the freshness of Wolfe's approach was welcome.

Harold Hayes gave Malcolm complete freedom to review what he wanted. Malcolm usually chose books that were topical, but his growing preoccupation with Christianity could be seen in reviews of books about Kierkegaard and medieval mystics. Some of Malcolm's more substantial essays in the 1960s first appeared in *Esquire*, such as his long reflection on Kim Philby in the light of the spy's defection to the Soviet Union. He would keep up his book reviewing assignment for over a decade.

Another American magazine with which he became familiar was *National Review*, edited by a brash young conservative named William F. Buckley, Jr. What attracted Malcolm to Buckley was his witty, cultivated prose and his ability to skewer the utopian fantasies of liberals. He found Buckley's attempt to run for mayor of New York in 1964, and his account of it in *The Unmaking of a Mayor*, highly amusing. He was to become one of the most frequent guests on Buckley's television programme, *Firing Line*. With Buckley, he shared a disdain for the myth that grew up around John F. Kennedy after his assassination. The legend of the Kennedy presidency – the Camelot with a youthful shining Arthur and his Round Table of Harvard-trained social planners – presented a bubble that Malcolm did not hesitate to prick. Among his more thoughtful essays for *Esquire* was a dissection of several hagiographical books on J.F.K. by former colleagues. The essay concludes:

> Let us hope that some other less engaged hand will some day write the Kennedy story; not as a paltry twentieth-century fantasy, with a golden youth and glamorous girl walking hand-in-hand into the White House, to discover together that life is real, life is earnest. Rather, in the manner of Greek Tragedy, in which the rage of the gods is called down on those who smile too often, too concertedly, and too determinedly.[13]

The most damning thing to be said about Malcolm's negative television documentaries is that they were not faithful to the truth as he knew it. Malcolm had always attacked people and institutions he felt to be in the wrong, but in the past there had been a fairly high ratio of inner conviction to outward condemnation. By the mid-1960s, it often seemed that Malcolm was using a bazooka, rather than poisoned arrows – the very sin he had counselled the editors of *Private Eye* to avoid. The same syndrome was turning up in his print journalism. As early as 1958, he turned on his friend Field Marshal Montgomery, describing him in an article as "cold, sharp, avidly egotistical little man with not much capacity for friendship or compassion".[14] A reporter read this passage out to Monty and received the curt reply: "Good." Continuing to read Malcolm's article, the reporter came to Malcolm's description of Monty's home, a "converted mill . . . arranged as a museum, with all his trophies and portraits of himself on display. It is macabre, and even touching, to think of him thus living, an exhibit among exhibits." At this point, Monty cut the reporter off. "I don't want to hear any more. No comment," he said and put down the phone.[15]

Another example of Malcolm turning on someone he had once felt affectionate about can be found in his essay on Max Beerbohm. Malcolm's admiration for Beerbohm had been similar to his love of P.G. Wodehouse: both men lived in the past, remained blissfully ignorant of the jaded present and retained a sort of endearing innocence. But in "The Legend of Max", Malcolm argues that the key to Beerbohm's personality was his "panic flight" from his Jewishness and his homosexuality. "The upper-class English are not, like their American equivalents, overtly anti-semitic, but they create a milieu in which Jews seem outlandish, and therefore feel alien and ill-at-ease. The worst thing we do to well-off Jews in England is to make them as stupid, snobbish and philistine as the well-off natives. This is our version of Dachau." What begins as a sharp-edged but debatable point ends in bizarre and thoroughly repulsive analogy. This is not an example of the satirist's legitimate indulgence in bad taste, but of callous insensitivity. It might be considered that the crassness of the analogy was evidence of anti-semitism on Malcolm's part. But the fact is that Malcolm had largely left his youthful anti-semitism behind, and his circle of Jewish friends had become wide and affectionate. A deeper problem lay beneath these cruel and arbitrary attacks. Malcolm had become fused with his persona; everyone and everything had become grist for his mill of scorn and invective.

Malcolm was acutely aware of his tendency to lose himself in trivial and unprofitable attacks. It was this self-consciousness that made his feelings of guilt so intense. Malcolm knew that he had, to use contemporary terminology, an addictive or compulsive personality. His lifelong attraction to the Simple Life – to abstemiousness and self-control – emerged from his need to renounce his compulsions and to regain some control over his life. In short, the only way he knew to combat his spiritual inertia was to start by disciplining his body. If he could break out of the fantasy world his addictions had caged him in, he would be able to live in reality. He would leave Legend behind and regain his citizenship in Life.

But the struggle to achieve the Simple Life was to take years, and only came late in Malcolm's life. Malcolm's most persistent compulsion, of course, was sex. Kingsley Amis, a writer with a talent for malicious gossip equal to or surpassing that of Malcolm, recounts in his memoirs an episode that illustrates Malcolm's compulsive sexual behaviour. Some time in the "early Sixties", Amis was asked to appear on an independent television programme dealing with "the state of the nation". There he met Malcolm, who was appearing on the same programme. When their duties were done, Malcolm invited Amis out to dinner, adding that they would be joined by Sonia Orwell. By the time dinner was over, all three of them had had a great deal to drink. But when Amis made noises about needing to get back to his home in Cambridge, Malcolm would have none of it. "Rubbish, dear boy. We're off to Sonia's flat for a last drink." Once there, Amis recalls, Malcolm said: "Come on, chaps, we're going to have an orgy." Amis thought that "orgy" overstated the case, since there were only the three of them. As the organiser of the evening, Malcolm claimed his right to go into Sonia's bedroom first. "After a time I tried not to measure, Malcolm came back into the sitting-room. His manner had lost its earlier decisiveness. He said to me without much expression, 'Afraid I couldn't manage anything in there. You go in and see what you can do.'" Amis, it turned out, couldn't manage anything either, so Malcolm gathered him up and brought him back to his London flat. The next morning, after having breakfast at the Waldorf with Malcolm, Amis made his way back to Cambridge.[16]

Even if one allows for a large measure of spitefulness on Amis's part – why else would he write about the incident? – there is a painful ring of truth to this story. There is something embarrassing and unsettling about witnessing a person caught in the grip of compulsive behaviour. A supremely self-conscious man, Malcolm was all too aware of how pathetic such moments were. Sex and death, passion and futility, compulsion and guilt were the poles of emotion that marked his sexual life, from beginning to end.

By the mid-1960s, however, Malcolm had achieved the goal for which he had longed for half a century: he finally embraced the Simple Life. Since he lived in the public spotlight, this change in his life immediately became a source of further controversy and criticism. In weighing Malcolm's character in the balance, it would be well for us to reject the simplistic notion that old age makes giving up fleshly appetites easy. Malcolm's struggle to curb his appetites was a real struggle, with real costs and sacrifices. The victory, though it came in stages, was complete; no territory was relinquished.

It seems that 1964 was something of a milestone in this struggle. Since the late 1950s, Malcolm and Kitty had become vegetarians by degrees. Meat had been given up first, but they continued to eat fish for a time before giving it up as well. Lunch invariably consisted of bread, cheese and salad, with ham being provided for guests. Supper included poached eggs, peas, carrots, rice and macaroni and cheese; guests were offered chicken. After several attempts to quit smoking, Malcolm managed to kick the habit in 1964. He was in America for the lecture tour that was being filmed for a BBC documentary. Confined to his hotel room for an entire day writing, he had filled several ashtrays with cigarettes before going out to his evening lecture. When he returned, he found that the air conditioning had broken down, and the stagnant air brought on a wave of disgust that enabled him to quit smoking for good. Drinking, it seems, was the last to go, but it too was left behind.[17]

Symbolic of this new spartan life was the last, and shortest, move of the Muggeridges' life. With the children now living on their own, Malcolm and Kitty decided that Salehurst Farmhouse was too big for them. They had taken a seven-year lease on the house, which expired in 1963. Just a few hundred feet away was Park Cottage, which they purchased and had improved. It was, by Kitty's calculation, the twenty-second move of their life together. Ironically, it was at this point in their lives that money was, for the first time, no longer a cause for anxiety.

Malcolm's newly achieved asceticism naturally attracted attention and comment. "After sixty," he told Godfrey Winn in an interview, "a man must decide either to curb his appetites or surrender to them. I have conquered mine."[18] Many people, including a number of friends and colleagues, found this climacteric surprising and rather off-putting, particularly when it came to the hints he made about giving up his "lechery". Malcolm's timing could not have been worse. On the one hand, he would for ever be open to the charge that he had given up sex, and begun to denounce it, when his own desires had withered on the vine. On the other hand, it was during the 1960s that the "sexual revolution" was at the height of its popularity – the great liberation that would usher in an era of honest pleasure, equality between the sexes and happy, healthy, well-adjusted psyches. Malcolm was on a collision course with the "Age of Aquarius" – dominated by the trinity of sex, drugs and rock music – which was then in the first flush of hedonistic optimism.

Malcolm's conversion to asceticism, combined with his unremitting denunciation of the permissive society, landed him, once again, in hot water. Bernard Levin, a fellow journalist, put the case against Malcolm in a way that would be repeated again and again. Malcolm's creed, Levin argued, began with the "extirpation of sex, from which all else follows". This, he concluded, was evidence of a "deeply disturbed psyche ... How sad was that decline, how sad that one of the bravest and most astringent minds of the time should now cower so cravenly in a corner, begging the world to stop trying to inflame his withered desires, lest the attempt prove successful!"[19]

With the passage of time, many of Malcolm's most unpopular opinions have been forgiven; some of those opinions have even been shown a little grudging respect, as in his criticisms of the former Soviet Union or his cautionary words about a "Royal Soap Opera". But if there is one sin that has not been forgiven, one accusation that threatens to vitiate his reputation, it is his late affirmation of the traditional Christian teachings about sexual morality. The unmistakable implication, evident in such critics as Bernard Levin, is that Malcolm was essentially an opportunist, in this case seizing the "opportunity" afforded by his declining sexual potency to turn against sex and proclaim himself a Christian prophet. To those who are convinced that Malcolm was a disturbed puritan, it is not difficult to demonstrate that he projected his own morbid, unhealthy guilt on to the lives of others. The Freudian option will always remain open. But the notion that Malcolm was an opportunist cannot be supported by the facts. His successful attempt to live an abstemious life had no direct association with Christianity, since at that time Malcolm continued to deny the truth of the most basic Christian doctrines, including the belief that Christ was the incarnate son of God.

Malcolm's attacks on the sexual revolution were, like so many of his opinions, directed in large part against himself. Read in that light, these opinions achieve a certain authenticity and force. One of his finest epigrams – "Sex is the mysticism of materialism" – looked back to his discipleship under D.H. Lawrence. Malcolm had always found that his sexual liaisons, far from leading to the extinguishing of his consciousness in mystical orgasm, left him bitterly alone and self-conscious. Writing about the cult of sexual freedom, which manifested itself in many ways, including the clinical studies of "sexperts" like Masters and Johnson, Malcolm concluded:

It would seem that the cycle is now complete. Sex begins in ecstasy, momentarily fusing two separate egos into union with one another and with all life; it ends in the total separation of one ego exclusively preoccupied with its own orgasm. Sex begins as a window on to eternity, and it ends in a dark cellar self-enclosed and boarded up with time. Sex begins as the sap rising in a tree to make buds and blossoms and leaves and fruit; it ends in Dr Masters's movie. Sex begins as a mystery out of which has come the art, the poetry, the religion, the delight of successive civilizations; it ends in a laboratory. Sex begins in passion which comprehends the concepts of both suffering and joy; it ends in a trivial dream of pleasure which itself soon dissolves into the solitude and despair of self-gratification.[20]

Malcolm knew that the ultimate justification for adultery was based on an appeal to the imagination. As he put it:

Of the Seven Deadly Sins, Lust is the only one which makes any serious appeal to the Imagination, as distinct from the Will, eroticism being a sort of *ersatz* transcendentalism which can easily be mistaken for the genuine article. It is easy to say, as contemporary moralists frequently do, that sins of the flesh are less heinous than those of the ego; even easier to transfer the whole issue from the individual to the collective, and in denouncing racial prejudice, or imperial arrogance, or economic exploitation with much sound and fury, to let Lust slip away unnoticed.[21]

One would think that the grim aftermath of the sexual revolution – including the exponential rise in divorce, teenage pregnancy, sexually transmitted disease, child abuse, pornography and abortion – might bring about a softening of the attacks on Malcolm's moral positions. But there are those who continue to insist that these problems are due to a lack of education, or to economic deprivation or some other social "sin" rather than to any inherent moral problem with sexual promiscuity. To Malcolm, education was the great "mumbo-jumbo and fraud" of the twentieth century, a panacea that was utterly unsuited to combatting what were, at root, moral issues. The cry for "more and better education", which Malcolm had heard on innumerable panel discussions, was founded on the liberal belief that people were inherently good and only needed the right information to make the right decisions. But this was to stake the entire social order on a fundamentally flawed understanding of human nature. By weakening the restraints, inhibitions and institutions of the Judeo-Christian tradition, liberalism opened the way for moral and social anarchy.

*

By 1965, Malcolm had won the battle with his bodily appetites, but he was still living a double life. In the realm of Legend, he was omnipresent, appearing ever more frequently on radio and television as interviewer, documentary host, and in general serving as the "pop Socrates". On the *Let Me Speak* series on the BBC, Malcolm confronted a variety of minority groups, from Jesuits in cassocks to bearded anarchists to the same Empire Loyalists who had vandalised his home during the monarchy row. The shows frequently broke down into shouting and name-calling, but were almost always entertaining. Malcolm's columns were appearing regularly in America's *Esquire* and England's *New Statesman* and *Observer*. He even had several books in the works. He wrote the text for a book, *London à la Mode*, that featured the drawings of illustrator Paul Hogarth. As an attempt to capture some of the raucous life of the city in the "Swinging Sixties", the book was fairly successful. Malcolm's text, which chronicles the life of the city through the course of the day, from morning to night, has a strong affinity with the fevered, symbolic language of *In a Valley of This Restless Mind*. Describing himself walking along the streets during the morning rush hour, he wrote:

> Moving with the others, my anxieties diminish. The floating dome of St Paul's increased them, picking out my ego like a spotlight to shrink and shiver in the glare. Now striding purposively from nowhere to nowhere, I am serene. Momentarily, I have attained the quest of mid-twentieth-century man, and lost my separate identity. These great cities with their sprouting aerials for dreaming spires, with their crowded streets and everlasting movement, meet an essential requirement of our time. London is an enormous vat, steaming and bubbling, into which egos can be thrown to make a single scalding brew.[22]

Jonathan Miller asked him to play the part of the Gryphon in his television version of *Alice in Wonderland*. With John Gielgud as the Mock Turtle, Malcolm, sprouting huge white eyebrows and whiskers, danced the Lobster Quadrille. In the *Guardian*, Geoffrey Moorhouse commented: "Mr Muggeridge's whole life has been leading up to the evening when he would dance a dab-toed quadrille before a carefully prepared audience, against a sky of gathering gloom."[23] The publisher Collins asked him for a collection of his recent essays, which was published in 1966 under the regrettable title, *Tread Softly for You*

Tread on My Jokes. With the exception of a few flashes of insight, this collection infects the reader with the world-weariness of its author. Those held up for ridicule – feeble politicians and intellectuals like Anthony Eden, the Fabians and C.P. Snow – hardly seem worth the effort. The following year saw the republication of *The Thirties* and a collection of his radio and television work, *Muggeridge Through the Microphone*. Both of these books sparkled with the vintage Muggeridge wit, but like all these efforts in the world of Legend, they looked backward, perpetuating the image of a Malcolm Muggeridge that the real Malcolm Muggeridge found increasingly uncomfortable to live with.

Perhaps the ultimate proof that he was indeed one of the mighty ones in the realm of Legend came in 1968, when Madame Tussaud's Waxwork Museum unveiled their Malcolm Muggeridge statue, which shared the room with Charles de Gaulle, Richard Burton, Elizabeth Taylor, Frank Sinatra, Twiggy, Alfred Hitchcock and the Beatles. The room they all shared was called: "Heroes – Live".[24] Malcolm, pondering on mortality and the fleeting nature of fame, wondered how long it would be before his image was melted down to make way for a new live hero.

Away from the arc-lights and waxworks, Malcolm continued to struggle with questions that were, at heart, religious. He had been looking towards the Christian faith with "sick longing" ever since he read that Bible (wrapped in brown paper) as a boy in Croydon, but he had also built up a number of prejudices and defence mechanisms regarding that faith. Having called a halt to the compulsive indulgence of his body, he now had to determine where he stood in terms of the spirit. He had publicly stated that, while he did not believe in the truth of the central Christian dogmas – including the Virgin Birth, Incarnation and Resurrection – he did believe that Christ's teachings had a luminosity and truth unsurpassed in human history.

Malcolm's low opinion of the institutional Church, though it proceeded from mixed motives, was not without justification. This was the Sixties, after all, when theologians, attempting to be hip, proclaimed the virtues of *The Secular City*, as the Harvard scholar Harvey Cox put it. The Bishop of Woolwich had penned *Honest to God*, a manifesto for anyone wanting to accommodate Christian teaching to the latest cultural trends. The World Council of Churches in these years was just becoming enamoured of Marxist regimes and terrorist rebels around the world, supplying them with money, guns and prayers.

Malcolm's opinions and attitudes toward Christianity were full of contradictions and unresolved dilemmas. Why, for instance, if he could not embrace traditional dogma, did he criticise the Churches for abandoning those very teachings? He might have responded that he was concerned largely with the moral teachings of the Church on matters like marriage, sexuality and abortion, which were crucial for the maintenance of the social fabric. But the connection between the retreat from belief in the supernatural and the loosening of moral restrictions had clearly gone hand in hand, as he had argued in the past. The fundamental contradiction in Malcolm's thought was that, in the area of religion at least, his thought was indistinguishable from that of a liberal. He had spent much of his life attacking the relativism of the liberal mind – the notion that since truth cannot be known, no one has the right to impose their "truth" on anyone else. Relativism, he thought, gave way to vagueness, inertia and chaos; it tended to live off the moral capital inherited from the Judeo–Christian tradition. But in denying the truth of Christian revelation, Malcolm had no grounds for criticising liberal clerics and theologians.

Since the late 1930s, Malcolm's attitude towards Christianity had been similar to that of his friend Hugh Kingsmill: a Johnsonian belief in the existence of evil and the corollary that human nature could never be perfected, combined with a conviction that truth, goodness and beauty were transcendent values incompatible with materialism. Unlike Kingsmill, who had found his religion primarily in the sublimities of Romantic poets like Blake and Wordsworth, Malcolm had sought for nourishment in the writings of the Christian mystics. The figure of Christ had always haunted his imagination, at least since those youthful days in India when the wild extravagances of the faith had enchanted him in the writings of G.K. Chesterton. Malcolm was also fascinated by the conversion stories of Augustine and Pascal, recognising his own evasions and excuses in their autobiographical writings. But he did not share their capacity for the type of abstract thought necessary to the pursuit of theology and philosophy. The development of Malcolm's religious position would, therefore, be incremental and intuitive, rather than logical or theological.

It was television, once again, that brought about an opportunity for Malcolm to confront Christian faith in a highly personal, concrete fashion. *Pilgrims to Lourdes*, a BBC documentary directed by Michael Tuchner, was broadcast in 1965. If it was just as personal and idiosyncratic as Malcolm's previous documentaries, it was radically different in tone. As befits the subject, the mood is quiet, plain, and Malcolm's personality is no longer in the foreground. The documentary followed a pilgrimage to the Catholic shrine of Lourdes in France, where the grotto of St Bernadette attracts the sick and the dying in the hope of a miracle, or at least spiritual nourishment. Witnessing the suffering and faith of the pilgrims, and the love of those who cared for them, was deeply moving to Malcolm. It brought him back to the days when he had seen, in India and the Ukraine, the human spirit shining out of poverty, degradation and oppression. Perhaps being with these pilgrims reminded him also of how far away he had drifted, in the intervening years, from a concern for the poor and the meek. Standing on the rail platform, Malcolm's opening monologue reflects on the anachronism of Christian pilgrims in search of healing in the late twentieth century. The atmosphere on the pilgrimage, he continued, far from being depressing, was like an outing that provided a lift to the spirits. "One dreads to sentimentalise men and women so afflicted," he continued. "I need not have worried. They are easy to talk to, and disarm mawkish pity by their robust attitude toward their misfortunes."

MAN WITH CRUTCHES: I'm suffering from disseminated sclerosis, it's a brain disease sort of thing, which affects the walking and movements of the legs.
MUGGERIDGE: Makes it more difficult to get around?
MAN: Yes, I can't get around without sticks and I go very slowly.
MUGGERIDGE: And you're hoping at Lourdes to throw these sticks away?
MAN: I'm hoping to wrap them around somebody's neck.
MUGGERIDGE: I give you full permission to wrap them around my neck. If you don't get a miracle will you still have been glad to come?
MAN: I will indeed because I think it's very spiritually refreshing.
MUGGERIDGE: What's that mean?
MAN: Well, refreshing from the point of view of the hereafter sort of thing.

Throughout the documentary Malcolm maintained a stance that is both sceptical and sympathetic. Stepping back from the pilgrimage itself, he reflected for the television audience on whether the terminally ill should have been aborted or, once born, be subjected to euthanasia.

337

Malcolm's growing interest in what might be called "life" issues was prophetic: abortion would be legalised in Britain within two years and euthanasia, though it would develop much more slowly, became a serious political issue by the 1980s. The Christian answer to these policies of "termination", he argued, was that everyone is part of God's family and was therefore created for a purpose. "I, as it happens, believe them more readily than I do the pronouncements of experts on population and eugenics. It can be argued, it seems to me, that no lives are worth living, or that all lives are worth living, but not that some lives are worth living and others not."[25]

Off screen, Malcolm really had been affected by the experience of making the documentary. Shrines, surrounded by peddlers offering saccharine souvenirs and doubtful relics, were not among his favourite places. But radiant faith in the midst of suffering he did find extraordinary. In an account written several years later, Malcolm recalled that there had even been "a tiny miracle for me" while filming. A woman on the pilgrimage asked Malcolm to see her sick sister.

> The sister was obviously at the point of death, and like any other glib child of twentieth-century enlightenment, I had nothing to say, until I noticed in the most extraordinarily vivid way, as in some girl with whom I had suddenly fallen in love, that her eyes were quite fabulously luminous and beautiful. "What marvellous eyes!" As I said this, the three of us – the dying woman, her sister, and I – were somehow caught up into a kind of ecstasy. I can't describe it any other way. It was as though I saw God's love shining down on us visibly, in an actual radiance.[26]

Malcolm had to develop his own response to the question of why God permits suffering. He had always believed that the frantic efforts of modern men and women to insulate themselves from suffering were fatuous and misguided. From his childhood, Shakespeare's *King Lear* had symbolised for Malcolm the truth that people learn the deepest lessons about human existence only through suffering. Lear's words at the end of the play – "Come, let's away to prison;/We two alone will sing like birds i' the cage . . . /And take upon's the mystery of things,/ As if we were God's spies" – embodied for Malcolm the mystical vision of a great artist.

The lives of the pilgrims at Lourdes were clearly tragic, but Malcolm could not help but see that many of them had moved beyond tragedy to a sense of redemption – a hope in the "hereafter sort of thing". That, in turn, led him to contemplate afresh the significance of the Cross, as he had in the first chapter of *In a Valley of This Restless Mind* thirty years before. As if in answer to prayer, it was around this time that he encountered the writings of Simone Weil, which focused on the question of suffering – or, as she put it, "affliction". Malcolm was introduced to Weil's books by his friend Sir Richard Rees, who had also been one of George Orwell's friends. Weil, a French Jew, had lived a short but passionate life, struggling intensely with religious and political questions.

Malcolm found in Weil a kindred spirit. She had longed to be a Christian, but at the time of her death she had not felt able to take the final step and join the Catholic Church. That she had worked for the Gaullists in London during the war also gave her a special place in Malcolm's heart. Her sacrificial love and mystical vision somehow seemed to redeem what he had known as a dark and confused period in French history. Though Weil's prose could be dense and elliptical, Malcolm found her writings on affliction as convincing as the drama of her life. Whenever one is separated from God, she wrote, one is subject to the realm of brute necessity, whether this be through physical pain, or the moral pain of following our appetites and descending into our animal nature. Affliction, though it can be devastating, is really part of the "apprenticeship" we must undergo in order to become obedient to God's will. Our willingness to accept affliction with love allows God to come into the soul. Affliction is like a nail being pounded into wood. "He whose soul remains ever turned in the direction of God while the nail pierces it, finds himself nailed on to the very centre of the universe . . . It is at the intersection of creation and its Creator. This point of intersection is the point of intersection of the branches of the Cross."[27]

Weil was, in the broadest sense of the word, an "existentialist" Christian, as were nearly all of Malcolm's favourite religious thinkers. He had no interest in theology or Christian apologetics: neither St Thomas Aquinas nor C.S. Lewis made much of an impression on him. The religious figures who spoke to Malcolm were men and women who not only possessed keen intellects but who also struggled through intense suffering and even rebellion against God, achieving in the end a mystical vision that encompassed both joy and suffering. Weil thus joined Augustine, Pascal and Blake in Malcolm's personal pantheon. He also discovered two other Christian existentialists at this time, the nineteenth-century Danish writer, Søren Kierkegaard and the German pastor, Dietrich Bonhoeffer, who had been executed by the Nazis at the end of World War II. Kierkegaard was a model of what a modern Christian prophet should be: capable of denouncing the decadence of bourgeois society, including the Church itself, but a passionate believer in the heart of the Christian message. Bonhoeffer played a special role in Malcolm's thinking because he had made the ultimate sacrifice for the truth: giving up his life in order to fight evil. Malcolm also found himself returning to his childhood hero, Tolstoy, with renewed appreciation: not for any of the Russian's wild ideas, but for his tragicomic attempt to live out the precepts of the Sermon on the Mount. Tolstoy's efforts to live a life of poverty and chastity were disastrous and yet retained a strange nobility. "There was a kind of grandeur in the very disparity between his aspirations and his performance – in his fantastic vitality and exuberance, in the glory of him; some relationship with life that made him, at one and the same time, inextricably part of life and yet immeasurably above it and beyond it."[28]

That his own "apprenticeship" had been far too long and rebellious Malcolm was now willing to accept. But even after his victory over his bodily appetites, Malcolm discovered, with a shock, that his soul suffered from its own forms of self-indulgence. One of the formative moments in his slow conversion to Christianity involved someone very close and very dear to him. This person had suffered from mental illness for a number of years, going through many episodes that required hospitalisation. Malcolm found the situation extremely painful and at the same time immensely frustrating – unlike Kitty, whose patience and love in the face of this suffering he found saintly, but which he could not emulate. Moreover, their son Leonard, a devout Christian, had also shown a remarkable serenity while working in a hospital for the mentally ill.

In a long and candid interview with Roy Trevivian, Malcolm felt impelled to talk about the situation. He admitted that, at one point, "I became violently angry with someone infinitely dear to me who had gone temporarily mad." The intractability of the illness – "the unreason, the animality, the . . . almost bestiality" of it – caused him to lose his temper. But "then I realized that this was an utterly evil thing to do, that it was a thing which damaged me, that it could only add to the pain and anguish of someone I loved sorely pressed by a terrible misfortune." The realisation that mental illness could not fit

into the simple categories of right and wrong – that it was an affliction
and not merely a matter of the will – was difficult for a moralist like
Malcolm to accept. Many of Malcolm's critics had pointed to his too
facile use of mental illness as an indicator of modern decadence. In his
remorse over this incident, he vowed never to give in to anger again,
and claimed in the interview that he had kept to his promise.[29]

Less than a year after the documentary on Lourdes, Malcolm's
public statements about religion were beginning to change. Early in
1966, he wrote a short essay in which he claimed that "God comes
padding after me like a Hound of Heaven."[30] A few weeks later, in an
essay for a collection called *What I Believe*, he took a tentative step
forward in his religious search. The essay begins with a list of what he
does not believe in: progressivism, utopian politics, science and
education. Then he elaborates the metaphor of "Life and the Legend".
But a new note is sounded when he turns to religion. "It is true that
these basic propositions of Christianity have got cluttered up with
dogma of various kinds that I find often incomprehensible, irrelevant
and even repugnant. All the same, I should be proud and happy to be
able to call myself a Christian; to dare to measure myself against that
sublimely high standard of human values and human behaviour."[31]

This statement, phrased in the subjunctive mood, was little more
than dipping his toe in the water. Over the course of the next two
years Malcolm dodged the Hound of Heaven without being able to
leave him behind entirely. He developed a pattern in which he used
his television documentaries to do "on site" exploration of the Christian
faith, while he sent out written dispatches to the *New Statesman* and
the *Observer* about the current state of his religious convictions. *The
English Cardinal*, aired on BBC1 in the spring of 1966, gave Malcolm
the opportunity to examine the life and beliefs of the Roman Catholic
Cardinal of Westminster, John Heenan. The two men had appeared in
a debate in 1959 and developed a friendly respect for one another.
Malcolm genuinely admired Heenan's strength of character and sense
of humour, which he thought stemmed from his origins as a child of
working-class Irish parents. The programme opened with Malcolm in
a facetious mood, asking Heenan if he enjoyed being waited on by
nuns. Heenan parried this by telling Malcolm that he would make an
excellent cardinal. Walking with Heenan in the Vatican gardens,
Malcolm questioned the cardinal about the liberalising forces in the
Church that had been unleashed by the Second Vatican Council.
Heenan proved to be a balanced and orthodox cleric, a far cry from the

trendy priests Malcolm frequently criticised.[32] Off camera, Malcolm asked Heenan why he had never attempted to convert him to Catholicism. Heenan replied with a laugh: "It would have been disastrous if you had!"[33]

Malcolm received a somewhat more pointed challenge from an Ursuline nun he interviewed for *The Road to Canterbury*, a programme about the diversity of religious quests in the modern era, broadcast in January 1967. Sister Mary Thomas told Malcolm that his own religious search posited too radical an opposition between flesh and spirit.

> [Y]ou're like a shipwrecked man who finds himself in the water, and when he finds an opposition between the water and his body, he panics and fights and tries to get out of the water, to climb out of the water into the air. Well of course he can't do this, and so he drowns. But if he just changes his attitude he finds that this opposition will remain between the water and his body, but he can make it creative and he can float and . . . he's saved.[34]

Malcolm's secular critics were rather less constructive, accusing him of hypocritical posturing and a Manichean hatred of the flesh. Writing in the *New Statesman*, Colin MacInnes noted that Malcolm's reflections on religion contain vague hints about his own unregenerate past, but that they lacked any true feeling of "confession and repentance. MM does not need a Peter to deny him thrice – he does it himself, and this betokens the absence of a real, and not just a wry and feigned, humility." While granting that Malcolm was compulsively readable, with an outstanding range of knowledge and experience, MacInnes held that he was far too vague about what sort of God he believed in. Moreover, MacInnes argued, Malcolm was diluting his message with so many appearances on television. "I feel that the time has come for MM to abandon, for a while, the enticing magazine columns and the alluring telly box, and retire to the hills there to meditate, and come up with the consequences of his reflections: in other words that a man of such great talents should write a *book*."[35]

MacInnes may not have been a sympathetic critic, but several of these shafts struck home. Malcolm recognised that his tendency to remain a detached observer was at odds with the essence of the Christian faith, which requires both an affirmation of belief and communion with fellow believers. He was now in an extremely awkward position: he was proposing Christianity as an answer to modern secularism and its discontents, but he could not even recite the Apostles' Creed with conviction. A glimpse into the emotional intensity of this unresolved conflict can be found in an essay on "The Crucifixion", published in the *Observer* on Easter Day, 1967. The thesis of the essay is that the Crucifixion constituted a "sublime mockery of all earthly authority and power". Instead of turning the essay into yet another occasion to pillory utopian politics, Malcolm concentrates more on the inward, personal meaning of the Cross. Drawing on his memories of the British Raj in India, Malcolm imagines the Crucifixion as a minor execution in an imperial province, not important enough to cause the Pilates to cancel their garden party in honour of the Emperor's birthday. But this obscure event had in fact stood the world on its head. "We are henceforth to worship defeat, not victory; failure, not success; surrender, not defiance; deprivation, not satiety; weakness, not strength."

In contrast to the essay's moving language about the Cross, Malcolm repeatedly states that for the twentieth-century "nihilist" like himself, Christian doctrines are "largely meaningless" and "beyond credibility". He concludes with the statement that even if Christ did not rise from the dead, the meaning of the Crucifixion was not altered. Perhaps, Malcolm suggests, a dim-witted body snatcher had heard of the death of the King of the Jews, and made off with the body of Jesus in the hopes of getting some expensive baubles.

> What a disappointment for him! This King of the Jews has no crown, no jewels, no orb, no sceptre, no ring; he is just a worthless, wasted, broken, naked body. The man contemptuously abandons the body to the vultures, who in their turn leave the bones to whiten in the sun – those precious, precious bones![36]

When the South African novelist, Alan Paton, read this essay, he found it unforgettable. As he wrote in a short devotional book, *Instrument of Thy Peace*, Malcolm suffered the pain of someone "who wants to believe and who cannot believe".[37]

As agonised as Malcolm's religious journey was by 1967, he managed to impress a variety of people as being more relaxed and kinder. He conducted two extensive television interviews that year – with Leonard Woolf and Sir John Reith – that were critically acclaimed. After the Woolf interview, a commentator in the *Listener* wrote that he had heard rumours of a "profound spiritual change" in Malcolm. What the commentator could see for himself was that Malcolm had no longer had a "high-pitched nagging voice" and that he had "lost the cadaverous look, and his face has quite filled out".[38] As if to prove that he could not please all the people all the time, Malcolm was even criticised for being too soft on Sir John Reith, the first Director-General of the BBC.

Around this time Malcolm was approached by his first love from his youth in Croydon, Dora Pitman Gould. Malcolm had met Dora only once since the 1920s – in an air raid shelter during the Blitz. When Dora contacted Malcolm in 1967, she had already been a widow for several years. With little in the way of financial resources, she had got into serious debt, and turned to Malcolm for help. Malcolm instructed his lawyers to pay Dora's rent, which had fallen into arrears, and any legal fees arising out of a dispute with her landlord. Dora was deeply grateful, and, a few years later, corresponded with Malcolm while he was writing his memoirs. This aid to Dora was not the first time Malcolm had proven his generosity. He had helped one of his brothers to emerge from debt in the late 1950s and had also provided financial help to his children whenever they needed it.

Another moment of happiness was the publication, in the autumn of 1967, of *Beatrice Webb: A Life*, written by Kitty and an author named Ruth Adam. The book proved what many friends of the Muggeridges had always known: that Kitty had a vivid intelligence and her own way with words. Writing the book had become possible only when the children had left home. In the book's prologue, Kitty wrote a graceful memoir in her own voice about "My Aunt Bo". If she was more sympathetic to the human dimension of Beatrice Webb's life than Malcolm had ever been, it was clear that she shared Malcolm's criticism of her aunt's political philosophy. The reviewers received the biography warmly. After the book was published, Kitty gave a number of interviews and public lectures, but she made it clear to her interviewers that she did not share Malcolm's enjoyment of life in the spotlight, and was quite happy to return to the peace of Park Cottage. She contemplated writing a biography of the Social Darwinist, Herbert Spencer, but nothing came of the idea. Nonetheless, publishing the biography gave her confidence, and she was to pursue a number of other literary projects in the coming years, much to Malcolm's satisfaction.

*

Meanwhile, Malcolm's religious quest was approaching a critical turning point. The tension so evident in his essay on "The Crucifixion" had to be resolved. He took the next step as one might expect a veteran journalist to do – by going "on location". He spent three weeks living with the Cistercian monks at Sancta Maria Abbey at Nunraw, in Scotland, making a documentary for the BBC, entitled *A Hard Bed to Lie On*, which was broadcast in August 1967. Several months before filming was to begin, Malcolm had to travel to the monastery to seek the permission of the monks to make the film. He was immediately impressed by the radiance of "inward sanctity" he noticed on the faces of many of the monks. When the time came to discuss the proposal, however, he found the monks' questions sharp and to the point. In the end, they proved to be common-sensical and cooperative, even relaxing their rule of silence to allow for interviews. They even agreed to a small deception for the benefit of the television audience: while out in the fields they were filmed wearing their habits. Normally they wore work clothes, but Malcolm explained that viewers might think they were merely farm-workers employed by the monks. Malcolm was given a private room for his stay at the abbey, but otherwise participated in most of the monastic prayers. Getting up for Mass at four-thirty in the morning was not difficult for him, since he usually rose a little after that. He had not lived in the midst of a daily liturgical life since his days at the Oratory of the Good Shepherd at Cambridge forty years earlier.[39]

A Hard Bed to Lie On is not on a par with his documentary on Lourdes; it was made around the same time as Malcolm's essay on "The Crucifixion" and bears some of the signs of his ambivalent mood. There were, of course, a number of scenes that caught, in quiet moments of revelation, the essence of the monastic life. A shot of an old brother tending to his lambs made the metaphor of the Lamb of God all the more vivid. Close-ups of monks singing Compline provide an array of different expressions, from strain to serenity. Much of the programme was taken up with discussions about the upheavals in Church and society that were creating pressures on the community. Malcolm was chided by some critics for commenting that the liberal (*Honest to God*) Bishop of Woolwich "has got into the woodwork", but he was entirely right to sense that even the monastic orders would be affected by the massive changes taking place in the Church. The older monks, many of whom came over from Ireland in 1946 to found the abbey at Nunraw, were easily the most persuasive. Brother Oliver gave the programme its title when he recalled the saying that "the Cistercian bed is hard to lie on, but it's sweet to die on." This was the type of epigram that normally would have delighted Malcolm, but he pressed on to other subjects.[40]

For sheer contrast with life at Nunraw, it would be hard to imagine anything better than the interview Malcolm conducted just a couple weeks after the broadcast of *A Hard Bed to Lie On*. It was with the Maharishi Mahesh Yogi, who had recently achieved fame as guru to the Beatles and the popular exponent of Transcendental Meditation. Throughout the entire interview, Malcolm tried to get the Maharishi to admit that the spiritual life required some form of sacrifice and self-restraint. But the guru would have none of it. Take the case of a man who ate far too much, Malcolm suggested. Shouldn't he limit his appetite?

> MAHARISHI: Not 'limit', actually. Only the senses should be so trained that they function very normally in a useful manner.
> MUGGERIDGE: Doesn't that imply some degree at any rate of restraint?
> MAHARISHI: I wouldn't say 'restraint'. I would say the culture of the senses in order that they function normally and bring fulfilment. Restraint is unnatural, mm?
> MUGGERIDGE: To me it's absolutely necessary. I have a greedy, sensual nature. If I allowed this greedy, sensual nature to have complete freedom, I should be like a pig in a trough.
> MAHARISHI: No. This will be when the greediness is not controlled in the natural way.
> MUGGERIDGE: But just what is a natural way?
> MAHARISHI: Natural way is that the man should be more sensible. Naturally he should think rightly.

And so on. Clearly, there was more than a language barrier standing between these two men.

Something more serious took place when Malcolm travelled to the Holy Land in the autumn of 1967 to spend two months filming a three-part programme entitled *A Life of Christ*. Once again the choice of subject was his; once again the BBC faithfully provided the requisite support. It was not a documentary: no experts were interviewed for their opinions of the historicity of the Gospels or the relationship of Christianity to other Jewish sects of the first century. This was to be another intensely personal project, an extended soliloquy by Malcolm about Christ.

He had been to the Holy Land before, but on his previous visits he had been distracted and self-absorbed. Even now his feelings were mixed. The brief but fierce Arab-Israeli war had been fought just a few months before Malcolm and his crew arrived; evidence of the war was everywhere. On the other hand, the tour buses continued to rumble along and, clustered around the holy places, myriad shops and stands sold kitschy souvenirs, relics and other religious paraphernalia. Malcolm began to think he was in a huge amusement park – "Jesusland".

He was reflecting in just this way – writing editorials in his mind – while sitting in the Church of the Nativity in Bethlehem. Hovering in the shadows of the crypt, Malcolm had to wait until the doors of the church were closed to the public before they could begin filming. It was during that waiting period that he began to notice the faces of those who approached the spot where Jesus was said to have been born. The faces, he thought, seemed to reflect the typical range of attitudes, from the pious to the merely curious. But, when they finally saw the spot, they *all* were transfigured: their faith in the Christian story, whether fervent or only residual, shone forth. Seeing their faith, Malcolm was suddenly seized "with a curious, almost magical, certainty" that Christ was present, that he had been born, lived, and died as the Gospels proclaimed. He had an impulse to kneel down with the worshippers, but the old Adam in him restrained him; he held back, fearing that the film crew would laugh.[41]

Nonetheless, this was the moment of illumination Malcolm had been searching for. Always the outsider, Malcolm came to faith only by seeing it in the faces of others. If he could not look directly at God, he could at least see his reflection in his fellow human beings. It was precisely because these people were not special in any way – they were neither theologians nor clerics nor television commentators – that he was able to register the genuine nature of their faith. He might have thought of Kierkegaard's distinction between an apostle and the genius. According to Kierkegaard, the genius claims to have a unique intelligence that enables him to discover truth, but there is always some inherent human limitation in the genius that causes us to doubt that he has the whole truth. The apostle, on the other hand, makes no claims to intelligence. The apostle simply says: "I have been told something important that I must pass on to you." And when he does, his words carry conviction. Malcolm had received the story from those who had no qualifications at all other than their common humanity.

That Malcolm had now become a believer and not just an agonised searcher can be seen in the completed film, which was not aired until April 1968. *A Life of Christ* marks a new phase in Malcolm's life. For the first time in decades, Malcolm's language became suffused with the ardour of his early idealism. The rhythms and cadences of his narration were almost musical; large sections of *A Life of Christ* achieve an effect close to that of blank verse. It was once said of Malcolm's rhetoric in his best television programmes that he spoke "in paragraphs, rather than sentences".[42] Nowhere is that more evident than in this film. For example, Malcolm imagines Christ reading in the synagogue at Nazareth the passage from the prophet Isaiah beginning, "The spirit of the Lord is upon me." But when Jesus finishes the passage and proclaims that this scripture has been fulfilled in him, he is thrown out of the synagogue.

> He made for Capernaum by the Sea of Galilee. I see him, a solitary figure, trudging along, until the sight of the lake opened up before him; with no luggage, no money, no prospects, no plans; only those magnificent words still ringing in his ears, and a sense of exaltation at the knowledge that he had, indeed, been chosen to give them a new, tremendous reality. Those who met him along the way must have marvelled to see one who was at once so poor and so uplifted.[43]

Even in Malcolm's tart and seemingly pessimistic comments there is a new spirit, a sense of things falling into place in his mind and heart.

> Christ withdrew alone to the desert to fast and pray in preparation for a dialogue with the Devil. Such a dialogue was inescapable; every virtue has to be cleared first with the Devil, as every vice is torn with anguish out of God's heart. Christ found the Devil waiting for him in the desert, but what took place between them was really a soliloquy. When we talk with the Devil we are talking to ourselves . . .
> What Christ had to say was too simple to be grasped, too truthful to be believed. Our faculties are like those smelting works that can take only ore of a high degree of impurity; when the light is too bright we cannot see . . .

Mystics and great artists know – what is often hidden from other men – that our free will is shaped by our passions into an inescapable destiny. Prometheus is both bound and free . . . Christ is the only liberator whose liberation lasts forever.[44]

Malcolm's impassioned words were well complemented by the film's cinematography. There were many shots of Israeli soldiers and burned-out tanks to give a contemporary feel to the film, but the most moving visuals were recorded out in the harsh countryside, where picnickers are shown scrambling up the hill where the Sermon on the Mount was preached and where fishermen pursue their trade on the Sea of Galilee much as they had in Christ's time. Perhaps the most visually memorable moment was a scene shot in a cave, where Malcolm's voice is distorted by echoes. As one television critic wrote of this scene: "[T]he camera, shooting from below, makes [Malcolm] appear, gaunt and white-haired, like some minor prophet."[45]

When he came to the final programme, entitled *The Road to Emmaus*, Malcolm returned to the subject of the Crucifixion and Resurrection that he had written about only months before. Rather than dwelling on body snatchers and bones whitening in the desert sun, he relegates such matters to the realm of "legitimate historical investigation". "[W]hat is not open to question is that today, two thousand years later, Christ is alive." Malcolm brings the film to a conclusion with the image of the two disciples walking on the road to Emmaus shortly after the Resurrection. They are joined by a stranger, "a third presence", who expounds God's plan of salvation with such insight that the disciples' hearts burned within them. "On every walk, Christ came to tell us, whether to Emmaus or Wimbledon or Timbuktu, there is the same stranger waiting to accompany us along our way, if we want him."[46]

Malcolm wanted him. Christ, he now believed, dwelled in and gave meaning to Life. By comparison, the realm of Legend, or even that of Café Limbo, seemed tawdry and false. He had known this all along. But now, with the mysterious stranger at his side, Malcolm felt less like a stranger. Emerging from the shadows of the crypt in the Church of the Nativity like Jonah from the mouth of the whale, Malcolm was no longer a detached observer, but a tentative participant, a prophet ready to confront his mission at last, a mission he had evaded for more years than he cared to remember. It would not take him long to find a pulpit from which to preach this long-neglected message.

« 18 »

A Door of Utterance
1968–1975

WITHIN A FEW WEEKS of his return from the Holy Land, Malcolm found himself embroiled in another public controversy, arising out of his duties as Rector of Edinburgh University. This was an office, it will be recalled, for which he had competed back in 1957, when another controversy – the monarchy row – had been in full swing. Back then, his supporters had been kidnapped and demonstrations against him had been organised. But in the spring of 1966, Malcolm was once again approached by a student delegation from Edinburgh, who asked him to contest the election. This time around, Malcolm's iconoclasm made a stronger appeal to Edinburgh's student population, whose restiveness was soon to explode into the political activism and anarchic mayhem that would characterise university politics throughout the Western world at the close of the decade. It would be an understatement to say that in electing Malcolm, they got more than they bargained for.

On November 10, 1966, Malcolm was elected Rector by a comfortable majority, outpolling J.P. Macintosh, MP for Berwick and East Lothian, Lord Birsay, chairman of the Scottish Land Court, and Quintin Hogg, who was then MP for St Marylebone. The polling was marked by the traditional student antics, including running battles between factions where soup, flour, vegetables, rotten eggs and fish heads were turned into projectiles.[1] These high spirits were fairly harmless, but they had the effect of pointing out the ambiguity surrounding the office of Rector. In all four of the oldest Scottish universities, the Rector is elected for a three-year term and, in addition to certain ceremonial functions, he is charged with the task of representing the needs and concerns of the student body to the university administration. He is assisted by the Rector's Assessor, who in Malcolm's case was an Edinburgh lawyer named Alan Frazer, who was also a committed Christian and a friend.

Malcolm had won the election both as a celebrity and an iconoclast; so what, exactly, was expected of him? Before he even took office, Malcolm wrote to the president of the Student Representative Council with his own interpretation of the Rector's role.

> The Rector's job, as I understand it, is to work with you and your colleagues. If ever I felt for any reason that my relations with the SRC precluded full cooperation I should at once resign. The purely ceremonial aspects of being Rector make less than no appeal to me, and if the job's usefulness as providing a liaison between you and the University authorities were to be limited or precluded I should resign.[2]

These strictures are rather testy for a relationship that had not even formally begun, but Malcolm was right to suspect that conflicts were looming ahead.

The investiture took place on February 16, 1967. Malcolm's address was, as might be expected, a shot across the bows, calculated to offend students, faculty and administrators alike. He attacked what he thought of as one of the central articles of faith among liberals: the notion that education was the antidote to every social problem, that human nature was essentially good and only needed the correct information to make wise choices. The corollary to this, he continued, is the "permissive" society, in which the individual is allowed to create his or her own morality. "When birth pills are handed out with free orange juice and consenting adults wear special ties and blazers, and abortion and divorce – those two contemporary panaceas for all matrimonial ills – are freely available on the public health, then ... it will be realized that this path, even from the shallow point of view of the pursuit of happiness, is a disastrous cul-de-sac." The great advantage to the crisis of the West, he concluded, was that it provided an opportunity to discard utopian schemes and return to the perennial truths that had undergirded our civilisation, and in particular to "the sublime truths of the Christian religion".[3]

There were no serious conflicts for the first eight months of Malcolm's tenure as Rector. Then, in October, the magazine *Student*, published by students at Edinburgh, carried an article calling for the use of the drug LSD to be legalised. This led the Discipline Committee of the university to suspend the editor of *Student*. But after members of the SRC cried "censorship", the editor was restored to his position with a "reprimand". As the students gained a sense of increased power, some of them went on the offensive, accusing Malcolm and Alan Frazer of failing to defend the editor of *Student* at the time of his suspension. The SRC made this accusation formal by passing a motion, on November 14, 1967, demanding that the Rector and Assessor express only the views of the SRC in their dealings with the university. Three weeks later, as if taking their cue from Malcolm's investiture address, the SRC passed another motion, calling on the university health authority to provide contraceptive pills on request to female students.

Both Malcolm and Frazer made it clear to the SRC that they would not be muzzled, nor would they do anything to further the motion requiring free distribution of "the Pill". A tense but orderly meeting was held on December 7, where each side stated its position. Malcolm said that if the students would not back down, he might resign and contest the election again to see if the majority of the student body supported the SRC. The first issue of *Student* published after the Christmas vacation carried a cartoon of Malcolm, depicting him as a decomposing head, with worms crawling out of his skull. The editorial, entitled "Who is Muggeridge?", concluded with an ultimatum: represent the SRC's wishes or resign.

The timing of Malcolm's response couldn't have been better. It so happened that Malcolm was scheduled to deliver the annual rectorial address on January 14, 1968, from the pulpit of St Giles', the High Kirk of Edinburgh. Word of the controversy had spread, and the church was not only crowded, but contained a substantial contingent from the media, including the BBC, which broadcast the address. Fresh from his experience in Bethlehem, Malcolm decided that he would deliver a sermon, rather than a speech, from the pulpit of St Giles'. Taking as his text Christ's words, "I am the light of the world," Malcolm began by comparing the late twentieth-century West to the decaying Roman Empire. In both eras, he contended, men were utterly credulous about the fantasies of materialism, while being sceptical about spiritual truth. He then focused on the controversy at the university:

> The students here in this university . . . are the ultimate benefici-
> aries under our welfare system. They are supposed to be the

spearhead of progress, flattered and paid for by their admiring seniors, an *élite* who will happily and audaciously carry the torch of progress into the glorious future before them. Now, speaking for myself, there is practically nothing that they could do in a mood of rebelliousness or refusal to accept the ways and values of our run-down, spiritually impoverished way of life for which I shouldn't feel some degree of sympathy or, at any rate, understanding. Yet how infinitely sad; how, in a macabre sort of way, funny, that the form their insubordination takes should be a demand for pot and pills, for the most tenth-rate sort of escapism and self-indulgence ever known! ... The resort of any old, slobbering debauchee anywhere in the world at any time – dope and bed.[4]

Since he could feel nothing but "contempt" for the students' course of action, and since the SRC demand that he represent their views was unconscionable, he and Alan Frazer would resign their positions, effectively immediately. The remainder of the sermon was devoted to the conflict between utopianism and Christianity. As far as he was concerned, this conflict boiled down to one stark choice: "It is Christ or nothing."

The resignation drew the now standard denunciations of Malcolm as a crazed puritan. One of these denunciations, however, came from a somewhat unexpected source: the Roman Catholic university chaplain. "The plain fact is that we do not find elderly journalists with a gift of invective useful allies in presenting Christian standards."[5] Malcolm predicted that the chaplain would go on to become a bishop, which in due course he did.

But Malcolm's flair for the dramatic gesture was quite effective in this instance. There was strong support for Malcolm's position. The Vice-Chancellor of Edinburgh University, Michael Swann, publicly announced his unqualified support. He would have made the same decision, he said. "It is plainly intolerable that any attempt should be made to force you or your Assessor to espouse causes ... that you do not believe in."[6] Two days later, Swann revealed that several major gifts and legacies that had been pledged to the university had been cancelled as a result of the controversy. Among the students there was considerable support for Malcolm. A debate was held in the student union on the proposition that "This house stands behind Malcolm Muggeridge." The motion was carried by 479 votes to 414. The SRC even attempted a little damage control by censoring *Student* magazine for a time. The same committee of students that had drafted Malcolm in 1966 asked him to run again. But the curtain had come down on this act; Malcolm felt the need to move on.[7]

In the spring of 1968 Malcolm went on another American lecture tour, but this time he spent the lonely moments in between talks contemplating the state of his soul. He had taken up the banner of the Christian faith in public, but his own mind and heart were still in transition. With the exception of his screen biography of Jesus, his faith remained rather abstract, a useful counterpoint to his attacks on secular liberalism. As the critic Colin MacInnnes had pointed out, there was in Malcolm's writings and speeches little sense of the personal dimension of conversion, of penitence and humility. Between his American lecture stops, he returned to his worn paperback copy of Augustine's *Confessions*, looking for guidance. On April 7, in Salem, Oregon, he composed a prayer and inscribed it on the flyleaf of the *Confessions*: "O God, stay with me. Let no word cross my lips that is not your word, no thought enter my mind that is not your thought, no deed ever be done or entertained by me that is not your deed."[8]

Not long after his return from America, Malcolm was informed that there was an opportunity to interview an Indian nun who worked with the poor in Calcutta. One of the BBC's religious broadcasting staff, Oliver Hunkin, had heard that this nun, Mother Teresa, was beginning to attract international attention for her tireless work with lepers, orphans, the dying and the hungry. On the train to London, Malcolm prepared for the interview by reading whatever Hunkin had managed to dig up on Mother Teresa. The order she had founded, known as the Missionaries of Charity, had spread from Calcutta to many other places in India, and was on the verge of seeding new efforts in Latin America and the Middle East. The habit of the order was made of the cheapest cotton fabric of the type used by Indian peasants, with a few small stripes of blue, symbolising the spiritual patronage of the Virgin Mary. The interview, for the *Meeting Point* series, was held at the Holy Child Convent in Cavendish Square. Mother Teresa was late, and Malcolm began to get impatient for her arrival. When she finally arrived, Malcolm wasted no time, whisking her off to the room where the camera had been set up. "Come along, Mother Teresa!"

Malcolm discovered that Mother Teresa was in fact Albanian, not Indian, though she had worked in India for many years. A tiny, wizened woman, she was not, in the traditional sense, photogenic. Malcolm, for whom the TV interview was a form of "hypnosis", was not impressed, though he later said that Mother Teresa's face had a radiance that was impossible to forget.

MUGGERIDGE: [A] tremendous lot of your work is to do with children.

MOTHER TERESA: These are either children from unwedded mothers or children that have been left anywhere and picked up either by the sisters or by the police or by anybody who has found a baby lying in the street. Sometimes we find them in the dustbins; sometimes wrapped up in newspaper and left near the door or under a bus seat.

MUGGERIDGE: Mother Teresa, will you explain one thing for me? The inspiration and strength for your work comes from the Mass, from your Catholic devotions, from your religious life. Now then, when you have people helping, don't you feel that you must put them in the way of having this same help?

MOTHER TERESA: Everyone, even the Hindus and the Mohammedans, has some faith in their own religion that can help them to do works of love.

MUGGERIDGE: Is that enough?

MOTHER TERESA: To begin with it's enough. And once they come in contact with this suffering, then by serving them, you see, love begets love, and it becomes very infectious.[9]

After the interview ended, Malcolm was afraid that Mother Teresa had been so soft-spoken and shy that she would not "come across" well. Some on the BBC staff wondered whether it should be shown at all, or if so, perhaps late at night. But Oliver Hunkin wanted the interview to be broadcast on a Sunday evening. He prevailed.

The response was immediate and overwhelming. Mother Teresa's love had been so infectious that both the BBC and Malcolm himself received letters filled with cash, cheques, money orders and even securities. The messages that accompanied the gifts said essentially the same thing, according to Malcolm: "This woman spoke to me as no one ever has, and I feel I must help her." A second screening of the interview produced another outpouring of moral and financial support. The total amount donated came to over £20,000. Malcolm, as he freely admitted, had not predicted this outcome. At the time of the interview, he had been thinking like a jaded media man, looking "with, not thro' the eye", to quote one of his favourite passages from Blake. Here, as in Bethlehem, it was the faith of common men and women that enabled him to see the spiritual significance of what lay before him. Within a few months, he would, with the BBC's blessing, seek to make a film about Mother Teresa's work.

In the autumn of 1968, Malcolm was given permission to seek Mother Teresa's approval for a film about the Missionaries of Charity. Her answer arrived by mail in December. She had decided against making a film, which she thought was an inappropriate way of spending her time; she also resisted anything that attempted to place her, rather than her work, in the spotlight. Malcolm sympathised with this, but in this instance he sided with the camera, and enlisted the support of his old friend Cardinal Heenan. Heenan's letter to Mother Teresa was gracious and disarming. It was enough to overcome her opposition, if not her scepticism. "If this TV programme is going to help people to love God better, then we will have it, but with one condition – that the Brothers and Sisters be included, as they do the work."[10]

The filming took place in the spring, under the direction of Peter Chafer. There was a great deal of pressure on the entire crew because they only had five days in which to complete the filming; if something turned out badly, there was no time to go back and do it again. Malcolm attended Mass daily with Mother Teresa. It was an emotional experience for him. Here, kneeling on a hard straw mat with the Sisters, several of the deepest emotional threads in Malcolm's life were braided together. Two of his earliest formative experiences – the spiritual and liturgical life at the Oratory of the Good Shepherd in Cambridge and his happy years in southern India – were encompassed by Mother Teresa's order. Here he saw the Simple Life lived with sincerity and authenticity: Western Christianity adapted to meet the needs of the East. Here high-caste Indian women lovingly bathed the leprous sores of the "untouchables" – an image of the human family united by love. Malcolm remembered another small, wizened figure, Gandhi, who also inspired millions with his call for personal moral change as the only way to achieve lasting social change.

Despite his own continuing resistance to institutional Christianity, Malcolm was acutely aware that Mother Teresa's faith was grounded in the most orthodox and traditional Catholicism. He respected this. The opposite tendency, that of liberalism, departed from the ancient dogma of the faith, substituting collective, political solutions for the personal and spiritual solutions of Christianity. Mother Teresa put the distinction into simple terms, when she recounted what a Hindu man had said to her. The social worker, he said, did what he did for *something*, while the Missionaries did what they did for *someone*. That someone, of course, was Christ. Working with the poorest of the poor enabled the Missionaries to see "Christ in his distressing disguise".[11] This was a significant revelation for Malcolm. One of the barriers that stood between Malcolm and a deeper commitment to faith was the ambivalence he felt about Jesus. He had spoken of the "third presence" ready to join us at any time, but still treated Jesus more as a sublime teacher than a personal saviour. There can be little doubt that Mother Teresa helped Malcolm to draw nearer to Jesus, as his writings after the filming of *Something Beautiful for God* testify.

The intensity of Malcolm's experience with Mother Teresa can be gauged by his earnest belief that "the first authentic photographic miracle" took place during the filming. It happened like this. When the time came to record scenes from Mother Teresa's Home for the Dying, it was getting dark. The photographer, Ken Macmillan, declared that he did not have the right film for such poor lighting conditions; whatever they shot would not come out. But, with a single small light, they went ahead and recorded some footage, adding some shots from the courtyard as insurance. When the film was developed, the interior of the Home for the Dying was "bathed in a particularly beautiful soft light", while the outdoor shots were "dim and confused". Macmillan was surprised by the outcome, though he would never go so far as to claim that a miracle had taken place. However, on his next assignment, Macmillan tried to reproduce the same lighting conditions as in the Home for the Dying. The result was too dark to be usable.

Soon after his departure, Mother Teresa replied to a letter from Malcolm: "I can't tell you how big a sacrifice it was to accept the making of the film – but I am glad now that I did so because it has brought us closer to God." She went on to say that she had given the Sisters an instruction on obedience, comparing Malcolm's obedience to his director, Peter Chafer, to the Sisters' obedience to God. The letter concluded: "Try to make the world conscious that it is never too late to do something beautiful for God."

It was not until December 1969, that *Something Beautiful for God* was broadcast. Without any question it is the finest documentary Malcolm ever made, a tribute not only to him, but to the skills of

Chafer and Macmillan as well. In depicting the work of the Mission-aries, the film relies heavily on visual images unencumbered by verbiage. For most of the film, Malcolm himself does not appear inside the camera frame; his voice can be heard, and occasionally a glimpse of his hand gesturing can be seen, but the focus remains fixedly on Mother Teresa and the people to whom she ministers. As in *Pilgrims to Lourdes*, Malcolm avoided sentimentalising the work of the Mission-aries. The Sisters and Brothers are brisk, earthy and efficient – virtues necessary for them to be able to work amidst the squalor and suffering around them. By stepping out of the camera's eye, Malcolm had made the most effective and moving film of his career. In the light of his newfound faith in Christ, this paradox made perfect sense.

When his publisher, Collins, asked Malcolm if he would be willing for them to publish a collection of his essays on his religious search, he was at first reluctant. Looking back over the last three years, he realised that these pieces were full of contradictions and inconsisten-cies. After all, they traced a series of shifting ideas and commitments, hardly providing the scheme of a coherent book. But Lady Collins persuaded him that the sincerity and passion of his religious quest would more than offset the lack of a coherent theological position. He acknowledged this in the foreword to *Jesus Rediscovered*. "Theology is one of those subjects, like algebra and thermodynamics, in which I have never been able to interest myself. I am a theological ignoramus, and likely to remain one to the end of my days."

What he knew of the Christian faith derived from the New Testament and his own set of mystical masters: St Augustine and St Francis, Bunyan and Blake, Pascal and Kierkegaard, Tolstoy and Dostoevsky, Bonhoeffer and Simone Weil. He recounted the mystical moment in Bethlehem when he became convinced of Christ's divinity. "[T]here really had been a man, Jesus, who was also God: I was conscious of his presence. He really had spoken those words. I heard them. He really had died on the cross and risen from the dead . . . The Cross is where history and life, legend and truth, time and eternity, intersect. There Jesus is nailed forever to show us how God could become a man and a man become God."[12]

There was one step, however, that he was not prepared to take. Despite his love of the Roman Catholic Church, he could not join it. Catholicism, he declared, was rushing to reproduce all the "follies and fatuities of Protestantism", and he would not climb on board a sinking ship. He acknowledged that his critics had attacked him for being a lecher-turned-puritan, and that he had "gone soft" and become a bore. These criticisms he could understand. But the one argument that he rejected outright was the notion that Christian faith "amounts to a kind of escapism, an evasion of the ardours and responsibilities of reality". To prove the point, he cited the example of Dietrich Bonhoeffer, who had returned to Germany under the Nazis and who opposed them in word and deed, only to be executed by them weeks before their surrender. Bonhoeffer made the ultimate sacrifice to oppose the idea that worldly power could bring any lasting liberation.

Nearly all of the essays reprinted in *Jesus Rediscovered* represented positions from which Malcolm had moved on. But the title essay, which appeared in the June 1969 issue of *Esquire*, sounded a truly new note. The essay is autobiographical, an attempt to trace what Blake called the "golden string" of God's grace through the story of his life. Malcolm begins by returning to his childhood and, more specifically, to his father. In contrast to the television documentary *A Socialist Childhood*, which treated his father and his youth with condescension and scorn, "Jesus Rediscovered" is gentle and affectionate in tone – a gesture towards reconciliation with his father. The idealism and unworldliness of H.T. are given their due as important factors in Malcolm's own spiritual pilgrimage. Here he also made public for the first time the fact that he had read the Bible secretly in his bed as a child. Three pages into the essay, Malcolm shifts into a direct address to God, in the manner of Augustine's *Confessions*. "I was to learn that You are to be found in the lowest, darkest depths, and that all who find You are thereby transported to the loftiest, brightest heights."

The tone of penitence which had been lacking in his earlier writings enters into "Jesus Rediscovered". He recalled that the symbol of the Cross had always filled him with an anguished sense that it comprehended the mystery of human existence – even when his eye picked its form out on a telegraph pole. But he had turned away from it, again and again.

As I remember this, a sense of my own failure lies leadenly upon me. I should have worn it over my heart; carried it, a precious standard never to be wrested out of my hands; even though I fell, still borne aloft. It should have been my cult, my uniform, my language, my life. I shall have no excuse; I can't say I didn't know. I knew from the beginning, and turned away. The lucky thieves were crucified with their Saviour; You called me, and I didn't go – those empty years, those empty words, that empty passion!

Later, when he describes his years in India at Union Christian College, he confesses that among "these good and dedicated men I was given my last chance to enlist definitively in Your service, but I turned away". This is a remarkable insight, another indication that Malcolm had always been ruthlessly honest about himself, whether or not he heeded the truths he discovered when he looked inwards, or confided them to others. But God had not been absent from Malcolm's life even when he was running away from him. There were glimpses, such as the little painted church in the woods at Kliasma near Moscow, or at the Easter service in famine-ravaged Kiev. There was the "old, coloured shoeshine man on a windy Chicago street one February morning, smiling from ear to ear; or a little man with a lame leg in the Immigration Department in New York, whose smiling patience as he listened to one Puerto Rican after another seemed to reach from there to eternity".[13]

The long interview with Roy Trevivian at the end of *Jesus Rediscovered* is also the most candid he had ever given. There he admitted that he had tried to commit suicide in Lourenço Marques in 1943, something he had publicly denied in 1966 when the historian David Irving had unearthed the fact from the wartime dispatches of the German spy, Leopold Wertz.[14] He also told Trevivian that his "lechery" had been largely responsible for the lateness of his Christian conversion. He had refused to publicly espouse the faith so long as he could not live up to the ethical standards of Christianity. The one sin he did not want to commit was that of hypocrisy. Finally, it was in this interview that he revealed how shocked he had been by his explosion of rage at the person so dear to him who suffered from bouts of mental illness.

That these were painful admissions, accompanied by genuine contrition, would seem impossible to deny, but many of Malcolm's critics were undeterred. Pundits like Bernard Levin would continue to portray Malcolm as a "pinchbeck Savonarola". To this day, this remains the most common tactic for dismissing Malcolm's ideas and his Christian witness. As recently as 1994, in a controversial Channel 4 documentary attacking Mother Teresa and her work, *Hell's Angel*,

Christopher Hitchens could speak of "that old mountebank, Malcolm Muggeridge".

But when *Jesus Rediscovered* was published in the summer of 1969, there were many who were won over by the honesty of Malcolm's religious quest. Among them was a young Jesuit, Peter Hebblethwaite, who edited a magazine called *The Month*. He was one of a group of religious journalists who met Malcolm when the book was published. Hebblethwaite's explanation of why so many clergy had a suspicious attitude towards Malcolm was simple: "Regular troops are mistrustful of guerrillas." But despite Malcolm's criticisms of the institutional Church, Hebblethwaite wrote, he listened patiently and graciously to the often hostile questions posed to him. One cleric suggested that Christian, in Bunyan's *Pilgrim's Progress*, should have lowered his gaze from the Celestial City and spent his time improving conditions in the City of Destruction. "Or perhaps," Malcolm added, "lingered in Vanity Fair and nationalized the brothels." "The oddest objection to Muggeridge," Hebblethwaite argued, "is that 'he was converted on television beneath the arc lights'. All one can say is that he happens to have worked in television and conversion happens where one is. Saint Paul preached in the market place. Television is the market place of the global village." The one criticism Hebblethwaite ventured had more than a grain of truth in it: Malcolm "is at his best not when he is denouncing the modern world or the antics of hipster clerics but when, in a phrase or an image or a parable, he throws light on the Gospel for today."[15]

Evidently a great many people shared Hebblethwaite's positive impression of *Jesus Rediscovered*, because it instantly became a best-seller, going into several printings, and eventually running to several hundred thousand copies in print. It soon became clear that Malcolm had become the most popular Christian apologist since the death of C.S. Lewis in 1963. He shared with Lewis a lucid and supple prose style and a willingness to champion Christian orthodoxy against the liberalism of the modern age. But in other respects the two men could not have been more different. Lewis was for most of his life a bachelor don, whose writings are filled with literary allusions to Chaucer and Dante and Milton. One side of Lewis was romantic, expressing his Christian faith in children's stories and fantasies; the other side was rational, producing ingenious theological arguments in books like *Mere Christianity*. Malcolm, on the other hand, was a grizzled journalist who had been all over the world, a cynical satirist whose conversion had come late in his life. His Christian writings were neither romantic nor rational, but existential, a mixture of prophetic attacks on decadence and arresting observations on the truth of "the Gospel for today". Malcolm never reached Lewis's level of popularity because his life was so much more complicated and his religious convictions were salted with doubt and astringent irony.

When Malcolm began his religious search through the medium of television in the mid-1960s he had received letters, some from critics, but many more from those who responded with appreciation. With the publication of *Jesus Rediscovered*, the trickle of letters turned into a flood, often brought to the door of Park Cottage in large sacks by the postman. There were far too many for him to be able to respond to individually, but they were often deeply moving. The letter he quotes in the foreword to *Jesus Rediscovered*, from a monk who said he prayed for Malcolm daily at Mass, was in fact representative of the prayers and good wishes he received. Easily the most surprising letter he received was from Svetlana Alliluyeva, the daugher of Joseph Stalin, who had emigrated to America in 1967. In the letter, Svetlana mentioned that she had been baptised and was sustained by her faith in Christ. "I am so glad you had written your book, Mr Muggeridge. It is a fine book for all those snobbish, sceptical intellectuals who are the plague of our time . . . I wish it could be translated into Russian too . . ."[16] Malcolm was deeply touched by this letter, and was later able to send Svetlana a copy of *Something Beautiful for God*, autographed by Mother Teresa, whom she too admired.

In addition to letters, there were now visitors who came to Park Cottage to sit at Malcolm's feet. Playing the role of sage or guru was not something that Malcolm relished. When people came to talk with Malcolm he preferred to engage them in conversation, asking as many questions as he was asked, rather than in making oracular pronoucements. Since Kitty had progressed towards Christianity along with Malcolm, she was an equal participant in these conversations, though her contributions were less frequent. Most visitors wrote or phoned to set up a time to make their visit, but some people just turned up at the door. Kitty often referred to the young man who knocked at the door, unannounced, and said simply: "I've come from Alaska to see Mr Muggeridge." A few were more disturbed, including the man who greeted the Muggeridges by saying: "I am Jesus." This demented messiah then went on to inform Malcolm that *he* was a reincarnation of St Paul, and that he would be glad to have such a mouthpiece to proclaim his good news. Despite a moment's regret – Jesus, after all, had been considered by many to be a madman – Malcolm asked the man to go on his way. But Malcolm and Kitty rarely turned pilgrims away. Frequently they were invited to share a meal at the long wooden table in the kitchen of Park Cottage. Those who came away from their trip to Robertsbridge referred not only to Malcolm's humour and conversation, but also to Kitty's serenity and quietly sacrificial love.

Malcolm and Kitty had reason to feel content in their private life. They were now unified in faith, the long, tortured years of struggle were behind them, and their children were all doing well. One of their great joys was that in 1969 their daughter Valentine married a Dutchman named Gerrit-Jan Colenbrander. The last of the three children to get married, Valentine met Gerrit-Jan in London while he was working for Shell; he subsequently left the world of business to become a professor of economics. Within a few years of their marriage, the Colenbranders would become the Dutch coordinators of Mother Teresa's Co-Workers, helping to organise supplies, money and volunteer efforts on behalf of the Missionaries of Charity. Malcolm's eldest son Leonard lived in Bedfordshire with his wife Sylvia and son Peter. They would have three more children. Leonard had earned a degree in theology from the London Bible College, and had gone to work for a time in a German psychiatric hospital. After returning to England, he became a schoolteacher and served as a lay preacher for the Plymouth Brethren. John had emigrated to Canada and married Anne Roche, a devout Roman Catholic, who was to become a writer and activist in her own right. John himself became a Catholic in 1962. The most literarily gifted of the children, John contributed articles and book reviews to a number of publications, including the *New Statesman* and the *American Spectator*, and became a schoolmaster and, later, a college professor, in Ontario.

Another joy was the return of Alec Vidler to Rye, a mere ten miles from Robertsbridge. He had retired as Dean of King's College, Cambridge, in 1967, a position he held for many years after his time as chaplain of Windsor Castle. When Malcolm was not abroad, he and Alec would get together twice a week, much as Malcolm and Hugh Kingsmill had in the late 1930s. Vidler lived in the oldest building in Rye used for a residence, an ancient building that was called Friars of the Sack, after the medieval monks who had first built it. His back garden, where Malcolm and Kitty used to sit with him in good weather, looked out over the mud flats leading to the sea. An avid beekeeper, Vidler introduced the Muggeridges to the fine art of maintaining an apiary. When Malcolm donned his protective suit, with its net-enclosed hat, to go out and deal with the bees, he liked to say that he was dressing "in drag".

Over the years Vidler had represented to Malcolm a sort of fixed point, a man whose faith was certain and yet not overly dogmatic. Vidler had little direct role in Malcolm's conversion – which was, in any case, a process that had been going on for many years, and which involved mystical and existential influences quite removed in spirit from Vidler's quiet, donnish Christianity. But Vidler's steadying presence was something that Malcolm counted on. Vidler had helped to encourage his fledgling Christian faith at Cambridge, and was still there, nearly half a century later, to calm the skittish Malcolm down. In a prayer of thanksgiving composed by Malcolm a few years after Vidler's return, Malcolm paid tribute to the three people who had meant the most to him in his life: Kitty, Hugh Kingsmill and Vidler himself.

> K., for undying love, given and received.
> H.K., for laughter and light.
> A.V., for the roots, the trunk, the branches and the leaves.
> For these incomparable blessings, I offer thanks to God, my Creator, Redeemer, and Father in Heaven. Amen. Madrid, January 6, 1971.

One form of fellowship which Malcolm and Kitty enjoyed with Vidler was a weekly Bible study group that met on alternate weeks at Vidler's home in Rye and at Park Cottage. The meetings would begin with a recording of sacred music. Then Vidler would expound the particular book of the Bible they were studying, followed by general discussion, and concluding with conversation over cups of tea. Another tradition was a carol service in the crypt of the ruined Cistercian abbey at Salehurst near Robertsbridge.[17]

Around the time that Malcolm had made his film biography of Christ, he conceived the idea of doing a similar series of programmes on St Paul. It occurred to him that in order fully to grasp St Paul's character and mission, it was important to know some of the historical and theological background. So he asked Vidler to be his on-screen partner in tracing the life and missionary journeys of St Paul. Malcolm would play the role of questioner and Vidler was to provide the answers. The BBC provided its customary support, enabling Malcolm and Vidler to spend two months in the spring of 1970 filming in the countries ringing the eastern Mediterranean, from Israel to Syria, Turkey, Greece and Italy.

The result was *Paul: Envoy Extraordinary*, broadcast in five parts in February and March of 1971. The conversational mode of presentation enabled Malcolm and Vidler to convey a great deal of information, speculation and insight without tedious exposition. Photographed amid the sun-drenched ruins and teeming cities of the region, the series is a visual delight. Their personalities complemented one another well: Malcolm, shifting from spiritual reflection to cynical debunking, and Vidler, ever judicious, providing the needed background and slapping Malcolm down when he went too far. Malcolm began the film by saying how strange it was that he and Vidler should be making a film on St Paul as white-haired old men, fifty years after they had first met at Cambridge. Another veiled reference to their relationship can be detected in a scene on the road to Damascus, where they discussed the nature of conversion.

> MALCOLM: Conversion is something that you as a priest must have met with often – a person being reborn, becoming a new man. Paul is said to have been blinded by the experience, but he was blind only because afterwards he truly could see whereas before he couldn't.
> ALEC: Paul's conversion does seem to have been sudden, but of course sudden conversions are seldom as sudden as they seem. I remember reading somewhere that our twentieth-century psychologist Jung had remarked that Paul had been a Christian for a long time before his conversion, only unconsciously.
> MALCOLM: You mean fighting against something he knew would ultimately captivate and capture him.[18]

The series was published in book form the following year, with a prologue by Malcolm and an epilogue by Vidler. There they paid tribute to each other. Vidler compared Malcolm's genius to that of St Paul, who

> was an intuitive thinker. He had the insights of a seer and was able to express what he saw with the confidence of a prophet and with the imaginative resourcefulness of a poet. It has been well

said that "to speak about God with any degree of adequacy one must be a poet or a prophet or a mystic" Paul, like other poets, prophets and mystics, had scant regard for the niceties of logic or of rational coherence. He never used words like "possibly", "probably" or "perhaps".[19]

Vidler's generous tribute provides ample evidence that Malcolm could inspire intense loyalty and affection in his closest friends.

Malcolm recognised that genuine faith demanded a commitment to action, not mere lip service; that "faith, if it hath not works, is dead, being alone," as the Epistle of St James has it. "My own difficulty – over which I brood from time to time – is a lack of participation and partisanship," he wrote around the time that *Jesus Rediscovered* was published. Being the outsider had taken its emotional toll over the years. In his journal he had noted that Christians were not as lonely as those outside of the faith.[20] Even though he was now a Christian, he remained an outsider, standing on the church steps, but refusing to go inside and kneel down with others. Because his conversion had been such a public event, he was now receiving dozens of requests to endorse good causes, speak at rallies, march in protest and deliver sermons. He tried to be selective in what he accepted, but inevitably he was becoming more and more a participant, rather than an observer.

Ironically, the costs were often heavy, in the sense that Malcolm opened himself up to fiercer ridicule than he had ever endured. There may indeed have been times when he wished he was once again a lone wolf. Take, for example, the national campaign for moral renewal in Britain, known as the Festival of Light. Its founder was a man named Peter Hill, who, when he returned to Britain after four years in India, was appalled by the triumph of the permissive society. Mr Hill, it seems, had a vision of young people marching in support of "positive values". So he had set about organising the Festival of Light. It was to be a non-denominational effort, directed at young people, and filled with pageantry and symbolism. To inaugurate the effort, two hundred beacon fires were to be lit across the country, and prayers were to be recited in churches on behalf of the Festival.

As such efforts go, the Festival of Light was probably no worse than many, and quite a bit better than most. Mr Hill and his associates were able to attract support from such well-known figures as the then Bishop of Stepney, Trevor Huddleston, as well as Mary Whitehouse and Malcolm. But the inherent limitations of moral crusades were demonstrated at the first meeting of the Festival participants, held at Central Hall, Westminster, on September 9, 1971. The meeting, consisting of four thousand people, including some who were watching on closed circuit television, was constantly disrupted by activists from the Gay Liberation Front, the Women's Liberation Movement and other activist organisations. When a man described as a "tall Dane" got up to testify to the deleterious effects of pornography in his country, he was shouted down. The choir was asked to sing in an effort to calm things down. Neither Bishop Huddleston nor Malcolm fared much better. Not long into his address, Malcolm watched while a number of young women dressed as nuns "cavorted across the hall" beneath the podium before they were ejected. Malcolm managed to complete some of his address, which began with the assertion that without moral order, a society can have no real order at any level. He went on to point out that sex and violence were the most effective ways for the entertainment industry and its financial backers, the advertisers, to sell their products. Television had even sensationalised news-reporting to the point where it was impossible for the public to get at the real issues. And what could words like "love" and "freedom" mean when those who championed them were really addicted to promiscuity and drugs?[21]

When the Festival of Light march from Trafalgar Square to Hyde Park took place on September 26, the same drama was enacted. Though the marchers numbered around thirty thousand, their opponents from the Gay Liberation Front and allied groups diverted attention by hurling stink bombs and insults. The Festival spokesmen urged the government to enact censorship laws that would protect the citizenry from pornography while still giving freedom to writers and performers. Both Malcolm and Mrs Whitehouse spoke at the rally.[22]

There was nothing fanatical in either of Malcolm's addresses, but by appearing in such forums he opened himself up for a tarring and feathering by pundits like Bernard Levin. Merely standing on the same platform as Mary Whitehouse was enough for Malcolm to be associated with her style of moral campaign. He had written in a preface to a book by Mrs Whitehouse that he differed with her in placing less hope in censorship and criminal prosecutions. "My own disposition is to regard them both as broken reeds."[23] Yet he agreed to stand beside her, despite the risks. Back in the 1930s, Malcolm had mocked the liberal disarmament marches and Peace Ballots for their sentimentality and self-righteousness. That he was now willing to take part in such collective activities, with all their faults and limitations, is one sign of how much he needed to join with others to act on behalf of his convictions.

Malcolm soon walked into an even larger minefield: the Longford Commission on Pornography, constituted in the spring of 1971. In this instance, it is clear that Malcolm's involvement was more a matter of personal friendship and loyalty than burning desire. The chairman of the commission, Lord Longford (Frank Pakenham), was, after Alec Vidler, Malcolm's closest friend. A well-known public figure, Longford had served for many years in Labour governments and as an active participant in the debates in the House of Lords. Though he was an aristocrat with a castle in Ireland, Longford was known primarily as an idealist. A convert to Roman Catholicism, he made no secret of the way his faith influenced his political convictions. The cause dearest to his heart was penal reform. His wife, Elizabeth, was a highly regarded historian and author, and several of his children, including Antonia Fraser and Thomas Pakenham, had also become accomplished writers. After moving to Robertsbridge in the late 1950s, the Muggeridges had become neighbours of the Longfords, who lived in the next village, Hurst Green. They usually had dinner together at weekends. Malcolm had been responsible for introducing the Longfords' daughter Rachel to her husband, the television producer Kevin Billington.

Malcolm's affection for Lord Longford was genuine. "If he hadn't been a clown and a bit of a saint as well," Malcolm said of his friend, "Frank would have been a very successful politician. He has an uncanny political flair. It's not so much the facts of politics that he's aware of, as their implications." While some of Longford's less sympathetic critics called him an eccentric and a sentimentalist, Malcolm thought of him as otherworldly, a struggling Christian pilgrim willing to make himself foolish in the service of humane causes. Unfortunately, Longford's chairmanship of the pornography inquiry lent itself to remorseless mockery. According to his biographer, Longford had not really been aware of the existence of pornography until 1970, and he was by nature something of a puritan. His fight against pornography was, at heart, a desire to shield the vulnerable from exploitation, especially children, but the issue was clouded by so many other matters that he found it nearly impossible to stick to this central thought. Photographs of Longford entering a porno cinema in Copenhagen with a thoughtful expression on his face were widely reproduced and became fodder for cartoonists. But aside from Longford's personality, the project was in trouble from the outset. The difficulty of proving the deleterious effects of pornography has always dogged the subject. Add to this the perennially controversial topic of censorship. Top it off with the spectacle of politicians and experts attempting a highly visible inquiry into public morals, and the mixture yielded a great deal of controversy without much constructive debate.[24]

The Longford Report was officially released on July 31, 1972 – a hefty tome that was signed by forty-seven members of the commission. It contained serious essays from such writers as Kingsley Amis, Elizabeth Jane Howard, Bishop Trevor Huddleston and Malcolm. Malcolm's role had been to chair the broadcasting committee and to write up the committee's conclusions. The resulting essay is not among Malcolm's best. Disregarding the setting of a public inquiry, based on the deliberations of many individuals, Malcolm wrote an utterly personal diatribe against decadence, greed and the BBC, making the issue hinge on the acceptance or rejection of Christianity. That he should have given in to a rant on this occasion is regrettable, because the essay contains a number of important insights. One of these concerned the influence of intellectual elites on the mass media. Malcolm's argument was that intellectuals had become alienated from traditional values, and had launched a sustained assault on the Western tradition, shielding themselves behind the rhetoric of tolerance and free speech. Malcolm also undermined the notion that the media ought to be neutral with regard to morality, except for a few absolutes, such as racism. He pointed to the recent spate of television dramas whose thesis was that problems like divorce and drug addiction were caused exclusively by poverty and injustice, contrasting them with Tolstoy's novel *Resurrection*. Tolstoy's novel also depicts a victim of social injustice, he noted, but it "related his human drama to the everlasting one of Good and Evil out of which all great art and all true enlightenment is born. Without this, compassion becomes sentimentality, and moral titillation is a substitute for virtue just as sexual titillation is for love."[25]

Malcolm's contribution to the Longford Report did his reputation little good, providing additional ammunition for those who wanted to dismiss him as a cranky, self-proclaimed religious prophet. His desire to join forces with fellow believers and fight for what he believed had been more complicated than he could have imagined.

Malcolm's efforts were far more inspiring when they were focused on individuals or small voluntary causes. This was, after all, his own philosophy: the larger the collective activity, the greater the distance between appearance and reality. Malcolm's laments about the decline and fall of Western civilisation, though they became his trademark, did not lead him to disengage from the world. The deeper his faith grew, the more he sought to help Christian organisations dedicated to serving the weakest and most vulnerable members of society. The single most dramatic contribution Malcolm made to any of these efforts came with the compilation of a book based on his film on Mother Teresa.

As a book, *Something Beautiful for God* is more than a mere transcription of the film, though it does contain an extended conversation Malcolm had with Mother Teresa that was shown, in abridged form, in the film. This conversation, along with a selection of Mother Teresa's own sayings, is sandwiched between two narrative sections written by Malcolm. In stark contrast to the film, Malcolm is at the centre of this narrative: his doubts and fears, his yearnings for communion, are entwined with the story of his encounter with Mother Teresa. But this is precisely what makes the book so effective: because he is an anguished but sympathetic outsider, Malcolm's tribute to Mother Teresa avoids a saccharine or hagiographical tone. He shows us a tough, practical woman, deeply spiritual but able to maintain a capacity for joy in the midst of suffering. One of his favourite stories of Mother Teresa was the offer she made to Air India to serve as a stewardess in exchange for free tickets. Imagining her as a stewardess gave Malcolm endless delight.

In Malcolm's narrative, Mother Teresa's faith is demonstrated not only in her work, but in her spiritual insights into Malcolm's condition. He quotes from her letters to him, the most perceptive including this comparison with the figure of Nicodemus from the Gospels, who came to Jesus "under the cover of night" to question him about salvation:

> I think I understand you better now . . . I don't know why, but you to me are like Nicodemus, and I am sure the answer is the same – 'Unless you become a little child . . .' Your longing for God is so deep, and yet He keeps Himself away from you. He must be forcing Himself to do so because He loves you so much . . . Christ is longing to be your Food. Surrounded with fullness of living food you allow yourself to starve. The personal love Christ has for you is infinite; the small difficulty you have re His Church is finite. Overcome the finite with the infinite. Christ has

created you because He wanted you. I know what you feel – terrible longing with dark emptiness. And yet He is the one in love with you.[26]

Malcolm often said that Mother Teresa wanted him to become a Catholic, and while this is undoubtedly true, it does not do full justice to what she had to say to him. In the letter quoted above and at other times she concentrated more on Malcolm's inner struggle between commitment and withdrawal than on the need to accept Church dogma. Nicodemus came to Jesus furtively in the night, and asked him questions to which he already knew the answer; Malcolm saw the aptness of the analogy.

Something Beautiful for God was published in England in April 1971, and was quickly translated into a dozen languages. Malcolm arranged for all profits from the book to be assigned to Mother Teresa's Missionaries of Charity. At the signing session that marked the book's publication, Lady Collins introduced Malcolm, and asked him to say a few words about the book. He returned to the theme that Mother Teresa was motivated by love for Christ, rather than a humanitarian altruism. "In all my travels around the world, I have never seen one leprosarium conducted by humanists." After the book signing, he spoke with a group of guests about putting in the section of Mother Teresa's words. "Mother Teresa will never write about herself or her work," Malcolm said. "When she is considered for the Nobel Prize, there should be something in print in her own words." Eileen Egan, a "co-worker" of Mother Teresa and the person who recorded these words, thought the comment about the Nobel Prize was misplaced. After all, the Peace Prize is won primarily by political figures, not nuns. When Mother Teresa won the prize in 1979, she recalled the prescience of Malcolm's words.[27]

While Malcolm was in New York to promote the American publication of *Something Beautiful for God*, Mother Teresa was able to join him there. They made a number of joint appearances on television talk shows. On one of the programmes Mother Teresa noticed that the commercials advertised food that tasted delicious but had few calories. Undoubtedly thinking of the starving people her order struggled to feed, she said in a quiet voice: "I can see that Christ is needed in television studios." When Malcolm looked through a copy of the *New York Times*, he showed Mother Teresa and Eileen Egan an advertisement for *Something Beautiful for God*, showing a picture of her face.

"There she is," Mother Teresa said, referring to herself in the third person. Here again Malcolm marvelled at her ability to see what had taken him so long to admit: that the self becomes an image or persona through the media. They made a joke of her comment, asking her over the next two days: "Would *she* be ready to leave to visit Cardinal Cooke? Will *she* please come to the telephone?"

Before he left New York, Malcolm came to the convent of the Missionaries of Charity located in the South Bronx. Malcolm joined them for a meal, eating nothing but a cheese sandwich that he had brought with him. He mentioned to Mother Teresa and the Sisters that he had received a cheque for the David Frost interview and wanted to know if he could put the money to some special use. Eileen Egan mentioned an Indian girl named Shadona, whose little brother had recently died. The Sisters felt that it was important that Shadona emerge from her grief and get married. Egan suggested that the cheque could pay for Shadona's dowry. Not long after he left, a letter arrived from Malcolm. "Enclosed is the David Frost cheque duly endorsed, and I hope that it will help Shadona to get a good husband."[28]

Malcolm became involved in other Christian missions, but he was particularly drawn to efforts to help the mentally ill and retarded. One of these was known as L'Arche (The Ark), founded by a French Canadian named Jean Vanier. The son of the nineteenth Governor General of Canada, Vanier had served as an officer in the Royal Canadian Navy and, later, as a professor at the University of Toronto. But when he visited a residence in France for thirty men with mental handicaps, run by a Dominican priest named Fr Thomas Philippe, Vanier was struck by the way these young men flourished when they were removed from an institutional setting and lived in a familial atmosphere where they were treated with respect and love. So he began by taking two mentally handicapped men into his own home. This was the beginning of L'Arche, which has grown over the years to more than seventy communities around the world. Malcolm was drawn to Vanier because his work, like that of Mother Teresa, grew out of a strong Christian faith.

When Malcolm received an unexpected financial windfall in 1974 (from an insurance policy that had matured), he used the money to build a cabin next to Park Cottage, calling it The Ark as a tribute to Jean Vanier. The Ark had a large open room, with a bed for guests, books, and other memorabilia that did not fit in Malcolm's small study in Park Cottage. It also proved useful for television interviews, since it had more open space than was afforded by the cottage.

Fr Paul Bidone, a priest of an order known as the Sons of Divine Providence, had introduced himself to Malcolm in 1971, when *Something Beautiful for God* was first published. Fr Bidone's order, founded by an Italian, Don Orione, early in the twentieth century, was devoted to serving the poor in a variety of ways. He had come to England in 1949, working tirelessly to establish homes for the elderly, who suffered a great deal under post-war austerity measures. Fr Bidone was a shrewd and effective organiser, but he was also an intelligent and cultivated man, with a love of literature, though this was not a side that many others saw. Fr Bidone enlisted Malcolm's support for a project known as the Molesey Venture, a home for retarded teenage boys. It was a vital addition to the order's work, because as the boys grew older, it was important that they were not always forced to live with the youngest children. Malcolm recorded a fund appeal for the project, which was broadcast on the BBC and brought in desperately needed donations. This formed the basis of a friendship that would have an important influence on Malcolm and Kitty. Fr Bidone was closer to the Muggeridges than either Mother Teresa or Jean Vanier; he was thus able to serve as something of a spiritual director.[29]

For a number of years, Malcolm's thoughts had been turning in the direction of his own life story. He had, since 1964, made several autobiographical films for the BBC, including episodes on his youth, his years in India and his stints as "our own correspondent" in Moscow and Washington. He had also laboured at a written autobiography. But the all-consuming intensity of his religious search had pushed the autobiography to the background for a number of years. Once he had put down roots into what C.S. Lewis called "mere Christianity", he was no longer so distracted. Indeed, his conversion made him even more committed to telling his life story. Like St Augustine, he needed to trace the hand of God in his life, to show that even in the worst of his life's "black moments" God was there in the shadows. Malcolm's autobiography would be both a *Confessions* and an *Apologia Pro Vita Sua*. He had known the title of his autobiography since 1933, when, in his diary, he had noted a phrase taken from one of Shakespeare's sonnets: *Chronicles of Wasted Time*.

Writing an autobiography usually requires some preparation to refresh the memory. Malcolm was never known for his efforts at fact-checking, but he did correspond with Dora Pitman and his old teacher, Helen Corke. He had also compiled over the years large scrapbooks of press cuttings, containing not only many of his published pieces, but reviews of his books and articles about himself. But the most important source of information was his diaries. From his weekly, diary-like letters sent home from India in 1924 until the early 1960s, with gaps ranging from weeks to several years, Malcolm had kept diaries filled with sharply-etched observations and intimate reflections. However, reading the diaries in the original holograph form would have proved a burdensome and frustrating effort. For a man nearly seventy years old, even his own handwriting was difficult to read, particularly in the case of fragile old notebooks whose ink had faded with the years. So Malcolm worked with a secretary to have all his major diaries typed, a Herculean effort that in the end came to about a million words. Significantly, these typed transcripts were not edited in any way; none of the painful or embarrassing passages were cut or altered. Nor were the diaries – type-scripts or originals – destroyed after he had made use of them. The complete set was among the papers he gave to Wheaton College in Illinois. Malcolm made no effort to place obstacles in the way of future bio-graphers. Ironically, on the first page of his autobiography, he speculated that his papers would end up at "some American university, grateful for any pabulum to fill its air-conditioned, dust-and-damp-proof vaults".[30]

The first volume of *Chronicles of Wasted Time*, subtitled *The Green Stick*, was published in 1972; it covered the years up to his return from the Soviet Union in 1933. *The Infernal Grove*, spanning the years from 1933 to 1945, appeared in the following year. The *Chronicles* were greeted by the critics – whether sympathetic or hostile – as his finest achievement, books "sparkling with wit, graceful with unexpected beauties, poignant revelations and a genuinely religious sense of life as a lost and bewildered stranger in this stained and impermanent realm", according to one reviewer in *The Times*. There was also near unanimity about the richness of Malcolm's prose style, so finely tuned that it could move with ease from the economy and pungency of an epigram to the rolling cadences of description, bringing alive scenes as diverse as a teeming Indian market and Depression-era Manchester. His character portraits of figures like the Webbs, Gandhi, Churchill and Montgomery were also singled out for their humour and insight. These books were an important reminder that Malcolm was not just "an electronic blob on a bright little screen", but a writer of the first order, with an extraordinary story to tell.[31]

There was less agreement about the opinions and ideas expressed in *The Green Stick* when it was published. The majority of reviewers were, naturally, offended by Malcolm's attacks on the progressive political agenda. A more telling criticism of *The Green Stick* was not that it swam against the ideological tides of the twentieth century, but that, as a narrative, it was interrupted far too frequently by editorial digressions that did not grow organically out of the story. The reviewer in *The Times* complained of the "tedious chunks of second-rate rhetoric, undigested hatreds and twitchingly intemperate sermonizing . . . "Take for example the following paragraph from *The Green Stick* condemning "modern art"; even if one felt inclined to identify with the intial comparisons offered, the concluding comment on Ernest Hemingway reduces the entire passage into a mean-spirited rant.

As for literature and the arts. . . listen to the *Missa Solemnis* after the Beatles, and be thankful to Cage for his soundless concertos and symphonies. Likewise, render hearty thanks to Beckett for his wordless, actionless, mindless play after taking a look at *Oh Calcutta!* Corbusier's high-rises are sweet, but those unbuilt are sweeter. After Bacon's canvases, blessings on those empty ones trendy curators delight to buy for vast sums of money and hang in their galleries! Where are the Parnassians of yesteryear; the dear, drunken Americans gathering in Paris at the Shakespeare bookshop with Sylvia Beach to care for them, Gertrude Stein or Alice B. Toklas to bore them? Alas, poor Scott, and poorer Zelda, and Ernest with a self-made hole in his head; the only shot he ever fired that found its target![32]

Samuel Johnson called Shakespeare's penchant for puns his "fatal Cleopatra". Something of the kind could be said for Malcolm's tendency to drop into these mini-editorials. Far from strengthening his argument, they alienate, or at least discomfit, all but the most enamoured of his readers. He is far more effective when, to take just one example, he describes the credulity of the Webbs about the Soviet Union, and then goes on to tell us exactly what he saw in the back alleys of Moscow and the corpse-strewn Ukrainian farmland. Whether Malcolm paid attention to these criticisms or not, he drastically reduced the amount of sermonising in the next volume, *The Infernal Grove*, making it easily the better of the two books.

What of the portrait Malcolm gives us of himself in the *Chronicles*?

In his own book reviews he had often complained about autobiographies that failed to provide any savour of the individual's inner life. When his friend and disciple, Christopher Booker, heard that Malcolm was writing his autobiography, he urged Malcolm to cast aside his hardened public persona and write honestly about his life, and in particular about the stages of his spiritual pilgrimage.[33] Malcolm acknowledged the problem in the introduction to *The Green Stick*: "The hazards in the way of telling the truth are, indeed, very great . . . Every man the centre of his own universe; insensibly, we sub-edit as we go along, to produce headlines, cross-heads, a story line most favourable to our egos . . ." He went on to use a series of metaphors drawn, appropriately enough, from television: "How take off my own motley, wash away the make-up, raise the iron shutter, put out the studio lights, silence the sound effects and put the cameras to sleep?"[34]

The answer is that the *Chronicles* are only partially and fitfully successful in giving us a portrait of the real Malcolm Muggeridge. On the positive side, the spirit of penitence that first appeared in his essay "Jesus Rediscovered" permeates the *Chronicles* as well. He frequently acknowledges his faults, and the pain they inflicted on others. Among these sins, he counts his "urge to be gone", his sexual obsessions and his propensity to "kick in the teeth institutions or enterprises I have served, as well as the individuals concerned in running them, at the moment of departure".[35] Reflecting on his motivation in leaving the Ministry of Information and seeking active duty in the Second World War, he writes in *The Infernal Grove* that he ran away from his responsibilities as husband and father. Throughout both volumes of the *Chronicles* are heartfelt tributes to Kitty's patience, sacrificial love and faithfulness. Above all, there is his conviction that in turning away from God he became trapped in the darkness of his own ego, wasting his time in pursuits that did not do justice to the gifts he had been given.

But there are significant gaps and evasions in these books, places where the persona remains intact and the sub-editing ego has done its work. While the portrait of his father is affectionate and balanced, there is no sign that he had any family life. He relates no anecdotes about his brothers, except for the death of his brother Stanley, and his mother is never shown in anything but a grotesquely comic light. His account of Stanley's death, and of his father's grief, would have been the natural place for Malcolm to say something about his feelings about the death of his son, Charles. But that tragic event remained an unmentionable subject. The depiction of his turbulent Cambridge years is perhaps the most distorted and scanty. It also contains the only outright lie in Malcolm's autobiography: the denial that he had ever had a phase of homosexual activity. His affair with Amrita Sher-Gil is made to look more idyllic than it really was; it gives a romantic glow to what were, in fact, his "black moments". Even the story of Malcolm's spiritual pilgrimage is not drawn out with the consistency that it requires. There is no recounting of his secret reading of the Bible while still an adolescent, nor is the intensity of his Christian conversion at Cambridge given its due, as Alec Vidler was to point out in his own autobiography.

The lasting value of *Chronicles of Wasted Time*, then, lies not so much in its revelations about Malcolm's personality as in the window it provides on the failed political and intellectual experiments of the twentieth century. Malcolm often derided the notion that the "eye-witness" to history inevitably had a firmer grasp of the true story; he had, after all, seen innumerable instances of journalists, from Walter Duranty onward, getting the story utterly wrong. But as the *Chronicles* remind us – in their brilliant reportage on such episodes as the twilight of the British Empire in India, Stalin's totalitarian nightmare and the moral ambiguities of the Liberation in France – Malcolm was more clear-sighted about the pretensions of power and ideology than almost any writer of his generation, including more celebrated figures like George Orwell or W.H. Auden.

A third volume in the *Chronicles* was planned but never completed. It was to be called "The Right Eye", from a saying in the *Theologica Germanica*: "The soul has two eyes, one of which, the right eye, sees into Eternity, and the other sees time and the creatures." Malcolm began the book, but got no further than a few manuscript pages. Why did he never write a book that was so eagerly anticipated by admirers of the first two volumes? Several of Malcolm's friends recall that he thought of this final volume as the work that would end his writing career. He wanted to put that moment off as long as he could. By the time he came to write it, he no longer possessed the stamina.

But the two published volumes of the *Chronicles* confirmed that Malcolm had, on the eve of his seventieth birthday, experienced a second spring. They brought an end to the long drought that had lasted since 1949, when his last full-length book, *Affairs of the Heart*, had been published. Malcolm had found his way back to the faith that had been such an important part of his youth, giving him something to celebrate – a positive vision to balance his "savage indignation". The final section of *Something Beautiful for God* was entitled "A Door of Utterance", from a passage in the Epistle to the Colossians in which St Paul prays "that God would open unto us a door of utterance, to speak the mystery of Christ". As the moving language of "Jesus Rediscovered", *Something Beautiful for God* and the *Chronicles of Wasted Time* proved, that door had finally opened for Malcolm.

« 19 »

One Word of Truth

1975–1980

ONE OF MALCOLM'S favourite propositions was that "highly imaginative people are invariably miserable when they are young, and, on the whole, grow progressively happier." In youth the imagination is a torture, because its hunger for perfection is thwarted by the world's myriad flaws. With the benefit of time and experience, the imagination is able to transcend imperfections and fears, bringing true consolation. He found a similar thought in a quotation from Marcel Proust: "A little knowledge separates us from God, much knowledge brings us back. One should never be afraid to go too far, for the truth is beyond." If it is possible to speak of a man as driven as Malcolm was as happy, it would be fair to say that, in his seventies, he had finally found a measure of happiness. If he was not quite "mild and cured", like Hugh Kingsmill's ham, the warring aspects of his personality had been united and brought into balance. His long religious and moral struggle had been resolved. Malcolm was now ready to leave autobiography behind and turn outward. There were causes and issues that he wanted to confront. But before addressing himself to controversial subjects, he turned his attention first to the one figure he had been keeping at arm's length for so many years, Jesus of Nazareth.

Jesus: The Man Who Lives, published in 1975, is arguably the book Malcolm was born to write. It is, without question, his literary masterpiece, a powerful fusion of his imaginative and iconoclastic talents. It is Malcolm's attempt to answer Jesus' question to Peter: "But whom say ye that I am?" In the years since his BBC film on the life of Christ, which had been completed in 1967, his faith had eventually come to centre on the figure of Jesus. His encounter with Mother Teresa had constituted an important breakthrough, helping him to see the face of Christ in the "distressing disguise" of the poor and outcast. This in turn had enabled Malcolm to develop a far more personal devotion to Jesus than he had ever known.

Jesus: The Man Who Lives is dedicated, appropriately enough, to Alec Vidler, who had vouchsafed to Malcolm his first vision of Christianity as a way of life. Like the character in a Chesterton novel who had to walk all the way around the world in order to find his own home, Malcolm felt that he had only now returned to the youthful intimations of faith he had experienced in Croydon, Cambridge and Alwaye.

Early on in *Jesus: The Man Who Lives*, Malcolm declares that his book stands in direct opposition to the nineteenth-century *Vie de Jésus* by Ernest Renan. Renan's book had shocked and intrigued its readers by presenting Christ as a Rousseauean hero of enlightened sentiments. This vision of a secularised saviour constituted a spiritual and intellectual watershed in the modern world and signalled the rise of liberalism. It was Renan's Christ whom H.T. Muggeridge and his socialist comrades had found worthy of their approbation. Malcolm's intention, by contrast, is to return to the traditional understanding of Jesus as the incarnate son of God. But, having positioned himself in the book's opening pages, Malcolm does not continue in a polemical mode. *Jesus: The Man Who Lives* is not marred by the sort of undigested editorial digressions that crop up in his autobiography. The narrative weaves spiritual reflections with Malcolm's enormous experience of the world into a seamless garment. By taking the historical story recounted in the New Testament and setting it against a contemporary backdrop, Malcolm is able to be arresting without being didactic, as in this passage on King Herod the Great. "These Herods, unlike Jesus, make their appearance in history. We have their dates, and details of their buffooneries, which interested chroniclers like Josephus, as they would today the Media. They trafficked in the stuff of news – murder, money, fornication, crime, violence and exhibitionism."[1]

If *Jesus: The Man Who Lives* has a thesis, it is the traditional, orthodox belief that Jesus Christ was both fully human and fully divine, and that we go astray when we attempt to reduce him to one or the other. Renan and his ilk made Jesus into an inspired teacher or political revolutionary, while religious fundamentalists made him into a figure too remote to touch our lives. Neither vision of Jesus has the power to transform the human heart and offer the hope that the City of God can be glimpsed and pursued from the City of Man. "As Man alone," Malcolm wrote, "Jesus could not have saved us; as God alone, he would not; Incarnate, he could and did."[2] Malcolm grants that the Incarnation is a mystery and a paradox, but, like G.K. Chesterton, he argues that the Incarnation alone has the power to give meaning to the human condition.

Malcolm's paradoxes are not as flashy (or as brittle) as those of Chesterton, but they have the same capacity to surprise us into assent. For example, Malcolm notes that Jesus wanted his followers to believe him because of what he said, rather than because of the miracles he performed. Nonetheless, in the face of the constant demands made on him to heal the sick and the dying, Jesus, sometimes with a sigh, attempts to alleviate the suffering around him. "Jesus was most human when, in performing his miracles, he seemed to be resorting to the supernatural, and ... his divinity showed most clearly in what will have appeared to his contemporaries as most ordinary – his day-to-day evangelism and giving out of love." In his discussion of Christ's humility in washing the feet of his disciples, Malcolm concludes: "When we want to adulate men, we say they are godlike; but when God became Man, it was in the lineaments of the least among men."[3]

Malcolm is most eloquent in treating the knotty subject of suffering. In a world separated from God by sin and imperfection, he argues, it is in suffering and dying that we truly live, while our frantic search for health and well-being leads to inner sickness and death. To support his argument, he points to the example of those human beings who are at the furthest remove from the Sunday magazine image of glamour and beauty, the mentally ill and retarded.

> Their blank faces and stumbling words, their clumsy gestures and movements, their very fury and violence, have a strange kind of inner beauty, and even grace, as their wild laughter and grotesqueries – exaggerated courtesies and formalities, like kissing hands very elaborately, bowing and scraping and uncovering, can seem, in a poignant sort of way, truly funny ... They are earthy mystics whose Cloud of Unknowing is a ground-mist rather than aerial.

The ultimate proof of the paradox of suffering lies in the passion of Christ, which offers us eternal life. But Jesus does not respond to mockery and derision with words. "Jesus is a silent hero; if he is portrayed with his mouth open (as in Graham Sutherland's superb drawing), it is in groaning, not orating. He is the anti-demagogue, the lord of silence and of suffering."

Balancing the confidence of Malcolm's assertions are a few moving glimpses into his own continuing sense of being a pilgrim *en route*. The Eucharist, he acknowledges, is a sacrament in which he cannot participate. Despite his Christian conversion, Malcolm could not take a seat at the Lord's Table. He felt mysteriously barred from communion, in both senses of that word: for the "communion" of the Eucharist is also the centre of the "communion" which is the institutional Church. But his faith is strong enough that he is able to experience moments of grace in the midst of his spiritual loneliness.

> I have often, myself, sat in darkness, and cried aloud for the Holy Spirit to deliver me from the fantasies that gather round a parched soul like flies round a rotten carcass in the desert. Likewise, sat tongue-tied, crying out to be given utterance, and delivered from the apprehensions which afflict the earth-bound. And never, ultimately, in vain. Jesus' promise is made good; the Comforter needs only to be summoned. The need is the call, the call is the presence, and the presence is the Comforter, the Spirit of Truth.[4]

Jesus: The Man Who Lives is a book that deserves to be ranked alongside G.K. Chesterton's *The Everlasting Man* and C.S. Lewis's *Mere Christianity* as a supremely imaginative defence of Christian orthodoxy. Soon after the book was published, Malcolm sent a letter to the one reader whose opinion mattered most to him. "I long to hear what you thought of my Jesus book sometime," he wrote to Mother Teresa. "In a sense I wrote it for you."[5]

About the time that *Jesus: The Man Who Lives* was published, Malcolm's most ambitious series of television documentaries was broadcast. *A Third Testament* was commissioned by the Canadian production firm of Nielsen-Ferns, and originally aired by the Canadian Broadcasting Corporation. In 1976, it was published as a handsomely illustrated book. *A Third Testament* was produced soon after such groundbreaking and enormously popular cultural documentaries as Kenneth Clark's *Civilisation* and Jacob Bronowski's *The Ascent of Man*. Both of those documentaries had manifested an essentially liberal, progressivist philosophy. With *A Third Testament* Malcolm had the opportunity to provide a Christian alternative.

The series enabled Malcolm to pay tribute to his personal pantheon of Christian heroes: St Augustine, Blaise Pascal, William Blake, Søren

Kierkegaard, Leo Tolstoy and Dietrich Bonhoeffer. Seen together, Malcolm held, these prophets and mystics form a third testament to God's providence in the world. In his introductory remarks, he likened this group to the "stay-behind" agents used by intelligence services, men and women who were "required to lie low until circumstances arose in which they could make themselves useful by collecting and transmitting intelligence, or organizing sabotage". It was much the same with those whom Malcolm called "God's spies", from the phrase in *King Lear* he had cherished for so long.[6]

The making of *A Third Testament* was as gruelling as any film project he had undertaken, requiring him to visit locations from North Africa to the Russian countryside, and including sequences in Copenhagen, Chartres and the sites of several German concentration camps. The entire process took nearly a full year, from 1972 to 1973, not including the post-production work. As in his film on Mother Teresa, there were moments during the production of *A Third Testament* when Malcolm felt that God's grace was manifest. For the episode on Pascal, Malcolm and producer Richard Nielsen sought to film a choir of cloistered nuns. The nuns agreed, but on three conditions: they receive no payment, they not be asked to rehearse and that they remain anonymous. When asked about the prohibition on rehearsal, the nuns replied that their singing was worship, and that God would accept the spontaneous results of the moment. Malcolm turned to Nielsen and said "If only we all practised what these nuns require as a rule of life!"[7]

After the series had been completed, Malcolm concluded that the most moving experience in the course of filming had been in Russia. After a timely intervention from the Canadian government, the Soviet authorities reluctantly agreed to allow the production crew to film the episode on Tolstoy on location. The Soviet official who monitored the project had no idea that Malcolm intended to focus on Tolstoy's Christianity. When this finally dawned on him, he screamed at Malcolm and director Pat Ferns for half an hour. But the official, it seemed, had launched into his harangue primarily to keep up appearances; later, he took Malcolm and Ferns aside and apologised. They would not be hindered, he said.[8]

Standing on the edge of the ravine at Tolstoy's estate, Yasnaya Polyana, Malcolm felt the intense contrast between the writer's intensely spiritual idealism and the dead weight of the totalitarian regime that still dominated the Russian people. While Malcolm recorded his thoughts at the graveside, the Russian translator, who was a Christian, was moved to tears. Malcolm thought of the interview he had done with a Soviet emigre named Anatoly Kuznetsov. In response to Malcolm's questioning, Kuznetsov had agreed that the Bible had been effectively banned from the Soviet Union. But, Kuznetsov continued, Stalin had made a mistake when he did not ban the works of Tolstoy and Dostoevsky, whose works breathed a Christian spirit that was also subversive. One of the other scenes in the Tolstoy episode was filmed in front of the Soviet Writers' Union, which, Malcolm later discovered, was at that time uniting to expel Aleksandr Solzhenitsyn from their ranks, the penultimate step before his departure into exile in the West.

After the original series of six films had been completed, Malcolm's thoughts returned to Russia. With the full support of Nielsen-Ferns, he filmed an additional episode about Dostoevsky. Once again the Soviet authorities seemed to discover Malcolm's Christian intentions only after filming had begun. This time, however, their response was more severe. The entire film crew was relegated to a hotel in Leningrad that was without food or heating. They had to stand in queues to get bread and yoghurt. This episode of involuntary asceticism delighted Malcolm, but the rest of the crew were not amused.[9]

Watching these films today, in an era of rapidly shrinking attention spans, one is struck by the density of the thought and reflection Malcolm put into them. Each of these episodes is a condensed biography, moving from the personal crises and tensions in their subjects' lives to the religious visions they wrested from the often painful circumstances in which they were enmeshed. Though he conveys the essential information about their lives and works, Malcolm makes no attempt to disguise his thoroughly personal approach to these writers. The Kierkegaard episode in particular seems an exercise in veiled autobiography, using the eccentric Danish founder of existentialism as a mirror on his own life. Kierkegaard, we are told, had a distant relationship to his mother, but had been extremely close to his father. At some point, however, a dark secret about his father had emerged and shattered their intimacy, sending the young Kierkegaard out into the world as a lonely outsider. A man with a "gregarious, dissolute side" to his personality, Kierkegaard found it necessary to "strip himself down until there was nothing, nothing at all, other than a sense of his own worthlessness". In Malcolm's eyes, this melancholy Dane was the quintessential outsider, given to pounding the streets of Copenhagen, only to be jeered at by his fellow citizens as a fool. "The two sides of his nature were at war, the imaginative and the polemical." Despite, or perhaps because of, this mystical schizophrenia, Kierkegaard had been vouchsafed prophetic insight into most of the twentieth century's dominant themes, from the power of mass communications to the dilution of Christianity into a form of liberal humanitarianism.[10]

The films on Tolstoy and Dostoevsky demonstrated Malcolm's continuing love for Russian history and culture, and his unflagging opposition to the Soviet regime. But it was the emergence of Aleksandr Solzhenitsyn on to the international scene as a writer and dissident that lent moral authority and authentic witness to the things Malcolm had been saying for so many years. Solzhenitsyn's chronicles of life in the *gulags* or Soviet prison camps – both in novels like *One Day in the Life of Ivan Denisovich* and *First Circle*, and in his painstaking history, *The Gulag Archipelago* – made clear the devastating human costs of totalitarianism. Even more compelling to Malcolm than the facts of torture and inhumanity was the phenomenon of spiritual rebirth in the *gulag*, as recorded by Solzhenitsyn and others. Stripped of his freedom, his possessions, his health and the last shreds of his human dignity, Solzhenitsyn found that there was one thing his gaolers could not take away: his soul. "It was in my prison," Solzhenitsyn had written in *The Gulag Archipelago*, "that for the first time I understood reality ... that the line between good and evil passes not between countries, not between political parties, not between classes, but down, straight down each separate human heart."[11] Malcolm was always haunted by the scene in *Ivan Denisovich* where a *zek*, or political prisoner, unfolds and pores over a tattered piece of paper on which the Gospels are written in tiny script – a scene taken directly from Solzhenitsyn's own experience.

Malcolm found the treatment of Solzhenitsyn by Western journalists and commentators painfully and ironically familiar. When Solzhenitsyn first went into exile, he was hailed as a political dissident and literary genius; his Christian faith, on the other hand, was largely ignored. But by the time he spoke at Harvard University in 1978, delivering his "A World Split Apart" speech, Solzhenitsyn made it clear that in his mind Christianity alone had the power to regenerate not only his shattered country, but also the decadent, materialistic West. The result of this prophetic warning was that many of his former admirers turned on

Solzhenitsyn, accusing him of being a simplistic and fanatical Slavo-phile, an enemy to democracy and other enlightened institutions. Malcolm admired Solzhenitsyn's courage in risking his fame and reputation to speak the truth as he saw it. He remembered back to the 1930s, when the Soviet writer Gorki, who had become a literary puppet for Stalin's views, was rewarded with an Italian villa and other perks. But to Malcolm's mind, Solzhenitsyn had earned the right to speak as a prophet. In his Nobel Prize address, Solzhenitsyn had concluded by quoting a Russian proverb that Malcolm adopted as a motto: "One word of truth outweighs the world."

Soon after Solzhenitsyn had delivered his "Warning to the West" speech, Malcolm discussed it on the American interview programme *Firing Line*, hosted by his friend, William F. Buckley, Jr. "He is the greatest man now alive in the world," Malcolm concluded. "It's rather sad to think that the president of the United States, who receives a great many people, didn't think it worthwhile, when [Solzhenitsyn] was there, to receive him – something that will be [recorded] in history books . . ."[12]

From this time on, Malcolm was eager to interview Solzhenitsyn himself, particularly on his religious convictions, but it would be several years before Solzhenitsyn was prepared to take up the offer. In a letter to Malcolm, Solzhenitsyn spoke of his "deep respect and sincere sympathy" for Malcolm's life and work. But he felt that his ideas – particularly those relating to faith – ought to be expressed in his literary works or not at all. Precisely because he was open to attack as a religious nationalist, Solzhenitsyn decided to cut out nearly all public appearances and speak only through his books. It was not easy for him to turn Malcolm down, because he was grateful not only for Malcolm's praise of his writings, but also for his decades-long opposition to the Soviet regime. But in 1983, when he travelled to London to receive the Templeton Prize, Solzhenitsyn finally agreed to an interview with Malcolm.[13] "In a strange way," Solzhenitsyn told Malcolm on the BBC2 broadcast, "I not only hope, I'm inwardly convinced that I shall go back."[14] Malcolm himself had been predicting the collapse of the Soviet Union since the mid-1970s, despite the persistence of the Cold War. Both men were to see their prophecies fulfilled.

Malcolm was, by the mid-1970s, in constant demand as a speaker for religious organisations around the world. After his experiences with the Festival of Light and the Longford Commission, he made an effort to be more selective in the invitations he accepted. But he was constantly on the move in these years. In 1976, he travelled to Australia and New Zealand, where he delivered a series of addresses, including the Olivier Beguin Memorial Lecture on "The Bible Today". After his visit, the Anglican Archbishop of Sydney, Dr Marcus Loane, described Malcolm as "the most significant layman since C.S. Lewis", a sentiment that was being echoed with increasing frequency by Malcolm's admirers.[15]

One of Britain's leading evangelicals, the Revd John Stott, invited Malcolm to deliver the "London Lectures on Contemporary Christianity", in November 1976. The subject Malcolm chose was "Christ and the Media". All three lectures were held at All Souls' Church, Langham Place, where Stott was rector. That the church was adjacent to the offices of the BBC was an irony that was not lost on Malcolm or his audience. Each night the church was packed to capacity. To give the event added spice and a touch of controversy, the chairmen for the first two evenings were Sir Charles Curran, then Director-General of the BBC, and Sir Brian Young, Director-General of the Independent Broadcasting Authority. On the second evening, Sir Brian was joined by Sir Michael Swann, who had been the Vice-Chancellor of Edinburgh University at the time of Malcolm's resignation as Rector, and was by the time of these lectures the Chairman of the Board of Governors of the BBC.

Sir Charles Curran opened the proceedings with a surprisingly venomous attack on Malcolm as a "Manichean pessimist". Without skipping a beat, Malcolm took the podium and thanked Sir Charles for presiding at the lecture. "It's a very friendly act on his part – especially as I gather it involves missing a Royal Command show at the Palladium . . ." He went on to acknowledge that he had been treated with indulgence by the BBC, but refused to admit that he was guilty of biting the hand that fed him.

I've always thought myself that there was a very close resemblance between the BBC and the established Church of England. So that our chairman here this evening would be the primate, and the Chairman of the Governors, Sir Michael Swann, would be the ecclesiastical commissioner, and the various department heads would be bishops, like there might be Alastair television and

Edward radio and so on, all entitled to manifest their standing by adding a tiny little microphone to their signatures.

He preferred to think of his own role, he said, as that of a "turbulent lay preacher".

Malcolm began his first lecture, entitled "The Fourth Temptation", by declaring the media, and TV in particular, to be the "greatest single influence" on society. But this influence was being exerted irresponsibly, without reference to any moral or intellectual principles. His own remarks, however, would be confined to the question of whether the "reality of Christ" could be adequately represented through the media. The answer, as might be expected, was emphatically in the negative. "Not only *can* the camera lie; it always lies." Malcolm's rhetorical strategy, as usual, had little to do with building layers of carefully structured arguments; rather, it involved a mixture of satire, personal anecdote and an appeal to common sense. After a humorous recounting of his own journalistic career, he wondered what would have happened if a Roman media tycoon, one Lucius Gradus (a transparent reference to the BBC impresario, Lew Grade), came across a provincial preacher named Jesus and decided that he had the potential to become a superstar. This scenario enabled Malcolm to string out a sequence of absurdities in which Jesus is subjected to the sort of packaging, marketing and hyping so common in the media. Gradus can see it all:

For the set they'd have fountains playing, a lush atmosphere, with organ music, a good chorus-line, if possible from Delphi, and some big names from the games – gladiators in full rig; also, if possible, priests and priestesses from the Aphrodite Temple, and maybe some from some of the Eastern cults becoming so popular with the young. Jesus himself would need something special in the way of a robe, and a hair-do and beard trim. He'd be the central figure, naturally, but for safety's sake his words would have to be put on autocue. Here a doubt seized Gradus. Could Jesus read? On reflection he decides it doesn't really matter. The show would have to be mimed anyway, and because of the language difficulty they'd have to use lip-sync. To avoid any impression of bigotry, there would be readings from different scriptures, including Hebrew, of course, and a discussion running to eight to ten minutes for which they'd get over some teachers and students from the Philosophy School in Athens – always good value.[16]

The second lecture, "The Dead Sea Videotapes", was also based on a fictional scenario: what if archaeologists from the future came upon our civilisation's record of itself through film. What would they imagine about our most cherished values and passions? How would they reconstruct our social life? This allowed Malcolm to take aim at some of his favourite targets, including progressivism, consumerism and the panaceas of education and sexual liberation. More relevant to his subject was his contention that the media were dominated by a false "consensus". Despite the protests of those in the media who paid homage to the idea of pluralism, Malcolm held that the media present an ideologically monolithic and predictable face to the world. This consensus – sometimes imposed, but more often a matter of conformism – is more liberal and more secular than the population as a whole. Magnified by the enormous power of the media, Malcolm contended, this bogus consensus has the power to affect the outcomes of wars, elections and parliamentary deliberations. Perhaps most pernicious of all, he thought, was the argument that the media had to be value-neutral, lest they attempt to impose a single viewpoint on others. But this policy represented a very definite point of view, that of moral relativism, and it could not help but corrode the traditional, Judeo-Christian system of values in society as a whole. Malcolm noted how convenient such a policy was. It was enough to make him almost nostalgic for the unctuous Calvinist rectitude of the BBC's first Director-General, Sir John Reith.[17]

In the final lecture, "Seeing Through the Eye", Malcolm finally responded to the hostile questioners who had complained that his criticisms of the media were far too vague and general. He became more specific about the ways in which the camera can lie. The chief problem with the camera, he began, was its undiscriminating gaze. Unlike the written word, which allows the individual time and a certain distance in which to reflect about what might be "between the lines", the TV screen is immersive: what it presents seems, for the time it is on the screen, to be the real thing. As Malcolm put it: "Thus news becomes, not so much what happened, as what can be seen as happening, or seems to have happened."

The sheer glut of news he likened to the constant drone of saccharine music heard in lifts and doctors' surgeries: instead of Muzak, the media offer Newzak. Moreover, the producers of news programmes, anxious about their ratings, increasingly lean towards the lurid and sensational. When it comes to what makes "good tape", there is an unwritten hierarchy: a plane crash, for example, is more morbidly fascinating than an earthquake, and so on. In the case of documentaries, a subject he knew something about, the temptation is to stage events when they are not dramatic enough. Within a few years of this comment, the rise of the "docu-drama" on television would give viewers instant history, such as terrorist incidents and sensational crimes, within weeks or months of their occurrence. That such docu-dramas were filled with speculation wherever the facts ran thin does little to dampen the public's enthusiasm for them. The impact of television on politics, Malcolm continued, was incalculable, amounting to a revolutionary change in the nature and process of democratic government. The revolution, he thought, was signalled by the US presidential campaign of 1960, when the telegenic John F. Kennedy debated with a perspiring Richard M. Nixon, and went on to win the election. Malcolm predicted that politics would be reduced to a war of carefully staged "sound bites" rather than serious deliberation.

After unleashing his prophetic denunciations, Malcolm closed the lectures on a note of conciliation and hope. Yes, he conceded, television could on rare occasions be used for morally and spiritually edifying purposes, as he had discovered in making films about Mother Teresa and other religious subjects. He also spoke of the joy he felt when, because of his media appearances, people would approach him and let him know that they shared the bond of Christian faith. Once, he recalled, while waiting for a train in the Underground station, a man came up to him and asked permission to shake his hand. The man said that he wanted Malcolm to know that some words of his on a radio programme had prevented him from committing suicide. Malcolm concluded the lecture by arguing that tactical pessimism about the decline of Western civilisation ought to be tempered with strategic optimism, for it was only when power was breaking down that its true nature was revealed, providing a new opportunity for Christ's message to be heard.

Thanking Malcolm for his lectures, the Revd John Stott declared him to be a "true prophet of the twentieth century". Prophets like Malcolm, he said, displayed extraordinary courage and perception, but they were "awkward fellows to live with", given to exaggerations and inaccuracies. In the Bible, Stott recalled, the prophet Elijah had miscalculated the number of the Lord's faithful servants by seven thousand. But this did not lead God to reject Elijah, according to Stott. "I believe that in the reckoning of God," Stott concluded, "prophetic faithfulness is more important than strict statistical accuracy."[18] Stott had another reason to be grateful to his speaker: Malcolm stipulated that all royalties from the publication of *Christ and the Media* should be donated to the Evangelical Literature Trust, which funds book clubs and other literary projects among missionaries in the Third World.

Much as Malcolm worried about the pervasive influence of the media, he felt there was an even greater urgency about what might be called the "life issues": abortion, contraception, genetic experimentation and euthanasia. Some critics assumed that Malcolm's positions on these issues were adopted only after his public conversion to Christianity. But as we have seen his convictions about these matters ran deep, dating back to the very beginning of his adult life.

A more telling attempt to undermine Malcolm's beliefs about the sanctity of life would point out the years when Malcolm took full advantage of contraception during his extra-marital affairs. The truth is that no one was more acutely aware of this than Malcolm himself. The guilt that haunted him throughout these affairs was grounded in his sense that they were sterile, escapist and self-indulgent, that they lacked the commitments and sacrifices of marriage and family life. A Freudian interpreter would no doubt conclude that Malcolm dealt with his guilt by projecting his own need for self-repression on to others. Malcolm preferred to be judged by the less ingenious but still workable terms of the Judeo-Christian tradition, including good and evil, conscience and guilt, repentance and rebirth.

Ironically, it was Malcolm who adopted a Freudian term to describe the inner dynamic of liberalism that had led to the legalisation of abortion and the real possibility of a similar relaxation of laws about euthanasia. He spoke of the liberal "death-wish", a fundamental alienation that drove liberals to dismantle the moral and cultural traditions of the West. Like T.S. Eliot and C.S. Lewis, Malcolm was convinced that the rise of modern philosophy, beginning with Descartes and gaining ascendancy during the Enlightenment, dethroned God and replaced him with man. The essence of modernity was the abandonment of the idea that man needed to conform to the moral laws God had written into his nature; instead, there arose the notion that we are the creators of our own laws and values. Moreover, the enormous power of modern science has given men the illusion that they have the wisdom to be masters of their own destinies. In political terms, modernity had given rise to the inhuman totalitarian regimes of

Nazi Germany and the Communist regimes in the Soviet Union and beyond. But Malcolm, like Lewis before him, felt that the real danger lay not in the nuclear bombs, but in the biological manipulation of life itself. Writing before the legalisation of abortion, Lewis had concentrated his fire, in his book *The Abolition of Man*, on the spectre of genetic engineering.

Malcolm felt that there were many examples in the late twentieth century of a coarsening attitude towards life. Two examples that he often singled out were the large number of automobile fatalities and the development of "factory farms" which raised livestock in horrendous conditions.

In the 1970s and 1980s, Malcolm became convinced that in the culture war between traditionalists and modernists, the front lines were the battles over who had control over life and death – the clash over the issues of abortion, infanticide and euthanasia. Abortion was to him the perfect illustration of the way liberalism begins in humanitarian acts of "compassion", but ends in the sanctioning of inhuman brutality. Just as liberal crusaders for the downtrodden like Shaw and the Webbs averted their eyes from Stalin's policies of genocide and terror, so contemporary liberals, in the name of compassion, do not look too deeply into the reality of abortion. Malcolm thought of abortion as "the humane holocaust", the title of an essay he wrote on the subject.

In lectures, speeches and editorials, Malcolm pointed out that the Holocaust had its roots not simply in Nazi ideology, but in the earlier policies of Weimar Germany, which had legalised "mercy-killing" for ostensibly enlightened and humanitarian reasons. Behind the lofty rhetoric of choice and freedom, Malcolm argued, was a moral decadence that no longer wanted to endure suffering or even inconvenience. "The logical sequel to the destruction of what are called 'unwanted children'," he wrote in *The Times*, "will be the elimination of what will be called 'unwanted lives' – a legislative measure which so far in all human history only the Nazi Government has ventured to enact."[19] Malcolm found a grim irony in the fact that the Nazi policy of euthanasia was one of the war crimes cited at the post-war Nuremberg trials. "So, for the *Guinness Book of Records*, you can submit this: that it takes just about thirty years in our humane society to transform a war crime into an act of compassion."[20]

Because Malcolm was convinced that the legalisation and extension of euthanasia would become the next major threat to human life, he thought a stage play would be an effective way of dramatising the issue and warning people of the larger moral and spiritual issues at stake. In 1975 he contacted the playwright Alan Thornhill about the possibility of collaborating on the writing of such a play. Having failed to get any of his plays staged since 1931, Malcolm recognised that Thornhill's technical skills would help to ensure a more tightly constructed script. The result was *Sentenced to Life*, which opened at the Westminster Theatre in London on May 17, 1978. Both the theatre, and the production company – Aldersgate Productions – were run by Christians who were well disposed towards Malcolm's message.

Unfortunately, *Sentenced to Life* turned out to be, in purely dramatic terms, a flop. Most theatre-goers understand that a play on a burning moral and political issue will be to some extent partisan, but in order to gain their sympathy, the play's advocacy has to be earned by a moving dramatic conflict. In the case of *Sentenced to Life*, the drama simply does not reach the level of intensity needed to carry off the play's argument. The story centres on Gerald Vickory, an Oxford don and crusader for progressive causes, and his wife Eileen, whose career as a concert pianist has been tragically ended by a disease that has paralysed most of her body. Succumbing to despair, Eileen begs Gerald to end her life by giving her poison, but without telling her when he is to do the deed. When he fails to show the courage of his enlightened convictions, she calls him an impotent intellectual. Observing this conflict is the Vickorys' German *au pair*, Anna, a devout Catholic girl who lovingly tends to Eileen's every need. Eileen experiences a change of heart, but before she can tell Gerald, she drinks a poisoned cup of coffee he has finally decided to give her. In Act III, Gerald returns home from his murder trial, which has resulted in a lenient two-year suspended sentence. Though he has been at the centre of a milestone euthanasia case, Gerald is broken and contrite. Anna offers him a Christian vision of suffering, forgiveness and redemption.

Sentenced to Life does not take enough emotional and psychological risks, and so it falls flat. Gerald's conversion experience happens off-stage, making it abrupt and unconvincing. Though the young actress who portrayed Anna was highly praised, her character becomes in the end merely a mouthpiece for religious consolation rather than a flesh-and-blood person caught in a morally and emotionally tangled situation. The characters are given to uttering undigested bits of vintage Muggeridge. Subtitling the play *A Parable in Three Acts* could not disguise the fact that it was written primarily as propaganda. If only this play had the tension and ambiguity of Malcolm's unpublished and unperformed play, "Liberation", it might have had the impact that he had hoped for.[21]

The play may not have been a success, but Malcolm's timing, as usual, proved to be prescient. Euthanasia was in fact becoming a hotly debated issue. At the same time that *Sentenced to Life* was running, another play, *Whose Life Is It Anyway?*, written by Brian Clarke and starring Tom Conti, was playing at the Mermaid Theatre. It made a passionate plea for the legalisation of euthanasia. It was also while *Sentenced to Life* was in rehearsal that a book titled *Jean's Way*, by Derek Humphry, was published. Humphry and his first wife Jean were in exactly the same position as the Vickorys in Malcolm's play. But rather than repent, Humphry had, after killing his wife, gone on to be the celebrated founder of the pro-euthanasia organization, Exit. On May 9, 1978, Malcolm debated with Humphry on the *Tonight* programme. They agreed about nothing, of course, but Malcolm conceded to Humphry that if one denies the existence of God, there really isn't any reason to oppose euthanasia.

For anyone tempted to attribute the failure of *Sentenced to Life* to some inherent limitation in Malcolm's ideas about euthanasia, a recent, dramatic revelation ought to give one pause for thought. Malcolm proved to be far more prophetic than he ever realised. In 1992, Derek Humphry's second wife, Ann, committed suicide. Humphry abandoned Ann soon after she was diagnosed as having cancer, and proceeded to have her barred from any contact with Exit, the organisation she had co-founded with him. In the last year of her life, while she struggled with despair, Ann befriended an opponent of euthanasia, Rita Marker, and revealed that she and Humphry had "sanitised" the story of Jean Humphry's death in *Jean's Way*. Jean had not died when the poison had been administered; Humphry had had to suffocate her.[22]

Malcolm's concern for the "life" issues was not something that emerged from a merely intellectual conviction. Whenever he heard the phrase "unwanted child" he remembered the tiny, wizened newborn that Mother Teresa had found in a dustbin in Calcutta. Holding up the child in the palm of her hands, Mother Teresa smiled: "See? There's life in her!" When he heard about cases of abortion or infanticide for children with mental and physical defects, he remembered the days he spent with the exceptional children at Jean Vanier's L'Arche and Fr Bidone's order near London. In Malcolm's documentary film on L'Arche, *An Ark for Our Time*, Vanier speaks of the humanity of those whom society prefers to ignore or to condemn as having an insufficient "quality of life". The men and women who are cared for in L'Arche, Vanier said,

> have been deeply, deeply wounded ... who are carrying in their body the violence of the world, the violence of rejection. They're really carrying in their body the sins of the world, all the hatred and the indifference and the rejections, and this has come into their whole being. But what we find is that the world of suffering and the world of joy are very close together. You see, the wonderful thing here is that we can all realise that we are weak and that we're poor and that we're hurt, but that we don't have to be frightened to pretend we're not.[23]

As he surveyed the Christian Churches, Malcolm found few such profoundly counter-cultural efforts as those of Mother Teresa or Jean Vanier. On matters such as abortion, he saw that a large number of Christians were abandoning their historic moral positions and drifting along with the *Zeitgeist*. The most ludicrous thing he came across was a prayer, composed by the Anglican Bishop of Winchester, for the occasion of an abortion. This prayer reminded him how difficult it was for the satirist in the late twentieth century to come up with exaggerations when reality was constantly outstripping his imagination. However, as the years passed, it became increasingly clear to Malcolm that despite the enormous spiritual and ideological upheavals within the Catholic Church, there was no sign that it was likely to drop its opposition to abortion, contraception and euthanasia. Malcolm never went more completely against the spirit of the times as when he publicly defended Pope Paul VI's encyclical, *Humanae Vitae*, which restated the Church's position on these issues, with special reference to contraception. Speaking to a conference in San Francisco, Malcolm said that he had come to understand sexuality as a sacrament. "[O]ut of ... the simple need of men to eat and drink came the Blessed Sacrament; and similarly, out of the creativity in men, their animal creativity, came the sacrament of love ... which created the Christian notion of family, of the marriage which would last, which would be something stable and wonderful ..."[24]

Here Malcolm is open to the charge, also levelled against the Catholic Church, that his position on contraception is baldly misogynistic, that he was nothing more than a reformed philanderer who wanted punish women by having them pregnant and in the kitchen. But Malcolm was not quite so crude as that. When Germaine Greer's feminist manifesto, *The Female Eunuch*, was published in 1971, he reviewed it appreciatively in *Esquire* magazine. Her "strictures on the romanticization of sex in the interests of salesmanship and sugar-daddy pleasures are apposite and apt", he wrote. He agreed that women had a right to complain of male exploitation, and of male neglect of their own experience of sexual pleasure. Her solutions he found less compelling. They included raising children in women's collectives and praise for groups like the Society to Cut Up Men (SCUM) and Women's International Terrorists Conspiracy from Hell (WITCH). Malcolm thought these organisations could only achieve a "pyrrhic or cockless victory". But he genuinely admired Greer's prophetic indignation against a materialistic society, comparing her to Florence Nightingale, Mary Wollstonecraft and, somewhat unexpectedly, to that eminently practical mystic, St Teresa of Avila.[25] Over a decade later, in her book *Sex and Destiny: The Politics of Human Fertility*, Greer sounded some of the very same notes that Malcolm had been making for years. In *Sex and Destiny* Greer continued her indictment of "consumerist" society, arguing that the notion of overpopulation is a myth, that government efforts at "family planning" are ill-conceived and counter productive, that attitudes towards Third World population control are often laced with the same racism that motivated the Nazi experts in eugenics. She even questioned artificial methods of birth control as being potentially harmful to women. While this hardly made Greer a Catholic, it did bear out Malcolm's intuition that they shared some common ground. When *Sex and Destiny* was published, Malcolm felt that his praise for Greer had been justified.[26]

By the late 1970s, interest in Malcolm's life was growing on both sides of the Atlantic. A Canadian professor of law named Ian Hunter, who had been corresponding with Malcolm since the early 1970s, came to the conclusion that very few people were aware of the consistency of Malcolm's religious and intellectual ideas. When he said this to Malcolm, the reply was immediate: "Well, why don't you put together a collection of my writings?" The result was *Things Past*, published in 1978, which goes back to Malcolm's earliest contributions to the *New Statesman* in the 1920s and moves up to the present. *Things Past* (the title is from Bunyan's *Pilgrim's Progress*) is the most valuable of the books that collect Malcolm's occasional pieces, because it demonstrates the unity of Malcolm's thought, despite the astonishingly diverse subjects he tackled over the years. In particular, his ardent essays from the 1930s, including "Time and Eternity" and "What Is My Life?", reveal the intensity of his religious search that was forced under ground both during and after the war.

In the course of preparing *Things Past*, Hunter spent some time at Park Cottage. One day, Malcolm took him up to the attic above the Ark and began to show Hunter where all his correspondence, diaries and other papers were located. When Hunter asked why he was being shown these materials, Malcolm said: "Why, because you're going to write my biography, dear boy." Hunter was stunned but flattered. To write the biography, he would need access to these papers. Malcolm had anticipated this. Since Malcolm's son John and his family lived in Canada, he proposed to Hunter that they swap houses for a year. Hunter would be free to make full use of his papers, and also be able to visit Malcolm's closest friends, Alec Vidler and Lord Longford. Malcolm and Kitty would be able to spend an extended period of time with John and his family.

One other detail was eventually added to the plan. Malcolm was invited to teach at the School of Journalism at Western University in Ontario. Although he was given an academic title as a "distinguished visiting professor", he preferred to be called the "Old Hack in Residence". In return for this position, he offered a free-ranging seminar on the subject of journalism. After his teaching stint was over, Malcolm wrote: "The only image I could think of . . . to describe my role at the school was to regard the 30 or so graduate students as so many debutantes lately released from a high-class finishing school, who had unaccountably decided to embark on a career of prostitution. As such they might benefit from the reminiscences of an old madam of many years' experience, who could perhaps give them useful guidance in dealing with the more awkward clients."[27]

Kitty spent much of the year in Canada working for her new translation of *The Sacrament of the Present Moment*, which was published by Collins in 1981. A guide to the spiritual life, the book was written by an eighteenth-century French Jesuit, Jean Pierre de Caussade. In it he calls on every Christian to experience God's presence and love in the here and now, rather than give in to restless worries about the past or the future. Malcolm, in particular, found de Caussade's words consoling. He and Kitty would often turn to one another and say: "Shall we de Caussade it?" Kitty's last book, *Gazing on Truth*, published in 1985, is a series of meditations for Lent, written at Malcolm's urging, and dedicated to him.

Living in Canada enabled Malcolm to launch out on a number of speaking engagements in the United States. He was now widely known in America as a Christian apologist and spokesman for the pro-life cause, hailed in churches and college campuses as "St Mugg" the Christian sage. Among those who were most receptive to his message were the sort of evangelicals who had become admirers of C.S. Lewis. Like Lewis, Malcolm was a British writer who employed wit, humour and a captivating prose style to defend Christian orthodoxy. The American edition of *Christ and the Media* even appeared with a foreword by Dr Billy Graham, the famous evangelist whom Malcolm had baited in his first television interview in 1954. But Malcolm's appeal to evangelicals on both sides of the Atlantic was more limited than that of Lewis. Malcolm's public sympathy for the Catholic Church, his astringent irony and his complicated personal past frightened off the majority of evangelicals. They much preferred Lewis, a bachelor don for most of his life, at once more romantic and more rationalistic than Malcolm. Whenever evangelicals asked Malcolm their favourite question – could he please recount the precise moment when he accepted Jesus Christ as his Lord and Saviour? – he replied, with literal accuracy, that his conversion had been a life-long process.

Those who encountered Malcolm on his many speaking engagements in the 1970s and early 1980s, both in North America and in Britain, found him not only charming, but also patient and cheerful as he faced questions he had been asked innumerable times. No questioner, however hostile or fanatical or naïve, was dismissed out of hand. Malcolm surprised many of his hosts by spending much of his time on these speaking tours asking questions himself – a legacy of his life as a journalist, but also a sign to many of his genuine interest in others. In his 1965 television programme, *Ladies and Gentlemen, it is my pleasure* . . ., Malcolm had mocked the earnest, sentimental and vacuous American lecture-goers he met on his cross-country tours. He now treated the same people with an almost courtly deference and sincere affection.

It was during his year in Canada that I met Malcolm for the first time. I had been given the job of driving Malcolm from his base in London, Ontario, back to my college in rural Michigan, where he was scheduled to participate in a week-long conference in February 1979. I was at the time a nineteen-year-old college student, with only a passing knowledge of Malcolm's writings and reputation. However, I was intrigued by what little I knew, and asked to be given the job of being his driver. Because the trip was about five hours long, it was agreed that I would stay overnight with Malcolm and Kitty before setting out with him on the return trip the next day. They met me at the door. After partaking of the simple dinner that was their regular fare, I joined them in the living-room, where Malcolm recited the Anglican service of Evening Prayer from memory and Kitty and I said the responses. The following morning, after breakfast, Malcolm recited the service of Morning Prayer. We talked the entire five-hour drive to the college, ranging widely from literary discussions about Dostoevsky and Solzhenitsyn to the current political scene. At one point during his stay at our college, I recall disagreeing, somewhat vehemently, with his prediction that the Soviet Union would soon collapse. For some reason I was convinced that the Soviet regime was, to all intents and purposes, eternal. Malcolm merely turned to me and said: "But, my dear boy, there are no Communists left in Russia; the only Communists knocking about today hold professorships at Western universities." A few days later, on the trip back to Ontario, our conversation was even more wide-ranging and more raucously funny. Somehow it did not seem strange for me to feel that, despite the huge difference in age and experience between us, I could now count Malcolm as a friend. In this respect, my experience was no different from that of dozens of others who came to know Malcolm in these years.

Two months later I travelled to Washington, DC, to hear Malcolm address another conference. On Saturday morning a group of about a dozen people had gathered around him. As it was about midday, Malcolm suggested to the group that, rather than going to a restaurant, we pick up some food at a nearby stand. Armed with our oranges, plums and apples, we sat on a small grassy patch of ground in the middle of downtown Washington. It might have been a gathering of disciples around their guru, except that Malcolm never acted the part of guru, steadfastly refusing to set himself up as a figure of authority. Most of the questions were directed to him, but he stirred up the conversation amongst the entire group.

Throughout his year in North America, Malcolm announced that this was his final trip abroad, that he was going to retire to Roberts-bridge, no longer to sally forth to the four corners of the earth. Of course, he had spent many years telling the world that he was going to live a monastic existence, but he had continued to find reasons for being up in London or abroad. *Private Eye* took to calling him "The Well-Known Recluse-About-Town". But there were practical as well as spiritual reasons for him to retire to Park Cottage. Age was beginning to take its toll. He no longer had the energy required for long-distance travel. Though he continued to rise at dawn or before, he now needed a long nap in the afternoon. Even his passion for walking was finally reined in. Instead of walking across the hop fields around Park Cottage, he and Kitty would stick to the nearby lanes, or walk around a few favourite places, like the ancient church at Winchelsea, perched dramatically on the Sussex coast, not far from Rye.

Malcolm's failing strength inevitably meant a lessening of creative energy. But he was still widely in demand, both as writer and speaker. Every time he gave a speech, some newspaper, magazine or journal would beg to publish it. Thus it was inevitable that Malcolm would begin to repeat himself, telling the same stories over and over again, often in the same words. Perhaps the most famous of these was the story he told, apropos the subject of death, of his nocturnal out-of-body experiences. To a man of his age, he would say,

> the queerest thing happens. You very often wake up about two or three in the morning and you are half in and half out of your body, a most peculiar situation. You can see your battered old carcass there between the sheets and it's quite a toss up whether you resume full occupancy and go through another day or make off where you can see, like the lights in the sky as you're driving along, the lights of Augustine's *City of God*. In that sort of limbo ... you have the most extraordinary confidence, a sharpened awareness that this earth of ours with all its inadequacies is an extraordinarily beautiful place.[28]

The story ends, of course, with Malcolm returning reluctantly to his battered old carcass, for Kitty's sake. The repetition of this and other stories lent itself to parody, some of it mean-spirited and vindictive. A rather mild example, from one of his more sympathetic critics, Auberon Waugh, came in the form of a mock obituary: "Many people will have been saddened to learn of the sudden death of Malcolm Muggeridge at the age of 150."[29] Others, less kind, preferred to shake their collective heads and mutter about this being only the latest symptom of Malcolm's general slide into senility. Was he now in the position of the aging Churchill, whom he had mocked in *Punch*? Was he, too, trying to prolong his literary powers, even while the pen slipped from his feeble fingers? Those close to Malcolm knew that the charge of senility was nonsense, that Malcolm was in many ways far more serene and more given to laughter than he had even been before. But even they recognised that a poignant drama was beginning to unfold: the painful tension between Malcolm's waning strength and his instinctive desire to produce copy and meet deadlines. Nor would Malcolm be able to meet death with anything like the clarity and conscious choice that his favourite story dwelled upon so humorously.

« 20 »

Jerusalem's Wall
1981–1990

WITH HIS USUAL blithe inconsistency, Malcolm began what was to be his final and permanent retirement with a flurry of activity. His old friend, Lord Longford, was struck by Malcolm's energy, noting in his diary at the beginning of 1981: "Malcolm is having a splendid Indian summer just now."[1] Most of this activity, it is true, was devoted to retrospective examinations of his life and career, but these brought with them a certain amount of satisfaction. Malcolm had survived long enough to become an institution in his own right. When Longford asked him about this, Malcolm recounted one of his favourite stories, one that he had heard on his first trip to India. "There was a Hindu festival which was held in a village near us every year, and a Scottish missionary who had been sent out to that particular area took it upon himself to stand in the street and shout abuse at the festival. Well, of course they threw sticks and stones and so forth at him, but he did it year after year regardless. Then when he died the Hindu leaders wrote to his mission, asking them to send another one."[2]

Within the space of a few months, Ian Hunter's biography of Malcolm and an edited version of Malcolm's diaries, entitled *Like It Was*, were published. There were inherent limitations in both books; since Malcolm was alive and well, neither book could delve too deeply into his private life. The diaries, heavily edited though they were, nonetheless gave readers great pleasure. Malcolm's portraits of public figures like Churchill and Montgomery, along with those of writers like Max Beerbohm and George Orwell, struck more than one reviewer as rivalling John Aubrey's *Brief Lives* for wit and insight. A number of reviewers acknowledged that the diaries proved that Malcolm's Christian faith was not an old man's conversion, but a lifelong struggle. Christopher Booker, who thought of himself as a close friend of

Malcolm, found reading the diaries a shock, "because the real inner story of his life that they revealed was so much more interesting and moving than the endlessly polished-up version he had come to present the world in later years."[3]

A literary luncheon was held at Foyle's to celebrate the publication of *Like It Was*. On arriving, Lord Longford was asked which trait of Malcolm's he found most irritating. His first reaction was to dismiss the question as ill-mannered, but he soon discovered that Malcolm had already "answered it himself with gusto, naming his tendency to belittle prominent persons". Longford then volunteered Malcolm's claim that he never read the newspapers, "while always knowing everything that's contained in them".

Of course, the ultimate retrospective on Malcolm's life took place on television. In 1981, the BBC ran an eight-week series of programmes, produced by Jonathan Stedall, tracing his television career. The series was called, waggishly, *Muggeridge: Ancient and Modern*, after the Anglican hymnal. Each of the programmes comprised the broadcast of one of Malcolm's documentaries, followed by his current thoughts about his television career. The first programme consisted of his autobiographical documentary, *A Socialist Childhood*. Viewers were thus treated to the spectacle of the Malcolm of the present commenting on the Malcolm who had made the programme fifteen years before, while that programme itself had commented on the Malcolm of forty or fifty years before that. The "modern" Muggeridge found much to atone for in the behaviour of his "ancient" alter ego. His reaction was immediate:

What a terrible man I was! There's a certain arrogance about myself as narrator – the way I lay down the law. I think it's rather horrible. I'd put it differently now. What is completely lacking is any humility ... I ought to have made it clear that I was one of five children, instead of giving the impression that I was an only child. But I was undoubtedly my father's favourite, and therefore went to Cambridge whereas my brothers didn't. But I leave them out, which is pure egotism ... I'm glad to have an opportunity of repudiating this figure of fifteen years ago, who to me is the most appalling S.O.B. I've seen in a long time.

He also acknowledged that the headmaster of his secondary school should have written a stiff note to the BBC, complaining of Malcolm's on-screen trashing of his alma mater.[4]

Along with Jonathan Stedall, Malcolm also filled in the un-televised gaps of his autobiography, taping brief reflections on editing *Punch*, appearing on *Panorama* and being caught up in the monarchy row. All this new material, along with selections from his post-1967 broadcasts, was added to the earlier collection *Muggeridge Through the Microphone*, and published in 1981 as *Muggeridge: Ancient and Modern*, with new illustrations by Trog.

Malcolm's career with the BBC might well have ended with this retrospective series, if he had not received a remarkable letter in the autumn of 1980. It was from Svetlana Alliluyeva, Stalin's daughter, who had written to Malcolm after reading *Jesus Rediscovered*. She explained that in the ten years since she had first written, she had married a second time, had a daughter at the age of forty-five, and then gone through a divorce. She had suffered terrible affliction since her childhood and her renewed correspondence demonstrated that she wanted to share her story with Malcolm, whom she continued to admire. Svetlana lived a reclusive life in the United States and had refused for many years to give interviews. Malcolm felt that her story was as newsworthy as anything he had ever covered and suggested to her that he interview her for the BBC. At first she refused, but eventually she relented. It was arranged that she would come to stay with Malcolm and Kitty for a week in the summer of 1981. There, in the friendly and informal atmosphere of their home, they would film her in conversation with Malcolm. It was to be her first trip outside the United States since her emigration there in 1967.[5]

A Week with Svetlana, broadcast on BBC 2 in March, 1982, traced the tragic story of her life, from her mother's suicide when she was only six to her estrangement from her father, to her eventual escape to the West, which completely cut her off from her two sons in Russia. Her testimony provided a unique window on some of the most horrifying events of this century.

Unfortunately, the sequel to Svetlana's visit was not as happy as the events leading up to it. While she had been at Park Cottage, Malcolm found her "an utterly tragic person, living a life beyond bearing . . . arrogant; but unstable . . ." This only increased his affection for her. But the instability manifested itself when Svetlana asked Malcolm's advice about the possibility of moving to England. When he told her that he did not think it was a wise idea, she took offence, imagining that he was rejecting her. Soon after, she wrote what Malcolm described as a "bitter and hurtful" letter that more or less ended their friendship.[6] Svetlana's restlessness and unhappiness manifested themselves a few years later when she returned to the Soviet Union with her daughter Olga, amidst a flurry of publicity. But Olga did not want to be pulled away from her life in the West, and Svetlana could not find peace in Russia. Two years later, she returned to the US. Malcolm watched the saga unfold, but was unable to restore his relationship with Svetlana.

Throughout the early 1980s Malcolm and Kitty continued to be marvellous hosts to the hordes of visitors who came to Park Cottage. The daily routine was still intact. Overnight guests would stay either in the Ark or in one of the little bedrooms at the top of the cottage. Breakfast would be eaten rather early, Malcolm having risen at his normal time of 5 a.m. Guests would often find themselves assaulted in the morning at 7 a.m. by the radio blaring at high volume. Though he might have had his television aerials removed, Malcolm remained addicted to radio news broadcasts. They provided him with his daily dose of political news, and became the occasion of much hilarity. The intense volume of sound from the radio was a consequence of his growing deafness.

After breakfast, Malcolm would retreat to his study to write. He would emerge for lunch, treating himself afterwards to his one gastronomic indulgence: a Fox's Glacier Mint. In the early afternoon there might be conversation and a walk or possibly an outing to Rye to visit Alec Vidler. Malcolm would drive through the country lanes of Sussex at breakneck speed, terrorising his passengers but keeping up a constant stream of conversation. Increasingly he took naps in the afternoon, emerging again for tea, served with a variety of cakes Kitty had prepared. Then dinner and a little more conversation, often while Malcolm played game after game of patience. As he was an early riser, Malcolm turned in for the night quite early.

Malcolm's insatiable hunger for gossip and outrageous stories never abated. Christopher Booker's description of the talk in the sitting-room of Park Cottage captures the experience of everyone who visited there:

> Always the themes were the same, a gossipy, half-serious, half-uproarious, always mocking ramble round the absurdities of the public drama of our time – what he called the "legend" – the self-deceiving follies of politicians and intellectual figures, as our poor

old civilization struggled on toward what he saw as its inevitable doom. How, in his derisive drawl, he liked to roll around his tongue such phrases as "the whole show is over"; such-and-such a thing (the monarchy, the BBC, the United Nations, Communism) "is all washed up"; some much-praised book of the moment was "pitifully thin stuff"; some famous writer was "irredeemably mediocre". He seemed to have known or at least met everyone, and spoke of them all in the same half-affectionate, half-scornful tones – "the trouble with poor old Lawrence was that he was impotent", "poor old Mailer – his trouble is that he is a rabbi manqué", "poor old Churchill – in the end he was just a power-crazed maniac like the rest of them". It was delivered with such gusto and good humour that it elevated us all – indeed, some of the best and driest lines came from Kitty.[7]

The most famous of Kitty's witticisims was a spontaneous comment on television personality David Frost. According to Kitty, Frost was a man who had "risen without a trace." On one occasion, when Kitty asked Malcolm who he had invited to lunch that day, he told her, somewhat mischievously, "one of those head-shrinking chappies". To which she responded: "In that case, we had better have Freud fish and Jung potatoes".[7]

One of Malcolm's prized conversation-pieces in these years was a framed photograph that hung above the fireplace in the sitting-room. It was a picture of the fire, started by a lightning strike, that burned one of the transepts of York Minster in 1984. The fire had taken place just four days after the consecration of the controversial liberal Bishop of Durham, David Jenkins. Bishop Jenkins had made headlines by his questioning of the literal truth of the Virgin Birth and the Resurrection. When I first pointed out the photograph, Malcolm leaned back and laughed. "The wrath of God, my dear boy, the wrath of God."

His habit of denigrating public figures – the sin he had confessed at the Foyle's luncheon – was not a sin he ever repented. There were times when this habit could just as easily become irritating as endearing. Richard Nielsen, the producer of Malcolm's television series *A Third Testament*, discovered one of the reasons why Malcolm issued such blanket condemnations. He once praised the Swedish film-maker Ingmar Bergman, only to hear Malcolm denounce him as obsessed with sex and Freudian psychology. This upset Nielsen, who considered Bergman to be one of the few directors to take religion seriously. He confided this to Kitty, who responded cheerfully: "Oh, I doubt Malcolm has actually ever seen a Bergman film. In fact, I'm sure he hasn't." Later it dawned on Nielsen that Malcolm dropped these verbal bombs in order to elicit from others what they really thought of a particular figure. "This was the way he kept up with what was going on," Nielsen concluded. But, like almost everyone else, Nielsen enjoyed the humorous possibilities of Malcolm's love of nasty gossip. When a biography of the American president Franklin Delano Roosevelt was published that revealed an affair F.D.R. had with his secretary, Missy LeHand, Malcolm was delighted. Turning to Nielsen, he said: "The good Lord did give us a clue, he did. We should have known." "What was that?" Nielsen asked. "Well," said Malcolm, "in view of Roosevelt's paralytic condition, her name, Missy LeHand, yes. The good Lord gave us a clue."[8]

For all the raucous laughter, observant visitors to Park Cottage noticed that Malcolm was increasingly depressed about his loss of creative energy. It took him longer to complete writing assignments, even short ones. Deadlines became more menacing than they had ever been, even at the outset of his journalistic career. Just as the printer's assistant at the *Manchester Guardian* waited for Malcolm to turn out his leader to rush it to the compositor, so, fifty years later, one of Malcolm's grandsons was enlisted to run an article up to London to meet a deadline. There was a widening gap between Malcolm's habits of a lifetime – his expectations of himself as a working writer – and his ability to fulfil them. This was the shadow that slowly but inexorably crept across Malcolm's last years.

In the autumn of 1982, Malcolm proved once again his flair for the dramatic gesture. On November 27, *The Times* carried an article by Malcolm entitled "Why I am becoming a Catholic". A note accompanying the article stated that Malcolm and Kitty Muggeridge were to be formally received into the Catholic Church that day. The news came as a shock to almost everyone who knew Malcolm, including his family.

This is how it came about. A few months earlier, Malcolm and Kitty received a letter from Fr Bidone. It was nothing more than a short, handwritten note. Aside from greetings and good wishes, the letter said only one thing: "It is time." The message was simple: it was time for Malcolm and Kitty to be received into the Roman Catholic Church. Over the years Fr Bidone had done little directly to recruit Malcolm into the Church, but at the same time he knew that Malcolm continued to agonise about his status as an outsider. He judged that Malcolm would have to make a commitment one way or the other before his health and mind began to fail. Fr Bidone gambled that a single direct appeal would elicit a positive response. He was right. Malcolm wrote back to Fr Bidone that he and Kitty had responded to his call "as one person without ever so much as discussing the matter". They wanted to be received as soon as possible.[9]

The only requirement that had to be fulfilled before they could be received was that Malcolm and Kitty receive instruction in the Church's teachings. Fr Bidone undertook this task himself. Though he was an orthodox and conscientious priest, he also recognised that Malcolm had little interest in theology or dogma. So the instruction period was abbreviated, taking place just a few weeks before the date of their reception.[10]

The whole process took such a short time that Malcolm did not bother to communicate the decision to many people. But he and Kitty did write to Mother Teresa, who received the news with joy. She apologised for not being able to be present at the occasion of Malcolm and Kitty's reception. "I . . . want to thank you," she wrote, "for all you have done for Jesus through your writings – still I get letters and meet people who say that they have come closer to God through reading *Something Beautiful for God*."[11]

The ceremony was held at the chapel of Our Lady, Help of Christians, in the village of Hurst Green on November 27, 1982. Lord and Lady Longford acted as their sponsors. The Mass was concelebrated by the Bishop of Arundel, Cormac Murphy O'Connor, Fr Bidone and the local priest, Fr Maxwell. Fr Bidone had brought with him a number of children from his home for retarded youth. At first this filled Malcolm with trepidation. "Trepidation because I foresee the children fidgeting, moving about, emitting strange sounds. In fact, when this actually happens, quite unexpectedly and mysteriously a great satisfaction possesses me, transforming what might otherwise be a respectable quiet ceremony into an unforgettable spiritual experience."[12] Kneeling at the altar rail next to Kitty, Malcolm received the sacrament. He was, at last, on the inside. In the article in *The Times*, he wrote that in becoming a Catholic he felt: "A sense of homecoming, of picking up the threads of a lost life, of responding to a bell that had long been ringing, of taking a place at a table that had long been vacant."[13]

News of Malcolm's conversion spread quickly. Once again the postman heaved large grey canvas sacks full of letters through the door of Park Cottage, just as he had after the publication of *Jesus Rediscovered*. Most of the letters came from Catholics who had been praying for his conversion, but many were simply letters of support and gratitude. There were the same disarming messages: an old woman who had prayed for him at daily Mass for twenty years, a man who had contemplated suicide, but was comforted by something Malcolm had written. Among them was a note from Graham Greene, Malcolm's companion during the Blitz, a Catholic convert whose relationship to the Church was complex. Greene wrote: "I don't know whether to congratulate you or to commiserate with you on making your decision, but I can sincerely wish you good luck and I can also hope that you will make a better Catholic than I have done . . ."[14]

Public reaction to Malcolm's conversion ran along predictable lines. To many of his critics his decision was nothing less than the final step in the decline and fall of Muggeridge: the anarchic scourge of every form of authority was now grovelling before the epitome of all authority, the Roman Catholic Church. But many of Malcolm's closest friends and family members were also stunned by the news. It is a subject that remains controversial, perhaps especially among those who had been close to him. There are those who still have their doubts about the sincerity and thoroughness of Malcolm's conversion.

Ever since his public profession of Christian faith in the late 1960s, Malcolm had declared that he would be, like Simone Weil, an outsider, gazing into the Church with longing, but for ever barred from entering. As he put it in *Something Beautiful for God*: "The Church, after all, is an institution with a history; a past and a future."[15] He would not place himself in a position of having to defend its historic sins and failures. For many years he did not think the Catholic Church had much of a future. Though he had long considered it the last bastion of Christianity in its fullest sense, the Church was now suffering from the ravages of liberalism that had long been plaguing Protestantism. This destructive force – unleashed by the Second Vatican Council, though not directly caused by it – attacked the core of the moral and spiritual teachings of the Church. The result of this attempt to adapt Catholicism to the spirit of the times, he argued, was catastrophic: it had, for example, decimated the ranks of the religious orders and the priesthood. Divided by dissent, the Church was no longer a sure guide to moral truth, Malcolm complained. He would not climb aboard a sinking ship.

What, then, made him change his mind? Pascal said that the heart has reasons of which the reason knows nothing. There can be little doubt that Malcolm's entrance into the Catholic Church was primarily a matter of the heart rather than the head, something that was influenced by forces deep within his psychic history. He certainly did not develop a newfound interest in theology, or gain new insight into the Catholic doctrine of Mary's Immaculate Conception. But it would be wrong to assume that Malcolm had no intellectual reasons for taking this step. He had, for example, been reading the works of John Henry Newman for several years, and had even wanted to add an episode on Newman to *A Third Testament*.[16] Kitty and Malcolm frequently read out loud to each other from an anthology called *The Heart of Newman*. Though Newman had a profound spirituality, he was not the sort of mystical writer that Malcolm normally preferred to read. His admiration for Newman grew out of the recognition that he had been an early and ardent foe of liberalism. Newman's response had been to defend Christian orthodoxy and, eventually, the Catholic Church. The central problem with liberalism, he concluded, was that it could not abide any form of authority. But this did not lead Newman, in practice, to become a mindless supporter of Papal infallibility. He had, in fact, been a champion of the legitimate rights and prerogatives of the laity.

Having studied Newman, Malcolm grew more sympathetic to the argument that the Church was the *only* institution on earth that was backed by a divine guarantee, and that this freed the Catholic to be critical not only of all secular authority, but of nearly everything that went on in the Church as well. According to the interviewer who probed most deeply into Malcolm's conversion, Malcolm was fond of Hilaire Belloc's more whimsical version of the idea. Belloc claimed, Malcolm told the interviewer, "that the Church must be in God's hands because, seeing the people who've run it, it couldn't possibly have gone on existing if there weren't some help from above."[17]

Malcolm found that he greatly admired Pope John Paul II. Karol Wojtyla shared many of the same experiences as another hero of Malcolm's, Aleksandr Solzhenitsyn. Wojtyla was "an admirable choice as Pope precisely because he has been a cardinal in a communist country and therefore knows at first hand what it means to be at the mercy of an atheistic, tyrannical regime". In 1983, while he was in Rome filming a television programme with William F. Buckley, Jr,

Malcolm met the Pope for a few moments at an audience. Malcolm came away with the impression that John Paul did not really understand England, and only had a rudimentary, phonetic grasp of English. But the Pope's campaign to shore up the teaching authority of the Church did not alarm Malcolm. His pontificate was a clear refutation of Malcolm's earlier predictions that the Catholic Church would soon abandon its central teachings and embrace the *Zeitgeist*. The Pope's efforts to protect those moral teachings, including those dealing with abortion, contraception and divorce, are "sorely needed in an irreligious, materialistic world, even at the cost of a certain conservatism".[18] Similarly, he had recognised the link between Mother Teresa's traditionalism and the power and practical effectiveness of her love.

Mother Teresa herself was an important influence on Malcolm's conversion to Catholicism. In *Something Beautiful for God* he had admitted that he was tempted to join the Church in order to please her; the prayers of a Mother Teresa are hard to resist. As her letters demonstrate, Mother Teresa did not always take the confrontational approach with Malcolm; she was able to empathise with his loneliness and sense of exclusion. But she was also capable of cutting Malcolm's self-justifications short. He frequently alluded to a conversation he had with Mother Teresa while walking along the Serpentine in London. As they strolled through the park, he explained to her that he shared Simone Weil's belief that God needed Christians outside the Church as well as inside. "No, he doesn't," she said to him tartly.[19] There was something about her simple confidence that seemed to him to cut through all his evasions. This was precisely the way Alec Vidler had spoken to Malcolm, ever since their Cambridge days.

Another person who loved Malcolm, but whose deep-seated convictions led her to frequent disagreements about the Church, was his daughter-in-law, Anne Roche Muggeridge, married to his son John. Malcolm regarded Anne, who came from an Irish Catholic family and who was an active leader in pro-life and traditionalist Catholic organisations, as the quintessential insider Catholic. When they were together and he had been sounding off on one of his ideas, he would often stop and ask her: "Darling, don't you think so?" Not easily cowed, Anne would often retort: "No, I think that's absolute nonsense." Usually this led to fits of laughter, but occasionally he and Anne would have what she calls "dust-ups". His invariable tactic when she was upset was to make her laugh, precisely when she didn't want to. But the connection between Anne's faith and her life as a mother of five children and an activist was not lost on Malcolm. He really did want to know what she thought.[20]

Malcolm's decision to enter the Catholic Church was, in the end, a matter of the heart, in Pascal's sense of the word. He had been an outsider and a non-participant for so long that his desire for communion finally outweighed his reluctance to join in. Holding himself aloof from institutions had enabled him to satirise and excoriate their failures and betrayals, but the danger in such a position was the sin of pride, of making himself the ultimate authority. Getting down on his knees with his fellow men was the final step toward communion and humility and away from loneliness and pride. At the altar rail in Our Lady, Help of Christians, he had come home. Having walked along the Emmaus Road for so long, he came to know his Lord in the breaking of bread.

In the article that appeared on the day of his conversion, Malcolm added a postscript to the effect that the decision had been made with Kitty, as if they were "one person". Actually, that is not strictly true. Kitty had in fact been prepared to become a Catholic for some time. But with her customary humility, she waited until Malcolm was ready to lead and then took her place by his side. No one who knew Kitty in these years doubted for a moment that though she always went last, she was, in reality, first.

The question naturally arises: did Malcolm's Catholicism "take"? If by this one means the practice of Catholic devotions and customs, the answer to that question has to be: no. Having been received into the Catholic Church on the eve of his eightieth birthday, Malcolm was not interested in learning to pray the rosary, participate in novenas or attend First Friday services. He freely admitted to interviewers that if he were to explain exactly how he understood certain doctrines, "it might not be considered totally orthodox; yet I do say them and I do believe them."[21] He spoke of Christianity as being grounded in "artistic truth rather than historical truth", arguing that efforts to ascertain the facts concerning the Virgin Birth and other biblical and dogmatic tenets would inevitably lead one away from the truth. How he separated this position from that of, say, Bishop Jenkins, was never entirely clear. But on most of the burning moral and political issues of the day, he remained firmly within the ranks of the orthodox, and adamantly opposed to the Bishop Jenkinses of the world.

The spirituality of Park Cottage remained largely as it was: Malcolm and Kitty said the Anglican services of Morning and Evening Prayer, read aloud from a variety of religious authors, from the anonymous medieval author of *The Cloud of Unknowing* to George Herbert and John Henry Newman. Becoming a Catholic meant for Malcolm a sense of belonging to a communion and of taking a stand on behalf of certain fundamental but unpopular truths.

The only point where the Church touched Malcolm's life in a way that was deeply meaningful to him was in the Eucharist. It was while he was at Cambridge in the 1920s that he had begged Alec Vidler to "explain the Blessed Sacrament" to him. Then, at the Oratory of the Good Shepherd in Cambridge, he found himself moved by the practice of daily Mass. In the intervening years, he had haunted many Catholic churches. He preferred Mass to be celebrated with simplicity and dignity, scorning the use of guitars and what he called "pop-like hymns".[22] Those who observed him at Mass, including his son John and daughter-in-law Anne, noticed his intense reverence and devotion throughout the service. When his health began to fail and he could not get out, the sacrament would be brought to him. Depending on the availability of a priest, he might not receive the sacrament for a few weeks at a time. Once, a lay minister showed up at the door of Park Cottage in blue jeans and a sweater and asked Malcolm if he wanted to receive the sacrament, which he pulled out of a container in his hip pocket. Malcolm grew incensed and threw him out, finding the man's casualness about the Eucharist a "shocking abomination".[23]

Though Malcolm had always shown nothing but contempt for the sort of honours bestowed by the Establishment – hell would certainly freeze over before the world ever encountered Sir Malcolm Mugger-idge – there were a few tributes he received that meant a good deal to him. One of these took place on the occasion of his eightieth birthday in 1983, when Richard Ingrams organised a special dinner at the Garrick Club to honour Malcolm. In addition to Alec Vidler and Fr Bidone, there were more than twenty friends and colleagues from Fleet Street, including Bill Deedes, James Cameron, Hugh Cudlipp, Terence Kilmartin, Auberon Waugh, Christopher Booker, Alan Watkins, Andrew Boyle and Jonathan Stedall of the BBC. Malcolm was presented with a framed cartoon by Trog, depicting him as St Mugg, in a monastic habit, holding a sign that doubles as the symbol for infinity and the number 8, while a halo over his head also functions as a zero.

A far more unexpected source of acknowledgment came to Malcolm from a sitting president of the United States, Ronald Reagan. The first message Malcolm received from President Reagan came one day in 1981, when a long black limousine from the American Embassy in London pulled up to Park Cottage. A member of the embassy staff emerged and hand-delivered an envelope containing a photograph signed by President Reagan. The photograph depicted Mother Teresa emerging with President and Mrs Reagan from the diplomatic gate of the White House. An accompanying letter explained that when a member of the press shouted out: "What did you talk about, Mr President?" Reagan replied: "We didn't talk. We listened." When Reagan was elected to the presidency, Malcolm had assumed that his anti-abortion and anti-Communist positions would quickly disappear as the power of the "consensus" swallowed him up.[24] But Reagan was not so easily swallowed up. Malcolm had the satisfaction of hearing Reagan declare the Soviet Union an "evil empire" – a phrase for which he received a great deal of opprobrium.

Even more impressive to Malcolm was Reagan's unwavering opposition to abortion and euthanasia. In the spring of 1983, Reagan published a long essay in *The Human Life Review*, a quarterly journal published in New York by James McFadden, who had become a close friend of Malcolm. In the essay, "Abortion and the Conscience of the Nation", Reagan quoted Malcolm twice. When the essay was published in book form, Malcolm's own essay, "The Humane Holocaust", was added as an afterword. Malcolm wrote to McFadden praising Reagan's "courage and honesty . . . There is no comparable figure on our side of the Atlantic who could be relied on to take a similar stand."[25] In fact, one of the reasons that Malcolm never thought much of Margaret Thatcher as Prime Minister was that she preferred to concentrate on her brand of *laissez faire* economics than to take a stand on such moral issues as abortion and euthanasia.

Malcolm's joking prophecy in the introduction to *Chronicles of Wasted Time* – that his papers might one day be preserved "at some American university, grateful for any pabulum to fill its air-conditioned, dust-and-damp-proof vaults" – was fulfilled when he was approached in the 1980s by a number of American colleges and universities.[26] In the end, despite his raillery on the subject, Malcolm made an agreement with two of these institutions. The Hoover Institution on War, Revolution and Peace, a research library and think-tank with the most extensive collection of materials on the history of the Soviet Union in the West, asked for Malcolm's papers. He had spent some time at the Hoover Institution, as had Solzhenitsyn, and decided to send his papers there. But after this agreement was signed, representatives from Wheaton College, in Illinois, approached him with the same request. Wheaton is an evangelical college whose most famous alumnus is Dr Billy Graham. The representatives from Wheaton persuaded Malcolm that their college would be a more appropriate repository for his papers than the Hoover Institution. It was arranged that the Hoover Institution would receive copies of everything that went to Wheaton.

Wheaton College, of course, is the home of the Wade Collection, containing materials relating to seven Christian writers: C.S. Lewis, J.R.R. Tolkien, Charles Williams, G.K. Chesterton, Owen Barfield, George MacDonald and Dorothy L. Sayers. Since the Wade Collection is restricted to those writers, Malcolm's papers are kept separately. Malcolm is an unlikely hero in the evangelical pantheon: his life and convictions are far more unruly than the average evangelical sensibility is prepared to accept. One wonders if Wheaton College knew just how unruly Malcolm was when they asked for his papers. In his biography of C.S. Lewis, A.N. Wilson writes about seeing Malcolm's typewriter at Wheaton College encased behind glass, "like the body of Lenin". Malcolm would have appreciated the irony, perhaps even the absurdity, of enshrining his typewriter as a quasi-sacred relic. But at the same time he had come to feel a genuine solidarity with those individuals at Wheaton who cared about defending their Christian faith. He could live – and die – with any of the attendant ironies.

By the mid-1980s, Malcolm's publications had slowed down to a trickle of short articles, mostly for Catholic newspapers. *Vintage Muggeridge*, a collection of religious essays dating from the late 1960s to the present was published in 1984. *My Life in Pictures*, a pictorial autobiography with brief comments and captions, appeared in 1987. Neither book received careful editing or broke any new ground. A more impressive event was the publication of Malcolm's novel about the *Manchester Guardian* – *Picture Palace* – more than half a century after it was suppressed.

It was around this time that Malcolm finally confronted the fact that he did not have the stamina to complete the third volume of his autobiography. He had not wanted to write the book that would "draw down the shades" on his life, but those shades began to descend anyway. As a substitute for the third volume, he decided to write a much shorter book, focusing exclusively on his spiritual pilgrimage. Even with this less ambitious proposal, the book still took several years for him to complete. The resultant volume, published in 1988 as *Conversion* in Britain and as *Confessions of a Twentieth-Century Pilgrim* in the US, is a poignant indication of Malcolm's physical and mental decline. Except for the brief introduction, about his reception into the Catholic Church, the book goes over the same territory as in *Chronicles of Wasted Time*. It is written in much the same form as Augustine's *Confessions* – a story that is also a prayer addressed to God. Referring to himself in the third person as "The Child", "The Adolescent", "The Foreign Correspondent", the narrative strives for, and fitfully achieves, a tone of genuine humility. But the narrative has been padded with dozens of quotations from spiritual authors, and excerpts from earlier essays are spliced in to fill out the book. A reader coming to this book with little or no knowledge of Malcolm's writing will find it a moving introduction to his life and thought, but for others it will remain a painful reminder of Malcolm's last years.

Malcolm had spoken for decades of the need to acknowledge our mortality and to face death with faith and hope. But he was not to be allowed to meet death in the way he would have liked.

Malcolm suffered from many of the common ailments of old age. He always had a weak chest and in cold weather he suffered from what he referred to as "catarrh". Both he and Kitty also suffered hearing loss and had to use deaf aids. Being averse to technology, they invariably found themselves caught up in comic scenes where the electronic gadgets in their ears would give off beeps and wails, and require endless fiddling. They also had problems with failing eyesight, including cataracts. Even though cataract surgery had become a routine operation, Malcolm refused to submit to it. Part of this was undoubtedly an aversion to going under the knife. But there was more to it than that. Malcolm had long opposed the use of new medical technologies, not because he was a Luddite, but because he felt that the attempt to circumvent the process of aging and death, from organ transplants to plastic surgery, had become the obsession of a decadent, materialistic society. Refusing something as simple as a cataract operation borders on the eccentric, but Malcolm preferred to practise a radical consistency in these matters. When word of Malcolm's decision to refuse this operation came out in the Peterborough column of the *Daily Telegraph*, it caused a flurry of letters to the editor, some supporting Malcolm and others chiding him. He had managed to make even his own declining health a matter of controversy.

Far more serious was the degeneration of Malcolm's mental faculties, a degeneration that crept up slowly. The onset of his condition
was gradual and its symptoms were not clear-cut, either to Kitty or to
other friends and family. Malcolm had manifested the normal memory-
losses of old age, but after 1985 more serious problems began to
emerge, including the inability to recognise people he knew quite well.
There were episodes when his speech became confused and incoherent,
though he showed no sign that anything was wrong. His son Leonard
remembers accompanying Malcolm to a talk he was asked to give in a
church around 1987 or 1988. Malcolm ascended to the pulpit and
began his address. What came out of his mouth was pure gibberish.
The minister and congregation were far too polite to give any sign that
anything was amiss, and so they thanked Malcolm afterwards for his
words of wisdom.[27]

By the time these symptoms had become unmistakable, it was
thought that Malcolm might be suffering from Alzheimer's disease.
But in the end the doctors concluded that Malcolm had experienced a
number of episodes of something known as TIA – a "transient ischemic
attack", or minor stroke. A TIA occurs when there is a temporary
deficiency in the blood supply to the brain. Most episodes last only a
few minutes and may only cause slight weakness or tingling, or a brief
loss of vision. It is possible that Malcolm was unaware when a TIA
had taken place. Each time the body undergoes a small stroke like this,
areas of brain cells are killed off. This in turn can lead to a condition
known as "multi-infarct dementia", which is characterised by progressive memory loss, disintegration of personality and increasing
depression.

Malcolm manifested all these symptoms in the last years of his life,
much to the distress of friends and family. Despite her own health
problems, Kitty struggled valiantly to keep the show on the road. She
felt that if Malcolm had enough stimulation, it would help to dispel
the cloudiness of his mind, so she accepted requests from journalists
who wanted to come down to Park Cottage. Sadly, some of the
reporters and interviewers who did come found Malcolm incoherent,
and had to leave without obtaining any *bons mots*. The one clear
message that Malcolm communicated in these years was a desire to
live alone with Kitty. The price of this continued independence was
that others might be called upon at any moment to deal with real
emergencies or false alarms. They had been given a special telephone
with a distress button that would alert neighbours. Kitty kept pressing

the button by accident, so that neighbours would rush over only to find nothing wrong.

Attempts to bring in a live-in nurse or companion inevitably ended in disaster. When one well-intentioned relative sent a young woman to Park Cottage, Malcolm became furious. She stayed just one night, but the next day he threw her out of the house. There was more than enough money to pay for such help, of course. But in his own confused way, Malcolm became fiercely protective of Kitty, imagining that strangers might be coming to hurt her. Malcolm was eventually moved into his study on the ground floor. He insisted on turning the heat up to stifling levels, which puzzled the family until they learned that stroke victims are susceptible to chills. His son Leonard tried to come to Robertsbridge on most weekends, spending hours sitting with his father. Malcolm would sit silently staring into space. He lost interest in bathing and shaving. There were those who thought that he had fallen into a condition of despair. It would be impossible to sort out how much of this depression had any real basis outside his physiological condition.

There came a time when almost everyone became a stranger to him and he did not even recognise family members. When Malcolm's son John arrived for a visit in the summer of 1989, Malcolm threw him out of the house as well, forcing him to stay with some long-suffering neighbours. Several attempts were made to get Malcolm and Kitty into some form of managed care facility, such as a rest home which was a step below a nursing home. Their daughter Val and her husband Gerrit-Jan came over from Holland and took them around to look at several different institutions in and around Sussex. Malcolm continued to resist these efforts. In the end it took a bit of subterfuge to persuade Malcolm to leave Park Cottage. By the spring of 1990, Kitty had decided that she was going to have her cataracts operated on. Since Malcolm could not be left alone, Kitty was able to persuade him to come into a rest home with her so that she could have the operation. Once the operation was completed, they simply stayed there. Leonard continued his regular visits and was soon joined by Malcolm's only surviving brother Jack, who had decided to give up his work for a charitable organisation in order to attend to Malcolm and Kitty's needs.

On July 27, 1990, Malcolm suffered a major stroke and was rushed to the intensive care unit at St Helen's Hospital in Hastings. The stroke was so serious that doctors were guarded in speaking of

Malcolm's chances for even a partial recovery. Leonard came down and was able to sleep in a room adjoining Malcolm's. Throughout the night, Leonard could hear his father shouting in a loud voice: "Father, forgive me! Father, forgive me!"

But the stroke did not prove fatal, at least not immediately. Malcolm recovered sufficiently to be brought back to the rest home. But the rest home was not equipped to deal with someone as frail as Malcolm was at this time; it lacked full-time medical staff and facilities. One night Malcolm got out of bed and began to wander around the rest home, going into nearly every room in the building. At one point, all twenty rooms were ringing their attention bells at the same time. A nursing home was found in Hastings that could take both Malcolm and Kitty.

Not long after they had settled into the nursing home, Malcolm had a fall that injured his hip and caused him severe pain. Within a couple of days, Kitty had a similar fall. The doctors decided that both of them needed to have their hips replaced. Kitty was able to have her operation almost immediately, but Malcolm's weak chest caused a delay. Once he received the hip replacement, he was sent to a rehabilitation hospital in Bexhill to regain the ability to walk. But after a few sessions of therapy, the doctors realised that Malcolm's strokes had impaired his capacity to learn and the rehabilitation effort was abandoned.

It was at the rehabilitation hospital that Malcolm's son John saw him for the last time and witnessed an event that seemed to balance the tortured cries for forgiveness that echoed through the night of July 27. While John was visiting, he saw a nurse arrive with a cart full of pills and medicines. Malcolm was to be given a tranquiliser in the form of a small pill no larger than a peppercorn. Malcolm could not be induced to take the pill. A nursing aide came over to help, but to no avail. Then the Charge Nurse took over. "Leave this to me," she said. "Come on, Malcolm, it'll make you better." This, too, ended in failure. In the end, Malcolm had to receive an injection. About half an hour later, "an apologetic little man in grey [trousers] and blazer" arrived. John took this man for a dentist, but it turned out that he was the hospital chaplain, come to give Malcolm Holy Communion. Having just witnessed the drama of the pill, John thought the chaplain's efforts would also come to naught. "But the priest lit a candle, said the usual prayers, gave a piece of the Host first to my mother and me and then to my father, who closed his eyes and consumed it reverently."[28]

Throughout the autumn, Malcolm's condition deteriorated. Before he had to return to Canada, John saw Malcolm straining to read the one-syllable words in the headlines of the *Daily Mirror*, but understanding nothing else. He refused to eat and consequently grew thin and weak. Kitty, Leonard and Jack continued their vigil by his bedside. The end came on the morning of November 14. The cause of death was listed as "bronchopneumonia", combined with the effects of the stroke in July.

Malcolm's funeral was scheduled for November 19. The arrangements were marked by confusion, something that would have greatly appealed to Malcolm's anarchic sense of humour. It was decided that the funeral service should be held at the local Anglican church of St Mary the Virgin in Salehurst, with Mass to be celebrated by Bishop Cormac Murphy O'Connor. Unfortunately, the organisers had forgotten that it is still a criminal offence to celebrate a Catholic Mass in any place of worship owned by the Church of England. At the last minute the word "Eucharist" on the funeral programme had to be scratched out, and Lord Longford's eulogy was substituted. "We have lost our greatest witness for the faith and we are all poorer and lower by the loss," Lord Longford began, quoting the words Cardinal Manning had used at the funeral of Cardinal Newman. He concluded by quoting Malcolm's description of the disciples walking along the road to Emmaus, "joined by a third presence". "Those of us who have known Malcolm longest," Lord Longford said, "will agree that all his life he was conscious of another world and in later years of another presence."

After the service, the funeral cortege proceeded to Whatlington, where Malcolm was buried next to his parents. The churchyard lies only a few hundred yards from Mill House, the house where he and Kitty and the children had lived in the years before the war and which had held happy memories for him. A wheelchair was offered to Kitty, but she insisted on walking, with human support, up the hill to the graveside. Once again no provisions were made for a Catholic service, so John Muggeridge and the local priest, Fr McLean-Wilson, said a few prayers over the grave. John found an old set of rosary beads in his pocket and threw them on the coffin.

Malcolm's oldest and dearest friend, Alec Vidler, outlived him by a few months, dying in 1991. It was decided that Kitty should go to live with John and his family in Canada. In the next few years she suffered some of the same mental clouding that had overtaken Malcolm, as if she had to share everything that Malcolm had experienced, both in sorrow and in joy. At her death in 1994, Kitty was conscious and peaceful.[29]

*

Now that Malcolm Muggeridge's life can be seen as a whole, it is time for a revaluation of his achievement and his place in the history of twentieth-century letters. Here, as in most other areas of life, Malcolm harboured few illusions. He knew well that literary reputations were made and broken by the reigning political and ideological forces of the time. To adapt a favourite phrase of his, he knew that literary history is written by the victors. At present, Malcolm's stock is extremely low when compared to his contemporaries, including Graham Greene, Evelyn Waugh and George Orwell. Yet he deserves to be ranked alongside these writers. As a master of English prose style, Malcolm easily holds his own in their company. Though he was not a literary artist of the calibre of Greene and Waugh, he articulated a Christian and Catholic critique of the modern era that equals theirs in depth of vision. In many ways, Malcolm's literary talents were closest to those of Orwell: a capacity for brilliant reportage, incisive essays, satirical parables. But despite the fact that Malcolm's political judgements and prophetic insights proved to be more accurate and reliable than those of his old friend, Orwell is considered a towering figure of moral authority while Malcolm is relegated by many critics to the status of an old hack who went dotty in his last years. Though he was often a spectator, Malcolm had extraordinary success as a man of action. As an intelligence agent, a campaigner against totalitarianism and abortion, a Christian apologist and a supporter of Christian works of compassion, Malcolm had more direct impact on his times than either Greene, Waugh or Orwell.

There is no question that much of Malcolm's output can be classed as "wasted time", including many hours in front of the cameras. But there is also much that lives, from *In a Valley of This Restless Mind* and *The Thirties* to the *Chronicles of Wasted Time* and *Jesus: The Man Who Lives*. There is also a rich vein of sardonic wit and arresting insight in his journalistic output that can be mined again and again, including brilliant dissections of liberalism and utopianism, the power and influence of the media and the amoral fantasies of a materialistic age.

If a prophet is to be judged by the accuracy of his predictions, Malcolm Muggeridge comes off better than most. So many of his early insights, from the collapse of the British Empire to the advent of the Second World War, have faded into historical record that we can lose sight of their genius. But if one looks simply at the world at the time of his death, the number of prophecies fulfilled is startling. The Soviet

Union and its empire in Eastern Europe have collapsed, as Malcolm long argued it would. Solzhenitsyn has indeed returned to his devastated land. Twenty-four-hour television news networks, such as CNN, now produce an endless stream of "Newzak". Parliamentary debates and even wars are televised live. In the Gulf War cameras were even fitted on to bombs, so that viewers could ride them down to their final conflagration. The notion that the media, and in particular television, have a massive, largely deleterious effect on the processes of democratic government is no longer a shocking allegation but something taken for granted. That we live in an "information age" that has lost sight of truth in an overload of facts is no longer considered a cranky statement. In the Netherlands an extremely permissive euthanasia law has been enacted, shocking even some of its moderate proponents. Similar laws are now under consideration around the world. The Royal Soap Opera has become even more interminable and more absurd than Malcolm could have imagined in 1955. "The imagination," Malcolm once wrote, "at however rudimentary a level, reaches into the future. So its works have a prophetic quality."[30]

As a twentieth-century Christian apologist, Malcolm Muggeridge stands beside G.K. Chesterton and C.S. Lewis. Malcolm's sensibility – more darkly satirical, more willing to balance doubt with faith, more deeply informed by a huge store of worldly experience – complements the romanticism of Chesterton and Lewis. His life was too unruly and too complicated for him to become the centre of a cult, a fate that has befallen Lewis. But in the long run this will certainly prove to be an advantage, since Malcolm will never be in danger of being made into a plaster saint. He was much more comfortable with the image of himself as the gargoyle on the church steeple. "Only clowns and mystics ever speak the truth," Malcolm was fond of saying. He was both.

On Malcolm's gravestone, in addition to his name, the dates of his birth and death, and the words *Requiescat in pace*, there is a single phrase: "Valiant for Truth." The idea for this came from his son John. The reference is to a character who appears near the end of Bunyan's *Pilgrim's Progress*.

> Then they went on, and just at the place where Little-faith formerly was robbed, there stood a man with his sword drawn, and his face all bloody. Then said Mr Great-heart, "What art thou?" The man made answer, saying, "I am one whose name is

Valiant-for-Truth, I am a pilgrim, and am going to the Celestial City."

Valiant-for-Truth is a much-battered but noble old soldier. His single-minded pursuit of truth is his greatest virtue. Though he has been constantly engaged in fights and struggles, Bunyan gives this old warrior one of the most beautiful lyrics in his book, a lyric that would later be adapted into a popular hymn. He sings it shortly before he crosses over to Jerusalem's Wall. The final stanza might serve as an extended epitaph for Malcolm Muggeridge, that restless pilgrim of the absolute.

> Hobgoblin, nor foul fiend,
> Can daunt his spirit:
> He knows, he at the end,
> Shall life inherit.
> Then fancies fly away,
> He'll fear not what men say,
> He'll labour night and day,
> To be a pilgrim.

NOTES

Malcolm Muggeridge's papers are held in the Special Collections section of the Buswell Library, Wheaton College, Wheaton, Illinois. The Muggeridge collection is listed as SC-4. All references in the notes to letters, diaries, and other unpublished works by Malcolm Muggeridge in the Wheaton College Special Collections contain the abbreviation WCSC.

Preface

1 *Christ and the Media* (Grand Rapids, MI: Wm.B.Eerdmans, 1977), pp. 47–8.
2 Christopher Booker, "Beneath the Carapace", *National Review*, December 31, 1990.
3 Anthony Powell, *To Keep the Ball Rolling* (London: Penguin Books, 1983), pp. 361–2.
4 "Recalling the Thirties", in *Things Past* (New York: William Morrow, 1979), p. 80.

Chapter 1

1 *Chronicles of Wasted Time, Vol.1: The Green Stick* (New York: William Morrow, 1973), p. 27.
2 Margaret Cole, *The Story of Fabian Socialism* (London: Oxford University Press, 1961), p. 4.
3 *The Green Stick*, p. 32.
4 *The Green Stick*, p. 41.
5 *Autumnal Face* (London: Putnam, 1931), pp. 11–12.
6 *The Green Stick*, p. 23.

7 Ian Hunter, *Malcolm Muggeridge: A Life*, (London: Collins, 1980), p. 18.

8 Conversation with the author, summer 1986.

9 *Jesus Rediscovered*, (New York: Doubleday, 1968) p. 31; memoir of Malcolm Muggeridge by Jack Muggeridge, WCSC.

10 *Jesus Rediscovered*, p. 41; *Tread Softly for You Tread on My Jokes* (London: Collins, 1966), p. 78; *Confessions of a Twentieth-Century Pilgrim* (San Francisco: Harper & Row, 1988), p. 24.

11 *The Green Stick*, p. 63.

12 *My Life in Pictures* (New York: William Morrow, 1987), p. 17.

13 Helen Corke to Malcolm Muggeridge, November 16, 1963, WCSC.

14 *The Green Stick*, p. 26.

15 *Malcolm Muggeridge: A Life*, p. 19.

16 *The Green Stick*, p. 47.

17 *The Green Stick*, p. 50.

18 *The Green Stick*, p. 50.

19 *In a Valley of This Restless Mind* (London: Routledge, 1938; London: Collins, 1978). See chapter 17, "The Adoration of Young and Beautiful Creatures for One Another".

20 *The Green Stick*, p. 40.

21 *The Green Stick*, p. 58.

22 Memoir by Jack Muggeridge, WCSC.

23 Unpublished manuscript, "A Portrait of Our Time, A Socialist Father", WCSC.

24 *The Green Stick*, pp. 52, 30.

25 *The Green Stick*, p. 13.

Chapter 2

1 Unpublished manuscript, "A Portrait of Our Time, A Socialist Father", WCSC.

2 *The Green Stick*, p. 67.

3 *The Green Stick*, p. 67.

4 *The Green Stick*, p. 71.

5 *Autumnal Face*, p. 22.

6 *The Green Stick*, p. 35.

7 *The Green Stick*, p. 35.

8 *Autumnal Face*, pp. 91–5.

9 "A Portrait of Our Time".

10 Michael Shelden, *Orwell: The Authorized Biography* (New York: Harper Perennial, 1992), p. 75.

11 *The Green Stick*, p. 78.

12 Unpublished diary entry, October 27, 1934, WCSC.

13 Unpublished diary entry, November 18, 1934, WCSC.

14 Unpublished diary entry, November 27, 1934, WCSC. In a documentary on his early life, produced by the BBC in 1966, Malcolm recalls Dora Pitman

carrying a dictionary marked "Dora P. Upper Fifth". *A Socialist Childhood*, BBC1, October 13, 1966. Reprinted in *Muggeridge: Ancient and Modern* (London: British Broadcasting Corporation, 1981), pp. 33–4.

15 *The Green Stick*, p. 73.
16 Unpublished diary entry, November 27, 1934, WCSC.
17 Unpublished diary entry, November 27, 1934, WCSC.
18 *The Green Stick*, p. 74.
19 *Autumnal Face*, pp. 45–6.
20 *Autumnal Face*, pp. 50–1.
21 *Jesus Rediscovered*, p. 79.
22 *Muggeridge: Ancient and Modern*, p. 34.
23 Jack Muggeridge, memoir of Malcolm Muggeridge, London P.E.N. Society, May 15, 1991.
24 *Confessions of a Twentieth-Century Pilgrim* (San Francisco: Harper & Row, 1988), pp. 28–9.
25 *The Green Stick*, p. 56.
26 *Confessions of a Twentieth-Century Pilgrim*, p. 30.
27 "A Portrait of Our Time".
28 "A Portrait of Our Time".
29 "A Portrait of Our Time".
30 *The Green Stick*, pp. 71–2.

Chapter 3

1 Alec Vidler, *Scenes from a Clerical Life* (London: Collins, 1977), p. 26.
2 Mercia Mason, *Blue Guide to Oxford and Cambridge* (London: Ernest Benn, 1958), pp. 28, 157.
3 Michael Grant, *Cambridge* (New York: Reynal, 1966), p. 158.
4 *The Green Stick*, p. 75.
5 *Scenes from a Clerical Life*, p. 26.
6 *The Green Stick*, p. 76.
7 Malcolm Muggeridge to Alec Vidler, 1921, passim, WCSC.
8 Jack Muggeridge, memoir of Malcolm Muggeridge, London P.E.N. Society, May 15, 1991.
9 *Scenes from a Clerical Life*, p. 33.
10 *Scenes from a Clerical Life*, p. 27.
11 *The Green Stick*, p. 81.
12 *Scenes from a Clerical Life*, p. 27.
13 Malcolm Muggeridge to Alec Vidler, April 5, 1921, WCSC.
14 Malcolm Muggeridge to Alec Vidler, July 18, 1921, WCSC.
15 H. T. Muggeridge to Alec Vidler, November 18, 1921, WCSC.
16 Malcolm Muggeridge to Alec Vidler, September 3, 1921, WCSC.
17 *Scenes from a Clerical Life*, pp. 33–4.

18 Malcolm Muggeridge to Alec Vidler, undated, but marked by Vidler as July 1921, WCSC.

19 Dora Pitman Gould to Malcolm Muggeridge, February 4, 1972.

20 Dora Pitman to Alec Vidler, March 2, 1923, WCSC.

21 *The Green Stick*, p. 78.

22 Unpublished diary entry, November 27, 1934; unpublished diary entry, April 14, 1950; Ian Hunter, *Malcolm Muggeridge: A Life*, p. 34, WCSC.

23 Malcolm Muggeridge to Alec Vidler, January 31, 1923, WCSC.

24 "Memoir", unpublished manuscript, WCSC.

25 Malcolm Muggeridge to Alec Vidler, October 1921 and undated, 1922, WCSC.

26 "A Portrait of Our Time".

27 *The Green Stick*, pp. 83–4.

28 Unpublished manuscript of sermon preached at Union Christian College, Alwaye, India, "The Atonement", WCSC.

29 Penelope Fitzgerald, *The Knox Brothers* (New York: Coward, McCann & Geoghegan, 1977), p. 159.

30 *The Knox Brothers*, p. 162.

31 *The Green Stick*, p. 81.

32 Malcolm Muggeridge to Alec Vidler, December 19, 1922, WCSC.

33 *The Knox Brothers*, p. 162.

34 *The Green Stick*, p. 82.

35 Malcolm Muggeridge to Alec Vidler, November 5, 1923, WCSC.

36 Malcolm Muggeridge to Alec Vidler, undated, November 1923, WCSC.

37 Malcolm Muggeridge to Alec Vidler, March 4, 1924, WCSC.

38 Malcolm Muggeridge to Alec Vidler, May 23, 1924, WCSC.

39 Alec Vidler to Malcolm Muggeridge, June 12, 1924, WCSC.

40 Malcolm Muggeridge to Alec Vidler, November 7, 1924, WCSC.

41 *The Green Stick*, p. 85.

42 *The Green Stick*, p. 90.

43 *The Green Stick*, p. 87.

44 *The Green Stick*, p. 86.

Chapter 4

1 *The Green Stick*, p. 93.

2 *The Green Stick*, p. 95.

3 Malcolm Muggeridge to Alec Vidler, undated, December 1924, WCSC.

4 *The Green Stick*, p. 99.

5 *The Green Stick*, p. 100.

6 *The Green Stick*, p. 101.

7 *The Green Stick*, p. 102.

8 *The Green Stick*, p. 103.

9 *Malcolm Muggeridge: A Life*, pp. 37–8.

10 Malcolm Muggeridge to Alec Vidler, February 10, 1925, WCSC.

11 Malcolm Muggeridge to Alec Vidler, April 27, 1925, WCSC.

12 Malcolm Muggeridge to Alec Vidler, April 27, 1925, WCSC.

13 Malcolm Muggeridge to H. T. Muggeridge, January 25, 1925, WCSC.

14 *The Green Stick*, pp. 109–10.

15 Malcolm Muggeridge to Alec Vidler, March 25, 1925, WCSC.

16 *Malcolm Muggeridge: A Life*, p. 40.

17 Unpublished manuscript, "Happiness is found strangely", July 22, 1927, WCSC.

18 *The Green Stick*, p. 106.

19 *The Green Stick*, p. 114.

20 *Malcolm Muggeridge: A Life*, p. 38.

21 *Malcolm Muggeridge: A Life*, pp. 39–40.

22 Malcolm Muggeridge to H. T. Muggeridge, January 31, 1925, WCSC.

23 Malcolm Muggeridge to H. T. Muggeridge, April 30, 1925, WCSC.

24 Malcolm Muggeridge to H. T. Muggeridge, March 2, 1926, WCSC.

25 Malcolm Muggeridge to H. T. Muggeridge, August 25, 1925, WCSC.

26 Malcolm Muggeridge to H. T. Muggeridge, December 31, 1924, WCSC.

27 Malcolm Muggeridge to H. T. Muggeridge, October 10, 1926, WCSC.

28 Malcolm Muggeridge to H. T. Muggeridge, January 31, 1925, WCSC.

29 Malcolm Muggeridge to Alec Vidler, April 22, 1925, WCSC.

30 Malcolm Muggeridge to H. T. Muggeridge, December 1, 1925, WCSC.

31 Malcolm Muggeridge to H. T. Muggeridge, August 6, 1926, WCSC.

32 Malcolm Muggeridge to H. T. Muggeridge, February 2, 1926, WCSC.

33 Malcolm Muggeridge to H. T. Muggeridge, August 25, 1925, WCSC.

34 *The Green Stick*, p. 115.

35 "On the Loneliness of Being a Sahib", *Calcutta Guardian*, March 25, 1926.

36 "The Compleat 'Bus Rider", *Calcutta Guardian*, August 12, 1926.

37 "On Trains", *Calcutta Guardian*, January 27, 1927.

38 "Along the Parur Road", *Calcutta Guardian*, November 4, 1926.

39 Malcolm Muggeridge to H. T. Muggeridge, undated, April 1925, WCSC.

40 Malcolm Muggeridge to H. T. Muggeridge, July 7, 1925, WCSC.

41 Malcolm Muggeridge to H. T. Muggeridge, November 26, 1926, WCSC.

42 *The Green Stick*, pp. 126–30.

Chapter 5

1 Malcolm Muggeridge to H. T. Muggeridge, February 7, 1927, WCSC.

2 *The Green Stick*, p. 37.

3 "A Portrait of Our Time".

4 *The Green Stick*, p. 131.

5 Unpublished manuscript, May 12, 1927, WCSC.

6 Unpublished manuscript, "God's Chastity", undated, probably 1927, WCSC.

7 Unpublished manuscript, July 2, 1927, WCSC.

8 Kitty Muggeridge and Ruth Adam, *Beatrice Webb: A Life* (New York: Knopf, 1968), pp. 11–12.

9 *The Green Stick*, p. 140.

10 *The Green Stick*, p. 140.

11 *The Green Stick*, p. 140.

12 *My Life in Pictures*, p. 24.

13 *The Green Stick*, p. 141.

14 *The Green Stick*, p. 141.

15 *The Green Stick*, p. 141.

16 *The Green Stick*, pp. 146–7.

17 *The Green Stick*, p. 149.

18 Malcolm Muggeridge to H. T. Muggeridge, April 27, 1926, WCSC.

19 Malcolm Muggeridge to H. T. Muggeridge, July 23, 1925, WCSC.

20 Malcolm Muggeridge to Alec Vidler, November 17, 1927, WCSC.

21 Malcolm Muggeridge to Alec Vidler, April 13, 1928, WCSC.

22 *The Green Stick*, p. 155.

23 *The Green Stick*, p. 156.

24 *Three Flats* (London: G. P. Putnam's Sons, 1931), p. 14. In the character of Dennis, Malcolm also caricatured some aspects of the writer Louis Wilkinson whom he had met in Belgium.

25 *Three Flats*, p. 32.

26 *Three Flats*, p. 101.

27 Beatrice Webb, *The Diary of Beatrice Webb, Vol. 4, 1924–1943* (Cambridge, MA: Harvard University Press, 1985), p. 193.

28 Carole Seymour-Jones, *Beatrice Webb: A Life* (Chicago: Ivan R. Dee, 1992), pp. 306–7.

29 Malcolm Muggeridge to H. T. Muggeridge, August 28, 1928, WCSC.

30 Malcolm Muggeridge to H. T. Muggeridge, November 23, 1928, WCSC.

31 Malcolm Muggeridge to H. T. Muggeridge, September 19, 1929, WCSC.

32 *Malcolm Muggeridge: A Life*, p. 66.

33 "Subject Peoples", *Young Men of India*, October 1928.

34 *The Green Stick*, p. 160.

35 *The Green Stick*, pp. 160–1.

36 Hugh Brogan, *The Life of Arthur Ransome* (London: Jonathan Cape, 1984), p. 308.

37 *The Green Stick*, p. 162.

Chapter 6

1 Malcolm Muggeridge, *Picture Palace* (London: Weidenfeld & Nicolson, 1987). The novel was republished in 1987, with an introduction by Richard Ingrams.

2 *The Green Stick*, p. 167.

3 Kingsley Martin, *Father Figures* (London: Hutchinson & Co., 1966), p. 167.

4 *Picture Palace*, p. 4.

5 *Picture Palace*, p. 9.

6 *Picture Palace*, p. 9.

7 *Picture Palace*, p. 151.

8 A. J. P. Taylor, *A Personal History*, (New York: Atheneum, 1983), p. 109. See also Adam Sisman, A.J.P. Taylor: *A Biography* (London: Sinclair Stevenson, 1994) pp. 90–2.

9 *The Green Stick*, p. 170.

10 *Picture Palace*, p. 29.

11 *Picture Palace*, p. 5.

12 *Manchester Guardian*, July 29, 1931.

13 David Ayerst, *Guardian: Biography of a Newspaper* (London: Collins, 1971), p. 470.

14 "The Government's India Policy", *Manchester Guardian*, June 28, 1932.

15 "This Side Idolatry", *Manchester Guardian*, April 23, 1932.

16 *The Green Stick*, pp. 183–4.

17 Hesketh Pearson and Malcolm Muggeridge, *About Kingsmill* (London: Methuen, 1951), p. 2.

18 *About Kingsmill*, p. 3.

19 *About Kingsmill*, p. 4.

20 *The Green Stick*, pp. 184.

21 *The Green Stick*, pp. 185–6.

22 *Autumnal Face*, p. 55.

23 *Autumnal Face*, pp. 188–9.

24 *Sunday Referee*, December 6, 1931.

25 Kingsley Martin, *Editor* (London: Hutchinson & Co., 1968), p. 2.

26 *A Personal History*, p. 112.

27 *The Green Stick*, p. 142.

28 Unpublished diary entries, August 18, 1933, and August 23, 1933, WCSC.

29 Unpublished diary entry, November 6, 1934, WCSC.

30 *Picture Palace*, p. 67.

31 *Picture Palace*, p. 68.

32 *Picture Palace*, p. 69.

34 Unpublished diary entry, November 20, 1934, WCSC.

35 Unpublished diary entries for November 9, 10, 20 and 21, 1934, WCSC.

36 *Picture Palace*, p. 72.

37 Unpublished diary entry, November 9, 1934, WCSC.

38 Unpublished diary entry, November 10, 1934, WCSC.

39 *Guardian: Biography of a Newspaper*, p. 471.

40 *Guardian: Biography of a Newspaper*, p. 471.

41 *The Green Stick*, p. 197.

42 *The Green Stick*, pp. 199–200.

43 "Death of Mr E. T. Scott", *Manchester Guardian*, April 23, 1932.
44 *The Diary of Beatrice Webb, Vol. 4*, p. 286.
45 *The Green Stick*, p. 203.

Chapter 7

1 *The Green Stick*, p. 205.
2 Malcolm Muggeridge, *Winter in Moscow* (London: Eyre and Spottiswoode, 1934), p. 207.
3 *A Personal History*, p. 111.
4 *Winter in Moscow*, p. 8.
5 *The Green Stick*, p. 211.
6 *The Green Stick*, p. 212.
7 Malcolm Muggeridge, *Like It Was: The Diaries of Malcolm Muggeridge*, selected and edited by John Bright-Holmes (New York: William Morrow, 1982), p. 14.
8 *The Green Stick*, p. 215.
9 *Like It Was*, p. 19.
10 *Like It Was*, p. 22.
11 *Like It Was*, p. 25.
12 *Winter in Moscow*, pp. 89–90.
13 *Winter in Moscow*, pp. 111–12.
14 Eugene Lyons, *Assignment in Utopia* (New York: Twin Circle, 1967 [1937]), p. 221.
15 *The Green Stick*, p. 228.
16 *Like It Was*, p. 38.
17 *The Green Stick*, p. 206.
18 *Like It Was*, p. 39.
19 "Too Much Venus", unpublished manuscript, p. 29, WCSC.
20 Unpublished diary entry, November 4, 1932, WCSC.
21 Unpublished diary entry, November 28, 1932, WCSC.
22 Quoted in *Winter in Moscow*, p. 87.
23 *Like It Was*, p. 30.
24 Alexander Woolcott, "A Personal Note on Walter Duranty", in *Duranty Reports Russia* (New York: Viking Press, 1934), p.*v.*
25 *The Green Stick*, p. 255.
26 *Winter in Moscow*, p. 68.
27 S. J. Taylor, *Stalin's Apologist: Walter Duranty, The* New York Times*'s Man in Moscow* (New York: Oxford University Press, 1990), p. 222.
28 *The Green Stick*, p. 244.
29 *Like It Was*, p. 53.
30 For a comprehensive account of this episode in Russian history, see Robert

Conquest, *The Harvest of Sorrow: Soviet Collectivization and the Terror-Famine* (New York: Oxford University Press, 1986).

31 *The Harvest of Sorrow*, p. 3.

32 *Stalin's Apologist*, pp. 202–3.

33 Quoted in *Guardian: Biography of a Newspaper*, p. 511.

34 *Like It Was*, p. 63.

35 *The Green Stick*, pp. 257–8.

36 *The Green Stick*, pp. 258–9.

37 Red-Orange Journal, Box 2, Journals, WCSC.

38 *The Green Stick*, pp. 259–60.

39 "The Soviet and the Peasantry; An Observer's Notes: I. Famine in North Caucasus; Whole Villages Exiled", *Manchester Guardian*, March 25, 1933.

40 "The Soviet and the Peasantry; An Observer's Notes: III. Poor Harvest in Prospect", *Manchester Guardian*, March 28, 1933.

41 *The Green Stick*, p. 268.

42 *The Green Stick*, pp. 263–5. See also the fictionalised account of this dinner in *Winter in Moscow*, pp. 213–17.

Chapter 8

1 *The Green Stick*, p. 267.

2 *The Green Stick*, p. 268.

3 "The Soviet's War on the Peasants", *Fortnightly*, May 1933.

4 "Russia Revealed. II. Crucifixion of the Peasants", *Morning Post*, June 6, 1933.

5 "Russia Revealed. III. Terror of the G.P.U.", *Morning Post*, June 7, 1933.

6 "Russia Revealed. IV. How the World is Deceived: Art of Gulling our Intelligentsia", *Morning Post*, June 8, 1933.

7 *The Green Stick*, p. 266.

8 *Winter in Moscow*, p. 93–4.

9 *Winter in Moscow*, p. 70–1.

10 *Assignment in Utopia*, p. 221.

11 "Father and Son. Piquant Difference of Opinion on Russia" [published article, source unknown], WCSC.

12 Malcolm Muggeridge to Beatrice Webb, February 8, 1933, quoted in Carole Seymour-Jones, *Beatrice Webb: A Life*, p. 314.

13 Quoted in Paul Hollander, *Political Pilgrims: Travels of Western Intellectuals to the Soviet Union, China, and Cuba* (New York: Harper Colophon, 1983), p. 146.

14 *Stalin's Apologist*, p. 210.

15 *Stalin's Apologist*, p. 220.

16 Quoted in *The Harvest of Sorrow*, p. 320.

17 "To the Friends of the Soviet Union", *English Review*, January 1934, reprinted in *Things Past* (New York: William Morrow, 1979), pp. 27–34.

18 *Stalin's Apologist*, p. 5.

19 Unpublished diary entry, August 16, 1933, WCSC.

20 Unpublished diary entry, August 18, 1933, WCSC.

21 *Scenes from a Clerical Life*, p. 87.

22 Malcolm Muggeridge, *Chronicles of Wasted Time. 2: The Infernal Grove* (New York: William Morrow, 1974), p. 8.

23 *The Infernal Grove*, p. 9.

24 Unpublished diary entry, October 10, 1933, WCSC.

25 Unpublished diary entry, October 11, 1933, WCSC.

26 Unpublished diary entry, December 2, 1933, WCSC.

27 Unpublished diary entry, December 9, 1933, WCSC.

28 Unpublished diary entry, February 2, 1934, WCSC.

29 *Like It Was*, p. 81.

30 *Like It Was*, p. 78.

31 *Like It Was*, p. 79.

32 "Towards a Repetition of 1914", typescript version, WCSC.

33 "Herr Hitler's Cold", *Calcutta Statesman*, March 1935, WCSC.

34 "The Revolt Against Mind", *Calcutta Statesman*, n.d., WCSC.

35 "Totalitarian Religion", *Calcutta Statesman*, October 21, 1934, WCSC.

36 *Like It Was*, p. 78.

37 "Portrait of a Poet", *AAAM International Review*, 1971, p. 11.

38 *The Infernal Grove*, p. 20.

39 Unpublished diary entry, October 25, 1934, WCSC.

40 Unpublished diary entry, November 6, 1934, WCSC.

41 Unpublished diary entry, November 15, 1934, WCSC.

42 Unpublished diary entry, October 26, 1934, WCSC.

43 Unpublished diary entry, November 26, 1934, WCSC.

44 Unpublished diary entry, March 14, 1935, WCSC.

45 *Like It Was*, pp. 104–5.

46 Unpublished diary entry, February 14, 1935, WCSC.

47 Ibid.

48 *Like It Was*, p. 114.

49 Unpublished diary entry, April 3, 1935, WCSC.

50 *Like It Was*, p. 117.

51 *The Infernal Grove*, p. 38.

52 *The Infernal Grove*, p. 44.

53 *Like It Was*, pp. 122–8.

54 Unpublished diary entries, June 6, 10 and 16, 1935, WCSC.

55 *Like It Was*, pp. 129, 131.

56 *Like It Was*, p. 134.

57 *God's Apology: A Chronicle of Three Friends* (London: Hamish Hamilton, 1986 [1977]), pp. 110–1.

58 *The Earnest Atheist: A Study of Samuel Butler* (London: Eyre and Spottiswoode, 1936), pp. *ix–x*.

59 *The Earnest Atheist*, p. 130.

60 *The Earnest Atheist*, p. 10.

61 *The Earnest Atheist*, p. 21.

62 *The Earnest Atheist*, p. 27.

63 *The Earnest Atheist*, p. 36.

64 *The Infernal Grove*, p. 49.

65 *Like It Was*, p. 135.

Chapter 9

1 *Like It Was*, p. 141.

2 *The Diaries of Sir Robert Bruce Lockhart, 1915–1938*, edited by Kenneth Younger (London: Macmillan, 1973), p. 329.

3 "The Londoner's Diary", *Evening Standard*, October 11, 1935.

4 *The Infernal Grove*, p. 59.

5 *The Infernal Grove*, p. 57.

6 *The Infernal Grove*, p. 52.

7 "Lord Beaverbrook", *New Statesman*, December 24, 1955.

8 *The Infernal Grove*, p. 54.

9 *The Infernal Grove*, p. 60.

10 Unpublished diary entry, April 16, 1936, WCSC.

11 Unpublished diary entry, April 17, 1936, WCSC.

12 *The Diaries of Sir Robert Bruce Lockhart, 1915–1938*, p. 375.

13 Interview with Malcolm Muggeridge, *Sunday Post*, March 8, 1970.

14 *In a Valley of This Restless Mind* (London: Collins, 1978 [1938]), p. 170.

15 *The Infernal Grove*, p. 62.

16 *Malcolm Muggeridge: A Life*, p. 108.

17 *About Kingsmill*, p. 74.

18 *About Kingsmill*, p. 22.

19 Richard Ingrams, *God's Apology: A Chronicle of Three Friends*, (London: Hamish Hamilton, 1986), p. 115.

20 *God's Apology*, p. 107.

21 Michael Holroyd, *Hugh Kingsmill: A Critical Biography* (London: Unicorn Press, 1964), p. 85.

22 *God's Apology*, pp. 114, 116.

23 *About Kingsmill*, p. 4.

24 *About Kingsmill*, p. 16.

25 *About Kingsmill*, p. 67.

26 *About Kingsmill*, p. 42–3.

27 *About Kingsmill*, p. 43–4.

28 Hugh Kingsmill and Malcolm Muggeridge, *Brave Old World: A Mirror for the Times* (London: Eyre and Spottiswoode, 1936), p. 3.

29 *Hugh Kingsmill: A Critical Biography*, p. 155.

Notes

30 Christopher Hawtree, editor, *Night and Day* (London: Chatto and Windus, 1985), pp. *vi–xiv*.

31 Unpublished diary entry, November 15, 1936, WCSC.

32 Unpublished diary entry, April 1, 1937, WCSC.

33 Unpublished diary entries, August 19 and 29, 1936, WCSC.

34 "What is My Life?" *Time and Tide*, June 12 and 19, 1937, reprinted in *Things Past*, pp. 57–66.

35 "Faith", *Time and Tide*, October 23, 1937, reprinted in *Things Past*, pp. 69–71.

36 *Things Past*, pp. 76–7.

37 "Time and Eternity", *Time and Tide*, February 6, 1937, reprinted in *Things Past*, pp. 72–7.

38 *The Infernal Grove*, pp. 68–9.

39 Unpublished diary entry, August 30, 1936, WCSC.

Chapter 10

1 Evelyn Waugh, "Desert Islander", *The Essays, Articles and Reviews of Evelyn Waugh* (London: Methuen, 1983), p. 233. Originally published in the *Spectator*, May 27, 1938.

2 "Memoir", unpublished manuscript, p. 6, WCSC.

3 "Memoir", unpublished manuscript, p. 7, WCSC.

4 "Memoir", unpublished manuscript, pp. 41–2, WCSC.

5 Introduction, *In a Valley of This Restless Mind* (London: Collins, 1978 [1938]), p. 11.

6 *In a Valley of This Restless Mind*, p. 15.

7 *In a Valley of This Restless Mind*, p. 40.

8 *In a Valley of This Restless Mind*, p. 94.

9 *In a Valley of This Restless Mind*, pp. 100–2.

10 *The Essays, Articles and Reviews of Evelyn Waugh*, p. 233.

11 *Forward*, April 30, 1938.

12 *Time and Tide*, June 4, 1938.

13 "Why I Am Not a Pacifist", *Time and Tide*, November 28, 1936, reprinted in *Things Past*, pp. 48–53.

14 *The Infernal Grove*, p. 72–3.

15 *The Infernal Grove*, p. 74.

16 *The Infernal Grove*, p. 77.

17 *The Infernal Grove*, p. 79.

18 *The Infernal Grove*, p. 84.

19 *The Infernal Grove*, p. 87.

20 *The Infernal Grove*, p. 85.

21 *The Infernal Grove*, p. 86.

22 *The Infernal Grove*, p. 87.

23 *The Thirties: 1930–1940 in Great Britain* (London: Hamish Hamilton, 1940), p. 29.

24 *The Thirties*, p. 47.

25 *The Thirties*, p. 105.

26 *The Thirties*, p. 258.

27 *The Thirties*, p. 169.

28 *The Thirties*, p. 31.

29 *The Thirties*, p. 314.

30 *The Thirties*, p. 269.

31 *The Thirties*, p. 148.

32 Rebecca West, "Ashes in Your Wine", *Time and Tide*, March 9, 1940.

33 Graham Greene, "The Last Decade", *Listener*, March 14, 1940.

34 George Orwell, "The Limit to Pessimism", *New English Weekly*, April 25, 1940.

35 *The Infernal Grove*, pp. 91–3.

36 *The Infernal Grove*, p. 98.

37 *The Infernal Grove*, p. 99–101.

38 *The Infernal Grove*, p. 104.

39 *The Infernal Grove*, p. 107.

40 *The Infernal Grove*, p. 105.

41 Malcolm Muggeridge to Kitty Muggeridge, undated, WCSC.

42 Malcolm Muggeridge to Kitty Muggeridge, undated, WCSC.

43 *The Infernal Grove*, p. 119.

Chapter 11

1 *The Infernal Grove*, p. 117. See also Norman Sherry, *The Life of Graham Greene, Vol. II: 1939–1955* (New York: Viking, 1945).

2 *The Infernal Grove*, p. 124.

3 *The Infernal Grove*, pp. 130–1.

4 *The Infernal Grove*, p. 125.

5 *The Infernal Grove*, p. 129.

6 *The Knox Brothers*, p. 237.

7 Anthony Masters, *Literary Agents: The Novelist as Spy* (Oxford: Basil Blackwell, 1987), p. 92.

8 *The Infernal Grove*, p. 132–3.

9 *Like It Was*, p. 168.

10 *Like It Was*, p. 168.

11 Unpublished diary entry, April 16, 1942, WCSC.

12 *Like It Was*, p. 177.

13 *The Infernal Grove*, p. 140.

14 Malcolm Muggeridge to Kitty Muggeridge, May 20, 1942, WCSC.

15 *Like It Was*, p. 185.

16 *Like It Was*, p. 187.

17 *The Infernal Grove*, p. 152.

18 *The Infernal Grove*, pp. 153–4.

19 *Literary Agents*, pp. 101–2.

20 *The Infernal Grove*, p. 170.

21 *The Infernal Grove*, pp. 173–4.

22 John Mockford to Malcolm Muggeridge, October 21, 1974, WCSC.

23 *The Infernal Grove*, p. 165.

24 Malcolm Muggeridge to Kitty Muggeridge, November 1942, WCSC.

25 John Mockford to Malcolm Muggeridge, October 21, 1974, WCSC.

26 Unpublished diary entry, July 17, 1943, WCSC.

27 *The Infernal Grove*, p. 180.

28 *The Infernal Grove*, p. 181.

29 "Public Thoughts on a Secret Service", *Tread Softly for You Tread on My Jokes* (London: Collins, 1966), p. 219.

30 Unpublished diary entry, July 17, 1943, WCSC.

31 *The Infernal Grove*, pp. 183–4.

32 *Daily Sketch*, April 14, 1966.

33 *The Infernal Grove*, p. 186.

Chapter 12

1 *The Infernal Grove*, p. 188.

2 Malcolm Muggeridge to Kitty Muggeridge, October 7, 1943, WCSC.

3 *Tread Softly for You Tread on My Jokes*, pp. 207–8.

4 *The Infernal Grove*, pp. 192–3.

5 *The Infernal Grove*, p. 205.

6 Malcolm Muggeridge to Kitty Muggeridge, December 25, 1943, WCSC.

7 *The Infernal Grove*, p. 195.

8 *The Infernal Grove*, p. 196.

9 Unpublished diary entry, April 18 [1944], WCSC.

10 *The Infernal Grove*, p. 199.

11 *The Infernal Grove*, p. 209.

12 *The Infernal Grove*, pp. 209–10.

13 *The Infernal Grove*, p. 211.

14 *The Infernal Grove*, p. 221.

15 *The Infernal Grove*, p. 216.

16 *The Infernal Grove*, p. 227.

17 *The Infernal Grove*, p. 225.

18 "Liberation", unpublished play, p. 57, WCSC.

19 "Liberation", p. 30.

20 Malcolm Muggeridge to Kitty Muggeridge, November 15, 1944, WCSC.

21 "What Price Glory?", *Tread Softly for You Tread on My Jokes*, p. 205.

Notes

22 Unpublished diary entry, May 1, 1945, WCSC.

23 *The Infernal Grove*, p. 237.

24 Kim Philby, *My Silent War* (New York: Grove Press, 1968), pp. 48, 97.

25 *The Infernal Grove*, pp. 258–9.

Chapter 13

1 Unpublished manuscript, "The Right Eye", WCSC.

2 Anthony Powell, *To Keep the Ball Rolling*, p. 263.

3 *Like It Was*, p. 193.

4 *The Infernal Grove*, p. 261.

5 *The Infernal Grove*, p. 259.

6 Unpublished manuscript, "The Right Eye", WCSC.

7 Unpublished manuscript, "The Right Eye", WCSC.

8 *Like It Was*, p. 208.

9 *Like It Was*, p. 194.

10 *Faces in My Time*, pp. 82-6.

11 George Orwell, "As I Please" in *The Collected Essays, Journalism and Letters of George Orwell, Vol.III, As I Please, 1943–45*, edited by Sonia Orwell and Ian Argus (New York: Harcourt, Brace & World, 1968), p. 63.

12 George Orwell, "Notes on Nationalism", *As I Please*, p. 372.

13 *Like It Was*, p. 195.

14 "George Orwell", *English Review*, March 1950, p. 218.

15 Julian Symons, "Orwell: A Reminiscence", *London Magazine*, September 1963, pp. 41–2.

16 *Like It Was*, p. 204–5.

17 Unpublished diary entry, March 28, 1946, WCSC.

18 *Like It Was*, p. 212.

19 *Like It Was*, p. 216.

20 Malcolm Muggeridge to Kitty Muggeridge, April 16, 1946, WCSC.

21 Malcolm Muggeridge to Hugh Kingsmill, May 12, 1946, WCSC.

22 Malcolm Muggeridge to Kitty Muggeridge, April 21, 1946, WCSC.

23 Malcolm Muggeridge to Kitty Muggeridge, April 24, 1946, WCSC.

24 *Like It Was*, p. 223.

25 *Muggeridge: Ancient and Modern* pp. 225–6.

26 *Muggeridge: Ancient and Modern*, p. 224.

27 *Like It Was*, p. 222.

28 Malcolm Muggeridge to Kitty Muggeridge, July 1, 1946, and September 30, 1946, WCSC.

29 Malcolm Muggeridge, "79th Congress Marked an Epoch in History of U.S.", *Daily Telegraph*, August 2, 1946.

30 *Muggeridge: Ancient and Modern*, p. 226.

31 Unpublished diary entry, April 18, 1946, WCSC.

32 Malcolm Muggeridge to Kitty Muggeridge, August 10, 1946, WCSC.

33 "Introduction", *Ciano's Diary*, (London: Heineman, 1947), reprinted in *Things Past*, pp. 91, 93.

34 *Like It Was*, p. 229.

35 *Like It Was*, p. 231–2.

36 *Like It Was*, pp. 234–5.

37 *Like It Was*, p. 236.

Chapter 14

1 *About Kingsmill* p. 24.

2 *Like It Was*, p. 243.

3 BBC broadcast, January 1, 1941.

4 Unpublished diary entry, April 4, 1948, WCSC.

5 *Like It Was*, p. 264.

6 Quoted in Myrna Grant, "An Historical Analysis of Biographical, Societal and Organizational Factors Shaping the Radio Career of Thomas Malcolm Muggeridge, 1948–1957", doctoral dissertation, Northwestern University, 1986, p. 151. Hereafter referred to as "Radio Career of Malcolm Muggeridge".

7 Quoted in "Radio Career of Malcolm Muggeridge", p. 137.

8 Harman Grisewood to H.D.T., June 3, 1948, WCSC.

9 G. B. Barnes to Malcolm Muggeridge, June 18, 1948, WCSC.

10 *Like It Was*, p. 280.

11 "Radio Career of Malcolm Muggeridge", p. 146.

12 Malcolm Muggeridge, "Lord Reith's Self-Portrait of a Disappointed Man", *Daily Telegraph*, November 17, 1949.

13 Malcolm Muggeridge, "My Life in the BBC", Reprinted in *Tread Softly*, pp. 191–8.

14 "Radio Career of Malcolm Muggeridge", pp. 147–8.

15 "Radio Career of Malcolm Muggeridge", p. 168.

16 Malcolm Muggeridge, *Affairs of the Heart* (New York: Dell, 1965 [1949]), pp. 11–12.

17 *The Diary of Beatrice Webb, Vol. 4*, p. 488.

18 Unpublished diary entry, June 26, 1950, WCSC.

19 *Affairs of the Heart*, p. 155.

20 Unpublished diary entry, March 24, 1948, WCSC.

21 *Hugh Kingsmill: A Critical Biography*, pp. 208–9.

22 *Like It Was*, p. 268.

23 Unpublished diary entry, January 20, 1949, WCSC.

24 *Like It Was*, p. 320.

25 *Like It Was*, p. 334.

26 *About Kingsmill*, pp. 112–3.

27 *About Kingsmill*, p. 170.

28 T.R. Fyvel, *Orwell: A Personal Memoir* (New York: Macmillan, 1982), pp. 164–5.

29 *Like It Was*, p. 375.

30 John Rodden, *The Politics of Literary Reputation: The Making and Claiming of 'St George' Orwell* (Oxford: Oxford University Press, 1989), pp. 142, 148.

31 Unpublished manuscript, "A Portrait of Our Time: A Socialist Father", WCSC.

32 *Like It Was*, p. 385.

33 Malcolm Muggeridge, "Britain's Decline in Prestige", *Daily Telegraph*, July 30, 1951.

34 Malcolm Muggeridge, "Communism and Christianity", *Daily Telegraph*, September 9, 1951.

35 *Like It Was*, p. 262.

36 Phillip Knightley, *The Master Spy* (New York: Knopf, 1989), p. 182.

37 Malcolm Muggeridge, "Senator McCarthy McCarthyised, or The Biter Bit", reprinted in *Tread Softly*, p. 131.

38 *Like It Was*, pp. 341–2.

39 *Like It Was*, pp. 401–2.

40 *Like It Was*, p. 440.

41 *Like It Was*, pp. 393–5.

42 *Like It Was*, p. 420.

Chapter 15

1 *My Life in Pictures*, p. 63.

2 *Malcolm Muggeridge: A Life*, p. 184.

3 Anthony Powell, *To Keep the Ball Rolling*, p. 353.

4 *Time*, September 14, 1953.

5 Claud Cockburn, *I, Claud* (London: Penguin. 1967), pp. 358–9.

6 *I, Claud*, p. 378.

7 *I, Claud*, p. 362.

8 *Punch*, April 29, 1953, p. 510.

9 *Muggeridge: Ancient and Modern*, p. 238.

10 *Things Past*, pp. 128–9.

11 *New Yorker*, May 23, 1953, p. 27.

12 *Like It Was*, p. 454.

13 "Advice to Diplomats" *Punch*, August 19, 1953, p. 220.

14 "Sponsored Escalation", *Punch*, July 29, 1953, p. 134.

15 *To Keep the Ball Rolling*, p. 358.

16 *Punch*, February 3, 1954.

17 *I, Claud*, p. 366.

18 *To Keep the Ball Rolling*, p. 360.

19 *Newsweek*, April 23, 1956.

20 *I, Claud*, p. 371.

21 *I, Claud*, p. 373.

22 Arthur Prager, *The Mahogany Tree*, (New York: Hawthorn Books, 1979), p. 28.

23 *Daily Telegraph*, January 18, 1951.

24 "Television – Commercial Competition?", *Listener*, February 11, 1954, pp. 251–2.

25 *Tread Softly*, p. 195.

26 *My Life in Pictures*, p. 72.

27 *Muggeridge: Ancient and Modern*, pp. 247–8.

28 *Muggeridge: Ancient and Modern*, p. 145.

29 *Tread Softly*, p. 308.

30 Peter Black, *The Mirror in the Corner*, (London: Hutchinson, 1972), p. 126.

31 *Like It Was*, p. 471.

32 *I, Claud*, pp. 370–1.

33 Malcolm Muggeridge, *Some Answers*, (London: Methueun, 1982), p. 42.

34 *Some Answers*, p. 74.

35 *Some Answers*, p. 85.

36 *Some Answers*, p. 465.

37 *Like It Was*, p. 487.

38 *Muggeridge: Ancient and Modern*, pp. 188–91.

39 *The Times*, March 14, 1956.

40 *The Times*, March 15, 1956.

41 *Truth*, March 29, 1956.

42 *The Times*, March 27, 1956.

43 *News Chronicle*, April 13, 1956.

44 Unpublished diary entry, September 13, 1948, WCSC.

45 Unpublished diary entries, December 17, 1949, and January 6, 1950, WCSC.

46 John Muggeridge to author.

47 *Like It Was*, p. 471.

48 Peter Black, *The Biggest Aspidistra in the World* (London: British Broadcasting Corporation, 1972), p. 155.

49 *The Times*, January 8, 1982. Michael Berry was made a Life Peer in 1968, and known as Lord Hartwell. Pamela Berry became Lady Hartwell.

50 Unpublished diary entry, January 14, 1954, WCSC.

51 *Like It Was*, p. 468.

52 Unpublished diary entry, March 28, 1957, WCSC.

53 Unpublished diary entry, March 30, 1957, WCSC.

54 *Like It Was*, p. 388.

55 *Like It Was*, p. 434.

56 Unpublished diary entry, January 21, 1962, WCSC.

57 *Like It Was*, p. 427.

58 *Like It Was*, p. 457.

59 *The Mahogany Tree*, pp. 248–9.

60 *The Mahogany Tree*, p. 249.
61 *Tread Softly*, p. 11.

Chapter 16

1 *People*, October 13, 1957.
2 "Royal Soap Opera", *New Statesman*, October 22, 1955.
3 "Does England Really Need a Queen?", *Saturday Evening Post*, October 19, 1957.
4 *Railway Review*, November 15, 1957.
5 Henry Fairlie, "An Anatomy of Hysteria", *Spectator*, November 8, 1957, pp. 600–1.
6 *The Times*, October 15, 1957.
7 *The Mirror in the Corner*, p. 125.
8 *The Times*, October 17, 1957.
9 "The Queen and I", *Encounter*, June 1961.
10 Alistair Cooke, *American Observed* (New York: Knopf, 1988), pp. 105–6.
11 "The Mike Wallace Interview", October 19, 1957, transcript, WCSC.
12 Quoted in *Time*, December 23, 1957.
13 *The Times*, October 17, 1957.
14 *Manchester Guardian*, November 15, 1957.
15 *I, Claud*, p. 398.
16 "The Queen and I".
17 *The Times*, January 23, 1958.
18 *The Times*, April 13, 1964.
19 *My Life in Pictures*, p. 68.
20 "The Queen and I"
21 Interview with Geoffrey Barlow, conducted by Myrna Grant, WCSC.
22 *My Life in Pictures*, p. 74.
23 "In Defence of Bad Taste", *Maclean's Magazine*, August 3, 1957, reprinted in *Things Past*, p. 120.
24 *Things Past*, p. 105.
25 *Things Past*, p. 122.
26 *Things Past*, p. 105.
27 Australian Broadcast Commission transcript, May 4, 1958.
28 *West Australian*, May 10, 1958.
29 *Tread Softly*, pp. 154–6.
30 *West Australian*, May 12, 1958.
31 *South China Morning Post*, June 9, 1958.
32 *Like It Was*, p. 492.
33 *Like It Was*, p. 493.
34 *Like It Was*, p. 495.
35 *Like It Was*, pp. 498–9.

36 *West Australian*, July 30, 1958.
37 *Like It Was*, p. 501.
38 *Sunday Pictorial*, November 11, 1958.
39 "Ten Days That Didn't Shake the World", *New Statesman*, March 14, 1959.
40 *Daily Mirror*, February 25, 1959.
41 "*Krokodil*", *New Statesman*, February 20, 1969, reprinted in *Things Past*.
42 "Pursuit of Happiness (International) Inc.", *New Statesman*, September 13, 1958.
43 "London Diary", *New Statesman*, February 8, 1958.
44 Unpublished diary entry, January 18, 1962, WCSC.
45 *Like It Was*, p. 520.
46 Alexander Walker, *Peter Sellers* (New York: Macmillan, 1981), p. 97.
47 *Like It Was*, p. 522.
48 *Muggeridge: Ancient and Modern*, p. 199.
49 Unpublished diary entry, August 15, 1961, WCSC.
50 *Like It Was*, p. 525.
51 *Like It Was*, p. 534.

Chapter 17

1 Malcolm Muggeridge, "What I Believe" in *What I Believe* (London: Allen and Unwin, 1966), reprinted in *Things Past*, pp. 161–6.
2 "Life and the Legend, Or Queen for a Day", unpublished play, WCSC.
3 "Life and the Legend" (essay), reprinted in *Tread Softly*, p. 319.
4 *Muggeridge: Ancient and Modern*, p. 181.
5 Richard Ingrams, *The Life and Times of* Private Eye, *1961–71* (London: Pressdram, 1971), pp. 7–11.
6 Christopher Booker, "Beneath the Carapace", *National Review*, December 31, 1990.
7 *The Life and Times of* Private Eye, p. 108.
8 "The Hollow Tooth", *New Statesman*, August 24, 1962.
9 *Muggeridge: Ancient and Modern*, pp. 65–76.
10 J. D. S. Haworth, "Documentary", *Listener*, October 27, 1966, p. 631.
11 *Muggeridge: Ancient and Modern*, pp. 182–3.
12 *Muggeridge: Ancient and Modern*, pp. 184–5.
13 *Tread Softly*, p. 130.
14 *New Statesman*, May 10, 1958.
15 *Malcolm Muggeridge: A Life*, p. 210.
16 Kingsley Amis, *Memoirs* (London: Hutchinson, 1991), pp. 232–5.
17 Jack Muggeridge, communication to Wheaton College Special Collections, June 11, 1994.
18 *Evening News*, December 3, 1965.

19 Bernard Levin, *Run It Down the Flagpole: Britain in the Sixties* (New York: Atheneum, 1971), pp. 89–98.

20 *Tread Softly*, p. 57.

21 Introduction, *In a Valley of This Restless Mind*, p. 10.

22 *London A La Mode* (London: Studio Vista, 1966), p. 17.

23 Quoted in *My Life in Pictures*, p. 85.

24 *Things Past*, pp. 203–4.

25 *Muggeridge: Ancient and Modern*, pp. 96-104.

26 *Jesus Rediscovered*, p. 109.

27 Simone Weil, *Waiting on God* (London: Fontana, 1950), pp. 93–4.

28 *Jesus Rediscovered*, p. 132.

29 *Jesus Rediscovered*, pp. 197–8.

30 *Jesus Rediscovered*, p. 83.

31 *Jesus Rediscovered*, pp. 104–5.

32 *Muggeridge: Ancient and Modern*, pp. 153–7.

33 *My Life in Pictures*, p. 78.

34 *Muggeridge: Ancient and Modern*, p. 187.

35 *New Statesman*, September 9, 1966, p. 360.

36 *Jesus Rediscovered*, pp. 93–9.

37 Alan Paton, *Instrument of Thy Peace* (New York: Seabury Press, 1968), pp. 23–4.

38 *Listener*, March 16, 1967.

39 *Jesus Rediscovered*, pp. 150–7.

40 *Muggeridge: Ancient and Modern*, pp. 200–5.

41 *Jesus Rediscovered*, pp. x–xi, 2; *My Life in Pictures*, pp. 92–3; "Londoner's Diary", *New Statesman*, September 12, 1969.

42 William Oddie to author.

43 *Jesus Rediscovered*, p. 10.

44 *Jesus Rediscovered*, pp. 8, 15, 21.

45 *The Times*, April 13, 1968.

46 *Jesus Rediscovered*, p. 26.

Chapter 18

1 *The Times*, November 11, 1966.

2 Malcolm Muggeridge to Brian McClelland, December 7, 1966, WCSC.

3 *The Times*, February 17, 1967.

4 *Jesus Rediscovered*, pp. 54–5.

5 *Jesus Rediscovered*, p. xii.

6 *The Times*, January 17, 1968.

7 *The Times*, January 19, 1968.

8 *Something Beautiful for God* (London: Collins, 1971), p. 39.

9 *Listener*, May 23, 1968.

10 *Something Beautiful for God*, p. 37.

11 *Something Beautiful for God*, pp. 114, 97.

12 *Jesus Rediscovered*, pp. x–xi.

13 *Jesus Rediscovered*, pp. 30–49.

14 *Daily Sketch*, April 14, 1966.

15 *The Times*, June 21, 1969.

16 *Listener*, March 4, 1982.

17 *Scenes from a Clerical Life*, p. 192.

18 *Paul: Envoy Extraordinary* (New York: Harper and Row, 1982), pp. 45–6.

19 *Paul: Envoy Extraordinary*, pp. 153–4.

20 *New Statesman*, September 12, 1969.

21 *The Times*, September 10, 1971.

22 *The Times*, September 27, 1971.

23 Quoted in Lord Longford, *The Grain of Wheat* (London: Collins, 1974), p. 229.

24 Mary Craig, *Longford: A Biographical Portrait* (London: Hodder and Stoughton, 1978), pp. 165–75.

25 *The Longford Report* (London: Coronet, 1972).

26 *Something Beautiful for God*, pp. 141–2.

27 Eileen Egan, *Such a Vision of the Street* (New York: Doubleday, 1985), pp. 194–5.

28 *Such a Vision of the Street*, pp. 208–9.

29 Fr John Kilmartin, F.D.P., to author.

30 *The Green Stick*, p. 11.

31 *The Times*, September 28, 1972.

32 *The Green Stick*, pp. 15–16.

33 Christopher Booker to Malcolm Muggeridge, August 5, 1970.

34 *The Green Stick*, pp. 19, 22.

35 *The Green Stick*, p. 126.

Chapter 19

1 Malcolm Muggeridge, *Jesus: The Man Who Lives* (London: Fontana, 1976), p. 37.

2 *Jesus: The Man Who Lives*, p. 31.

3 *Jesus: The Man Who Lives*, pp. 97, 153.

4 *Jesus: The Man Who Lives*, p. 162.

5 Malcolm Muggeridge to Mother Teresa, July 31, 1975.

6 *A Third Testament* (Boston: Little, Brown, 1976), p. 14.

7 Richard Nielsen to author.

8 Pat Ferns to author.

9 Pat Ferns to author.

10 *A Third Testament*, pp. 119–45.

11 Quoted in *The End of Christendom* (Grand Rapids, MI: Wm.B.Eerdmans, 1980), p. 43.

12 "The Vision of Solzhenitsyn", *Firing Line* transcript, March 27, 1976.

13 Aleksandr Solzhenitsyn to Malcolm Muggeridge, January 25, 1982, and March 7, 1983.

14 *The Human Life Review*, Winter/Spring 1985.

15 *Christ and the Media*, p. 121.

16 *Christ and the Media*, pp. 40–1.

17 *Christ and the Media*, pp. 51–3.

18 *Christ and the Media*, p. 122.

19 *The Times*, February 2, 1975.

20 *Vintage Muggeridge* (Grand Rapids, MI: Wm.B.Eerdmans, 1985), p. 63.

21 *Sentenced to Life* (Nashville, TN: Thomas Nelson Publishers, 1983).

22 Rita Marker, *Deadly Compassion* (New York: William Morrow, 1993).

23 *An Ark for Our Time*, typescript commentary, WCSC.

24 *Vintage Muggeridge*, p. 59.

25 *Things Past*, pp. 218–9.

26 Germaine Greer, *Sex and Destiny: The Politics of Human Fertility* (New York: Harper and Row, 1984).

27 *The Canadian*, October 13/14, 1979.

28 *The End of Christendom*, p. 24.

29 Quoted in *Malcolm Muggeridge: A Life*, p. 241.

Chapter 20

1 Lord Longford, *Diary of A Year* (London: Weidenfeld and Nicholson, 1982), p. 7.

2 *Varsity*, May 13, 1967.

3 *National Review*, December 31, 1990.

4 *Muggeridge: Ancient and Modern*, pp. 37–9.

5 Excerpts from Svetlana's letters to Malcolm were printed in the *Listener*, March 4, 1982.

6 *My Life in Pictures*, p. 99.

7 "Beneath the Carapace", *National Review*, December 31, 1990; *The Times*, June 14, 1994.

8 "Truth vs. Facts", *Idler*, July & August 1991.

9 Malcolm Muggeridge to Fr Bidone, n.d. [1981 or 1982].

10 Robert Nowell, "The Spiritual Pilgrimage of Malcolm Muggeridge", *St Anthony Messenger*, November 1983.

11 Mother Teresa to Malcolm Muggeridge, October 31, 1982.

12 *Confessions of a Twentieth-Century Pilgrim*, p. 11.

13 *The Times*, November 27, 1982.

14 Graham Greene to Malcolm Muggeridge, November 3, 1982.

15 *Something Beautiful for God*, p. 56.

16 *The End of Christendom*, p. 59.

17 Conversation between Malcolm Muggeridge and author.

18 *My Life in Pictures*, p. 104.

19 "Malcolm Muggeridge: A Memoir", *Touchstone*, March, 1991.

20 Anne Roche Muggeridge to author.

21 "The Spiritual Pilgrimage of Malcolm Muggeridge".

22 "The Same Stance, Yet Five Years a Catholic", *Catholic Herald*, March 18, 1988.

23 John and Anne Roche Muggeridge to author.

24 *Listener*, December 18 and 25, 1980.

25 Ronald Reagan, *Abortion and the Conscience of the Nation* (Nashville, TN: Thomas Nelson Publishers, 1984), p. 11.

26 *The Green Stick*, p. 11.

27 Leonard Muggeridge to author.

28 John Muggeridge, "Dilemma of a Pre-Conciliar Convert", *The Latin Mass*, Winter 1995.

29 The section on Malcolm's last years is derived from conversations with Jack Muggeridge, Leonard Muggeridge, and John and Anne Roche Muggeridge.

30 *The Green Stick*, p. 14.

BIBLIOGRAPHY

Books by Malcolm Muggeridge

Three Flats. London: G. P. Putnam's Sons, 1931.

Autumnal Face. London: Putnam, 1931.

Picture Palace. London: Eyre and Spottiswoode, 1934, withdrawn. London: Weidenfield and Nicolson, 1987.

Winter in Moscow. London: Eyre and Spottiswoode, 1934. Grand Rapids, MI: Wm.B.Eerdmans, 1987.

The Earnest Atheist: A Study of Samuel Butler. London: Eyre and Spottiswoode, 1936.

Brave Old World: A Mirror for the Times (with Hugh Kingsmill). London: Eyre and Spottiswoode, 1936.

Next Year's News (with Hugh Kingsmill). London: Eyre and Spottiswoode, 1938.

In a Valley of This Restless Mind. London: George Routledge and Son, 1938. London and Cleveland: Collins, 1978.

The Thirties: 1930–1940 in Great Britain. London: Hamish Hamilton, 1940. London: Collins, 1967. London: Weidenfield and Nicholson, 1989. Published in the US as *The Sun Never Sets: The Story of England in the 1930s* (New York, 1940).

Affairs of the Heart. London: Hamish Hamilton, 1949. New York: Dell, 1965.

About Kingsmill (With Hesketh Pearson). London: Methuen, 1951.

Tread Softly for You Tread on My Jokes. London: Collins, 1966; in United States, *The Most of Malcolm Muggeridge*. New York: Simon and Schuster, 1966.

London à La Mode (with Paul Hogarth). London: Studio Vista, 1966.

Muggeridge Through the Microphone. London: BBC Publications, 1967; London: Fontana, 1969.

Jesus Rediscovered. London: Fontana, 1969. London: Hodder & Stoughton, 1995. New York: Doubleday, 1969

Something Beautiful for God. London: Collins, 1971. New York: Harper and Row, 1971

Paul: Envoy Extraordinary (with Alec Vidler). New York: Harper and Row, 1972.
Chronicles of Wasted Time:
The Green Stick. London: Collins, 1972. New York: William Morrow, 1973
The Infernal Grove. London: Collins, 1973. New York: William Morrow, 1974
Jesus: The Man Who Lives. London: Collins, 1975.
A Third Testament. Boston: Little, Brown and Co., 1976.
Christ and the Media. London: Hodder and Stoughton, 1976. Grand Rapids, MI: Wm.B.Eerdmans, 1976.
Things Past. London: Collins, 1978. New York: Wm. Morrow, 1979.
Some Answers. London: Methuen, 1982.
Muggeridge: Ancient and Modern [revised and amplified edition of *Muggeridge Through the Microphone*]. London: BBC Publications, 1981.
Like It Was: The Diaries of Malcolm Muggeridge. London: Collins, 1981. New York: William Morrow, 1982.
Vintage Muggeridge: Religion and Society. Angel Press, 1985. Grand Rapids, MI: Wm. B. Eerdmans, 1985.
Conversion: A Spiritual Journey. London: Collins, 1988; published in the US as *Confessions of a Twentieth-Century Pilgrim.* San Francisco: Harper and Row, 1988.

Books edited by Malcolm Muggeridge

Ciano's Diary. London: Heinemann, 1947.
Ciano's Diplomatic Papers. London: Odham's Press, 1948.
Ciano's Hidden Diary. London: F. P. Button, 1953.
Mother Teresa, *A Gift for God.* London: Collins, 1975.

Other Sources

Claud Cockburn, *I, Claud.* London: Penguin, 1967.
Michael Holroyd, *Hugh Kingsmill: A Critical Biography.* London: Unicorn Press, 1964.
Richard Ingrams, *God's Apology: A Chronicle of Three Friends.* London: Andre Deutsch, 1977. London: Hamish Hamilton, 1986.
Ian Hunter, *Malcolm Muggeridge: A Life.* London: Collins, 1980.
Anthony Powell, *To Keep the Ball Rolling.* London: Penguin, 1983.
Michael Shelden, *George Orwell.* New York: HarperCollins, 1991.
Norman Sherry, *The Life of Graham Greene, Vol. I: 1904–1939.* New York: Viking, 1989. *Vol. II: 1939–1955.* New York: Viking, 1995.
Martin Stannard, *Evelyn Waugh: Vol. I: The Early Years.* New York: W.W. Norton, 1987. *Vol. II: The Later Years.* New York: W.W. Norton, 1992.

INDEX

Index

Index

Index

Index

Index

Index

Masters, William H. and Johnson, Virginia
E., 332
Mathail (Indian sadhu), 52, 62, 72
Maugham, W. Somerset, 276
Mauriac, François, 218
Maxwell, Elsa, 316
Maxwell, Father Vincent, 407
Mayhew, Christopher, 276
Mayor, Andreas, 183–4, 237
Meeting Point, 354
Melk, Austria, 74–5
Menzies, Sir Stuart ("C"), 190–1
Methuen (publishers), 176
Metropolitan-Vickers Electrical Company
(Metro-Vic), 115
MI6, 188–90, 206, 260
Mike Wallace Interview, The, 298
Miller, Arthur, 316
Miller, Jonathan, 321, 334
Minia, Egypt: Government Secondary
School, 71–3
Missionaries of Charity, 354, 356, 363, 371–2
Mockford, John, 200
Molesey Venture, 373
monarchy: MM criticises, 293–302, 350
Monkhouse, Alan, 87
Monkhouse, Allan, 115
Monkhouse, Paddy, 84, 95
Montgomery, Field Marshal Bernard Law,
1st Viscount, 195, 261–2, 328, 401
Month, The (magazine), 361
Montherlant, Henri de, 218
Moore, Dudley, 321
Moorhouse, Geoffrey, 334
Moral Rearmament movement, 155, 166
Morea, SS, 47–8
Morning Post (newspaper), 119–20, 124, 224
Morris, William, 4
Moscow, 101–2, 105, 360
Mother Teresa's Co-Workers, 363
Mountbatten, Louis, 1st Earl, 273
Mozambique *see* Lourenço Marques
Muggeridge: Ancient and Modern (MM), 316,
402, 403
Muggeridge, Anne Roche (John's wife), 363,
410, 412
Muggeridge, Annie (*née* Booler; MM's
mother): marriage, 5–6; appearance, 8;
and husband's absences, 18; sexual
attitudes, 18–19; depicted in MM's *Three
Flats*, 75; home bombed in war, 185, 193;
and husband's decline and death, 192; in
MM's autobiography, 376
Muggeridge, Charles (Kitty's son by
Vyvyan): born, 141–2; character, 228–30;
relations with MM, 228–9, 286–7; carves

MM's name into *Punch* Table, 268; killed
while skiing, 286–7, 290, 376
Muggeridge, Douglas (MM's brother), 7, 17,
27
Muggeridge, Eric (MM's brother), 7, 23
Muggeridge, Henry Ambrose (MM's
grandfather), 2
Muggeridge, Henry Thomas (MM's father):
and MM's birth, 1; relations with MM,
1–2, 6–8, 10, 15–16, 25–6, 64, 89, 94, 139,
192–3; background and career, 2–3;
political and religious views, 3–6, 24, 31,
80, 380; marriage, 5–6; and MM's
schooling, 9; reading, 10–11; discussion
groups and meetings, 11–12, 14; as
Croydon Councillor, 14–16, 18, 26, 95;
designs house, 14; as Member of
Parliament, 14, 26, 76; and World War I,
17–18; absences from home, 18; and MM
at Cambridge, 27–9, 31, 33–4, 36; and son
Stanley's death, 37, 376; quarrel over
MM's debts, 40, 60; sees MM off to India,
46; letters from MM in India, 54–7, 60,
63, 71; criticises MM's short stories, 58;
declines offer of directorship, 63; meets
MM in Italy, 63; unworldliness, 64; not
invited to MM's wedding, 69; and Webbs,
69–70; depicted in MM's writings, 75–6,
89–90; sees MM's *Three Flats*, 88; loses
parliamentary seat (1931), 94–5; admires
USSR, 117; and MM's *Winter in Moscow*,
122; MM dedicates *The Earnest Atheist* to,
149; health decline and death, 185, 192–3
Muggeridge, Jack (MM's brother), 7, 23, 31,
417
Muggeridge, John (MM's son): born, 114,
118; childhood, 142; relations with MM,
228; education, 287; emigrates to Canada
and marries, 363; MM visits in Canada,
397; on MM's religious observances, 412;
and MM in old age, 417–18; at MM's
funeral, 419; suggests MM's tombstone
epitaph, 421
Muggeridge, Katherine (*née* Dobbs, Kitty;
MM's wife): MM meets, 44–5; and MM's
absence in India, 61; background, 66–8;
courtship and marriage, 68–9; in Egypt,
71–2; marriage relations, 72, 91–4, 124–5,
127, 134, 141, 158, 191, 229, 249–50,
363–4; pregnancies and children, 72, 76,
101, 105–7, 114, 118, 127–8; near-
miscarriage, 75–6; depicted in MM's
Autumnal Face, 89–90; sexuality, 91, 124;
affairs, 93; in USSR, 97, 98–9, 101;
contracts typhus, 105–7; leaves USSR,
108; Vyvyan falls for, 108, 125; meets MM
on return from USSR, 118, 124; affair

Index

with biography of MM, 397; at MM's
8oth birthday, 412; explains Eucharist to
MM, 412; death, 419
Vintage Muggeridge (MM), 414
Volkov, Anna, 183
Vyvyan, Michael: infatuation with Kitty, 108,
125; MM meets in Moscow, 108; Kitty's
affair with, 133; qualities, 139; fathers
Kitty's child (Charles), 141

Waddell, Helen: *The Wandering Scholars*, 289
Wade Collection, Wheaton College, Illinois,
414
Wadsworth, A. P., 95
Wafd (Egyptian nationalist party), 74, 77
Wallace, Henry, 236
Wallace, Mike, 298–300
Warburg, Fredric, 253
Washington, DC, 229–37
Watkins, Alan, 412
Watson, Alfred, 129, 223
Watson, Arthur, 223–4, 256
Waugh, Auberon, 400, 412
Waugh, Evelyn, 7, 156, 163, 168–9, 184, 210,
215, 227, 240, 248; satirical writings, 322,
420; *The Ordeal of Gilbert Pinfold*, 248;
Scoop, 144
Webb, Beatrice (*later* Lady Passfield): and
MM's father, 12, 69–70; view of USSR,
27, 117, 122–3, 209, 243, 375, 392; and
Dobbs family, 44, 61, 66; influence on
sister Rosy, 44; character and appearance,
67, 70; and Kitty, 67–8; MM on, 70, 179;
social manner, 71; and MM's *Three Flats*,
75, 77; praises MM, 80; and Kitty in
USSR, 97; status in USSR, 106; MM
satirises, 155; in MM's *In a Valley of This
Restless Mind*, 167; MM broadcasts on,
243–4; diary, 249; on MM's attraction to
Catholicism, 249; Kitty's life of, 344; *Our
Partnership* (with Sydney), 243; *Soviet
Communism: a New Civilisation?* (with
Sydney), 123
Webb, Sidney (*later* Baron Passfield): and
Fabian Society, 4; visits MM's home, 12;
idealises USSR, 27, 117, 122, 209, 375,
392; appearance, 67, 70–1; praises MM,
80; status in USSR, 106; MM satirises,
155; in MM's *In a Valley of This Restless

Mind, 167; and scientific socialism, 179;
MM broadcasts on, 243
Week with Svetlana, A, 403
Weil, Simone, 339, 358, 408, 410
welfare state, 225, 241
Welles, Orson, 246
Wells, H. G., 12, 89, 253, 255
Wertz, Leopold, 195–7, 201, 204, 360
West, (Dame) Rebecca, 180
Western University, Ontario, 397
Westminster Theatre, 393
What I Believe (MM), 341
'What Is My Life?' (MM), 159, 397
Whatlington, Sussex, 146, 148, 163, 171, 256;
419
Wheaton College, Illinois, 374, 413–14
White, Antonia, 268
Whitehouse, Mary, 366–7
'Why I am becoming a Catholic' (MM), 406
'Why I am Not a Pacifist' (MM), 170
Wilkinson, Louis and Nan, 45
Williams, Alan, 187
Williams, Charles, 148, 414
Willingdon, Freeman Freeman-Thomas, 1st
Marquess of and Marie, Marchioness of,
135
Wilson, A. N., 414
Wilson, (Sir) Angus, 268
Wilson, Trevor, 208, 212
Winn, Godfrey, 331
Winter in Moscow (MM), 99–100, 104, 110,
120–2, 128, 131, 134, 177
Wodehouse, P. G., 214–15, 269, 329
Wolfe, Tom, 327
Woolf, Leonard, 343; *Quack! Quack!*, 130
Woollcott, Alexander, 109
Wordsworth, William, 157, 241–2
Wordsworth, William Christopher, 129–30,
173
World Council of Churches, 335

Yalta Conference (1945), 257, 263
Yarwood, Mike, 304
Yeats, W. B.: *Autobiography*, 8
York Minster: 1984 fire, 405
Young India (newspaper), 51, 58
Young Men of India, 76
Young, Sir Brian, 387

Zaghlal, Saad, 77
Ziman, H. D., 224
Zinoviev, Grigori Ye., 169